JESUS IN EUROPEAN
PROTESTANT THOUGHT

STUDIES IN HISTORICAL THEOLOGY 1

General Editor: David C. Steinmetz, Duke University

JESUS IN EUROPEAN
PROTESTANT THOUGHT

1778–1860

COLIN BROWN

THE LABYRINTH PRESS
Durham, North Carolina

Library of Congress Cataloging in Publication Data

Brown, Colin, 1932-
    Jesus in European Protestant thought, 1778-1860.

    (Studies in historical theology ; 1)
    Revision of thesis (doctoral)—University of Bristol, England, 1969.
    Bibliography: p.
    Includes index.
    1. Jesus Christ—History of doctrines—18th century.
2. Jesus Christ—History of doctrines—19th century.
3. Jesus Christ—Historicity—History—18th century.
4. Jesus Christ—Historicity—History—19th century.
I. Title   II. Series: Studies in historical theology
(Durham, N.C.) ; 1.
BT198.B826 1984   232.9′09′033   84-20111
ISBN 0-939464-18-7 (lib. bdg.)

Printed in the United States of America

TABLE OF CONTENTS

Acknowledgments

I wish to express my gratitude to the librarians and staff of the University of Bristol, England, and the McAlister Library of Fuller Theological Seminary, Pasadena, California, without whose help and resources this work would not have been possible. I am also indebted to the following libraries for making available books which would otherwise have been inaccessible: the Universities of Aberdeen, Berlin, Copenhagen, Cologne, Glasgow, Liverpool, London, the University of California Los Angeles, Münster, Tübingen, the Bodleian Library, Oxford, the School of Theology at Claremont, California, Columbia Theological Seminary, the Selly Oak Colleges, Birmingham, Trinity College, Bristol, Dr. Williams's Library, London, the London Library, the municipal libraries of Bristol, Düsseldorf and Middlesborough, and the Huntington Library, San Marino, California.

I have endeavored to give full details of published works in the end-notes, and in quoting have sought to obtain the appropriate permission from the owners of copyrights. If through oversight or inability to trace the owner I have omitted to obtain the requisite permission, I ask their indulgence. I wish to record my thanks to the following in granting permission to quote from their respective books: the Abingdon Press, W. G. Kümmel, *The New Testament: The History of the Investigation of its Problems*, translated by S. McLean Gilmour and Howard Kee, English translation copyright © 1972 by Abingdon Press, used by permission; Adam and Charles Black, Publishers, *Lessing's Theological Writings*, edited by Henry Chadwick, 1956, John Locke, *The Reasonableness of Christianity etc.*, edited I. T. Ramsey, 1958, and J. N. D. Kelly, *Early Christian Doctrines*, 1978; Basil Blackwell, Ludwig Wittgenstein, *Philosophical Investigations*, translated by G. E. M. Anscombe, 1958; Bobbs-Merrill Educational Publishing, Immanuel Kant, *Critique of Practical Reason*, translated by Lewis White Beck, copyright © 1956, and *Foundations of Metaphysics of Morals*, translated by Lewis White Beck, copyright © 1959, reprinted with permission of the publisher ITT Bobbs-Merrill Educational Publishing, Inc., Indianapolis; the Syndics of the Cambridge University Press, B. Orchard and T. R. W. Longstaff, eds., *J. J. Griesbach: Synoptic and Text-Critical Studies*, 1978, Horton Harris, *David Friedrich Strauss and his Theology*, 1973, N. H. Palmer, "Lachmann's Argument," *New Testament Studies* 13, 1966-67, Owen Chadwick, *The Secularization of the European Mind*, 1975, J. G. Fichte, *Science of Knowledge (Wissenschaftslehre)*, edited and trans-

translated by T. M. Greene and H. H. Hudson, reprinted by permission of The Open Court Publishing Company, La Salle, Illinois, copyright © by The Open Court Publishing Company, copyright © 1960 by Harper & Brothers; Oxford University Press, John Locke, *An Essay Concerning Human Understanding*, edited by A. S. Pringle- Pattison, 1924; David Hume, *Enquiries*, edited by L. A. Selby-Bigge, revised by P. H. Nidditch, 1975, R. G. Collingwood, *The Idea of History*, 1946, G. W. F. Hegel, *Phenomenology of Spirit*, translated by A. V. Miller, with Analysis of the Text and Foreword by J. N. Findlay, copyright © Oxford University Press, quoted by permission of Oxford University Press, Soren Kierkegaard, *The Present Age and Two Minor Ethico-Religious Treatises*, 1940, Soren Kierkegaard, *Christian Discourses*, 1940, Stephen Neill, *The Interpretation of the New Testament*, 1961-1961, 1964, Horton Harris, *The Tübingen School*, 1975, Peter C. Hodgson, editor and translator, *Ferdinand Christian Baur on the Writing of Church History*, copyright © Oxford University Press, Inc., 1965, Claude Welch, editor and translator, *God and Incarnation in Mid-Nineteenth Century German Theology: G. Thomasius, I. A. Dorner, A. E. Biedermann*, copyright © Oxford University Press, Inc., 1956; Princeton University Press, Soren Kierkegaard, *Either/Or*, translated by Walter Lowrie, copyright © 1944, 1959, Princeton University Press, *Kierkegaard: Letters and Documents*, *Kierkegaard's Writings*, vol. 25, translated by Henrik Rosemeier, copyright © Princeton University Press, 1978, Kierkegaard, *Philosophical Fragments*, originally translated and introduced by David F. Swenson, new introduction and commentary by Niels Thulstrup, translation revised and commentary translated by Howard V. Hong, copyright © 1936, 1962, Kierkegaard, *Concluding Unscientific Postscript*, translated by David F. Swenson, completed and provided with introduction and notes by Walter Lowrie, copyright © 1941, Kierkegaard, *Training in Christianity*, translated with introduction and notes by Walter Lowrie, 1941; Routledge & Kegan Paul, Friedrich Schleiermacher, *On Religion: Speeches to its Cultured Despisers*, translated by John Oman, reprint edition copyright © 1958 by Harper & Brothers, reprinted by arrangement with Routledge & Kegan Paul Ltd., London, Ludwig Feuerbach, *The Essence of Religion*, translated by George Eliot, 1854, Introductory Essay by Karl Barth and Foreword by H. Richard Niebuhr, copyright © Harper & Row, reprinted by arrangement with Routledge & Kegan Paul, Alastair Hannay, *Kierkegaard*, copyright © Alastair Hannay, 1982, G. W. F. Hegel, *Lectures on the Philosophy of Religion*, translated by E. B. Spiers and J. Burdon Sanderson, 3 vols. 1895, reprint edition, 1962, published by Routledge & Kegan Paul, London, and the Humanities Press, Atlantic Highlands, N.J.; Scholars Press, Friedrich D. E. Schleiermacher, *On the Glaubenslehre*, translated by James Duke and Francis Fiorenza, copyright © The American Academy of Religion, 1981, G. W. F. Hegel, *The Christian Religion*, edited and translated by Peter C. Hodgson, copyright © The American Academy of Religion, 1979; S.C.M. Press Ltd., Karl Barth, *Protestant Theology in the Nineteenth Century*, translated by Brian Cozens, John Bowden, *et. al.*, copyright © 1952, 1972, S.C.M. Press, London, Judson Press,

Valley Forge, P.A.; and Mrs. Nancy Perrin for permission to quote from her late husband Norman Perrin's book *The Kingdom of God in the Teaching of Jesus*, Philadelphia: Westminster Press and London: S.C.M. Press, 1963. The Bible text in this publication is (apart from where authors give their own translations) from the Revised Standard Version of the Bible, copyrighted 1946, 1952 © 1971, 1973 by the Division of Christian Education of the National Council of Churches of Christ in the U.S.A., and used by permission. Finally, I would like to express my special thanks to Michael Stribling and Janet Gathright of the Word Processing Office of the School of Theology, Fuller Theological Seminary, for word processing my typescript. Together they produced the computer tape from which the type for this book was set.

Abbreviations

ADB	*Allgemeine Deutsche Bibliothek.*
AW	*Ausgewählte Werke.*
Bekenntnisschriften	*Die Bekenntnisschriften der evangelisch-lutherischen Kirche. Herausgegeben im Gedenkjahr der Augsburgischen Konfession 1930*, 3rd ed. (Göttingen: Vandenhoeck & Rupprecht, 1956).
BHT	*Beiträge zur historischen Theologie.*
CG	F. D. E. Schleiermacher, *Der christliche Glaube... Siebente Auflage auf Grund der zweiten Auflage und kritischer Prüfung des Textes neu herausgeben und mit Einleitung, Erläuterungen und Register versehen von* Martin Redeker, 2 vols. (Berlin: Walter de Gruyter & Co., 1960).
Copleston	F. Copleston, *A History of Philosophy*, 9 vols. (London: Burns, Oates, and Search Press, 1946–75).
DNB	*Dictionary of National Biography*, 63 vols., ed. Leslie Stephen, continued by Sidney Lee (1885–1900); and *Supplements* and *Errata* (New York: Macmillan; London: Smith, Elder & Co., 1904).
DTC	*Dictionnaire de Théologie Catholique, contenant L'Exposé des Doctrines de la Théologie Catholique, Leurs Preuves et leur Histoire. Commencé sous la direction de A. Vacant, E. Mangenot, continué sous celle de E. Amann*, 15 vols. (Paris: Letouzey et Ané, 1930–50).
EB	*Encyclopaedia Britannica.*
EKL	*Evangelisches Kirchenlexikon. Kirchlich-theologisches Handwörterbuch, herausgegeben von H. Brunotte und O. Weber*, 3 vols., 2nd ed. (Göttingen: Vandenhoeck & Rupprecht, 1955–62).
EP	Paul Edwards, ed., *The Encyclopedia of Philosophy*, 8 vols. (New York: Macmillan and the Free Press; London: Collier Macmillan, 1967).

Exp. T.	*The Expository Times.*
FGLP	*Forschungen zur Geschichte und Lehre des Protestantismus.*
FKD	*Forschungen zur Kirchen- und Dogmengeschichte.*
FSOT	*Forschungen zur systematischen und ökumenischen Theologie.*
FSTR	*Forschungen zur systematischen Theologie und Religionsphilosophie.*
Geschichte	Albert Schweitzer, *Geschichte der Leben-Jesu-Forschung* (Tübingen: J. C. B. Mohr [Paul Siebeck]. 1906; 6th ed., 1951).
GS	*Gesammelte Schriften.*
GW	*Gesammelte Werke.*
Hennecke-Schneemelcher	*New Testament Apocrypha*, ed. E. Hennecke and W. Schneemelcher, 2 vols. (London: Lutterworth Press, 1963–65).
Hirsch	Emanuel Hirsch, *Geschichte der neuern evangelischen Theologie*, 2nd ed., 5 vols. (Gütersloh: Gütersloher Verlagshaus Gerd Mohn, 1960).
HJKCH	H. Ristow and K. Matthiae, eds., *Der historische Jesus und der kerygmatische Christus*, 2nd ed. (Berlin: Evangelische Verlagsanstalt, 1962).
JSNT	*Journal for the Study of the New Testament.*
JTC	*Journal for Theology and the Church.*
JTS	*Journal of Theological Studies.*
Kraus	Hans-Joachim Kraus, *Geschichte der historisch-kritischen Erforschung des Alten Testaments von der Reformation bis zur Gegenwart*, 2nd ed. (Neukirchen-luyn: Neukirchener Verlag, 1969).
Kümmel	Werner Georg Kümmel, *The New Testament: The History of the Investigation of its Problems* (Nashville and New York: Abingdon Press, 1972).

Lachmann-Muncker	G. E. Lessing's *Sämtliche Schriften*, ed. K. Lachmann and F. Muncker, 23 vols. (Berlin-Stuttgart-Leipzig: J. G. Goschen, 1886–1924; reprint ed., Berlin, 1968).
LCC	*Library of Christian Classics.*
LTK	*Lexikon für Theologie und Kirche. Herausgegeben von J. Höfer und K. Rahner*, 2nd ed., 10 vols. plus index and 3 supplements (Freiburg: Herder, 1967–68).
Neill, Interpretation	Stephen Neill, *The Interpretation of the New Testament, 1861–1961* (London: Oxford University Press, 1964).
NTS	*New Testament Studies.*
NZSTh	*Neue Zeitschrift für systematische Theologie.*
ODCC	*The Oxford Dictionary of the Christian Church*, 2nd ed. edited by F. L. Cross and E. A. Livingstone (London: Oxford University Press, 1974).
PT	Karl Barth, *Protestant Theology in the Nineteenth Century: Its Background and History* (London: S.C.M. Press, 1972).
Quest	Albert Schweitzer, *The Quest of the Historical Jesus: A Critical Study of its Progress from Reimarus to Wrede* (1910), Eng. trans. with an Introduction by J. M. Robinson (New York: Macmillan, 1969).
RE	*Realencyklopädie für protestantische Theologie und Kirche. Begründet von J. J. Herzog. In dritter verbesserter und vermehrter Auflage unter Mitwirkung vieler Theologen und Gelehrten herausgegeben von Albert Hauck*, 24 vols. (Leipzig: J. C. Hinrichs'sche Buchhandlung, 1896–1913).
RGG³	*Die Religion in Geschichte und Gegenwart. Handwörterbuch für Theologie und Religionswissenschaft. Dritte neu bearbeitete Auflage in Gemeinschaft mit Hans Frhr. v. Campenhausen, Erich Dinkler, Gerhard Gloege und Knud E. Løgstrup, herausgegeben von Kurt Galling*, 6 vols. and *Registerband* (Tübingen: J. C. B. Mohr [Paul Siebeck], 1957–65).
Richardson, History	Alan Richardson, *History, Sacred and Profane*, Bampton Lectures for 1962 (London: S.C.M. Press, 1964).

Sacramentum Mundi	Karl Rahner et al., eds., *Sacramentum Mundi: An Encyclopedia of Theology*, 6 vols. (New York: Herder and Herder; London: Burns and Oates, 1968–70).
S-B	H. Strack and P. Billerbeck, *Kommentar zum Neuen Testament aus Talmud und Midrasch*, 5 vols. (Munich: C. H. Beck, 1926–; reprint ed., 1956–61).
SDST	*Studien zur Dogmengeschichte und Systematischen Theologie.*
SJT	*Scottish Journal of Theology.*
Stephan-Schmidt	Horst Stephan, *Geschichte der deutschen evangelischen Theologie seit dem deutschen Idealismus*, 2nd ed., ed. M. Schmidt (Berlin: Alfred Topelmann, 1960).
STGNJ	*Studien zur Theologie und Geistesgeschichte des Neunzehnten Jahrhunderts.*
SW	*Sämtliche Werke.*
TC	Karl Barth, *Theology and Church* (New York: Harper; London: S.C.M., 1962).
TF	*Theologische Forschung.*
ThStKr	*Theologische Studien und Kritiken.*
TKT	*Texte zur Kirchen- und Theologiegeschichte.*
TRE	*Theologische Realenzyklopädie*, ed. Gerhard Krause, Gerhard Müller, et al. (Berlin: Walter de Gruyter, 1976–[proceeding]).
Typen	Christian Walther, *Typen des Reich-Gottes-Verstandnisses. Studien zur Eschatologie und Ethik im 19. Jahrhundert*, FGLP 10. Reihe, Band 20 (Munich: Chr. Kaiser Verlag, 1961).
Types	H. R. Mackintosh, *Types of Modern Theology: Schleiermacher to Barth* (Digswell Place: Nisbet, 1937).
WUNT	*Wissenschaftliche Untersuchungen zum Neuen Testament.*
ZKG	*Zeitschrift für Kirchengeschichte.*
ZTK	*Zeitschrift für Theologie und Kirche.*

INTRODUCTION

The Christian Church has gone through many crises of faith. But two in particular overshadow all the rest, for in them the issue at stake is that which sets Christianity apart from other religions and beliefs—the identity of Jesus Christ. The first of these crises began with the appearance of Jesus and lasted into the fifth century. It went through numerous phases and had several focal points. In the fourth century, the Niceno-Constantinopolitan Creed met the challenge of Arianism by asserting the divinity of Jesus in terms of his consubstantiality with the Father. The Council of Chalcedon (A.D. 451) laid down the parameters of orthodoxy for Western Christendom which were to endure for over a millennium. Its definition was a patchwork of phrases drawn from the rival schools of Antioch and Alexandria, ruling out the heresies of the respective schools, and affirming Jesus Christ to be "of one substance with the Father as touching the Godhead, the same of one substance with us as touching the manhood, like us in all things apart from sin." The nice distinctions which were appended asserted the integrity of his divine and human natures and their union in the person of Jesus. They did not resolve the difficulties of how to conceive of the identity of Jesus, but they provided guidelines for thinking which only very few people questioned until relatively modern times. In the mainstream of Western Christianity the orthodoxy of the creeds remained unchallenged until the eighteenth century when fresh doubt began to be cast on the historicity of the Church's beliefs about Jesus and, in particular, its claims concerning his divinity. Thus began the second major crisis of faith concerning the identity of Jesus Christ. It is with the genesis of this crisis that this book is concerned.

In his great book *The Quest of the Historical Jesus*, Albert Schweitzer saw this crisis as an endeavor—often misguided—to recover the Jesus of history. His account was a chronicle of the enterprise from Hermann Samuel Reimarus in the late eighteenth century to William Wrede in the twentieth century—or, perhaps more accurately, to Schweitzer himself, for Schweitzer concluded with his own solution to the riddle of Jesus as the only effective answer to Wrede's skepticism. Few doctoral dissertations have matched the book's narrative verve. It remains the classic guide to the highways and byways of German scholarship. As Norman Perrin has observed, the book

> was so written as to give the reader the impression that he is travelling down a long and difficult road with Albert Schweitzer as his guide. The traveller is continually faced with forks in the road, either-or alternatives, until he comes to the last and final fork: either the thorough-going scepticism of Wilhelm [*sic*] Wrede or the thorough-going eschatology of Albert Schweitzer. In no case does the guide fail to point out the fork that is to be taken, least of all in the case of the last one![1]

Schweitzer found fault with the work of his predecessors in their almost total neglect of the eschatological thought-world of Jesus and the role it played in shaping Jesus' understanding of his mission. Schweitzer himself gave no more credence to first-century eschatology than his liberal predecessors did, but he held that it was of decisive importance for understanding Jesus. He portrayed Jesus as a man obsessed with the idea of the Kingdom of God which he believed that he could bring about through his own messianic suffering. The Kingdom did not come in the way that Jesus envisaged, and his first-century eschatological beliefs must now be regarded as mistaken. Nevertheless, Schweitzer closed his work on a somewhat enigmatic, mystical, and even existential note which called into question the whole enterprise of attempting to recover the historical Jesus as a basis for faith. He concluded that as a concrete historical personality Jesus remains a stranger to our time, but his spirit which lies hidden in his words is known in simplicity. He comes to us "as One unknown." His identity remains "an ineffable mystery." But those who obey his call and follow him, performing the tasks he sets, "shall learn in their own experience Who He is."[2]

To many people, Schweitzer's work seemed to put a stop to the whole enterprise of recovering the historical Jesus. Quite apart from whether his conclusions were satisfactory, Schweitzer appeared to have said all that could reasonably be said. However, despite the comprehensiveness of his account and the importance of his recognition of the significance of eschatology for understanding the New Testament, Schweitzer's work was not without its limitations. Schweitzer deliberately restricted his investigation to critical scholarship concerned with the historical Jesus and then concluded that the whole enterprise was misconceived. His own attention was confined largely to German Protestant Biblical scholars, with occasional references to French writers. The work of the great German philosophers of the period fell outside his purview, despite their manifest concern to reassess the significance of Christ within the context of their philosophical schemes. It was perhaps inevitable that Schweitzer should have nothing to say about Kierkegaard, for at the time when he was writing, the work of the Danish thinker was scarcely known outside his native land. But for us today the thought of Kierkegaard must occupy a central place in any account of nineteenth-century thought, especially in the area of Christology. Moreover, Schweitzer displayed no interest in the systematic theology of the period, despite the concern of many thinkers to reappraise the role of Christ in their theology. Three quarters of a century have elapsed since the appearance of Schweitzer's work. A great deal of critical work has been done in many areas of theology and philosophy that relate to Jesus in nineteenth-century thought. The present book is an attempt to reassess thought about Jesus in the light of modern scholarship in the crucial period between 1778 and 1860.

The period under review embraces the Golden Age of German literature and philosophy. It was the age of Goethe, Herder, Kant, Fichte, Hegel, and Schelling. It was an age of revolutionary ideas in theology no less than in the arts and in philosophy. It was the age of Schleiermacher, Strauss, Baur, and a host of lesser thinkers. Whatever their differences, there was an awareness among an increasing number of theologians of the need to come to terms with—or provide an effective answer to—contemporary philosophy and current historical techniques. The dates 1778 and 1860 span the period from Lessing's publication of Reimarus's *Fragment* "On the Intentions of Jesus and his Disciples" to the death of Ferdinand Christian Baur. It was a time of great intellectual ferment and profound change. In 1778 Lessing had yet to write his dramatic poem *Nathan the Wise*, and Moses Mendelssohn and Immanuel Kant had still to discuss what it meant to live in the Age of Enlightenment. By 1860 Romanticism had been transcended. All the great protagonists of Idealism were dead, and D. F. Strauss had long since ceased to see in it a means of rescuing Christianity from the ravages of historical criticism. When Strauss published his second *Life of Jesus* in 1864, a work designed for popular consumption as a German rival to that of Renan, he reverted to Spinoza and Kant for guidance in discerning the true meaning of Christ.

The intense debate about Jesus was by no means confined to historical questions asked by Gospel critics. The need to reappraise the identity and significance of Jesus was felt by poets, philosophers, and theologians. To some, the enterprise represented a quest of the historical Jesus; to others, it was more a quest for the real Christ. In short, the nineteenth-century quest to recover Jesus did not follow a single, albeit tortuous, road leading ultimately to Albert Schweitzer. It was more like a series of paths in a forest which were sometimes connected and sometimes not, and which led the perplexed traveller out of the forest at different places.

In the study that follows I have tried to map out some of those paths. Five areas seem to me to be of particular significance. For the sake of organization I have termed them as follows: I. The Fragments Controversy: A Chapter in the Theology of the Enlightenment; II. Philosophical Idealism and Rational Religion; III. New Perspectives in Religion; IV. The Life of Jesus and Critical History; V. Orthodoxy Modified. Within each of these main divisions, separate chapters focus attention on individual thinkers or movements.

In beginning with the "Fragments Controversy" I have begun at the same point as Albert Schweitzer, which scholars (following Schweitzer) have come to regard as the beginning of the quest of the historical Jesus. It concerns the publication by G. E. Lessing of anonymous extracts from an unpublished work by the recently deceased H. S. Reimarus. The latter called into question the whole fabric of Christian belief, not only by denying the divinity and resurrection of Jesus but also by imputing to the disciples the fraudulent invention of the resurrection message and Christ's Second Coming. The ensuing furor gave Lessing the opportunity to chastise critics and air his own views on the relevance of history to religious belief. In retrospect, Reimarus's views do not appear (as they did to Schweitzer) like a bolt from the blue but the German expression of a Deism which Reimarus himself had got to know at first hand in England over half a century previously and which was already well known in German intellectual circles.

The section on "Philosophical Idealism and Rational Religion" examines the thought of Kant, Herder, Goethe, Fichte, Hegel, and Schelling. In its broadest sense Idealism denotes those philosophies which seek to transcend both the enlightenment and orthodox Christianity with a world view that is ultimately rational and spiritual. But Idealist philosophers differed among themselves over their understanding of reason. Kant was concerned with the critical reappraisal of the main areas of human activity in the light of the individual subject's rational faculties which he maintained were incapable of grappling with anything beyond the objects of their own immediate apprehension. Fichte, Hegel, and Schelling, on the other hand, endeavored to develop rational philosophies of the structure of the universe. Not only did these thinkers influence the theology of their own and later generations, but they themselves were concerned to restate what they considered to be the true character of Christianity and the role of Jesus within their schemes of thought. The latter was largely determined by the attitude of the thinker in question to reason. In Kant's case Jesus was an enlightened teacher of rational and moral truths. The Gospel account of his life represents their ideal embodiment in human nature. The systems of Absolute Idealism are not so much interested in envisaging a historical Jesus as in speculating about the ontological role of Christ. In his early unpublished, theological writings Hegel began with a Kantian view of religion and Jesus, but as he progressed to Absolute Idealism, his understanding of religion and Jesus correspondingly changed.

Herder and Goethe have also been included in this section because of their Idealist approach to religion. Herder differed from other Idealist thinkers insofar as he was interested in a critical and historical appreciation of Jesus. This was bound up with his concern for a kind of pan-history and the place of Christianity within it. His approach to the Gospels anticipated some of the points of later Form Criticism, but his work attracted comparatively little attention among theologians at the time, perhaps because he was not a professional theologian himself. Goethe presents what might be termed a post-Christian interpretation of Christ in terms of a non-theistic world view.

The section on "New Perspectives in Religion" groups together Schleiermacher, Feuerbach, and Kierkegaard. The reason for this grouping does not lie in any material similarities of methods or conclusions. It is partly a matter of convenience. But it also gives recognition to the fact that each of the three presented a new perspective as a radical alternative to previous thinking. In a sense, both Schleiermacher and Kierkegaard could be said to be attempting to outflank Kant's embargo on the cognitive status of religious pronouncements. At the same time, they sought to reflect more deeply on the essence of Christianity. Schleiermacher offered a comprehensive reinterpretation of the Christian faith, including Christology, in terms of his analysis of the content of Christian experience. According to Schleiermacher, Jesus' experience of God was so profound that it might be said to constitute an existence of God in human nature. In this way Schleiermacher sought to affirm the divinity of Christ while avoiding the difficulties of the traditional two-natures doctrine. Kierkegaard, on the other hand, was both more conservative and more radical in his thinking. In his beliefs he remained traditionally orthodox. At the same time he produced what might be called a grammar of belief which sought to give due recognition to the transcendence of God. No previous Christian thinker saw so clearly God's transcendence, even in revelation. Consequently, Kierkegaard saw the Incarnation as the expression of the Absolute Paradox in which God remains incognito in the very act of manifesting himself in human form. By contrast, Feuerbach represents an early form of the secularizing of Idealism. His analysis of the essence of Christianity presented theology as a form of anthropology and religious beliefs as the projection of deep-seated human longings. Like Schleiermacher and Kierkegaard, Feuerbach lived in the shadow of Hegel. But for none of the three did Hegel's Idealism provide either a viable philosophy or pose an ultimate threat. For Feuerbach, Hegel's Absolute Spirit was replaced by man. To Schleiermacher and Kierkegaard, the Hegelian system failed to do justice to the realities posited by Christian existence.

The section dealing with "The Life of Jesus and Critical History" traces the progress of Gospel Criticism from the late eighteenth century down to the time of Renan's *Life of Jesus*. Competing theories of Gospel origins are discussed together with the work of D. F. Strauss and F. C. Baur. In the work of both these scholars the influence of Hegel is apparent, but in neither was it decisive. The crucial factor in Strauss's early work on Jesus was his concept of myth which had already been used by other scholars and which Strauss saw in the application to Jesus of Old Testament prophecies and categories. In a sense his work was an early essay in Form Criticism and a History of Religions approach to the Gospels. He invoked Hegelianism in his first *Life of Jesus* in order to salvage some significance for Jesus and the Christian faith. The idea of Incarnation was the symbolic expression of the entrance of the Absolute Spirit in human life posited by Hegel. But even this was dropped in Strauss's second *Life of Jesus* which appeared a generation after the first *Life*. F. C. Baur's work is not to be seen as the application of Hegelian philosophy to New Testament criticism but as the expression of a tendency criticism which Baur developed independently of Hegel. When Baur philosophized about the meaning of history and the development of dogma he spoke like a Hegelian, but his characteristic views were developed before he came into contact with Hegelian thought. Baur's views on Jesus were reached against the background of his rejection of supernaturalism, and they bear traces of Schleiermacher's influence.

The fifth and final section, which is entitled "Orthodoxy Modified," examines the response to the above developments among the more orthodox theologians, especially in the field of dogmatics. Two main movements are considered: Confessionalism, which was partly a reaction to modern trends, partly a revival of nostalgia inspired by the tercentenary of the Reformation, and partly a continuation of pietistic revivalism; and Mediating Theology, which sought to build bridges between Christian faith and modern thought.

In some cases the Confessionalists responded by retreating into evangelical piety. Others, like Tholuck, were aware of critical developments, and even indulged in controversy as part of their pastoral concern. But although learned, Tholuck's work tended to be solid and devotional rather than creatively historical. The most original work among the Confessionalists was done by the Erlangen theologians, Hofmann and Thomasius. Both significantly altered the orthodox Lutheran understanding of Jesus, the former chiefly in the sphere of the work and the latter in the sphere of the doctrine of the person of Christ. Hofmann modified the penal view of atonement. Thomasius tried to meet the charge that the orthodox view of Christ failed to treat him as a real man by developing a doctrine of *kenōsis*. But although Thomasius was concerned with the humanity of Jesus, the answer that he gave was about the Christ of faith rather than the Jesus of history. The validity of the thought of both Hofmann and Thomasius was closely tied to the validity of the belief system within which they worked.

The Mediating Theologians, on the other hand, sought to mediate between orthodoxy and modern thought. Although not slavishly tied to Schleiermacher, the first generation of Mediating Theologians did not stray far from the paths trod by their former teacher and colleague. Ullmann's view of Jesus pursued the thought of a sinless man who by his unique position was the mediator between God and man, as opposed to following the orthodox two-natures christology. The later Mediating Theologians, Rothe and Dorner, were more indebted to speculative Idealism which they used to interpret the significance of the incarnation.

Inevitably, any survey like the present book must remain a torso. It covers only a segment of eighteenth- and nineteenth-century thought. It ends with the conclusions of scholars of a bygone age. It has been undertaken in an attempt to understand what moved them to reach their conclusions rather than assess what is valid for us today. If there is any one obvious conclusion that may be drawn, it is that there is no single direction in which the thought of the age was moving. Although there was a manifest concern for the historicity of the foundations of Christian beliefs and a growing interest in the life of Jesus, such concerns by no means displaced more orthodox piety. The stream of books which poured forth from the theological presses of Europe is evidence of the ready market for new ideas concerning Jesus as well as the reaffirmation of old ideas. But the present study has made no attempt to assess the acceptance of ideas in the Church and public at large. It has merely tried to analyze the ideas contained in the printed books of the age. It would be interesting to pursue the question of the relationship between politics and theology in the German universities. It would be fascinating to examine the connections between geography and theology in this period and ask whether some states were more receptive than others to new ideas. Clearly, state censorship was a factor to be reckoned with in the eighteenth century, and governments played a part in the appointment of professors. At times it seems as if a new form of *cuius regio eius religio* plays a part in shaping the course of nineteenth-century theology.[3] However, the exploration of such questions lies outside my scope. My aim has been the more modest one of trying to identify ideas and relate them to the theological and philosophical presuppositions and methods employed in their genesis.

I have not attempted to draw together a series of general conclusions. This is partly because each of the five main areas of thought that I have investigated is relatively self-contained. The observations that I have made and the conclusions that I have drawn can be found in the respective separate chapters. However, the temptation is strong to emulate Albert Schweitzer and write a concluding chapter which sets aside the work of the scholars discussed and offers its own alternative solutions. It is a temptation which I have resisted, not least because a final chapter in a book of this kind is not the place to embark on stating a fresh approach to Christology. But perhaps a few isolated observations are in order.

The first is to repeat what becomes abundantly apparent at numerous places in this survey that the question of the identity of Jesus is not one which can be settled either on a historical, critical level or on a philosophical or theological level. Whatever conclusions we draw about Jesus involve an interplay of judgments which pertain to each of these various disciplines. If I were pressed to confess my own philosophical preferences, I would have to admit that, despite the contemporary resurgence of interest in them, Hegel and Absolute Idealism appear to offer no intelligible, viable approach to understanding reality. By contrast, I find myself endorsing Wittgenstein's observation that "Kierkegaard was by far the most profound thinker of the last century. Kierkegaard was a saint."[4] Rightly understood, Kierkegaard may yet present the twentieth century with better conceptual tools for approaching theology than any other thinker of his age.

When we turn to the theologians and New Testament critics, certain sins of omission can scarcely be overlooked. There is an almost universal lack of interest in the Jewishness of Jesus and his background. Few scholars appear to take much interest in Jewish writings or see the possible relevance of the Jewish world to understanding Jesus. To some extent, Reimarus and Semler present exceptions to this. D. F. Strauss displayed a far more extensive knowledge of the Old Testament than many of his contemporaries. But by and large the scholars of the period appear to treat Jesus as someone like themselves, separated from them only by the lapse of centuries. Doubtless, there were two sides to this lack of concern for the Jewishness of Jesus. Positively, there was a desire to see the universal significance of Jesus. Negatively, there was a wide gulf between Christian and Jewish culture and an even wider one between Christian and Jewish theology. This implicit polarizing of Christian and Jewish consciousness affected people in different ways. Some advocated the transcendence of all particular religions, while others expressed views on the place of Judaism in universal history which verged on anti-Semitism. What appears to have been largely overlooked in the process was the relevance of Jewish studies to the understanding of Jesus and his times. Admittedly, a number of writers offered wild conjectures about the Essenes. But these were made largely in the interests of rationalistic accounts of Jesus' activities. The attempt to see Jesus as a Jewish figure in Jewish history seems in retrospect to be at best half-hearted.

Few scholars appear to appreciate the significance of references to the Holy Spirit in the Gospel accounts of Jesus. Schleiermacher saw an analogy between the indwelling of the Spirit in believers and the divine presence in Christ. But Schleiermacher himself did not explore in any detail the biblical testimony to the Spirit of God. Most thinkers—including both the defenders and opponents of orthodoxy—operated with what was virtually a tritheistic view of God which treated each member as a separate, self-contained divine person. In the Incarnation the second of the three persons left the other two behind in order to become a man. For the orthodox, this was the view to be defended. For the rest, this was the view to be attacked and replaced. The Enlightened alternative was to depict Jesus as a moral teacher or the ideal embodiment of a humanity that was well-pleasing to God. Absolute Idealism saw Jesus as the expression in human life of the immanent divine reality. Schleiermacher's account was a form of Unitarianism in all but name. A virtually tritheistic approach to the Trinity lay behind the kenotic Christologies of the more orthodox whose views were designed to explain the conceivability of the Incarnation. In practice, kenotic Christology merely compounded the problems of orthodoxy. In retrospect it would seem that the nineteenth-century thinkers felt themselves confronted by the choice of defending a virtually tritheistic view of the Trinity or of abandoning Trinitarian and even theistic thinking altogether. The possibility of working with an alternative model of the Trinity, such as Augustine's understanding of the threefold oneness of God, and of using it to interpret Christology does not seem to have been seen as a serious option. But such a possibility might have occurred if theologians pondered Calvin's teaching on the Trinity, or had been prepared to examine in depth the biblical testimony to the Spirit and reexamine the New Testament pronouncements on the Spirit in relation to Christology.

I have attempted to explore this question more fully at the conclusion of my study on *Miracles and the Critical Mind*.[5] Perhaps one further observation may be permitted here which is also more fully examined in that book. It concerns the miracle stories. In the period under review, the miracle stories were already being dislodged from their place as the foundation of apologetics. The rationalists sought natural explanations. Strauss put them down to the myth-making tendency in religion. Even the more orthodox were becoming increasingly inclined to construct their Christologies first and justify their belief in the biblical miracles afterward in the light of the Incarnation. From the English Deists onward, the figure of Apollonius of Tyana was repeatedly brought forward as an example of a Hellenistic, miracle-working divine man whose feats paralleled those of Jesus. The implication was drawn that the miracles of Jesus were modeled on those of Apollonius and similar divine men on the principle that anything a Hellenistic divine man could do, Jesus could do better. Recent investigation into the figure of Apollonius and the concept of the divine man has set serious question marks against these conjectures. Some recent scholars now favor a sociological approach to the miracle stories of the Gospels.[6] But it may be doubted whether the miracle stories were invented by Christians in times of persecution in order to cheer each other up.

There are grounds for thinking that, instead of belonging to the later strata of the Gospel tradition, the miracle and exorcism stories belong to its earliest stratum and that they constitute the essential factor which explains not only the course of Jesus' career but also the attitude of Jesus' Jewish opponents. The thirteenth chapter of the Book of Deuteronomy gives instruction as to what to do with a prophet who performs signs and wonders in order to lead the people of Israel astray. The people of Israel were not only to give no heed to the prophet, they were to put him to death: "So shall you purge the evil out of the midst of you." A strong case can be made for thinking that the Jewish leaders perceived Jesus to be such a person and that they concluded at a very early stage in Jesus' ministry that he should be removed in the manner prescribed by the Torah. If this is so, the miracle stories belong not to the Hellenistic world but to the Palestinian milieu. The crucial question then becomes that of whether the evangelists were correct in portraying Jesus as the awaited Spirit-anointed Messiah or whether the Jewish leaders of the day were correct in seeing Jesus as a blasphemous pretender who was in league with Satan and who practiced black arts. But these are questions for us today. They are not the questions which scholars asked in the eighteenth and nineteenth centuries. Their views should be read, not as providing definitive answers to our questions, but on their own terms, sharing with us the questions and the insights of their day.

The present book had its origins some twenty years ago when I began doctoral research in the University of Bristol, England. The dissertation was completed in September 1969, and the degree was awarded the following year. The present work is the outcome of substantial revision and updating. Wherever possible I have made use of existing translations, so as to enable the reader to pursue questions further in texts that are accessible. Where no translation was available, I have given my own rendering of the original. I have kept titles of books, articles, and journals in their original languages, but where translations are available I have given the English title in the footnotes. In order to save space I have not included a bibliography. However, titles of works may readily be found via the index.[7] It remains for me to thank Professor and Mrs. David Steinmetz for their kindness and interest in the publication of my research, and my colleagues at Fuller Theological Seminary for their stimulus and encouragement. I owe a special debt of love and gratitude to my wife, Olive, for her unfailing help in revising the text, proof reading and compiling the index. I wish to dedicate this book to Verity, Matthew, and Stephanie who were growing up while their father was coming of age as a student of theology.

Pasadena, California,
Christmas 1983

I

THE FRAGMENTS CONTROVERSY: A CHAPTER IN THE THEOLOGY OF THE ENLIGHTMENT

1. REIMARUS AND HIS CRITICS

Since the publication in 1906 of Albert Schweitzer's *Von Reimarus zu Wrede*, it has been customary to date the quest of the historical Jesus from Hermann Samuel Reimarus.[1] The year 1778 saw the publication of a study by Reimarus which Schweitzer hailed as "perhaps the most splendid achievement in the whole course of the historical investigation of the life of Jesus, for he was the first to grasp the fact that the world of thought in which Jesus moved was essentially eschatological."[2] Indeed, after Reimarus "the whole movement of theology down to Johannes Weiss, appears retrograde" (in view of its neglect of eschatology). Whether the work ever quite merited the academic laurels that Schweitzer was prepared to lavish upon it, and whether it was even quite as original as Schweitzer thought it to be, are questions which require fuller discussion later on. What is beyond doubt is that the work itself and the controversy it provoked were portents of the many storms which were to rage throughout the nineteenth century and which even today give little indication of subsiding.

The study in question, "Von dem Zwecke Jesu und seiner Jünger," purported to be an examination of the intentions of Jesus and his disciples. It was the last of seven anonymous pieces published by G. E. Lessing between 1774 and 1778 as *Fragmente eines Ungenannten*.[3] The circumstances of their publication throw light not only on their author and editor but the age out of which they grew. The seven *Fragments* were really part of a much larger work by Reimarus in defense of the rational worshipers of God, *Apologie oder Schutzschrift für die vernünftigen Verehrer Gottes*. The sheer size of this work has defeated generations of would-be publishers, and it was only in 1972 that a critical edition finally appeared.[4] The author's identity remained shrouded in mystery until 1814 when his son, Dr. J. A. H. Reimarus, donated manuscripts to the State and University Libraries of Hamburg and Göttingen.[5]

Hermann Samuel Reimarus and the Fragments of an Unnamed Author
Outwardly, Hermann Samuel Reimarus (1694–1768) was a learned, if somewhat rationalistic, orthodox Christian. He came from an old clergy family. He

taught briefly in the philosophy faculty at Wittenberg and as a schoolmaster in Wismar. Between these two posts he spent some time in Holland and England. His home was a center of intellectual life in his native Hamburg, where he spent his last forty years as a teacher of oriental languages at the Gymnasium Johanneum. To the last Reimarus attended the worship and sacraments of the Lutheran church. The formidable list of his learned, if now forgotten, published writings indicates his respect for reason and Christianity as a rational religion, but it gives little hint of the doubts he had long nursed about revealed religion, the historical worth of the Bible and the origins of Christianity. These he reserved for his *magnum opus*, written to clarify his personal doubts and destined not to be seen except by a small circle of intimate friends.

However, in the year before Reimarus's death, Gotthold Ephraïm Lessing moved to Hamburg in the capacity of drama critic to the newly established National Theatre. Somehow he got wind of the manuscript, and on assuming the post of librarian to the Duke of Brunswick's library at Wolfenbüttel in 1770 (after the collapse of the theatrical venture), Lessing took a version of the manuscript with him.[6] Two obstacles stood in the way of publication. One (which repeatedly defied would-be publishers) was the inordinate length and diffuse argument of the complete work. The other was the controversial nature of the book which intensified the Reimarus family's reluctance to have the father's name besmirched through any controversy that might arise. Lessing surmounted both by publishing extracts as if he had recently discovered them in the Ducal Library in a series *Zur Geschichte und Literatur. Aus den Schätzen der Herzoglichen Bibliothek zu Wolfenbüttel.*

For good measure, Lessing attempted to throw witch-hunters off the scent by naming Johann Lorenz Schmidt as the putative author.[7] The credibility of this conjecture was heightened, not only by the fact that Schmidt was a well-known Deist and heretic, but also by the fact that he had spent the last two years of his life at Wolfenbüttel. Moreover, Lessing had the foresight to obtain from the Duke of Brunswick in February 1772 exemption from censorship for the whole series, provided that he did not attack religion. This privilege was forfeited in 1778 because of the controversy he had provoked, and Lessing was obliged to surrender his manuscript to the Duke.

The first *Fragment* bore the title *Von der Duldung der Deisten*. It gave more than a hint of what was to come. Jesus was a teacher of rational, practical religion. Anyone who was rational and followed his ethical teaching was entitled to call himself a Christian.[8] Unfortunately, the teaching of Jesus had been distorted almost beyond recognition by the apostles who had foisted on to it Jewish ideas of the Messiah and the divine inspiration of the Hebrew Scriptures. They had substituted a religion full of mysteries for the simplicity of Jesus. And now, though Jews and pagans are tolerated, Deists are not. Rationalists should be accorded the same toleration as that God commanded the Israelites of old to grant to the stranger within their gates. The succeeding *Fragments* developed themes which had been rallying cries for the English Deists over half a century previously.

The first *Fragment* attracted little attention, and it was not until 1777 that any further installments were published. But in that year five *Fragments* appeared together, and these succeeded in mobilizing the counterattack of the orthodox. The second and third pleaded the case for rational religion,[9] and the next two launched a bitter attack upon the Old Testament.[10] The sixth *Fragment, Ueber die Auferstehungsgeschichte*, saw inconsistencies in the Gospel narratives of the resurrection and concluded that since the evangelists disagreed as to the circumstances, they were also mistaken as to the fact of the resurrection of Jesus.[11]

On the Intention of Jesus and His Disciples

It was against this background of rationalism and historical skepticism and the hue and cry that they provoked that Lessing proceeded to launch the notorious seventh *Fragment, Von dem Zwecke Jesu und seiner Jünger*.[12] The earlier *Fragments* each occupy between twelve and thirty pages of Lessing's collected writings; this last one takes up well over a hundred. The earlier ones assaulted the outer walls of the Christian edifice; the final one attempted to storm the inner citadel itself.

In attempting to discern the original teaching of Jesus, Reimarus pointed out that we are hampered by the fact that Jesus left no personal record of his own teaching. We have no option but to rely upon the records of the evangelists, regardless of whether they might have forgotten or kept back something important. Nevertheless, Reimarus was confident that he had detected the original message of Jesus in the exhortation of Mark 1:15b: "Repent and believe the gospel!" The original implication was twofold. In contrast with the Sadducees and what Reimarus took to be the teaching of the Old Testament, Jesus preached a gospel of personal immortality. In contrast with the pettifogging legalism of the Pharisees, Jesus strove for the moral elevation of mankind. Unfortunately, the exhortation to repent was also charged with Jewish overtones which eventually colored Jesus' whole outlook. To the Jewish mind the transition from repenting to preparing for an earthly theocratic kingdom to be inaugurated by a Messiah was but slight. Very early on Jesus took the small but fatal step of confusing the two ideas.

In a manner evocative of the English Deists, Reimarus insisted that no "mysteries" were involved in Jesus' teaching.[13] Jesus himself remained a Jew and intended that his followers should remain Jews likewise. The missionary journeys of the disciples had no other purpose than to proclaim the advent of Jesus as the political Messiah. The notions of a triune God and redemption through a God-man never once entered Jesus' head but were the inventions of a later age. Even when the expression *Son of God* was found on Jesus' lips, it meant no more than what Reimarus thought it meant in the Old Testament,

"God's Beloved." At most it meant that Jesus identified himself with the Messiah; it could not signify that he thought of himself as more than human.[14]

Basic to Reimarus's view was the contention that Jesus introduced neither new teaching nor new ceremonies into the Jewish religion.[15] Even when Jesus condemned Pharisaic hypocrisy and urged the need for moral change, he left the ceremonial law intact. He took part in the worship of synagogue and Temple, and announced that he had not come to destroy the law but to fulfill. Heaven and earth would pass away before the least letter of the law would fall unfulfilled (Matt. 5:18). Turning to the Christian sacraments, Reimarus insisted that baptism was simply the revival of a familiar Jewish practice by which candidates publicly announced their adherence to the Mosaic Law.[16] The Last Supper was essentially a Passover meal.[17]

The first major turning point in Jesus' career came when he allowed himself to be sidetracked into embracing political messianism.[18] The second came when Jesus decided to force through this program at all costs.[19] One false step led to another, and the end came rapidly. Jesus chose the Passover to display his hand and force a decision. Unfortunately for him, he had completely miscalculated popular support. The Baptist was no more. The disciples' pull over the people was far too weak. He himself had alienated the Pharisees by his refusal to prove himself by a miracle. The disturbance he created in the Temple simply confirmed the authorities in their decision to have him liquidated. At the crucial moment even the disciples deserted him. Had he been able to perform a miracle at the eleventh hour, things might have been different. As it was, he died a broken man. His last words express his disillusionment with God, who had failed him.[20]

The entire Christian religion might well have ended there but for the imagination and duplicity of the disciples. In the course of a few weeks they completely transformed the picture by means of two bold masterstrokes. The first was the claim that Jesus had risen from the dead; the second was the promise that he would return to complete the work of establishing the messianic kingdom. Both were equally fraudulent, but together they constitute the foundation of Christianity.

Reimarus's main critique of the resurrection narratives had already appeared in the *Fragment, Ueber die Auferstehungsgeschichte*. He now reiterated the argument that the watch set upon the grave (Matt. 27:62–66) was obviously a fraud invented by Matthew—the only evangelist who records the episode—to cover up the disciples' own theft of the corpse.[21] This was a necessary first step toward making the resurrection story credible. Even so, the disciples deemed it wise to wait fifty days before putting out their story, thereby allowing time for incriminating evidence to disappear.[22] The next principal target of Reimarus's criticism was the alleged eyewitnesses. Was it not highly suspicious that only believers saw the risen Christ? Would it not have furthered the interests of truth if Jesus had appeared to all and sundry?[23] In addition to the contradictions of the resurrection narratives,[24] there is the apostles' perverted use of Old Testament prophecy. The latter simply make themselves ridiculous by applying to Jesus utterances torn from an entirely unrelated context.[25]

Shrewdly realizing that to spiritualize their former message or even to postpone Christ's return indefinitely would mean suicide for their cause, the disciples set about proclaiming that Christ's second advent was at hand. Nor were they lacking in sayings of Jesus which were readily adaptable for their purposes. Had he not promised that there were those among his followers who would not taste death until they saw the Son of Man come in his kingdom?[26] The only difficulty was that Jesus had not mentioned his intervening death and resurrection. But even this proved no insuperable obstacle for the disciples. They revived the ancient tradition found in the Book of Daniel, Justin's *Dialogue with Trypho* and certain rabbinic sayings, that the Messiah would come twice—once in human lowliness and again in the clouds of heaven.[27]

The disciples themselves realized that this explanation was only a stopgap solution, raising difficulties as acute as those which they solved. When confronted by members of the Thessalonian congregation as to why the promised second advent was so long in coming, the apostle Paul was pushed into an indefinite postponement (2 Thess. 2:1–12). Rather more deftly, Peter parried the objection by reminding his readers that in the last days scoffers would come and that with the Lord a thousand years were but as a day (2 Pet. 3:1–8; cf. Ps. 90:4). In the meantime, he tacitly omitted giving a direct answer. Once this initial storm was weathered, the rest was comparatively clear sailing. Few people since then have remembered that the promised time is long past. They thus fail to realize that this major item of the primitive church's teaching is palpably false, which in turn means that the second remaining pillar propping up Christianity has crumbled away under their eyes without their noticing.[28]

Nor may the tottering edifice of Christianity be rescued by the traditional appeal to miracles.[29] Even though the New Testament miracles are less exaggerated than those of the Old Testament, they are scarcely less improbable. The New Testament writers themselves admit that Jesus performed no miracles in the presence of the more educated sections of the community. When the latter asked for proof, they met with nothing but abuse. Moreover, the narratives were written down some thirty to sixty years after the alleged events, when those who had known Jesus were no longer alive and able to question their veracity. Finally, Reimarus pointed out what David Hume had argued in 1748, that all religions appeal to the miraculous, and therefore they all cancel each other out on that score.[30]

Reimarus was equally unimpressed by the New Testament's appeal to prophecy.[31] Some of the texts adduced as prophecy were patently false, while others were obscure and ambiguous. To the former category belongs the saying, "Out of Egypt have I called my son" (Matt. 2:15 = Hos. 11:1). To apply Hosea's prophecy to the infant Jesus was to read into the passage a meaning never intended by the prophet. But there was a further group of prophecies of which Zechariah 9:9 (= Matt. 21:5; John 12:15) presents an example. Here the event of Jesus' entering Jerusalem upon an ass was deliberately contrived so that it would appear to be the fulfillment of prophecy.

It only remained for Reimarus to complete his case by unmasking the motives of the disciples. The latter had originally followed Jesus in the hope of material gain. These aspirations had been rudely shattered by the arrest and crucifixion of Jesus. When this happened, they were so petrified that they remained in hiding behind locked doors, lest a similar fate should befall them. They even left the burial of their master's corpse to the women and Nicodemus. Yet things turned out far better than they had dared to hope. The authorities had no intention of instigating a general persecution. As the days passed, their thoughts turned to the future. It dawned upon them that they were being confronted with the stark alternatives of returning to their former hard ways of life before they had thrown in their lot with Jesus or of finding some means of perpetuating their apparently lost cause. Reluctant to return to their former insignificance and, perhaps even worse, to having to earn their livings, and having little to lose and everything to gain, the disciples hit upon the plan detected and outlined by Reimarus.[32]

Undoubtedly, they were helped by the inactivity of the police, the indifference of the Romans, their own welfare work with its promise of future rewards, their sheer nerve and the spiritual blackmail practiced upon Ananias and Sapphira (Acts 5). They had also picked up from Jesus the trick of appearing to perform miracles.[33] The great testing time came with Pentecost when the disciples launched their fraud upon the public. While Reimarus was able to explain away the events described in Acts 2, most of the general public were not.[34] Thus Christianity became an institution which had fraudulently perpetuated itself down the centuries.

Such was the work which Schweitzer hailed as "perhaps the most splendid achievement in the whole course of the historical investigation of the life of Jesus."[35] In fact, it bore no small resemblance to Schweitzer's own treatment of the subject, not only in its conclusions but also in its presuppositions and method. Although both Reimarus and Schweitzer seized on eschatology as the key to understanding the Gospels, neither of them gave any credence to it. Schweitzer's high estimate of Reimarus was not, however, shared by the majority of Reimarus's immediate contemporaries who took a distinctly less favorable view of the whole enterprise.[36]

The Pamphlet War

The second batch of *Fragments*, published in 1777, had already provoked replies from various quarters. The first was the polite and respectful paper of Johann Daniel Schumann of Hanover, *Ueber die Evidenz der Beweise für die Wahrheit der christlichen Religion* (September 1777), which restated the traditional arguments from miracles and prophecy. The same year the Lutheran super-intendent at Wolfenbüttel, Johann Heinrich Ress, published a harmonization of the Gospel narratives, *Die Auferstehungsgeschichte Jesu Christi, gegen einige im vierten Beytrage ... gemachte neuere Einwendungen verteidigt.* But the most celebrated champion of orthodoxy in the conflict was the minister of the Lutheran Church of St. Catherine at Hamburg, Johann Melchior Goeze,[37] who directed his shafts more at Lessing than at the *Fragments* themselves.

To Goeze the publication of the *Fragments* represented a threat to the faith of believers. He took the view that Lessing would have been better advised to have published what he had found in Latin translation so that it could be discussed calmly by scholars without attracting the attention of the general public. Such a view clearly underestimated Lessing's real intentions, as did his naive request that Lessing should state frankly what he believed. Lessing was far too adroit an adversary to comply with such a plea. To the church-going public of the day a complete revelation of what Lessing thought would have served only to damn Lessing without more ado. Lessing's own views were diametrically opposed to the orthodoxy of the Chief Pastor who identified the Bible with revelation. To Goeze, Scripture represented the oral teaching and witness of the apostles. It was through Scripture alone that the Spirit spoke. In short, "The letter is the Spirit and the Bible is religion."

In the meantime Lessing suffered two grievous personal blows. On December 24, 1777, Lessing's wife Eva, whom he had married the previous year, gave birth to a child. The child died within hours and Eva died on January 10, 1778. Goeze bore the full brunt of Lessing's bitterness. To those so minded, pun and innuendo could be read into Lessing's references to his name. The Modern High German "Götze" means "idol." In earlier ages it was used as a familiar name, carrying the sense of "Dummkopf." Such meanings would hardly have been lost on Lessing.[38]

Lessing wasted little time in making his replies. He had already appended to the *Fragments* of 1777 his own *Gegensätze des Herausgegebers* which dis-claimed responsibility for the views expressed but endorsed the propriety of making them. He turned upon Schumann in *Ueber den Beweis des Geistes und der Kraft. An Den Herrn Director Schumann, zu Hannover* and the appended *Das Testament Johannis. Ein Gespräch* (1777) and against Ress in *Eine Duplik* (1778), which mocked his work as a "Harmony of wax noses, which will rescue each and every evangelist in every syllable." To attempt to harmonize the evange-lists was to ridicule them. Did not an enterprise "mock an honest historian, who is supposed to recount such stuff and nonsense ... just because the Holy Spirit guided his pen?" To this Ress replied in *Die Auferstehungsgeschichte Jesu Christi ohne Widersprüche gegen eine Duplik* (1779). However, it was Goeze who was the repeated target of Lessing's vituperations in *Eine Parabel. Nebst einer kleinen Bitte, und einem eventualen Absagungsschreiben an den Herrn Pastor Goeze, in Hamburg; Axiomata, wenn es deren in dergleichen Dingen giebt. Wider den*

*Herrn Pastor Goeze, in Hamburg; Anti-Goeze. D. i. Nothgedrungener Beyträge
zu den freywilligen Beyträgen des Hrn. Past. Goeze ERSTER. (Gott gebe, letzter!)*
and its ten successors; *Gotthold Ephraim Lessings nöthige Antwort auf eine sehr
unnöthige Frage des Herrn Hauptpastor Goeze, in Hamburg* and its sequel. All
these appeared in 1778.

These works raised issues far more significant than the immediate context of
Lessing's personal feuds might suggest. They will be considered later when we
turn to Lessing. In the meantime, on 13 July 1778 (while Lessing's most recent
assault upon Goeze was still in the press) the Duke of Brunswick informed him
that all his future religious writings would be subject to the censor. Lessing was
now obliged to return to his "former pulpit, the theater"[39] in order to veil his
continued polemics and disseminate his theological ideas. In the meantime the
Fragments drew into the debate not only the prominent Neologian, J. C.
Döderlein, but also the most formidable theological figure of the age, J. S.
Semler.

The Neologians

The term *Neologie* denotes a movement which reached its zenith in the
half-century between 1740 and 1790. In general, the Neologians sought to transcend both orthodoxy and pietism by restating the Christian faith in the light of
modern thought. To them, revelation was a confirmation of the truths of reason.
They drew a distinction between religion and theology, and between dogmas and
the Bible. In a sense they were pioneers of a moderate biblical criticism, maintaining that Jesus deliberately accommodated his teaching to the beliefs and
understanding of his hearers. Among the prominent Neologians were J. F. W.
Jerusalem, G. Less, F. V. Reinhard, A. F. W. Sack and J. J. Spalding. J. J.
Griesbach, J. G. Eichhorn, J. G. Herder, J. D. Michaelis and J. S. Semler are
also sometimes counted among their number. Neology found classic expression
in J. C. Döderlein's *Institutio Theologi Christiani in Capitibus Religionis Theo-
reticis nostris Temporibus accommodata* (1780; 6th ed., 1797). In dealing with
the two natures of Christ, Döderlein abandoned the traditional Lutheran doctrine
of the *communicatio idiomatum* and represented Jesus as a man bound to the
divine Logos by the bonds of love. But in dealing with the *Fragments*, Döderlein,
who was the only Neologian in the strict sense of the term to write a full-scale
refutation, was not prepared to tamper with orthodoxy. In his *Fragmente und
Antifragmente* (1778–79) he laid down the alternatives: "Either Jesus is risen or
he is a deceiver."[40] This choice of alternatives was, in fact, to accept the
Fragmentist's basic formulation of the problem but to reverse his verdict.

The Fragmentist's treatment of the resurrection prompted J. D. Michaelis's
Eklärung der Begräbnis- und Auferstehungsgeschichte Christi (1783) which was
followed by *Das 5. Fragment selbst mit Anmerkungen* (1785). By this time
Lessing was dead, and the controversy had lost its initial frenzy. In the meantime
the whole debate received the considered attention of the *Allgemeine Deutsche*

Bibliothek and its principal reviewer, F. G. Lüdke. The *Allgemeine Deutsche Bibliothek* had been founded in 1765 by C. F. Nicolai and ran through 268 volumes before it was terminated in 1806. It was probably the single most influential organ of the German Enlightenment. Lüdke ministered at the Church of St. Nicolai in Berlin and had clashed with Goeze on the subject of the dogmatic authority of the confessions in *Vom falschem Religionseifer* (1767). Reviewing Döderlein's work, Lüdke attempted to steer a middle course between the Fragmentist's skepticism and the latter's insistence upon the historicity of the Gospel narratives. Döderlein had gone too far in a conservative direction. Lüdke believed that the spiritual significance of the Gospels could be salvaged without having to defend every part as historical. The disciples may have allowed their senses to be deceived, but Jesus was no deceiver. In a manner perhaps anticipating Tillich and Bultmann, he insisted that, "His resurrected corpse actually helps us in nothing, but his glorified Spirit will help us eternally, if we live, have patience and hope according to his gospel."[41]

In general, the Neologians viewed the debate with a detached and even patronizing air, though not all remained so aloof as J. W. F. Jerusalem who, despite the pleas of a Jewish convert, refused to intervene.[42] As the battle dragged on, Lüdke and the *Allgemeine Deutsche Bibliothek* awarded prizes and black marks for the points made, regularly reminding its readers that much of what was being said had already been said before.[43] Although much of what the Fragmentist was saying might sound new and shocking to German ears, similar views had been expressed in England half a century before by Deistic writers like Woolston and Collins.

The plea of the first *Fragment* for reason to be given freer rein was already outdated. The author's dependence upon the English Deists was calmly pointed out. His attacks upon the authors and heroes of the Bible were put down to his vexation over the doctrine of verbal inspiration. His complaints against the Old Testament could only be regarded as somewhat naïve. Had not scholars like Jerusalem, Michaelis, Eichhorn and Herder already pointed out that the latter belonged to the infancy of humanity and therefore was to be understood not as philosophy but as poetry? The Fragmentist had fallen into the error of failing to relate the biblical personalities to their historical background, which in turn had led him into the error of judging them by modern, enlightened standards. At the same time, he failed to perceive the moral values inculcated by apparently morally offensive stories like the sacrifice of Isaac (Gen. 22:1–12).

Turning to the New Testament, the Fragmentist was to be faulted for his lack of method in evaluating its sources. In particular, he was taken to task for his circular argument: that the evangelists were deceivers because they represent Jesus the politician as a harmless moralist, and this picture of Christ was false precisely because they were deceivers. Moreover, the Fragmentist's reconstruction of events was psychologically impossible. The compound of deceit and sublimity, which he attributed in part to Jesus but above all to the apostles, was beyond credibility. At best the *Allgemeine Deutsche Bibliothek* damned with faint praise. Its attitude might be compared with Lessing's verdict on Voltaire: "The first step of wisdom is to understand the false; the second is to perceive the true." Unfortunately, the second step had not been taken.[44]

Semler

Of all the replies that were made to the *Fragments* the weightiest both in bulk and prestige was that of J. S. Semler. Johann Salomo Semler (1725–91) has been credited with being "the founder of the historical study of the New Testament"[45] and with bringing about "the historical change from old to modern Protestant theology."[46] Two years after his death the Old Testament scholar, J. G. Eichhorn, wrote, "In church history the newest epoch of our times began with Semler." He was "the first reformer of our theology, the boldest and the most widely read, the theologian richest in research and results."[47]

In his student days at Halle, Semler found refuge from the pietism of his home background in the person of his teacher, S. J. Baumgarten, whose rational and historical investigations pointed in the direction of the modern critical approach but whose conservatism kept him tied to the traditional outlook. After his death, Semler felt that the time had come to cut loose from orthodox dogmatism. But he did not do so without inner turmoil. In his autobiography he recalled, "I have made myself many an anxious hour, so that I could pit my own perception which is only in early stages against so many books."[48] In 1752 Semler became professor of theology at Halle. Under his leadership Halle became one of the leading, if not the dominant, center of liberal, critical theology in the eighteenth century.

Semler was one of the first to talk about *liberal theology*.[49] Freedom of thought and conscience belonged to the Protestant principle.[50] In his pro-grammatic, epoch-making *Abhandlung von freier Untersuchung des Canon* (4 parts, 1771–75)[51] Semler drew a sharp distinction between "Holy Scripture" and "Word of God," and could lament how little this distinction was recognized even by theological teachers in his own day.[52] All Scripture was not equally the Word of God; not every part taught *moral* truths valid for all mankind of every age. The Jews had their own *Mythologie* just like other nations.[53] In the light of historical development one could no longer appeal to the doctrine of inspiration as a guarantee of the text of Scripture as the Word of God.[54] Nor indeed may appeal be made to the teaching of Jesus and the apostles who accommodated their teaching to their hearers' presuppositions and limitations.[55] The Gospels themselves were not intended to be universally valid, definitive histories, but each grew out of a particular historical context.[56]

In making these points, Semler was conscious that he was building on foundations already laid by others. Baumgarten, William Whiston (on whom he had written his master's dissertation) and others had taught a doctrine of accommodation.[57] The Catholic theologian, Richard Simon, whose teaching

Semler helped to propagate, had pioneered a historical and critical appraisal of Scripture.[58] What Semler urged—and in no small measure achieved—was a general, reverent and judicious acceptance of the new critical approach to Scripture. It was precisely these qualities that were lacking in the final *Fragment* which was causing dismay and bewilderment among theological students, some of whom were even seeking other vocations.[59] At first Semler hesitated about replying. But his answer was not long in coming, and when it came it dealt a sledge-hammer blow. The *Beantwortung der Fragmente eines Ungenannten insbesondere vom Zweck Jesu und seiner Jünger* (1779) numbered 452 pages and was accompanied by an *Anhang zur Beantwortung der Fragmente des Unge-nannten. Bekant gemacht von D. Joh. Salomo Semler* (1779) of 32 pages. Although he described the Fragmentist's manner as "repugnant, frivolous, wholly mocking and thoroughly hostile,"[60] he paid him the compliment not only of producing a revised version,[61] but also of examining the Fragmentist's argument almost sentence by sentence. In the manner of Origen's *Contra Celsum*, Semler reproduced his adversary's text section by section and dealt with him point by point.

From time to time Semler exploited the faulty logic and self-contradictions of the Fragmentist, as when the latter wrote,

> Just as there can be no doubt then that Jesus directed men (Jews and non-Jews) to the true, great goal of a religion, viz. an eternal blessedness, so only the question remains for us what goal Jesus himself had in his teaching and actions.

Semler acidly commented,

> As important as is the first part of this utterance, that Jesus led men to the true goal of a religion, to an eternal blessedness, by his teaching and actions, so strange is then the following thesis: *so only the question remains for us*—who can conceive *another* totally *opposed goal that Jesus had*, if it is beyond *doubt*, that Jesus led men to the true goal of a religion, to an eternal blessedness?[62]

But such criticisms could only expose the chinks in his opponent's armor. By themselves they did not demonstrate the impregnability of the Christian faith. This could only be done by painstaking exegesis and historical criticism. It was to this task that the bulk of Semler's reply was devoted.

The Fragmentist had made much of the command to repent and believe the gospel of the kingdom, which, in the absence of any qualifying explanations, he took to mean the establishment of an earthly theocracy under a messiah. Semler countered by denying that the meaning of the kingdom was left unexplained. Passages like Matthew 3, 5 and 19 showed that it had moral significance, quite different from the accepted ideas of Jesus' contemporaries.[63] On the question of whether Jesus wanted to found a new religion different from Judaism, Semler used his knowledge of Philo and rabbinics to show that the idea of a spiritual religion superseding Judaism was not something invented by the apostles.[64] Later on Semler explained that Jesus kept the ceremonial law in order to invest it with a spiritual significance.[65]

Turning to the Fragmentist's contention that the doctrine of the Trinity was utterly foreign to Jesus' thinking, Semler admitted that *homoousios* and the Trinitarian vocabulary of later ages were not to be found in the New Testament. Nevertheless, the substance of the thought was there. But here as elsewhere in the book, Semler's argument falls short of carrying complete conviction. Instead of producing the proof, Semler contented himself with exploring the historical significance of the terms without defending them by a fresh evaluation of biblical evidence.[66] The same is to some extent true of his treatment of the term *Son of God*. Semler conceded that the Fragmentist's interpretation was broadly correct so far as the Old Testament was concerned. But the term had a more specialized meaning outside Palestinian Judaism. It was the apostles who perceived the real significance of the term.[67] Here again a crucial link in the argument seems to be missing. Semler's discussion leaves open the question of whether Jesus himself knew of the wider context of the term, or deliberately used it in a special sense, and what historical justification the primitive church had for its use of the term.

An important part of Semler's strategy was his attempt to outflank the Fragmentist by showing that not only did Jesus transcend Judaism, but that messianic expectation did so as well. The Fragmentist had argued that the Trinitarian baptismal formula of Matthew 28:19 was the invention of the church. Semler dismissed this as an argument *a silentio ad negationem*. In any case, Jesus had spoken of the Father and the Holy Spirit long before (John 3 and 7).[68] Semler's approach is epitomized by a remark summing up his discussion of the baptismal formula.

> I have shown above that the Jews expected exactly from the messiah *a new and special religion*. The Unnamed Author wanted, however, to denigrate equally by his work the Christian and Jewish religions, in order to establish himself as a Deist.[69]

If Semler fell short of conclusively demonstrating the historicity of the Gospel narratives, he succeeded in raising serious questions about the Fragmentist's motivation and explanations. The linchpin of the Fragmentist's case was the assertion that Jesus understood himself in terms of certain Jewish, semi-political expectations and no more. By showing that Jewish expectations were by no means so materialistic as the Fragmentist made out, Semler had at least given a feasible alternative interpretation of Jesus' actions.

Semler's *Beantwortung* painstakingly worked its way through the main events of the Gospels, offering at each point an alternative explanation to that of the *Fragment*. A special interest attaches to Semler's treatment of Old Testament prophecy and the resurrection of Jesus, not only in view of the Fragmentist's dismissal of both as spurious with the corollary that Christianity was therefore fraudulent, but also in view of Semler's own more liberal approach to the Bible. Semler wanted to defend both but not quite on the same grounds as the orthodox.

A distinct note of caution can be detected in Semler's handling of prophecy. It was legitimate for the early Christians to use the Old Testament in the way they did, for this was their common ground with the Jews.[70] But for the educated man of the eighteenth century, the situation had changed. Christianity was to be vindicated not by the fulfillment of predictions but by its basic truths.

> The *New Covenant* has partly already overthrown Judaism and paganism and partly superseded it, certainly with regard to its content. Thus it is spread increasingly among men. And this is also the sole purpose of Christian teachers *in still appealing* to these prophecies which are there among the Jews in such documents. But *we do not prove from prophecy the content of Christianity*, or the *basic truths* which constitute the Christian religion and elevate it above Judaism and paganism. We know them from the teaching of Jesus and the apostles. And now people either accept or reject this content.[71]

Needless to say, Semler would not attempt to use the argument from fulfilled prophecy against the Deists.[72]

In the last analysis, the question of whether any given prophecy has been fulfilled is a matter of private opinion. Both the prophecy and the fulfillment may be symbolic. What was significant for the Jewish mind may no longer be so for us today. The use of Hosea 11:1 in Matthew 2:15 and the play on the word "Nazarene" in Matthew 2:23 were cases in point. The facts of the Exodus and Jesus' childhood in Egypt were true. But Hebrew hermeneutics loved riddles and the detection of hidden meanings in the text. Therefore, both passages were significant and valid for Jewish readers but not necessarily for others.[73] In other words, Semler's treatment of prophecy was an extension of his principle of accommodation. The validity of a point depended not only, or even primarily, upon the point itself but upon the presuppositions of the speaker and especially of the hearer.

On the subject of the resurrection of Jesus, Semler insisted that many of the Fragmentist's objections had to do with surface details. These would indeed be fatal to the old doctrine of inspiration, but they prove trivial when historical techniques are applied. Semler was not interested in harmonizing every detail.[74] It had to be remembered that the Gospels were written under different circumstances and at different times, the earliest perhaps some thirty years after the death of Jesus. In the circumstances discrepancies were only to be expected. Indeed, the later evangelists like Mark and Luke could easily have touched up the text to produce a harmony if their intentions had been to propagate a fabricated story that was consistent in every detail. But the modern reader may safely bypass all this. The resurrection does not depend "on this or that set of circumstances." The apostle Paul does not even mention the women in his account in 1 Corinthians 15. Since the apostles themselves did not commit any contradictions and since there were many thousands of preachers and Christians before the Greek text of the narratives got into such disarray, *"the ground of the Christian religion stands now as before."*[75]

To Semler, the resurrection of Jesus was "no mere *physical* event," capable of being seen by the human eye.

> It is a *supernatural event*, the intrinsic possibility of which was granted by the Pharisees and many others. But it does not at all follow that the Risen One must necessarily strike the senses, just as a tree, a mountain, a bird, etc. It stands firmly in his particular will, to whom he will appear. Only he can see him.... All these objections and long-winded answers—the speculation and invention of the human mind—fall at once away, because the resurrection of Jesus was no natural event, subject to the laws of motion and the senses. It constituted a free effect of the living Jesus which he himself determined and ordered for his ultimate purpose.[76]

For this reason the objection was irrelevant that only believers witnessed the risen Christ, for in the nature of the case it could hardly be otherwise. So too was Edelmann's view that the body of Jesus was never found because it was buried by the earthquake that shook Jerusalem after his death.[77] Semler himself could think up other possible explanations, such as that Jesus did not actually die but was revived by Joseph of Arimathea.[78]

However, all this inverted the true order of faith. One does not believe because of some irrefragable historical evidence. Belief in the risen Christ follows from acceptance of his teaching and Christian experience. In reply to the Fragmentist's contention that Jesus' resurrection and ascension were invented by the apostles to fit the course of events and thus became the fraudulent "foundation stone of their new doctrinal edifice," Semler retorted,

> This last point is utterly and thoroughly false. The precepts of Jesus concerning general religion and participation in the Holy Spirit were *preserved* by them as the ground of *their doctrinal* edifice. And now they have added to it the precept of their own experience, even the Jesus who taught this, who you executed on account of it, and is risen from the dead. Firmly they believed it and told it everywhere....And now Christians endorse even this historical precept, *but as a consequence* of the teaching of Jesus. Anyone who did not believe the teaching of Jesus could believe this historical precept as a consequence and proof of the Pharisaical system, as is told of Herod that he believed that John was risen again. And he was from the ground of Christianity even more far removed.[79]

Elsewhere Semler continued in similar vein, drawing a sharp distinction between historical and spiritual truths.[80] It was on this note that he rounded off his work. Even if all the contemporaries of Jesus had seen and touched him, it would not have fitted God's purposes. For seeing and touching belong to the realm of nature and the senses.

> This is quite different from belief in those truths, to the content of which all the senses contribute nothing....Have we Christians really said here anything so unreasonable? Enough that we believe and practice the Christian religion according to the precepts of Christ in a spiritual way, therefore, so that it comes to all men likewise in their own experience in all times and places as long as the world stands.

We compel no Deist to this faith, because it is utterly impossible. But neither can any Deist tear from our soul this true Christian faith.[81]

With the publication of Semler's *Beantwortung*, the *Fragments* controversy began to fizzle out. Albert Schweitzer put this down not so much to the effectiveness of Semler's answer as to "the respect in which Semler was held, and the absolute incapacity of contemporary theology to overtake the long stride forward made by Reimarus." The result was that Reimarus's work "was neglected, and the stimulus which it was capable of imparting failed to take effect." Indeed, the fact was that "Semler had nothing in the nature of a complete or well-articulated argument to oppose him." But Reimarus had posthumous revenge by shaking Semler's faith in historical theology and the freedom of science, which finally induced him to give approval to Wöllner's edict for the regulation of religion (1788).[82]

Such a verdict is unjust and misleading. Semler may not have achieved a spectacular knockout, but at least he had earned a solid points victory. His painstaking examination of the Gospel narratives achieved two things: it showed that Reimarus's interpretation was frequently at variance with the text of the New Testament and that in the light of the latter's background a more or less traditional interpretation was at least feasible. If the Fragmentist could appeal to the notion of the kingdom and say that it had quasi-political associations, Semler could point to Philo and strands of rabbinic and Hellenistic teaching to show that spiritual interpretations of religion also belonged to the background of the Gospels. This type of reply is apt to induce a feeling of stalemate because it stops short of proving that one's opponent's view is inadmissible and that one's own is the only one tenable.

To later generations Semler's reply would also fail to carry complete conviction because of its significant omission to evaluate sources. In dealing with the resurrection, Semler suggested that Matthew might well have been written some thirty years after the death of Jesus and the other Gospels still later. Matthew and John were disciples; the other evangelists were not. Each work had been written under different circumstances and for different purposes. All this could well explain the differences between the various resurrection narratives and adequately account for the difficulties so eagerly seized upon by the Fragmentist as proof that the whole affair was a fraud. The same point had been used in his treatment of the canon to show that the Gospels were not intended to be universally valid, definitive histories. But neither here nor later on did Semler show any interest in source criticism. He failed — as did the Fragmentist[83] — to grasp the significance of an evaluation of the authorship, date, intentions and method of a work as a necessary condition of a proper evaluation of its contents. The program of a historical appreciation of the Bible for which Semler had campaigned so much of his life was only partially carried through.

Nevertheless, Semler had made a valid point when he pleaded for a sympathetic hermeneutic that would not prejudge prophecy by modern standards, but that would seek to understand the minds of its original recipients. Moreover, he had raised the question of history and faith. Admittedly, Semler did not get much beyond the reiteration that the two were quite different. Certain of his utterances could be construed as typical expressions of Enlightened belief that what matters in religion is rational, moral teaching and the appropriate response. Such pronouncements could well have been lifted straight out of Lessing. But for Semler, Jesus was more than a teacher of moral religion. If belief in his resurrection stems mainly from his teaching, which in turn predisposes one to certain views of history, there is something in that teaching which generates belief and gives the believer a new outlook in a way which historical data do not. Semler stopped well short of saying that history was simply the occasion and expression of eternal ideas. But he did not elaborate on why he accepted a supernatural framework for history, though clearly it was not prompted by the miraculous as such, and the supernatural pertains more to the metaphysical framework of history than to the events which occur within it.[84] It would almost seem to be a matter of existential involvement in the teaching of Jesus that was the deciding factor in Christian belief and one's general outlook. This view could not be forced upon the Deist; but neither could the Deist undermine it. But the fact was that Semler was no philosopher. He did not progress far beyond affirming these basic ideas. It fell to Lessing, whom Semler belabored for publishing the *Fragments*[85] and whom Schweitzer largely ignored, to take up this crucial aspect of the debate.

2. LESSING AND THE RELEVANCE OF HISTORY

Although a layman, Gotthold Ephraïm Lessing (1729–81) was no novice in theological matters. The son of a Saxon pastor, he was brought up in the atmosphere of orthodoxy charged with the pietism of Herrnhut. At school in Meissen, he spent twenty-five hours a week on religious studies, and in 1746 he went to Leipzig to study theology. However, his absorbing interest was the stage for which he abandoned his theological studies. Already in Leipzig he imbibed the popular philosophy of the Enlightenment. At Berlin (1748–60) he got to know personally numerous leaders of enlightened thought. Among them were the Neological author and founder of the *Allgemeine Deutsche Bibliothek*, Friedrich Nicolai, and the prominent Jewish enlightened thinker, Moses Mendelssohn.

The middle period of Lessing's life saw him emerge as an eminent literary critic and dramatist, whose work played a major part in the creation of modern German literature. During his years at Breslau (1760–65) he not only wrote his comedy *Minna von Barnhelm* and his essay on poetry and painting, *Laokoon*; he also made a study of Leibniz, Spinoza and the church fathers. In 1767 Lessing moved to Hamburg as consultant and critic to the short-lived National Theater. It was in this period that he developed his friendship with the Reimarus family. In

1769 the Duke of Brunswick offered Lessing the post of librarian in the Ducal Library at Wolfenbüttel. In 1771 he became a Freemason. His patron at Wolfenbüttel was Grand Master of the German lodges. The *Beiträge zur Geschichte und Literatur aus den Schätzen der Herzoglichen Bibliothek zu Wolfenbüttel*, into which the *Fragments* were judiciously inserted, commenced publication in 1773. It was only at this late stage in his career that Lessing entered the arena of public theological debate. Lessing had sought and failed to obtain the censor's approval to publish the whole work in Berlin in 1771. He now tried a new tack. On the grounds of their alleged historical interest the Duke exempted the *Beiträge* from censorship. Under the shelter of this umbrella Lessing took the opportunity to join in the fray. When the exemption was revoked, he carried on the battle with his drama, *Nathan der Weise* (1779) and *Ernst und Falk. Gespräche für Freymaurer* (1778–80).

In publishing the second set of *Fragments*, Lessing appended a series of *Gegensätze des Herausgebers*.[1] These were in part a disclaimer of parenthood of the doctrines contained in the *Fragments* and in part a blast against the clergy who were opposed to them. The role which Lessing cast for himself in the whole affair oscillated between that of a midwife and that of an advocate. Although his comments on particular issues make it far from clear whether he saw himself in the latter capacity as counsel for the defense or counsel for the prosecution, Lessing's opening remarks indicate the general direction in which his mind was moving.

> And now enough of these fragments. Any of my readers who would prefer me to have spared them altogether is surely more timid than well instructed. He may be a very devout Christian, but he is certainly not a very enlightened one. He may be wholehearted in his upholding of his religion; but he ought also to have greater confidence in it.
>
> For how much could be said in reply to all these objections and difficulties! And even if absolutely no answer were forthcoming, what then? The learned theologian might in the last resort be embarrassed, but certainly not the Christian. To the former it might at most cause confusion to see the supports with which he would uphold religion shattered in this way, to find the buttresses cast down by which, God willing, he would have made it safe and sound. But how do this man's hypotheses, explanations, and proofs affect the Christian? For it is simply a fact—the Christianity which he feels to be true and in which he feels blessed. When the paralytic feels the beneficial shocks of the electric spark, does it worry him whether Nollet or Franklin or neither of them is right?
>
> In short, the letter is not the spirit, and the Bible is not religion. Consequently, objections to the letter and to the Bible are not also objections to the spirit and to religion.
>
> For the Bible obviously contains more than is essential to religion, and it is a mere hypothesis to assert that it must be equally infallible in this excess of matter. Moreover, religion was there before a Bible existed. Christianity was there before the evangelists and apostles wrote. A long period elapsed before the first of them wrote,

and a very considerable time before the entire canon was complete. Therefore while much may depend upon these writings, it is impossible to suppose that the entire truth of the religion depends upon them. If there was a period in which it had already spread far and in which it had gained many souls, and when, nevertheless, not a letter of that which has come down to us had yet been written down, then it must also be possible that everything which the evangelists and apostles wrote could have been lost, and yet that the religion which they taught would have continued. The religion is not true because the evangelists and apostles taught it; but they taught it because it is true. The written traditions must be interpreted by their inward truth and no written traditions can give the religion any inward truth if it has none.

This, therefore, would be the general answer to a large part of these fragments, as I have said, in the worst case.[2]

This was perhaps the nearest that Lessing ever came to making a public confession of faith. It contains much that deliberately raises (and begs) questions that were to recur in his polemical pamphlets. Lessing's thought may best be brought into focus if we consider in turn three related issues: (1) Lessing's view of reason, revelation and history; (2) his view of historical religion; and (3) his view of Christian origins.

Reason, Revelation and History

It was not long before Lessing again took up the question of revelation and history. He did so in his reply to Schumann in the brief but significant essay *Ueber den Beweis des Geistes und der Kraft* and the appended dialogue *Das Testament Johannis*. Together these works develop the twofold thesis announced in the *Gegensätze*. On the one hand, historical testimony can never be more than tenuous and doubtful. But on the other hand, the truth of religion does not depend upon it. The central truths of religion are, in fact, self-evident to those who practice religion. The two works were complementary, each concentrating on one aspect of the main thesis.

Ueber den Beweis des Geistes und der Kraft examined a weapon familiar in the armory of the Christian apologist since the second century and which ultimately derives from the New Testament: the proof of Christianity from prophecy and miracle.[3] As we shall see in the next chapter, it was precisely this which was the focal point of the English Deists' attack on orthodox Christianity. Lessing's title took up a phrase from Origen's *Contra Celsum*, which in turn echoed the apostle Paul's claim that his speech and message were not in plausible words of wisdom "but in demonstration of the Spirit and power" (1 Cor. 2:4). Ironically it was designed to underline the contrast between orthodoxy and what Lessing considered to be the truth. Origen had observed that, "the proof of power is so called because of the astonishing miracles which have happened to confirm the teaching of Christ."[4] Lessing complained that miracles and prophecy no longer constitute a proof of power because they are no longer admissible as evidence. Had he lived in the days of Christ and had direct experience of the events in question, he would have had no difficulty in believing. Alternatively, if miracles had continued down to the present day, as Origen apparently believed that they did in his, there would again be no difficulty. The trouble with history is that it comes to us at second, third, fourth and fifth hand (and so on almost *ad infinitum*). As such, it cannot be binding. Even so, the deliciously ironical qualifications that Lessing applied to historical events, had he himself been an eyewitness, set a great question mark against what may be inferred from them. His own views turned out to resemble more those of Celsus than of Origen's. To be more precise, the negative criticisms of Reimarus were an eighteenth-century counterpart to the negative criticisms of Celsus, whereas the positive views of Lessing on religion were not unlike the philosophy of Celsus.

All this takes us a step beyond Hume's argument against miracles of some thirty years previously which itself was propounded nearly twenty years after the height of the Deistic controversy.[5] While deliberately refraining from mentioning the Gospel miracles or the resurrection of Jesus, Hume argued that miracles were contradictions of the laws of nature. The actual testimony to them was weak since they were invariably performed in obscure corners of the globe and witnessed by ill-educated persons of uncertain character and intelligence. It was irrational to accept miracles or, for that matter, prophecy (which was only a form of miracle). Hume concluded with the ironical comment that Christianity was founded on faith, not reason.

At this stage Lessing made no attempt to evaluate criteria for establishing the historicity of miracles or of anything else. His views on the origin and value of the New Testament writings were not to be published during his lifetime. Lessing did not deny (at least for the purposes of argument) that "the reports of miracles and prophecies are as reliable as historical truths ever can be." What he did deny was that such reports could ever be compelling or even relevant for the foundation of religious belief. He crowned his argument with the celebrated axiom,

> If no historical truth can be demonstrated, then nothing can be demonstrated by means of historical truths.
> That is: *accidental truths of history can never become the proof of necessary truths of reason.*[6]

In propounding this part of his thesis, Lessing had not so much presented a reasoned chain of arguments as restated the same point in a number of different ways. The crucial term was the word "demonstrated." Lessing did not entertain the question of whether events in the past might be established beyond all reasonable doubt by means of evaluating historical evidence. Nor was he concerned with the verification of propositions by means of controlled experiment. Rather, Lessing was reiterating an axiom of continental rationalism since Descartes, that only clear and distinct ideas may serve as the basis of a system of thought. The ideal of knowledge was geometry with its self-evident definitions, axioms and logically necessary deductions. The thought was exemplified in Spinoza's *Ethica Ordine Geometrico Demonstrata* (1677) with its repeated *Q.E.D.* at the end of each argument. The ideal of rationality lay behind Spinoza's critique of miracles and revealed religion and also of the Deists' critique. Leibniz had explained the point underlying Lessing's axiom in numerous places, including an essay on "Necessary and Contingent Truths" (ca. 1686), his *Nouveaux Essais sur l'entendement humain*, 1, 1, 5 (1704) and his *Monadologie*, 33 (1714). Lessing's distinction between "accidental truths" and "necessary truths" corresponds to the distinction that Kant made between "synthetic" and "analytic judgments" in his *Kritik der reinen Vernunft* (1781), which was published in the year of Lessing's death. Lessing's argument was not the introduction of a new thought into philosophy. Its novelty lay in Lessing's application of the idea within the internal polemics of Protestant theology.

To Lessing the situation could be compared with the discovery of "a very useful mathematical truth" through "an obvious fallacy."[7] Recognition of the fallacious means of discovery would not invalidate the truth. As Lessing's argument develops, two main reservations concerning historical assertions may be discerned. The first is the intrinsic uncertainty about all historical claims which may turn out to be ill-founded. Thus, Alexander's conquest of Asia may be founded "on a mere poem of Choerilus just as the ten-year siege of Troy depends on no better authority than Homer's poetry."[8] The second difficulty concerns the status of truth-claims handed down by history. Lessing had no problem in believing that such and such a historical person believed this or that. The crucial question was whether their beliefs and assertions could be binding on subsequent generations.

> If on historical grounds I have no objection to the statement that this Christ himself rose from the dead, must I therefore accept it as true that this risen Christ was the Son of God?
> That the Christ, against whose resurrection I can raise no important historical objection, therefore declared himself to be the Son of God; that his disciples therefore believed him to be such; this I gladly believe from my heart. For these truths, as truths of one and the same class, follow quite naturally on one another.
> But to jump with that historical truth to a quite different class of truths, and to demand of me that I should form all my metaphysical and moral ideas accordingly; to expect me to alter all my fundamental ideas of the nature of the Godhead because I cannot set any credible testimony against the resurrection of Christ: if that is not a *metabasis eis allo genos*, then I do not know what Aristotle meant by this phrase.[9]

Lessing's view was to be echoed by generations of German theologians down to Günther Bornkamm who asserted that "the last historical fact" available to scholars is not the resurrection but "the Easter faith of the disciples."[10] The observation drew from Alan Richardson the reply that the historian cannot admit any "last facts," for they would be "causeless events." To Richardson, history was a "causal nexus" and no events were "in principle inexplicable," even if one had to look for metaphysical and theological explanations.[11] But for Lessing, truth-claims based on appeals to history presented "the ugly broad ditch which I cannot get across, however often and however earnestly I have tried to make the leap. If anyone can help me over it, let him do it, I beg him, I adjure him. He will deserve a divine reward of me."[12] Despite these protestations, Lessing saw no need to leap across the ditch. For the basis of religion did not lie in history. Anyone who got the point of what Lessing was saying would see that it was itself *a necessary truth of reason.* Lessing concluded his remarks with the triumphant announcement that it was the teachings of Christianity that bound him and the enigmatic wish, "May all who are divided by the Gospel of John be reunited by the Testament of John. Admittedly it is apocryphal, this testament. But it is not on that account any less divine."[13]

The fact that what Lessing called *The Testament of John* is woven around an apocryphal story gives it added point. Its historical origin is contained in a remark of Jerome which Lessing appended to his dialogue.[14] When the disciples of the aged John became bored with the same old daily exhortation, "Little children, love one another," they asked him why he always said the same thing. To this the apostle replied, "Because it is the Lord's command; because this alone, if it is done, is enough, is sufficient and adequate."[15] This, Lessing added, was the Testament of John. It was practical. It was an axiom which was self-evident to all rational men. It did not depend upon the shifting sands of history. Nor was it bound up with the dogmas of the church. Love of one's fellow was the essence of revelation and the basis of true religion.

Historical Religion

This view of history at once raises questions about the truth and value of religion in its historical forms. For his contemporaries it was by no means easy to discover what precisely Lessing believed. His polemical works invariably threw a smokescreen around Lessing's private beliefs,[16] and his most personal pronouncements were written down in fragments first published posthumously by his brother, Karl. Here he appears to oscillate between Deism and pantheism. In some notes *Ueber die Enstehung der geoffenbarten Religion*, he leaned toward the former.[17] But in *Ueber die Wirklichkeit der Dinge ausser Gott*[18] and *Das Christentum der Vernunft*,[19] Lessing spoke like a pantheist. In the latter he declared,

> 1. The one most perfect Being has from eternity been able to be concerned only with the one consideration of what is the most perfect thing.
>
> 2. The most perfect thing is himself; and thus from eternity God has only been able to contemplate himself.

On the meaning of the term *Son of God* Lessing commented,

> 6. This being is called in Scripture the Son of God, or, which would be still better, the Son-God. A god because he lacks none of the attributes which belong to God. A

Son because according to our ideas that which conceives a thing has a certain priority to the conception.

7. This being is God himself and is not to be distinguished from God because one thinks of it as soon as one thinks of God, and one cannot think of it without God; that is, because one cannot think of God without God, or because that would be no God at all from whom one could take away his own conception.

The practical outcome of all this is the recognition that *moral beings* are beings which follow a law.

26. This law is derived from their own nature, and can be none other than: *Act according to your individual perfections.*

Such thinking was virtually an echo of Spinoza's *Ethics*.[20]

From Lessing's death to the present day, friends and foes have keenly debated whether Lessing was a theist, a Deist or a Spinozist.[21] In public he adopted the stance of an enlightened well-wisher of the Protestant faith. Perhaps this was as far and as wise as he deemed prudent to go. But even in his private professions of Spinozism among friends, Lessing may have been playing the devil's advocate — at least in part.[22] During a visit to Wolfenbüttel in July 1780, F. H. Jacobi had shown Lessing a copy of Goethe's poem *Prometheus*, assuming that Goethe's irreverence would shock him. However, Lessing declared that "orthodox ideas of the deity" were not for him. His own creed was contained in the pagan Greek formula *Hen kai Pan* ("One and all") which also fitted Goethe's sentiments. In subsequent conversation Lessing went on to endorse Spinoza and to declare Leibniz to be a Spinozist at heart.

Jacobi's revelation of Lessing's professed pantheism and affinity with Spinoza in open letters addressed to Mendelssohn shocked the enlightened public and drew angry protests from the Jewish scholar.[23] However, these posthumous disclosures were preceded by the professions of faith contained by the dramatic poem *Nathan der Weise* (1779) and the essay *Die Erziehung des Menschengeschlechts* (1780). Both were concerned with the truth, function and value of religion within the framework of history.

Lessing had completed the main outline of *Nathan der Weise* by November 1778. In making his final revisions he sent a copy to Mendelssohn, whose suggestions were incorporated in the final form. The hero was in fact modeled on Mendelssohn. Although there was a good deal of Lessing in him, Alexander Altmann remarks with justice that, "*Nathan* without Mendelssohn would have been like *Hamlet* without the Prince of Denmark."[24] Other characters were identifiable, including Goeze as the Patriarch. The play was Lessing's first to be written in verse. He now modified the rule that he had laid down in his *Hamburgische Dramaturgie*: that reasoning should be reserved for comedy and passion for tragedy. The play was neither a comedy nor a tragedy. For this reason he provided it with the description *Ein dramatisches Gedicht*.

In *Nathan der Weise* the three great religions are represented by the three main characters: Nathan the Jew, Saladin the Moslem and the Knight Templar. The climax comes in Act III, scene 7, where Saladin asks Nathan which of the three religions is true. The latter replies with an allegory adapted from Boccaccio's *Decameron* and other sources. There was once an ancient ring which had the power to bestow upon its owner the gift of being loved by God and man. This gift was passed on to the favorite son of the original owner and so on down many generations, until it came into the possession of a father who had three sons, all equally dear to him. To resolve his dilemma he had two replicas made and gave a ring to each son. After his death all three claimed to possess the true ring. But, as with religion, the original cannot be traced. Historical investigation is of no avail. A judge, brought in to arbitrate, suggests in exasperation that perhaps none of them is genuine. Perhaps the father no longer wanted to tolerate "the tyranny of the one ring" over his house. It is clear that none of the brothers at present is beloved by all, which raises doubt as to whether any of them possesses the ring. However, the judge advises the brothers each to behave as if he possessed the true ring and thereby prove the truth of his claims. The play ends with the discovery of mutual kinship and joyful reconciliation.

There is here the familiar eighteenth-century enlightened plea for tolerance and recognition that the truth transcends all creeds and particular forms of religion. Rousseau had made such a plea nearly two decades earlier in his *Émile*.[25] There is more than a hint of Lessing's freemasonry with its kindred appeal for universal brotherhood and transcendence of the positive religions. But above these themes an existential note may also be heard. True religion is not a body of dogmas demanding mental assent, but truth discovered in life. It cannot be verified *a priori* by rational argument or appeal to history, but only *a posteriori* and experimentally. The practice carries with it its own justification, and to that extent its truth is self-evident. This note was already sounded in the *Gegensätze des Herausgebers*, where Lessing argued that the letter was not the spirit, and compared religion with the therapeutic shock treatment. It did not matter whose particular theories were right, so long as the treatment worked. The argument recurred in *Das Testament Johannis* and in a celebrated passage in *Eine Duplik* where Lessing argued,

> It is not truth, the possession or imagined possession of which, that makes the worth of a man, but honest pains to get behind the truth. For it is not through possession, but through the persistent search for truth that his powers expand, in which alone consists all his ever-growing perfection. Possession makes a man complacent, lazy, proud.
>
> If God held closed in his right hand all truth and in his left the single ever active drive to truth, even with the qualification of having to err continually for ever, and said to me, "Choose!" I would fall with humility on his left and would say, "Father, give! The pure truth is yours and yours alone."[26]

It was because of this insight into the fragmentary and existential character of religious truth that Lessing was reluctant to jettison positive religion in favor of an enlightened abstract religion. To his enemies this doubtless seemed to be just another piece of Lessing's prevarication. Yet for Lessing it had its justification in his belief that history presented the occasion but not the ground of religious truth, and that therefore this truth was not bound absolutely to any one form of religion, but neither was it to be divorced from religion in its historical forms. Furthermore, religion in its historical forms had its part to play in the education of the human race.

Die Erziehung des Menschengeschlechts (1780) was Lessing's last major theological essay to be published in his lifetime. The first fifty-three paragraphs had in fact already appeared, appended to Lessing's comments on the *Fragments*[27] in reply to the contention that the Books of the Old Testament were not written to reveal a religion. Lessing did not abandon the basic Deistic belief in an ultimate rational and moral religion, independent of creeds, ceremonies and dogmatic sanctions. Rather, he superimposed the thesis that the positive religions aid and even accelerate progress toward that goal, though in so doing they do nothing that man cannot do for himself.[28] In a sense Lessing was inverting the thesis of the Deists, the *philosophes*, Rousseau, Voltaire, Reimarus, and possibly his own version of the parable of the ring, that positive religion was a corruption of primitive natural religion.[29] Lessing contended that Old Testament religion represented a fairly advanced stage in the evolutionary progress of mankind[30]—a view which relieved him of the dilemma of having to defend the Old Testament against all comers or to abandon it wholesale because it failed to square with enlightened ideas. It was, in short, an *elementary primer* which could be dropped in due course when Christ came.[31] Jesus himself inaugurated a new stage in the education of mankind, being "the first *reliable, practical* teacher of the immortality of the soul."

> 59. The first *reliable* teacher. Reliable, by reason of the prophecies which were fulfilled in him; reliable by reason of the miracles which he achieved; reliable by reason of his own revival after a death by which he had put the seal to his teaching. Whether we can still *prove* this revival, these miracles, I put aside, as I leave on one side *who* the person of Christ was. All *that* may have been at that time of great importance for the first acceptance of his teaching, but it is now no longer of the same importance for the recognition of the *truth* of his teaching.

> 60. The first *practical* teacher. For it is one thing to conjecture, to wish, and to believe in the immortality of the soul, as a philosophic speculation: quite another thing to direct one's inner and outer actions in accordance with it.

> 61. And this at least Christ was the first to teach. For although, before him, the belief had already been introduced among many nations, that bad actions have yet to be punished in the life to come; yet they were only such actions as were injurious to civil society, and which had, therefore, already had their punishment in civil society

too. To preach an inward purity of heart in reference to another life, was reserved for him alone.[32]

But just as the value of the Old Testament was practical but transient, so too was that of the New. And by implication, so too was that of Jesus whom almost every other word of Lessing's discussion damned with faint praise. For all practical purposes, Jesus was just another great teacher who had had his day. The stories about him were politely but skeptically put on one side. His central teaching, which was described as that of the immortality of the soul, but the cash value of which seemed to be doing good for its own sake, could readily be seen to be valid. It did not require his personal sanction to give it authority. The merit of Jesus was that he was the first to teach it. It certainly did not mean that he was divine. If we relate this conclusion to what Lessing had earlier said about the Son of God in *Das Christentum der Vernunft*, it could mean that the man Jesus had some apprehension of the divine *Son-God* manifestation. However, Lessing stopped short of a Spinozist metaphysical explanation. The picture of Jesus that he chose to give to the public was that of an enlightened teacher whose altruistic rational insights were ahead of his time.

The great goal of humanity lay in the future, where man would no longer have to bolster his hopes upon past events and future rewards. He would do what was right for its own sake. In a manner anticipating Kant, Lessing proclaimed his belief in a morality which superseded the sanctions of religion.

> 85. No! It will come! it will assuredly come! the time of the perfecting, when man, the more convinced his understanding feels about an ever better future, will nevertheless not need to borrow motives for his actions from this future; for he will do right because it *is* right, not because arbitrary rewards are set upon it, which formerly were intended simply to fix and strengthen his unsteady gaze in recognizing the inner, better, rewards of well-doing.

> 86. It will assuredly come! the time of a new eternal gospel, which is promised us in the primers of the New Covenant itself![33]

In other words, religion is not true because the evangelists taught it; they taught it because it is true. The truth of religion is neither accidental nor in the last analysis historical. It carries with it its own rational necessity. History merely presents occasions for grasping it.

Christian Origins

In addition to his philosophy of history, Lessing also gave thought to the question of the historicity of Christian origins. *Eine Duplik* (1778) joined issue with J. H. Ress over the resurrection narratives. Ostensibly Lessing took a middle course between Reimarus who denied the resurrection altogether and Ress who denied discrepancies in the narratives.[34] He would keep the resurrection along with the discrepancies. But the wording of the reply was so framed that the objections to Ress were tantamount to an endorsement of the Fragmentist. Throughout Lessing heaped abuse upon the anonymous Ress. Critical discussion was confined to noting ten crucial difficulties in the resurrection narratives.[35] Each was stated in its acutest form, and every attempt to resolve them was greeted with the derision that Lessing usually managed to muster in theological debate.

But the problem of Christian origins also prompted Lessing to attempt his own positive reconstruction. This took the shape of various essays, none of which were published in Lessing's lifetime. The most complete and, in its author's estimation, both his best theological writing and his most formidable attack upon orthodoxy,[36] was the *Neue Hypothese über die Evangelisten als blos menschliche Geschichtschreiber betrachtet*.[37] It was a primitive essay in source criticism, exploring ground which the other main disputants in the *Fragments* controversy had hardly ventured upon.

Lessing's thesis was that, behind the canonical Gospels, there lay a single primitive Hebrew or Aramaic Gospel which remained in use for some thirty years, or as long as Christianity was confined to the Palestinian Jews. Towards the end of this phase there was increasing demand for translations to meet the needs of Gentile converts.[38] Fastening on to, but modifying, the testimony of Eusebius, Papias and Jerome, Lessing held that Matthew was the first of the canonical Gospels.[39] But whereas these fathers believed that Matthew had composed his Gospel in Hebrew (or Aramaic), Lessing inverted their testimony and claimed that Matthew had merely selected and translated into Greek extracts from an already existing Gospel. Never at a loss for a conjecture, Lessing put down this mistake about the language to the chronological proximity of the extracts and the original and to the fact that people expected Matthew to write in Hebrew.

> 31. Indeed, the original of Matthew was certainly Hebrew, but Matthew himself was not the actual author of this original. From him, as an apostle, many narratives in the Hebrew original may well derive. But he himself did not commit these narratives to writing. At his dictation others wrote them down in Hebrew and combined them with stories from the other apostles; and from this human collection he in his time made merely a connected selection in Greek. But because his selections, his translation, followed quickly on the original, because he himself could equally well have written in Hebrew, because in view of his personal circumstances it was more probable that he in fact wrote in Hebrew, it is not surprising that to some extent the original was confused with the translation.[40]

Mark and Luke simply followed suit. Luke had before him "the Hebrew document, the Gospel of the Nazarenes" and transferred most of its contents "only in a rather different order and in rather better language."[41] Mark, "who is commonly held to be only an abbreviator of Matthew, appears to be so only because he drew upon the same Hebrew document, but probably had before him a less complete copy."[42]

John, on the other hand, knew of this source, but radically adapted it in order to give his Gospel universal appeal and cater to mankind's need of a divine-human mediator.

> 51. And John? It is quite certain that John knew and read that Hebrew document, and used it in his Gospel. Nevertheless his Gospel is not to be reckoned with the others, it does not belong to the Nazarene class. It belongs to a class all of its own.

> 62. If therefore Christianity was not to die down again and to disappear among the Jews as a mere Jewish sect, and if it was to endure among the Gentiles as a separate, independent religion, John must come forward and write his Gospel.

> 63. It was only his Gospel which gave the Christian religion its true consistency. We have only his Gospel to thank if the Christian religion, despite all attacks, continued in this consistency and will probably survive as long as there are men who think they need a mediator between themselves and the Deity; that is, for ever.

> 64. That we accordingly have only two Gospels, Matthew and John, the Gospel of the flesh and the Gospel of the spirit, was long ago recognized by the early Church Fathers, and is actually denied by no modern orthodox theologian.[43]

It is at this point that the christological significance of Lessing's thesis emerges. The divine son of the Fourth Gospel is a pragmatic necessity created at the expense of history. He is a projection of the imagination, meeting the practical needs of the Christian religion for a distinctive tenet and the psychological need of certain sections of humanity for a mediator. The closing paragraphs spell out Lessing's belief that the Jesus of the first Jewish Christians and his hypothetical source document was no more than a human messiah.

> 57. The former, even if our consideration goes back to their origins, could not possibly have intended to keep also the Mosaic law if they had regarded Christ as more than an extraordinary prophet. Indeed, even though they held him to be the true, promised Messiah, and as Messiah called him Son of God; yet it is beyond dispute that they did not mean by this title a Son of God who is of the same essence as God.[44]

The clear, but unuttered, implication was that the whole fabric of orthodox Christology was without historical basis. The end result was substantially the same as that of the Fragmentist, though Lessing had reached it by a very different route. Eschatology played no significant part in this reconstruction. There was no need to impute to the apostles the motives of fraudulent deceit. Orthodox beliefs were based on a misunderstanding of language and a failure to appreciate sources.

> 61. In a word: Orthodox and Sectaries all had of the divine person of Christ either no idea at all or a quite wrong idea, as long as there existed no other Gospel but the Hebrew document of Matthew or the Greek Gospels which flowed from it.[45]

Lessing's reconstruction of primitive Christology turned on two significant points. The first of these Lessing shared with the Fragmentist. It was his conviction that the term "Son of God" was not a divine title in Palestinian Judaism. In making this judgment Lessing was doubtless correct.[46] But Lessing did not pause to ask whether there were other grounds for asserting Christ's divinity or indeed for asking what might be entailed in this belief. Instead, he proceeded to his second point which was the assumption that primitive Christology could be ascertained by referring to the beliefs of the Ebionites (whom Lessing took to be a representative sample of Jewish Christians before the fall of Jerusalem),[47] Cerinthus[48] and Carpocrates.[49] It was these heretics, rather than the canonical evangelists, who preserved the teaching of the original Matthaean Gospel posited by Lessing.

For Lessing there were two forms of Christianity. There was ecclesiastical orthodoxy which was derived from the Fourth Gospel, "the Gospel of the Spirit"; and there was the faith of the Ebionites and others which was derived from "the Gospel of the flesh." Clearly the latter beliefs corresponded to the historical Jesus. Mark and Luke (who likewise knew only "the Gospel of the flesh") were retained by the early church, partly because they filled certain gaps and partly because the former was the pupil of Peter and the latter the pupil of Paul.[50] The fact that when the fathers contrasted John with the other evangelists, they did not draw Lessing's inference that John was unhistorical and the others were ignorant of Christ's divinity, was passed over without explanation or comment.[51]

It remains to be noted that Lessing prefaced his hypothesis with a speculation about how the primitive Hebrew source came into being in the first place. His starting point was the fact that the primitive Jewish Christians were known as the Nazarenes.[52] Coupled with this was the further fact that a *Gospel of the Nazarenes* in Syriac or Aramaic was known in the fourth century and was even prized by no less a figure than Jerome, who translated it and used it to explain the Greek text of the existing Gospels.[53] This Gospel, Lessing thought it safe to assume, was written down soon after the death of Jesus,[54] and subsequently became the basis of the work used by Matthew. The pivot of Lessing's argument —which is lost sight of amid the patristic allusions and numerous secondary propositions—was the double assumption that the earlier Nazarenes were the same as the later Nazarenes who came to be bracketed with the Ebionites and that they taught an Ebionite Christology.[55] How ill-founded the whole argument was is shown by recent reconstructions of the Gospel on the basis of references in Jerome and other writers. These indicate that the work was dependent upon Matthew. Moreover, the text is so sparse that no distinctive Christology can be reconstructed.[56]

Lessing's christological conclusions were restated, but not re-argued in a brief paper (occupying less than a page in translation) entitled *Die Religion Christi*.[57] The religion of Christ and the Christian religion were two entirely different things.

> 3. The former, the religion of Christ, is that religion which as a man he himself recognized and practised; which every man has in common with him; which every

man must so much the more desire to have in common with him, the more exalted and admirable the character which he attributes to Christ as a mere man.

4. The latter, the Christian religion, is that religion which accepts it as true that he was more than a man, and makes Christ himself, as such, the object of its worship.[58]

The two religions were indeed to be found in the same book. But whereas the former "is therein contained in the clearest and most lucid language," the latter "is so uncertain and ambiguous, that there is scarcely a single passage which, in all the history of the world, has been interpreted in the same way by two men."[59] What Lessing stated so succinctly here was not a new program. It might almost have been a summary of the central tenets of English Deism whose zenith virtually coincided with the year of Lessing's birth.

3. THE FRAGMENTS CONTROVERSY IN RETROSPECT

Readers of Schweitzer's *Quest of the Historical Jesus* may well be pardoned, if they conclude that Reimarus was a bolt from the blue. Schweitzer stated categorically that,

> He had no predecessors; neither had he any disciples. His work is one of those supremely great works which pass and leave no trace, because they are before their time; to which later generations pay a just tribute of admiration, but owe no gratitude.[1]

Examination of the historical background makes it impossible to endorse Schweitzer's judgment except on the single point that Reimarus left no disciples. Over half a century before Schweitzer, D. F. Strauss had pointed out how Reimarus's views on the Old Testament were anticipated by Spinoza and Pierre Bayle and that his views on religion in general and on Jesus in particular were positively indebted to the English Deists.[2] Subsequent research has confirmed this view.[3] Apart from urging his readers not to dismiss Reimarus as a Deist, Schweitzer largely overlooked the fact that Reimarus set out his views on Jesus in what was ostensibly an apology for the rational worshipers of God. In order to see Reimarus in perspective, his thought would have to be examined against the broader background of European skepticism, rationalism and the Age of Enlightenment generally and against the narrower background of English Deism. Adequate exploration of the labyrinthine character of this background would clearly require a series of separate studies. The aim of the present chapter is the more modest one of taking note of criticisms of orthodoxy in Britain and the Continent prior to Reimarus and of asking what impact they may have had on German thought.

Criticisms of Orthodoxy from Servetus to Spinoza

If one casts about for precedents for questioning the orthodox Christian doctrine of the incarnation and for denying the Trinity, one does not have to look very far or hard. The case of Michael Servetus was certainly the most notorious but by no means unique instance of denial of the Trinity and the divinity of Jesus. Nor was Servetus the only thinker to pay for such views with his life. Prior to his death at the stake in Geneva in 1553, Konrad in der Gassen had been executed at Basel in 1530 for denying that Jesus was true God and true man. Servetus had set out his views in his *Christianismi Restitutio* (1553), but such was the thoroughness of the attempt to eradicate his heresy that only three copies of the original edition are known to exist today. However, the fact that a partial edition was reprinted in London in 1723 and a complete edition was published in Nuremberg in 1790 is some indication of renewed interest in his thought in the eighteenth century.[4]

Servetus had previously questioned the tenets of orthodoxy in *De Trinitatis Erroribus Libri Septem* (1531) and *Dialogorum de Trinitate Libri Duo* (1532).[5] Perusal of these texts reveals Servetus to be a man of a very different stamp from either Reimarus or Lessing. He was certainly an enthusiast for his ideas. In a sense it could be said that he was an enthusiast for the historical Jesus. But the Jesus that he saw in Scripture was the product of a modalistic adoptionism, reminiscent of earlier heresies.[6] Servetus took Scripture as authoritative and at its face value. For him, orthodoxy had erred in misunderstanding biblical language concerning God, his Word and his Spirit, and patristic language concerning "Nature" and "Persons."[7] There was no question of fraudulent deceit on the part of the biblical writers or of a merely human understanding of Jesus as with Reimarus. What was at issue was the correct understanding of the God revealed in Scripture.

Servetus was only one among many questioners of Trinitarianism and forerunners of Socinianism.[8] The latter found credal expression in the Racovian Catechism, published in Polish at Rakow in 1605 and followed by versions in German (1608), Latin (1609), English (1652) and Dutch (1665). The work was hardly a catechism in the customary Reformed sense of the word. It was more like an extensive treatise on the person of Christ, preceded by preliminary discussions of the authority of Scripture, salvation and the knowledge of God, with a postscript on the church. Its discussion of Christ followed the characteristic Calvinistic pattern of examining the three offices of prophet, priest and king. But the interpretation was radically different from Calvin's. Although Jesus was "the only begotten Son of God" who was conceived by the Holy Spirit "without the intervention of any human being,"[9] he was a man who "had not existed from eternity."[10] "God is but one person."[11] Christ is God's agent in man's salvation. In honoring him, God is honored. Although the "testimonies of the Old Testament, spoken of God, were applied to Christ . . . it would not hence follow that he possessed a divine nature."[12]

Two observations may be made concerning Socinianism, the Racovian Catechism and their relevance to the quest of the real Jesus. The first concerns the fact that while the Catechism viewed Jesus as a human, historical figure, it did not question the divine authority of Scripture. The Holy Scriptures were sufficient, authentic and perspicuous. The Socinian case in the sixteenth and seventeenth centuries turned on the failure of the orthodox to see what God was so clearly saying about the person of Christ. The second observation concerns the extent and influence of Socinianism. Although the Reformers for a time wrestled with the question of whether to retain the Trinitarian conceptual apparatus of the ecumenical councils and although anti-Trinitarians, Arians and Socinians coexisted for a time in the Reformed churches, by the beginning of the seventeenth century the Socinians in Europe were a sect apart. They flourished in Poland, Transylvania and to some extent in Holland, where toleration was practiced more freely than in other Reformed countries. In Germany the religious laws effectively prevented them from gaining any substantial foothold. Where they existed, they formed separate groups with their own self-conscious identities. In England Socinian ideas were disseminated among Dissenting congregations, but it was half a century after the height of the Deistic controversy that Unitarianism emerged as a distinctive form of worship and belief. When Deism emerged, Socinians repudiated it. Despite apparent similarities of theological views, Deism and Unitarianism maintained separate identities.[13] The Deistic views of Reimarus and Lessing and the anti-trinitarian Christology of the Socinians and their Unitarian successors were not close kin but distant relatives. Although traces of Socinian influence may be detected in Deism, the Deistic critique of Christianity was far more radical. It was Deism, rather than Socinianism, which inspired the *Fragments* controversy.

The questions of Servetus and the Socinians were posed within the framework of a revealed theology based on Holy Scripture. The questions of Reimarus and Lessing were questions which attacked the very idea of revelation. To appreciate them in their broadest context would require a comprehensive analysis of the Enlightenment and the changing attitudes to science, history and philosophy, together with their impact on theology.[14] The new outlook was epitomized by the advent of Pyrrhonism which played no small part in the emergence of philosophical rationalism and Deism.[15] In both cases it gave impetus to the quest for certainty, rationality and objective knowledge. The movement was named after the Greek skeptic, Pyrrho. In the hands of sixteenth-century Catholic apologists it became a "new engine of war," forged for the destruction of Calvinism. By questioning its truth-claims based on the Word of God and the internal testimony of the Holy Spirit, Catholic Pyrrhonists sought to clear the ground for accepting the authority of the church. But it was readily apparent that Pyrrhonism could be turned against such fideism and indeed against all claims to knowledge. The rationalism of Descartes and his successors was an attempt to develop a philosophy based on self-evident premises and logically related ideas that would be immune to such doubt.

Such a philosophy sought to exhibit the rational structure of reality, co-ordinating the knowledge of God with the natural sciences and ethics. Descartes himself saw no real conflict between his rationalism and orthodox Catholic theism. Likewise many Protestant thinkers viewed their rationalism as the philosophical foundation of Protestant orthodox theism. Characteristic of the German Enlightenment was Christian Wolff's *Vernünftige Gedanken von Gott, der Welt und der Seele des Menschen auch allen Dingen überhaupt* (1720, 5th edition 1733). It was succeeded by sundry other *Vernünftige Gedanken* on the purposes of natural things, the use of the parts of human and animal bodies, and reflections on natural theology. It was to this genre of writing that Hermann Samuel Reimarus contributed his respected reflections on natural theology, animal behavior and the use of reason.[16] Such writings were ostensibly vindications of orthodoxy. Although they stressed reason, they gave little hint of the destructive criticism that Reimarus was privately nurturing. The most explicit indication of anything that might disturb the equilibrium of rationalistic orthodoxy was his disavowal of miracles. In *Die vornehmsten Wahrheiten der natürlichen Religion* (1754) Reimarus had observed that miracles contradicted the order of creation and could not be accepted by a rational man.[17] However, he did not choose to enlarge upon this. In any case, the question of miracles and their relevance to the truth-claims of Christianity had already been well ventilated in the course of the Deistic controversy which was becoming increasingly familiar in German intellectual circles.[18]

The title of *Die vornehmsten Wahrheiten der natürlichen Religion* was itself evocative of the age of Deism. The book was in part a reply to the atheistic materialism of La Mettrie's *L'Homme machine* (1747) and the rationalistic pantheism of Spinoza. The latter had openly criticized miracles in his *Tractatus Theologico-Politicus* (1670), where he judged the root error to lie in imagining "the power of God to be like that of some royal potentate, and nature's power to consist in force and energy."[19] For Spinoza there was a single, supreme reality which could be called God or nature, *Deus sive natura*. The roots of Spinoza's thought may be traced to Cartesian rationalism and Jewish medieval thought. However, in his discussion of miracles Spinoza adopted the language in which Calvinistic divines spoke of the divine immutability and God's eternal decrees in salvation, and applied it to the laws of nature. "Now, as nothing is necessarily true save only by Divine decree, it is plain that the universal laws of science are decrees of God following from the necessity and perfection of the Divine nature." Hence, a miracle as a "contravention to the laws of nature" would involve God acting against his nature, and would therefore be "an evident absurdity."[20] On the other hand, "the laws of nature . . . extend over infinity, and are conceived by us, after a fashion, eternal, and nature works in accordance with them in a fixed and immutable order; therefore, such laws indicate to us in a certain degree the infinity, the eternity, and the immutability of God."[21]

Spinoza confined his discussion of miracles largely to the Old Testament, the subsequent misunderstanding of biblical language and the neglect of natural factors patently present in its account of signs and wonders. He noted that in John

9 "certain acts are mentioned as performed by Christ preparatory to the healing of the blind man," and hinted that there were "numerous instances showing that something further than the absolute fiat of God is required for working a miracle."[22] But the implications of his argument for Christian apologetics would not have been lost on his readers. By 1670 the question of the rationality of religion and the role of miracles as divine accreditation of special revelation was already exercising some of the acutest minds of the age. If miracles could be attributed to mistakes of fact or to man's inadequate grasp of the workings of nature, the apologists' appeal to objective divine attestation of the Christian revelation would be undermined and with it the personal deity of Christ.

Underlying Spinoza's critique of miracles was his view of reality. Spinoza's specific objection to miracles as incompatible with the laws of nature was one which was to be repeated countless times in the course of the next two centuries by many who did not share his pantheistic world view. But his view of reality with its emphasis on the rational unity of form and being and its exclusion of a theistic view of God as the transcendent, personal ground of all beings was one which was to have profound effects of subsequent thought. To some contemporaries and immediate successors Spinoza's thought seemed to be a form of atheism. Among them were Pierre Bayle and David Hume.[23] It demanded considerable courage to confess oneself to be a Spinozist. But following F. H. Jacobi's revelations of Lessing's alleged Spinozism[24] it became increasingly easy to profess Spinozism.[25] As we shall see in subsequent chapters, his thought affected Schleiermacher, Goethe and Idealism generally. Hegel, who defended Spinoza from the charge of atheism and had a share in publishing the Jena edition of Spinoza, saw him as a precursor of his own Idealism which corrected the Jewish thinker's onesidedness.[26] The significance of Spinoza for subsequent Christology emerged fully only after the *Fragments* controversy. The replacement of theistic Trinitarianism by an immanent dynamic ground of the world's being could not but radically affect the way one viewed the divinity of Christ.

The World of Newton and Locke

In Britain Thomas Hobbes suggested in his *Leviathan* (1651) that popular belief in miracles was largely due to "ignorance and error" over "natural causes."[27] He allowed that a Christian state might require assent to them in the interests of the public good, but maintained that a man, in private, was free to believe in accordance with his reason. Hobbes is sometimes thought of as a pioneer of empiricism, but in many ways his thought was a transplant of continental skepticism onto British soil. In England he found himself at variance with the *virtuosi* of the Royal Society on account of his contempt of inductive methods. In both France, where he spent his most productive years, and England he was widely suspected of atheism.

The views of Spinoza and Hobbes were not shared by the founding members of the Royal Society of London for the Improvement of Natural Knowledge, which received its charter in 1662 from King Charles II. The Royal Society became the most prestigious scientific body in Europe. Many of its early leaders were not only members of the established church but were themselves clerics, for whom neither miracles nor theism posed any serious problem.[28] Sir Robert Boyle (1627–91), the "father of chemistry," observed that "the use we ought to make of a doctrine in judging of a miracle is not to deny the historical part, if it be substantially attested, but to distinguish whether it be likely to come from some evil spirit than from God." In the manner of orthodox apologetics, he argued that "if the revelation backed by a miracle proposes nothing that contradicts these truths, . . . and much more if it proposes a religion that illustrates and confirms them; I then think myself obliged to admit both the miracle, and the religion it attests."[29] In his will, Sir Robert left the sum of £50 per annum to establish a series of lectures against unbelievers to be delivered in London churches. However, the need to establish the "Boyle Lectures" was itself a testimony to the growth of unbelief.

The leading scientist of the age, Sir Isaac Newton (1642–1727), was also intensely interested in theological questions. He privately questioned the doctrine of the Trinity, but remained a conforming churchman. Among his personal papers were twenty-three *Queries regarding the Word Homoousios*.[30] He mused at length over *Paradoxical Questions concerning the Morals and Actions of Athanasius and His followers*.[31] His own framework of belief was essentially a theistic one which saw God as the one who

> made the world and governs it invisibly, and hath commanded us to love, honour and worship him and no other God . . . and to honour our parents, masters, and governors, and love our neighbours as ourselves, and to be temperate, modest, just and peaceable, and to be merciful even to brute beasts.[32]
>
> Jesus Christ, a true man born of a woman, was crucified by the Jews for teaching them the truth, and, by the same power by which God gave life at the first to every species of animals, being revived, he appeared to the disciples.[33]

Having explained to men that he was the Messiah, Servant, Son of God and Holy One, prophesied by the Old Testament, Jesus "is gone into the heavens to receive a kingdom and prepare a place for us, and is mystically said to sit at the right hand of God." Following the creeds, Newton expressed his belief in the return of Christ, the judgment and the place of the visible church in the divine scheme.[34]

However, all these thoughts were consigned to private papers. It was Newton's view of the physical universe which transformed the thinking of the age. Even in his scientific writings, Sir Isaac Newton remained a convinced theist. He conceived infinite space as the divine sensorium in which God perceived his creatures, but repudiated the suggestion that the world might be thought of as the body of God.[35] Nevertheless, Newton's mechanics and his view of the absolute fixed character of time and space which he set out in his *Philosophiae Naturalis Principia Mathematica* (1687) profoundly affected both natural science and philosophical theology. It posed the question of whether God could be thought of as a being who interacts with the world. More specifically, it raised the question of whether God could be thought of as one who might become incarnate.

Newtonianism exercised enormous influence on eighteenth-century continental thought, as did the sensationalism of Newton's friend, John Locke (1632–1704).[36] In common with predecessors and other contemporaries Locke set a high premium on reason in both philosophy and religion. In his *Essay Concerning Human Understanding* (1690) Locke retained much of the vocabulary of rationalism. But he rejected the rationalistic doctrine of innate ideas and stressed that, "All ideas come from sensation or reflection."[37] For Locke rational religion was based on sense experience, and there was no tension between Christian orthodoxy and rational religion. Whereas the Cambridge Platonists verged on reducing the former to the latter,[38] Locke drew a sharp distinction between ideas that were *according to reason, above reason* and *contrary to reason.*

> (1) *According to reason* are such propositions whose truth we can discover by examining and tracing those ideas we have from sensation and reflection, and by natural deduction find to be true or probable. (2) *Above reason* are such propositions whose truth or probability we cannot by reason derive from those principles. (3) *Contrary to reason* are such propositions as are inconsistent with or irreconcilable to our clear and distinct ideas. Thus the existence of one God is according to reason; the existence of more than one God is contrary to reason; the resurrection of the dead above reason.[39]

On this basis Locke proceeded to lay down that,

> *Reason* is natural *revelation*, whereby the eternal Father of light, and Fountain of all knowledge, communicates to mankind that portion of truth which he has laid within the reach of their natural faculties. *Revelation* is natural *reason* enlarged by a new set of discoveries communicated by God immediately, which reason vouches the truth of, by the testimony and proofs it gives that they come from God.[40]

Locke developed these thoughts further in *The Reasonableness of Christianity* (1695) and *A Discourse of Miracles* (1706). To Locke miracles and fulfilled prophecy were credentials which validated the claims of revelation. Thus a miracle was "a sensible operation, which, being above the comprehension of the spectator, and in his opinion contrary to the established course of nature, is taken by him to be divine."[41] Although doubt might be entertained by this or that particular Gospel miracle as the possible product of chance or natural causes, the Gospels themselves were not to be impugned, and the miracles as a whole could not be gainsaid. "By all which it is plain, that where the miracle is admitted, the doctrine cannot be rejected; it comes with the assurance of a divine attestation to him that allows the miracle, and he cannot question its truth."[42] However, it was precisely the plausibility of the Gospel records and the fulfillment of prophecy (as a form of miracle) that the Deists were soon to question with increasing openness. In so doing, they initiated the modern quest of the historical Jesus, as they sought to detect a human Jesus behind the supernaturalism of the Gospels and the credal formulations of orthodoxy. Although Locke's empiricism was to have a long-term effect on the course of Western thought, it was his epistemology rather than his theological apologetics that attracted attention. It was the English Deists that gave the precedent, the impetus and many of the essential critical ideas to Reimarus's questioning of orthodox Christian belief.

The Deist Controversy

In his celebrated *Dictionary of the English Language* (1755), Dr. Samuel Johnson defined Deism as "The opinion of those that only acknowledge one God, without the reception of any revealed religion." The term has been traced back to Pierre Viret in the sixteenth century, who used it to denote an unidentified group of thinkers who professed belief in God but rejected Christ and his teaching. A number of anti-Christian writings of such a character date from the late sixteenth and early seventeenth centuries.[43] Among them is the autobiographical work of Uriel da Costa who is mentioned by Reimarus in his *Apologie*. Da Costa was a convert to Judaism who found himself at variance with his new faith. Like Spinoza's family he came from Portugal to Holland. He lived for a time in Amsterdam and Hamburg, and is sometimes regarded as a precursor of Spinoza.

In the year that Lessing published the first of the *Fragments*, F. G. Lüdke offered to German readers a definition of Deism that was in essential agreement with Dr. Johnson's: "The Deist does indeed believe in God and the natural religion of reason, but not in the special revelation of God in the Bible."[44] In the first of the Boyle Lectures preached on "The Folly of Atheism, And (what is now called) DEISM; Even with Respect to the *Present Life*" (1692), Richard Bentley claimed to have "detected the mere *Deists* of our Age to be no better than disguised *Atheists*."[45] When these words were uttered, the Deistic controversy had not yet reached its climax. Moreover, the full impact of Deism on the understanding of Jesus still lay in the future.

Lord Edward Herbert of Cherbury (1583–1648) is generally regarded as "the father of English deism."[46] Lord Herbert served for a time as the English ambassador in Paris, where he published *De Veritate, Prout distinguitur a Revelatione, a Verisimili, a Possibili, et a Falso* (1624). It was in part a reply to French Pyrrhonian skepticism and in part an alternative to Protestant and Catholic orthodoxy. Like the rationalists, Lord Herbert believed in innate ideas. In the first edition he contented himself with describing varieties of truth and the faculties of the mind. In the enlarged edition of 1645, he elaborated on the Common Notions of religion and criticized the idea of revelation, urging the historical investigation of all religions and their testing by the Common Notions of monotheism and morality. He was critical of bibliolatry and the idea of an infallible church. While acknowledging Christianity to be the best religion, he urged priests to abandon mysteries, prophecies and miracles in support of unworthy beliefs. These themes received further elaboration in *De Causis Errorum*, including *De Religione Laici* and an *Appendix ad Sacerdotes* (London, 1645), and *De Religione Gentilium Errorumque apud Eos Causis* (Amsterdam, 1663; English version, 1705).

A zealous propagator of Deistic ideas was the disciple of Lord Herbert and follower of Thomas Hobbes, Charles Blount (1654–1693). In 1680 he published a collection of sayings from Hobbes criticizing religion and an attack on priest-craft entitled *Great is Diana of the Ephesians* and *The First Two Books of Philostratus Concerning the Life of Apollonius Tyaneus, written originally in Greek with philological notes on each chapter*. The significance of the latter work lay in the fact that Apollonius was a reputed holy man and miracle worker of the first century A.D. whose activities appear to diminish the uniqueness of Jesus. The figure of Apollonius has hovered in the background of discussions of Christology throughout the nineteenth and twentieth centuries. Philostratus's work has been widely taken as evidence of pagan influence on Christology, though there is reason to think that the work itself was a product of pagan counter-propaganda.[47] The *Life of Apollonius* was followed in 1683 by a tract ascribed to Blount, *Miracles No Violations of the Laws of Nature*, which was actually a paraphrase of chapter 6 of Spinoza's *Tractatus Theologico-Politicus*. An English translation of the latter work appeared in 1689. Among Blount's other writings was *The Oracles of Reason* (1693).

The former Irish Catholic and private scholar who enjoyed connections at the Prussian court, John Toland (1670–1722), claimed to be popularizing Locke in his *Christianity Not Mysterious, Showing that there is Nothing in the Gospel Contrary to Reason, nor above it; And that no Christian Doctrine can properly be call'd a Mystery* (1696).[48] In fact, his work proved to be a decisive step towards the position adopted by Reimarus and was indeed used by him. As his subtitle indicates, Toland held that there is nothing in Christianity beyond the grasp of reason. Jesus himself preached a simple moral religion. The so-called mysteries of Christianity were due to the intrusion of pagan ideas and priestcraft.[49] Citing Romans 10:4 and Matthew 5:17, Toland pronounced Jesus to be the end and fulfillment of the law,

> for he fully and clearly preach'd the purest Morals, he taught that reasonable Worship, and those just Conceptions of Heaven and Heavenly Things, which were more obscurely signifi'd or design'd by the Legal Observations. So having stripp'd the Truth of all those external Types and Ceremonies which made it difficult before, he rendered it easy and obvious to the meanest Capacities.[50]

Although the converted Jews continued "mighty fond of their *Levitical* Rites and Feasts," it was only later that Christianity was corrupted by Gentile fondness for mysteries, vestments and elaborate sacraments.[51] "Mystery prevail'd very little in the first Hundred or Century of Years after *Christ*."[52]

In 1698 Toland published a *Life of Milton* in which doubt appeared to be cast on the authenticity of the New Testament. Its sequel the following year, *Amyntor: Or, A Defence of Milton's Life*, contained an early discussion of the canon in the light of patristic evidence under the title of "A Catalogue of Books attributed in the Primitive Times to Jesus Christ, his Apostles and other eminent Persons: With several important Remarks and Observations relating to the Canon of Scripture." Toland's *Nazarenus: Or, Jewish, Gentile, and Mahometan Christianity. Containing The History of the antient Gospel of Barnabas... The Original Plan of Christianity occasionally explain'ed in the history of the Nazarens, wherby diverse Controversies about this divine (but highly perverted) Institution may be happily terminated* (1718) anticipated Lessing's views about institutional religion and his theory about the *Gospel of the Nazarenes*. Most of the Jews and Gentiles "mistook the design of Jesus" who did not come to abolish the law, but recognized its moral validity, just as did Cicero.[53] Toland went on to argue that since the Nazarenes or Ebionites were the first Christians, their view of Jesus must be the authentic one.[54] The Gospels and the other New Testament writings could not be taken as authentic without more ado against the views of the Nazarenes.[55] Indeed, "the Mohametan may not improperly be reckon'd and call'd a sort or sect of Christian."[56] The clear implication was that the Gospel accounts of Jesus paint an unhistorical and falsely supernatural picture of Jesus. Toland's work prompted a swift response from the future Göttingen church historian, J. L. Mosheim, *Vindicia Antiquae Christianorum disciplinae contra Tolandi Nazarenum* (1720).

Toland's *Letters to Serena* (1704), who was in fact Sophie Charlotte, the wife of Friedrich I of Prussia, contained an attack on Spinoza. But his *Socinianism truly Stated* (1705) not only gave currency to the word "pantheist" but was essentially an argument for pantheism. His *Tetradymus* (1720) was a collection of four essays, the first of which argued the thesis that the Exodus cloud and pillar of fire were "not miraculous but, as faithfully relat'd in Exodus, a thing equally practis'd by other nations, and in those places not onely useful but necessary,"[57] and the last defended his *Nazarenus* against the counterattack of the Bishop of London's chaplain. Toland's *Pantheisticon. Sive Formula Celebrandae Sodalitatis Socratae* (1720) has been variously interpreted as "a serious exposition of the philosophy of pantheism, a literary hoax, a sort of litany in derision of Christian liturgies, a mask to disguise atheism, a modernized version of the secret doctrines of Freemasonry, and a device to stimulate new thinking."[58]

While Toland was making his pilgrimage from Romanism to pantheism via free-thought, Anthony Collins (1676–1729) was making a frontal assault on one of the main buttresses of Christian apologetics, the idea of fulfilled prophecy. Collins belonged to the landed gentry and was a justice of the peace. He was a friend and trustee of Locke. Like Locke, he spent some time in Holland where he enjoyed contact with men of intellect. Toland dedicated several of his writings to Collins. Alan Richardson has observed that ever since his day "free-thinking has generally been employed as a synonym for 'atheist.' "[59] In 1713 he published anonymously (as he did his other writings) *A Discourse of Free-Thinking, Occasion'd by The Rise and Growth of a Sect call'd Free-Thinkers*. In it he urged that,

> The Subject of which Men are deny'd the Right to think by the Enemys of *Free-Thinking*, are of all others those of which Men have not only a *Right to think*, but of which they are oblig'd in duty to think; *viz.* such as *of the Nature and Attributes of the Eternal Being* or God, *of the Truth and Authority of Books esteem'd Sacred*, and *of the Sense and Meaning of those Books*; or, in one word, *of Religious Questions*.[60]

Collins himself sought to meet this obligation in *A Discourse on the Grounds and Reasons of the Christian Religion* (1724), which provoked so many replies that a sequel was required which Collins entitled *The Scheme of Literal Prophecy Consider'd; In a View of the Controversy, Occasion'd by a late Book, intitled, A Discourse of the Ground and Reasons of the Christian Religion* (1727). Collins was certainly known to Reimarus who in his *Apologie* approved of his late dating of the Book of Daniel.[61] The *Discourse* was, as its subtitle indicated, in two parts.[62] The first part examined the nature of prophecy in the light of the use made of it in the New Testament. The second part considered and rejected Whiston's literal hermeneutic. The *Scheme of Literal Prophecy* prosecuted in detail the exegesis of the *Discourse* in the light of the massive criticism that he had provoked.[63]

The main thrust of Collins's argument was that the messianic claims of the New Testament were based exclusively upon fulfilled prophecy. Even the argument from miracles is subordinate to the argument from prophecy.[64] Without actually saying that the messianic interpretation of prophecy was forced and false, Collins implied as much by insisting that the messianic significance could not be read out of its literal meaning. The prophetic writings referred primarily to events in the lifetime of the prophets. The New Testament writers wrote *typically* and *allegorically* in accordance with rabbinic exegesis.[65] In both works he considered the concept of fulfillment in five key passages in Matthew (Matt. 1:22–23; cf. Isa. 7:14; Matt. 2:15; cf. Hos. 11:1; Matt. 2:23; 11:14; cf. Mal. 4:5; and Matt. 13:34–35; cf. Isa. 6:9).[66] In none of these instances could Jesus' messiahship be proved by literal interpretation of the prophecies.

Collins claimed that the key to understanding the use of prophecy in the New Testament had been discovered by the Amsterdam Hebraist, Surenhusius,[67] whose attention had been drawn to rabbinic exegesis in the Talmud by a friendly rabbi. Following Surenhusius, he declared that "the jewish doctors are used to detach passages from their connection, and put a sense upon them, which has no relation to what goes before or follows after."[68] In answer to the objection "*that the allegorical reasonings of the apostles were not design'd for absolute proofs of Christianity, but for proofs* ad hominem, *to the Jews that were accustomed to that way of reasoning*," Collins insisted that this way of thinking was common in the ancient world. "If therefore christianity is grounded on *allegory*, converted gentiles must be convinc'd by allegory, and become *allegorists* or *mystical Jews*, no less than converted Jews. For the religion itself, to which they were converted, was *allegory*, or Christianity as taught *allegorically* in the Old Testament."[69] Collins left it to his readers to draw from this whatever inferences they would.

The learned but eccentric mathematician and translator of Josephus, William Whiston,[70] had experienced difficulty in reconciling the wording of prophecy quoted in the New Testament with its form given in the Old. He attempted to solve the problem by claiming that the Old Testament in its present form had been mutilated by the rabbis in order to obscure the original messianic references. Collins used Whiston's work as a chopping block. The result was the most daring and dangerous attack yet made on the authenticity of the Gospels and by implication on the orthodox view of Jesus.

At the end of *The Scheme of Literal Prophecy* Collins promised a *Discourse upon the miracles recorded in the Old and New Testament*. It fell, however, to the Cambridge don, Thomas Woolston (1670–1733), to launch the major assault on the miracles and resurrection of Jesus. He did this in a series of six *Discourses on the Miracles of our Saviour, in View of the Present Controversy between INFIDELS and APOSTATES*, which were published by himself between 1727 and 1729. Each one was prefaced by an ironic dedication to a bishop of the established church. His early study of Origen opened up the possibilities for him of an allegorical interpretation of Scripture. Some years before the *Discourses*, questions had been raised about his mental stability, and in 1720 he was deprived of his fellowship at Sidney Sussex College. In 1725 an unsuccessful attempt was made to prosecute him for his heterodox religious writings. The *Discourses* reveal a lucid, learned and witty mind, which perceived orthodoxy as a fabric of artificiality and did not shrink from saying so.

In the first *Discourse* Woolston remarked, "If ever there was a useful Controversy stated, or revived in this Age of the Church, it is *this* about the *Messiahship* of the Holy Jesus, what the *Discourse of the Grounds*, etc. has of late rais'd."[71] He added that such allegorical demonstration from prophecy "is the only way to prove him to be the Messiah, that great Prophet expected by the *Jews*, and promised under the Old Testament." In pressing allegorical interpretation, Woolston professed his aim "to honour Jesus" and to reduce the clergy "to the good old way of understanding Prophecies, which the Church has unhappily apostasis'd from."[72] There was "no Sanctuary" to be found in the miracles of Jesus. Indeed, they *"were never wrought, but are only related as prophetical and parabolical Narratives of what will be mysteriously and more wonderfully done by him."*[73] In similar vein, Woolston concluded the first Discourse with the plea,

> Be not longer mistaken, *good Sirs*. The History of *Jesus's* Life, as recorded in the *Evangelists*, is an emblematical Representation of his spiritual Life in the Soul of Man; and his Miracles are Figures of his mysterious Operations. The Four Gospels are no Part a literal Story, but a System of mystical Philosophy or Theology.[74]

In all, Woolston examined fifteen miracle stories, culminating in the resurrection of Jesus. Some of them were touched on more than once.[75] In general, the miracle stories were pronounced absurd, incredible and even immoral. Commenting on the miracle at Cana, Woolston observed that, "If *Apollonius Tyanaeus*, and not *Jesus*, had been the Author of this Miracle, we should have reproached his memory with it."[76] The star of Bethlehem was compared with "a Will-a-Whisp."[77] In some instances Woolston suggested psychosomatic factors and natural explanations. The woman in Luke 13 who is said to have been bound by Satan for eighteen years was pronounced "freed from the whimsical imagination of being *Satan ridden*."[78] "Reasonably then speaking, there was not much in the Disease and Cure of this Woman."[79] However, the episode of the woman by the well of Samaria in John 4 was "a silly story."[80] The account of Jesus' cursing the fig tree provided Woolston with occasion to ridicule Jesus' lack of knowledge and Judas's lack of foresight, as the disciple responsible for the material needs of the band.[81] The account of the man in John 5 by the Pool of Bethesda "absolutely destroys the Fame and Credit of *Jesus* for a Worker of Miracles" because of his omission to heal the rest of the afflicted.[82] Woolston went on to see allegorical significance in the five porticoes mentioned in John 5:2.[83] The clay made of dust and spittle in John 9:6 "would sooner put a Man's Eyes out than restore a blind one to his Sight."[84] But the story is really an allegory.

And the Cure of Mankind of the Blindness of his Understanding, by the *Spirit*'s being temper'd with the *Letter* of the Scriptures, which is the most mystical *Eye-Salve*, will not only be a most stupendous Miracle, but a Proof of *Jesus's Messiahship* beyond all contradiction, in as much as by such opening of the Eyes of our Understandings, which have been hitherto dark, we shall see, how he is the Accomplishment of the Law and the Prophets.[85]

As the *Discourses* proceeded, Woolston, introduced "a satirical Invective of a supposed Jewish *Rabbi*."[86] In the final *Discourse* the rabbi promises to become a Christian, if the resurrection of Jesus is proved to him. But the accounts of it are soon pronounced to be a "Romance" which put the author in mind of Robinson Crusoe who filled "his Pockets with Biskets, when he had neither Coat, Waistcoat nor Breeches on."[87] Indeed, the resurrection of Jesus was "the most manifest, the most bareface, and the most self evident Imposture ever put upon the World."[88]

Woolston contended that the disciples and the priests had made an agreement to open the tomb on the third day, so that the prophecy of Jesus' resurrection might be tested in public. But the disciples stole the body the previous night.[89] Only three or four soldiers were on guard. In any case, they had been bribed or in some way prepared, and were probably drunk.[90] According to the narratives themselves, Jesus appeared only to his own disciples, and they were known deceivers.[91] Eventually they themselves came to believe it.[92] To Woolston it was belief in the resurrection which is the true miracle.[93] He himself looked to "*That Happiness* of the state of Nature, Religion and Liberty, which may be looked for upon the coming of our *Messiah*, the allegorical Accomplisher of the Law and the Prophets."[94]

Unlike Reimarus, Woolston was a martyr for his views. In 1729 he was tried for blasphemy by the Lord Chief Justice in the Guildhall and sentenced to a year's imprisonment and a fine of £100. He refused to retract or cease to write. When he died he was still technically a prisoner, despite the efforts of Samuel Clarke, the rationalistic Anglican divine, to procure his release.[95]

There were, however, others who replied less savagely and more effectively on intellectual grounds. Among them was the Bishop of Bangor, Thomas Sherlock (1678–1761), to whom Woolston had dedicated his fifth *Discourse*. Sherlock wrote with the verve and self-assurance of an eighteenth-century C. S. Lewis. His work, *The Tryal of the Witnesses of the Resurrection* (1729), became a minor classic in both Britain and the Continent.[96] The arguments for and against the resurrection had thus been well ventilated a good many years before Reimarus's final *Fragment* was published.

Sherlock took his cue from Woolston's trial, but reversed the roles. The scene was a friendly discussion among gentlemen of the Inns of Court. The whole case was re-opened, with one of the company acting as judge, another as counsel for Woolston and a third as counsel for the apostles. With regard to Woolston's view of the sealing of the tomb, the counsel for the defense observed that, "It is surprising to hear these circumstances made use of to prove the resurrection to be a fraud, which could not but happen, supposing the resurrection to be true."[97] The argument that prophecy was not fulfilled, since Jesus was not three full days in the tomb, was met by the rejoinder that "after three days" means "inclusive days" in Jewish chronology.[98]

As the judge observed in his summing up, the charges against the apostles fell into two main categories. The first (which anticipated Reimarus) was that the whole story was a piece of fraud and deceit. The second (which anticipated Hume and Lessing) was that the evidence adduced was "insufficient to support the credit of so extraordinary an event."[99] To Sherlock decisive proof of the apostles' integrity was their continued affirmation of Jesus' resurrection in the face of threats, torture and death. Although Woolston's counsel pointed out that it was common for men to die for false opinions, the judge observed that "every mistaken man is not a cheat."[100] The apostles might have been sincerely mistaken, but Woolston's case (like that of Reimarus) required them to be demonstrable cheats.

The validity of the second charge turned upon presuppositions and expectations based on past experience. At this point Sherlock drew upon an analogy used by Locke before him and Butler, Hume and others after him, concerning the feasibility for someone living in a tropical climate of water ever becoming solid. The counsel for the apostles carried the day with the argument that his opponent's case turned on the presupposition that the testimony of others ought not to be admitted, but in such matters as appear probable, or at least possible to our conceptions. For instance: a man who lives in a warm climate, and never saw ice, ought on no evidence to believe that rivers freeze and grow hard in cold countries; for this is improbable, contrary to the usual course of nature, and impossible according to his notion of things. And yet we all know that this is a plain manifest case, discernible by the senses of men, of which therefore they are qualified to be good witnesses. A hundred such instances might be named, but it is needless; for surely nothing is more apparently absurd than to make one man's ability in discerning, and his veracity in reporting plain facts, depend on the skill or ignorance of the hearer. And what has the gentleman said, on this occasion, against the resurrection, more than any man who never saw ice might say against a hundred honest witnesses, who assert that water turns to ice in cold climates?[101]

Sherlock's work was a piece of popular apologetics, combining history and philosophy with the drama and logic of the law court. It was not, however, critical history in the strict sense. It appraised the evidential significance of the testimony contained in the Gospels but made no attempt to examine the Gospels as historical documents. But then neither had Woolston. On the other hand, Sherlock recognized the resurrection as a historical question that was not exempt from historical scrutiny by reason of its status as an article of faith. He grappled with the question of historical criteria in a way which confirmed the believing theist in his belief that he had nothing to fear from free, unbiased inquiry in the historical basis of his faith. Like Locke a generation earlier, Sherlock saw in the events reported in the Gospels the divine accreditation in history of Christian beliefs.[102]

At the height of the controversy over Woolston and miracles, Matthew Tindal (1655–1733) published a work which came to be regarded as "the Bible of Deism." Tindal has been described as one who "sheltered himself during a long life behind the corner of a comfortable fellowship."[103] In 1678 he had been elected to a law fellowship at All Souls' College, Oxford. He was a Doctor of Civil Law and an authority on ecclesiastical law. He was past seventy when he published *Christianity as Old as the Creation: Or, the Gospel, a Republication of the Religion of Nature,* Volume 1 (1730). The work was translated into German in 1741 by Johann Lorenz Schmidt, whom Lessing had named as the putative author of the *Fragments.*

Although Tindal referred to earlier authors, including Locke, he remained aloof from the current controversy. It must remain a matter of conjecture whether this was due to circumspection or whether Tindal actually joined the battle in a second volume which Dr. Edmund Gibson, the Bishop of London, procured and burned. Gibson was the bishop to whom Woolston dedicated his first *Discourse.* It is not without significance that the title of Tindal's work was drawn from a sermon by the orthodox Thomas Sherlock who had declared that, "The Religion of the Gospel, is the true original Religion of Reason and Nature. — And its Precepts declarative of that original Religion, which was as old as the Creation."[104] Similar statements abounded in the utterances of the more rationally minded divines of the age. But whereas Sherlock proceeded to draw the same inference that Locke drew, Tindal inverted the argument and claimed that the gospel must not be made to teach anything beyond the dictates of reason and nature. The only basic difference between natural and true revealed religion lay in their mode of communication. "The One being the Internal, as the Other the External Revelation of the same Unchangeable Will of a Being, who is alike at all Times infinitely Wise and Good."[105]

But this very fact gave rise to a grave problem when rational, natural religion was contrasted with historic Christianity. Although Tindal described himself as a "Christian Deist," he made it plain that the two were not coterminous. Certain Christian doctrines were highly expendable. High on the list were those of the fall, original guilt, and vicarious atonement. "If Men alike, at all Times, owe their Existence to God, they at all Times must be created in a State of Innocence, capable of knowing, and doing all God requires of them."[106] Asceticism and priestcraft were alike the products of superstition, and Tindal devoted much of his work to a withering attack on them.

Tindal anticipated Hume's argument that nothing could be proved from miracles, because all parties appealed to them, claiming their own to be "divine" and those of their opponents "diabolical."[107] "If the Doctrines themselves, from their internal Excellency, do not give us a certain Proof of the Will of God, no traditional Miracles can do it; because one Probability added to another will not amount to Certainty."[108] In arguing on these lines, Tindal also anticipated Lessing. Central to his argument was his thesis "That the Religion of Nature consists in observing those Things, which our Reason, by considering the Nature of God and Man, and the Relation we stand in to him and one another, demonstrates to be our Duty; and those Things are plain."[109] Whereas Lessing was to argue that the gospel was not true because the evangelists taught it but vice versa, Tindal remarked that "It's an odd Jumble, to prove the Truth of a Book by the Truth of the Doctrines it contains, and at the same Time to conclude those Doctrines to be true, because contain'd in that Book."[110]

In similar vein, Tindal argued that rational, altruistic religion transcended the rites of the church. Modes of worship should be judged by their fitness to promote human happiness. The idea that God desired worship for his own sake was an irrational superstition.[111] In a manner recalling Spinoza and anticipating Lessing and Kant, Tindal declared that happiness consisted in living in accordance with reason and man's nature and that duty consisted in seeking "the Good of the governed."[112] Such teaching might be found in the instruction of Jesus and the sayings of the Sermon on the Mount, though Tindal qualified this with the remark "that such like Texts have, by being interpreted literally, run Men into monstrous Absurdities."[113] Just as Lessing was to find truth in Judaism and Islam, Tindal observed, "I am so far from thinking the Maxims of *Confucius* and Jesus Christ to differ; that I think the plain and simple Maxims of the former, will help to illustrate the more obscure Ones of the latter, accommodated to the then Way of Speaking."[114]

Deism reached its zenith with Tindal. His work provoked over 150 replies discussing the relationship between natural and revealed religion.[115] But the specific battle over miracles and their relevance to the person of Jesus continued to be fought in an open way by Deists of lesser rank like Peter Annet and Thomas Chubb and in an indirect way by Conyers Middleton and David Hume.

It was widely agreed that Sherlock had vindicated the apostolic witness to the resurrection, but fifteen years later Peter Annet re-opened Woolston's case in a series of pamphlets.[116] Peter Annet (1693–1769) has been variously described and assessed. Sir Leslie Stephen, who was not exactly unsympathetic to the Deists, compared him with "an abusive Old Bailey barrister," cross-examining the evangelists. "He spares no imputations, sticks at no cavils, and bullies and browbeats as if he had to deal with convicted felons."[117] Emanuel Hirsch, on the other hand, considered that his writings exhibit "acute observation, critical reflection and a scientific method outstanding for his time. He is the originator of scientific criticism of the Easter stories and thereby gave impetus to the field of New Testament criticism as a whole."[118]

Hirsch reached his verdict on three counts. First, he held that Annet had proved his case for maintaining that Jesus' prophecies of his resurrection were really a later invention put into his mouth. In the second place, Annet had shown the sealing of the tomb to be a Matthean invention. Thirdly, he had demonstrated that the evangelists contradict each other. The Fourth Gospel was legendary, and the Synoptics contradict each other both over the resurrection appearances and over the ascension.[119]

Annet endorsed Woolston's point that it would have been more convincing had the resurrection witnesses been either hostile or neutral.[120] But he felt that Woolston was inconsistent and did not go far enough.[121] Annet felt the need to explain what had happened to Jesus' corpse. He resolved the dilemma by claiming that Jesus was not really dead. For evidence Annet turned to the Gospels, which he had found so untrustworthy on other matters. He detected a clue in Pilate's surprise that Jesus took so short a time to die.[122] Although the Fourth Gospel might be legendary, Annet was prepared to take at face value its testimony that no bones of Jesus were broken.[123] But the mention of the wound in his side must be treated with caution. Moreover, it must be remembered that Jesus was a young man in his prime. On the other hand, his loss of blood and sufferings changed his appearance beyond all recognition, so that even his disciples could recognize him only by his wounds.[124]

This solution to the problem of the resurrection created another which Reimarus later tried to resolve by enlarging upon the fraudulent motives of the disciples and treating their eschatological preaching as a gigantic confidence trick. However, other German writers, like Bahrdt, Venturini and Paulus, adopted the thesis that Jesus did not really die. In one other respect Annet anticipated certain later critics in teaching that Christianity was largely the creation of Paul.[125] In the meantime the orthodox arguments for the resurrection were restated by Gilbert West whose work was duly translated into German.[126] Both Sherlock and West were known to Lessing who complained that the former did not attempt to deal with the discrepancies in the narratives. The latter did so, but his multiplication of events and personalities was incredible.[127]

Another writer who attacked orthodox views of Jesus was the self-educated working man, Thomas Chubb (1679–1746), although the comparative mildness of his writings and his lack of formal education meant that he was overshadowed by men like Collins, Woolston and Tindal. Nevertheless, his views on free will attracted the attention of Jonathan Edwards in America and his tracts were discussed in Germany by S. J. Baumgarten.[128] In 1715 he attracted the attention of Whiston and others with his tract, *The Supremacy of the Father Asserted: Or, Eight Arguments from Scripture to prove, that the Son is a Being inferiour to the Father, and the Father alone is the Supreme God*. It was republished together with thirty-four others in *A Collection of Tracts on Various Subjects* (1730). In 1738 Chubb published *The True Gospel of Jesus Christ Asserted*, which he further defended in *The True Gospel of Jesus Christ Vindicated* (1739).

Chubb depicted Jesus as a positive Deist. His command to keep the two great commandments is identified with "that law or rule of actions, which is founded in the reason of things and which is summarily contained in the ten commandments."[129] The gospel was not a historical report of facts such as that Jesus died, rose again and ascended into heaven. It was preached to the poor before all these things.[130] Jesus addressed his fellow men as free beings and taught them to conform to "that eternal and unalterable rule of actions which is founded in the reason of things" which will render men pleasing and acceptable to God.[131] As a corollary, Chubb rejected the doctrine of vicarious atonement and imputed righteousness. The posthumous *Works of Mr. Thomas Chubb* (2 volumes, 1748) included the author's "Farewell" to his readers, which summarized his arguments, presenting the mission of Jesus as divine, but rejecting his personal divinity.

Among the later Deists was the Welshman, Thomas Morgan (d. 1743), who took up medicine on his dismissal as a Dissenting minister.[132] He described his tracts as "Christian deistical" and designated himself as an "M.D. and Moral Philosopher." He espoused the Common Notions of Lord Herbert and pioneered Pentateuchal criticism. His work ranged widely over the whole field of religion, but in our present context perhaps the most significant feature of his thought was his contention that the disciples had grossly distorted the teaching of Jesus. However, Paul, "the great freethinker of that age," and Christ, "the bold and brave defender of reason against authority," taught the pure religion of nature.[133] After the latter's death, Paul defended this doctrine against the fanatical Judaizers led by Peter. Unfortunately, sacerdotalism gained the upper hand in the hierarchy of the early church, and the true Christians who followed private judgment were reviled as Gnostics and followers of Simon Magus.[134]

By the 1740s the Deistic controversy was past its peak, but the Deists' case received indirect support from the pens of Conyers Middleton and David Hume. Both writers launched major assaults on miracles. Although neither of them deal directly with the Gospel miracles, their arguments sought to undermine the appeal to the miraculous. Middleton did it with a massive critique of miracles in the patristic church. Hume questioned the credibility of miracles in general and their evidential value in apologetics. Both writers were at pains to avoid mentioning the miracles of Jesus, but a simple extension of their arguments implied serious questions about the historical value of the Gospels and the supernatural character of Jesus' activities.

Conyers Middleton (1683–1750) was a redoubtable figure in the politics and debates of Cambridge University. His chief work was a life of Cicero, but he also wrote elegantly and polemically on ecclesiastical and theological questions.[135] In a posthumous essay entitled *Reflections on the Variations, or Inconsistencies which are found among the Four Evangelists In their Different Accounts of the same Facts*, Middleton raised the question of verbal inspiration. As historical documents, the four Gospels confirm each other by their trifling discrepancies. But an historical approach to them is undermined by the theory that represents the evangelists as mere "organ pipes" for conveying the utterances of the Divine Spirit. The doctrine of "the perpetual inspiration and infallibility of the Apostles and Evangelists" has imported "such difficulties and perplexities into the system of the Christian religion, as all the wit of man has not been able to explain."[136] Sacred history should be treated on the same footing as secular history.

> The case is the same in Theological, as in natural enquiries; it is experience alone, and the observation of facts which can illustrate the truth of principles. Facts are stubborn things, deriving their existence from nature, and tho' frequently misrepresented and disguised by art and false colors, yet cannot possibly be totally changed or made pliable to the Systems which happen to be in fashion, but sooner or later will always reduce the opinions of men to compliance and conformity with themselves.[137]

This principle was elaborated and applied to miracles in *A Free Inquiry into the Miraculous Powers which are supposed to have subsisted in the Christian Church, from the Earliest Ages through several successive centuries. By which it is shown that we have no sufficient authority to believe, upon the authority of the primitive fathers, that any such powers were continued to the church, after the days of the Apostles* (1749).[138] The subtitle indicated the scope and conclusions of the book. It was devoted to a detailed discussion of post-biblical miracles. In a formal sense Middleton was arguing the case of Reformed apologetics that miracles ceased with the apostolic age, and therefore no credence could be given to Catholic truth-claims that were based on continued miracles in the church.[139] Middleton himself insisted that this was his only intention. However, Middleton's relentless impugning of the testimony of early Christian writers left his readers wondering whether the application of the same cross-questioning to the New Testament writers would result in the same devastating results. On reading the work John Wesley observed that Middleton had contrived to "overthrow the whole Christian system."[140]

Whereas earlier writers had made a strong point of accepting the veracity of the testimony of honest eyewitnesses, however improbable, Middleton refused to take such testimony at its face value. The attitude underlying all his criticisms of testimony to the supernatural and extraordinary in history from the post-apostolic age down to the miracles alleged to have been wrought at the tomb of François de Pâris within the previous twenty years[141] is contained in the following statement:

> Ordinary facts, related by a credible person, furnish no cause of doubting from the nature of the thing: but if they be strange and extraordinary, doubts naturally arise, and in proportion as they approach towards the marvellous, those doubts still increase and grow stronger: for mere honesty will not warrant them; we require other qualities in the historian; a degree of knowledge, experience, and discernment, sufficient to judge of the whole nature and circumstances of the case: and if any of these be wanting, we necessarily suspend our belief. A weak man, indeed, if honest, may attest common events as credibly as the wisest; yet can hardly make any report, that is credible, of such as are miraculous; because a suspicion will always occur, that his weakness, and imperfect knowledge of the extent of human art, had been imposed upon by the craft of cunning jugglers. On the other hand, should a man of known abilities and judgement, relate to us things miraculous, or undertake to perform them himself, the very notion of his skill, without also of his integrity, would excite only the greater suspicion of him; especially, if he had any interest to promote, or any favorite opinion to recommend, by the authority of such works: because a pretention to miracles, has in all ages and nations, been found the most effectual instrument of impostors, towards deluding the multitude, and gaining their ends upon them.[142]

Sir Leslie Stephen observed that,

> Middleton's covert assault upon the orthodox dogmas was incomparably the most effective of the whole deist controversy. It indicates the approach of a genuine historical method. Middleton was the first to see, though he saw dimly, that besides the old hypotheses of supernatural interference and human imposture, a third and more reasonable may be suggested. The conception is beginning to appear, though still obscured by many crude assumptions, of a really scientific investigation of the history of religious developments. Middleton is thus the true precursor of Gibbon.[143]

What Sir Leslie Stephen appears to conceive by "scientific investigation of religious developments" is a steadfast refusal to entertain the supernatural in history, accompanied by a determination to seek other explanations or remain agnostic if none be forthcoming. In this Middleton was the precursor of many who engaged in the nineteenth-century quest of the historical Jesus. Without actually formulating the methodological principle of analogy in the manner of Ernst Troeltsch,[144] underlying all Middleton's discussion was the conviction of the essential homogeneity of events and the consequent need to interpret accounts of the past in the light of his understanding of the present.

The same conviction received philosophical expression in David Hume's celebrated essay "Of Miracles" which he inserted as Section X in his *Enquiry Concerning Human Understanding* (1748).[145] Today Hume's essay is regarded as the classic critique of miracles. However, in his own day Hume was mortified "to find all England in a ferment, on account of Dr. Middleton's Free Enquiry, while my performance was entirely overlooked and neglected."[146] Unlike the Deists and Middleton, Hume refrained from discussion of specific historical cases, apart from those examples drawn from Catholic piety (like the miracles associated with François de Pâris) and pagan antiquity that he knew that his Protestant readers would reject.[147] Like the latter, Hume refused pointblank to believe. But the grounds of his disbelief were such as would include disbelief in the Gospel miracles. His argument crystallized into historical canons the objection which the Deists had levelled against the orthodox Christian apologetic for revelation. Miracles were contrary to the experience of the rational man who is guided by his knowledge of the laws of nature. Hence miracles provided no compelling argument for revealed religion and truth-claims about God.

The premises of Hume's argument were his convictions that, "A wise man...proportions his belief to the evidence," that experience is "our only guide in reasoning concerning matters of fact,"[148] and therefore in weighing evidence his rule was "always to reject the greater miracle."[149] Thus, even with considerable historical testimony, certain events might prove so incredible, that it was easier to accept the incredibility of the witnesses than the credibility of the event.

> A miracle is a violation of the laws of nature; and as a firm and unalterable experience has established these laws, the proof against a miracle from the very nature of the fact, is as entire as any argument from experience can possibly be imagined.[150]

In other words, miracles were by definition impossible. On the basis of present experience, the ground was cut from underneath all historical testimony to the miraculous.

In the second part of his essay, Hume reflected upon certain common characteristics of historical testimony. The latter failed on four counts. In the first place, there was a lack of "a sufficient number of men, of such unquestioned good sense, education and learning, as to secure us against all delusion in themselves."[151] Secondly, there was a general human propensity to exaggerate which "will be found to diminish extremely the assurance, which we might, from human testimony, have in any kind of prodigy."[152] Thirdly, Hume observed that miracles generally occurred in obscure, uncivilized places in the remote past. "It is strange, a judicious reader is apt to say, upon the perusal of these wonderful historians, *that such prodigious events never happen in our days!*"[153] Hume's fourth reason concerned rival testimony, particularly that of rival religions that in appealing to miracles to support their truth-claims cancelled each other out.[154] This led to the reflection that miracles destroy the credit of the witnesses and therefore undermine, rather than confirm, belief in a religion based on them. "Our most holy religion is founded on *Faith*, not on reason; and it is a sure method of exposing it to put it to such a trial as it is, by no means, fitted to endure."[155]

Deism and the Quest of the Historical Jesus

If we look at Reimarus's work against the background of late seventeenth-century and early eighteenth-century thought, it no longer appears, as it did to Albert Schweitzer, as something new, revolutionary and epoch-making. It was an expression of a development that was already considerably well advanced. It was merely one, and not a particularly original one at that, of the many sides of the movement known as the Enlightenment. Wilhelm Dilthey saw the characteristic features of the Enlightenment to be everywhere the same: "the autonomy of reason, the solidarity of intellectual culture, confidence in its unimpeded progress and the aristocracy of the spirit."[156] Ernst Troeltsch believed that the unifying factor in Enlightened thinking was the rejection of supernaturalism[157] and that Deism was the religious philosophy of the Enlightenment.[158] R. G. Collingwood saw the Enlightenment characterized by the endeavor "to secularize every department of human life and thought. It was a revolt not only against the power of institutional religion but against religion as such."[159]

Elements of truth in each of these definitions may be seen in the *Fragments* controversy and its antecedents. Even the opponents of the Deists sought to demonstrate the rationality of their beliefs and their solidarity with what Dilthey called "intellectual culture." Although the definitions of Troeltsch and Collingwood would exclude from the Enlightenment thinkers who belonged to the Age of Enlightenment, the attempt to desupernaturalize and secularize religion in general and Jesus in particular was a characteristic of the Deists as it was of Reimarus and Lessing.

Sir Leslie Stephen drew a sharp distinction between "Constructive Deism" and "Critical Deism."[160] It is questionable whether such a distinction can be sustained. The two best-known Deists who might qualify as being "constructive" were Toland and Tindal. In fact, their thought was essentially critical. It differed from that of "critical" Deists like Collins, Woolston and Annet, chiefly by being less specific. Whereas the latter were openly critical of biblical prophecy and miracles, the so-called "constructive" Deists reduced the Bible to rational truths.

Whether Deism may ever be said to have had a common, coherent distinctive philosophy and faith is questionable. What the Deists had in common were shared convictions about the power of reason, the acceptance as self-evident of certain moral values and a professed belief in an ultimate divine being. Beyond that, it was their negative attitude to the Bible and the Christian revelation that distinguished the Deists from other rationalists, but which they shared with Spinoza, who was himself regarded as a Deist in some quarters.[161] The affinities of the Deists with Spinoza were based more on the biblical criticism of the

Tractatus than the metaphysics of the *Ethica*. Of the leading English Deists, only Toland went on to embrace the pantheism of the latter. For the rest, the Deists shared with Spinoza a common rejection of the Christian theistic view of a personal God whose interaction with the world culminated in the incarnation. Like Spinoza, their approach to God was intellectual and moral. It provided a theoretical basis for their critique of orthodox Christian beliefs.

By the time that Lessing published the first of the *Fragments* in 1774, the critical issues and key personalities were already well known in Europe. The skeptic, Voltaire, had firsthand knowledge of the Deistic controversy through his visit to England from 1726 to 1729. His personal library included many Deistic works, which he drew upon in writing his own works.[162] Many of the writings of the Deists and their opponents were translated into French and German.[163] Prior to 1741, when J. L. Schmidt published his translation of Tindal's *Christianity as Old as the Creation*, German interest in Deism was historical and only occasionally polemical.[164] After that date Deistic questions became increasingly significant in German discussions of philosophy and theology, not least because of the climate created by Wolffianism.[165]

For half a century before the publication of the *Fragments* Deism had been discussed in Germany. C. M. Pfaff, who had studied in England and Holland, had discussed it in a dissertation (1716) and in his inaugural disputation at Tübingen (1717). Pfaff has been described as "next to Mosheim the most brilliant theological figure in the eighteenth century."[166] The latter gave an early account of Toland's life and writings which he prefaced to his *Vindicia Antiquae Christianorum Disciplinae Contra Tolandi Nazarenum* (1720). Woolston was discussed by C. Lemker in *Historische Nachrichten von Th. Woolstons Schicksalen, Schriften und Streitigkeiten* (1740) and by C. C. Woog in *De Vita et Scriptis Thomae Woolstoni* (1743). In 1734 C. Kortholt wrote a dissertation on Tindal and Christian Gottlieb Jöcher lectured on him at Leipzig. Toland, Tindal, Collins and Woolston, together with Lord Herbert, Newton, Locke and Spinoza were among the notables deemed worthy of inclusion in the original four volumes of Jöcher's *Allgemeines Gelehrten-Lexicon* (1751). Although German translations of replies to Deism sometimes preceded the Deists' writings themselves and were sometimes regarded as more important, Jöcher evidently did not esteem Sherlock's reply worthy of mention or regard him as a significant enough scholar to merit an entry.

A number of works offered surveys of the field of debate. G. W. Alberti published *Briefe betreffend den allerneusten Zustand der Religion und der Wissenschaften in Gross-Brittanien* (1752–54). John Leland's two-volumed *View of the Principal Deistical Writings* (1754–56) appeared in the translation of Heinrich Gottlob Schmid and Johann Heinrich Meyenberg with the title *Abriss der vornehmsten deistischen Schriften* (1755–56). Leland's work was reviewed by Lessing in his *Briefe die neueste Literatur betreffend* (1754).[167] In 1755 Urban Gottlob Thorschmid published a *Critische Lebensgeschichte Anton Collins*. This was followed by Thorschmid's *Versuch einer vollständigen Engelländischen Freydenker-Bibliothek, in welcher aller Schriften der berühmtesten Freydenker nebst den Schutzschriften für die christliche Religion . . . entgegengestellt werden,* (4 volumes, 1765–67). In 1759 J. A. Trinius published a *Freydenker-Lexikon, oder Einleitung in die Geschichte der neuern Freygeister, ihrer Schriften, und deren Widerlegungen.* Other contemporary sources of information were the *Allgemeine Deutsche Bibliothek,* the *Göttingsche gelehrte Anzeigen* and S. J. Baumgarten's *Nachrichten von einer Hallischen Bibliothek* (8 volumes, 1748–51) and *Nachrichten von merkwürdigen Büchern* (12 volumes, 1752–58).

In short, the ground was very well prepared for the *Fragments* controversy. The novel element lay not in the introduction for the very first time of new and shocking ideas that threatened to undermine Christianity at its foundation but in the open espousal of the criticism. Previous writers had reported on debates that had gone on in England. Now Lessing undertook to publish the work of a deceased German critic of the Gospel and defend the validity of his questions. From time to time indications have been given of the acquaintance on the part of both Reimarus and Lessing with English Deistic literature. It remains to be pointed out that Reimarus himself studied in Holland and England in 1720–21. Little is known of Reimarus's activities there, but it seems that he came to know of Deism at that time and proceeded to study Deistic writers in the course of the next two decades.[168] He made use of Toland, Shaftesbury, Collins, Tindal and Morgan, as well as Conyers Middleton.[169] His personal library included most of the writings of the English Deists.[170] A notable exception was Peter Annet's *The Resurrection of Jesus Considered* (1744) whose theory that Jesus only appeared to die seems to have escaped his notice. Among continental writers whom Reimarus defended was Gabriel da Costa, but Reimarus's thought seems to be more indebted to the English Deists than to any European writers.[171]

It is possible that Reimarus's thinking was influenced by ideas of considerably greater antiquity than English Deism, with which as an orientalist and antiquarian he could well have been familiar. Reimarus's treatment of the term "Son of God" was in line with Jewish and Islamic views. The Qur'ān seems to throw doubt on Jesus' death and resurrection,[172] and the story that the disciples stole the body of Jesus long survived in Jewish tradition.[173] However, if there was a connection between these ideas and Reimarus, it was not made explicit in the *Fragments.*

Reimarus was a child of the Enlightenment in his relentless endeavor to desupernaturalize and secularize religion. He was also the synthesizer and translator of English Deism in a form in which it directly challenged German Protestant orthodoxy. However, in one important respect he appears not to have pressed a point stressed by Collins and Woolston, and in another respect he went beyond the Deists. In common with Collins and Woolston, Reimarus regarded as false the orthodox Christian understanding of fulfilled prophecy. The suggestion of Collins and Woolston that the Christian application of Old Testament prophecy to

Jesus might be allegorical or mystical (though strictly unwarranted) anticipated D. F. Strauss's view of myth-making in religion. However, it was not taken up by Reimarus who preferred to represent the use of prophecy as sheer fraud. On the other hand, Reimarus went beyond the English Deists in developing a comprehensive alternative account of the origins of Christianity. The Deists had contented themselves with raising specific objections. Reimarus put forward an alternative explanation that introduced eschatology as the key to understanding the mistaken and fraudulent character of Christianity.

The themes of Christ's second coming and the last judgment were familiar in Reformation and post-Reformation theology.[174] Rationalization and even rejection of them, in the manner of Spinoza, was now becoming increasingly familiar in Enlightened circles.[175] Reimarus broke new ground by directing critical attention to their place in the mission and message of Jesus. But the significance of his insight was largely overlaid by the polemical capital that he tried to make out of it. Strictly speaking, he was not interested in eschatology (any more than Albert Schweitzer was after him).[176] Neither Schweitzer nor Reimarus made any deep penetration into the thought-world of apocalyptic. Little attempt was made to understand the nature of eschatological language. Instead, certain apparent predictions were fastened upon and interpreted in a literalistic manner. The Gospel narratives were then reinterpreted within a strictly naturalistic framework. The resultant hypothesis was a brilliant piece of cynical ingenuity. But it was not scientific history. Reimarus's interest in the Jewish background extended no further than his interest in reducing Jesus' mission to a messianic political coup. The question of how far the supernatural might be admissible in historical reconstruction was not even discussed (though in this Reimarus was no different from many others who joined in the quest of the historical Jesus). As with Schweitzer, the eschatological element in Jesus' teaching was taken as proof that the message of the New Testament was incredible.

Reimarus made no attempt to understand the religious experience of the early Christians. Everything had to be explained away in terms of fraud and credulity. Either of these alternatives might conceivably fit this or that piece of individual testimony. But they hardly accounted for the early church's universal belief in the resurrection and its explanation of itself and its experiences in terms of encounter with the risen Christ. This, however, was not a question which perturbed the rational thinker of the eighteenth and nineteenth centuries. For at bottom he believed that all intelligent men, including Jesus, held the same rational beliefs. Anything they believed over and above this could be put down to circumstances and dismissed as peripheral. This tacit dismissal of the alien and the strange was doubtless a major factor in the neglect of eschatology in critical investigation until well into the second half of the nineteenth century.

From one modern standpoint, a remarkable feature of the controversy was the lack of discussion of sources and documents. Semler conceded the point that the four Gospels had been written considerably after the events and for different reasons, and therefore we ought not to expect them to tally in every detail. Lessing alone seems to have seen the full significance of the bearing of the authorship, date and character of the sources on one's estimate of Jesus, and he alone put forward a theory. Perhaps the lack of debate on this subject was due to the level on which the battle was fought. It was a case of the rational credibility of the stories in themselves versus a rationalistic alternative explanation. Even with Lessing it was on the plane of reason and not that of historical investigation that his attitudes both to Jesus and to history were basically decided. Klaus Scholder has argued that the initial advances in biblical criticism were made more in the realm of philosophy than in that of theology.[177] This he ascribes not so much to the reluctance of the clergy to face new ideas as to the fact that it was in the realm of philosophy that the tensions were first felt. In the first instance Scholder was talking about the seventeenth century. As we saw in our discussion of Semler and the Neologians, a historical and critical approach to the Bible had gained a firm foothold in Germany by the mid-eighteenth century. Even so, the significance of a critical evaluation of the authorship, date and character of the source documents had not become fully apparent even to Semler.

But even Lessing's *Neue Hypothese* has the air of a hypothesis constructed in the interests of a preconceived theory. Whatever internal evidence Lessing might have found in the Gospels to support his views, he certainly spared his readers the trouble of sifting it. The Lucan prologue indicates the existence of written sources behind the third Gospel, but in no way does it endorse Lessing's particular thesis concerning the relation of the canonical Gospels to a single primitive Hebrew or Aramaic source. Lessing's handling of external evidence was arbitrary, and much of it looks suspiciously like window dressing, produced to support a thesis arrived at on other grounds.

In several ways Lessing's essay, like his treatment of history in general, anticipated the methods and conclusions of succeeding generations. The separation of John from the first three Gospels, the quest for sources, insistence that the Gospels should be treated on a par with all other historical documents, and the implied questioning of the divinity of Christ—all these were points which figured in Lessing's essay. But it has to be added that none of them were examined with any consistency or detail. Lessing's contribution was not so much to work out firm conclusions as to state problems.

The suggestion is attractive that Lessing's original motive in publishing the *Fragments* was not so much to convince the public that Reimarus was right, but to open up discussion and above all give himself the opportunity to fly his own theological kites. Weight is lent to it by some of Lessing's own remarks and by his methods of conducting debate. What he bequeathed to posterity was not a well worked-out theology but a collection of seminal ideas, though the fact that they ranged more widely than those of his contemporary professional theologians does not make them any less fragmentary or any more true.

To Goeze, Lessing boasted that he was a "lover of theology and not a theologian."[178] He might with equal frankness have confessed that, although history figured in his writings, he was not a historian either. Indeed, he was not a lover of history at all. The main thrust of so much of his writing was to show that history was unreliable. Where it suited his purpose, as in the *Neue Hypothese*, he would argue that the results of historical investigation show that accepted ideas about history are unhistorical. Historical research could yield useful negative results. But Lessing's main interest in history centered not in the historical as such, but only insofar as it exemplified truths which transcended particular circumstances.[179] In this, Lessing was a true son of continental rationalism. But he was by no means the last of the line. In treating historical Christianity as the expression of some higher rational truth, Lessing was also a herald, in the Age of Enlightenment, of the Idealist approach to religion and Christian origins.

II

PHILOSOPHICAL IDEALISM AND RATIONAL RELIGION

4. FROM KANT TO GOETHE

The term Idealism is both elastic and elusive. In its narrowest sense it is used as shorthand for the speculative systems of Absolute Idealism, but in its widest sense it embraces that movement of thought from Kant to Hegel and his successors which superseded the Enlightenment. Ernst Troeltsch spoke of it as

> that form of modern knowledge and outlook on life which emerged from the Enlightenment and the English and French culture that was built on it. But under the peculiarly German circumstances it produced a quite different and in many ways opposite way of thinking and feeling. If the Enlightenment was characterized by dogmatism, empiricism, "Common-Sense" and skepticism, by utilitarian and individualistic-atomistic ethics, by mechanistic-atomistic natural science, and by the dominating influence of this conception of nature on all areas of thought, Idealism was characterized by a formal and material Idealism founded upon critical epistemology and convictions concerning feeling, by an ethic concerned with generally valid, universal rational values, by a genetic-objective view of history, and by an organic-dynamic view of nature, that subjected nature to the spiritual purposes of the universe.[1]

Although Idealism is linked with the names of some of Germany's greatest philosophers, it was more than a set of philosophical systems. It embraced an outlook on life which had philosophical and religious implications. As such it was shared by many who were not philosophers in the technical sense. The age of Idealism might equally well be called the Age of Goethe. H. A. Korff, the eminent student of German literature, claims that

> the system of ideas of Idealism, in which the spirit of the Age of Goethe unfolded, was on the one hand the overthrow of Christianity and the Enlightenment and on the other hand the uniting of them into a higher synthesis. Christianity and the Enlightenment both appear to us to be transcended in the Age of Goethe, that is they are both preserved and abandoned. Thus it appears possible to speak of the Age of Goethe as the hour of birth of a new religion, provided that one understands the concept of religion in a very broad sense. But this demands the further recognition that German Idealism can be regarded only in this broad, extended sense as a "religion." In fact, it is only a religious form of a philosophical world view, which must necessarily give up what is specific in a *genuine* religion. Indeed, German Idealism wants to be

precisely a world view without religion, *a philosophy and not a religion*. Thus, however much the Age of Goethe is to be conceived as an age of religious ferment, its profoundest characteristic, which it inherited in its blood from the Enlightenment, is, nevertheless, the *emancipation from religion* (in the strict sense of this word). And if, in spite of this, it has a religious character, it is that of a *free religiosity*, in which the idea of "religion" is actually destroyed.[2]

The ideas which Troeltsch and Korff describe here affected thinking about Jesus. In the present chapter we shall focus attention on Kant, Herder and Goethe; in the next chapter, the Absolute Idealism of Fichte, Hegel and Schelling. Of these thinkers only Herder had any claim to be considered a theologian, and he is better remembered for his contributions to literature. Nevertheless, the views of these writers exerted considerable influence on nineteenth-century religious thought.

Kant

Three years after publishing his *Kritik der reinen Vernunft* (1781), Immanuel Kant (1724–1804) asked and answered the question, "What is Enlightenment?" His reply was that

Enlightenment is man's release from his self-incurred tutelage. Tutelage is man's inability to make use of his understanding without direction from another. Self-incurred is this tutelage when its cause lies not in lack of reason but in lack of resolution and courage to use it without direction from another. *Sapere aude!* "Have courage to use your own reason!"—that is the motto of enlightenment.[3]

Kant went on to say that no generation should be bound by the creeds and dogmas of bygone ages. To be so bound was an offense against human nature, whose destiny lies in progress. Admittedly, the age that Kant lived in was not yet an *enlightened age*, but it was the century of Frederick the Great and the *Age of Enlightenment*. "We have clear indications that the field has now been opened wherein men may freely deal with these things and that the obstacles to general enlightenment or the release from self-imposed tutelage are gradually being reduced."[4]

These reflections sound a *Leitmotiv* in the thinking of Kant who increasingly dominated German philosophy from 1770 when he assumed the chair of Logic and Metaphysics at Königsberg. Already in the *Kritik der reinen Vernunft* he had observed that, "Our age is, in an especial degree, the age of criticism, and to criticism everything must submit."[5] Neither metaphysics nor religion were exempt. Although it might have appeared in recent times that the claims of metaphysics to the title of Queen of all the sciences had been vindicated "through a certain *physiology* of the human understanding—that of the celebrated Locke," it had turned out otherwise.[6] Moreover, religion "cannot claim the sincere respect which reason accords only to that which has been able to sustain the test of free and open examination."[7]

In the *Kritik der reinen Vernunft* Kant used reason to scrutinize the scope and limits of human understanding. He broke with rationalistic metaphysics and sought to delineate an epistemology that was compatible with the mechanistic world view of Newtonian science without succumbing to the skepticism of David Hume. Insofar as religion presumed to pronounce upon the transcendent, it was attempting to perform the impossible. For the human mind was not equipped to grapple with anything beyond the range of immediate experience.[8] Once the human mind tried to press beyond this, it found itself embroiled in "Antinomies" or unresolvable self-contradictions.[9] The existence of God over and above the universe is rationally indemonstrable, and significant discourse about divine activity was precluded.

> Now I maintain that all attempts to employ reason in theology in any merely speculative manner are altogether fruitless and by their very nature null and void, and that the principles of its employment in the study of nature do not lead to any theology whatsoever. Consequently, the only theology of reason which is possible is that which is based upon moral laws or seeks guidance from them. All synthetic principles of reason allow only of an immanent employment; and in order to have knowledge of a supreme being we should have to put them to a transcendent use, for which our understanding is in no way fitted.[10]

Kant allowed that we *undoubtedly* assume "a wise and omnipotent Author of the world." But in answer to the question whether we thus "extend our knowledge beyond the field of possible experience," he replied,

> *By no means.* All that we have done is merely to presuppose a something, a merely transcendental object, of which, as it is in itself, we have no concept whatsoever. It is only in relation to the systematic and purposive ordering of the world, which, if we are to study nature, we are constrained to presuppose, that we have thought this unknown being *by analogy* with an intelligence (an empirical concept); that is, have endowed it, in respect of the ends and perfection which are to be grounded upon it, with just those properties which, in conformity with the conditions of our reason, can be regarded as containing the ground of such systematic unity. This idea is thus valid only in respect of the *employment* of our reason *in reference to the world.* If we ascribed to it a validity that is absolute and objective, we should be forgetting that what we are thinking is a being in idea only; and in thus taking our start from a ground which is not determinable through observation of the world, we should no longer be in a position to apply the principle in a manner suited to the empirical employment of reason.[11]

In short, Kant considered the idea of God to be a *Regulative Principle* (as opposed to a *Constitutive Principle*). It was useful in giving cohesion to thought, but no content whatsoever could be given to it.

In the realm of ethics Kant worked out an enlightened approach to morality in works like the *Grundlegung zur Metaphysik der Sitten* (1785), *Kritik der praktischen Vernunft* (1788) and *Die Metaphysik der Sitten* (1797). Ethics should be based, not upon sanctions and laws imposed upon man from outside, but upon principles which were self-evident to man's practical reason. The formal principle of all duty resides in what Kant called the Categorical Imperative: "Act only according to that maxim by which you can at the same time will that it should become a universal law."[12] In this way Kant sought to lay a new foundation for ethics, removing it from the provinces of theology, law and custom, and planting it firmly in the area of what is rational to the enlightened mind. It centered on "the principle of the *autonomy* of the will" in contrast with all other principles which Kant classified under the category of *heteronomy*.[13]

In view of all this it might seem that Kant was ready to abandon religion altogether. Certainly he studiously avoided going to church. Even on the *dies academicus*, when the university solemnly processed to worship, Kant made a point of quitting its ranks as it reached the church door and going off home round the back. So far as can be seen, even when dealing with Christianity, Kant never allowed himself to put pen to paper in order to write the names Jesus or Christ. Yet religion still had a place, though it too must be reinterpreted in an enlightened, rational way. Indeed, Kant had long conceived a grand scheme in which he proposed to subject religion and anthropology to the same critical reappraisal that he had given to epistemology and ethics. In May 1793 Kant wrote to the Göttingen professor of theology and advocate of Kantianism, Carl Friedrich Stäudlin,

> My longstanding plan for the reappraisal, incumbent upon me in the field of pure philosophy centered on dealing with three tasks: (1) What can I know? (Metaphysics) (2) What should I do? (Ethics) (3) What may I hope? (Religion); whereupon the fourth should follow: What is man? (Anthropology; on which I have annually delivered a course for more than 20 years)—With the accompanying book *Religion innerhalb der Grenzen* etc. I have sought to complete the third division of my plan. In this work conscientiousness and true respect for the Christian religion, but also the principle of a proper freedom of thought, have led me to conceal nothing. On the contrary, I have presented everything openly, as I believe I see the possible union of the latter with the purest practical reason.[14]

The book which accompanied this letter was *Die Religion innerhalb der Grenzen der blossen Vernunft* (1793). As its title suggests, it sought to define the role of religion within the limits prescribed by reason. Kant had already thrown out hints as to how he would reappraise religion. The *Kritik der reinen Vernunft* treated the idea of God as a "regulative principle." The *Kritik der praktischen Vernunft* treated the ideas of God, freedom and immortality as "postulates of pure practical reason."[15] But Kant remained adamant that such postulates were non-cognitive.

> The postulates of pure practical reason all proceed from the principle of morality, which is not a postulate but a law by which reason directly determines the will. This will, by the fact that it is so determined, as a pure will requires these necessary conditions for obedience to its precept. These postulates are not theoretical dogmas but presuppositions of necessarily practical import; thus, while they do not extend

speculative knowledge, they give objective reality to the ideas of speculative knowledge in general (by means of their relation to the practical sphere), and they justify it in holding to concepts even the possibility of which it could not otherwise venture to affirm.[16]

At the heart of the Kantian scheme lies this paradox: morality is autonomous and stands in no need of the idea of God; on the other hand, it points to religion and God. This theme constituted the climax of the *Kritik der praktischen Vernunft*. In *Die Religion innerhalb der Grenzen der blossen Vernunft* it set the key for the whole work:

So far as morality is based upon the conception of man as a free agent who, just because he is free, binds himself through his reason to unconditioned laws, it stands in need neither of the idea of another Being over him, for him to apprehend his duty, nor of an incentive other than the law itself, for him to do his duty.[17]

Yet the idea of God provides men with "a special point of focus for the unification of all ends."[18] Only God can unite duty and happiness. Morality points to "the idea of a highest good in the world for whose possibility we must postulate a higher, moral, most holy, and omnipotent Being which alone can unite the two elements of this highest good."[19]

It has been disputed whether this introduction of God is logically consistent with Kant's program of making man autonomous, guided only by what is self-evident to his reason. It has also been vigorously debated whether Kant himself recognized this and in his last years eliminated God altogether from his scheme of thought.[20] Nevertheless, he did not do so in his published work. And it was in this frame of mind that he proceeded to throw every Christian doctrine into the melting pot in his reassessment of religion within the limits of reason alone. What emerged from the anti-metaphysical, rationalistic, moralistic mold was something which bore a resemblance to Christianity, but which had marked affinities with Deism. Revealed religion was, as the Deists, Lessing and Rousseau had already insisted, a particular form of rational, natural religion. The picture that Kant painted of such a religion was that of a Pelagianism of a fairly pure strain. It recognized an evil inclination in man.[21] But the salvation that it proferred was one of self-help and unflinching duty. Because of man's propensity to a passive faith, it must be repeatedly inculcated that

true religion is to consist not in the knowing or considering of what God does or has done for our salvation but in what we must do to become worthy of it. This last can never be anything but what possesses in itself undoubted and *unconditional* worth, what therefore can alone make us well-pleasing to God, and of whose necessity every man can become wholly certain without any Scriptural learning whatever.[22]

Kant maintained that the ideal of a humanity pleasing to God "resides in our morally-legislative reason. We *ought* to conform to it; consequently we must *be able* to do so."[23] This, for Kant, was the central concern of the Christian religion, which he stated in the following passage concerning *"The Personified Idea of the Good Principle"*:

> *Mankind* (rational earthly existence in general) *in its complete moral perfection* is that which alone can render a world the object of a divine decree and the end of creation. With such perfection as the prime condition, happiness is the direct consequence, according to the will of the Supreme Being. Man so conceived, alone pleasing to God, "is in Him through eternity,"[24] the idea of him proceeds from God's very being; hence he is no created thing but His only-begotten Son, "the *Word* (the *Fiat!*) through which all other things are, and without which nothing is in existence that is made"[25] (since for him, that is, for rational existence in the world, so far as he may be regarded in the light of his moral destiny, all things were made). "He is the brightness of His glory."[26] "In him God loved the world,"[27] and only in him and through the adoption of his disposition can we hope "to become the sons of God,"[28] etc.
>
> Now it is our universal duty as men to *elevate* ourselves to this ideal of moral perfection, that is, to this archetype of the moral disposition in all its purity — and for this the idea itself, which reason presents to us for our zealous emulation, can give us power. But just because we are not the authors of this idea, and because it has established itself in man without our comprehending how human nature could have been capable of receiving it, it is more appropriate to say that this archetype has *come down* to us from heaven and has assumed our humanity (for it is less possible to conceive how man, by nature *evil*, should of himself lay aside evil and *raise* himself to the ideal of holiness, than that the latter should *descend* to man and assume a *humanity* which is, in itself, not evil). Such union with us may therefore be regarded as a state of *humiliation* of the Son of God[29] if we represent to ourselves this godly-minded person, regarded as our archetype, as assuming sorrows in fullest measure in order to further the world's good, though he himself is holy and therefore is bound to endure no sufferings whatsoever. Man, on the contrary, who is never free from guilt even though he has taken on the very same disposition, can regard as truly merited the sufferings that may overtake him, by whatever road they come; consequently he must consider himself unworthy of the union of his disposition with such an idea, even thought this idea serves him as an archetype.[30]

This passage has been quoted at some length because it reproduces *in nuce* Kant's Christology. Perhaps Christology is too strong a word. For neither here nor in the rest of the work is the title *Christ* referred to directly. What Kant ostensibly describes is the personified idea of the good principle. It is a piece of thinking aloud about a hypothetical moral being, posited by reason, regardless of whether the figure bears any resemblance to any character known in history. "We need, therefore, no empirical example to make the idea of a person morally well-pleasing to God our archetype; this idea as an archetype is already present in our reason."[31] On the other hand, the passage is replete with biblical allusions. Christological terms and concepts are lifted out of the New Testament, but are secularized, rationalized and demythologized in all but name. Kant's own term for this process was to describe it as divesting the vivid, popular mode of representation of its "mystic veil." When duly carried out—and this was one of the major tasks of the theologian[32]—the result was the rediscovery of the universally binding, rational and moral principles that underlie religion.

> Once this vivid mode of representation, which was in its time probably the only *popular* one, is divested of its mystical veil, it is easy to see that, for practical purposes, its spirit and rational meaning have been valid and binding for the whole world and for all time, since to each man it lies so near at hand that he knows his duty towards it. Its meaning is this: that there exists absolutely no salvation for man apart from the sincerest adoption of genuinely moral principles into his disposition.[33]

At one point Kant admitted that the ideal of moral perfection "made its appearance in an actual human being, as an example to all others."[34] But for the most part he preferred to speak in general terms of an unnamed third party who was not unique, but only a particular case of a potentially recurring phenomenon.[35] From time to time Kant paused to deal with items which presumably helped to make up the now obsolete and undesirable "mystic veil." We are not to think of the archetypal figure as being more than human. To demand belief in his capacity to perform miracles is itself a form of "moral unbelief."[36] To ascribe divinity to this person would be self-defeating, for a divine person could not be presented to us "as an *example* for our imitation."[37] To speak of an incarnation was permissible, provided that it be understood to refer to "the ideal of goodness" displayed in his life and teaching. And even this is restricted to the "disposition which he makes the rule of his actions."[38] Elsewhere Jesus is described as "the *wise* Teacher" of rational religion.[39]

Kant declared himself not unsympathetic to the motives which have prompted men to think of a virgin birth, but these must pale into insignificance when compared with the "symbol of a mankind raising itself above temptation to evil (and withstanding it victoriously)."[40] In dealing with the death of the archetypal figure, Kant showed himself aware of recent controversy. In a footnote he spurned the "fancifully imagined" theory of C. F. Bahrdt that Jesus deliberately sought suicide as a sensational means of furthering his cause. Death might come accidentally in pursuance of some end, but one could not morally dispose of one's life as a means in this way.[41] In the same footnote Kant went on to assail the *Wolfenbüttel Fragments* for imputing to the "Master" merely political and unlawful intents which miscarried. Kant's alternative explanation was certainly more moral, but scarcely less rationalistic. "This death (the last extremity of human suffering) was therefore a manifestation of the good principle, that is, of humanity in its moral perfection, and an example for everyone to follow."[42]

This death did not, in fact, conquer the evil principle, but it broke the hold of evil over those who do not wish it. Kant sought to harmonize his view with the church's view of atonement, but he felt compelled to preface the harmonization with the candid admission that the two systems of salvation were radically different.

The acceptance of the first requisite for salvation, namely, faith in a vicarious atonement, is in any case necessary only for the theoretical concept; in no other way can we *make comprehensible* to ourselves such absolution. In contrast, the necessity for the second principle is practical and, indeed, purely moral. We can certainly hope to partake in the appropriation of another's atoning merit, and so of salvation, only by qualifying for it through our own efforts to fulfil every human duty—and this obedience must be the effect of our own action and not, once again, of a foreign influence in the presence of which we are passive. For since the command to do our duty is unconditioned, it is also necessary that man shall make it, as maxim, the basis of his belief, that is to say that he shall begin with the improvement of his life as the supreme condition under which alone a saving faith can exist.[43]

At best, traditional Christian teaching was a graphic and garbled way of teaching morality. It was no substitute for the Categorical Imperative which it may even obscure with its stress on help from outside and faith instead of works. For Kant it was the Categorical Imperative which was the ground and means of salvation and which constituted the burden and substance of "the Teacher's" instruction.

Although Kant made no express references to the Deists and their critique of Christianity, his own restatement of religion, based on his critical epistemology and his rationally self-evident ethics, reached essentially the same view of religion. As his work reached its climax, Kant presented a statement of "The Christian Religion as a Natural Religion":

Natural religion, as morality (in its relation to the freedom of the agent) united with the concept of that which can make actual its final end (with the concept of *God* as moral Creator of the world), and referred to a continuance of man which is suited to this end in its completeness (to immortality), is a pure practical idea of reason which, despite its inexhaustible fruitfulness, presupposes so very little capacity for theoretical reason that one can convince every man of it sufficiently for practical purposes and can at least require of all men as a duty that which is its effect. This religion possesses the prime essential of the true church, namely, the qualification for universality, so far as one understands by that a validity for everyone (*universitas vel omnitudo distributiva*), i.e., universal unanimity. To spread it, in this sense, as a world religion, and to maintain it, there is needed, no doubt, a body of servants (*ministerium*) of the invisible church, but not officials (*officiales*), in other words, teachers but not dignitaries, because in the rational religion of every individual there does not yet exist a church as a universal *union (omnitudo collectiva)*, nor is this really contemplated in the above idea.[44]

Within this scheme Kant encouraged his readers to entertain the supposition that

there was a teacher of whom an historical record (or, at least, a widespread belief which is not basically disputable) reports that he was the first to expound publicly a pure and searching religion, comprehensible to the whole world (and thus natural). His teachings, as preserved to us, we can in this case test for ourselves.[45]

From the description of this unnamed teacher Kant drew the conclusion that

> one will not fail to recognize the person who can be reverenced, not indeed as the
> *founder* of the *religion* which, free from every dogma, is engraved in all men's hearts
> (for it does not have its origin in an arbitrary will), but as the founder of the first true
> *church*.[46]

Following a brief interpretation of the Sermon on the Mount and the parables of
the kingdom, Kant saw in Jesus' teaching concerning the Two Great Commandments an understanding of the basis of morality which was virtually identical
with his own.

> Finally, he combines all duties (1) in one *universal* rule (which includes within itself
> both the inner and the outer moral relations of men), namely: Perform your duty for
> no motive other than unconditioned esteem for duty itself, *i.e.*, love God (the
> Legislator of all duties) above all else; and (2) in a *particular* rule, that, namely,
> which concerns man's external relation to other men as universal duty: Love every
> one as yourself, *i.e.*, further his welfare from good-will that is immediate and not
> derived from motives of self-advantage. These commands are not mere laws of
> virtue but precepts of *holiness* which we ought to pursue, and the very pursuit of
> them is called *virtue*.[47]

In reaching this conclusion Kant identified love of God with "unconditioned
esteem for duty itself." He also glossed over the fact that in the Gospels Jesus was
not concerned with self-evident maxims for morality, but the interpretation of the
Torah of Yahweh, the God of Israel who relates to men in a personal, cognitive
way.

Kant's reappraisal of religion was not dissimilar to Lessing's. The accidental
and historical was neither proof nor substitute for the eternal truths of reason. At
best it exemplified in a partial and transitory way that which was self-evident to
the enlightened, rational mind. It was merely a passing phase in the progress of
humanity. Kant's position is outlined in a section entitled, "The gradual Transition of Ecclesiastical Faith to the Exclusive Sovereignty of Pure Religious Faith is
the Coming of the Kingdom of God."[48] But unlike Lessing, Kant did not pursue
the vision of a universal, rational religion, arising like a phoenix out of the ashes
of the present world religions. He remained true to his basic principle of refusing
to speculate on that of which we have no direct experience, insisting that in any
case moral faith was a private affair always likely to be at variance with institutional religion.[49]

Whereas Lessing's Christ was an enlightened teacher, Kant's was a symbolic incarnation of the Categorical Imperative who preached what he practiced.
In its own way Kant's view of Jesus was scarcely less radical than that of the
Fragmentist. The latter had launched a broadside attack upon the integrity of the
Gospels, denouncing everything dear to orthodoxy as a fraud. Kant's view was
presented as a reinterpretation of Christianity, ostensibly bringing out its own
basic inner principles in the light of a modern world view. Although he had dealt

some heavy blows to orthodox beliefs, Kant had refrained from attacking the Bible itself openly. Nevertheless, the validity of the New Testament message was clearly impugned. Kant's assault did not escape the attention of the minister for religion, Wöllner.[50] It drew upon Kant the personal censure of Friedrich Wilhelm II who threatened the philosopher with the most unpleasant consequences if he persisted in propagating such views.[51] In his reply Kant promised the king that he would refrain from the public discussion of religious issues. However, when the king died in 1797 Kant felt himself released from his promise, and the book was already in its third edition.[52]

Subsequent generations of nineteenth-century Protestants took a somewhat more favorable view of Kant. D. F. Strauss compared him with the early fathers who were not so much interested in the details of history as the idea involved in it,[53] though Kant's method unfortunately revived the old allegorical interpretation of Scripture and compelled him to read into it his own moral ideas. Later still, Julius Kaftan and Friedrich Paulsen hailed Kant as the philosopher of Protestantism.[54] Kant was seen as the philosophical continuator of the line begun by Luther of rejecting external authorities and making the individual's response the determining factor in religion. Personal morality mattered more than dogmas and ceremonies. Today it is impossible to endorse these verdicts. Kant's teaching was a complete reversal of Luther's. Justification by faith was replaced by justification by the Categorical Imperative. His whole system was a repudiation of the reformers' doctrine of grace. Whereas the latter operated within a framework of biblical supernaturalism which they had inherited from the medieval and early church, Kant dismissed the supernatural to the realm of the unknowable. Revelation through Scripture is replaced by ostensibly rational, self-evident principles. The result is a Pelagian Deism in which Kant has neither a Jesus of history nor a Christ of faith. Instead he has a symbolic figure of ideal humanity practicing rational moral religion and hovering between history and vision. What Kant says about this figure has the air of a compromise between his philosophical system and historic Christianity. On the one hand, his philosophical premises required him to say that a life based upon the Categorical Imperative was perfectly possible. On the other hand, he had gone as far as he dared in criticizing the Christian religion, and he had to fit the figure of Christ in somewhere. Under the circumstances it is not surprising that the resultant figure was highly attenuated and lacking in historical substance. Kant had a philosophy of history, but he was not interested in history as such. Like Enlightened thinkers before him and Idealist philosophers after him, Kant was more concerned with reading into history his preconceived rational world view.

In one respect Kant was the philosopher of Protestantism, but it was the liberal, anti-metaphysical, anti-dogmatic Protestantism of Ritschl and the Neo-Kantians in the second half of the nineteenth century.[55] In other respects Kant might more accurately be described as the philosopher of Deism. But it was an agnostic, critical Deism, which not only criticized revealed religion, but the nature and status of its own truth-claims. As Kant saw it, he was steering a course between the dogmatism of Wolff's rationalism and the skepticism of David Hume. For him, "The *critical* path alone is still open."[56] Kant's immediate philosophical successors went their own different ways. Even though they may have taken Kant as their starting point, in one way or another they found illumination in Spinoza. Hegel, Schleiermacher, Fichte and Schelling were all influenced by Kant. But in the end, what they accepted from him was not his philosophical system but his anti-supernaturalistic attitude toward philosophy and religion. And even this—like the nineteenth century liberal stress on the moral aspect of Christianity—was not something unique to Kant. It was part of the legacy of the Age of Enlightenment. Kant's contribution was his attempt to fulfill his self-imposed task of giving that legacy a consistent, philosophical formulation. The result was a bridge between the age of Enlightenment and the age of Idealism. It was an agnostic Idealism. It posited an ideal realm, but insisted that nothing certain could be said about it. All its positive affirmations were thoroughly rationalistic.

Herder

Johann Gottfried von Herder (1744–1803)[57] was a man of almost universal interests and many parts. He was a critic, poet, philosopher, educator, preacher and amateur theologian. In Schweitzer's *Quest of the Historical Jesus*, he merited only two or three pages and was bracketed (though with some hesitation) with the older rationalists.[58] Karl Barth, on the other hand, called him "the inaugurator of typical nineteenth-century theology before its inauguration by Schleiermacher."[59]

From 1762 to 1764 Herder studied theology and philosophy at Königsberg, where he attended Kant's lectures. But it was the pre-critical Kant, and although the young Herder acquired from him an enthusiasm for geography, anthropology and even philosophy, including that of British writers, it was J. G. Hamann (who worked in the excise office at Königsberg) who proved to have the more decisive influence. Hamann turned his attention to poetry and literature. Herder began to read the Old Testament not as a series of specially revealed propositions but as a primitive literature that as such was revelation. As Alexander Gillies has pointed out, "Any elements of a system which Kant might have taught Herder were destroyed by the influence of this incoherent but stimulating writer."[60]

While teaching at Riga, Herder wrote his *Fragmente über die neuere deutsche Literatur* (1767), which established his reputation as a literary critic. He was ordained in the same year. But his interest in popular culture led him to travel. He conceived it his mission in life to study the history of mankind from its primitive beginnings in order to see the path of society in the future. His enthusiasm for Shakespeare and folk poetry, which he conceived as the unrepressed utterance of human creative genius, contributed to the *Sturm und Drang* movement in German literature.

In 1771 he became court preacher to the Count of Schaumburg-Lippe at Bückeburg. In 1776 he moved to Weimar, the cultural capital of Germany, as Generalsuperintendent of the Lutheran Church and court preacher. Doubts were raised about his orthodoxy, but the appointment was confirmed, partly through the influence of Goethe. However, by 1793 the friendship with Goethe had waned. Herder's greatest works belong to the earlier part of the Weimar period, his *Volkslieder* (1778–79) and his *Ideen* (1784–91). In the last decade of his life he produced five collections of *Christliche Schriften* (1794–98) in which he reappraised Christianity in general and orthodox beliefs about Jesus in particular.

Early on in his career Herder dreamed of becoming the Newton of history.[61] He sought to realize this ambition through two works. The first bore the somewhat barbed title of *Auch eine Philosophie der Geschichte zur Bildung der Menschheit, ein Beytrag zu vielen Beyträgen des Jahrhunderts* (1774). It had as its target the many philosophies of history written by Enlightened thinkers who were totally lacking in historical sense. However, it was superseded by *Ideen zur Philosophie der Geschichte der Menschheit* (1784–91).[62] It was an evolutionary history of mankind which saw human progress as the product of man's reaction to his environment.

> What is the principal law which we observe in all great phenomena of history? It seems to me to be this: *That which comes to be in every place on our earth, which can come to be upon it, does so partly in accordance with the situation and needs of the place, partly in accordance with the circumstances and occasions of the time, partly in accordance with the innate or acquired character of the peoples.*[63]

The cosmos was not to be explained on the basis of a literal reading of Genesis. Herder had already made it clear that he regarded the First Book of Moses as a human document, to be read as poetry and not as a scientific treatise.[64]

But the divine was not altogether eliminated. It was naturalized and channeled into man's gifts and the processes of nature. Herder's fullest statement of his views on God appeared in *Gott: Einige Gespräche* (1787). In the second edition of 1800 the subtitle was enlarged to make it more descriptive: *Einige Gespräche über Spinoza's System; nebst Shaftesburi's Naturhymnus.*[65] The dialogue form served partly as an insurance against being pinned down to any definite opinion. At the same time it provided opportunity to modify and develop Spinoza's deterministic pantheism into a dynamic panentheism. Almost invariably Theophron (the defender of Spinoza) gets the best of the argument, while Philolaus (who has the task of setting up objections) admits with monotonous regularity that his queries have been fully answered.

Philolaus at first finds difficulty with Spinoza's proposition, "There is but one Substance, and that is God. All things are but modifications of it."[66] However, Theophron reassures him that he must not be misled by the word *Substance*.

> What is Substance but a thing which is self-dependent which has the cause of its existence in itself? I wish that this pure meaning of the word could have been

introduced into our philosophy. In the strictest sense, nothing in the world is a
Substance, because everything depends on everything else, and finally on God, who
therefore is the highest and only substance.

Philolaus soon concedes that "so many pathetic declamations against
Spinoza" suddenly dwindle to nothing.[67] Whereupon Theophron presses home
the rationality of Spinoza's position with the question,

> Then you will also find it no blasphemy, when Spinoza calls the Independent Being
> the immanent and not the transitive cause of all things?

The question is answered in turn by further questions.

> PHILOLAUS: How could I find it so, when, on the contrary, it is impossible to think
> of God as a transitive cause of things? How and when and to what is He transitive? A
> creature without His support is nothing, and how can He be transitive who has no
> place, leaves no place, in whom there can be no change nor alteration?
>
> THEOPHRON: But what if God dwells out of the world?
>
> PHILOLAUS: Where is there a place out of the world? The world itself, and space
> and time therein, the sole means by which we measure and count things, all exist
> only through Him, the Infinite One.
>
> THEOPHRON: Excellent, Philolaus.[68]

Herder was not simply a Spinozist. He found confirmation and insight in
other rationalist systems. His translator, F. H. Burkhardt, saw in Herder "a loose
synthesis of Leibniz and Spinoza, in which the doctrines of the one were used to
augment and modify those of the other."[69] Spinoza needed to be made more
dynamic and be brought into line with more recent science. As Herder himself
put it, "Truth quietly marches on. Spinoza's times were the childhood of natural
science, without which metaphysics only builds castles in the air or gropes about
in the dark."[70] Herder's naturalism and pantheism—or more precisely panentheism—were complementary. God was not to be eliminated; he was the immanent ground of all things. Without God nothing would exist. But if we are to find
him, we must look for him not in the supernatural but in the natural. It was
against this background that Herder made his study of Jesus and the Gospels.

Herder's chief contributions to New Testament criticism were made in the
last decade of his life. They are to be found in the second and third collections of
his *Christliche Schriften: Vom Erlöser der Menschen. Nach unsern drei ersten
Evangelien* (1796) and *Von Gottes Sohn, der Welt Heiland. Nach Johannes
Evangelium. Nebst einer Regel der Zusammenstimmung unsrer Evangelien aus
ihrer Entstehung und Ordnung* (1797). The titles themselves make it plain that
John and the Synoptics require different treatment.[71] Both in this and his treatment of numerous other points Herder anticipated the conclusions of later
generations.

The opening remarks of *Vom Erlöser* propose that the prior question to be
asked, before anything can be said about Jesus himself, is, "What are the

Gospels?'' In a manner anticipating Bultmann, Herder drew attention to the great gulf between the thought-world of the secular writer and that of the evangelists.

> There he saw events arise out of natural causes and issue in natural effects. He heard on them the judgments of understanding. The author was at pains to show the cause in the effect, and the effect in the cause, and considered it the purpose of his work to develop this connection, either through the juxtaposition of events themselves or through discourse and judgments. Here he finds himself in another world. Heavenly powers have their visible play on the earth. Angels and the Son of God, opposed by the demons of hell, engage in conflict against each other, so that almost no human motive remains *merely* natural, and thus comprehensible and capable of being seen. The Son of God, whom angels announced, whom the demons recognize, works wonders, and promises the gift of wonders to all who believe on him. Born supernaturally, he lives supernaturally, and ascends to heaven. Here can the devotee of purely human history say: I have here much to amaze me, much to wonder at, but little to understand. I am not in history but in the land of poetry, surrounded by divinity and supernature.[72]

The unusualness of much that is in the Gospels rules it out as history. But Herder was not simply concerned with *a priori* rationalism. He was also concerned with the lack of confirmation by other New Testament writers.

> No single apostle has endorsed with his name the historical narrative of his colleague or apostle among the evangelists. Paul did not confirm the Gospel of Luke, and Peter the Gospel of Mark. In no writing of the N.T. does there even occur a mention of written Gospels. . . . Precisely for that reason they remain late compositions, not confirmed by the apostles.[73]

Nor had Herder much confidence in the critical judgment of the early fathers as guarantors of the historical accuracy of the Gospels.[74] His own critical judgment detected contradictions of fact, style, manner of speech and reporting, which made harmonization impossible. "Whom should we now trust? Whose picture is true? Did Jesus speak as John represents him, or as the three others paint him?"[75]

Nevertheless, Herder recognized a "striking similarity" between the Gospels. He rejected the idea of an *Urevangelium* and also the theories of mutual literary dependence which were to become textbook orthodoxy in later years.[76] He doubted whether it could be shown when and for whom the Gospels were first written.[77] But Herder did not despair of a solution. His doubts were intended to clear the ground for saying that the evangelists were not classical historians or biographers, but writers in the primitive poetic, Jewish tradition,

> The historical style of the Hebrews belongs, like their poetry, to *the infancy of the human race*. . . . Therefore, forgetting everything foreign, we must get into the character of a *nation which knew no foreign literature and dwelt in its ancient holy books . . . as in the sanctuary of all wisdom*. In them every letter was divine, every parable a heavenly mystery, and whoever wrote anything composed in this frame of mind.[78]

The Gospels were not themselves the foundation of the gospel. In the beginning was the sermon. "Christianity did not begin with Gospel writing, but with the proclamation of past and future things *(kērygma, apokalypsis)*, with exposition, doctrine, consolation, exhortation, preaching."[79] This preaching found clearest expression in the Fourth Gospel.

> Above all it was the concern of our evangelists that the notion should be grasped in the right sense of what it was to be *God's Son* and how he gives *eternal life* as the *Savior of the world*. For as this expression was the symbol of Christianity and faith, in which all Christians hoped for the salvation of the world (Acts 2:38, 39; 4:12; 8:37), this teaching was also the Gospel of John's *only dogma* (John 20:31).[80]

This was in fact the motive which turned the original oral Gospel into four written Gospels. The similarities were to be explained by the fact that over the years certain patterns or—to use Herder's term with its associations of folk poetry—*apostolic sagas* were established.

> To be sure these oral evangelists must have got through their instruction a *circle (Cyklus)*, within which their account obtained, and this it was which the apostles themselves had at the beginning of their preaching. It is indicated in the Acts of the Apostles (1:21–22; 2:23–36; 10:36–43). As all the stories came from one source, the apostles, and at that time everything was close together (2:34; 4:32), the instruction of disciples was the primary occupation of the apostles (6:3–7). Thus through this and the accompaniment of the apostles, evangelists were formed. In our three Gospels, e.g., occur *the same* parables, miracles, stories and discourses. From this it appears that the general tradition of these *Gospel Rhapsodists* (if this name be permitted me) kept mainly to these stories. They are often told with the same words. For it is often the nature of the case in an oral, oft told and oft repeated, especially *apostolic saga*, as we note it in Peter's sermons and the letters of the apostle himself. They were *fixed, holy sagas*.[81]

Werner Georg Kümmel credits Herder with recognizing for the first time the form-critical problems of the Gospels.[82] It may have been that Herder was influenced by the ideas of F. A. Wolf whose *Prolegomena ad Homerum*, vol. 1 (1795) had been published in the year prior to *Vom Erlöser der Menschen*. But this seems unlikely. Although Herder had read Wolf's essay, he had long had similar theories of his own on Homer in particular and on folk poetry and community literature in general.[83] His two essays on the Gospels do not read like hastily dashed off bright ideas, but like the convictions of many years. Herder was applying to the Gospels his long held views on the origins of popular, primitive literature. What he said here about oral tradition, the thought-world of the primitive church, the role of the community, the paraenetic character of the documents and their theological tendencies anticipated the views, not so much of the nineteenth but of the twentieth century.

Herder's treatment of John also broke with current views. The Fourth Gospel was not to be regarded as history. It was a series of "speaking pictures" held together by editorial cement of the loosest texture. No historical sequence was intended.[84] John himself practiced demythologization in all but name. John was concerned with "the reality of idea" and not the letter of the word.

> He shows in what consists this liberation, help, power, this sonship, this Word of *God*, as it revealed itself in humanity and goes on revealing itself. Consequently, it is the *living meaning* of the ancient Palestinian expression. Necessarily there belonged to it the rejection of Jewish wrappings and forms. Providence itself has torn apart and laid aside these swaddling-clothes; Christianity had outgrown them.[85]

John was not interested in the earthly Jesus but in his spiritual significance.

> Therefore it is precisely this *unveiling of Christ*, the *pure glorification of him*, that is the most precious in John. Indeed, it is his whole meaning, his soul. He forgot, if I may say so, the earthly character of his Palestinian friend, bound to place and time, in order to depict the heavenly, the eternal in him, that transcends place and time and unites him with all humanity.... To this end his *divine support (paraklētos)* was to live in them and lead them through act and experience from truth to truth.[86]

How far John's picture of Jesus remained valid for Herder's readers was not exactly clear. In *Vom Geist des Christenthums* Herder spoke of the continuing illumination of the Spirit that works in the community of mankind in accordance with the rules of reason.[87] In *Vom Erlöser* Herder declared that the creeds and dogmas of the church were external symbols and signs.[88] What mattered was "the gospel itself; this concerns the *teaching*, the *character of Jesus* and his *work*, that is, the institution which he wanted to carry out for the benefit of mankind."[89] Although Herder did not speak expressly of "the historical Jesus," the summary that he gave of the mission of Jesus was almost identical in substance with that of Harnack who culminated a century of liberal theology, much of which was devoted to the quest of the historical Jesus. "*The teaching of Jesus* was simple, and capable of being grasped by all men: *God is your Father*; you should all be brothers to each other."[90]

As with Deism and later liberal theology, this altruistic message banished from true religion every kind of empty ceremonial and all speculation about the deity. It was a gospel which embraced the ideals of eighteenth-century Freemasonry. The practical realization of the brotherhood of men was the fulfillment of true piety and the manifestation of divinity. "The same notion, that God is the Father of all men, *binds the human race to each other as brothers*, as brothers of a noble stock of *divine nature and origin*."[91] Herder's view was in a sense a secularization of the gospel and a divinization of secular history.

> That which made the teaching of Christ in so few words into a *universal, sovereign attitude of mind* and an *endless endeavor*, the character of Jesus expressed as completely as it did simply in his two names. *He was called Son of God and Son of Man.* To God's Beloved the *will of the Father* was the highest rule and motive of all his acts, even the most burdensome to the offering of his life. Respect, honor, wealth,

unmerited shame and contempt were all the same to him. There was a work to be completed, to which he bore the vocation in himself, the *work of God*, that is the true, eternal business of providence with our race, to save it and make it blessed. This work he did as Son of Man, that is out of pure duty and for the highest goal of mankind.[92]

This work begun by Jesus was the ongoing work of mankind.[93]

These pronouncements contain echoes of Kant and earlier Enlightened thinkers. But Herder was not simply an Enlightened philosopher. His interest in the origins of literature and his application of literary theories about folk literature to the Bible set him apart. Nevertheless, his work was not exactly critical, historical investigation. It was more an imaginative reconstruction based upon certain presuppositions: oral tradition, independent production of the Gospels, belief that the authorship of the Gospels cannot be known and the need to reinterpret the thought-world of the New Testament in modern secular terms. The final reconstruction of the mission and message of Jesus appears, however, like a bolt from the blue, arbitrary, preconceived and distinctly reminiscent of earlier Enlightened views. Perhaps it would not be amiss to apply to Herder an observation that Renan passed upon his own *Vie de Jésus*. It sought to discard what the author deemed impossible and present in its place a picture of one of the ways in which things might have happened.[94]

Herder's Idealism hovered in the background. In retrospect Herder seems to have had a good deal in common with the academic Idealist philosophers that were soon to dominate German philosophy. They believed in an immanent world spirit that was the ground of all history. They were united in rejecting the traditional, orthodox, Christian views of religion and reality. Whereas Herder expressed his views concretely, Fichte, Hegel and Schelling were more concerned with the underlying metaphysical explanation. They might seem to us today to be the two sides of the same coin. But it did not seem so to the Hegelians. They rejected Herder's thought in its entirety. E. Gans observed in the preface to his edition of Hegel's *Vorlesungen über die Philosophie der Geschichte* that Herder's *Ideen* contradict their title by disdaining all metaphysical speculation.[95] As late as 1895 W. Wundt could complain that philosophers still failed to recognize the value of Herder's pioneer work. Part of the reason was that Herder was a non-academic. To carry weight among professional scholars in Germany one had to be a scholar oneself.[96]

Albert Schweitzer felt that Strauss was the next logical step after Herder.[97] He ascribed the time lag of some forty years to the need for some prosaic spirit like Paulus to question miracles from a purely historical standpoint. But in questions of history, the logical is not always the next step or even the next step but one. By the time that he wrote his *Christliche Schriften* Herder was already passé. By the time that the dust of the Napoleonic Wars had settled down Herder was long dead and new voices clamored to be heard.

Goethe

To examine Goethe's thought about Jesus and religion involves a detour from the main stream of theological development. Johann Wolfgang von Goethe (1749–1832)[98] was neither a philosopher nor a theologian, yet philosophy and theology permeated his thought. He is read and remembered as Germany's greatest poet and writer. What he had in common with the Idealists was his religious and spiritual understanding of reality. It was an approach which transcended both the Enlightenment and traditional Christianity. It is aptly summed up by Heinrich Hoffmann:

> Goethe has this in common with the other representatives of the great epoch of German philosophy, poetry and music, with Lessing, Herder and Kant, with Beethoven, with Schleiermacher, Fichte, Schelling and Hegel. They had all torn loose from the ecclesiastical Christianity of the pre-Enlightenment age, but in contrast to the radical French Enlightenment and in contrast to the wave of materialism and positivism that swept over Europe from about 1830, they were all firmly rooted in religion.[99]

Goethe devoted none of his many writings to the person of Christ. It would be difficult to show that his views on Christ directly influenced later theology. But they are significant as a reflection of the spirit that was infiltrating the intellectual life of the times. In turn they helped to condition the cultural ethos of the nineteenth and twentieth centuries.

Like other contemporary men of letters, Goethe dabbled in biblical criticism.[100] In his youth he had been deeply impressed by pietism.[101] But the God that he eventually came to believe in was neither that of the Bible nor that of latterday evangelical piety. Goethe's mode of expression was far removed from the abstract reasoning of Spinoza and Hegel, but like them he did not revere a transcendent God over and above the universe, but one who manifests himself in every part of it. As Hoffmann observes, "The close connection in which God and nature are placed is the characteristic mark of Goethe's religion."[102]

Goethe could be struck by the immanence of the divine by contemplating a piece of granite.

> Here on the most ancient, eternal altar, that is built directly upon the depth of creation, I bring an offering to the Being of all beings.[103]

Whereas the Idealist philosophers put forward metaphysical explanations of the Being of all beings, Goethe expressed his thoughts in personal language. God was to be found *in herbis et lapidis*, "only in and out of *rebus singularibus*."[104] In *Gott, Gemüt und Welt* Goethe declared,

> Will you into the Infinite stride,
> Go to the finite on all sides.[105]

The outlook is reminiscent of Herder's *Ideen*.[106] The multiplicity and simplicity of nature give the decisive command "to prostrate ourselves in devotion before the mysterious original ground of all things."[107]

With Goethe, feeling after the Infinite in the finite was more important than conceptual thought. Like Herder and Schleiermacher, he was deeply impressed by Spinoza. Following Jacobi's disclosures concerning Lessing's alleged Spinozism, Goethe wrote to Jacobi, "I cling more and more firmly to the reverence for God of the atheist."[108] But it was the seminal ideas of Spinoza that Goethe admired; he did not imitate his way of philosophizing. Goethe himself did not readily conform to any fixed set of beliefs. He oscillated between systems according to the needs of the moment. He once set out his beliefs in the following scheme.[109]

	We are	
In the exploration of nature	In writing poetry	In morals
Pantheists	Polytheists	Monotheists

But even this self-imposed pigeonholing was not quite accurate. It left out of account the role of feeling and dependence which lay at the heart of Goethe's religion.

> For even the individual may manifest his kinship with the divinity only as he subjects himself and adores. [110]

Hoffmann comments, "The feeling of dependence *Abhängigkeitsgefühl* which Schleiermacher regarded as the kernel of religion, stood out strongly in Goethe."[111]

All this did not mean—or at least Goethe did not take it to mean—a total repudiation of the Christian faith. Rather, Goethe was practicing his own, free, private form of religion, which incorporated elements of Christianity. He honored Christ, but rejected the church. He did not attend formal worship, and pronounced church history to be a mishmash of error and power politics.[112] Apart from his encounters with the church, he may have been inclined to these views by his pantheism and erstwhile pietism. Perhaps it was a combination of these influences which determined Goethe's attitude to the supernatural and to Jesus. As with many who shared a similar outlook, rationalism and pantheism were two sides of the same belief.

However much he reverenced the mysterious, Goethe drew a sharp distinction between mysteries and miracles.[113] In a letter to J. K. Lavater, Goethe proclaimed that all events happened according to laws, and that wonders were a blasphemy against God and his revelation in nature.[114] To Goethe the cross was a negation of life. It was one of the four things which were as repugnant "as poison and snakes." The fact that the other three were tobacco smoke, bugs and garlic only heightens Goethe's disdain.[115] Goethe dismissed the atonement as a theory designed to fit unwelcome facts.[116] The resurrection and the empty tomb were pure deception: "Rogues, you took him away."[117] To Herder he wrote on September 4, 1778, that "the fairy tale [*Märchen*] of Christ" could retard human progress for ten thousand years.[118] A year previously Goethe remarked of Herder's *Ideen*, "Since I have no Messiah to await, this is to me the dearest gospel."[119]

Later on Goethe adopted a somewhat more benevolent attitude, but it was no nearer to orthodoxy. In the *West-östlicher Divan* (1819), a collection of poems marked by oriental influence, Jesus was depicted as a man who was supremely aware of God. To elevate anyone to the rank of God was against his will.[120] This outlook was perhaps more typical of Goethe both in youth and old age.[121] It also harmonized with his fundamental religious attitudes. God was not to be found above nature, or in the abstractions of theological speculation, but in nature by those who feel and plunge into life. This theme is sounded in Goethe's greatest work, *Faust*, whose composition spanned much of Goethe's life. In it Goethe revived the legend of the scholar who dabbled in magic and sold himself to the devil. When Faust first appears, he is in his study despairing of his life's work. He has studied philosophy, law, medicine and "unfortunately also theology." Wretched fool that he is, he is just as clever as before, and sees "that we can know nothing." Presently he feels the need of revelation which is to be found par excellence in the New Testament. Whereupon he begins to translate the Gospel of John.

> 'Tis writ, "In the beginning was the Word!"
> I pause, perplex'd! Who now will help afford?
> I cannot the mere Word so highly prize;
> I must translate it otherwise,
> If by the Spirit guided as I read.
> "In the beginning was the Sense!"
> Take heed, The import of this primal sense weigh,
> Lest thy too hasty pen be led astray!
> Is force creative then of Sense the dower?
> "In the beginning was the Power!"
> Thus should it stand: yet, while the line I trace,
> A something warns me, once more to efface.
> The Spirit aids! from anxious scruples freed,
> I write, "In the beginning was the Deed!"[122]

This translation of *logos* in John 1:1 is exegetically unwarrantable, but it accorded with Goethe's philosophy of religion.[123] The ground of the universe is not to be sought in *logos* Christology or trinitarian theology, but in the dynamic, immanent spirit of the universe. It is in practical action that Faust finally finds salvation. This, the Chor Mysticus points out in the final lines of the poem, is beyond all rational comprehension, though man may feel it and participate in it through selfless action:

> Everything mortal
> Is but a parable;
> The unattainable

Here becomes event;
The ineffable
Here it is done;
The Eternal-Womanly
Draws us above.[124]

Strictly speaking, Christology is here superfluous. A place might be found for Jesus in this religious scheme. But in the last analysis he is on the same plane as Faust. In modern terms (though they derive from nineteenth-century Idealism) Jesus might be said to be a man who was at one with the dynamic ground of his being. He differed from Faust in that he was more completely integrated and did not commit the mistakes or undergo the vicissitudes of Faust.

But this was not quite Goethe's last word on religion. Eleven days before he died he had a lengthy conversation with J. P. Eckermann in which he declared that there were two approaches to religion and the Bible, the natural (or higher and purer) and the institutional:

There is the standpoint of a form of original religion [*Urreligion*], that of pure nature and reason, which is of divine origin. This will remain eternally the same, and will last and hold true as long as there are divinely gifted people. But it is for chosen people, and is much too exalted and noble to become common. Then there is the standpoint of the church, which is of a more human form. It is frail, transitory and is grasped in transition. Yet it too will endure in eternal metamorphosis, as long as there are weak human beings. The light of unclouded, divine revelation is much too pure and brilliant, to be adapted and borne by poor and utterly weak humans. But the church enters as a benevolent mediator, to subdue and moderate, so that all may be helped and all the many healed. Through the presence of the faith of the Christian church, through liberating from the burden of sin as the follower of Christ, the church is a very considerable power. It is an outstanding goal of the Christian priesthood to abide in this power and esteem and so to preserve the ecclesiastical edifice.[125]

On these terms Goethe could accept the Gospels as a revelation, despite their faults. He could reverence Christ as the revelation of the highest moral principle. But he could also reverence the sun as a revelation of the power of being.

For the rest "genuine" or "non-genuine" are quite strange questions concerning the things of the Bible. What is "genuine" but that which is utterly excellent, that stands in harmony with purest nature and reason and even today serves our highest development.... Should the genuineness of a biblical writing be decided by the question, whether nothing but truth is conveyed to us, one could even doubt the authenticity of the Gospels in a few points on which Mark and Luke have written not on the basis of immediate eyewitness and experience, but only late and according to oral tradition, and the last Gospel, by the disciple John, only in very old age. However, I consider the Gospels, all four, to be thoroughly genuine, for there is working in them the reflection of a majesty, which emanated from the person of

Christ, and is of such a divine manner, as the divine has only ever assumed on earth. If you ask me, whether it is in my nature to show him worshipful reverence, I say "Certainly!"—I bow before him, as the divine revelation of the highest principle of morality. If you ask me, whether it is in my nature, to honor the sun, I say again, "Certainly!" For it is likewise a religion of the highest, and indeed the mightiest that it is granted us children of earth to perceive. I worship in it the light and the generative power of God, by which alone we live, strive and exist, and all plants and animals with us.[126]

In saying this, Goethe was adopting a position akin to that of his contemporary Idealist philosophers. Like them, he was a member of a world come of age which was not afraid to use its own understanding in its reappraisal of traditional beliefs. He had not worked out a formal system of speculative metaphysics. But like the philosophers he rejected the idea of biblical revelation and its superstructure of orthodox theism. Together they saw the world as the material outworking of a spiritual reality.[127] Within this scheme they found a place for institutional religion, though it was but the imperfect form of something higher. Goethe's conversation with Eckermann contained echoes of Kant and Deism in its identification of religion with morality whose ultimate source is reason and nature. Within the broad spectrum of Idealism, thinkers differed among themselves over what to do with Jesus. Goethe, like Kant, saw him as the incarnation of morality. Goethe and Kant had a place for Jesus, but had no real Christology, whereas Hegel was almost the reverse, having a Christology but little room for Jesus. Even so, Goethe's Jesus was a shadowy figure, a symbol of moral and religious humanity. Goethe paid lip service to history, but in practice he had no interest in the historical Jesus. Historical research might serve to show flaws in the records, but one's basic attitude to religion and reality was not determined by history. In common with the Idealist philosophers, Goethe did not begin with the historical documents, but read (or ignored) what he found in the New Testament in the light of his world view. The result added little to the thought of those involved in the *Fragments* controversy. It merely shifted around the metaphysical scenery behind the Jesus of the Enlightenment. In doing this it encouraged the view that orthodoxy was obsolete and that history had little positive contribution to make. At best history might serve to show the inadequacy of traditional belief and to illustrate rational truths. Decisive attitudes in philosophy and religion were to be determined on other grounds.

5. ABSOLUTE IDEALISM

The words "Idealism" and "Idealist" came to be used as philosophical terms in the eighteenth century.[1] Kant referred to his own views as "transcendental" or "critical idealism." But already in his lifetime a new generation of philosophers was growing up who believed that Kant's system stood in need of correction. They came to be known as Absolute Idealists on account of their view of the ultimately spiritual or mental character of reality. In this chapter we shall consider the three leading representatives of Absolute Idealism, Fichte, Hegel and Schelling, and the bearing of their thought on the interpretation of Jesus.

Fichte

Johann Gottlieb Fichte (1762–1814)[2] began his career as a student of theology at Jena, from whence he moved to Wittenberg and Leipzig. His anonymous *Versuch einer Kritik aller Offenbarung*,[3] which was published at Königsberg in 1792, was widely attributed to Kant in the belief that the Königsberg philosopher had written a new critique. Chronologically it anticipated by a year Kant's own statement of *Die Religion innerhalb der Grenzen der blossen Vernunft*. Kant disowned authorship of the new *Kritik* but praised its author. In its second edition the work was dedicated to Franz Volkmar Reinhard, the professor of theology at Wittenberg and chief court chaplain. Reinhard's own rationalistic and moralistic reinterpretation of Jesus had been published in 1781.[4] Fichte's work attracted the attention of Goethe who recommended his call to the chair of philosophy at Jena (1794). He was, however, obliged to leave Jena in 1799 on account of his alleged atheism. His Sunday lectures antagonized local clergy, and his work *Ueber den Grund unseres Glaubens an eine göttliche Weltregierung* (1798) identified God with the moral world order. After teaching briefly at Erlangen and Königsberg he moved to Berlin, where in 1810 he was made dean of the newly formed philosophical faculty. For a while he was rector of the university. While at Berlin he took part in the national struggle against Napoleon. He died prematurely of typhus.

In his student days Fichte was influenced by Lessing's championship of toleration and freedom. The study of Lessing led him to Spinoza, though he came to regard the latter's determinism as inconsistent with ethical freedom. The most decisive influence on Fichte's thinking was Kant, whose radical revision of the current conceptions of philosophy had been widely misunderstood by his contemporaries. Fichte saw it as his life's work to carry forward Kant's discoveries, though in a manner completely independent of him.[5] He held that every science must have a basic *Grundsatz* which determined its character.[6] His own philosophy was based on the concept of the I or Ego. In individual experience the I is more fundamental than any particular experiences or perceptions. In the context of his philosophy, when Fichte spoke of the I, he meant not only the individual (which clearly could not create the universe and all the experiences within it); he maintained that "the One immediate spiritual life itself is the Creator of all appearances, and thus of all appearing individuals."[7] This view led Fichte into the mainstream of Absolute Idealism and into a dialectic which is often said to be the characteristic of Hegel, his successor at Berlin. Already in his *Grundlage der gesamten Wissenschaftslehre* (1794) Fichte had formulated what he called the third basic proposition of philosophy: "*In the self I oppose a divisible not-self to the divisible self.*"[8] Fichte saw reality in terms of a personal dynamic process of Thesis, Antithesis and Synthesis.

> First: the self posits itself absolutely as *infinite* and unbounded. Second: the self posits itself absolutely as *finite* and *bounded*. And there would thus be a higher contradiction in the very nature of the self—as evidenced by its first and second acts—from which the present contradiction derives. Once the former is resolved, we also resolve the present contradiction which depends on it.
>
> All contradictions are reconciled by more accurate determination of the propositions at variance; and so too here.[9]

In his Berlin lectures of 1806 on *Die Anweisung zum seligen Leben oder auch die Religionslehre* Fichte spoke of God in terms of absolute being. "Being —Being [*Seyn*], I say, and Life is again One and the same."[10] The thought was reminiscent of Spinoza's doctrine of substance, but Fichte deemed it necessary to press beyond the latter's dogmatism to a more dynamic view of Being coming to self-consciousness. In itself life is one, indivisible and unchanging. But it expresses or manifests itself externally.

> Being—is there; and Being-there [*Daseyn*] is necessarily consciousness or reflexion according to definite laws that lie in consciousness itself and which are to be developed out of it: this is the ground of our entire teaching which has by now been thoroughly discussed from all sides.[11]

The converse of this proposition also holds good. "Knowing is above all not a mere knowing of itself...but it is a knowing of a single *Being*, namely of the One Being that truly is, God."[12] Knowledge of *Being* is not knowledge of a particular object only. For *Being*, and correspondingly knowledge, is splintered into the multiplicity of forms in which *Being* is manifested. Pure *Being* is never known in itself. It is the task of philosophy to demonstrate its forms.

> Now this sole possible object of knowledge never occurs purely in actual knowledge, but always broken by utterly necessary forms of knowledge which are to be demonstrated in their necessity. The demonstration of these forms is precisely philosophy or epistemology.[13]

Fichte claimed that his teaching was the metaphysical counterpart to Christian belief. In his early *Aphorismen über Religion und Deismus* (1790) he could say:

> These first basic theses of religion are grounded more on feelings than on convictions: on the need to become one with God; on the feeling of one's sinful wretchedness and culpability etc. The Christian religion, therefore, seems more intended for the heart than for the understanding; it will not impose itself by demonstrations, it desires to be sought out of need; it appears as a religion of good, simple souls.[14]

Already this makes it clear that Fichte did not accept Christianity in an orthodox, traditional sense. A quarter of a century later he restated his pantheism in his

Berlin lectures on religion and in the next breath affirmed that this was none other than the inner meaning of Christianity.

> There is no Being and no Life at all outside the immediate divine life. This Being is veiled and clouded over in the consciousness in manifold ways by the particular, ineradicable laws of this consciousness which are grounded in its own being. But it again emerges free from those veils, and now only yet modified by the form of infinity, in the life and action of the man yielded up to God. In this action it is not man that acts but God himself in his original Being and Essence, who acts in him and works his work through man.... This doctrine ... is in particular the doctrine of Christianity, as it still lies to this moment before our sight in its most authentic and pure source, the Gospel of John.[15]

Indeed, Christianity is true only insofar as it is the expression of reason thus conceived.

> And likewise Christianity must prove itself, even as agreeing with reason and as the pure and complete expression of this reason, apart from which there is no truth, if it wants to lay claim to any kind of validity.[16]

Fichte defended his appeal to the Fourth Gospel on the ground that, "the apostle Paul and his party, as the originators of the opposed Christian system remained half Jews and allowed to stand in peace the fundamental error of Judaism as well as of paganism." John, on the other hand, respected reason and appealed to the only proof permitted to the philosopher, the inner proof of reason.

> Only with John can the philosopher come together, for he alone has respect for reason, and appeals to the proof which the philosopher alone can allow as valid: the inner. "If anyone will do the will of him who has sent me, he will know inwardly that this teaching is of God" [cf. John 7:17]. But this will of God is, according to John, that one can rightly know God and him whom he has sent, Jesus Christ. The other preachers of Christianity, however, build on external proofs through miracles, which for us at least prove nothing. Furthermore, John alone among the evangelists contains what we seek and desire, a doctrine of religion.[17]

Fichte's reading of the Fourth Gospel could hardly be described as a piece of historical, critical exegesis. He justified it by what he called his "principle of interpretation":

> so to understand them therefore, as if they had wanted to say something, and, so far as their words allow, had said what is right and true.[18]

It would seem to be an unabashed attempt to read into the text as much as he could of his philosophy. On this basis Fichte proceeded to argue that John rejected the Jewish theistic idea of creation in favor of the ultimacy of the Logos. In non-pictorial language John meant to say,

> Since, apart from God's inner and hidden being that we can conceive by thought, he is also there over and above what we can merely factually grasp, he is thus neces-

sarily there through his inner and absolute Essence. And his Being-there, which is separated only by us from his Being, is in and of itself not to be separated from it; but this Being-there is originally, from all time and without all time, with his Being, inseparable from Being and itself Being.[19]

F. C. Copleston calls this lecture an "essay in demythologization."[20] It is so in all but name. The Fourth Gospel is turned into an embryonic statement of Absolute Idealism, couched in the language of post-classical culture. But Fichte's interpretation of Christianity did not end there. The lecture closed with a brief reassessment of the man Jesus.

> Without doubt Jesus of Nazareth possessed the loftiest perception of the absolute identity of mankind with God, which contains the ground of all other truths....[21]
> The manner and mode of this perception...may best be characterized by contrast with the manner and mode by which the speculative philosopher comes to the same perception.
> The latter proceeds to explain existence as a task imposed by his thirst for knowledge, which in itself is alien and profane to religion.... But this is not the case with Jesus. He did not proceed initially simply from any kind of speculative question.... Only in union with God is reality.... It was absolute reason come to immediate self-consciousness, or in other words, religion.[22]
> In this absolute fact Jesus now reposed, and was merged in it. He could not think, know or say otherwise, but that he just knew that it was so, that he knew it immediately in God, and that he knew even this too, that he knew it in God.[23]

In other words, Jesus was an Idealist, but of a practical rather than of a speculative bent. His uniqueness lay in his unique awareness of the ultimate absolute identity of God and man. Historically Christianity arose because Jesus was the first to realize and practice this.

> With regard to the present case one takes the primary fact of Christianity historically and purely as a fact, when one accepts, what is patently clear, that Jesus knew, what he indeed knew, earlier than any other knew it, and taught and lived as he did.[24]

This was no mere general knowledge that "the whole of mankind proceeds from the divine being"; he knew it "as an individual."[25] This knowledge was unique in history. Jesus thus pioneered the idea of union between God and man as a practical reality to be experienced.

In the First Introduction to his *Wissenschaftslehre* Fichte declared that, "I have long asserted, and repeat once more, that my system is nothing other than the *Kantian*; this means that it contains the same view of things, but is in method quite independent of the *Kantian* presentation."[26] It would be easier to grasp this assertion if Fichte had written *Spinozist* instead of *Kantian*. For on the one hand, Fichte's view of Being seems to have much more in common with Spinoza's notion of Substance than with Kant's view of *das Ding an sich*. On the other hand, Fichte's system posited the rejection of Kant's radical distinction between analytic and synthetic judgments.[27] Whereas Kant was resolutely opposed to metaphysical speculation on the basis of analytic judgments which conveyed no knowledge of reality, Fichte used logical analysis to penetrate the structure of Being. This method in turn provided him with the instrument for interpreting knowledge and being as a unified, dynamic and comprehensive scheme of reality.

Although Fichte laid great stress on ethics in his various writings, his picture of Jesus was not that of the enlightened upholder of rationalistic, moral principles. In portraying Jesus as a unique man who was supremely conscious of the ultimate ground of religion, Fichte had more in common with the views that Schleiermacher was developing than he had with Kant's view of Jesus.[28] In his analysis of the opposing tendencies of Jewish and Hellenistic Christianity and their resolution in Johannine theology, Fichte was anticipating the thought of F. C. Baur. Indeed, there is evidence to suggest that it was Fichte and Schelling (and not Hegel, as is widely thought) that provided Baur with his decisive impetus in his formative years.[29] Fichte's premature death at a crucial stage in philosophy and theology doubtless contributed to the comparative obscurity into which he fell as the nineteenth century proceeded. His influence gave way to that of Hegel and Schelling. But it was like a stream that went underground and emerged somewhere else in a different form. The rediscovery of Fichte at the turn of the twentieth century left its mark on the philosophical theology of Paul Tillich.[30]

Hegel

Georg Wilhelm Friedrich Hegel (1770–1831)[31] carried Idealism to its absolute limits. His disciples saw in his system a comprehensive account of the structure of reality; his adversaries dismissed it as esoteric nonsense. Hegel lived to see himself the acknowledged leader of German philosophy, but not quite long enough to see the uses to which his teaching would be put by German theologians like D. F. Strauss and F. C. Baur. After his death Hegelianism was split by rival schools of left and right. Within a decade Kierkegaard in Denmark was condemning his malign influence, and Marx was busy secularizing and adapting Hegel to his own ends. In the second half of the century Hegel found champions in Oxford and the Scottish universities and manses. But generally speaking, in the Anglo-Saxon world Hegel's posthumous fortunes have waxed and waned in inverse proportion to those of the empiricists.

Although he read theology at Tübingen, Hegel did not fulfill his parents' wishes and become ordained. Instead, he took posts as private tutor first at Bern (1793–96) and then at Frankfurt (1797–1800). Although outwardly uneventful, these years proved to be formative. The fruit of Hegel's thinking is to be found in some essays on the origins and essence of Christianity which were first published in 1907 in a volume edited by Hermann Nohl, entitled *Hegels Theologische Jugendschriften nach den Handschriften der Kgl. Bibliothek in Berlin*.[32] If these essays were not to exert any influence on the public history of thought for more than a century after their composition, the effect they produced on their author was profound. They mark a transition from a Kantian sketch of the life of Christ to a transcended Kantianism in which *Geist* is the reality behind all phenomena.

Among Hegel's fellow students were Schelling and the future poet, Friedrich Hölderlin. His studies included Kant and Plato. Lessing was already one of his heroes. Hegel was interested in the "Pantheismusstreit" concerning Lessing's alleged Spinozism. There is reason to think that already at this time Hegel himself used the formula *hen kai pan* to denote what H. S. Harris calls "this living unity of all organic life, this immortal equilibrium of unstable, mortal elements, sustained by the universal power of life."[33] Underlying this view was a Platonic conception of the World-Soul which manifested itself in the workings of nature. In 1793 Fichte visited Tübingen, where Hegel and his friends were already discussing the *Kritik aller Offenbarung*, which had been published the previous year.

In 1801 Hegel became Privatdozent at Jena, where Schelling was already a professor. It was not until 1806 that, thanks to Goethe's intervention, he received his first stipend of one hundred thalers. But the Battle of Jena soon deprived him even of this modest income, and he was glad to accept the post of editor of the *Bamberger Zeitung* (1807–8), which he left for the more acceptable appointment of rector of the Aegidiengymnasium in Nuremberg (1808–16).

In the meantime Hegel began to publish his major works. His first book was a comparison of Fichte and Schelling under the title *Differenz des Fichte'schen und Schelling'schen Systems der Philosophie in Beziehung auf Reinhold's "Beyträge zur leichtern Übersicht des Zustands der Philosophie zu Anfang des neunzehnten Jahrhunderts"* (1801).[34] *Phänomenologie des Geistes*[35] appeared in 1807. It was followed by *Die objektive Logik* (3 vols., 1812–16). His reputation won him offers of chairs at Erlangen, Berlin and Heidelberg. In 1816 he accepted the offer from Heidelberg but left after two years to take up the renewed offer of the chair at Berlin that was still vacant after Fichte's death. At Heidelberg he produced his *Encyclopädie der philosophischen Wissenschaften im Grundriss* (1817; 2nd ed., 1827; 3rd ed., 1830), an exposition of his system for use in lectures. At Berlin he published *Naturrecht und Staatswissenschaft im Grundrisse* (1821). But thereafter Hegel devoted himself almost entirely to his lectures.

Some of his most influential works grew out of lecture courses. They were not published as books in his lifetime but were put together by former students after his death. These were based partly on the students' notes and partly on Hegel's own. The editing sometimes left much to be desired. They included *Vorlesungen über die Philosophie der Religion* (1832),[36] *Vorlesungen über die Geschichte der Philosophie* (1833),[37] and *Vorlesungen über die Philosophie der Geschichte* (1837).[38] In 1830 Hegel was made rector of the University of Berlin. He died in 1831 after a day's illness in a cholera epidemic.

Hegel's early theological writings date from the period 1790–1800, though it is not possible to date them with exact precision.[39] Up to 1795 Hegel was still strongly under the influence of Kant, but by 1797 other influences had become increasingly apparent. To the former period belong *Das Leben Jesu* and the first two parts of *Die Positivität der christlichen Religion*. To the latter belong the third part of *Die Positivität* and, most significant of all, *Der Geist des Christentums und sein Schicksal* together with the brief *Systemfragment von 1800*.

"Hegel," Richard Kroner has observed,

> became a Kantian the moment he understood the revolution brought about by Kant's Critical Philosophy; and he remained a Kantian throughout his life, no matter how much he disputed many of Kant's doctrines and even his fundamental position. Hegel would never have found his dialectical method without the "Transcendental Dialectic" in Kant's *Critique of Pure Reason*.[40]

However true this latter point may be, Hegel's Kantianism reached its highwater mark in these early years, and Kant's religion found its purest expression in Hegel's *Leben Jesu*.[41]

The opening words of *Leben Jesu* proclaim the gospel of the deity of reason:

> Pure reason, incapable of all bounds, is the Godhead itself. — According to reason, therefore, is the plan of the world in general ordered (John 1). Reason it is that acquaints man with his destiny, an unconditioned purpose of his life. Often indeed is it obscured, but it has never been completely extinguished. Even in the darkness a weak glimmer of it has always endured.[42]

From here Hegel proceeded to sketch the life and teaching of John the Baptist and Jesus himself. The historical outline was lifted directly out of the New Testament, but the spirit that filled it was Kant's. Even the vocabulary used in expressing the principle underlying the Sermon on the Mount was lifted straight from Kant.

> What you could will that "it" should hold general law among men, even against you, act according to such a maxim. This is the fundamental law of all morality, the content of all law giving and of the sacred books of all peoples.[43]

But if this was the voice of Kant, it also spoke with the accents of Lessing and enlightened thinkers generally.[44] It gives a reminder that the essential truths of the great positive religions point in the same direction: the grand goal of all religion is the attainment of virtue. The hard sayings of Matthew 7 are paraphrased in a way more reminiscent of Act II of *The Magic Flute* than of first-century Palestinian Judaism.

> Enter through this portal of Right into the Temple of Virtue. This portal is indeed narrow, the way to it full of danger, and your companions shall be few. All the more sought is the Palace of Vice and Ruin, whose gates are wide and whose road is level.[45]

Hegel's narrative wends its way through the sayings and incidents of the Gospels without pausing to discuss sources. It harmonizes the Synoptics with John and gives everything a moralistic slant. When Hegel finally comes to the Last Supper, the harmonizing techniques are clearly evident and the theme of the morality uppermost. Jesus is thus paraphrased:

Keep me in your remembrance, who gave up his life for you, and let my remembrance, my example, be to you a mighty source of strength for virtue. I see you around me like the shoots of a vine, which bear fruit that is nourished by it, and even now, though separated from it, bring the good to maturity through your own life-power. Love one another, love all men, as I loved you. That I give up my life for the "benefit" of my friends is the proof of my love.[46]

The sacrificial overtones of the New Testament are eliminated. The Gospel narrative is followed as far as the burial in the tomb of Joseph of Arimathea. And there the story ends. Not a word is said about the resurrection. No hint of a Christology is given.

If *Das Leben Jesu* was a Kantian paraphrase of the Gospel narratives, *Die Positivität der christlichen Religion* sought to explain how institutional Christianity had managed to obscure the original message. It is again axiomatic, "that the aim and essence of all true religion, our religion included, is human morality." From this it follows

that all the more detailed doctrines of Christianity, all means of propagating them, and all its obligations (whether obligations to believe or obligations to perform actions in themselves otherwise arbitrary) have their worth and sanctity appraised according to their close or distant connection with that aim.[47]

And again we have the same picture of Jesus. Finding the moral life of the nation at a very low ebb, he undertook the task of reformation, and "recalled to the memory of his people the moral principles in their sacred books."[48]

As in the *Leben Jesu* Hegel again virtually eliminated the supernatural and the miraculous in the Gospel accounts of Jesus.

He was a Jew; the principle of his faith and his gospel was not only the revealed will of God as it was transmitted to him by Jewish traditions but also his own heart's living sense of right and duty. It was in the following of this moral law that he placed the fundamental condition of God's favor.[49]

Jesus found himself "compelled for his own purposes to speak a great deal about himself, about his own personality. He was induced to do this because there was only one way in which his people were accessible."[50] Among these compelling factors was the expectation of a Messiah and the conjecture that Jesus might fit the bill. Jesus tried to ward this off and also cash in on it.

Jesus could not exactly contradict them, for this supposition of theirs was the indispensable condition of his finding an entry into their minds. But he tried to lead their messianic hopes into the moral realm and dated his appearance in his glory at a time after his death.[51]

In this way Hegel took cognizance of the eschatological element which so arrested Reimarus, if only to dismiss it as a more or less harmless piece of sophistry.

The miracles receive slightly more attention but scarcely more serious consideration. Here again they are dismissed as a means to an end. The Jews could not do without them. As to whether they actually happened, Hegel ostensibly sits on the fence. What is important is that the disciples believed that they did. Nothing contributed so much to making Christianity a positive religion as the belief in miracles and their use to underwrite authority.[52] Eventually recognition of this authority came to be confused with the divine will.[53] To some extent Jesus himself was responsible for this with his appointment of a fixed number of disciples and the institution of sacraments which drew a sharp line of demarcation between the believer and the unbeliever, the saved and the damned.[54] In all this Jesus compares rather unfavorably with Socrates whose disciples loved him "because of his virtue and his philosophy, not virtue and philosophy because of him."[55] The inversion of the Socratic method was a first step towards turning Jesus' teaching into a positive religion.

For Hegel the tragedy of positive religion arose from the way in which God was transformed from subject to object through the ascription of materialistic ideas and practices. Such a transformation took place in the Greco-Roman world, and the Christian church was by no means exempt from it. Commenting on the ideas which the early Christians ascribed to God, Hegel declared,

> The purpose which the Christians ascribed to this Infinite Being was poles apart from the world's *moral* goal and purpose; it was whittled down not simply to the propagation of Christianity but to ends adopted by a single sect or by individuals, particularly priests, and suggested by the individual's passions, by vainglory, pride, ambition, envy, hatred, and the like. . . .

> Thus the despotism of the Roman emperors had chased the human spirit from the earth and spread a misery which compelled men to seek and expect happiness in heaven; robbed of freedom, their spirit, their eternal and absolute element, was forced to take flight to the deity. [The doctrine of] God's objectivity is a counterpart to the corruption and slavery of man, and it is strictly only a revelation, only a manifestation of the spirit of the age. This spirit was revealed by its conception of God as objective when men began to know such a surprising amount about God, when so many secrets about his nature, comprised in so many formulas, were no longer whispered from ear to ear but were proclaimed on the housetops and known to children by heart. The spirit of the age was revealed in its objective conception of God when he was no longer regarded as like ourselves, though infinitely greater, but was put into another world in whose confines we had no part, to which we contributed nothing by our activity, but into which, at best, we could beg or conjure our way. It was revealed again when man himself became a non-ego and his God another non-ego. Its clearest revelation was in the mass of miracles which it engendered and which took the place of the individual's reason when decisions were made and convictions adopted. But its most dreadful revelation was when on this God's behalf men fought, murdered, defamed, burned at the stake, stole, lied, and betrayed. In a period like this, God must have ceased altogether to be something subjective and have entirely become an object, and the perversion of the maxims of morality is then easily and logically justified in theory.[56]

The interest of this passage does not lie in its adequacy as an account of the early church but in the fact that it constitutes a link between the enlightened philosophies of history and the full-blown philosophy of the mature Hegel. Here is Hegelianism in embryo. The past is seen like pieces of a jigsaw which are to be fitted together in order to reconstruct the movement of the Spirit in history. The whole picture only becomes clear when the pieces are fitted together. Examination of the individual pieces in accordance with strict historical criteria is conspicuous by its absence. Hegel is not a historian but a philosopher of history. As yet the characteristic Hegelian dialectic is lacking. But the thought of the deity as absolute subject becoming objectified in temporary manifestations should not pass unnoticed. It was soon to be decisive in Hegel's reappraisal of Christianity.

Richard Kroner has pointed out that the author of *Die Positivität* might have been a contemporary of Mendelssohn, Lessing or Kant; the author of *Der Geist des Christentums und sein Schicksal* was evidently a contemporary of Herder, Fichte, Schelling and the Romantics. Hitherto, Hegel had argued rationally as a representative of the Enlightenment; now he writes as "a Christian mystic, seeking adequate speculative expression."[57] In the earlier work he had been openly hostile to Christianity, contrasting Christianity unfavorably with the Greco-Kantian ethic; now he saw Christianity in the light of a new synthesis of love. In this synthesis there has been a re-shuffling of roles. The opposites are no longer the free, rational Greek spirit versus the church, but Christianity and Judaism. But perhaps the most striking aspect of the essay is the way in which everything is worked out in terms of the spirits which express themselves in nations and individuals.[58]

The fate of the Jewish nation was not like that of a Greek tragedy, inspiring terror or pity at the spectacle of a beautiful character overtaken by fate.

> The fate of the Jewish people is the fate of Macbeth who stepped out of nature itself, clung to alien Beings, and so in their service had to trample and slay everything holy in human nature, had at last to be forsaken by his gods (since they were objects and he their slaves) and be dashed to pieces on his faith itself.[59]

Jesus came on the scene at a point in history when this self-chosen fate was about to overtake the Jews. He alone of his contemporaries understood what was really happening. He tried to avert the impending disaster by altering course, by replacing contempt for the world with love for humanity. He failed in the short-term venture because something more than preaching was needed in the situation, but his religion was bound to find response in the rest of the world which was not dominated by the Jewish anti-worldly spirit.

Over against the anti-worldly theism of the Jews, Jesus stood for a religious humanism. Judaism was ugly. It thrived on the tension between religion and the world. In its service to humanity the religion of Jesus reconciled the two and manifests the spirit of beauty.

> Over against commands which required a bare service of the Lord, a direct slavery, an obedience without joy, without pleasure or love, i.e., the commands in connection with the service of God, Jesus set their precise opposite, a human urge and so a

human need. Religious practice is the most holy, the most beautiful, of all things; it is our endeavor to unify the discords necessitated by our development and our attempt to exhibit the unification in the *ideal* as fully *existent,* as no longer opposed to reality, and thus to express and confirm it in a deed. It follows that, if that spirit of beauty be lacking in religious actions, they are the most empty of all; they are the most senseless bondage, demanding a consciousness of one's annihilation, or deeds in which man expresses his nullity, his passivity.[60]

A few pages later on Hegel expresses this antithesis in terms of a pair of concepts which he used in his previous essay: *subject* and *object.* It is a contrast between the personal and the impersonal, or at any rate the freedom of humanity set free by love and life lived on a purely physical level.[61] And later still he uses these cumulative contrasts to repudiate his erstwhile Kantianism. The Sermon on the Mount is not about objective commands but about life which transcends them. The imperative presupposes a cleavage between duty and inclination. But love unites the two.

> The opposition of duty to inclination has found its unification in the modifications of love, i.e., in the virtues. Since law was opposed to love, not in its content but in its form, it could be taken up into love, though in this process it lost its shape.[62]

Similarly faith is a knowledge of spirit through spirit which transcends the estrangements of experience. It is through faith that one knows the transcendent power of life.

> Jesus too found within nature [i.e., in "life"] the connection between sins and the forgiveness of sins, between estrangement from God and reconciliation with him. . . .
> He placed reconciliation in love and fulness of life and expressed himself to that effect on every occasion with little change of form. Where he found faith, he used the bold expression [Luke vii.48]: "Thy sins are forgiven thee." This expression is no objective cancellation of punishment, no destruction of the still subsisting fate, but the confidence which recognized itself in the faith of the woman who touched him, recognized in her a heart like his own, read in her faith her heart's elevation above law and fate, and declared to her the forgiveness of her sins. A soul which throws itself into the arms of purity itself with such full trust in a man, with such devotion to him, with the love that reserves nothing for itself, must itself be a pure or a purified soul. Faith in Jesus means more than knowing his real personality, feeling one's own reality as inferior to his in might and strength, and being his servant. Faith is a knowledge of spirit through spirit, and only like spirits can know and understand one another; unlike ones can know only that they are not what the other is.[63]

Hegel's exposition of the Godhead and Jesus' relationship with the Father was largely a reinterpretation of the Fourth Gospel in the light of these concepts.

> The relation of a son to his father is not a conceptual unity (as, for instance, unity or harmony of disposition, similarity of principles, etc.), a unity which is only a unity in thought and is abstracted from life. On the contrary, it is a living relation of living beings, a likeness of life. Father and son are simply modifications of the same life,

not opposite essences, not a plurality of absolute substantialities. Thus the son of God is the same essence as the father, and yet for every act of reflective thinking, though only for such thinking, he is a separate essence.[64]

Thus the term *Son of God* is a conceptual expression for a particular manifestation of life. Conceptual thought requires men to think of the Father and the Son as separate entities, but in reality they are not. Indeed, in order to know this, there must be a divine element in the individual believer who is thus also a "modification of the Godhead."[65]

The final section of the essay was devoted to the fate of Jesus and the church. The opening words which recapitulate Hegel's conclusions make clear his view that Jesus was a divinely inspired man. Both terms are operative. Jesus possessed, or, rather, was possessed by a new spirit. At the same time he was essentially a man, different from other men in the degree of his spirituality and in his revolutionary message, but not otherwise. The glowing terms in which Hegel describes the mission and achievement of Jesus reveal all too clearly the gulf between Hegel and orthodoxy.

> With the courage and faith of a divinely inspired man, called a dreamer by clever people, Jesus appeared among the Jews. He appeared possessed of a new spirit entirely his own. He visualized the world as it was to be, and the first attitude he adopted toward it was to call on it to become different; he began therefore with the universal message: "Be ye changed, for the Kingdom of God is nigh." Had the spark of life lain dormant in the Jews, he would only have needed a breath to kindle it into flame and burn up all their petty titles and claims. If, in their unrest and discontent with things as they were, they had been conscious of the need for a purer world, then the call of Jesus would have found belief, and this belief would have immediately brought into existence the thing believed in. Simultaneously with their belief the Kingdom of God would have been present. Jesus would simply have expressed to them in words what lay undeveloped and unknown in their hearts.[66]

As it was, the "genius" of the Jewish people at that time gave to Jesus "a very impure sort of attention." However, "a small group of pure souls" attached themselves to him. With great magnanimity (*"Gutmütigkeit"*) and with the faith of a pure dreamer (*"eines reinen Schwärmers"*), Jesus "interpreted their desire as a satisfied heart, their urge as a completion, their renunciation of some of their previous relationships, mostly trivial, as freedom and a healed or conquered fate."[67] The lofty hopes of Jesus for Judaism were doomed to be thwarted. It soon became apparent that Jesus had to align himself with Judaism and sacrifice his "beauty" or reject Judaism and suffer the consequences. In neither case would he enjoy fulfillment, but the latter was the higher course.[68]

The church, on the other hand, was not quite so high-minded. It sometimes fell prey to the same spirit as Judaism.[69] This manifested itself in the need to objectify Jesus after his death.

> Jesus' need for religion was satisfied in the God of the *whole*, since his sight of God was his flight from the world, was each of his constant collisions with the world. He

needed only the opposite of the world, an opposite in whom his opposition [to the world] was itself grounded. He was his father, he was one with him.[70]

The church sought to objectify God. When Jesus died, the disciples attached their hopes to his person as an object of veneration.

He had taken everything into the grave with him; his spirit had not remained behind in them. Their religion, their pure life, had hung on the individual Jesus. He was their living bond; in him the divine had taken shape and been revealed. In him God too had appeared to them. His individuality united for them in a living being the indeterminate and the determinate elements in the [entire] harmony. With his death they were thrown back on the separation of visible and invisible, reality and spirit.[71]

The vacuum left by the manifestation of life in Jesus was filled by the thought of the risen, deified Christ. "The need for religion finds its satisfaction in the risen Jesus, in love thus given shape."[72] Belief in the resurrection of Jesus was not a historical but a religious necessity. But in the last analysis it was (like belief in miracles) a superficial necessity, for it substituted something finite, conceptual and objective for life itself.

In all the forms of the Christian religion which have been developed in the advancing fate of the ages, there lies this fundamental characteristic of opposition in the divine, which is supposed to be present in consciousness only, never in life.[73]

It is on this note—the church's attachment to the finite and particular, instead of love and life itself, and the consequent tensions—that the essay comes to an end.

Walter Kaufmann sees the essay as an attempt to read the "Sittlichkeit" of the Greeks and Goethe into the teaching of Jesus.[74] It replaces the Kantian "Moralität" of the earlier essays, but carries scarcely greater conviction. This was the reason why Hegel filed it away in a drawer where it belonged. Kaufmann's verdict hardly does justice to the originality of the work and its place in Hegel's development. It is somewhat removed from the conventional picture of Hegel, the abstract, system-building professor. The materials for the system are there. But they are suffused with a passion for a total vision of history and reality, from which Hegel seeks the key to interpret all experience. Here is an existential Hegel, finding the meaning of existence in involvement in life itself, and rejecting as inauthentic any philosophy or religion which stops short of life itself and becomes satisfied with some aspect, idea or (worst of all, as in the case of Judaism) a negation of life. It might be said that the young Hegel had a modern counterpart in Paul Tillich, with his insistence that God is not *a* being but *being itself*. In both cases Jesus is not the God-man of the creeds. He is not to be venerated for his own sake. His miracles and resurrection are not to be taken seriously from a scientific standpoint. Rather, he is, in Tillich's phrase, the *Bearer of the New Being*. He is the mediator of life insofar as he knew the power of life in himself.[75]

But if this is a far cry from the traditional picture of Hegel the philosopher, it is equally far from the biblical picture of Jesus of Nazareth and the Christ of the early church. It is true that at certain points Hegel attempts to relate his views to the New Testament. It might be said that here is a thinker who is trying to penetrate beneath the surface of the New Testament and relate what he finds there to religious experience in general. But the links which bind this picture of Christ to the Jesus of the New Testament are very tenuous. It is a Christ that is read into the Gospels rather than read out of them. It is a Christ-idea which has been molded by the presuppositions of a system. It has little to do with the historical realities of first-century Palestinian Judaism. A similar Christology was to be developed by Schleiermacher in much greater detail in the next twenty-five years. But Hegel himself turned his back on this line of thought in favor of a comprehensive version of Absolute Idealism.

In his *Encyklopädie der philosophischen Wissenschaften* Hegel complained that "Kantian criticism" was "merely a philosophy of subjectivity, a subjective Idealism."[76] It differed from Empiricism only with respect to the question of what constituted experience. However, it was in basic agreement with Empiricism in its contention that

> reason apprehends nothing beyond sensation, nothing rational and divine. It remains in the finite and untrue, namely in an apprehension that has only subjectively an externality and a Thing-in-itself as its condition, which is the abstraction of the formless, an empty beyond.

Hegel's solution was to interpret reality in terms of the absolute self or divine "I."[77]

The mature Hegel could speak of this absolute self in various ways. Sometimes he spoke of "the Idea [*die Idee*]." If the terminology was reminiscent of Plato, its content was conceived in a dynamic, personal, monistic way.

> *The Idea is the True in and for itself, the absolute unity of concept and objectivity.* Its ideal content is no other than the concept in its determinations; its real content is only its representation, which it gives itself in the form of external being.[78]

The Idea could also be understood as "Reason, the Subject-Object, the unity of the ideal and the real, of the finite and infinite, of soul and body, as possibility which has reality within itself."[79] It could also be conceived in terms of *Geist,* a word which carries with it connotations of both "spirit" and "mind." In the last analysis *Geist* alone possesses reality. Although Hegel continued to use the word "God," it has to be understood within the framework of his thought about *Geist,* the dynamic ground of all reality. In his *Phänomenologie des Geistes* Hegel declared,

> That the True is actual only as system, or that Substance is essentially Subject, is expressed in the representation of the Absolute as *Spirit*—the most sublime Notion and the one which belongs to the modern age and its religion. The spiritual alone is the *actual*; it is essence, or that which has *being in itself*; it is that which *relates itself to itself* and is *determinate,* it is *other-being* and *being-for-self,* and in this determinate-

ness, or in its self-externality, abides within itself; in other words, it is *in and for itself*. — But this being-in-and-for-itself is at first only for us, or *in itself*, it is spiritual *Substance*. It must also be this *for itself*, it must be the knowledge of the spiritual, and the knowledge of itself as Spirit, i.e. it must be an *object*, reflected into itself. It is *for itself* only for *us*, in so far as its spiritual content is generated by itself. But in so far as it is also for itself for its own self, this self-generation, the pure Notion, is for it the objective element in which it has its existence, and it is in this way, in its existence for itself, an object reflected into itself. The Spirit that, so developed, knows itself as Spirit, is *Science*; Science is its actuality and the realm which it builds for itself in its own element.[80]

Whether we think of nature, history or thought, everything is the outworking of *Geist*. The sum total of human knowledge is the Absolute Mind thinking its thoughts through finite minds. Conversely, history, nature, human thought and religion are expressions of *Geist* coming to self-consciousness. It has long been customary to think of Hegelianism in terms of a dialectic of thesis, antithesis and synthesis. But as J. N. Findlay has pointed out, these terms are more characteristic of Fichte.[81] However, the notion of the all-embracing dialectic is paramount in Hegel.

In his lectures on *The Philosophy of History* Hegel traced the emergence of freedom from oriental despotism, through Greco-Roman democracy and aristocracy to the Prussian monarchy. The grand climax of world history was Protestant Germanic culture which had emerged from these earlier stages according to the inner laws of the spirit. Whether many practicing historians could be found today to endorse Hegel's conclusions and methods is more than doubtful. But such thoughts did not deter Hegel from attempting to explain the course of history on the basis of this thesis. But like other enlightened thinkers of the previous half-century, Hegel had no qualms about philosophizing about the inner meaning of history without subjecting himself to the arduous discipline of historical research. It was sufficient merely to supply from history illustrations for a thesis that owed its origin to other sources.

But political history was only one particular manifestation of *Geist*. Hegel invoked the same basic ideas in order to explain religion which, since it also occurred in history, had a historical dimension. Indeed, religion could be called "the self-consciousness of God."[82]

We define God when we say that he distinguished himself from himself and is an object for himself but that in this distinction he is purely identical with himself, is in fact Spirit....We have here, accordingly, the religion of the manifestation of God, since God knows himself in finite Spirit. God is absolutely open or manifest: this is here the essential condition. The transition was our having seen that the knowledge of God as free Spirit is still tinged, so far as its substance is concerned, with finitude and immediacy. This finitude had further to be discarded by the labor of Spirit; it is nothingness, and we have seen how this nothingness has been made manifest to consciousness.[83]

As recent writers like Fackenheim and Yerkes have stressed, Hegel did not see himself as a purely abstract theorist.[84] His interpretation presupposed the historical existence of Christianity. What he now proposed was an interpretation of its inner meaning and existential significance. Hegel's language retained lingering echoes of orthodox Christian vocabulary. He could say that, "The Christian Religion is the religion of *revelation*."[85] But revelation is something which does not take place merely in external history; it occurs in the consciousness of Spirit. Hegel could speak of the worshiping community or church (*Gemeinde*). But this community too has to be understood as the band of enlightened spirits who perceive the truth of Idealism. It cannot be equated with the visible Christian church.

Hegel also taught a form of trinitarianism. But *Geist* was not to be identified with the *Heiliger Geist,* the Holy Spirit. The persons of orthodox trinitarianism should be understood as pictorial and figurative images of the one *Geist*.

> The Trinity has been set forth in the relationship of Father, Son, and Spirit. This is a childlike relationship, a childlike form. Understanding has no such categories or relations that would be comparable in regard to their suitability. But it must be recognized that this expression is merely figurative; Spirit does not enter into such a relationship. Love would be more suitable, for Spirit is by all means the truth.

> The abstract God, the Father, is the universal—eternal, encompassing, total universality. We are on the level of Spirit; the universal here includes everything within itself. The other, the Son, is infinite particularity and appearance; the third, the Spirit is individuality as such—but all three are Spirit. In the third, we say, God is the Spirit; but it is also presupposed that the third is the first. This is essential to maintain and is explained by the nature of the concept [of Spirit]; it comes to the fore with every goal and every life process.[86]

To say that these images are pictorial (*bildlich*) is not the same as saying that they are mythical and unhistorical. It is essential that the Christ be historical, for everything in history turns on the manifestation of *Geist* in history. In the course of his earlier discussion of the religious attitude Hegel noted the mythical way in which Homer spoke of Jupiter and other gods. Such allusions were reported in a historical way, but were not to be taken seriously as history.

> But then besides this there is something historical which is a divine history, and of such a nature that it is regarded as in the strict sense a history, the history of Jesus Christ. This is not taken merely as a myth in a figurative way, but as something perfectly historical. That accordingly is something which belongs to the sphere of general ideas, but it has another side as well. It has the Divine for its content, divine action, divine timeless events, a mode of working that is absolutely divine. And this is the inward, the true, the substantial element of this history, and it is just this that is the object of reason. In every narrative, in fact, there is this double element; a myth, too, has a meaning in itself. There are, it is true, myths in which the external form in which they appear is of the most importance, but usually such a myth contains an allegory, like the myths of Plato.[87]

As this statement indicates, Hegel drew a sharp distinction between a picture (*Bild*), the mental concept, representation or image (*Vorstellung*) and the Idea (*Idee*) itself.[88] The Idea manifests itself in and through pictures and mental concepts, but transcends them. In making these provisos Hegel was clearing the ground for his reinterpretation of the gospel story. The titles of Son of man and Son of God, the teaching of the Kingdom of God, and the death of Jesus all constitute important elements. The sonship of Jesus was not to be explained away in any general sense, such as that all human beings were children of God. The life and teaching of Jesus is to be understood as the manifestation of the Idea.

> In these and other passages, it cannot be a matter of exegesis flattening out these expressions [in a manner such as the following: Jesus was] well-pleasing to God; all [human beings are] God's children, just as all the stones and animals are his creation; [Jesus was a] pious sage. Rather [the words of Christ] confirm the truth of the Idea of what he has been for his community; they confirm the higher Idea of truth, which appeared in him in his community.[89]

There was an ontological necessity for the incarnation and for the death of Jesus. *"In order for this divine-human unity to become certain for man, God had to appear in the world in the flesh."*[90] On one level, Jesus lived and died as a martyr to the truth. Outwardly the course of his life was comparable to that of Socrates.[91] But formal comparison with the latter ends with his death. For Hegel, the death of Jesus was the focal point (*Mittelpunkt*) of the dialectic of Spirit coming to consciousness and realizing itself in the world. The thought could be expressed in more or less traditional theological language.

> *God has died, God is dead*: this is the most frightful of all thoughts, that everything eternal and true does not exist, that negation itself is found in God. The deepest anguish, the feeling of something completely irretrievable, the abandoning of everything that is elevated, are bound up with this thought.
>
> However, the process does not come to a halt at this point; rather, a reversal takes place: God, that is to say, maintains himself in this process, and the latter is only the death of death. God rises again to life, and thus things are reversed.
>
> The resurrection is something that in essence belongs equally to faith. After his resurrection, Christ appeared only to his friends. This is not an external history suitable for unbelief; rather the appearances occur only for faith. The resurrection is followed by the glorification of Christ, and the triumph of his ascension to the right hand of God concludes this history, which, as understood by believing consciousness, is the explication of the divine nature itself.[92]

However, the above quotation makes it plain that this is no mere "external history." The death, resurrection and glorification of Jesus are to be understood in terms of the dialectic by which the Spirit negates itself in manifesting itself, and in the process universalizes and transcends itself.

What Hegel says in these various passages drawn from his lectures on the philosophy of religion restates what he earlier wrote at the conclusion of his

Phänomenologie des Geistes. The death of the mediator was not merely—or even primarily—a soteriological necessity. It was an ontological necessity occasioned by the emerging self-consciousness of the absolute Spirit.

> The death of the Mediator as grasped by the Self is the supersession of his objective existence or his particular being-for-self: this *particular* being-for-self has become a universal self-consciousness. On the other side, the *universal* has become self-consciousness, just because of this, and the pure or nonactual Spirit of mere thinking has become *actual.* The death of the Mediator is the death not only of his *natural* aspect or of his particular being-for-self, not only of the already dead husk stripped of its essential Being, but also of the *abstraction* of the divine Being. For the Mediator, in so far as his death has not yet completed the reconciliation, is the one-sidedness which takes as *essential Being* the simple element of thought in contrast to actuality: this one-sided extreme of the Self does not as yet have equal worth with essential Being; this it first has as Spirit. The death of this picture-thought contains, therefore, at the same time the death of the *abstraction of the divine Being* which is not posited as Self....

> This Knowing is the inbreathing of the Spirit, whereby Substance becomes Subject, by which its abstraction and lifelessness have died, and Substance therefore has become *actual* and simple and universal self-consciousness.

> In this way, therefore, Spirit is *self-knowing Spirit;* it knows *itself;* that which is object for it, *is,* or its picture-thought is the true, absolute *content*; as we saw, it expressed Spirit itself. It is at the same time not merely the content of self-consciousness, and not merely object *for it,* but it is also *actual Spirit.*[93]

Hegel was one of the first European thinkers—though not absolutely the first—to speak of the death of God. But for him it did not mean what it meant for Jean Paul or Nietzsche, that God does not exist, and that henceforth men must leave the notion of God out of their reckoning.[94] Rather, it means that God has transcended himself in the death of Christ. Spirit is no longer abstract. In becoming concrete, the abstract idea of God over and above the world has died. This conclusion entails the abandonment of the orthodox view of divine transcendence. It was popularized in the 1960s by Thomas J. J. Altizer in *The Gospel of Christian Atheism.*[95] Perhaps the climate of opinion, convention and his own temperament deterred Hegel from flaunting his "atheism" in the same way as Altizer. But both do away with the transcendence of God in the confidence that they have thereby saved the gospel.

Karl Barth has called Hegel's teaching "the philosophy of self-confidence."[96] It is well known that Hegel saw his own age as the culmination of world history. If his own philosophy was not quite the philosophy to end all philosophies, at least he had seen the Promised Land. As he indicates in the closing words of *Phänomenologie des Geistes,* he had glimpsed the *goal* of "Absolute Knowing, or Spirit that knows itself as Spirit," which "has for its path the recollection of the Spirits as they are in themselves and as they accomplish the organization of their realm."[97] It might be said that Hegel never demonstrated; he only explained. This was his strength and his weakness. As Barth observed,

> Hegel puts his confidence in the idea that his thinking and the things which are thought by him are equivalent, i.e., that his thinking is completely present in the things thought by him, and that the things thought by him are completely present in his thinking.[98]

The difficulty is that his thinking is compatible with everything, and is incapable of verification or falsification. Everything may be taken as an illustration and be made to fit into the system; but nothing ever amounts to proof.

There is a sense in which Hegel fuses together the spirits of Romanticism and of the Age of Enlightenment.[99] He had a yearning for a total vision and a comprehensive explanation. His scheme encompassed everything in a quasi-mystical whole. Hegel produced an answer to the skepticism that he detected in Kant by articulating an evolving, logical and spiritual vision of reality. To his followers it was a vision which offered a comprehensive explanation of the sciences and of the empirical reality of the Christian religion. But to others who do not share the vision it was otherwise. One does not have to be a thoroughgoing Kantian to feel that Kant's comment on the ontological argument might equally well be extended to Hegel: "We can no more extend our stock of [theoretical] insight by mere ideas, than a merchant can better his position by adding a few noughts to his cash account."[100] Such sentiments might well have been echoed by a host of scholars from Schleiermacher to Kierkegaard and beyond as they pursued the quest for understanding Jesus.[101]

Schelling

Friedrich Wilhelm Joseph von Schelling (1775–1854)[102] was the son of a Lutheran pastor. A precocious youth, he was admitted to the Tübinger Stift at the age of fifteen, where he became the friend of Hegel and Hölderlin, both of whom were five years older than himself. All three championed the French Revolution. They also eagerly discussed the philosophies of Spinoza, Kant and Fichte. In his early days Schelling was a disciple of Fichte, a fact indicated by the title of *Vom Ich als Prinzip der Philosophie* (1795). In the same year he published *Philosophische Briefe über Dogmatismus und Kritizismus*, the former being represented by Spinoza and the latter by Fichte. Later he became dissatisfied with Fichte's view of nature simply as an instrument for moral action. But like Fichte, he developed the idea of reality as the manifestation of the absolute emerging into consciousness in and through man. His early works included *Ideen zu einer Philosophie der Natur* (1797) and *Von der Weltseele* (1798).

In 1798 Schelling was appointed to a chair at Jena. He was only twenty-three, but his writings had already won the commendation of Goethe and Fichte. At this time he was friendly with the Romantics, and in 1803 he married Caroline Schlegel after the dissolution of her marriage with A. W. Schlegel. Schelling lectured at Würzburg between 1804 and 1806, and from then onwards at Munich. For a time he collaborated with Hegel in editing a philosophical journal. The latter was comparatively unknown until 1807 when he published his *Phänomenologie des Geistes*. This work not only brought him fame but shattered the friendship with Schelling who regarded it as an inferior version of his own philosophy. Schelling's own writings at this period include *System des transcendentalen Idealismus* (1800), *Darstellung meines Systems der Philosophie* (1801), *Bruno oder über das göttliche und natürliche Princip der Dinge. Ein Gespräch* (1802), *Philosophie und Religion* (1804), *Darlegung des wahren Verhältnisses der Naturphilosophie zu der verbesserten Fichteschen Lehre. Eine Erläuterungsschrift der ersten* (1806), *Vorlesungen über die Methode des akademischen Studiums* (1803), and *Philosophische Untersuchungen über das Wesen der menschlichen Freiheit und die damit zusammenhängenden Gegenstände* (1809).

Schelling moved to Erlangen in 1821 but returned to Munich in 1827 to occupy the chair of philosophy and apply himself to the task of undermining Hegel's influence. Hegel's system seemed to him to be negative and abstract. A positive philosophy treating concrete existence was required. Ten years after Hegel's death Schelling assumed his chair at Berlin (1841). He began lecturing as the prophet of a new era. His audience included professors, statesmen and several younger hearers who were to become famous—Kierkegaard, Burckhardt, Engels and Bakunin. But the lectures were not successful, and the audiences began to dwindle. The experience prompted Kierkegaard's comment,

> The fact that philosophers talk about reality is often just as deceptive as when a man reads on a sign-board in front of a shop, "Ironing done here." If he were to come in with his linen to get it ironed, he would be making a fool of himself, for the sign-board was there only for sale.[103]

Schelling abandoned lecturing in 1846 apart from occasional discourses at the Academy of Sciences. He retired to Munich, where he occupied himself with preparing epoch-making works, which he failed to publish. He died in 1854. His *Philosophie der Mythologie* (1857) and *Philosophie der Offenbarung* (1858), which contain material delivered in his last lectures and represent a position somewhat different from that taken up half a century earlier, were published posthumously.

Schelling never quite lived up to his early promise. Like many of his generation he published too much. One recent writer has endorsed Hegel's view that Schelling carried out his education in public.[104] In the first decade of the century he taught a form of Absolute Idealism. Like Fichte, he sought to outflank Kant's critical philosophy by basing his teaching not on the individual I and the individual's reason, but upon the absolute I and the absolute reason which was the ground of all reality. He called his philosophy "das absolute Identitätssystem."[105] It sought to unite subject and object in the one single reality of "absolute Reason." *"Outside Reason is nothing, and in it is everything."* "The existence of absolute Identity is an eternal truth, for the truth of its existence is like the truth of the proposition $A = A$." *"The absolute Identity is not cause of the universe, but is the universe itself.* For everything that is is the absolute Identity itself. But the universe is everything that is, etc."[106]

In arguing in this way Schelling set aside the distinction that Kant drew between synthetic and analytic propositions and the corollary that the latter are not existential but are mere tautologies.[107] The *Darstellung* is set out like a series of theorems from which conclusions are drawn from allegedly self-evident axioms in the manner of Spinoza's *Ethica*. But similar conclusions could easily be multiplied from his other writings that were not cast in this form.[108] The result was that Schelling himself felt that he was standing on the threshold of a new era in which his own Absolute Idealism had overcome the old subject-object dualism.[109] In its place it put a philosophy of being that also replaced the Christian theistic view of God over against the world. It stressed the aliveness of nature in a more dynamic way than Spinoza's deterministic pantheism.

It was Schelling's abolition of the subject-object dualism which I. A. Dorner later found so suggestive in pointing to a new approach to Christology.[110] Although he could not give Schelling his unqualified approval, Dorner seized on the thought as a means towards understanding the union of the divine and human in Christ. The ideas of growth and the ultimately personal character of reality also commended themselves,[111] though again Dorner withheld his full endorsement on account of the self-contradictory idea of a growing God. Whether it is possible to say that Schelling had a Christology at this time is a debatable point.[112] In his *Vorlesungen über die Methode des akademische Studiums* he was at pains to point out that Christianity is not to be understood merely empirically. "From the idea of the Trinity it is clear that, if it is not conceived speculatively, it is utterly without sense."[113] Christianity is to be seen in terms of the world process of the integration of the finite and the infinite.

> Reconciliation of the finite, fallen away from God, through its own birth in finitude is the first thought of Christianity and the fulfilment of its entire purpose, of the universe and its history in the idea of the Trinity, which precisely on that account is utterly necessary in it. As is well known, Lessing has sought to unveil the philosophical meaning of this doctrine in his writing *The Education of the Human Race,* and what he has said about it is perhaps the most speculative thing that he has ever written. But in my opinion it still fails in relating this idea of the history of the world, which consists in the fact that the eternal Son of God, born from the being of the Father of all things, is himself the finite, as it is in the eternal contemplation of God, and which appears as a suffering God subjected to the fateful circumstances of time, who at the pinnacle of his appearance, in Christ, closes the world of finitude and opens up the sovereignty of infinitude or of the Spirit.[114]

In his speculative restatement of Christianity, creation and fall appear to coincide.[115] The finite is the eternal Son of God. It is this finitude which proceeds from God that manifests itself in Christ, putting an end to the world of finitude and inaugurating that of infinitude or spirit. In this process a dialectic of finite and infinite has replaced the traditional dialectic of sin and redemption. The same points were developed in Schelling's *Philosophische Untersuchungen* where an attempt was made to restate eschatology[116] and a historical incarnation justified on the grounds that a particular and personal union was required to effect the union of the finite and infinite in general.

> And indeed it appears, in order to oppose personal and spiritual evil likewise in personal and human form, and as mediator to restore the relationship of the creation with God on the highest level. For only the personal can heal the personal, and God must become man, so that man may come back to God.[117]

Schelling's language here employs traditional theological vocabulary in such a way as to suggest that he is purporting to talk about substantial realities. Elsewhere, however, he insists that the absolute can only be described in negative terms,[118] and that religion has to make use of mythological and symbolic ideas.[119] Schelling returned to this theme in his lectures on *Philosophie der Mythologie* and *Philosophie der Offenbarung*. By this time the subject of myth had become notorious through Strauss's *Leben Jesu* (1835–36). Schelling now said that revealed and mythological religions both contain mythology "precisely because the religions that grow out of mythology (the wild-growing ones) and the revealed are both religions." Nevertheless, a distinction was to be drawn.

> *The* great difference between the two must thus be recognized, in that the ideas [*Vorstellungen*] of mythology are products of a *necessary* process, of a movement of the natural consciousness, left entirely to itself, upon which, when once it is given, no free cause *outside* the consciousness has any further influence. Revelation, on the other hand, must expressly be thought of as something which presupposes an *act* outside the consciousness and a relationship that the freest cause, God, gives or has given, not necessarily but utterly voluntarily, himself to human consciousness. Both mythology and revelation are related to each other like outer process and inner history. In the process there is mere necessity, in the history is freedom.[120]

The mythological represents the religious view of the processes of nature. The revealed has to do with the inner processes of history. The former is bound by necessity; the latter is the realm of moral freedom. Sometimes the two overlap. A case in point is the practice of circumcision which (in the light of pagan antiquity) has "its initial occasion likewise in this mythological idea." But already in Deuteronomy 10:16, 30:6 and Jeremiah 4:4 the rite is demythologized insofar as "circumcision is explained to some extent morally."[121]

When Schelling finally reached the incarnation in the thirtieth lecture of his *Philosophie der Offenbarung,* he pronounced it to be "a *mysterium imperscrutabile*... an utterly unfathomable mystery... that for just that reason one should not try to plumb, or to seek for it a scientific elucidation would be in itself presumptuous."[122] But the acknowledged impossibility of the undertaking in fact did not deter Schelling from trying to plumb the mystery. He did so in terms of a spirit-matter dialectic, recalling his earlier treatment of creation.

> The primary *ground* for the humanity of Christ is thus laid by the second potency materializing itself against the higher. Naturally it is not personality as *such* (whereby there would be nothing to think), it is the *potency,* it is the natural, the substantial of

personality, that materializes itself in such a way . . . to determine that personality not merely as *personality*, but also as *natural potency*, to confer on it a *substantial* existence. But with mere materialization it would not yet be *creaturized*, and only with it—with the assumed *creaturely form*—is it completely divested of extra-divine divinity. "It materializes itself" thus means: it makes itself the material of an *organic* process, naturally of the highest organic process precisely because it should stand in the place of man and be instead of man.[123]

The Idealist explanation of the logic of the incarnation was set in the context of an exposition of the Christ-hymn in Philippians 2:6–10. When Schelling turned to the work of Christ in his next lecture, he returned to more traditional language but not necessarily to a more orthodox explanation.

That Christ bore punishment in our stead would be according to our modern concep-tion essentially a pure fiction. For from God's side the punishment was actually only given and was not necessary. Christ actually assumed it only lest we should draw a false conclusion to the detriment of the law from not being punished. Thus he actually assumed it merely in appearance.[124]

Despite this pronouncement with its overtones of Grotius[125] and anticipation of later liberalism, Schelling found himself compelled to admit, "That Christ suffered in our *stead* is indeed the most decisive assertion of the Christian documents." He declared that he had "no interest in being orthodox. . . . To me Christianity is only a phenomenon that I seek to *explain*."[126] The explanation that Schelling proferred combined allusions to biblical texts with talk about "a prin-ciple belonging to the life of God himself".[127]

By the time these lectures were published (and even while they were being delivered), Schelling was already a voice from the past. When he came to Berlin to assume the chair vacated by Fichte and Hegel, he enjoyed enormous prestige as the surviving philosopher of the golden age of Idealism. Schelling's own lectures hastened its demise. He exerted some influence over Dorner and over a number of Catholic theologians. But it was the earlier Schelling of the pre-Berlin period.[128] Although Schelling's thought enjoyed a certain repristination in the twentieth century, not least through the mediation of Paul Tillich, contemporaries of Schelling's later years found him less persuasive and relevant.

With an eye on Schelling, the historian Leopold von Ranke declared himself to be more concerned with understanding historical periods in accordance with the available data than with philosophizing about the inner spiritual dynamic of history. He criticized the Idealist philosophers of cosmic and terrestrial history who could not distinguish cosmogenic and theosophical myths from historical events.[129] Kierkegaard complained that Schelling's "main point is always that there are two philosophies, one positive and one negative. The negative is given, but not by Hegel, for Hegel's is neither negative nor positive but a refined Spinozaism. The positive is yet to come."[130] Although he spent much time writing down Schelling's lectures and making fair copies,[131] he finally gave up. He complained to his friend, Emil Boesen, that "Schelling talks endless nonsense both in an extensive and an intensive sense."[132] To his brother Peter he confided, "I am too old to attend lectures, just as Schelling is too old to give them. His whole doctrine of potencies betrays the highest degree of impotence."[133]

Conclusion

In the past two chapters we have reviewed the ideas of a number of thinkers under the general heading of "Philosophical Idealism and Rational Religion." What they have in common is a belief that orthodox Christian theism must be restated and transcended by a more rational world view that nevertheless leaves room for religion. Where they differ is over their attitude to reason. Paul Tillich drew a distinction between "technical" and "ontological" reason.[134] The former is reason in the sense of the capacity for reasoning; the latter is reason as it determines the ultimate structure of the universe. On the basis of our analysis, it may be said that Kant and, to a certain extent, Herder and Goethe were more concerned with "technical" reason. It may be added that all three believed in what Tillich called "the depth of reason," "something that is not reason but which precedes reason and is manifest through it."[135] Kant was concerned with a critical reappraisal of the scope and limits of reason. He rejected all speculative metaphysics and reappraised religion accordingly. Both Herder and Goethe subjected Christian orthodoxy to rational criticism, but especially in Goethe's case there were more things in his world view than the strictly rational. They were not to be apprehended by metaphysical speculation but through intuition and action. On the other hand, Fichte, Schelling and the mature Hegel were all concerned with what Tillich called "ontological" reason and the rational structure of the universe.

Broadly speaking, the Christologies of these thinkers correspond to their attitude to reason. In the last analysis, the Jesus of Kant, Herder and Goethe (together with that of the young Kantian Hegel) was an enlightened man with keen rational and moral insights who preached an altruistic humanitarian message. Through his life and teaching he brought mankind into contact with the divine. In the Absolute Idealist teaching of Fichte, Hegel and Schelling, Christ was seen as a manifestation of the rational, ontological principle of the universe. For ontological reasons this manifestation was a historical one, though the precise reasons and significance of the manifestation differed somewhat in each case. Fichte stressed the rationality of Being. Hegel developed a philosophy of *Geist* coming to self-consciousness. Schelling's Idealism was ultimately personal and religious. But, with the exception of Herder, none of the Idealist thinkers whom we have considered were interested in the details of historical investigation, especially in the area of Christian origins. Perhaps the reason for this was that they were at heart heirs of the rationalist tradition which sought to avoid the shifting sands of history for the apparently sure rock of the rational and the eternal. Even Kant was no exception to this. Although he maintained that a rational metaphysics was indefensible, he nevertheless sought to base his philosophy upon the self-evidently rational.

For Lessing it was axiomatic that "accidental truths of history can never become proof of the necessary truths of reason." It was an axiom that Kant could have endorsed and that Herder and Goethe found acceptable, though not a complete statement of the truth of religion. For the Absolute Idealists the "accidental truths of history" might not have been "proof of the necessary truths of reason," but they were certainly its necessary expression. They give the impression that further study of such accidental truths would be otiose. But this was a view that was not shared by the majority of their contemporaries or successors.

III

NEW PERSPECTIVES IN RELIGION

6. SCHLEIERMACHER AND RELIGIOUS AWARENESS

Goethe once observed that there is nothing more illogical than absolute logic for it gives rise to unnatural phenomena that finally collapse.[1] As we shall have cause to see in succeeding chapters, Hegelianism fragmented after Hegel's death in 1831. But even during his lifetime, philosophical Idealism was being challenged not only by the orthodox but by a philosopher and theologian who had been instrumental in bringing Hegel to Berlin.[2] That thinker was Friedrich Schleiermacher who possessed the most creative religious mind of the age.

Schleiermacher's Life and Works

In order to see Schleiermacher's thought in perspective, some account of his life and works must be given. Friedrich Ernst Daniel Schleiermacher (1768–1834)[3] came from a religious and pietistic background. Both his grandfathers were pastors, and his father was an army chaplain and Reformed minister in Silesia. In 1783 Schleiermacher entered the Moravian school at Niesky from which, two years later, he entered the seminary at Barby. In later life he could describe himself as "a Herrnhuter again, only of a higher order" and speak with gratitude of the awareness of a higher world he had received which preserved him from skepticism.[4] But at the time it seemed that his father's hopes of saving him from the eroding influences of rationalism by sending him to a Moravian institution were to be rudely shattered. Schleiermacher was irked not only by the inadequate teaching but by the stifling intellectual outlook. His inner conflicts were intensified by his failure to apprehend for himself the elusive experiences of grace which colored the Moravian outlook. Eventually, the father gave way to his son's pleas to be allowed to transfer to the nearby university of Halle, if only because the situation had become mutually intolerable and without a higher education the way to any profession would be barred.

Schleiermacher entered Halle in 1787. Semler was still writing, but the more distinguished younger biblical scholars were elsewhere. It was not theology but the debates between the Kantians and the Wolffians, led by his teacher, J. A. Eberhard, that claimed the young student's interest. Perhaps, as Dilthey has suggested, it was to the detriment of his later competence as a biblical critic that Schleiermacher did not take the opportunity to ground himself in the biblical languages and historical techniques.[5] But it was philosophical subjects that preoccupied his mind and pen for the next few years, and it was in the realm of philosophical theology that Schleiermacher was to make his chief contributions.

After taking his theological examinations at Berlin in 1790, Schleiermacher spent three years as a private tutor at Schlobitten. Despite attacks of skepticism, Schleiermacher did not abandon the Christian faith. As early as 1789 he preached an advent sermon on the theme "That Christ alone is our Savior and we have to await no other."[6] Schleiermacher was ordained in 1794. After two years as assistant to his uncle, he was appointed chaplain of the Reformed Church at the Charité Hospital at Berlin where in the course of the next six years he was drawn into the brilliant circle of Romantic writers and poets who constituted the *avant garde* intellectuals of the time.[7] It was in this period that Schleiermacher published his first major work, *Ueber die Religion. Reden an die Gebildeten unter ihren Verächtern*,[8] which appeared anonymously in 1799 and which was followed the next year by the anonymous *Monologen*.[9] Both works were later described by their author as impromptu pieces prior to the regular concert.[10]

In 1804 Schleiermacher was appointed Ausserordentlicher Professor of Theology at Halle where he published the first volume of his translation of Plato.[11] He began lecturing on hermeneutics and philology, ethics, theological encyclopaedia and dogmatics. He revised the *Reden*[12] and reissued his printed sermons. He applied to the New Testament epistles the techniques he had used on Plato in *Ueber den sogenannten ersten Brief des Paulus an Timotheus* (1807).[13] But the work of this period which bears most directly on Schleiermacher's theological method and understanding of Christ is *Die Weihnachtsfeier* (1806).[14]

The years at Halle were overshadowed by the Napoleonic wars. By the Peace of Tilsit (1807) Halle was severed from the rest of Prussia. At first there was talk of transferring the university to Berlin. But as time went on, this gave way to the more brilliant prospect of founding a new university at Berlin as part of the program of national renewal. Schleiermacher was the first dean of its theological faculty. One of the first works written in connection with his teaching was his *Kurze Darstellung des theologischen Studiums zum Behuf einleitender Vorlesungen entworfen* (1811; 2nd ed., 1830).[15] Over the years Schleiermacher gave courses on hermeneutics, ethics, dialectics, philosophy, various branches of theology, and the life of Jesus, which were posthumously published, though the lectures on *Das Leben Jesu* did not appear until 1864.[16]

At Berlin Schleiermacher came to the fore as the great patriotic preacher of German nationalism. From 1809 until his death he was the Reformed minister of the Dreifaltigkeitskirche, where he shared the pulpit with the Lutheran, P. K. Marheineke. Throughout this period Schleiermacher was an active member of the Königliche Akademie der Wissenschaften to which he delivered papers on classical, philosophical and historical subjects.

An event of profound significance for German Protestantism was the proposed union of the Lutheran and Reformed Churches in Prussia, which was encouraged by the king for both religious and political reasons.[17] Schleiermacher supported the union. His greatest work, *Der christliche Glaube nach den Grund-sätzen der christlichen Kirche im Zusammenhange dargestellt* (1821; 2nd ed., 1830–31)[18] could well be regarded as the first dogmatics of the Union Church. In the foreword to the first edition Schleiermacher wrote,

> If I am now the first to draw up a theology [Glaubenslehre] according to the tenets of the evangelical church, as if it were One, and thereby explain that to me there seems to stand no dogmatic dividing wall between the two ecclesiastical communities, I hope that this will be justified by the act. For I have endeavored to represent the essence of the evangelical view of faith and life in its particular boundaries as the same in both Confessions and to assign to the different views of both Confessions their place within this area.[19]

The attempt to penetrate outer forms and express the essence of the Christian faith in a manner relevant and acceptable to the modern mind was the dominating characteristic of Schleiermacher's theology. *Der christliche Glaube* was both preceeded and followed by various shorter writings clarifying and amplifying Schleiermacher's position. They included *Ueber die Lehre der Erwählung, besonders in Beziehung auf Herrn Dr. Bretschneiders Aphorismen* (1819), *Ueber den Gegensatz zwischen der sabellianischen und der athanasianischen Vorstel-lung von der Trinität* (1822), and *Ueber seine Glaubenslehre. An Herrn Dr. Lücke, Zwei Sendschreiben* (1829).[20]

Schleiermacher's Early Christology

It is a matter of debate how far Schleiermacher's addresses *Ueber die Religion* may be regarded as a theological expression of Romanticism. It certainly broke with the rationalistic and moralistic approach to religion of Kant and the thinkers of the Enlightenment. Schleiermacher appeared as an impassioned preacher, albeit not of the characteristic doctrines of the Moravians and reformed orthodoxy. Nor was his appeal couched in the language and imagery of pietistic devotion. The work might be regarded as an essay in apologetics and philosoph-ical theology, but it was not the natural theology so recently demolished by Kant. Rather it was a religious interpretation of life which strove to show that life was incomplete without religion.

> True science is complete vision; true practice is culture and art self-produced; true religion is sense and taste for the Infinite. To wish to have true science or true practice without religion, or to imagine it is possessed, is obstinate, arrogant delusion, and culpable error. It issues from the unholy sense that would rather have a show of possession by cowardly purloining than have secure possession by demanding and waiting. What can man accomplish that is worth speaking of, either in life or in art, that does not arise in his own self from the influence of this sense for the Infinite? Without it, how can anyone wish to comprehend the world scientifically, or if, in some distinct talent, the knowledge is thrust upon him, how should he wish to exercise it? What is all science, if not the existence of things in you, in your reason? What is all art and culture if not your existence in the things to which you give

measure, form and order? And how can both come to life in you except in so far as there lives immediately in you the eternal unity of Reason and Nature, the universal existence of all finite things in the Infinite?[21]

The object of religion was not a particular being or activity above or alongside others. Like the Absolute Self of the Idealists and Tillich's "Ground of Being" or "Being itself," Schleiermacher's God was not to be thought of as a self-contained, immutable being over and above the world. The traditional theistic way of thinking about God was "seldom entirely pure and always inadequate."[22] Schleiermacher was conscious that his train of thought had much in common with Spinoza. In a passage that prompted hostile criticism, he urged his readers to offer a tribute to "the holy, rejected Spinoza" who was pervaded by "the high World-Spirit."[23] However, Schleiermacher's own approach did not proceed, as it did with Spinoza and the Absolute Idealists, by way of deductive inference from ostensibly self-evident axioms. The given for Schleiermacher was the feeling-states of the individual. God's existence was not inferred from man's self-consciousness. It was given with it.

> Seeing then that I have presented nothing but just this immediate and original existence of God in us through feeling, how can anyone say that I have depicted a religion without God? Is not God the highest, the only unity? Is it not God alone before whom and in whom all particular things disappear? And if you see the world as a Whole, a Universe, can you do it otherwise than in God? If not, how could you distinguish the highest existence, the original and eternal Being from a temporal and derived individual? Otherwise than by the emotions produced in us by the world we do not claim to have God in our feeling, and consequently I have not said more of Him.[24]

The thought anticipates Schleiermacher's later definition of faith: "Glaube ist besonders die im Selbstbewusstsein gesetzte Gewissheit vom dem Mitgesetzten."[25] What was thus posited in the self-consciousness was not necessarily to be conceived on an anthropological model. Indeed, God was not so much a "personally thinking and willing" being, as the Highest Being "exalted above all personality," "the universal, productive, connecting necessity of all thought and existence."[26]

This approach, Schleiermacher believed, transcended the fixed positions of orthodoxy. He disparaged "the vain juggling with analytical formulas, in which, whether categorical or hypothetical, life will not be fettered"[27] and the systems of the schools which are often "mere habitations and nurseries of the dead letter."[28] It also superseded orthodox supernaturalism, enabling Schleiermacher to retain miracle, revelation, inspiration and grace, but treat them as religious ways of looking at natural phenomena.[29] As with Herder and Goethe, who were both influenced by Spinoza, the pantheistic or panentheistic approach to religion was the reverse side of a naturalistic approach to nature and history.

It was almost as a kind of tailpiece in the fifth and final *Rede* that Schleiermacher introduced a discussion of the uniqueness and value of Christianity and the place of Christ in religion. The former lay in its "ursprüngliche Anschauung" of the tension between the finite and the infinite.

> It is just the intuition of the Universal resistance of finite things to the unity of the Whole, and of the way the Deity treats this resistance. Christianity sees how He reconciles the hostility to Himself, and sets bounds to the ever-increasing alienation by scattering points here and there over the whole that are at once finite and infinite, human and divine.[30]

It is precisely this insight into alienation and reconciliation which gives Christianity its polemical and evangelistic character.[31] Christ's place in this proclamation does not derive from his high moral teaching. For this is shared by all spiritually-minded men. Rather it derives from the idea which possessed his soul that everything finite requires mediation and restoration.

> But the truly divine element is the glorious clearness to which the great idea He came to exhibit attained in His soul. This idea was, that all that is finite requires a higher mediation to be in accord with the Deity, and that for man under the power of the finite and particular, and too ready to imagine the divine itself in this form, salvation is only to be found in redemption.[32]

Schleiermacher had already touched upon the existence of mediators as "interpreters of the Deity and His works, and reconcilers of things that otherwise would be eternally hidden."[33] What distinguished Jesus from all other such mediators was the unparalleled degree in which he was able to do this in virtue of his unique communion with the infinite. It was this which constituted his mediatorship and it was in these terms that Schleiermacher construed his divinity. The divine God-man of the creeds and orthodox theology is replaced by a figure who fits easily into the naturalistic-panentheistic framework of Schleiermacher's thought. It is the kind of figure that is more readily comprehensible to the modern mind that rejects supernaturalistic premises—the expert in his specialized field. Jesus had a unique awareness of the infinite. It was this which constituted his mediatorship and what previously had been understood as his personal divinity.

> If all finite things require the mediation of a higher being, if it is not to be ever further removed from the Eternal and be dispersed into the void and transitory, if its union with the Whole is to be sustained and come to consciousness, what mediates must not again require mediation, and cannot be purely finite. It must belong to both sides, participating in the Divine Essence in the same way and in the same sense in which it participates in human nature. But what did He see around Him that was not finite and in need of mediation, and where was aught that could mediate but Himself? "No man knoweth the Father but the Son, and He to whom the Son shall reveal Him." This consciousness of the singularity of His knowledge of God and of His existence in God, of the original way in which this knowledge was in Him, and of

the power thereof to communicate itself and awake religion, was at once the consciousness of His office as mediator and of His divinity.[34]

Entirely consistent with this view, Schleiermacher visualized the theoretical possibility that Christianity and Christ might one day be superseded, though the possibility was remote.[35] In the meantime, Jesus foresaw the need for mediation, and provided for it in the shape of the church and its sacraments.[36]

H. R. Mackintosh has observed that one could no more understand modern theology without Schleiermacher's *Christliche Glaube* than one could understand modern biology without Darwin.[37] The comparison might be both extended and modified. Just as Darwin was not the first to discover evolution but the first to give the hypothesis comprehensive and cogent expression, so Schleiermacher did not invent modern, liberal theology. Just as Darwin expanded the thought of the *Origin of Species* (1859) in various later works, so Schleiermacher amplified his approach in numerous works, above all in *Der christliche Glaube*. But it was the *Reden* which formally inaugurated Schleiermacher's characteristic method of approaching theology neither as a body of received doctrines nor as a system of metaphysical and ethical ideas, but as the analysis of man's religious consciousness. In the words of Rudolf Otto, "Here in the *Speeches*...one will find the original concepts which were systematically elaborated in his later works, where they were assimilated to theology and received the imprint of traditional churchly form."[38]

Schleiermacher's next work, the *Monologen. Eine Neujahrsgabe* (1800) related the religious concepts of the *Reden* to ethics. For a while Schleiermacher was preoccupied with the *Lucinde* affair, occasioned by F. Schlegel's novel, and his translation of Plato. He returned to the theme of Christianity and religion in *Die Weihnachtsfeier. Ein Gespräch* (1806). Richard R. Niebuhr aptly summarizes it when he writes,

> *The Christmas Eve* is not a finished essay and comes to no explicit conclusion, but like its Platonic prototype is designed to involve its readers in the movement of thought and—something more—to awaken in them a deep feeling of the irresistible, humanizing stream of life that breaks forth in the Christ child and elicits from every sentient being an irrepressible rejoicing.[39]

The scene is the home of a cultivated, middle-class German family. It is Christmas Eve, and the circle of friends are gathered for the festivities. One by one we are introduced to each member: the hosts, Eduard and Ernestine, and their children, especially the musical, religious, precocious, but well-behaved Sofie. Ernst and Friederike are an engaged couple. There is also a young wife named Agnes; an unmarried lady, Karoline; the skeptical Leonhardt; and the somewhat enigmatic Josef who makes his appearance at the end to pronounce (like a Greek chorus) the moral of the tale.

Barth's comment on Leonhardt, that he is "the product of the theological rather than the literary imagination,"[40] applies, in fact, to the whole work. *Die*

Weihnachstfeier is a theological essay. But while its substance is Christian, its formal antecedents are pagan. In casting the work in dialogue form, Schleiermacher was adopting techniques and insights which he admired in Plato. In dialogue truth is not static. Nor is it confined to any one speaker. It emerges as the dialogue proceeds. There is a sense in which all the speakers represent some stage of the author's mind, even though Josef may be recognized as the author's self-portrait in the same way as a painter may be identified with some character in the corner of a medieval painting.[41] But even though Josef pronounces the last word, the finality of that word is only relative. This final word—like any single utterance in a dialogue—is not complete in itself. For the truth of the Christian message does not lie in words, but in the experiences to which the words point and into which Josef exhorts the company to enter through adoration, fellowship and music.

> I have not come to deliver a discourse, but to make myself glad with you.... To me all forms have become too stiff, and all discoursing too tedious and cold. The unspeakable subject demands and even produces in me an unspeakable joy; in my gladness I can only exult and shout for joy like a child.... I feel myself at home, and as it were new born in the better world, in which pain and sorrow have no more a meaning, nor a place.... For you know well that to me you are the dearest of all. Come, then, and bring the child above all things, if she is not yet asleep; and let me see your glories; and let us be glad, and sing something pious and joyous.[42]

The route which leads to this climax is circuitous. It passes through three main stages. The first sets the scene: the room, the decorations, the gifts, the singing, the lighted model of the crib, the child Sofie's piety and singing, all of which give rise to a welter of apparently disconnected observations on life and religion. The dialogue enters its second stage when the ladies accede to the men's request to recount experiences of bygone Christmas Eves. The theme which connects them all is that of mother and child. Friederike is reluctant to speak but readily obliges with impromptu piano accompaniment to the narratives. In the third stage the three men expound their views of Christmas. Leonhardt is the critical rationalist; Ernst the man of calm, inner experience; and Eduard the speculative mystic. While they are still debating, Josef makes his brief appearance and pronounces the conclusion.

What is the message of Christmas which these characters are intended to evoke by their cumulative words and actions? Certainly, it is concerned with the truth of religion, a truth which defies apprehension in precise propositional formulae, a truth which has to be caught rather than taught. It may also be said that it is concerned with the apprehension of Christ, but it is a Christ who does not come to men directly but is refracted in universal human experience and the tradition of Christmas. Three motifs recur in the narrative: music, woman and motherhood, and the meaning of Christmas.

We have already had occasion to note the part played by music in the dialogue. Schleiermacher admitted to a friend that he conceived the work while listening to Dülon's flute concerto.[43] To the modern reader little Sofie's talent for music, especially that composed "im grossen Kirchenstil,"[44] and Friederike's impromptu accompaniment might suggest a touch of "Schmalz." But Schleier-macher did not simply intend it as background music to heighten the effect. It falls to Eduard to remind the company,

> Every beautiful feeling only comes completely forth when we have found the right tone for it: not the spoken word, for that at any time can only be an indirect expression . . . but the musical tone in the proper sense. In fact, music is most closely related to the religious feeling . . . . What the word has made clear, the tones of music must make alive, or must convey, and fix as a harmony, into the whole inward nature.[45]

These reflections stand in sharp contrast with Reformed orthodoxy with its emphasis on preaching, its insistence on mental assent to carefully defined dog-matic propositions based upon propositional revelation.

But music was not the only medium of religion. Nor was it the sole object of Josef's commendation. While the men have been arguing, the ladies preferred to sing. And they, Josef observes, have chosen the better part.[46] The point begins to emerge that women *as* women have a profound and immediate apprehension of the divine and are, to use an expression from the *Reden* "interpreters of the Deity and His works, and reconcilers of things that otherwise would be eternally hidden." The point comes out in a carefully contrived artless remark of Sofie who sees her mother (and indeed all saintly women) as another Mary.[47]

Music, motherhood and the pious, festive mood mediate the meaning of Christmas. By contrast historical knowledge is comparatively meager and less significant. This emerges as the conversation turns to the question of the ascertain-able facts about the first Christmas and Jesus' earthly life. Leonhardt readily assumes the role of devil's advocate. He observes that custom and habit are more important to ordinary people than historical and intellectual precision.[48] The readiness of people to accept the historicity of an event often depends upon how far their minds have been conditioned by popular belief which has in turn been fed by religious feasts. Belief is as much inclined to create and embellish events as vice versa.

Leonhardt then proceeds to apply these considerations to the question of the historical Jesus.

> I allow Christianity to be regarded as unquestionably a strong and powerful present fact, but the earthly personal activity of Christ appears to me to be far less connected with it than most people rather assume than believe. In particular, what rests upon Him in reference to the reconciliation of our race, is connected by all of us specially with His death; and in this connection—as I think—more turns upon an eternal decree of God than upon a particular individual fact; and on this account we ought to connect these ideas not so much with one particular moment of time, but rather to extend them beyond the temporal history of the Redeemer, and hold them as symbolical.[49]

This observation leads to the thought that Paul was more the founder of the church than Jesus, who stood closer to John the Baptist than to the primitive community.

> Indeed it remains doubtful whether it was at all in accordance with Christ's will that such an exclusive and organized Church should be everywhere formed, although without it our present Christianity— and consequently also our festival, the subject of my discourse—cannot be conceived of. On this account the earthly life of Christ was also put greatly in the background in the first proclamation of Christianity; and as most people now believe, it was only proclaimed in part by subordinate persons.[50]

Moreover, there is much in the Gospel narratives that does not ring true. Obvious instances are Jesus' royal genealogies and supernatural birth.[51] The resurrection, ascension and deity of Christ are all highly questionable.[52] These conclusions might well seem to damn, but Leonhardt has some praise to offer. If it sounds faint, it nevertheless rescues Leonhardt from complete skepticism.

> In short, what is presented in experience and history regarding the personal existence of Christ, has become so uncertain by the diversity of opinions and doctrines maintained on the subject, that if our festival must be pre-eminently regarded as the foundation of the belief which has been maintained in common regarding Him, it is thereby glorified all the more, and there is demonstrated a power in it bordering closely upon that fact already mentioned, namely, that history itself is sometimes really made by such usages.[53]

How far does Leonhardt represent Schleiermacher himself? In a letter replying to questions about the book Schleiermacher acknowledged the work's "Platonic form," but professed Leonhardt's speech to be "essentially frivolous in nature."[54] Moreover, as Barth pointed out,[55] the way in which he softened and clarified the speech in the 1826 edition is an indication that it was not given merely to be refuted. Nor was it refuted by any of the characters in the dialogue. Friederike calls Leonhardt "the unbelieving knave,"[56] but she chides him less for the content of his speech than for misconstruing her own. In response to her request to take Leonhardt to task, the faithful Eduard admits that she is right, but ruefully adds that "it would be difficult to get at him; for he has taken care to plead his cause like a true advocate."[57] Ernst declines the opportunity to refute him on the grounds that it "would draw me away to other subjects, and I might then myself become liable to a penalty."[58] When Josef at last pronounces judgment, he carefully avoids pronouncing on the truth or falsehood of Leonhardt's views on history. The burden of his remarks is that rationalistic, intellectual (and historical) arguments are inadequate and even irrelevant to the real matter in hand.[59]

Leonhardt is not Schleiermacher, though Schleiermacher is acutely aware of the rising tide of historical skepticism. Wilhelm Dilthey saw in Leonhardt an anticipation of D. F. Strauss not only in his historical skepticism but in his recognition of the myth-making power of the cult.[60] However, Schleiermacher himself adopted a more positive attitude to both these factors. Dilthey went on to see in the figure of Eduard a representation of Schelling and other advocates of Christian speculative thought. Whereas Leonhardt had dealt with the "historical," Eduard proposed to deal with the "mystical" which he finds expressed in the Fourth Gospel. The meaning of Christmas was bound up with the idea of the Word of God becoming flesh.

> The flesh, however, as we know, is nothing else than our finite, limited, sensible nature. The Word, on the other hand, is the thought or consciousness; and its becoming incarnate is therefore the appearing of this original and divine thing in that form. Accordingly what we celebrate is just what we are in ourselves as a whole; in other words, it is human nature, or whatever you may call it, contemplated and known from the divine principle.[61]

Concretely, Eduard argued, Christ was "the starting point for this communication."

> For we, indeed, are born again through the Spirit of the Church. But the Spirit Itself only goes out from the Son, who requires no new birth, but is born originally from God. Thus He is the Son of Man absolutely. All that was before Him was a prefiguration of Him, and was related to Him; and only through this relation was it good and divine. Yet in Him we celebrate not only ourselves but all who will yet come, as well as all who have ever been; for they were only anything in so far as He was in them and they in Him. In Christ, then, we see the Spirit, according to the kind and manner of our earth, primordially take the form of self-consciousness in the individual. The Father and the Brethren dwell equably in Him, and are one in Him; devotion and love are His very being. Therefore every mother who feels that she has borne a man, and who knows by a heavenly annunciation that the Spirit of the Church, the Holy Ghost, lives in her, forthwith presents her child on that account with all her heart to the Church, and she claims to be allowed to do this as a right; and such a mother sees Christ also in her child, and this is just the inexpressible mother-feeling which compensates for all else.[62]

What Eduard is saying here was the answer of speculative Idealism to historical skepticism, expressed in the language of orthodoxy and picking up the theme of motherhood. But it was not quite Schleiermacher's last word. The dialectic of dialogue enabled him to reintroduce Josef to make the final pronouncement which we have already noted. The work itself was not Schleiermacher's last word on Christology. In the preface to the 1827 edition he conceded somewhat enigmatically that "most of what is here does not have the same truth as before." Nevertheless, it set out in a non-polemical way "the most diverse conceptions of Christianity," reminding its readers that "the letter kills and only the Spirit makes alive."[63] By the time he wrote this Schleiermacher had dropped Eduard's Idealist Christology and had both mitigated and made more explicit Leonhardt's skepticism. His Christology was now fully developed along the lines of his earlier thought of Christ as the *Urbild*, the original, perfect image, who mediates the divine.[64]

Christology and Method in "Der christliche Glaube"

Der christliche Glaube (1821; 2nd ed., 1830–31) contains Schleiermacher's definitive exposition of the Christian faith. It clarifies and amplifies the concepts of the *Kurze Darstellung des theologischen Studiums* (1811; 2nd ed., 1830). This earlier work had presented Schleiermacher's anatomy of theology, laying out its subject like the parts of a dismembered corpse, neatly dissected and labelled in the form of 338 propositions. Although suggestive, the brief paragraphs of the *Kurze Darstellung* left little room for discussion and argument. Now the bare bones were clothed with flesh. At the same time, Schleiermacher did not abandon the strict schematic presentation. The work is divided into two main parts, prefaced by two introductory chapters, all of which are divided into sections and subsections and numbered paragraphs. The two introductory chapters deal with the nature and method of dogmatics (secs. 2–31). The heading of Part I gives more than a hint as to how Schleiermacher intends to proceed: "The Development of that Religious Self-Consciousness which is always both presupposed by and contained in every Christian Religious Affection" (secs. 32–61). It contains an analysis of man's self-consciousness in relation to God and the world. Part II deals with the believer's awareness of sin and grace under the heading, "Explication of the facts of the religious self-consciousness, as they are determined by the antithesis" (secs. 62–169). A brief conclusion deals with the "The Divine Trinity" (secs. 170–172).

In the *Reden* Schleiermacher had defined religion almost exclusively in aesthetic and metaphysical terms as a "sense and taste for the infinite." *Die Weihnachtsfeier* had presented a series of variations on this theme, illustrating how it worked out in the lives of the cultured middle class. It had also given it a more positively Christian orientation. *Der christliche Glaube* returned to the theme to give it more precise analysis and definition within the context of the evangelical churches of the Union. Schleiermacher's basic position is summarized succinctly in the thesis of section 3:

> *The piety which forms the basis of all ecclesiastical communions is, considered purely in itself, neither a Knowing nor a Doing, but a modification of Feeling, or of immediate self-consciousness.*[65]

His meaning is brought out in section 3.4:

> For, indeed, it is the case in general that the immediate self-consciousness is always the mediating link in the transition between moments in which Knowing predominates and those in which Doing predominates, so that a different Doing may proceed from the same Knowing in different people according as a different determination of self-consciousness enters in. And thus it will fall to piety to stimulate Knowing and Doing, and every moment in which piety has a predominant place will contain within itself one or both of these in germ.[66]

What Schleiermacher gives here is not only a concept of religion but also a corresponding concept of psychology. The ultimate *locus* of religion is neither activity (*Tun*) nor knowledge (*Wissen*), but something which underlies and unites both: that continuum of feeling or awareness (*Gefühl*) which we call self-consciousness (*Selbstbewusstsein*).

But not all self-awareness is religious. Piety is a determination or particular case (*Bestimmtheit*) of self-consciousness.

> *The common element in all howsoever diverse expressions of piety, by which these are conjointly distinguished from all other feelings, or, in other words, the self-identical essence of piety, is this: the consciousness of being absolutely dependent, or, which is the same thing, of being in relation with God.*[67]

At this point English discussions of Schleiermacher have often been hampered by a somewhat constricted and rigid rendering of Schleiermacher's terminology. In translating the word *Gefühl* as *feeling* in their edition of *The Christian Faith*, Mackintosh and Stewart have only been following older exegetes like G. P. Fisher.[68] They were, in fact, giving a dictionary equivalent. The translation suggests that Schleiermacher was preoccupied with subjective religious feelings. It would, however, correspond more closely to his intentions and perhaps render his thought more realistic to the modern mind, if, instead of translating his key concept of *das schlechthinnige Abhängigkeitsgefühl* as *the feeling of absolute dependence*, it were rendered as *awareness*, *sense* or *consciousness of absolute*, *utter* or *ultimate dependence*. These alternatives are linguistically permissible, and the context often suggests a wider range of meaning than is conveyed by the word *feeling*.[69]

In point of fact, the sense of ultimate dependence is not a particular feeling; it is contained in every aspect of Christian experience. It is not one possible way to God; it is *the* medium of revelation.

> *The immediate feeling of absolute dependence is presupposed and actually contained in every religious and Christian selfconsciousness as the only way in which, in general, our own being and the infinite Being of God can be one in self-consciousness.*[70]

> *This feeling of absolute dependence, in which our selfconsciousness in general represents the finitude of our being (cf. sec. 8, 2), is therefore not an accidental element, or a thing which varies from person to person, but is a universal element of life; and the recognition of this fact entirely takes the place, for the system of doctrine, of all the so-called proofs of the existence of God.*[71]

Indeed, this proof of the existence of God is given in and with our awareness of ourselves in the world.

> The feeling of absolute dependence is contained in every Christian religious affection, in proportion as in the latter, through its co-determining stimuli, we become conscious that we are placed in a universal nature-system, i.e. in proportion as we are conscious of ourselves as part of the world.[72]

Schleiermacher's concept of dogmatics is the logical corollary of his conception of religion. It is the descriptive analysis of the faith of those within the church.

> *Dogmatic Theology is the science which systematizes the doctrine prevalent in a Christian Church at a given time.*[73]

Dogmatic statements are in principle descriptions of human feeling-states.

> *All propositions which the system of Christian doctrine has to establish can be regarded either as descriptions of human states, or as conceptions of divine attributes and modes of action, or as utterances regarding the constitution of the world; and all three forms have always subsisted alongside of each other.*[74]

Schleiermacher's method cut across that of traditional Protestant dogmatics with its deductive reasoning based upon axiomatic propositions divinely revealed in Scripture. His work contains scarcely any exegesis of biblical passages (despite the fact that some eight hundred are referred to in the course of the work). But Schleiermacher also broke with the speculative philosophical approach of the rationalists and the Idealists. He rejected the Kantian attempt to reduce religion to that which is conceivable within the limits of reason alone. His positive method was to analyze religious experience with a view to determining its essence. On the other hand, he virtually accepted Kant's embargo on the treatment of anything beyond the scope of direct human experience.

This last point is exemplified by Schleiermacher's insistence that we ought not to think of the divine attributes as objective realities but as part of the description of particular aspects of our subjective feeling-states.

> *All attributes which we ascribe to God are to be taken as denoting not something special in God, but only something special in the manner in which the feeling of absolute dependence is to be related to Him.*[75]

Similarly, sin must be understood in terms of self-consciousness. Basically it may be defined as "a positive antagonism of the flesh against the spirit."[76] Another way of putting it is "to reckon everything as sin that has arrested the free development of the God-consciousness."[77] Sin is a clouding over of our sense of absolute dependence, the attempt to be free and autonomous. The following extract from the chapter on "Sin as the State of Man" is significant not only because it crystallizes Schleiermacher's thought, but also because it betrays his embarrassment with certain aspects of orthodoxy.

> This explanation of sin as an arrestment of the determinative power of the spirit, due to the independence of the sensuous functions, is certainly reconcilable with those explanations which describe sin as a turning away from the Creator, though less so with those which interpret sin as a violation of the divine law. But it cannot be of any great consequence to insist on a reconciliation with the latter, for in the sense in which God and the eternal law might be distinguished—as if one could turn away from the latter as from a single and perhaps arbitrary act of God without turning away from Himself—law is not an originally Christian term and must therefore be merged in a higher.[78]

This was not the only point at which Schleiermacher found himself in tension with the older orthodoxy. The notion of original sin (*Erbsünde*) also calls for reappraisal. The idea of posterity inheriting Adam's guilty, sinful nature is highly artificial, indemonstrable, unjust and incapable of being derived from the conception just outlined. Instead, stress should be laid upon the universal incapacity for good which is present in all and which is exemplified by the story of Genesis 3.[79]

What has been said so far gives some idea of how Schleiermacher's ideas of God and man have been shaped by his method in general and by his understanding of religious experience in particular. These in turn supply the framework into which is fitted Schleiermacher's conception of Christ. Taking *Der christliche Glaube* as a whole, one cannot fail to be impressed by the thoroughgoing christocentric character of his approach. But equally striking is the way in which Schleiermacher's Christ is molded by the basic notion of *das schlechthinnige Abhängigkeitsgefühl*.

The main exposition of Christ's person and work appears in Part II. But some hint of what was to come was already given in the preliminary survey in section 11, where Christianity is defined as follows:

> *Christianity is a monotheistic faith, belonging to the teleological type of religion, and is essentially distinguished from other such faiths by the fact that in it everything is related to the redemption accomplished by Jesus of Nazareth.*[80]

The redemption (*Erlösung*) which Jesus is here said to accomplish means two things. On the one hand, it is a figurative way of describing the passage from an evil condition to a better one. And on the other hand, it points to the help given in this process by someone else.

> The term itself is in this realm merely figurative, and signifies in general a passage from an evil condition, which is represented as a state of captivity or constraint, into a better condition — this is the passive side of it. But it also signifies the help given in that process by some other person, and this is the active side of it.[81]

The really significant step in this procedure comes to light when Schleiermacher defines more precisely what he means here by man's "evil condition." He sees it not with the patristic writers as enslavement by the Devil and the powers of evil;[82] nor with Anselm as a debt incurred by sin;[83] nor yet with Calvin and Luther[84] as bondage under the Law. Rather, he explains it entirely in terms of our consciousness of God and the lack of it.

> But now apply the word to the realm of religion, and suppose we are dealing with the teleological type of religion. Then the evil condition can only consist in an obstruction or arrest of the vitality of the higher self-consciousness, so that there comes to be little or no union of it with the various determinations of the sensible self-consciousness, and thus little or no religious life. We may give to this condition, in its most extreme form, the name of *Godlessness*, or, better, *God-forgetfulness*. But we must not think this means a state in which it is quite impossible for the God-consciousness to be kindled.[85]

In the last analysis, evil is "Godlessness," or, to be more precise, "God-forgetfulness."

Against this backcloth of humanity's self-will and forgetfulness of God and all that they entrain, the figure of Christ stands out as the incarnation of all that the rest of humanity is not. The attitude of absolute dependence upon God is perfected in him. No cloud of self-will ever came between him and God. Jesus is, of course, thoroughly human. But sin is no essential part of human nature. Rather, it is a disturbance of that nature.[86] Indeed, it is his sinlessness, his close dependence upon God which makes Jesus what he is and constitutes a breakthrough in human history. Jesus had a unique experience of God which might even be called *an existence of God in human nature* and a mediation of *all existence of God in the world.*

> So that originally it is found nowhere but in Him, and He is the only "other" in which there is an existence of God in the proper sense, so far, that is, as we posit the God-consciousness in His self-consciousness as continually and exclusively determining every moment, and consequently also this perfect indwelling of the Supreme Being as His peculiar being and His inmost self. Indeed, working backwards we must now say, if it is only through Him that the human God-consciousness becomes an existence of God in human nature, and only through the rational nature that the totality of finite powers can become an existence of God in the world, that in truth He alone mediates all existence of God in the world and all revelation of God through the world, in so far as he bears within Himself the whole new creation which contains and develops the potency of the God-consciousness.[87]

Jesus' awareness of God marks a new beginning for humanity. It shows that human nature is capable of receiving a new implanting of God-consciousness. Jesus has not only broken the nexus of selfish, godless living which has become the common lot of mankind; he has also made it possible for men to share the higher life.

> He can only be understood as an original act of human nature, *i.e.* as an act of human nature as not affected by sin. The beginning of His life was also a new implanting of the God-consciousness which creates receptivity in human nature; hence this content and that manner of origin are in such a close relation that they mutually condition and explain each other. That new implanting came to be through the beginning of His life, and therefore that beginning must have transcended every detrimental influence of His immediate circle; and because it was such an original and sin-free act of nature, a filling of His nature with God-consciousness became possible as its result. So that upon this relation too the fullest light is thrown if we regard the beginning of the life of Jesus as the completed creation of human nature. The appearance of the first man constituted at the same time the physical life of the human race: the appearance of the Second Adam constituted for this nature a new spiritual life, which communicates and develops itself by spiritual fecundation.[88]

Jesus thus represents the completion of human nature. He is not only an example (*Vorbild*); he is the archetype, the original, the source (*Urbild*) of humanity rightly related to God through his awareness of God.[89]

In this way Schleiermacher achieved a radical integration and reinterpretation of Christ's person and work. While it does not exclude the supernatural (in the sense of transcendent spiritual reality), it is compatible with a closed view of the universe which rules out supernatural incursions into the universe. It is not surprising, therefore, that Schleiermacher inserted into his work a section arguing the thesis *"The ecclesiastical formulae concerning the Person of Christ need to be subjected to continual criticism."*[90] Moreover, this section is followed by four more sections reappraising Christ's person[91] and six, his work.[92]

The essentials of Schleiermacher's position have already been stated. Jesus was a normal, or, to be more exact, *the* normal human being. The difference between him and us lies in the constancy and potency of his awareness of God, which was *a veritable existence of God in him.*

> *The Redeemer, then, is like all men in virtue of the identity of human nature, but distinguished from them all by the constant potency of His God-consciousness, which was a veritable existence of God in Him.*[93]

Schleiermacher recognized that this thought had not always been uppermost in ecclesiastical formulae that were often "products of controversy," shot through with "Jewish or heathen elements."[94] Two rules must therefore be adopted in all critical reappraisal.[95] As against those who were preoccupied with obsolete, hair-splitting definitions Schleiermacher proposed recognition that, "A thing no longer really exists, but becomes mere matter of history, when it can exercise no further activity owing to the situation to which it properly belonged no longer being present." On the other hand, those who would oversimplify and cling to non-committal assertions were reminded that,

> If we go back to formulae which are simple, but just on account of their simplicity are too indefinite for didactic purposes, we gain a merely apparent satisfaction, which lasts only until the disagreement which has remained hidden under the identity of the formula breaks out somewhere or other.[96]

In the ensuing pages Schleiermacher outlined the kind of revision that he had in mind. In section 96 he scrutinized various credal pronouncements on the unity of the divine and human natures in one person. While claiming that they were really trying to say the same thing that he was, Schleiermacher objected to the intellectual contortions which their terminology forced upon the believer by compelling him to think in terms of *persons* and *natures*.

> For how can divine and human be thus brought together under any single conception, as if they could both be more exact determinations, co-ordinated to each other, of one and the same universal? Indeed, even divine spirit and human spirit could not without confusion be brought together in this way....
>
> Now if 'person' indicates a constant unity of life, but 'nature' a sum of ways of action or laws, according to which conditions of life vary and are included within a fixed range, how can the unity of life coexist with the duality of natures, unless the one gives way to the other, if the one exhibits a larger and the other a narrower range, or unless they melt into each other, both systems of ways of action and laws really

becoming one in the one life?—if indeed we are speaking of a person, *i.e.* of an Ego which is the same in all the consecutive moments of its existence. The attempt to make clear this unity along with the duality naturally but seldom results in anything else than a demonstration of the possibility of a formula made up by combining indications out of which it is impossible to construct a figure.[97]

The same applies when one thinks in terms of the *will*.[98] In place of all this Schleiermacher urged a fresh look at the whole question of the person of Christ that would get beyond the scholasticism taken over by the Reformers and ultimately produce a new Protestant statement.

> We hope that above we have laid the foundation for such a revision, which attempts so to define the mutual relations of the divine and the human in the Redeemer, that both the expressions, divine nature and the duality of natures in the same Person (which, to say the least, are exceedingly inconvenient) shall be altogether avoided. For if the distinction between the Redeemer and us others is established in such a way that, instead of being obscured and powerless as in us, the God-consciousness in Him was absolutely clear and determined each moment, to the exclusion of all else, so that it must be regarded as a continual living presence, and withal a real existence of God in Him, then, in virtue of this difference, there is in Him everything that we need, and, in virtue of His likeness to us, limited only by His utter sinlessness, this is all in Him in such a way that we can lay hold of it. That is to say, the existence of God in the Redeemer is posited as the innermost fundamental power within Him, from which every activity proceeds and which holds every element together; everything human (in Him) forms only the organism for this fundamental power, and is related to it as the system which both receives and represents it, just as in us all other powers are related to the intelligence.[99]

Such was Schleiermacher's basic position. Three further points are, however, worth noting, since they throw Schleiermacher's Christology into even sharper relief. They concern the Virgin Birth, the work of Christ, and the doctrine of the Trinity.

In line with his view that Jesus was thoroughly human, Schleiermacher insisted that his conception was a normal, physical one.[100] Moreover, the historical testimony to the Virgin Birth in the New Testament is thin. The church's creeds—whether they be those of the early centuries or those of the Reformation era—scarcely hint of a dogmatic purpose in the story. Nor is the idea necessary to secure Christ's sinlessness, for then we should have to posit the sinlessness of Mary and her ancestors. The story teaches in a figurative way the higher influence that was at work in Christ.

Thus Schleiermacher attempted to combine a realistic, scientific and historical approach with the essentials of traditional doctrine. The same might be said about his treatment of the work of Christ. Once again it is construed in terms of God-consciousness, as his introductory thesis announced. *"The Redeemer assumes believers into the power of His God-consciousness, and this is His redemptive activity."*[101] Schleiermacher went on to relate Jesus' primary awareness of God to his person-forming activity in the believer and with it to the renewal of the world, claiming that this was the meaning of the biblical language about being dead to sin and the new creation. In an embryonic way Schleiermacher anticipated Karl Barth's christocentric understanding of creation since the goal and ground of creation was the same purposeful divine activity that found focal expression in Christ.

> Now, if every activity of the Redeemer proceeds from the being of God in Him, and if in the formation of the Redeemer's Person the only active power was the creative divine activity which established itself as the being of God in Him, then also His every activity may be regarded as a continuation of that person-forming divine influence upon human nature. For the pervasive activity of Christ cannot establish itself in an individual without becoming person-forming in him too, for now all his activities are differently determined through the working of Christ in him, and even all impressions are differently received—which means that the personal self-consciousness too becomes altogether different. And just as creation is not con-cerned simply with individuals (as if each creation of an individual had been a special act), but it is the world that was created, and every individual as such was created only in and with the whole, for the rest not less than for itself, in the same way the activity of the Redeemer too is world-forming, and its object is human nature, in the totality of which the powerful God-consciousness is to be implanted as a new vital principle. He takes possession of the individuals relatively to the whole, wherever He finds those in whom His activity does not merely remain, but from whom, moving on, it can work upon others through the revelation of His life. And thus the total effective influence of Christ is only the continuation of the creative divine activity out of which the Person of Christ arose.[102]

Christ's redemptive activity was further defined in terms of the traditional Calvinistic conception of the three offices of prophet, priest and king. But if the orthodox vocabulary remained, its meaning was radically revised. The prophetic office consisted in *"teaching, prophesying, and working miracles."*[103] But the element of prediction was eliminated, and what remains is subsumed under the heading of teaching.[104] Similarly the miracles which figure so prominently in the Gospels dwindle in significance almost to vanishing point. Miracles cannot be fitted into a modern scientific world view. "For we cannot include these phe-nomena in the field of nature familiar to us without recourse to presuppositions such that the trustworthiness of the whole body of our records concerning Christ is imperiled."[105] But even in his own day "Christ never availed Himself of His miraculous power in any definite connection with the demands He made or His statements about Himself."[106] What counts are Christ's spiritual achievements. The external marvel is superseded by the spiritual miracle.

> For in Christ's miracles we have nothing which definitely raises them, in and by themselves, above other similar miracles of which we have stories from many various times and places. But if we consider the total spiritual miracle, then we must declare Him to be the climax, all the more definitely that we recognize that—apart from

Him—this total spiritual miracle could not have been achieved by all the powers of spiritual nature as we know it. But equally certainly Christ is also the end of miracle. For the surer it is that by Christ redemption has been completed, so that whatever is yet in store for the human race, so far as fellowship with God is concerned, is to be regarded only as a further development of Christ's work, not as a new revelation, the more reason we have for rejecting everything that claims to offer miraculous evidence for a new achievement in the sphere of spiritual life.[107]

In a similar way, the exposition of Christ's priestly work is relieved of its sacrificial and penal overtones and divested of the character of a metaphysical transaction. In common with the younger Hegel and the later Schelling, Schleiermacher insisted that Jesus did not die *"in our place."*[108] Rather, Christ is to be seen as our "satisfying representative" (*genugtuender Stellvertreter*)

in the sense, first, that in virtue of His ideal dignity He so represents, in His redemptive activity, the perfecting of human nature, that in virtue of our having become one with Him God sees and regards the totality of believers only in Him; and, second, that His sympathy with sin, which was strong enough to stimulate a redemptive activity sufficient for the assumption of all men into His vital fellowship, and the absolute power of which is more perfectly exhibited in His free surrender of Himself to death, perpetually serves to make complete and perfect our imperfect consciousness of sin.[109]

Likewise, the kingly office is also modernized and spiritualized, so that it comes to mean, *"that everything which the community of believers requires for its well-being proceeds from Him."*[110]

The corollary of this view of the work of Christ is that salvation is to be understood in terms of assumption into living fellowship with Christ. When viewed from man's side, it may be described as conversion, i.e., a changed form of life. When viewed from God's side, it may be described as justification, i.e., a changed relation to God.[111] But none of this demands belief in the literal resurrection and ascension of Christ. Schleiermacher himself neither explicitly denied nor affirmed belief in the resurrection. He conceded that Paul grounded his teaching on redemption in the death and resurrection of Jesus. He also admitted that to cast aspersion upon the veracity and competence of the alleged witnesses reflected indirectly upon the one who called them to be witnesses to him. However, belief in the resurrection, ascension and return of Christ do not arise directly from Schleiermacher's view of God's activity in Jesus and his sinlessness. "Rather they are accepted only because they are found in the Scriptures."[112]

Schleiermacher's teaching on the Trinity is striking both for its brevity and for its position in *Der christliche Glaube* where it appears virtually as an appendix. But on Schleiermacher's premises this is amply justified. Again he looked at the doctrine in the light of Christian selfconsciousness and concluded that, *"this doctrine itself, as ecclesiastically framed, is not an immediate utterance concerning the Christian selfconsciousness, but only a combination of several such utterances.*"[113] The doctrine is designed to express the being of God in Christ and subsequently in the church as the bearer of redemption. As such, it is "the coping-stone of Christian doctrine."[114]

> An essential element of our exposition in this Part has been the doctrine of the union of the Divine Essence with human nature, both in the personality of Christ and in the common Spirit of the Church; therewith the whole view of Christianity set forth in our Church teaching stands and falls. For unless the being of God in Christ is assumed, the idea of redemption could not be thus concentrated in His Person. And unless there were such a union also in the common Spirit of the Church, the Church could not thus be the Bearer and Perpetuator of the redemption through Christ. Now these exactly are the essential elements in the doctrine of the Trinity, which, it is clear, only established itself in defence of the position that in Christ there was present nothing less than the Divine Essence, which also indwells the Christian Church as its common Spirit, and that we take these expressions in no reduced or sheerly artificial sense, and know nothing of any special higher essences, subordinate deities (as it were) present in Christ and the Holy Spirit. The doctrine of the Trinity has no origin but this; and at first it had no other aim than to equate as definitely as possible the Divine Essence considered as thus united to human nature with the Divine Essence in itself.[115]

But this is almost at once qualified by the observation that,

> at this point we would call a halt; we cannot attach the same value to the further elaboration of the dogma, which alone justifies the ordinary term. For the term "Trinity" is really based on the fact that each of the two above-mentioned unions is traced back to a separate distinction posited independently of such union, and eternally, in the Supreme Being as such; further, after the member of this plurality destined to union with Jesus had been designated by the name "Son," it was felt necessary to posit the Father in accordance therewith as a special distinction. The result was the familiar dualism—unity of Essence and trinity of Persons. But the assumption of an eternal distinction in the Supreme Being is not an utterance concerning the religious consciousness, for there it never could emerge.[116]

If, therefore, the whole scheme of thinking about God in terms of unity of essence and trinity of persons is artificial and based upon wrong premises, the whole formulation of the doctrine, including the question whether the Sabellians were right after all, requires thorough reconsideration.[117] Schleiermacher himself did not venture to anticipate the results of such a fresh investigation. He contented himself with two concluding reflections. On the one hand, he hoped that it would be possible to devise formulae that will avoid asserting eternal distinctions within the supreme being, but that will at the same time express the union of the divine being with human nature in the personality of Christ and in the church.[118] On the other hand, he wondered whether the terms Father, Son and Holy Spirit might not ultimately be synonymous.[119] This question, like Schleiermacher's whole reconstruction, follows logically from his premises. But it also raises the further question, whether in the meantime the traditional Christian doctrine of the Trinity had not died the death of a thousand qualifications.

Christology and Schleiermacher's Critical Writings

Schleiermacher was one of the first Protestant theologians to make a special study of hermeneutics. Hitherto hermeneutics had been seen as a means of supporting, securing and clarifying an accepted understanding.[120] In one sense, the thinkers whom we have already been considering were practicing a new hermeneutic insofar as they were interpreting Christian teaching in the light of their philosophical understanding. In many cases the result was artificial and forced, because the thinkers were more interested in philosophical ideas than in the historical texts that they were ostensibly interpreting. Schleiermacher, however, marked a new departure. On the one hand, he was interested in the historical texts; and on the other hand, he devoted time and thought to working out a theory of hermeneutics.

Recent critical work on Schleiermacher's manuscripts indicates a shift from a hermeneutics oriented toward language to one oriented toward the subjective understanding and intentions of the author.[121] Schleiermacher saw hermeneutics as an art of understanding which was related to criticism in such a way that "the practice of either one presupposes the other."[122] In the published form of his *Hermeneutik*, edited by Friedrich Lücke, the fundamental question of hermeneutics is formulated as "What is the true inner kernel of the work, the decision in the life of the author?"[123]

Der christliche Glaube might be regarded as an attempt to express "the inner kernel" of the Christian faith in the life of evangelical Protestantism. Unlike so many attempts to express the essence of Christianity, Schleiermacher's work was accompanied by a great deal of historical and critical investigation. It is by his exegesis and hermeneutics of this material that Schleiermacher's view of Christianity stands or falls. In this section we shall look at his lectures *Ueber die Schriften des Lukas*, *Einleitung in das Neue Testament* and *Das Leben Jesu*, with a view to determining Schleiermacher's approach to the historical sources of Christianity and his reconstruction of the historical Jesus.

In his introduction to *Ueber die Schriften des Lukas* (1817)[124] Schleiermacher pointed out that the subject of Gospel criticism was already being hotly debated. His own approach shows him to have brought to it the same independent, radical mind that he brought to dogmatic theology. He rejected Hug's statement of the traditional theory that the later evangelists used the earlier ones as sources, and also rejected Eichhorn's view that the first three evangelists used a common source independently of each other.[125] Schleiermacher asked the following questions: Why did the evangelists omit some things and insert others? Who were the original recipients of the *Urevangelium*? Why did Matthew (whom Eichhorn regarded as both an apostle and the author of the Gospel which bears his name) rearrange the material? How was it that the *Urevangelium* was so soon lost? If it were not the work of an apostle, how did it come to be the exclusive source of the written Gospels? In the light of these questions, Schleiermacher concluded that it was much more satisfactory to drop the idea of a single, original written source in favor of a number of individual sources which came into being over the years and which were used independently by the evangelists.[126]

Not unlike later Form Critics, Schleiermacher envisaged an early period when there were no written traditions and when men were more interested in the Spirit of Christ than biographical details. The latter were written down only later in order to satisfy the curiosity of those who had never known Jesus. The result was that over the years numerous collections of different kinds of material came into being, and were used perhaps in worship or perhaps merely to satisfy private interest.[127] A case in point was the infancy narratives of Luke 1 and 2 which have a quite different style and outlook from the rest of Luke. The travel narrative of Luke 9:51–19:48 was another block or "Masse" which Schleiermacher thought was inserted more or less *in toto* by the third evangelist into his Gospel.[128] Schleiermacher concluded that Luke

> is neither an independent author, nor has he worked from several manuscripts which cover the whole of the life of Jesus. For too often there can be detected isolated sections which stand in no relation to the rest. The character of the individual parts is too diverse for it to be a case of one or the other. But from beginning to end he is only a collector and orderer of existing writings which he allows to pass through his hands unchanged. His merit as such is however twofold. It is partly that of ordering, but this is the lesser merit. For as he found much already set in order, the correctness of the ordering is partly due to his predecessors, and much can stand in the wrong order without him being to blame. But the ordering was also partly now much easier, than if he had found everything in individual fragments. However, the far greater merit is this, that he took over almost nothing but eminently genuine and good material. For this is certainly not the work of chance, but the fruit of determined research and definitely superior choice.[129]

The same approach was applied to the other Synoptic Gospels in Schleiermacher's *Einleitung in das Neue Testament*, which was published posthumously in 1845 on the basis of lecture notes. The *Urevangelium* theory was again rejected in favor of oral tradition that crystallized (especially after the scattering of the church following the death of Stephen) into a number of disconnected written fragments. Gradually two types of Gospel emerged, the Synoptics and John. The former consists of collections of isolated fragments differing considerably not only in content but on points of geography, chronology and order.[130] Only John with his orderly and precise chronological outline and lengthy monologues (which could hardly be preserved in the same way as the synoptic fragments) might properly be called a biography.

> In the Gospel of John, on the other hand, the biographical character is stamped in the most definite way. Everything is related to definite times, naturally not with the

intention of delivering a chronicle of the life of Christ, but nevertheless giving the whole development of events from his public appearance onwards. If we add to this the fact that, with John, what stands out most in the discourses of Christ which is most difficult to preserve in tradition, the dialogue material, then we see that this composition could only be given by someone who had lived with Jesus. A later writer would have had to pursue precise, critical researches, which would easily be noticed in the Gospel. A biographical Gospel, if it is to be genuine, could only be reported by a companion of Christ, or at most by someone at second hand.[131]

The Synoptic Gospels were not to be attributed to the persons whose names they bear. They were not eyewitness narratives or even consecutive biographies, but relatively late collections of assorted material, the historical value of which varied considerably.[132]

The full significance of this point emerges only when Schleiermacher turned to the life of Jesus. In his posthumously published lectures on *Das Leben Jesu* (1864), Schleiermacher started from the premise that "strictly speaking we have to say that *so far as our four canonical Gospels are concerned, we have actually only two different sources*. The Gospel of John is the one, and the other three taken together are the other."[133] As Schleiermacher explained in the course of his discussion of the resurrection narratives,

> I know no rule to set up except this: The Gospel of John is an account by an eyewitness, and the whole Gospel was written by one man. The first three Gospels are compilations of many accounts that earlier stood by themselves.[134]

Because of chronological and topological gaps and discrepancies, Schleiermacher conceded that, "when we are thinking in terms of a historical view—our sources cause us much embarrassment."[135] Nevertheless, a broad outline was possible, and Schleiermacher divided his survey into three main phases: Jesus' life before his public appearance, his public life up to his arrest, and the period from the arrest to the ascension.

Perhaps the most striking feature of *Das Leben Jesu* is Schleiermacher's combination of highly critical argument with an almost uncritical attempt to read into the Gospel narratives his own particular Christology. D. F. Strauss drew attention to the latter point in an extended critique which appeared soon after the publication of Schleiermacher's work, *Der Christus des Glaubens und der Jesus der Geschichte. Eine Kritik des Schleiermacher'shen Lebens Jesu* (1865).[136] The point is exemplified in the first of Schleiermacher's three divisions where he subjects the infancy narratives to rigorous scrutiny, questioning how they came into being and concluding that they are not to be taken as strict history.[137]

It was not only the fragmentary nature of the sources which were a source of embarrassment. As a modern man, Schleiermacher felt tension between the miracle stories in the Gospels and his modern world view. He found some relief in the observation that Jesus did not make use of his wonder-working powers to disturb or interfere with human relationships. His actions "conform to the rules of human morality, as does Christ's entire ministry."[138] This somewhat Kantian note was echoed in Schleiermacher's concluding comment on Jesus' miracles.

> Although we are not able to form a final judgment on all instances of Christ's miracle-working activity, it is nevertheless true that for our task, that of viewing the life of Jesus in its unity and totality, there remain no gaps, to the extent that we have been able to point out adequately the moral motivation involved in all these acts of Christ. Where this has not been possible we have said: So far as that which cannot be explained by these maxims is concerned, we believe it must have had some other context. We have also pointed out that such an existence as we assume was that of Christ makes possible effects in the area of human life such as no other man could have achieved. The only difficulty is that we can not determine the limits of Christ's unique power. So we have obtained a clear picture of the way Christ exercised his miracle-working powers, and that is all that is necessary for our task.[139]

In saying this, Schleiermacher was shifting the emphasis away from the traditional orthodox view which saw miracles as proof of Jesus' personal divinity to a view which focused on the potential of human nature, when indwelt by the divine.[140] Schleiermacher was clearly aware that his account of the life of Jesus involved a revision of orthodoxy. He replaced the traditional view of the two natures of Christ by an emphasis on Jesus' sinless God-consciousness. Indeed, sinlessness and God-consciousness were two sides of the same reality. Moreover, the model for understanding the divine and the human in Jesus was (as it was for D. M. Baillie in more recent times) the believer's experience of God.

> If in addition we take the fact into consideration that in Christian faith Jesus' development is believed to have been sinless—which does not mean that there was no human element in Jesus, for we never reckon sin as belonging to the essence of man, but which necessarily follows from a presupposed original divine indwelling—then in comparison to others Christ must have become conscious of his condition as a specific one, but that consciousness was not yet a consciousness of the divine in him. If we wish to ascribe to him such a self-consciousness as the creedal conception usually requires, a consciousness of a singular, pretemporal preexistence of the divine in him, then we must wholly do away with the human element. The exegetical basis of this assumption is very weak. If we hold fast to our canon, namely, the analogy of the indwelling of the Holy Spirit in us, then we find this only in what is most inward, in the principle of the pure volition of the divine will, consequently back of the actual consciousness, for every individual decision always involves human imperfection. Now Christ became aware of this in himself as a living being of God in him. The relationship of Father and Son is comprehensible as a consequence of the comparison of son (full-grown) and servant, the entire divine will, but also as a consciousness that gradually developed until it assumed definite form (greater works manifest it), namely, the entire will with respect to men. So he was able to say, I am the Son of God. According to the creedal conception he would have had to say, I have the Son of God in me.[141]

This characterization of Jesus was an attempt to portray him realistically in modern terms compatible with the believer's experience, as opposed to the con-

structions in the creeds which Schleiermacher dismissed as exegetically unten-
able and logically unthinkable. At the same time it was ostensibly based on the
Fourth Gospel. However, it failed to satisfy D. F. Strauss who observed that,
"With this interpretation Schleiermacher occupies the standpoint of the worst
Socinian-rationalist exegesis."[142] To Strauss, Schleiermacher's Christology was
arbitrary and eclectic. His emphasis on divine indwelling was utterly at variance
with the high Johannine Christology of the incarnation of the eternal Creator-
Word. Strauss's criticism of Schleiermacher's work is summed up in the fol-
lowing passage.

> Schleiermacher, we can say, is a supernaturalist in Christology but in criticism and
> exegesis a rationalist. His Christ, however many of the miraculous attributes of the
> old confession may have been removed, still remains essentially a superhuman,
> supernatural being. In contrast, his exegesis, as far as it pertains to the miraculous in
> the Scripture, is distinguished from that of Paulus only by somewhat more spirit and
> subtlety—a difference which precisely in the main points, such as the resurrection
> story, becomes imperceptible. The one appears to contradict the other; rather,
> however, the one is the basis for the other. Because Schleiermacher wants to remain a
> supernaturalist in Christology he must be a rationalist in criticism and exegesis. In
> order not to lose the supernatural Christ as a historical personality he cannot sur-
> render the Gospels as historical sources. But in order to avoid a supernatural Christ
> in the sense in which the supernatural is unacceptable to him, he must remove
> exegetically from the Gospels the supernatural which offends him. Indeed, he retreats
> to one Gospel, the Johannine, and appears to let the other three go. However, they
> still have too much in common with John, with regard to content and standpoint, to
> be separable in this way. Whoever thinks that in the miracle stories of the Fourth
> Gospel he has the facts in the report of an eyewitness will also assume facts in those
> of the first three, even if in more indirect tradition; and since he no longer believes in
> actual miracles, apart from the miraculous personality of his Christ, he will have to
> explain also these in a rationalist way.[143]

Schleiermacher's ambivalence is further illustrated by his discussion of the
Last Supper, the passion and the resurrection narratives.[144] It shows that he was
acutely aware of critical questions. But the decisive factor in Schleiermacher's
reconstruction was whether the event in question was susceptible of a moral and
spiritual interpretation. Schleiermacher was even prepared to entertain the question of whether Jesus had really died. On the one hand, "the only certain
indication of death is *the decomposition of the body*."[145] Information is lacking
on whether Jesus' body had begun to decompose. On the other hand, we are not
in a position to prove that an "absolute miracle" took place in the resurrection.
For this would require

> *an infinite amount of investigation that can never be brought to completion. We can*
> *therefore regard this whole matter as one of no importance and consider the details*
> *without prejudice and without any definite interest in proving one hypothesis or the*
> *other. However, we are concerned that the picture of Christ that we have formed*
> *should be continuous and remain the same to the last moment.*[146]

A premise vital to maintaining the consistency of that picture was the contention that

> It is not necessary for the satisfaction of the divine righteousness that one must believe that Christ's death was simply a physical event, without any moral or spiritual content. When we say that what satisfies the divine righteousness must be something spiritual, rather than something physical, we conclude that it can make no difference to the divine righteousness whether Christ's was a real death or a state similar to death. Once the act of dying had taken place in its spiritual significance, whether the physical part of death had been completed or not seems to me to be of no importance whatever.[147]

In saying this, Schleiermacher had preserved a relationship between the cross and divine righteousness but at the price of repudiating the traditional view of the need for atonement. The light-handed dichotomy made here between the spiritual and the physical was to characterize many later liberal discussions of atonement, though few went so far as to wonder whether Jesus really died.

Schleiermacher's Achievement

It has almost become a platitude to apply to Schleiermacher the words that he himself applies to Frederick the Great: "He did not found a school but an era."[148] Even in his own day voices were to be heard that anticipated this verdict. After reading *Der christliche Glaube*, J. C. Gass wrote to its author, "No one will dissuade me from believing that with your dogmatics a new epoch will begin not only in this discipline but in the whole of theological study."[149]

The justice of these verdicts might not have been immediately apparent to students of theology living in the middle of the nineteenth century. Schleiermacher's lectures were well attended. If he did not found a school, his influence could be recognized in his successor at Berlin, August Twesten, and others like Carl Immanuel Nitzsch and Alexander Schweizer who were representatives of the movement known as *Vermittlungstheologie*. But few New Testament scholars endorsed Schleiermacher's conclusions. In the world of philosophy Schleiermacher was overshadowed by Hegel—a fact made painfully clear to Schleiermacher by a chance remark of the young D. F. Strauss. On hearing from Schleiermacher of Hegel's death, Strauss blurted out, "It was for his sake that I came here."[150] Nevertheless, in the long term, Schleiermacher fulfilled Gass's prophecy.

What distinguished Schleiermacher from his contemporaries was not only his original view of Christianity, but the range and depth of his perception of the questions that Christian faith posed for modern man. To understand the significance of Christ was a multi-dimensional problem. It could not be answered simply on a historical or philosophical level. Ever since his own day a debate has raged over whether Schleiermacher's thought was a disguised form of Idealism or even pantheism.[151] Strauss claimed that if the key themes of the first part of *Der christliche Glaube* were translated into Latin, they would turn out to be formulations of Spinoza.[152] The radical F. C. Baur and the orthodox E. W. Hengstenberg were agreed in at least one respect: Schleiermacher's orthodoxy was a deception which destroyed the Christian faith.[153] To Hegel, Schleiermacher's preoccupation with "Gefühl" fell well short of his own philosophical understanding of the dialectic of *Geist*. Indeed, on Schleiermacher's premises a dog would be the best Christian, for it lived on the level of feeling.[154]

In his second *Sendschreiben* to Lücke, Schleiermacher confessed that he saw no harm in drawing upon philosophical language "for use in dogmatics, without leading to confusion in the representations of unconscious philosophizing."[155] But he noted that the philosophies of Leibniz, Wolff and their successors tended to "dogmatize very strongly." "Because of the subject matter, the philosophies of Kant and Fichte cannot offer great resources." He was mildly amused at the suggestions that his work was based on Jacobi or Schelling.[156] But all things considered, Schleiermacher saw "very little of philosophy or of philosophers" in his work. He did not even profess to throw down the gauntlet to speculative theology; he was willing to let it go its own way. There was a value in philosophy, "But I could never confess that my faith in Christ is derived from knowledge or philosophy, be it this philosophy or any other."[157]

In terms of philosophical language some affinity may be detected with Fichte's and even Hegel's talk of consciousness. But Schleiermacher refused to speculate about the inner nature of divine self-consciousness. Although he expressed enthusiasm for Spinoza in his earlier writings, Schleiermacher's mature thought stood in sharp contrast with the monistic pantheism of Absolute Idealism. In a sense, the influence of philosophy was a negative one. Schleiermacher worked within the parameters laid down by Kant, with one major difference. Kant placed an embargo on speculation beyond the limits of immediate experience. Schleiermacher tacitly accepted the embargo, but insisted on recognizing the importance of religious awareness as the basic datum of theological reflection. To that extent he adopted an empirical approach to religion.

It was not without significance that Schleiermacher placed on the title page of *Der christliche Glaube* the words of Anselm, "Neque enim quaero intelligere ut credam, sed credo ut intelligam." "Nam qui non crediderit, non experietur, et qui expertus non fuerit, non intelliget."[158] Whether he understood these words in the same way as Anselm is another matter. What was given for Schleiermacher was Christian experience, and this together with its implications had to be understood and interpreted in a way which was compatible with a modern scientific world view. The essence of Schleiermacher's method was to examine religious experience in order to discover a common denominator. It in turn became a yardstick by which Schleiermacher proceeded to measure all other doctrine. What did not fit was regarded as peripheral and non-essential. The common denominator was *das schlechthinnige Abhängigkeitsgefühl*.

Today a fundamental question that arises out of Schleiermacher's method is not whether he was too empirical, but whether he was empirical enough. Nowhere did he attempt a critical, analytical examination of religious experience in the manner of a work like William James's *The Varieties of Religious Experience* (1902).[159] The latter examined in some detail a wide range of cases and opinions and classified them under a number of distinct categories. Schleiermacher's *Christliche Glaube* examines no particular case in detail. It appears to be based on his own introspection. The result was the reduction of the essence of religion to one single ultimate idea. In so doing, Schleiermacher appears to treat the *schlechthinnige Abhängigkeitsgefühl* as if it were a kind of self-evident truth that only needs to be isolated and identified for its veracity to be perceived. Whatever differences he may have had with previous continental thinkers, Schleiermacher appears at this point to be continuing the quest begun by Descartes and Spinoza, and continued in their different ways by Lessing, Kant and Hegel for an autonomous, self-authenticating basis for his thought. Whereas others had failed to do justice to religion by producing highly speculative and abstract accounts, Schleiermacher's *schlechthinnige Abhängigkeitsgefühl* was readily recognizable as an element in Christian experience. But like all attempts to find a single key it had strong reductionist tendencies.

Schleiermacher himself repeatedly refused to reply to malicious and hostile criticism. But he found it necessary to remonstrate with his wife and daughter for adopting "a way of speaking constantly of the Saviour and placing God quite in the background.... Dearest heart, do try to hold fast the belief that *with* Christ and *through* Christ we are to rejoice in his and our Father."[160] In more recent times the principal editor of the English translation of *The Christian Faith*, H. R. Mackintosh, observed with regret that Schleiermacher expounded "as the Christian view of salvation what too often is but the attenuated creed of idealistic Monism."[161] These last mentioned extremes —a kind of Jesusolatry and an attenuated monism—were in fact complementary. Schleiermacher strove against both, but from his position it is easy to slip into either. His comments on the doctrine of the Trinity at the end of *Der christliche Glaube* raise the question of whether Schleiermacher retains any genuine Trinitarian conception of God.

In defense of Schleiermacher it might be said that he was endeavoring to practice a hermeneutic which interpreted the essentials of the Christian faith in a relevant and credible manner. But Schweitzer's comment on Schleiermacher's handling of the New Testament data is not without some justice.

> Schleiermacher is not in search of the historical Jesus, but of the Jesus of his own system of theology; that is to say, of the historic figure which seems to him appropriate to the self-consciousness of the Redeemer as he represents it. For him the empirical has simply no existence. A natural psychology is scarcely attempted. He comes to the facts with a ready-made dialectic apparatus and sets his puppets in lively action.... He is like a spider at work. The spider lets itself down from aloft, and after making fast some supporting threads to points below, it runs back to the centre and there keeps spinning away. You look on fascinated, and before you know it, you are entangled in the web.[162]

7. FEUERBACH AND THE REDUCTION OF
THEOLOGY TO ANTHROPOLOGY

The suggestion has been made that what gives unity to a historical period is not that its leaders think alike but that their thought is directed to the same problems.[1] Doubtless this suggestion needs to be qualified by the fact that classification of such periods is always relative to the interests of the historian. What constitutes a historical period from one standpoint does not necessarily hold for other standpoints. It is a patent fallacy to assume that all modern, educated men at any given period think alike. The most that can be said is that questions, or clusters of questions, can be seen to occupy the attention of acute minds at given periods and that certain favored lines of approach gain acceptance.

By the 1830s there was a consensus among the thinkers whom we have considered that the traditional orthodox approach to theology and Christology was untenable and that radical revision was called for. This conviction gave rise to the new orthodoxies taught by Hegel and the Idealists, on the one hand, and Schleiermacher, on the other hand. But these hardly came into being before they began to disintegrate. The early 1830s saw the deaths of Hegel, Goethe and Schleiermacher. As Heinrich Heine, the poet and sardonic commentator on German culture, observed when Goethe died, *"Les dieux s'en vont.* . . . It seems as if in that year Death had suddenly become aristocratic, and would distinguish the notable men on earth by sweeping them into the grave."[2] The deaths of Hegel and Schleiermacher created vacuums which no one could fill. Within less than a decade, D. F. Strauss was speaking of the differences between the Hegelian right and the Hegelian left.[3] The right consisted of Old Hegelians occupying academic positions who were dedicated to the preservation, propagation and application of the Hegelian system. They included Ludwig von Henning, H. G. Hotho, Philipp Karl Marheineke, Karl Daub and Hermann Hinrichs. The majority of the editors of Hegel's *Werke* belonged to this group. In the center were others like Karl Rosenkranz, Eduard Gans and K. L. Michelet. The left-wing consisted of Young Hegelians who were largely excluded from academic appointments on account of their radical views, which were unacceptable to the conservative governments that controlled the universities. In many respects they were a heterogeneous bunch, characterized by the conviction that Hegelianism required radical modification. Their number included Karl Marx (who had not actually been a student of Hegel), Arnold Ruge, D. F. Strauss, Bruno Bauer and Ludwig Feuerbach.

The thought of Strauss and Bauer will be examined later in connection with Gospel criticism and the life of Jesus. However, Ludwig Feuerbach stood apart. In asking what was Feuerbach's place in the history of theology, Karl Barth observed that he was never classed with the Idealists, but was usually bracketed with the sensualists, positivists, and even materialists — always in the section farthest removed from theology.[4] Nevertheless, Feuerbach was deeply concerned with theology. He protested that religion and theology were the "central concern of my thinking and my life."[5] They figured in all his writings and his knowledge of them was far more extensive and penetrating than that of most philosophers. His thought represents both a culmination of and a reaction to Idealism; and the point of tension lay in the realm of theology.

Background and Writings

Ludwig Feuerbach (1804–72)[6] studied theology at Heidelberg under the rationalist H. E. G. Paulus and the Hegelian Karl Daub. He found Paulus "in his exegesis unbearable, but in his church history no less so."[7] A few years later he castigated the conclusions of rationalist theology in the epigram,

> At long last, by means of the critical-historical standpoint They have actually proved to the world that water never becomes wine.[8]

Disappointed with theology, he resolved to study philosophy with the philosopher par excellence at Berlin, Hegel himself. He wrote to his father,

> What with Daub was still obscure and incomprehensible to me, or at least appeared unfounded, I have on my own already in the course of the few lectures that I have so far heard from Hegel clearly perceived and recognized in its necessity. What glimmered in me as tinder, I see already flaring up in bright flames.[9]

In 1828 Feuerbach presented a dissertation conceived in the Hegelian manner entitled *De Ratione, Una, Universa et Infinita*. He differed from Hegel solely on the point that, "Christianity cannot thus be conceived as the complete, absolute religion; this can only be the realm of the reality of the Idea and of present Reason *[der daseienden Vernunft]*."[10] Feuerbach obtained the post of Privatdozent at Erlangen, but all hopes of an academic career were wrecked by his anonymous *Gedanken über Tod und Unsterblichkeit* (1830)[11] which rejected individual immortality in favor of the human spirit as a whole and which replaced divine transcendence by that of humanity.

For the next few years he was unsettled. Although he lectured and wrote articles, he failed to find an academic post. His marriage in 1837 enabled him to live in semi-retirement at Bruckberg, though after 1860 he was forced to live in reduced circumstances at Rechenberg near Nuremberg. Although his *Gedanken* had taken a positive step towards his characteristic position, it was not until his lengthy article "Zur Kritik der Hegelschen Philosophie" (1839) that he broke with Hegel.[12] His subsequent major works dealt largely with aspects of religion. They include *Das Wesen des Christenthums* (1841),[13] which was followed by *Erläuterungen und Ergänzungen zum Wesen des Christenthums* (1846); *Grundsätze der Philosophie der Zukunft* (1843);[14] *Das Wesen des Glaubens im Sinne Luthers* (1844),[15] *Das Wesen der Religion* (1845),[16] *Vorlesungen über das Wesen der Religion* (delivered at Heidelberg in 1848 and published in 1851);[17] and

Theogonie nach den Quellen des classischen, hebräischen und christlichen Alterthums (1857).

Critique of Hegelianism and Christianity

Three main phases have been discerned in Feuerbach's thinking.[18] The first, which extended down to 1838, was characterized by his Hegelianism. The public break with Hegel in 1839 introduced a brief phase lasting to 1843 in which Feuerbach employed the tools of Hegelianism in his secularizing critique of both Hegel's Idealism and Christianity. The third phase, which began in 1844, was marked by a growing disenchantment with humanity in general and an increasingly positivistic, empiricist, scientific materialism.

In 1846 Feuerbach concluded the foreword to the first *Gesammtausgabe* of his writings with the affirmation that,

> Whoever says and knows of me nothing more than that I am an atheist says and knows of me as much as *Nothing*. The question whether there is a God or not, the opposition between theism and atheism, belongs to the eighteenth and seventeenth but no longer to the nineteenth century. I negate God. That means with me: I negate the negation of man. I put in the place of the illusory, fantastic, heavenly affirmation of man, which in real life is necessary for the negation of man, the sensuous, real and as a necessary consequence also the political and social affirmation of man. The question of the existence or non-existence of God is simply with me only the question of the existence or non-existence of man.[19]

Like the Idealists, Feuerbach was proposing to transcend theism. But already he was in a different world. Although the conceptual tools of Hegelianism remained, the Absolute Idea was already at an advanced stage of secularization and demystification. The divine had become humanized. The new gospel was stated not in lengthy abstract definitions; it was proclaimed with a prophetic vehemence. Its theme was the dethronement of God and the enthronement of man.

Feuerbach became as critical of Idealism as he was of Christianity. In the preface to the second edition of *Das Wesen des Christenthums* he declared that he was presenting his work as a specimen of a new philosophy. Although this philosophy could be seen as "the incarnate result of prior philosophical systems," it was "the direct opposite of speculation" which put "an end to it by explaining it."

> This philosophy has for its principle, not the Substance of Spinoza, not the ego of Kant and Fichte, not the Absolute Identity of Schelling, not the Absolute Mind of Hegel, in short, no abstract, merely conceptional being, but a *real* being, the true *Ens realissimum*—man; its principle, therefore, is in the highest degree positive and real. It generates thought from the *opposite* of thought, from Matter, from existence, from the senses; it has relation to its object first through the senses, *i.e.*, passively, before defining it in thought.[20]

The argument is ironically cast in the form of Hegelian dialectic, but it is intended as a repudiation of Hegelianism. Feuerbach's discussion of the cosmic role of the Second Person of the Trinity is a parody of Hegel's doctrine of the Trinity. It employs Hegelian language and dialectic only to make it clear that the entire train of thought is a product of the imagination.

> The second Person, as God revealing, manifesting, declaring himself (*Deus se dicit*), is the world-creating principle in God. But this means nothing else than that the second Person is intermediate between the noumenal nature of God and the phenomenal nature of the world, that he is the divine principle of the finite, of that which is distinguished from God. The second Person as begotten, as not *à se*, not existing of himself, has the fundamental condition of the finite in himself. But at the same time, he is not yet a real finite Being, posited out of God; on the contrary, he is still identical with God, — as identical as the son is with the father, the son being indeed another person, but still of like nature with the father. The second Person, therefore, does not represent to us the pure idea of the Godhead, but neither does he represent the pure idea of humanity, or of reality in general: he is an intermediate Being between the two opposites. The opposition of the noumenal or invisible divine nature and the phenomenal or visible nature of the world, is, however, nothing else than the opposition between the nature of abstraction and the nature of perception; but that which connects abstraction with perception is the imagination: consequently, the transition from God to the world by means of the second Person, is only the form in which religion makes objective the transition from abstraction to perception by means of the imagination. It is the imagination alone by which man neutralises the opposition between God and the world. All religious cosmogonies are products of the imagination.[21]

As the argument proceeded, Feuerbach developed an *I-Thou* philosophy, but it was not a quasi-religious doctrine of the personal character of being. It was the contention that man becomes conscious of himself over against other human beings and that there is nothing over and above nature and man.

> The *ego*, then, attains to consciousness of the world through consciousness of the *thou*. Thus man is the God of man. That he is, he has to thank Nature; that he is man, he has to thank man; spiritually as well as physically he can achieve nothing without his fellow-man.[22]

In this middle period Feuerbach's thought of the "human species" (*die menschliche Gattung*) occupies an important place. After 1844 Feuerbach dropped the concept.[23] But it had served it purpose in helping to build a bridge for the equation of theology with anthropology:

> That which comes from God to man, comes to man only from *man in God*, that is, only from the ideal nature of man to the phenomenal man, from the species to the individual. Thus, between the divine revelation and the so-called human reason or nature, there is no other than an illusory distinction; — the contents of the divine revelation are of human origin, for they have proceeded not from God as God, but from God as determined by human reason, human wants, that is, directly from

human reason and human wants. And so in revelation man goes out of himself, in order, by a circuitous path, to return to himself! Here we have a striking confirmation of the position that the secret of theology is nothing else than anthropology—the knowledge of God nothing else than a knowledge of man![24]

The point was reiterated in the third of Feuerbach's *Vorlesungen über das Wesen der Religion.*

Theology is anthropology: in other words, the object of religion, which in Greek we call *theos* and in our language God, expresses nothing other than the essence of man; man's God is nothing other than the deified essence of man, so that the history of religion or, what amounts to the same thing, of God—for the gods are as varied as the religions, and the religions are as varied as mankind—is nothing other than the history of man.[25]

When Feuerbach launched his attack on Christianity, D. F. Strauss had already published his *Leben Jesu.* The notion of myth was already well known. But Feuerbach's demythologizing was, if anything, even more drastic than Strauss's. For Strauss had left some room for the metaphysical. What Strauss took away by negative criticism was not exactly restored by an appeal to speculative Hegelianism. But at least comfort was drawn from the reflection that "If God and man are in themselves *one,* and if religion is the human side of this unity: then must this unity be made evident to man in religion, and become in him consciousness and reality."[26] This conviction prompted Strauss to reappraise the truth of Christian beliefs on Hegelian lines. The course that Feuerbach took was more drastic. Theology was anthropology not only in the sense that the study of man now replaced the study of God. Theology was itself to be seen as the projection of human consciousness.

God is the Love that satisfies our wishes, our emotional wants; he is himself the realised wish of the heart, the wish exalted to the certainty of its fulfilment, of its reality, to that undoubting certainty before which no contradiction of the understanding, no difficulty of experience or of the external world, maintains its ground. Certainty is the highest power for man; that which is certain to him is the essential, the divine.[27]

In a sense, Feuerbach was preaching an inverted Hegelianism. Instead of the absolute mind or Spirit coming to self-consciousness in religion, it was man's consciousness which created religion.

The consciousness of the divine love, or what is the same thing, the contemplation of God as human, is the mystery of the Incarnation. The Incarnation is nothing else than the practical, material manifestation of the human nature of God. God did not become man for his own sake; the need, the want of man—a want which still exists in the religious sentiment—was the cause of the Incarnation. God became man out of mercy: thus he was in himself already a human God before he became an actual man; for human want, human misery, went to his heart. The Incarnation was a tear of the divine compassion, and hence it was only the visible advent of a Being having human feelings, and therefore essentially human.[28]

In short, "the idea of the Incarnation is nothing more than the human *form* of a God, who already in his nature, in the profoundest depths of his soul, is a merciful and therefore a human God."[29]

To Feuerbach there was nothing unique about Christ. All human beings could be Christ by living in a loving way and could thus make the Christ of the Christian religion redundant.

> It is the species which infuses love into me. A loving heart is the heart of the species throbbing in the individual. Thus Christ, as the consciousness of love, is the consciousness of the species. We are all one in Christ. Christ is the consciousness of our identity. He therefore who loves man for the sake of man, who rises to the love of the species, to universal love, adequate to the nature of the species,* he is a Christian, is Christ himself. He does what Christ did, what made Christ Christ. Thus, where there arises the consciousness of the species as a species, the idea of humanity as a whole, Christ disappears, without, however, his true nature disappearing; for he was the substitute for the consciousness of the species, the image under which it was made present to the people, and became the law of the popular life.

> * Active love is and must of course always be particular and limited, *i.e.*, directed to one's neighbour. But it is yet in its nature universal, since it loves man for man's sake, in the name of the race. Christian love, on the contrary, is in its nature exclusive.[30]

The question might be asked whether Feuerbach has not overlooked the specificity of history. But he anticipated the objection by approaching the Gospels in the same spirit that he adopted toward religion in general. The events recorded in the Gospels were themselves products of the religious imagination. A case in point was the miraculous which could not be appealed to as supernatural attestation of divine intervention. Anticipating the charge of superficiality, Feuerbach leveled the countercharge of superficiality against all believers in miracles.

> If the explanation of miracles by feeling and imagination is superficial, the charge of superficiality falls not on the explainer, but on that which he explains, namely, on miracle; for, seen in clear daylight, miracle presents absolutely nothing else than the sorcery of the imagination, which satisfies without contradiction all the wishes of the heart.[31]

The resurrection of Jesus was similarly construed as "the satisfied desire of man for an immediate certainty of his personal existence after death, — personal immortality as a sensible, indubitable fact."[32]

To Feuerbach the Christian sacraments constituted a sacralizing of nature and of man himself.

> Water is the readiest means of making friends with Nature. The bath is a sort of chemical process, in which our individuality is resolved into the objective life of Nature.[33]

> If in water we adore the pure force of Nature, in bread and wine we adore the

supernatural power of mind, of consciousness, of man. Hence this sacrament is only for man matured into consciousness; while baptism is imparted to infants. But we at the same time celebrate here the true relation of mind to Nature: Nature gives the material, mind gives the form. The sacrament of Baptism inspires us with thankfulness towards Nature, the sacrament of bread and wine with thankfulness towards man. Bread and wine typify to us the truth that Man is the true God and Saviour of man.[34]

In his *Epigrams* Feuerbach was particularly disparaging of the Holy Spirit.[35] In *Das Wesen des Christenthums* his discussion combined Hegelian with patristic language, but emptied both of their meaning. Instead of expressing God in his loving movement toward his creation, the Spirit is the creation of man in his vain movement toward God.

The Holy Spirit owes its personal existence only to a name, a word. . . . In so far as the Holy Spirit represents the subjective phase, he is properly the representation of the religious sentiment to itself, the representation of religious emotion, of religious enthusiasm, or the personification, the rendering objective of religion in religion. The Holy Spirit is therefore the sighing creature, the yearning of the creature after God.[36]

The essence of Feuerbach's critique of the essence of Christianity was contained in his contention that,

The belief in God—at least in the God of religion—is only lost where, as in scepticism, pantheism, and materialism, the belief in man is lost, at least in man such as he is presupposed in religion. . . . The vital elements of religion are those only which make man an object to man. To deny man is to deny religion.[37]

Feuerbach's method could hardly be called scientific criticism. Whatever evidence Feuerbach might have had to support his contentions tended to be deposited in notes and explanations at the back of his books. But these had more the character of an anthology of utterances than that of a critical evaluation of data. This is true even of his *Theogonie* which purported to be an examination of sources. The actual discussion of Christian origins was thin, and modern Christian writers are inclined to dismiss his conclusions as trite.[38] Regarded from the viewpoint of a critical examination of Christian origins and the phenomena of religious experience, the verdict is just. But Feuerbach might be defended against such a judgment by pleading that he was not trying to produce learned treatises. His theological writings are the work of a prophet rather than a scholar. They do not present the assured results of scientific criticism, but proclaim a new hermeneutic for evaluating everything to do with religion—including scientific criticism. Admittedly, the hermeneutic was not exactly brand new. Indeed, like many a German theologian before and since, Feuerbach claimed Luther was an ally. For the latter had initiated the process of turning theology into anthropology by turning attention away from what God is in himself to what he is for men.[39] But in the last analysis, Feuerbach was not meeting the orthodox theologians on their own ground and fighting them with their own weapons. He was trying to cut the ground from under their feet.

In doing this, Feuerbach was following in the tradition of Idealism. But he had gone further. He had made a pilgrimage from theology to the philosophy of Hegel, and from Hegel to his own kind of naturalism and positivism. Both God and the Absolute had become secularized and naturalized. Like Schleiermacher, Feuerbach had become a theologian of experience.[40] But he went far beyond Schleiermacher. In the last analysis, the latter was a theologian of experience of the supernatural. Feuerbach's religious experience was of the natural. In this pilgrimage he had taken his Christ with him. Schleiermacher's Christ was a symbolic figure who mediated awareness of God. The Christ of Kant and the early Hegel had been a moral, enlightened teacher. The Christ of the mature Hegel was a moment in the dialectic of the Absolute Spirit coming to self-consciousness. The Christ of Feuerbach's *Das Wesen des Christenthums* retained an ethical element. But above all he was the projection of man's wish fulfillments, the creation of his feeling of utter dependence, the expression of the self-consciousness of man in his vain movement toward a reality which could only be found in man himself.

8. KIERKEGAARD AND THE REENTRY OF TRANSCENDENCE

It is one of the ironies of history that one of the most influential figures in twentieth-century theology was a nineteenth-century thinker who was little known outside his own country during his lifetime. The irony is less stark when it is remembered that the thinker in question, Søren Aabye Kierkegaard (1813–55),[1] wrote in Danish. For although Denmark was far from immune to outside influences in the early nineteenth century, the traffic of ideas was almost exclusively one way owing to the rest of Europe's ignorance of the Danish tongue. Even within Denmark, Kierkegaard stood so much outside the mainstream of thought that he attracted little significant attention.[2]

Background and Writings

Kierkegaard was born and died in Copenhagen. His whole life was over-shadowed by national turmoil. Rampant inflation accompanied the Napoleonic wars, and the country was declared bankrupt in the year of his birth. The political power and prestige of Denmark shrank progressively. Culturally the country was overshadowed by Germany. Throughout Kierkegaard's life the Danish Lutheran Church was struggling to come to terms with the modern world and cope with the advent of democracy. The efforts of the church leaders to secure a place for the church in Danish life resulted in Kierkegaard's growing alienation from Christendom in his last years. However, there was no such estrangement in his early years. His father, Michael Pedersen Kierkegaard, who was fifty-six when Søren was born, had risen from poverty to middle-class security. He was a prominent figure in the Lutheran Church and a personal friend of Jakob Peter Mynster, who prepared Søren for confirmation in 1828 and who became Bishop of Sjaelland and Primate of Denmark in 1834. In 1837 Søren recalled,

> I was brought up on Mynster's sermons—by my father. This is the trouble; of course it could never have occurred to my father to take those sermons otherwise than literally. Brought up on Mynster's sermons—by Mynster; yes, a problem.[3]

As with Schleiermacher, there was an element of Herrnhut piety in his family background, and this fact may well have intensified the introspective, melancholy piety of both father and son. Throughout his life Michael Pedersen Kierkegaard was haunted by a sense of guilt and divine retribution, which was passed on to his children.[4] Ten years after his father's death Søren recalled, "I am indebted to my father for everything from the very beginning. Melancholy as he was, when he saw me melancholy, he appealed to me: Be sure that you really love Jesus Christ."[5] Even this remark was not without its barbs. Its weight falls not upon Christ's redemptive love but upon his overwhelming demand.

Søren Kierkegaard matriculated at the University of Copenhagen in 1830. But the course of his studies was not so orderly as that of his elder brother, Peter Christian, the future Bishop of Aalborg, who had already taken his doctorate at Göttingen with a dissertation *De Notione atque Turpitudine Mendacii Commentatio*. It took Søren ten years to get his degree, though he soon followed it up with a dissertation for the degree of Magister Artium *Om Begebet Ironi (The Concept of Irony, With Constant Reference to Socrates)* (1841).[6] One of his early tutors was H. L. Martensen who in 1854 succeeded Mynster as Bishop of Sjaelland.[7] At the time Martensen was a rising theologian. When Schleiermacher visited Copenhagen in 1833 Martensen delivered a poem in his honor.[8] The following year he introduced Kierkegaard to the themes of *Der christliche Glaube*.[9] But Martensen was also a protagonist of Hegel. Kierkegaard's open hostilty to Hegel had not yet developed, but already he was drawing a clear distinction between philosophy and Christianity. In his *Journal* he reflected privately that *"Philosophy and Christianity can never be united."*[10] Christianity is concerned with redemption from past sins; philosophy calls upon man to forget the past. Moreover, Kierkegaard was already critical of the basic approaches of both Schleiermacher and Hegel.

> What Schleiermacher calls "religion" and the Hegelian dogmaticians "faith" is, after all, nothing else than the first immediacy, the prerequisite for everything—the vital fluid—in an emotional-intellectual sense the atmosphere we breathe—and which therefore cannot properly be characterized with these words [*faith* and *religion*].[11]

Another influence which dates from this period is the posthumous one of J. G. Hamann.[12] But the most positive influence of Kierkegaard's student days was that of Paoul Martin Møller, the professor of philosophy, who in contrast to Hegel stressed subjectivity and who suggested the theme of irony as the subject for Kierkegaard's dissertation. Following the defense of his dissertation and the breaking of his engagement, Kierkegaard went to Berlin (October, 1842 to March, 1843), where he heard Schelling lecture and began his own *Either/Or*. He now broke completely with Idealism. He paid further brief visits to Berlin in 1843, 1845, and 1846. But most of his life was spent in his native Copenhagen.

Some idea of the thought-world of the mature Kierkegaard is revealed by the auction catalog of April, 1856, which lists the contents of his library.[13] Some 2,200 books were listed, chiefly literature, philosophy and some theology. Apart from Shakespeare and a few English classics, the literature was dominated by German works. About 1,200 books were in German as against some 750 in Danish. Much of the German literature consisted of works by Goethe, Lessing, the romantics and their contemporaries. Plato, Aristotle, Kant, Fichte, Hegel, and Schelling were well represented. The theological section included writings by Luther, Augustine, and Schleiermacher (including the *Glaubenslehre*, the *Reden* and sermons). From 1837 to his death, apart from a wartime break, Kierkegaard subscribed to I. H. Fichte's *Zeitschrift für Philosophie und spekulative Theologie*.

However, books were not the sole influence on Kierkegaard's mind. On May 19, 1838, he recorded in his *Journal* a deep religious experience which he described as *"indescribable joy."*[14] Numerous attempts have been made to explain Kierkegaard in terms of physical deformity[15] or psychological imbalance.[16] He appears to have suffered from depression, alternating with exaltation. The manner of his courtship of Regine Olsen and his breaking of their engagement after a year in October, 1841, together with his continued attachment to her and his decision not to seek ordination after years of aspiration might suggest some form of compulsive detachment behavior. A case has been argued for regarding Kierkegaard as a self-conscious poseur.[17] At the same time it is difficult to dismiss his actions and to see interpretations of them as mere rationalizations. It may be that Kierkegaard was haunted by sins of youth, which he came to regard as the grounds of a divine imperative that barred him from marriage and ordination.[18] There are also grounds for thinking that his father had contracted syphilis and that this was the secret behind what he called "the great earthquake."[19] This possibility might explain a number of veiled allusions in his writings, the premature deaths in the family, and a possible fear that Søren might be a carrier of the disease, which would thus make marriage impossible. It is conceivable that such knowledge might have intensified Kierkegaard's antipathy to the erotic and aesthetic, whenever they are allowed to usurp the place of religion.

Kierkegaard's work falls into two broad categories: the "pseudonymous" or "aesthetic" writings published between 1841 and 1845 and the later Christian literature[20] or, perhaps more accurately, works attacking Christendom. These broad categories are not completely watertight, for the earlier works were accompanied by *Christian Discourses*, which stated in a more direct way what was stated indirectly in the "pseudonymous" writings. In the posthumously published *Synspunktet for min Forfatter-Virkomshed (The Point of View for my Work as an Author)*[21] Kierkegaard insisted that his intention from the beginning was to write as a Christian author. He saw his life under "Divine Governance." The aesthetic writings were a form of indirect witness, designed to shake the illusions of Christendom by exploring the hollowness of the merely aesthetic. "The problem itself is a problem of reflection: to become a Christian . . . when one is a Christian of a sort."[22]

The "aesthetic" writings were characterized by the "maieutic" method of indirect communication. The term derives from the Greek *maieutikos*, "one skilled in midwifery," and was already used by Plato in describing the Socratic method of teaching.[23] In his dissertation on *The Concept of Irony* Kierkegaard observed that Socrates "assisted the individual to an intellectual delivery, severed the umbilical cord of substantiality. As an *accoucheur* Socrates was unsurpassed, but more than this he was not. He assumed no real responsibility for his disciples' subsequent lives."[24] In his papers Kierkegaard noted that

> Socrates said he could not give birth but could only be a midwife. That is, every man possesses the ethical and the one who has been born cannot be born again (here the Christian rebirth enters in—as a relationship not between man and man but between God and man, a new creation).[25]

The concept of the witness and teacher who assists at the birth of insight and perception plays an important part not only in Kierkegaard's understanding of truth on a philosophical level but also in his understanding of Jesus.[26]

Bound up with his view of the teacher's role was Kierkegaard's attribution of the works of this period to various pseudonymous authors who represent different standpoints but who each have a part in the dialectical process of understanding. The major writings of this period include *Enten/Eller (Either/Or. A Fragment of Life. By Victor Eremita* [1843]);[27] *Frygt og Baeven (Fear and Trembling. A Dialectical Lyric by Johannes de Silentio* [1843]);[28] *Philosophiske Smuler (Philosophical Fragments, or a Fragment of Philosophy. By Johannes Climacus. Responsible for Publication S. Kierkegaard* [1844]);[29] *Begrebet Angest (The Concept of Dread. A Simple Deliberation on Psychological Lines in the Direction of the Dogmatic Problem of Original Sin. By Vigilius Haufniensis* [1844]);[30] *Stadier paa Livets Vej (Stages on Life's Way, Studies by Sundry Persons, Collected, forwarded to the Press and published by Hilarius Bookbinder* [1844]);[31] and *Afsluttende uvidenskabelig Efterskrift (Concluding Unscientific Postscript to the Philosophical Fragments. A Mimic-Pathetic-Dialectical Composition. An Existential Contribution. By Johannes Climacus. Responsible for Publication S. Kierkegaard* [1846]).[32]

With the publication of the *Postscript* Kierkegaard felt that he had rounded off his chief literary work and that he might retire to a country living.[33] He even discussed the plan with Mynster. But he was still oppressed by melancholy and guilt. He suddenly found himself attacked in a scurrilous weekly called *The Corsair*. He was forced to new depths of introspection. In Holy Week, 1848, a deep religious experience led him to record in his *Journal*, "My whole nature is changed. My concealment and inclosing reserve are broken—I am free to speak."[34] But by Easter Monday he reflected that his "inclosing reserve still cannot be broken."[35] He was increasingly oppressed financially, not least because of the cost of publishing his books. However, he continued to write, though he now largely abandoned the pseudonyms. The object of his attack was no longer Christianity as typified by Hegelianism. His writing became more direct and devotional. Among the books of this period were *Kjerlighendens Gjerninger (Works of Love, [1847])*,[36] *Christelige Taler (Christian Discourses*, [1848]),[37] and *Indøvelse i Christendom (Training in Christianity. By Anti-Climacus. Parts I, II, III. Edited by S. Kierkegaard*, [1850]).[38]

Although Bishop Mynster came to personify all that Kierkegaard objected to in Christendom, he long cherished the hope that the Bishop might change.[39] Following Mynster's death in 1854 Martensen delivered an address in which he hailed Mynster as a "witness to the truth." In Kierkegaard's opinion this was what Mynster precisely was not. Kierkegaard proceeded to launch a polemic in *Faedrelandet* which he continued in a series of tracts that have been collected and translated as *Kierkegaard's Attack upon "Christendom."*[40] In a sense, he was now saying openly what he had previously implied, but it was in a highly personal and extreme form. While the uproar was at its height, Kierkegaard collapsed in the street and was taken to Frederiks Hospital. He declined to see his brother and refused communion on the grounds that the minister was "the King's official," even though the latter was his oldest friend, Emil Boesen. He died prematurely, an old man at the age of forty-two, a martyr to his convictions, leaving barely enough money to pay the hospital bill and funeral expenses.

Kierkegaard's Approach

Kierkegaard's approach was dictated by his reaction to Hegel and all that he stood for in his mind; his debt to Greek thought, especially to Socratic irony; his sense of the otherness of God; and an overpowering awareness of the personal character of New Testament Christianity in contrast to the easy conformism of latterday Christianity. Not all these elements were equally present in his writings. Much depended upon the subject under discussion. We have already noted changes of focus, emphasis and style.

Kierkegaard's criticisms of Hegelianism may be summed up by saying that it was indemonstrable, irrelevant and based on a confusion of categories. It is vividly illustrated by the following passage from the *Concluding Unscientific Postscript*.

> The Hegelian philosophy, by failing to define its relation to the existing individual, and by ignoring the ethical, confounds existence.

The most dangerous form of scepticism is always that which least looks like it. The notion that pure thought is the positive truth for an existing individual, is sheer scepticism, for this positiveness is chimerical. It is a glorious thing to be able to explain the past, the whole of human history; but if the ability to understand the past is to be the summit of attainment for a living individual, this positiveness is scepticism, and a dangerous form of it, because of the deceptive quantity of things understood.... But a philosophy of pure thought is for an existing individual a chimera, if the truth that is sought is something to exist in. To exist under the guidance of pure thought is like travelling in Denmark with the help of a small map of Europe, on which Denmark shows no larger than a steel pen-point—aye, it is still more impossible. The admiration and enthusiasm of the youth, his boundless confidence in Hegel, is precisely the satire upon Hegel. This is something that would long ago have been perceived, if the prestige of pure thought had not been bolstered by an over-awing opinion, so that people have not dared to say that it is anything but excellent, and to avow that they have understood it—though this last is in a certain sense impossible, since this philosophy cannot help anyone to an understanding of himself, which is surely an absolute condition for all other kinds of understanding. Socrates said quite ironically that he did not know whether he was a human being or something else, but an Hegelian can say with due solemnity in the confessional: "I do not know whether I am a human being—but I have understood the System." I for my part would rather say: "I know that I am a human being, and I know that I have not understood the System."[41]

In his study of *Kierkegaard's Relation to Hegel* Niels Thulstrup has shown that Kierkegaard's language is redolent of Hegelian terminology and allusions. If his knowledge of Hegel and his disciples was not an exhaustive one, it was complete and accurate on the points that concerned him.[42] Detailed exploration of this thesis falls outside the scope of the present study. However, the observation may be made that Kierkegaard's fundamental objection to Hegel and Idealism turns on the Kantian distinction between synthetic and analytic statements, which the Idealists refused to recognize.

The questionableness of the "Method" becomes apparent already in Hegel's relation to Kant. A scepticism which attacks thought itself cannot be vanquished by thinking it through, since the very instrument by which this would have to be done is in revolt. There is only one thing to do with such a scepticism, and that is to break with it. To answer Kant within the fantastic shadow-play of pure thought is precisely not to answer him. The only thing-in-itself which cannot be thought is existence, and this does not come within the province of thought to think. But how could pure thought possibly vanquish this difficulty, when it is abstract? And what does pure thought abstract from? Why from existence, to be sure, and hence from that which it purports to explain.[43]

However, the distinction was not exclusively a Kantian one. The manner in which Kierkegaard chose to explore it in the *Postscript* took the form of a discussion of "Theses Possibly or Actually Attributable to Lessing."[44] In the course of it Kierkegaard ranged widely over the *Fragments* controversy and the "Pantheismusstreit." In the third thesis he discussed the proposition that, "Lessing has said that accidental historical truths can never serve as proofs for eternal truths of the reason; and that the transition by which it is proposed to base an eternal truth upon historical testimony is a leap."[45] His discussion culminated in the assertion of two theses: "(A), a logical system is possible; (B), an existential system is impossible." At bottom the systems of Idealism rested upon a confusion. "The systematic Idea is the identity of subject and object, the unity of thought and being. Existence, on the other hand, is their separation."[46]

Taken together, the *Philosophical Fragments* and the *Concluding Unscientific Postscript* might be called Kierkegaard's *Critique of Pure Reason*. They constitute a reappraisal of the nature and scope of reason in philosophy and religion from Kant and Lessing down to Hegel. The *Fragments* addresses the question stated on the title page, "Is an historical point of departure possible for an eternal consciousness; how can such a point of departure have any other than a merely historical interest; is it possible to base an eternal happiness upon historical knowledge?" The question is evocative of both the Hegelian concept of the self-consciousness of the absolute Spirit and Lessing's historical skepticism. Kierkegaard had evidently come across Lessing's *Über den Beweis des Geistes und der Kraft* via the translation, made by his relative Hans Brøchner, of D. F. Strauss's *Die christliche Glaubenslehre* (two volumes, 1840–41). This discovery prompted him to acquire Lessing's *Sämmtliche Schriften*.[47]

The titles of the *Philosophical Fragments* and the *Concluding Unscientific Postscript to the Philosophical Fragments* stand, like other titles of Kierkegaard's books, in ironic contrast to the imposing scientific, system-building implied by the titles of Hegel's writings. The title of the *Philosophical Fragments* is partly explained by the quotation from Plato's *Hippias Major*, 304 A, which he inserted as a motto in the Postscript: "But really, Socrates, what do you think this all amounts to? It is really scrapings and parings of systematic thought, as I said a while ago, divided into bits." However, it is tempting to speculate whether it might not also have been influenced by the *Fragments* published by Lessing. Like Lessing, he was the editor of the work. The central theme of both works may be said to be the intentions of Jesus and his disciples.

Although Kierkegaard knew of the *Fragments* controversy and Strauss's skepticism concerning the New Testament and the question of the historical Jesus, Kierkegaard's response did not take the form of a direct reply. It was more a philosophical reflection on the nature of truth in relation to God and history. What followed was an oblique reply both to the Hegelians and to the growing body of those preoccupied with the quest of the historical Jesus.

The oblique character of this and other writings by Kierkegaard was dictated partly by his conviction that Hegelianism should not be attacked directly on its own terms and partly by his conviction that God cannot be talked about directly. Accordingly, Kierkegaard's pseudonymous author Johannes Climacus begins his work with what he calls "A Project of Thought," which asks the question, "How far does the Truth admit of being learned?" It poses the Socratic dilemma:

> One cannot seek for what he knows, and it seems equally impossible for him to seek for what he does not know. For what a man knows he cannot seek, since he knows it; and what he does not know he cannot seek, since he does not even know what to seek.[48]

The Greeks tried to resolve the dilemma with the doctrine of recollection of truth known in a previous existence. Socrates played the role of a midwife in eliciting knowledge, "for between man and man the maieutic relationship is the highest, and begetting belongs to God alone."[49] But Platonic thought dissolves the historicity of existence in its perception of the eternal. Moreover, the question moves beyond the plane of intellectual puzzle, when the questions of sin[50] and the knowledge of God are introduced.[51]

Knowledge of the existence of God is not inferential or demonstrable. The so-called proofs of the existence of God are really the development of "the content of a conception."[52] "The works of the God are such that only the God can perform them. Just so, but where then are the works of God? The works from which I would deduce his existence are not directly and immediately given."[53] It is impossible to provide a final, conclusive proof of the wisdom of God in nature. In trying to develop a proof from nature

> I merely develop the ideality I have presupposed, and because of my confidence in *this* I make so bold as to defy all objections, even those that have not yet been made. In beginning my proof I presuppose the ideal interpretation, and also that I will be successful in carrying it through; but what else is this but to presuppose that the God exists, so that I really begin by virtue of confidence in him?[54]

The most fundamental difference between Kierkegaard and Hegel turns on their respective attitudes to reason and its relationship to God. To Hegel, nature and history were the expression of the reason of the absolute mind. Reason achieves the "mediation" of infinite and finite. Thus, to discern the movement of reason in the system of nature and history was to know God. To Kierkegaard this was merely fanciful dogmatic system-building which bore no real reference to reality. To use the language of twentieth-century Dialectical Theology, Kierkegaard believed that God was Wholly Other. He speaks of him as "the Unknown." At the heart of Kierkegaard's scheme of thought lies the distinction between time and eternity, the finite and the infinite, the immanent and the transcendent. Man and the world belong to the spatio-temporal realm. So does man's reason. As he later put it in the *Postscript*,

> God does not think, he creates; God does not exist, He is eternal. Man thinks and exists, and existence separates thought and being, holding them apart from one another in succession.[55]

In the *Fragments* Kierkegaard asked,

> For how should the Reason be able to understand what is absolutely different from itself? If this is not immediately evident, it will become clearer in the light of the consequences; for if the God is absolutely unlike man, then man is absolutely unlike

the God; but how could the Reason be expected to understand this? Here we seem to be confronted with a paradox. Merely to obtain the knowledge that the God is unlike him, man needs the help of the God; and now he learns that the God is absolutely different from himself. But if the God and man are absolutely different, this cannot be accounted for on the basis of what man derives from the God, for in so far they are akin. Their unlikeness must therefore be explained by what man derives from himself, or by what he has brought upon his own head. But what can this unlikeness be? Aye, what can it be but sin; since the unlikeness, the absolute unlikeness, is something that man has brought upon himself.[56]

There is thus a deep irony that is intrinsic to the human condition of knowing God. The difference between man and God is both metaphysical and moral.[57] It finds expression in the double paradox that merely to know that God is unlike man, man needs the help of God, and that revelation further discloses the absolute unlikeness of God. The difficulty presented by this paradox is countered by the Absolute Paradox of the Incarnation.

We have expressed this in the preceding by saying that man was in Error, and had brought this upon his head by his own guilt; and we came to the conclusion, partly in jest and yet also in earnest, that it was too much to expect of man that he should find this out for himself. Now we have again arrived at the same conclusion. The connoisseur in self-knowledge was perplexed over himself to the point of bewilderment when he came to grapple in thought with the unlike; he scarcely knew any longer whether he was a stranger monster than Typhon, or if his nature partook of something divine. What then did he lack? The consciousness of sin, which he indeed could no more teach to another than another could teach it to him, but only the God—if the God consents to become a Teacher. But this was his purpose, as we have imagined it. In order to be man's Teacher, the God proposed to make himself like the individual man, so that he might understand him fully. Thus our paradox is rendered still more appalling, or the same paradox has the double aspect which proclaims it as the Absolute Paradox; negatively by revealing the absolute unlikeness of sin, positively by proposing to do away with the absolute unlikeness in absolute likeness.[58]

In one sense the paradox is irrational, but reason requires it in its "paradoxical passion" which "precisely desires its own downfall."[59] Reason cannot break out of the closed circuit of finite rationality, but at least rational reflection leads to the recognition of the limitations of reason. The paradox does not resolve the problem on a rational level. Rather, it "unites the contradictories, and is the historical made eternal, and the Eternal made historical. Everyone who understands the Paradox differently may keep the honor of having explained it, which honor he won by not being content to understand it."[60] Moreover, "Faith is not a form of knowledge. . . . No knowledge can have for its object the absurdity that the Eternal is the historical. . . . But the disciple is in Faith so related to his Teacher as to be eternally concerned with his historical existence."[61]

The Absolute Paradox of the Incarnation involves a simultaneous unveiling and veiling of God. For God to be known at all there must be the unveiling of revelation. But for man to be able to perceive this in any way, God must encounter man in terms of his own rational, spatio-temporal conceptuality. Hence, the revelation is veiled in human, finite form.[62] The transcendent God cannot be described directly. The approach can be made only indirectly in terms of "A Project of Thought" which speaks of "the God" in a hypothetical way, and in which Kierkegaard is "like the man who collected a fee for exhibiting a ram in the afternoon, which in the forenoon could be seen gratis, grazing in the open field."[63] But the real issue is not the authorship of the thought, but the thought itself.

History and the Incarnation

In the *Philosophical Fragments* Kierkegaard argues that, "the God cannot be conceived; it was for this very reason that he appeared in the form of a servant. And yet the servant-form is no deception."[64] To form any conception of God, the learner must receive the condition from God himself. There is a divine "incognito" which cannot be penetrated "without receiving the condition from the Teacher."[65] What matters is that God should give "to the disciple the condition that enables him to see him, opening for him the eyes of Faith."[66] This does not mean that Kierkegaard was indifferent to "the outward figure," which was what the disciple "has seen and his hands have handled."[67] However, Christ is no longer physically present, and in any case to have been a contemporary in a merely temporal and physical sense is no guarantee of perception. What matters is to be a contemporary in the non-immediate sense, who in faith discerns, affirms, and responds to the Teacher.

> A contemporary may for all that be a non-contemporary; the real contemporary is such not by virtue of his immediate contemporaneity; *ergo*, it must also be possible for a non-contemporary (in the immediate sense) to be a contemporary, by virtue of that something which makes the contemporary a real contemporary. But the non-contemporary (in the immediate sense) is of course the member of a later generation, whence it must be possible for an individual so situated to be a real contemporary. Or what do we mean by being contemporary? Is it perhaps this kind of a contemporary that we praise, one who can speak as follows: "I ate and drank in his presence, and he taught in our streets. I saw him often, and knew him for a common man of humble origin. Only a very few thought to find something extraordinary in him; as far as I am concerned, I could see nothing remarkable about him, and I was certainly as much of a contemporary as anybody." Or is this what we mean by calling anyone a contemporary, and is he a contemporary to whom the God must say if they meet in another life, and he seeks to urge his contemporaneity: "I do not know you"? And so it was in truth, just as it was equally true that such a contemporary could not have known the Teacher. Only the believer, i.e., the non-immediate contemporary, knows the Teacher, since he receives the condition from him, and therefore knows him even as he is known.[68]

By itself empirical perception is not enough. Historical evidence is not and cannot be of such a kind as to compel belief in the gospel. For the historical and the empirical cannot mediate (in Hegel's sense) the transcendent. The transcendent is present in history, but history is the occasion for encountering the transcendent. The transcendent can never be reduced to the question of objective historical facts. Therefore the contemporary concern with the historicity of the New Testament facts does not touch the central issue. We ask the wrong question, when we ask about credibility, for credibility can belong only to a historical fact.

> But what historical fact? The historical fact which can become an object only for Faith, and which one human being cannot communicate to another, i.e., which can indeed be communicated to another but not so that the other believes it; and which if communicated in the form of Faith is so communicated as to prevent the other, so far as possible, from accepting it immediately. If the fact spoken of were a simple historical fact, the accuracy of the historical sources would be of great importance. Here this is not the case, for Faith cannot be distilled from even the nicest accuracy of detail. The historical fact that the God has been in human form is the essence of the matter; the rest of the detail is not even as important as if we had to do with a human being instead of with the God.... If the contemporary generation had left nothing behind them but these words: "We have believed that in such and such a year the God appeared among us in the humble figure of a servant, that he lived and taught in our community, and finally died," it would be more than enough. The contemporary generation would have done all that was necessary; for this little advertisement, this *nota bene* of a page of universal history, would be sufficient to afford an occasion for a successor, and the most voluminous account can in all eternity do nothing more.

> If we wish to express the relation subsisting between a contemporary and his successor in the briefest possible compass, but without sacrificing accuracy to brevity, we may say: The successor believes *by means of* (this expresses the occasional) the testimony of the contemporary, and *in virtue of* the condition he himself receives from the God....

> There is no disciple at second hand. The first and the last are essentially on the same plane, only that a later generation finds its occasion in the testimony of a contemporary generation, while the contemporary generation finds this occasion in its own immediate contemporaneity, and in so far owes nothing to any other generation.[69]

Perhaps this is the most frequently quoted passage in the whole corpus of Kierkegaard's writings. On a superficial reading Kierkegaard seems to be arguing a historical skepticism as complete as Strauss's or Bultmann's.[70] But in fact, Kierkegaard was not arguing the case for historical skepticism or trying to salvage what he could of Christian faith from the debris left behind by Reimarus and Strauss. Kierkegaard was not interested in critical study as such. His theological training had included scarcely any modern theological criticism. He knew of D. F. Strauss, F. C. Baur and Bruno Bauer, but he had no time for their critical work.[71] Occasionally Kierkegaard alluded to historical criticism, but he rejoiced in the fact that "this beautiful dream of critical theology is an impossibility, because even the most perfect realization would still remain an approximation."[72]

However, Kierkegaard's verdict on the value of history was not the result of historical research but the presupposition which he brought to history. It applied equally to a minimal view of the historicity of the Bible as to a maximal one. In fact, in other contexts Kierkegaard himself took the Bible at its face value as history. What Kierkegaard wrote in the *Philosophical Fragments* was not a denial of the historicity of the Gospel records but a statement concerning the place and importance of history. It was intended as a prerequisite for the proper understanding of the place of history in Christian faith and experience.

In the *Concluding Unscientific Postscript* which was actually a much longer work than the *Philosophical Fragments*, Kierkegaard turned his attention to the questions of how the eternal could be related to the temporal in the believer and how eternal happiness could be grounded in history. The work was an extensive repudiation of objective thinking which, though appropriate in mathematics and "historical knowledge of different kinds," always leads away from the subject, "whose existence or non-existence, and from the objective point of view quite rightly, become infinitely indifferent."[73] But to Kierkegaard, God was neither an abstract logical truth nor an object that existed in time and space that could be known objectively.

> The existing individual who chooses to pursue the objective way enters upon the entire approximation-process by which it is proposed to bring God to light objectively. But this is in all eternity impossible, because God is a subject, and therefore exists only for subjectivity in inwardness.[74]

The subjective element was therefore central to Christianity. Kierkegaard concluded the work with a series of reflections on "Subjective Christianity" in which he offered the following definition of "Subjectively, what it is to become a Christian":

> The decision lies in the subject. The appropriation is the paradoxical inwardness which is specifically different from all other inwardness. The thing of being a Christian is not determined by the *what* of Christianity but by the *how* of the Christian. This *how* can only correspond with one thing, the absolute paradox. There is therefore no vague talk to the effect that being a Christian is to accept, and to accept, and to accept quite differently, to appropriate, to believe, to appropriate by faith quite differently (all of them purely rhetorical and fictitious definitions); but *to believe* is specifically different from all other appropriation and inwardness. Faith is the objective uncertainty due to the repulsion of the absurd held fast by the passion of inwardness, which in this instance is intensified to the utmost degree. This formula fits only the believer, no one else, not a lover, not an enthusiast, not a thinker, but simply and solely the believer who is related to the absolute paradox.

> Faith therefore cannot be any sort of provisional function. He who from the vantage point of a higher knowledge would know his faith as a factor resolved in a higher idea has *eo ipso* ceased to believe. Faith *must* not *rest content* with unintelligibility; for precisely the relation to or the repulsion from the unintelligible, the absurd, is the expression for the passion of faith.[75]

The protest against the illusion of objectivity in religion and the vain attempt to find objective, compelling proofs from history were recurrent motifs in Kierkegaard. In *Training in Christianity* Kierkegaard asked and answered the following questions:

> Can one learn from history* anything about Christ?
>
> No. Why not? Because one can "know" nothing at all about "Christ"; He is the paradox, the object of faith, existing only for faith. But all historical communication is communication of "knowledge," hence from history one can learn nothing about Christ. For if one learns little or much about Him, or anything at all, He [who is thus known] is not He who in truth He is, i.e. one learns to know nothing about Him, or one learns to know something incorrect about Him, one is deceived. History makes out Christ to be another than He truly is, and so one learns to know a lot about... Christ? No, not about Christ, for about Him nothing can be known, He can only be believed.
>
> * By "history" is to be understood throughout profane history, world-history, history as ordinarily understood, in contrast to sacred history. S.K.

> Can one prove from history that Christ was God?
>
> Let me first put another question: Is it possible to conceive of a more foolish contradiction than that of wanting to prove (no matter for the present purpose whether it be from history or from anything else in the wide world one wants to *prove* it) that a definite individual man is God? That an individual man is God, declares himself to be God, is indeed the "offence" *kat' 'exochēn*. But what is the offence, the offensive thing? What is at variance with (human) reason? And such a thing as that one would attempt to prove! But to "prove" is to demonstrate something to be the rational reality it is. Can one demonstrate that to be a rational reality which is at variance with reason? Surely not, unless one would contradict oneself. One can "prove" only that it is at variance with reason. The proofs which Scripture presents for Christ's divinity—His miracles, His Resurrection from the dead, His Ascension into heaven— are therefore only for faith, that is, they are not "proofs," they have no intention of proving that all this agrees perfectly with reason; on the contrary they would prove that it conflicts with reason and therefore is an object of faith.[76]

Later on in the work, Kierkegaard reflected on what he considered to be perversions of Christianity.

> They make Christ a speculative unity of God and man; or they throw Christ away and take His teaching; or for sheer seriousness they make Christ a false god. Spirit is the negation of direct immediacy. If Christ is very God, He must also be unrecognizable, He must assume unrecognizableness, which is the negation of all directness. Direct recognizableness is precisely the characteristic of the pagan god.[77]

Although *Training in Christianity* might be classed as one of Kierkegaard's more devotional works, an undercurrent of polemic may be detected. The idea of

Christ as "a speculative unity of God and man" is clearly Hegelian, as is the language of "negation," "immediacy" and "Spirit." But the terms are used in an anti-Hegelian sense. Moreover, Hegelianism is not the only form of paganism. The theology reaching back into the Enlightenment, which valued Christ only for his moral teaching, and docetic orthodoxy also fall under the same condemnation. What they have in common is the desire to objectify the divinity or essence of Christ in one way or another and turn it into something identifiable.

In the same year that Kierkegaard published *Training in Christianity* (1850) he set out in his private papers what he called *The Dialectic Oriented Toward Becoming a Christian.*

> Socrates did not first of all try to collect some proofs for the immortality of the soul in order then to live, believing by virtue of the proofs. Just the opposite. He said: The possibility of immortality occupies me to the point that I unconditionally venture to wager my whole life unconditionally upon it, as if it were the surest thing of all. And this is the way he lived—and his life is a proof of the immortality of the soul. He did not first of all believe by virtue of the proofs and then live; no, his life is the proof and not until his martyr-death is the proof complete. — You see, this is spirit. It is a little embarrassing for mimics and all those who live second-hand and tenth-hand lives, those who are result-hunters, and those with cowardly, effeminate natures.
>
> Used with discrimination, this may be applied to becoming a Christian.
>
> First of all comes, quite properly, Lessing's doubt that one cannot base an eternal happiness upon something historical.
>
> But here there is [*existerer*] something historical, the story of Jesus Christ.
>
> But is it historically entirely certain? The answer to this must be that even if it were the surest thing in all history, this does not help; no *direct* transition from the historical can be made as the basis for an eternal happiness. This is something qualitatively new.
>
> What do we do now? This—A man says to himself, *à la* Socrates: here is [*existerer*] something historical which teaches me that for my eternal happiness I must turn to Jesus Christ. I must beware of taking the wrong turn into scientific rummaging and reconnoitering to see if it is historically entirely certain; for it surely is historical —that is, if it were ten times as certain even to the minutest detail, it still would not help me—for I cannot be helped *directly.*
>
> Then I say to myself: I choose; the historical here means so much to me that I resolve to venture my whole life on this *if.** And—then he lives on. He lives filled by this thought alone, venturing his life for it; and his life is the proof that he believed. He did not have a few proofs and thereupon he believed and then began to live. No, just the opposite.
>
> * (In margin) This is to be found in Christ's words as well: If anyone will follow my teaching, that is, live according to it, that is, act according to it, he will experience, etc. This means that there are no advance proofs—nor is he satisfied that accepting his teaching means: I give my word.

This is called *venturing*, and without venturing faith is an impossibility. *Relating oneself to spirit means to be up for examination*;** to believe, to will to believe, means to change one's life, to be up for examination; the daily examination is the tension of faith. — Yet one can preach about this to cowardly, effeminate, unspiritual natures until the end of the world—they do not grasp it, they do not want to grasp it. They actually think it is all very well for someone else to stick his neck out and then they attach themselves to him—and make assurances. But to venture out—no thanks!

But with regard to becoming a Christian there is a dialectical difference from Socrates which must be remembered. Specifically in the relationship to immortality—a person relates himself to himself and the idea—no further. But when a man chooses upon an *if* to believe in Christ—that is, chooses to wager his life upon that, then he has permission to address himself directly to Christ in prayer. Thus the historical is the occasion and still also the object of faith.

But all unspiritual natures turn the matter around. They say: To wager everything upon an *if* is a kind of skepticism; it is fancifulness, not positivity. It is because they will not "venture." And this is the unspiritual crowd which Christianity has taken in tow and which has finally done away with Christianity.

** (In margin) This comes from the fact that man is a synthesis of physical-psychical and spirit. But "spirit" establishes the division—whereas in every case the soft character wants to haul along the baser side of life and have its consent. This explains the anxiety about "venturing." The unspiritual man always wants "probability." But "spirit" will never concede it. "Spirit" is the examination: Will you relinquish probability, will you deny yourself, forsake the world, etc.[78]

Once again Kierkegaard takes up the themes of Socrates, Lessing, history, "Spirit" (with its implied contrast with Hegelianism) and Christ. History provides the challenge and occasion for belief. But it demands choice and response. However, the Socratic model has its limitations. It does not allow for the recourse that the believer has to Christ in prayer. Such recourse inevitably belongs to the subjective side of religion. It would scarcely count at all in the "scientific" objective approach of the Hegelians. But the devotional side of Christianity was for Kierkegaard the essential element. It provided the basis for his philosophical approach.

The Divine Incognito and the Imitatio Christi

In his short piece of 1848 entitled *Has a Man the Right to Let Himself be Put to Death for the Truth?*, Kierkegaard observed that,

To believe is to believe in the divine and the human together in Christ. To *comprehend* Him is to comprehend His life humanly. But to comprehend His life *humanly* is so far from being more than believing, that (if there is no faith besides) it means to lose Him, since His life is what it is for faith, the *divine*-human.[79]

In the companion piece, *Of the Difference between a Genius and an Apostle*, he reflected,

> Between God and man, then, there is and remains an eternal, essential, qualitative difference. The *paradox-religious relationship* (which, quite rightly, cannot be thought, but only believed) *appears when God appoints a particular man to divine authority*, in relation, be it carefully noted, to that which God has entrusted to him.[80]

Although Kierkegaard sometimes spoke disparagingly of Luther and was critical of the way in which Lutheranism had become an institutionalized state religion,[81] his christological teaching is strongly reminiscent of the early Luther's.[82] It sought to reaffirm and appreciate concretely the significance of the Incarnation. To do this it bypassed the vocabulary of Chalcedon and orthodoxy in favor of a personal realism, while at the same time accepting a two-natures doctrine of the person of Christ.

Jesus' humanity is pictured in concrete terms. Jesus knew hunger, thirst, suffering and death.[83] Even more important than the physical were the psychological tensions that arose from human situations, as when Jesus found himself obliged to rebuke Peter.[84] Then too there were the temptations of Jesus[85] and the mental agony of his desolation.[86] But all this suffering is not so much a denial of his divinity as an expression of it. Kierkegaard did not follow Schleiermacher and many other nineteenth-century writers at this point and use this data to reinterpret the divinity of Christ as a profound awareness of the divine in the most perfect man. Rather, he followed Luther in his doctrine of the divine incognito[87] and Pascal in saying that God is more hidden in the Incarnation than in the creation.[88]

> Behold where he stands—the God! Where? There; do you not see him? He is the God; and yet he has not a resting-place for his head, and he dares not lean on any man lest he cause him to be offended. He is the God; and yet he picks his steps more carefully than if angels guided them, not to prevent his foot from stumbling against a stone; but lest he trample human beings in the dust, in that they are offended at him.... But the servant form is no mere outer garment, and therefore the God must suffer all things, endure all things, make experience of all things.... Every other form of revelation would be a deception in the eyes of love; for either the learner would first have to be changed, and the fact concealed from him that this was necessary (but love does not alter the beloved, it alters itself); or there would be permitted to prevail a frivolous ignorance of the fact that the entire relationship was a delusion.[89]

Paul Sponheim has called this "a kind of daily kenosis."[90] But it is not the kind of kenotic doctrine that seems designed to explain how Jesus' views could be at variance with nineteenth-century critical ideas.[91] Nor does it offer a speculative theory about the divestment of divine attributes. The act of becoming a man—a particular man—necessarily involves an act of will on the part of God to be a particular man, which in turn means that the divinity is hidden in the humanity. But this in turn is an expression of divinity, revealing God to be that kind of God.

> Christ does not will to be God. In an omnipotent decision he has forced himself into being a single human being and must now very concretely suffer the total impotence of wretchedness with the cause of humanity upon his heart, must suffer being a poor individual man—and at every moment it is his voluntary decision that constrains him; he does, after all, have the power to break through and be God.[92]

> It was Christ's free will and determination from all eternity to be incognito. So when people think to do Him honour by saying or thinking, "If I had been contemporary with Him, I should have known Him directly," they really insult Him, and since it is Christ they insult, this means that they are blasphemous. . . . Oh, loftiest height of self-abnegation when the incognito succeeds so well that even if He were inclined to speak directly no one would believe Him. . . . And now in the case of the God-Man! He is God, but chooses to become the individual man. This, as we have seen, is the profoundest incognito, or the most impenetrable unrecognizableness that is possible; for the contradiction between being God and being an individual man is the greatest possible, the infinitely qualitative contradiction.[93]

This type of *kenōsis* and this doctrine of divine incognito inevitably arise out of a theology which sees God as wholly other. As in the Dialectical Theology of the 1920s and 1930s, God is so different from the creation that he cannot be expressed in it. He may touch it, but the point of contact is like a tangent touching a circle.

> Christ veritably relates tangentially to the earth (the divine cannot relate in any other way): He had no place where he could lay his head. A tangent is a straight line which touches the circle at only one single point.[94]

Because there is an infinite qualitative difference between God and man, God cannot express himself directly. The Incarnation is a real incarnation, but it means the incognito of the divine. The only way for Christ to be approached and affirmed is by faith.

> sense He can do no otherwise, and He would do no otherwise. As God-Man He is qualitatively different from every other man and therefore must refuse direct communication. He requires that He become the *object of faith*. . . . So inseparable from faith is the possibility of offence that if the God-Man were not the possibility of offence, He could not be the object of faith. So the possibility of offence is assumed in faith, assimilated by faith, it is the negative mark of the God-Man. For if the possibility of offence were lacking, direct communication would be in place, and thus the God-Man would be an idol. Direct recognisableness is paganism.[95]

Kierkegaard's view of Christ was no mere protest against self-sufficient theologizing. Nor was it merely a solution to a metaphysical puzzle overlooked by the Idealists. It was an expression of Kierkegaard's acute awareness of the personal demands of New Testament Christianity—both in what it called for from him and in what it wanted to give him. The Christian is summoned to learn obedience from Christ as a way to personal freedom.

> That obedience is the way to this end he has learnt and learns from Him who is the Way, from Him who Himself learned obedience and was obedient, obedient in all things, obedient in giving up all (the glory He had before the foundations of the earth were laid), obedience in doing without all (even that upon which He might lay His head), obedient in taking all upon Himself (the sin of the race), obedient in submitting to everything in life, obedient unto death.[96]

This kind of *imitatio Christi* is writ large in works like *Christian Discourses, Works of Love* and *Training in Christianity*. It might almost be said to be the characteristic Kierkegaardian emphasis.[97] But for Kierkegaard, Christianity was not merely an *imitatio Christi*.

> Therefore it is not simply a matter of Christ's being the prototype and that I simply ought to will to resemble him. In the first place I need His help in order to be able to resemble Him, and, secondly, insofar as he is the Savior and Reconciler of the race, I cannot in fact resemble him.[98]

The *imitatio* is not a substitute for, but the corollary of, the objective work of Christ. Here again Kierkegaard follows in the footsteps of traditional Protestantism in seeing Christ's death as an atonement making satisfaction for sin, drawing the sharpest possible distinction between Christ's work and ours.

> The fellow-worker with Christ in relation to the atonement thou canst not be, not in the remotest way. Thou art wholly in debt, He wholly makes satisfaction. So much the clearer is it that the blessing is everything. For what is the blessing? The blessing is what God does; everything that God does is the blessing. The share of the work with reference to which thou callest thyself a fellowworker is the share God does, that is the blessing. But at the altar Christ is the blessing. The divine work of reconciliation is Christ's work, and in relation to that man can do only less than nothing—so then the blessing is everything. But if the work is Christ's, then Christ is the blessing.[99]

This stress on Christ being everything and man nothing, coupled with the high view of the Lord's Supper hinted at in the above quotation, might be said to be characteristically Lutheran. But whereas in the sixteenth century this was an electrifying discovery, by the mid-nineteenth century it had become a truism in Protestant circles. Free grace had become (if one might borrow a phrase from Bonhoeffer) cheap grace.[100] Kierkegaard's burden was to open men's eyes to see that grace was both free and costly. He attempted to do this partly by drawing attention to the otherness of God and partly by showing that a mere historical knowledge of Christ was utterly inadequate.

Postscript

In many ways, Kierkegaard was swimming against the stream of nineteenth-century thought. Basically, he was maintaining an orthodox view of Christ without using the vocabulary, categories and arguments of orthodoxy. His view of Christ was not based upon "proofs" from Scripture, current critical theories, or fashionable philosophical world-views. With greater justice than Schleiermacher, he could have cited Anselm's "credo ut intelligam" as the key to understanding.[101] For belief in the divinity and humanity of Christ was the hermeneutical presupposition for understanding the Christ of the Gospels and also Christian experience. In a sense Kierkegaard was a theologian of experience. But Christian experience was not what it was for Schleiermacher, a means of determining a common denominator for understanding and reinterpreting dogma. Kierkegaard did not reinterpret, in the sense of restating Christian beliefs in modern terms. What Wittgenstein said of philosophy and language might also be said of Kierkegaard's philosophy of religion: "It leaves everything as it is. . . . The work of the philosopher consists in assembling reminders for a particular purpose."[102] Kierkegaard did not undertake a revision of orthodoxy. His work consisted in assembling reminders about what Christian orthodoxy really was and what it entailed.

Although Kierkegaard was less of a theologian in a technical sense than Schleiermacher, Scripture played a more normative part in his philosophical scheme than it did in Schleiermacher's *Der christliche Glaube*. Kierkegaard accepted the Bible in a pre-critical way. Admittedly the Old Testament appears to play relatively little part in his thinking, apart from furnishing the example of Abraham's offering of Isaac which figured prominently in *Fear and Trembling*, the story of Adam in *The Concept of Anxiety,* and the example of Job in *Repetition* and *Edifying Discourses*. Abraham served as a paradigm for Kierkegaard's reflections on the nature of faith and its relation to the ethical. Kierkegaard's use of Scripture was both selective and pre-critical. At the same time it was highly sophisticated. For although he took the biblical text at its face value, he did not treat Scripture as a corpus of revealed truths. Theology was not simply a matter of drawing inferences from Scripture and setting them out in an orderly system. The texts of Scripture provided occasions for reflection and for meditating upon and responding to the Absolute Paradox.

In a curious way Kierkegaard came near to the Idealists and to the more radical thinkers like Strauss in his elimination of the supernatural from the historical. But he did so for entirely opposite reasons. Strauss rejected the supernatural as a part of the mythical world view of the early church. In his earlier period he offered a Hegelian interpretation; in his later period he was more of a Kantian. Whereas Hegel and the Idealists subsumed the supernatural under the natural, treating nature and history and the concrete expression of Spirit in the world, Kierkegaard expunged the transcendent from critical history in order to preserve its integrity and inviolability. What may be seen in history is merely a succession of events; the transcendent is nevertheless hidden in them. Men may bear witness to the supernatural. The witness is purely human. The witness is open to historical investigation. But its content lies beyond.

Although Kierkegaard was sometimes critical of Kant,[103] there is a sense in which he could be said to be following in the Kantian tradition. His thought coincided with the parameters laid down by Kant concerning what could be identified and known objectively in time and space. The transcendent could not be metamorphosed into the immanent in the manner of Hegel and the Absolute Idealists. But whereas Kant reduced religion to ethics based on self-evident moral principles, and dismissed as incoherent self-contradictions all attempts to make truth-claims about the transcendent, Kierkegaard maintained that it was the occurrence of the transcendent in history that was the essence of religion. Kierkegaard's religion began at the point where Kant's ceased.

To some it might seem that Kierkegaard's portrait of Jesus was that of a Nestorian Christ and a teacher without a subject-matter. Certainly he held the two natures of Christ apart, affirming the reality of both in the person of Jesus, while denying any communication of the attributes of one to another. Kierkegaard's view of Christ as a teacher was certainly shaped by his view of Socrates and the maieutic method. What the teacher says is not the real content of his message but the means of getting the learner to see for himself. In the very nature of the case the divine cannot be objectified. What the teacher does is to bring the learner to the point where he can see for himself. In a sense Kierkegaard's Christology was profoundly orthodox. Like the Council of Chalcedon, it did not resolve the problem. Rather, it restated it in a more acute form.

IV

THE LIFE OF JESUS
AND CRITICAL HISTORY

9. EARLY GOSPEL CRITICISM

Early Lives of Jesus

The attempt to rewrite the life of Jesus as a piece of history (which by implication would be compatible with modern, rational ideas) was a characteristic of nineteenth-century theology. But such an enterprise was not exactly new. Already in 1768–even before the *Fragments* controversy burst upon the public—Johann Jakob Hess published the first volume of his *Geschichte der drei letzten Lebensjahre Jesu*. Admittedly, the treatment was not so drastic as that of Reimarus, but Hess's work enjoyed a far greater longevity,[1] and the impulses toward a rational interpretation of Jesus were marked, though somewhat muted.

Hess was born in 1741 and died in 1828. He was a pillar of the church at Zürich throughout the French Revolution and the Napoleonic Wars. Hess called his life of Jesus a "paraphrasing history." The description was apt. Hess harmonized, modernized and explained everything to make it as credible as possible to the man of his day. Touches of local color were carefully added, but Hess took care not to stray far from the narrative. His approach is illustrated by his account of the confrontation between John the Baptist and the Pharisees, which is transposed into the language of minor officials of an eighteenth-century petty state. The Pharisees began,

> We are under order to question you in the name of our superiors: whom do you present yourself as? Since at this time the Messiah is expected, and the people appear not disinclined to regard you as the same, we would like all the more to explain yourself concerning your calling and your person.

To this the Baptist replied, "One could have inferred from my speeches that I am not the Messiah. Why do people get such big ideas about me?"[2]

Hess admitted the miraculous. If Jesus had been only a moral teacher, miracles would have been unnecessary. But he was the Son of God. Nevertheless, we must not prize them for their own sake, but look for their moral significance. Where it is possible to give a natural explanation, Hess did so. It was not demons but the sick Gadarenes themselves that caused the stampede by rushing among the pigs. Hess's work was neither profound nor critical. It was, in fact, preaching.

It endeavored to explain and popularize, but stopped short at explaining away. Hess did his best to accommodate the Gospel narratives to the idiom of his day without sacrificing the gospel itself. His success in popular, if not in critical, esteem may be judged by the fact that his work found a market for over half a century despite the number of competitors who followed in his footsteps.

Versuch über den Plan, welchen der Stifter der christlichen Religion zum Besten der Menschheit entwarf (1781),[3] by Franz Volkmar Reinhard (1753–1812), was also the work of an ecclesiastic who was prominent in his own day, but who is now largely forgotten. He taught philosophy and theology at Wittenberg, where he became provost of the castle church. He became chief court preacher at Dresden, and at the height of his powers he attracted congregations of three to four thousand. His published sermons filled fortythree volumes. It was to Reinhard that Fichte later dedicated the second edition of his *Versuch einer Kritik aller Offenbarung* (1793). Reinhard's work had the aim of presenting Jesus in a credible, attractive light. To this end, miracles were accepted in principle, but were virtually eliminated in practice. While the divinity of Christ was affirmed, the book contented itself with demonstrating that the founder of Christianity was an extraordinary divine teacher. Jesus was compared with the great men of the past with a view to showing how much more he benefited mankind than they.

Jesus embraced Judaism, but only in the intention of implementing a general beneficial change for mankind. He took over the Jewish language about the kingdom of God and the kingdom of heaven but invested them with quite a different meaning. His plan did not depend upon political power. He never based his claims upon Davidic descent (which was the reason why he held aloof from his family). Even the entry into Jerusalem had no messianic significance. Jesus' death was the consequence and confirmation of his plan for a moral, as opposed to a political, revolution. Jesus sought to effect his mission by tying together religion and the loftiest ethics. Jesus' religion was not only for the church but for the whole of humanity. It did not depend upon special revelations. It was self-evidently rational, moral and spiritual.

In his attempt to make Jesus credible and significant, Reinhard had already taken several steps beyond Hess in the direction of enlightened rationalism. Neither book was a work of scientific history. Both sought to make Jesus realistic to the contemporary mind, and both adopted the procedure of digging out of the Gospel narratives material which appealed to the authors themselves. Hess repainted the whole story in modern colors. Reinhard stressed the moral element in Jesus' life and teaching, which he presented as self-evident and valid. The appeal of his work was to the enlightened, moral sympathies of his public. However, it stopped well short of Kant's attempt to reduce religion to rational morality and depict Jesus simply as an enlightened teacher. It kept the framework of the biblical narratives essentially intact. But before the close of the century two fictitious lives of Jesus had been written which offered a thoroughly rationalistic explanation for everything and filled in any gaps by dint of free invention.

Like Reinhard, Carl Friedrich Bahrdt (1741–92) did not attempt to write a full-scale biography. His lengthy *Ausführung des Plans und Zwecks Jesu. In Briefen an Wahrheit suchende Leser* (11 vols., 1784–92) was more an exposure of Christian origins after the manner of Reimarus. It was planned as a sequel to his *Briefe über die Bibel im Volkston. Eine Wochenschrift von einem Prediger auf dem Lande* (1782). Throughout his chequered career Bahrdt had been the center of endless controversies.[4] His work combines the air of a disillusioned man who has seen through everything with a kind of masonic interpretation of life. It is a flamboyant mixture of skepticism and fantasy with a plot worthy of a first-century James Bond.

Albert Schweitzer has retold Bahrdt's reconstruction at some length.[5] It hardly merits repeating in any detail. The whole story was the result of an Essene plot to transform Jewish society. The plotters had a vast and secret organization in which Nicodemus and Joseph of Arimathea were the link men. In order to deliver the nation from its messianic, political hopes (which would only bring disaster) they looked for a messiah who would lead the people into more peaceful ways. The secret order is none other than the Essenes. As a boy Jesus attracted their attention. He discussed with them Plato and Socrates in dialogues a hundred pages long and already desired to emulate the latter's martyr death. In the market place at Nazareth a mysterious Persian gave him two remedies—one for eye-infections and the other for nervous disorders. Further medical knowledge was gained from Luke, the physician. A host of imaginary characters become involved in the narrative—Haram, Schimah, Avel, Limmah, and the like.

The miracles were easily disposed of. The five thousand were fed by secret supplies of bread. Jesus was really floating on a raft and not walking on the water. The *tour de force* was, of course, the resurrection. The crucifixion was rigged by Nicodemus. Luke had already given Jesus pain-killing drugs. As soon as Jesus was taken down from the cross Luke set about the task of resuscitation in the cave where Joseph of Arimathea had arranged to have him placed. Jesus duly appeared from time to time to convince people that he had risen from the dead. He then retired from public life, making only the rarest appearances (as to Paul on the Damascus road), but continued to direct operations until he died. His teaching fell into two categories: the simple and the obscure. The former was for general public consumption to communicate spiritual ideas to the people. The latter was for the initiates of the order. The sayings about spiritual rebirth concern admission to the highest degrees of the brotherhood.

The Essenes also played a prominent part in Venturini's *Natürliche Geschichte des grossen Propheten von Nazareth* (4 vols., 1800–1802). Indeed, Karl Heinrich Venturini (1768–1849)[6] seems to have been indebted to Bahrdt for many of his ideas.[7] Again the miraculous was explained away. Jesus never healed without medicaments and always carried with him his "travelling pharmacy." The resuscitations were really cases of coma. The miracle at Cana was explained by the suggestion that Jesus had brought some jars of good wine along as a wedding present. Old age and the fact that John himself may have had too much to drink led him to think that a miracle had actually occurred.

Although the details were different, Venturini attributed the course of Jesus' ministry to the Essene plot to direct the destinies of Israel. The Essenes planned a kind of spiritual *coup*, which misfired when Jesus began to talk about hard and perilous times to come. The people began to doubt, and Jesus was arrested and put to death. This was not rigged, as in Bahrdt's account. But Joseph of Arimathea had a vague premonition that prompted him to ask for Jesus' body. The brotherhood held a wake in the tomb, and Jesus revived. After forty days Jesus took his leave.

It was Schweitzer's opinion that all the fictitious "Lives" of the nineteenth century went back directly or indirectly to the type that Venturini created. Although practically unknown by name, it was almost a case of Venturini's work being reissued annually.[8] There is a certain amount of hyperbole in this suggestion. As Schweitzer's own account shows, the next thirty years saw a trickle but hardly a stream of biographies of Jesus. The stream (which soon reached full spate) began in 1835 with the first volume of Strauss's *Leben Jesu*. In the meantime, various Idealists had restated the role of Jesus within the framework of their philosophies, Schleiermacher had worked out his own distinctive approach to Christianity and the significance of Christ, and a couple of clergymen and a couple of professional theologians tried their hand.

The two clergymen followed the lines marked out by Reinhard. Ernst August Opitz published his *Geschichte und Charakterzüge Jesu* at Leipzig and Jena in 1812. Four years later the Superintendent at Waltershausen, Johann Adolph Jacobi published *Die Geschichte Jesu für denkende und gemütvolle Leser*. Opitz gave rather more weight to the miraculous, while Jacobi followed Reinhard in toning it down. He did not eliminate it altogether, and expressed mistrust in thoroughgoing rationalism whose explanations often seemed more wonderful than the miracles themselves. Nevertheless, his own position was that miracles did not belong to the accreditation of Jesus's teaching, but followed from his life. Although he had not denied the miraculous, Jacobi had parted company with the traditional approach that treated prophecy and miracles as proof of the divinity of Christ.

The works of the two professional scholars were more important, not least because of the weight of their authors' office. From 1811 to his death in 1851, H. E. G. Paulus (1761–1851) held a chair of theology at Heidelberg, where he was the leading representative of rationalism in theology. As a student at Tübingen he was influenced by the writings of Semler and Michaelis. In 1789 he was called to Jena, where he taught oriental languages and biblical exegesis. He was a friend of Goethe, Schiller and Wieland, and in his capacity as pro-rector of the university defended Fichte in the atheism controversy. At Jena he made a study of Kant and also edited Spinoza's *Opera* (1802), which included an account of his life. When the Jena circle began to break up, he moved to Würzburg, where he hoped to establish a Protestant center of learning. Instead he spent four years on school reform. Paulus wrote copiously on a wide range of subjects, including commentaries on the Old and New Testaments. His *Philologisch-kritischer Commentar über das Neue Testament* (1800, onwards) provided the basis for Greiling's *Das Leben Jesu von Nazareth. Ein religiöses Handbuch für Geist und Herz der Freunde Jesu unter den Gebildeten* (1813). Among his later works were his three-volume *Exegetisches Handbuch zu den drei ersten Evangelien* (1830–33). Paulus was a bitter anti-Semite. He also maintained a protracted quarrel with Schelling, whom he had known at Jena and Würzburg. When Schelling was called to Berlin, Paulus had his lectures taken down and proceeded to publish them under the title *Die endlich offenbar gewordene Philosophie der Offenbarung, der allgemeinen Prüfung vorgelegt durch Dr. H.E.G. Paulus* (1842). Schelling took Paulus to court. Paulus defended himself on the grounds that it was a public duty to unmask Schelling's attack on sound reason. Paulus was not only acquitted, but succeeded in bringing about Schelling's resignation.

Schleiermacher's lectures on the life of Jesus (1819–20, 1821, 1823, 1829–30) were the first on this subject by a German professor. Paulus's massive *Das Leben Jesu als Grundlage einer reinen Geschichte des Urchristentums* (2 vols., 1828)[9] inaugurated a new era in being the first work of its kind to be published by a leading professor of theology. It represented what Schweitzer called "fully developed rationalism."[10] But it was not the kind of rationalism which denied God altogether. Rather, it consistently sought to explain all phenomena in a rational way, while leaving God to be the ultimate cause of all. In so doing, it transferred the center of interest from the supernatural and divine to the natural and the human.

Paulus explained in his preface:

> *My greatest wish is that my views on the miraculous narratives should by no means be taken for the chief matter.* O, how empty would be devotion or religion, if the truth depended on whether one believed in miracles or not.[11]

> The great *aim of Jesus* and of all his people is this: Always to begin with calls to change the habitual sensuous outlook of men and through godlike improvement of the will of the individual bring about in reality also an external state of affairs, which a true divinity could approve, a reign of God or theocracy for man. This aim is the living germ, the essence of early Christianity....*The miraculous about Jesus is himself*, his pure and serenely holy disposition, but which nevertheless was a genuinely human example for human spirits to imitate and emulate.[12]

From time to time Paulus lapsed into poetry and the second volume closed with a verse which made it clear where the true significance of Jesus lay for him.

> Rejoice with godly devotion, if ye be granted
> To follow from afar after centuries
> His world-transforming course, so brief it was.
> Consider, believe and follow the Example's path.[13]

If Kant had written verse, he could hardly have summed up better the conception of a positive, practical religion, conceived within the limits of reason alone.

Paulus devoted little time to the critical investigation of sources. He did not believe that it was possible to write a complete, consecutive life of Jesus. The original traditions concentrated on his person.[14] The earliest reports relied on memory, and they reflect the impact of his "most God-worthy exemplary life." The Gospels related "more the effects than the causes." The Fourth Gospel was the work of the apostle John at the age of ninety. Matthew, which was the "first collection," came nearest to "the Jewish popular mind." Luke was also Jewish, but written by a foreigner influenced by Paul. Paulus believed that Mark was written at a later time when there was need of a shorter summary.

The main exposition discussed the Gospels synoptically, dividing them into separate episodes that were treated as substantially historical. On the other hand, the supernatural interpretations of certain events, whether supplied by the evangelists themselves or inferred by the readers of later ages, were invariably explained away. Jesus' miraculous cures resulted either from his spiritual power or from his skillful use of medicines known only to himself.

> In the most striking illnesses, which people were wont to attribute to the influence of evil, departed spirits in different human bodies, it is most readily apparent how much faith (or steadfastness), which for us is no longer a recognizable precondition for an evil spirit to yield bodily before a holy man, could bring about miraculous help, in cases where people began to recognize Jesus as the Messiah. Then the results themselves retroactively strengthened this faith. Whoever looks closely at the Gospels, soon notices that the majority of those graciously healed were of this class. In all other forms of illness, of which examples of healing by Jesus have been preserved, we are completely ignorant of where the means of healing came from. But the use of means is expressly indicated here and there. And even the complaint, that often there was not even time to eat on account of the throng of such patients, indicates to every alert observer, that the healing was not brought about merely through will and word. Equally clear is the complaint that thereby *work was done on the sabbath day.*[15]

Simple explanations of the nature miracles were ready to hand. Jesus was not walking on the waves but standing on the shore, his features and position being partially obscured by the mist.[16] The five thousand were fed by those with provisions who were shamed into following the example of Jesus and the disciples who shared their own food with those sitting nearest to them.[17] Paulus followed Bahrdt in explaining the resuscitations as the emergence from coma, preceded by a prematurely pessimistic diagnosis.[18] Paulus was in his element explaining the resurrection of Jesus.[19] Jesus' physical appearances after the event precluded the possibility of spiritual visions. In fact, he was on the cross for a relatively short time. Jesus was revived by the cool atmosphere of the tomb, the spices and the earthquake. Stripping off the grave clothes, he found the gardener's things, which explained the failure of Mary Magdalene to recognize him.[20] In the gathering darkness on the Emmaus road the disciples failed to recognize the once familiar face, now transfigured by suffering.[21] Jesus' resuscitation was not a fraud. The apostles came to regard it as fulfillment of the prophecy that God would loose him from the pangs of death.[22] The accounts of Jesus' physical presence were evidence that he was still alive.[23] Jesus remained with the disciples another forty days, but he was already considerably weakened by his ordeals.[24] When he felt that the end was drawing near, he called his disciples together for the last time, and after blessing them he went away into the mist[25] and departed this life. Shortly afterwards two Galilean disciples returned to the others with the news that Jesus was now in the state of eternal bliss.[26]

Paulus's work excited considerable controversy, but it was soon eclipsed by that of Strauss who maintained that Paulus's naturalistic explanations were far-fetched and superfluous in the light of his own mythical explanation.[27] While allowing that there must be room for some natural explanation, Schweitzer concluded that,

> The method is doomed to failure because the author only saves his own sincerity at the expense of that of his characters. He makes the disciples of Jesus see miracles where they could not possibly have seen them; and makes Jesus Himself allow miracles to be imagined where He must necessarily have protested against such a delusion. His exegesis, too, is sometimes violent. But in this, who has the right to judge him? If the theologians dragged him before the Lord, He would command, as of old, "Let him that is without sin among you cast the first stone at him," and Paulus would go forth unharmed.[28]

With the brief textbook on *Das Leben Jesu zunächst für akademische Vorlesungen* (1829) by Karl August von Hase (1800–90) we are brought back to a more restrained rationalism. Evidence of the demand for such a text is given by Hase's observation in the preface to his fourth edition (1853) that there was scarcely a Protestant university in Germany where lectures were not read upon the life of Jesus.[29] Hase himself further revised the work and republished it as *Geschichte Jesu. Nach akademischen Vorlesungen* (1876). By that time Hase had established himself as the leading church historian of the day. He had studied at Tübingen and been a Privatdozent at Leipzig before accepting a call to Jena, where he remained for the rest of his career. His *Lehrbuch der Kirchengeschichte* (1834) reached its twelfth edition in 1900. His account of church history has prompted the comment that it "dissolved the entire course of events into individual pictures which verged on the anecdotal; it is distinguished by picturesque language and represents the counter pole to exact philological and historical knowledge and use of sources."[30]

To some extent this criticism was true of his handling of the life of Jesus which consisted largely of reflections on a concatenation of self-contained episodes. It was prefaced by some brief comments on the Gospels as sources. Like Schleiermacher, Hase believed that it was John who gives a precise chronological record in the absence of chronology in the Synoptics.

> The first three Gospels, up to the last Passover, follow no chronological order which can be distinctly traced, though they intend to relate the events in a certain succession of time. (See Luke i.3.) But the fourth Gospel indicates the order of time by means of the journeys made to attend certain festivals. The first three Evangelists, until they come to the final Passover, contain only the life of Jesus in Galilee: John describes particularly what occurred at the festivals in Jerusalem. These chiefly give his miracles and his discourses bearing on the universal condition of man, — social, moral, and religious: John records his spiritual discourses, and what he says of his own relation to God. The Synoptics produce the impression of a period of joy and hope: John, from the first, has the dying Messiah in his view, as the climax of the long conflict between light and darkness. The Synoptics describe the Christ chiefly in relation to the Jewish nation: John speaks of him as the religious Saviour of the world. Finally, the Synoptics appear to give the events as they learned them, without much selection: John selects those events which will contribute to the idea he means to give of the Christ.[31]

Although Hase distinguished the Synoptic Gospels from John, he regarded them as complementary sources sharing a "common origin."[32] Drawing on the testimony of Papias in Eusebius's *Historia Ecclesiastica*, 3, 39, Hase argued that John the apostle must have been the author of the Gospel that bears his name until criticism proves otherwise. He drew on "the traditional Evangelical narrative, either in its oral form or as written down by the Synoptics." This tradition was supplemented by personal reminiscence. Hase concluded his observations on John with the reflection that,

> A constant feeling in the Church has regarded his view of the Master as more deep and interior than those of the others, yet his Gospel fluctuates between the popular conception of the Messiah and the most spiritual view. And, moreover, for the perfect understanding of Jesus, we also need those other accounts which bear the stamp of strong national actuality.[33]

From time to time Hase indicated where his views differed from those of other scholars. He noted, for example, the suggestions of Strauss and Woolston that the appearances of the risen Christ might have been visions.[34] But here, as elsewhere, the view was countered by drawing attention to its inherent improbability. As the work passed through its successive editions, it was altered to include response to Strauss. But, as he noted in the preface to the third edition, Hase contented himself with noting the points where Strauss was to be contradicted. He ventured to think that "the scientific study of the life of Jesus has really been promoted by the merciless criticism of Strauss, and that he has sharpened our eye to notice the points upon which pure historic criticism depends."[35]

With regard to the question of myth, Hase contended that "If the narrations of the Gospel are to be proved unhistorical, then they must be regarded either as fabulous reports or sacred myths."[36] He allowed that it was conceivable that Christian beliefs might be colored by Jewish expectations that could have produced sacred legends. He was even prepared to allow their presence in the Synoptic Gospels.

> But the fourth Gospel, so long as its genuineness cannot be disproved, will make the admission of such myths impossible, unless it can be proved, in any case, that John was not present, or except it can be made probable that his historic judgment has been disturbed by personal feelings, or feelings imbibed from the Church.[37]

Moreover, the established traditions, insofar as they constituted the foundations of the Synoptics, "took their place in the Church under the eyes of the Apostles and of eyewitnesses" and "are very different things from the poetic, popular legends which spring up accidentally from seed scattered carelessly and without a purpose."

> The fundamental traits of the character and the work of Jesus, which were opposed as well to Jewish expectations as to Apostolic prejudices, conclusively prove that this character was his own, and not imagined by the Church. . . . Nor is the mere resemblance of a New Testament event to one in the Old Testament in itself any evidence of the legend, for such resemblances might well have occurred of design, especially among a people so closely bound to its past. . . . But if a single legendary portion of the Gospels is discovered, the whole must be studied in reference to this element, with no narrow prejudice, and no fear mistaking itself for piety. But the credibility of the four Gospels having been established by external and general reasons, we are by no means bound to prove the truth in detail of each single matter of fact, for such a demand would overturn all history. The burden of proof rests upon criticism, to show, if it can, with respect to any single fact, that, notwithstanding this general credibility of the Gospels, there are internal reasons why it could not have happened.[38]

Hase's appeal was to an intrinsic rational cogency which he found in the Gospel stories as a whole. History was a matter of making sense of the documents in the light of general knowledge and inner rationality. After examining any given episode from various angles, Hase selected the most credible explanation and then pronounced on what was historical and what was unhistorical in the account. For example, in dealing with the Transfiguration Hase made concessions to the mythical interpretation and the earlier view of Bahrdt and Venturini that a secret society was implicated. Hase concluded that,

> According to the Evangelical narrative, it is a matter of fact that Jesus appeared to the Apostles in unwonted splendor in the company of two unknown persons. That they were Moses and Elias is a conclusion not sufficiently supported, considering the situation of the eyewitnesses; especially according to Luke. The command to be silent, and the abrupt conclusion, indicate some secret circumstances in the history. But this matter of fact, historically established, contains nothing remarkable as history, nor ideally important. This came in through the mode in which the Apostles conceived it; in which, unconsciously to themselves, the idea of a spiritualized Messiah, standing on a national basis, took form. Accordingly, the Synoptic narratives show the innocent birthplace of a myth resting on an historic foundation.[39]

Hase admitted natural explanations, but did not always insist upon them. Where possible, he coordinated the physical and the spiritual.

> Perhaps all cures are confined to the region where the power of will over the body exists; which is often noticed in single cases and in less degree. These cures, therefore, are not without analogies in all ages and times. (Compare Matt. vii.22, xxiv.24; Mark xiii.22; 2 Thes. ii.9; Acts xiii.12.) A resemblance is afforded us in animal magnetism only so far as it contains a mysterious power over disease, arising out of the great life of nature; and perhaps, moreover, the means which Jesus used may have stood in some relation to magnetic phenomena. But the miraculous power of Jesus appears far more like intelligent mastery of nature by the soul. The soul of man, originally endowed with dominion over the earth, recovered its old rights by the holy innocence of Jesus, conquering the unnatural power of disease and death. Here, therefore, there was no violation of the laws of nature, but, on the contrary, the disturbed order of the world here recovered its original harmony and truth. Even the wonderful power exercised over external nature may be reduced under the same law, and be understood according to the analogy of an accelerated process of nature.[40]

Hase clearly preferred natural explanations, if they did not do obvious violence to the text. He balked, however, at Venturini's suggestion that the change of water into wine at Cana was an illusion, F. C. Baur's view that it was poetic fiction, and the idea that the whole story was borrowed from the mysteries of Bacchus. He considered the supposition of "the water being animated into the apparent qualities of wine."[41] In the end, however, he conjectured that the story was not originally about a miracle, and that John had preserved it as a miracle story in the light of his later feelings and views. But he doubted whether the final truth would ever be known. Hase entertained similar conjectures about the feeding of the multitudes.[42]

Hase's endeavor to discover a rationale for the Gospels' account of Jesus reached its climax in his discussion of the resurrection. He shunned the explanations of Gfrörer and Paulus,[43] but conceded that "It is impossible to demonstrate absolutely the death of Jesus, since there is no certain criterion of death in any case except the commencement of decay, or the destruction of an organ essential to life."[44] He felt it right to accept the church's testimony that Jesus had died but qualified this by saying that "we can only say, according to a universally recognized truth (Acts ii.31, xiii.35 &c.), that the organic principle of the body is not released till the lower powers of decay commence their work. In the case of Jesus this decay of the body had not begun."[45] In saying this, Hase laid the foundation for his explanation of the resurrection.

> We might expect beforehand that the wonderful power of healing which was at the command of Jesus would have certainly powerfully manifested itself in his own person. We can scarcely venture to give an account of the first revival of his consciousness. Yet the thought immediately occurs that death, as violent dissolution of the body, could not originally belong to the nature of an immortal being, but first arose through sin; and therefore that He who was untouched by sin could not have

been subject to this element not natural to death. At all events, it is historically certain that Jesus himself did not, by any combinations, produce a merely apparent death, but seriously expected to die. And therefore his resurrection, in whatever way it occurred, is a manifest work of Providence. Christianity in its essence—that is, as a perfect religion, essentially true—does not depend on the resurrection. But Christianity in its existence does; for it was victoriously established, and the Church actually founded upon the grave of the risen Master.[46]

Being thus able to offer a rationale for the central tenets of the faith, Hase felt able to make concessions concerning more peripheral matters, especially where the Synoptic Gospels were concerned. He readily surrendered the "Legends of Infancy," which were "opposed to every rigorous historic conclusion."

Their form is Poetry, by Matthew treated in simple, popular style, —by Luke, in idyllic style, with lyrics imitated from the Old Testament; finally, the historic aspect seems only the unconscious symbol of religious ideas.[47]

The angels and the miracles attending the resurrection "seem to belong to early legendary additions to the Gospels."[48] Luke's account of the ascension of Jesus "is to be regarded as a mythical expression of his return to his Father."[49]

Even the non-miraculous side of the Gospel narratives was furnished with rationalistic explanations. Thus Hase felt obliged to comment on Jesus' celibacy.

It might, indeed, appear that Jesus, like the Baptist, preferred the unmarried state from ascetic reasons, borrowed from the Essenes. (Matt. xix.12.) But such a one-sided view is inconsistent with the pure, human majesty of life. If, therefore, the true reason does not lie concealed in some unknown events of his youth, we may allow a conjecture that he, from whose religion that ideal view of marriage unknown to antiquity has proceeded, found no soul living in his time equal to his own, and capable of such a bond.[50]

Like Paulus, Hase detected two types of speech in Jesus, though his explanation was different. Hase saw two phases in the ministry of Jesus prior to the passion. In the first phase Jesus employed the messianic language of his age. But when he saw where this was leading, he spoke increasingly in the language preserved in the Fourth Gospel that brought out the religious and spiritual character of his intentions.[51] The messianic, eschatological language of the Synoptic Gospels should be interpreted in this sense.

Albert Schweitzer credited Hase with creating "the modern historico-psychological picture of Jesus."[52] The present writer would not preclude Hase's predecessors from the credit of having initiated this enterprise. On the other hand, none of these early attempts to reconstruct the life of Jesus could be called scientific history. All these early attempts to get at the history behind the Gospel narratives were conscious of the problems of the supernatural and miraculous for modern man. Some were conscious of historical difficulties, like the difference between John and the Synoptics. Several with their references to "thoughtful readers" and the like in their subtitles hinted that the time had come when the intelligent modern man could no longer accept the Gospels at face value. What they endeavored to do was not to make a rigorous investigation of sources and criteria, but to suggest answers that might explain (and, in some cases, explain away) the contents of the Gospels. What Hirsch says of Paulus applies in differing degrees to them all: "He wanted scientific historical writing without criticism."[53] There was a dividing line between the rational and the supernatural that some might cross and others not. But for the most part, the acid test of an explanation was whether it was natural and rational. Consequently, the Essenes could be invoked to provide a motivating force, although little was actually known about them beyond their name. But therein lay their value. They at least belonged to the realm of the natural. With these early lives of Jesus we are in the province of rational history writing, but we are not yet in the domain of scientific history.

Early Source Criticism

In the early church the basic test of whether a Scripture was canonical was apostolicity. "Unless a book could be shown to come from the pen of an apostle, or at least to have the authority of an apostle behind it, it was peremptorily rejected, however edifying or popular with the faithful it might be."[54] While the broad outline of the canon was fixed by the end of the second century, opinions differed among the fathers as to how the Gospels came to be written. Clement of Alexandria stated that the Gospels with genealogies were written before those without.[55] Augustine held that they were written in the order that we have them in the Bible, that the later ones knew of the existence of the earlier ones, and that Mark was the epitomizer of Matthew.[56] Papias, on the other hand, believed that Mark was the interpreter of Peter, that his Gospel contained, although not in order, all that the latter recalled about Jesus, and that Matthew compiled the *logia* in the Hebrew language, but everyone interpreted them as he was able.[57] Although there were varied opinions in the early church, they did not constitute major conflicts. While non-canonical Gospels were argued over and finally rejected, it was assumed that the four canonical Gospels could readily be harmonized to produce an authentic, historical, and indeed inspired record of the words and works of Jesus.[58] This attitude continued down to post-Reformation times.[59]

In the half-century or so that followed the *Fragments* controversy, the most wildly contradictory theories about the composition and authorship of the Gospels were put forward. Lessing argued for a single, primitive Hebrew or Aramaic source. Herder rejected the idea of an *Urevangelium* in favor of oral tradition. Neither writer set much store by the historicity of the Fourth Gospel. Schleiermacher also rejected the *Urevangelium* theory in favor of oral tradition, but came down firmly for the priority and fundamental historicity of John as opposed to the Synoptics. F. C. Baur subsequently concluded that the tendencies of the Gospels indicated the priority of Matthew but placed it a century after the death of Jesus. These views inevitably affected their holders' estimate of Jesus. In the meantime, others adopted different positions. In this section we shall attempt to fill in the background and survey the views of scholars so far not discussed.

One of the first scholars to attempt a thoroughly historical approach to Scripture was Johann David Michaelis (1717–91), the son of the classicist and orientalist, C. B. Michaelis. After studying at Halle he visited England (1741–42), where Deistic influence alienated him from pietism. He moved to Göttingen in 1746, where from 1750 onward he was professor of oriental languages. He was one of the leading scholars of his day. In 1750 he published his *Einleitung in die göttlichen Schriften des Neuen Bundes.*[60] Originally the work was an elaboration of the critical, textual studies of the French Catholic scholar, Richard Simon. But by the time it reached its two-volume fourth edition of 1788, it had become a comprehensive presentation of the historical problems of the New Testament and its individual books. In doing this, it inaugurated the science of New Testament introduction.[61] Michaelis discussed questions of language, textual criticism and the origin of individual books. He laid down the principle that

> The question, whether the books of the New Testament are inspired, is not so important, as the question whether they are genuine. The truth of our religion depends upon the latter, not absolutely on the former. Had the Deity inspired not a single book of the New Testament, but left the Apostles, and Evangelists without any other aid, than that of natural abilities to commit what they knew to writing, admitting their works to be authentic, and possessed of a sufficient degree of credibility, the Christian religion would still remain the true one. The miracles, by which it is confirmed, would equally demonstrate its truth, even if the persons, who attested them were not inspired, but simply human witnesses; and their divine authority is never presupposed, when we discuss the question of miracles, but merely their credibility as human evidence.[62]

Indeed, Michaelis questioned whether Mark and Luke were inspired in the same way as Matthew and John.

> Beside those books of the New Testament, which we have shewn to be inspired as having been written by Apostles, there are three which were written by their assistants, viz. the Gospels of St. Mark and of St. Luke and the Acts of the Apostles. The question is, what are the grounds for placing these likewise in the canon?

> I must confess, that I am unable to find a satisfactory proof of their inspiration, and the more I investigate the subject, and the oftener I compare their writings with those of St. Matthew and St. John, the greater are my doubts.[63]

Michaelis devoted considerable time to discussing the question of inspiration and historicity, which had been made all the more acute by the Wolfenbüttel *Fragments.* He readily granted the presence of discrepancies in the Gospels, but insisted that this did not mean that the main substance of their accounts was false. The evangelists were on the whole good historians.[64] He also conceded that the text of Matthew may have been corrupted in the process of translation into Greek.[65]

Michaelis rejected the idea of literary dependence among the evangelists, tracing their shared characteristics to their common use of "several apocryphal Gospels," which were among the accounts mentioned in Luke 1:1.[66] Michaelis also detected an antignostic polemic in John, and speculated that John had taken over the Logos idea from the gnostics[67] and had written his Gospel to "confute the errors of Cerinthus" and "the errors of the Sabians, or the Sect which acknowledged John the Baptist for its Founder."[68] Michaelis was thus the first modern critic to relate the Fourth Gospel to the gnostic thought-world.[69]

Among the influential biblical scholars who came from Göttingen in the latter half of the eighteenth century was Johann Gottfried Eichhorn (1752–1827). Eichhorn studied under Michaelis and the classical philologist, C. G. Heyne. He became professor of oriental languages at Jena (1775) and professor of philosophy at Göttingen (1778). Eichhorn was a pioneer of Pentateuchal criticism. His numerous works include his *Einleitung ins Alte Testament* (3 vols., 1780–83), *Einleitung in die apokryphischen Bücher des Alten Testaments* (1795) and his *Einleitung in das Neue Testament* (5 vols., 1804–27). Eichhorn and his pupil, Johann Philipp Gabler, related Heyne's concept of myth to the Old Testament, and were thus instrumental in acclimatizing the public to the idea of myth in the Bible.[70] The first volume of Eichhorn's *Allgemeine Bibliothek der biblischen Literatur* (1787) contained a 137-page review of *Uebrige noch ungedruckte Werke des Wolfenbüttelschen Fragmentisten. Ein Nachlass von Gotthold Ephraim Lessing. Herausgegeben von* C. A. E. Schmidt. It acknowledged the Fragmentist's acuteness and learning, but regretted his lack of historical understanding.

Eichhorn developed the idea suggested earlier by LeClerc and backed by Michaelis that our evangelists made use of earlier sources no longer extant.[71] By the early nineties Eichhorn's lectures on the question were arousing considerable interest, and in 1793 the Göttingen faculty made the synoptic problem the subject of a competition.[72] Eichhorn published his own solution the following year in an article "Ueber die drey ersten Evangelien."[73] He posited several sources all going back to a single Aramaic Gospel which in its own turn had been subjected to revision. The details of his hypothesis were complicated. Matthew used edition A, and Luke edition B. A version made out of A and B, designated C, was the basis of Mark. A further revision, D, was used by Matthew and Luke where they agreed with one another but differ from Mark. There were further manuscript sources from which they also drew. Ten years later Eichhorn presented an even more refined and complicated version of his solution in the first volume of his *Einleitung in das Neue Testament.* But such complications were inevitable if the premises were accepted that the evangelists were not eyewitnesses, that they worked from written sources, but that these sources were not themselves identical with any of our present Gospels.

Eichhorn's work brought into focus two critical questions.[74] On the one hand, there was the problem of the original form of Jesus' words which Eichhorn tried to solve by positing an original Aramaic (or Hebrew) source. On the other hand, he realized that the agreements of Matthew and Luke posed a special problem which seemed to posit a common written source. This paved the way for the idea of Q. Moreover, Eichhorn realized that this was more than a merely academic question. It concerned the truth of Christianity and the validity of its ideas and traditions about Jesus.

> This discovery of the Primal Gospel is of great importance for the explanation of the words used by the evangelists and the proper understanding of their meaning, for the criticism of the New Testament in general and of the evangelists in particular, indeed, for all theology.

> To make a beginning with the uses that the last-mentioned [i.e., theology] derives from this theory: by this discovery we are directed to those parts of the life of Jesus which the first teachers of Christendom regarded as alone essential for the establishment of the Christian faith among their Jewish contemporaries. And this is one of the most important of the preliminary questions for the simplification of Christian dogma, and one on which German theology for forty years has worked so assiduously....

> The reconstruction of the Primal Gospel demonstrates that neither that which Matthew nor that which Luke reworked had anything to say of the conception, birth, and youth of Jesus; and it was only later times, from which we cannot expect any reliable information about these matters, that enlarged the Primal Gospel with them: And can they therefore be regarded as anything more than sagas which, to be sure, may have a basis in fact, but a basis which can no longer be distinguished from the embellishments with which tradition has clothed it?...By this freeing *of the Primal Gospel from its accretions* countless doubts with which Jesus, his life, and his teaching have been assailed become completely meaningless....By this separation of the apostolic from the nonapostolic which higher criticism—if only its gift be not spurned—recommends for the most important of reasons, the means are found to establish the credibility and truth of the gospel story on unshakable foundations.[75]

In the century and a half which have elapsed since Eichhorn's day it may be doubted whether higher criticism has ever achieved such a consensus of opinion that could assure the inner credibility and truth of Gospel history, which Eichhorn sought. But few outside the circles of fundamentalism would question the value of a historical approach to the Gospels.

In the meantime an alternative proposal to the question of Gospel relationships was developed by Johann Jakob Griesbach (1745–1812). Griesbach advocated the priority of Matthew and argued that Mark was a late composition which drew on both Matthew and Luke. The Griesbach hypothesis exercised profound influence on German scholarship in the first half of the nineteenth century. It was accepted by F. C. Baur and D. F. Strauss whose radical views may have contributed to the disfavor into which the theory fell.[76] Griesbach himself could hardly have anticipated the radical conclusions drawn by Baur and Strauss. He clearly did not adopt the tendency criticism of the former or the theory of myth of the latter.

Griesbach himself was a student of J. S. Semler at Halle. He actually lived with Semler both in his student days and after he returned from his extensive European tour, which he undertook in order to acquaint himself with the methods of different professors and to examine the New Testament manuscripts housed in the great libraries of London, Oxford, Cambridge, and other centers of learning. Griesbach was a scholar in the tradition of Semler, who encouraged him to research the textual criticism of the New Testament. On returning to Halle in 1771, he laid the foundations of his great editorial work. In 1775 he accepted a call to Jena, where he became a dominant figure in the university. Goethe was a frequent visitor to his home and Schiller actually resided with him. He was a friend and colleague for a time of H. E. G. Paulus, but by no means shared the latter's rationalism. In theology he took what August Tholuck called the "supernaturalistic line."[77] For Griesbach the basic affirmations of the New Testament concerning the incarnation, the miracles, redemption, and the resurrection of Jesus were given data concerning the gracious acts of God in Jesus Christ.[78] However, it was not his dogmatic work but his critical work that affected the course of theology.

Even before the *Fragments* controversy Griesbach had taken the first steps, if not to repudiate the value of Gospel harmonies, at least to put them on a more scientific basis. In 1774 he published the first volume of his critical text of the New Testament in the form of a synopsis, *Libri historici Novi Testamenti Graece. Pars prior, sistens synopsin Evangeliorum Matthaei, Marci et Lucae*. It was in fact the first synopsis. In 1776 Griesbach republished his work as a separate volume with the title *Synopsis Evangeliorum Matthaei, Marci et Lucae, Textum Graecum ad fidem codicum, versionum et patrum emendavit et lectionis varietatem adiecit Io. Iac. Griesbach, Prof. Publ. Halae*. The significance of Griesbach's work was far-reaching, even though the inferences which he himself drew were comparatively mild. The mere fact that he had produced a critical text to rival the Received Text was a signal of the impending overthrow of the latter.[79] In Griesbach's opinion it was impossible to produce a Gospel harmony without first making a precise study of the text on the basis of a synopsis. Even then it was impossible to fit every detail into a chronological pattern, for the Gospels themselves did not provide the necessary information. He observed in the preface to the second edition (1797),

> I frankly acknowledge and wish my readers to keep in mind that under no circumstances will one find a so-called "harmony" in this little book. Although I am quite aware of all the trouble learned men have taken to prepare a harmony in accordance with the rules they have laid down, I believe, nevertheless, that not just a little but almost no profit at all can be derived [from their harmonies] that my synopsis —despite its inexactitude —does not offer. Furthermore, I doubt very much whether a harmonistic account can be composed from the books of the evangelists that with respect to chronological sequence agrees sufficiently with reality and is built on sure foundations. How could that be done? When none of the evangelists anywhere exactly follows the temporal sequence? And when there does not exist sufficient evidence from which to deduce who deviates from the chronological order and at what point he does so? And to this heresy I confess.[80]

Griesbach clearly did not invent the synoptic problem. However, Griesbach's separation of the first three Gospels from the fourth gave rise to the classification of the former as the Synoptic Gospels,[81] which in turn accentuated the questions of literary relationships and historicity. Among the early scholars who addressed themselves to the problem was the Göttingen professor, J. B. Koppe, whose *Marcus non Epitomator Matthaei* (1782) argued that the canonical evangelists made use of earlier sources such as those mentioned by Luke in his preface.[82] He claimed that Mark sometimes deviated from Matthew in a way in which no epitomizer would, and that when he did so he consistently agreed with Luke. He believed that none of the evangelists copied from the work of another. In 1786 Christian Gottlob Storr published his treatise *Ueber den Zweck der evangelischen Geschichte und der Briefe Johannis*. Storr was the leader of the old, conservative Tübingen School. He connected Mark with the testimony of Peter and held it to be the earliest of the extant Gospels. He believed that it was written in the period described in Acts 11:17–30, and that it was used by Luke and later by Matthew. Storr did not argue in detail the case for literary dependence of Luke and Matthew on Mark. He maintained that it was difficult, if not impossible, to account for Mark's omissions if Mark had used either of the other Gospels. However, this objection was not deemed to be insuperable by Griesbach.

Griesbach had already given a preliminary outline of his solution in an investigation of the resurrection narratives presented for the celebration of Easter *Paschatos Solemnia pie celebranda civibus indicit Academia Jenensis. Inquiritur in fontes, unde Evangelistae suas de resurrectione Domini narrationes hauserint* (1783). But his full exposition appeared some years later in his *Commentatio qua Marci Evangelium totum e Matthaei et Lucae commentariis decerptum esse monstratur* (Jena, 1789, 1790).[83] In essence it had been anticipated by Henry Owen in England and Anton Friedrich Büsching in Germany, but Griesbach made no mention of their names.[84] After briefly reviewing the theories of Lardner, Koppe, Storr and Eichhorn, Griesbach stated his thesis:

> That Mark when writing his book had in front of his eyes not only Matthew but Luke as well, and that he extracted from them whatever he committed to writing of the deeds, speeches and sayings of the Saviour.[85]

Griesbach proceeded to define this thesis more precisely by fifteen propositions which may be summarized as follows:[86] (1) Mark generally followed Matthew. (2) But occasionally he preferred Luke. (3) Where he stuck closely to Matthew, he did not lose sight of Luke, and vice versa. (4) He sought brevity. (5) This goal led him to omit things that did not pertain to Jesus' public office as a Teacher. (6) He passed over the longer sermons contained in both Matthew and Luke, thus omitting an entire third of Luke. (7) He wrote for non-Jewish readers, for whom the rules and regulations of Palestinian Jews and especially the Pharisees were hardly known. (8) For this reason he cut out of Matthew and Luke things concerning Jews alone or related to their way of thinking. (9) He was more sparing in his quotation of Old Testament texts. (10) But he added for the sake of illustration things that he thought useful. (11) He often preserved the same formulas, phrases, and constructions. (12) But Mark did not copy their books word for word, for he told in his own way what he read in them. (13) Mark frequently paraphrased and said in his own words more briefly and distinctly what was handed down to him. (14) He added to that material details which he thought would be of interest to his readers. (15) He also added a few, brief stories of his own, for reasons that the reader could readily discern.

Griesbach supported his argument by making three major observations. He noted first that, apart from twenty-four verses, all Mark's material could be found in either Matthew or Luke, and that various reasons could be discerned to explain his alternate use of his sources. He always returned to the place where he left off and followed the order of his sources. Secondly, Griesbach observed that almost the whole of Mark is contained in Matthew and Luke. He suggested that Mark was the son of a woman whose house was used by the Jerusalem church. He would have had contact with Peter and Paul and also opportunity to collect additional material. However, his restrained use of that material was dictated by the needs of his readers. Griesbach's third observation concerned the alternating agreement with Matthew and Luke. Although Mark leaps suddenly from one to the other, he soon returns to his former guide. But this would not be possible if Mark did not have before him the two other Gospels as sources. Finally, Griesbach addressed a number of anticipated objections.[88] He dismissed the testimony of Papias as untenable. It was inconceivable that the apostle, Matthew, should choose as his guide for handing on the story of Christ a writer who had not been present at the events themselves. Griesbach conjectured that Mark's Gospel had survived intact except for the lost verses of the final chapter, the ending for which had been supplied by another hand. He repudiated the attempts to produce a harmony on the grounds that none of the evangelists were interested in strict chronology. He concluded with the following observations whose shafts were directed both at the orthodox and the followers of Lessing.

> Mark understood the purpose and use of the Gospels quite differently from most theologians of later times. And if he had intended to illustrate Matthew by an accurate commentary, he would indeed have produced one quite unlike any of the customary commentaries. Undoubtedly such a work would have pleased the followers of Lessing and those who, by their study of *belles lettres*, have sharpened and polished their natural disposition and have learnt by long practice the right method of dealing with ancient literature; but it would not have pleased the authors of harmonies and tiresomely industrious commentators.

> Those who argue that Mark wrote under the influence of divine inspiration must surely regard it as being a pretty meagre one![89]

The Griesbach hypothesis found widespread acceptance in the first half of the nineteenth century, where it was sometimes linked with considerable skepticism concerning the historical value of Mark. It was adopted by H. E. G. Paulus in his influential *Philologisch-kritischer Commentar über das Neue Testament* and numerous others including K. G. W. Theile, *De trium evangeliorum priorum necessitate* (1825), Heinrich Saunier, *Über die Quelle des Evangeliums des Marcus. Ein Beitrag zu den Untersuchungen über die Entstehung unsrer kanonischen Evangelien* (1825), Karl August Fritzsche, *Matthaeus recensuit et cum commentariis perpetuis* (1826) and *Marcus recensuit et cum commentariis perpetuis* (1830), Heinrich August Schott, *Isagoge hist. crit. in libros novi foederis sacros* (1830).[90] Schleiermacher agreed that Griesbach was correct in placing Mark as the latest of the Gospels.[91] But, as we have already seen, Schleiermacher placed great emphasis on oral tradition behind the Synoptics and favored John as the only Gospel which provided firm biographical information. Friedrich Ludwig Sieffert pressed the point still further in *Über den Ursprung des ersten kanonischen Evangeliums. Ein kritisch Abhandlung* (1832). Sieffert argued that Matthew was written after the eyewitness period, and thus none of the Synoptic Gospels could be eyewitness accounts. In their different ways, both D. F. Strauss and F. C. Baur combined the Griesbach hypothesis with their particular radical views, which led them to profound skepticism about the historical value of Mark as the last of the Synoptic Gospels. Their views will be examined in the next two chapters.

In the meantime the Griesbach hypothesis was espoused by W. M. L. de Wette and Friedrich Bleek who were both more moderate critics. Wilhelm Martin Leberecht de Wette (1780–1849) was a pupil of Herder at the *Gymnasium* at Weimar, where he also heard his sermons. He was a pupil of Griesbach and Gabler at the University of Jena, where he became a Privatdozent in 1805. De Wette moved to Heidelberg in 1807 and to Berlin in 1810, where he helped to establish the new faculty there. He was, however, dismissed on account of a letter he wrote to the mother of the murderer of Kotzebue, and, after teaching privately for three years in Weimar, moved to Basel in 1822. De Wette used Griesbach's theory in his *Einleitung in das Neue Testament* (1826, 6th ed. 1860).[92] It was also adopted by Friedrich Bleek (1793–1859), who was a student of de Wette, Neander and Schleiermacher at Berlin. Bleek taught at Berlin between 1820 and 1829. His later career was spent at Bonn. His *Einleitung in das Neue Testament* (1862) was published posthumously by his son Johannes Friedrich Bleek.[93]

De Wette and Bleek argued that Mark was dependent upon Matthew and Luke, but they were in turn dependent upon an *Urevangelium* which provided a reliable link with earlier eyewitness tradition. This *Urevangelium* was not, however, an *Ur-Markus*, since both scholars reconstructed it from the material common to Matthew and Luke, arguing that neither evangelist knew the other.[94]

W. R. Farmer sees the critical significance of de Wette and Bleek less in the value of their conclusions than in the precedent that they set.

> Holtzmann depended heavily upon their work. We may say that their crucial importance for subsequent developments was their unique combination of Lessing's Ur-gospel hypothesis with that of Griesbach. This new creation did not endure, but it

facilitated the new synthesis which was to be achieved by Holtzmann. It represents a transitional stage in the thinking of critics. Whereas, formerly, critics were divided as to whether the phenomenon of literary dependence called for direct access of one Evangelist to the work of another, or whether this phenomenon could be satisfied by the notion that they independently copied an earlier Gospel; now one and the same critic could combine both ideas in a single hypothesis.[95]

To Farmer this was a retrograde step, for it meant that scholars were soon to lose sight of the Gospels as literary wholes. The distinctive intentions of each evangelist began to be obscured among the vague talk about "Synoptic-tradition," though this was not true of either de Wette or Bleek. Nevertheless, it signaled the beginning of a trend "which can only be described as eclectic. In accordance with this eclecticism, incommensurate elements of originally divergent wholes are combined."[96]

De Wette was not only a biblical critic. Next to Baur he has been regarded as the leading historian of dogma of his day.[97] He was the author of a *Biblische Dogmatik Alten und Neuen Testaments*, which formed the first volume of his *Lehrbuch der christlichen Dogmatik, in ihrer historischen Entwicklung dargestellt* and which he dedicated to Schleiermacher.[98] The work in fact antedated Schleiermacher's own *Der christliche Glaube*, but it shared certain common positions both with Schleiermacher and the Kantian, J. J. Fries.[99] He could say with Fries that the *Verstand* (or *Reflexion*) plays its part in supplying the categories of understanding and in critical reflection.[100] But it was feeling *(Gefühl)* that was the locus of religion. "Only in feeling, according to the law of presentiment, that the eternal comes to manifestation in the temporal, can we subordinate things under religious ideas."[101] Citing the support of Schleiermacher's *Reden* and Fries's *Kritik*, de Wette concluded,

> The religious world view presents itself immediately to man, when he apprehends the beauty and majesty of nature and life with pious feeling, so that the world becomes for him a mirror of the revelations of God and the higher world-order (Rom. 1:20).[102]

De Wette understood the task of his "biblical dogmatics" in the following terms:

> To conceive the religious elements that appear in the Old and New Testament, insofar as they appear in dogmas, in their particular relationship to *religious conviction* and pure *faith*, divested from the veiling that is partly alien to them; and insofar as they appear in symbols and myths, also to determine what belongs therein to conviction and faith; finally to relate all this, together with what appears in purely aesthetic form to the religious *temper of feeling*.[103]

The recovery of authentic Christian faith was like stripping numerous coats of varnish from an old painting. De Wette's analysis was not dissimilar to Baur's. Though the details might vary considerably and though de Wette was much more conservative than Baur, it could be said that his general outlook anticipated Baur by two decades.

> In view of their different conception and treatment of Christianity the New Testament books may be divided into the following two classes: I. *Jewish-Christian*, to which belong the first three Gospels, Acts in part, the Letters of Peter, James, Jude and the Apocalypse. Their character is intimate connection of Christianity with Jewish christology, hence chiliastic ideas, proof of the worth of Jesus from miracles and the like. In Luke and particularly in 1 Peter Pauline elements are evident. II. *Hellenistic*, in which a freer, purer spirit prevails, but among which further divisions must be made: 1. the Alexandrian *Letter to the Hebrews* with its allegorization; 2. the Johannine writings with the Alexandrian philosophical system of the Logos and the ideal-mystical view of Christ; 3. the *Pauline Letters*, to which Acts are partly related, with the ideal-rational view of Christ and the doctrine of faith and Christian freedom.[104]

This analysis led de Wette to insist on drawing a sharp distinction between Jewish, Alexandrian, and Pauline Christianity. He also insisted that we must "distinguish the teaching of Jesus from the conception of it in the apostles and the evangelists" and went on to note a lengthy list of recent works relevant to this task.[105]

De Wette also anticipated D. F. Strauss in claiming that certain aspects of New Testament teaching were mythological, insofar as they read into it alien ideas. He urged that a distinction be drawn between myth, symbol, and dogma, and their conscious and unconscious use, and proposed rules to that end.[106] (1) "Dogma is a matter of the understanding, symbol of feeling, and myth of the imagination; the first expresses itself in the concept, the second in the aesthetic picture, the third for preference in history." Whereas the first was the object of faith and the second of pious awe, the third was originally neither of these but the product of poetry. (2) Every religion should be seen as a whole and its spirit discerned out of its component parts, which include purely spiritual ideas and pictorial images. (3) If the form of a doctrine is alien, accommodation may be assumed as in the case of demonology and messianic ideas in Christianity. (4) If form and content stand in gross conflict, the conjecture may be allowed that the former is pictorial.

Nevertheless, de Wette stopped well short of Strauss's mythical interpretation of the Gospels. Although myth was an expression of the religious life, it applied more to the Old Testament than the New. In any case, the symbolic was not necessarily a synonym for unhistorical. Moreover, comparison of the first and second editions of his work suggests that he toned down some of his observations in the second edition. In the first edition de Wette roundly declared that "We cannot prove from what Jesus said that he taught a doctrine of the atonement. Jesus' death was credited with this very important significance first by the apostles."[107] In the second edition he noted the application of Isaiah 53 to Jesus' death and the concept of covenant sacrifice in Exodus 24. He added that out of such considerations "developed the apostolic doctrine of reconciliation and justification."[108] In the first edition de Wette observed that

> The genuine Christian independence was lost in part by the apostles, due to the fact that, although filled with the Spirit, they could not free themselves entirely from faith in authority. The principle of their religion is consequently revelation faith and Christolatry. To be sure, to the extent that they freely took over and developed Jesus' teaching, their independence had still some elbowroom, but for later Christians this became increasingly restricted. One unhappy consequence of this religious attitude even as early as the times of the apostles was the dogmatic and mythological treatment of religion.[109]

In the second edition de Wette observed that the apostles did not originally possess the divine revelation in Christ but received "the religious life" in a mediated form.

> And since they too could attain the freedom and purity of spirit that was in Jesus only gradually, and were obliged to be mingled more or less with the earthly, human spirit, it could not be otherwise that the copy remained more or less removed from the original. Their genuinely religious *faith in revelation and Christ* is thus mingled with faith in authority, and ideas of the senses and the understanding *(Dogmatism)* are applied to the genuinely ideal vision. Less with them than with their disciples did *mythology* also find entrance.[110]

W. G. Kümmel makes the observation that de Wette was the first to distinguish the proclamation of Jesus from apostolic teaching and to differentiate various subgroups within the latter.[111] De Wette's discussion of myth was largely confined to the identification of mythical elements alongside non-mythical ones. The mythical element consisted in such beliefs as the Virgin Birth[112] and redemption conceived in terms of rescue from the power of Satan.[113] Although he did not place angels in quite the same category, de Wette indicated that there was much in the language of the Gospels concerning them that was allegorical and parabolical and that Jesus' pronouncements about them had no dogmatic significance.[114] But when such elements were removed, the picture that de Wette presented was more akin to that of Schleiermacher than that of Strauss. Jesus fulfilled his redemptive work as he proclaimed "the word of truth," summoned men to a higher life, and through his self-sacrificial death freed men from the power of sensuality by reuniting them with God.[115] Like Schleiermacher, de Wette drew a distinction between the ecclesiastical doctrine of the Trinity and the teaching of Jesus "which was not only speculative, but conceived in faith and feeling."[116] In describing the revelation of God in Christ, de Wette's thought moved in the same direction as Schleiermacher's, and likewise drew heavily on the Fourth Gospel.

> He is *God's Son* (John 3:16; 10:36), is one with the Father (John 8:19; 10:30); the Father *loves* him (John 5:20), because he does his will (John 7:29) and is without sin and error (John 7:18; 8:46).[117]

He concluded his summary of the teaching of Jesus with an appendix of its "Significance for feeling" in which he again cited with approval Schleiermacher's *Reden* and declared that

> The history of Jesus is not only a moral mirror for the Christian but also symbol and example for pious feeling in contemplation as well as in art and poetry.[118]

K. R. Hagenbach, who in 1850 published an *Akademische Gedächtnisrede* for de Wette, applied to him the description, "In understanding a rationalist, in temperament a mystic or pietist." More recently Karl Barth has suggested that what Bultmann was to Heidegger, de Wette was to Fries.[119] But just as Bultmann was no mere theological interpreter of Heidegger, de Wette was no mere theological interpreter of a philosophical system. He acknowledged his debt to Schleiermacher and also anticipated, at least in print, some of the ideas which came to be regarded as characteristic of Schleiermacher. He was not so radical as either Strauss or Baur, but in some respects anticipated their ideas. If he was overshadowed by Schleiermacher and regarded eventually as a figure of second rank in the theological world, one factor might have been his comparative moderation. Another factor might have been his premature removal from the German university scene and his move to Basel, where he continued to write, teach, and enjoy great prestige in the city and university but where he was no longer in the main stream of German academic theology.

10. STRAUSS AND THE QUESTION OF MYTH

David Friedrich Strauss (1808–74)[1] was born and died at Ludwigsburg in Swabia. Most of his life was spend in south-west Germany. His modest, middle-class family circumstances permitted him to be sent to school at Blaubeuren, where F. C. Baur was one of his tutors. After four years there he gained admission to the Tübinger Stift (1825). The following year the faculty at Tübingen was reconstituted, and Baur (who was then thirty-four) and another tutor at Blaubeuren, F. H. Kern, were made full professors. The curriculum prescribed two years of philosophy, philology, and history to be followed by three more devoted to theology. The tuition in philosophy proved uninspiring, and Strauss and his friends fell back on their own devices. They turned to the nature philosophy of Schelling and the romantic poetry of Novalis and Tieck. Nor did the theology of the old Tübingen school hold much attraction for Strauss. He endured the lectures of J. C. F. Steudel, the senior member of the faculty and a devout supernaturalist, for four weeks and then gave up.[2] The most impressive of his teachers was Baur, who was still feeling his way towards his later characteristic teaching. At the time both Strauss and Baur were impressed by two men who were then at Berlin and at the height of their powers, Schleiermacher and Hegel. Neither Strauss nor Baur were to be mere imitators of either, and in later life they criticized Schleiermacher for his unhistorical attitude. But for the time being they were impressed by his approach to religion.

In the Fall of 1830 Strauss concluded his studies with a brilliant examination. His first post as Vikar to a country pastor at Klein Ingersheim, near Ludwigsburg, gave him leisure for further study. He was already wrestling with the question posed by parishioners as to what to believe about the devil and the "fantastic" miracles of the New Testament.[3] He partially resolved it on Hegelian lines, drawing a distinction between the philosophical concept *(Begriff)* and the theological representation *(Vorstellung)* containing the popular, erroneous form of belief. But this distinction did not answer the question of what to say to the congregation. At this time Strauss favored moving slowly and educating the people gradually to the new scientific ideas.

During this period Strauss resolved to apply for a doctorate. For a student who had passed his examinations with such high grades it was necessary only to submit a relatively brief dissertation. To this end Strauss proposed to submit a prize essay on the resurrection of the dead, which he had previously submitted anonymously to the Catholic Faculty in 1828. Strauss had been a joint-winner but had not received the prize when it was learned that he was a Protestant. He now asked the Catholic faculty to return the essay, but the work could not be found. Whereupon he submitted a brief essay of some twenty-eight pages, composed during his curacy, on the universal restoration of all things in the light of the history of religious development. It drew on Schleiermacher, Baur, Hegel, and other modern thinkers. It ranged widely from Yoga and Origen to Spinoza. The work was long thought to be lost. However, it was discovered during the Second World War and has been published together with a critical discussion by Gotthold Müller in his study *Identität und Immanenz*.[4] The work hardly foreshadows Strauss's later critique of Christian origins. Nevertheless, it prompted Müller's comment that

> Strauss never became or was at all a *theologian* in the full sense of the word, but only attempted to apply his *philosophical* presuppositions to theological questions, an undertaking that could produce no positive result, since thereby essential differences between the two fields were not seen and observed.[5]

Even before the dissertation was approved, Strauss was on his way to Berlin for further study with Hegel. He arrived in November, 1831, and met Hegel briefly and heard two lectures from him. The eminent philosopher was delighted to find so keen a student of his ideas. But on November 15, during his first visit to Schleiermacher, the latter informed him that Hegel had died the previous day of cholera. Strauss's spontaneous response, "But it was for his sake that I came here," was taken as a personal slight by Schleiermacher, and the two were never on cordial terms thereafter. Strauss contemplated leaving Berlin, but stayed on and became acquainted with other members of the Hegelian school.[6] He also attended Schleiermacher's sermons and lectures.

Although Schleiermacher was not lecturing at the time on the life of Jesus, Strauss obtained the notes previously taken by two students, from which he made his own draft. He determined to give his own lectures on the subject on returning to Tübingen. In a lengthy letter to Christian Märklin dated February 6, 1832,[7] Strauss outlined his views, expressing dissatisfaction with the view that the Gospels were eyewitness accounts, the "supernaturalism" of Schleiermacher, and the "vulgar rationalism" of Paulus. He already spoke of the "mythical element in the history of Jesus," and expressed his confidence that he could "as soon as something is destroyed critically—also in the individual details—immediately restore it dogmatically, whereby the whole would lose much of its hardness and offensiveness." This restoration was to be achieved by an interpretation on Hegelian lines that saw in the life of Jesus "the consciousness which the church has of the human spirit objectified as divine spirit." In his interpretation of the death and resurrection of Jesus, "the Spirit attains the true positivity, the divine life—indeed the sitting at God's right hand—only through the negation of its negation, which is naturalness."

Schleiermacher announced that he would again lecture on the life of Jesus in the summer term. But Strauss had already had enough of Schleiermacher. He acknowledged to Vatke that Schleiermacher had "greatly stimulated" him, but that he only went "half way." He was determined to return to Tübingen, where he would write his own life of Jesus according to his own ideas.[8] In the Spring of 1832 Strauss returned to Tübingen as a Repetent or junior tutor. The following year he wrote to Gustav Binder,

> In my theology, philosophy so completely dominates that my theological view can only be developed by thoroughly working through philosophy, and I will now pursue this course undisturbed, regardless of whether it will lead me back to theology or not. . . . When I examine myself closely, my attitude to theology is this: what interests me in theology is offensive, and what is not offensive does not matter to me. For this reason I have given up reading theological lectures.[9]

The background to this situation was the right which the Repetent at Tübingen enjoyed to lecture on philosophy. Strauss took the opportunity to teach Hegel as well as Plato to the joy of the students (among them Strauss's biographer and Baur's future son-in-law, Eduard Zeller) and the chagrin of the philosophy faculty, which eventually had the lectures stopped.

Further impetus to write a life of Jesus was provided by the rejection by the Hegelian *Journal für wissenschaftliche Kritik* of a review that Strauss had written of Hase's *Leben Jesu*. Strauss's own work was completed by October, 1834, but the Tübingen publisher, C. F. Osiander, was busy with F. C. Baur's work on *Gnosis*, and the first volume of Strauss's *Leben Jesu kritisch bearbeitet* did not appear until 1835. The second volume was actually ready by the end of 1835, although it bore the date 1836. The work plunged Strauss into the center of controversy and effectively destroyed his academic prospects.

Steudel secured Strauss's removal from the Stift. He was transferred to a teaching post at Ludwigsburg, but was glad to resign within a year and move to Stuttgart. Here he lived for several years replying to his critics in various *Streitschriften*[10] and preparing fresh editions of the now infamous life. The third edition of 1838–39 did, in fact, make a number of concessions. It expressed hesitations about former doubts after further study of the Fourth Gospel, de Wette's commentary and Neander's *Leben Jesu-Christi* (1837). But this "compliance" was swept away in the next edition (1840), where the author declared himself resolved to whet "my good sword, to free it from the notches made in it rather by my own grinding than by the blows of my enemies."[11] He also turned his attention to writing *Vergängliches und Bleibendes im Christentum* (1839), which reappeared the following year under the irenic title of *Friedliche Blätter*. For a brief period it seemed as if a rehabilitation might be effected, and Strauss was offered the chair of dogmatics at Zürich. But the opposition compelled the authorities to withdraw the offer, and Strauss was pensioned off.

Die christliche Glaubenslehre in ihrer geschichtlichen Entwicklung und in ihrem Kampfe mit der modernen Wissenschaft was published at Tübingen and Stuttgart in two volumes in 1840–41. Originally it had been planned as a sequel to *Das Leben Jesu*. Though always overshadowed by it, it was no less radical than its predecessor. It insisted that the teaching of the Bible cannot be harmonized with rationalism and modern speculative theology. In its place Strauss proposed a pantheistic, Platonic-Hegelian solution that would allow the historical and critical study of dogmas, but treat their particular expression as merely transitory, outer form. For the next twenty years Strauss turned his back upon theology and devoted his literary labors to other themes. His success in politics was modest, and his marriage broke down.

Strauss's study of *Hermann Samuel Reimarus* (1862) paved the way for a return to theology. A second life of Jesus intended for a wider public—*Das Leben Jesu für das deutsche Volk bearbeitet*—appeared in 1864.[12] It was followed by his remorseless critique of Schleiermacher's recently published lectures on the life of Jesus, *Der Christus des Glaubens und der Jesus der Geschichte. Eine Kritik des Schleiermacherschen Lebens Jesu* (1865).[13] He belabored "Vermittlungstheologie" and orthodoxy in *Die Halben und die Ganzen. Eine Streitschrift gegen die HH. DD. Schenkel und Hengstenberg* (1865). In 1870 he published his lectures on *Voltaire*. His last book was devoted to a reappraisal of the post-Darwinian theological situation, *Der alte und der neue Glaube. Ein Bekenntniss* (1872).[14] Although the work went through sixteen editions by 1904, there were many, both among the theologians and the skeptics, who declared the author to be bankrupt of ideas. Before he died, Strauss found himself the victim of the young Nietzsche's withering sarcasm, which was poured out in the latter's

Unzeitgemässe Betrachtungen: I, David Friedrich Strauss, der Bekenner und Schriftsteller (1873). Strauss was also a minor poet. Shortly before he died he wrote the following verse, which expresses the pathos of his resignation.

> Feeble still, and waning,
>   Yet bright, and pure, and wise,
> Be this expiring glimmer,
>   This echo as it dies.[15]

He was buried without Christian ceremony.

Das Leben Jesu kritisch bearbeitet

The bulk of Strauss's 1,480 pages was devoted to a detailed examination of the events of the Gospels, episode by episode. But the exposition was prefaced by a seventy-six-page introduction on the "Development of the Mythical Point of View in Relation to Gospel Histories." It performed the double function of surveying the inadequate approach of his predecessors and of explaining the methodology about to be applied.

Strauss devoted little time to the question of literary sources. It sufficed to observe that it had been "clearly demonstrated by Griesbach" that

> our second Gospel cannot have originated from recollections of Peter's instructions, i.e., from a source peculiar to itself, since it is evidently a compilation, whether made from memory or otherwise, from the first and third Gospels.[16]

It was only in his second life of Jesus, published in 1864, that Strauss felt the need to amplify his position with supporting arguments.[17] He did this partly in response to F. C. Baur's criticism that Strauss's work wanted to give "a critique of Gospel history without any critique of the Gospels."[18] In his first *Life of Jesus* Strauss showed little interest in literary criticism. The Griesbach hypothesis served him well at a point at which his own construction was vulnerable. For if credence could be given to Papias's testimony that Mark was Peter's interpreter and that he had written down Peter's recollections of Jesus' discourses and actions,[19] Strauss's own theory of inventive myth-making would have been undermined. Strauss's interest lay, not so much in literary sources, as in denying the value of external testimony. With regard to Strauss's actual treatment of the Gospel material, C. M. Tuckett has pertinently observed that, "In contrast to Baur, whose *Tendenzkritik* foreshadows modern redaction criticism, Strauss's work was more the precursor of modern form-criticism, with its main interest in the *pre*-literary development of the tradition."[20]

If Strauss may be said to have anticipated form-criticism, he also pioneered a history-of-religions approach to Gospel interpretation. The main thrust of this book was to interpret the Gospels in the context of what Strauss conceived to be the process of myth-making in general and of religion in particular, with a view to showing that the Gospels were shaped by this general development. As Peter C.

Hodgson has shown, there were two aspects to Strauss's method, a negative and a positive.[21] Negatively it consisted in the rejection of the *prima facie* supernaturalism of the Gospels themselves and all attempts to provide rational explanations of the supernatural. Positively it consisted of the mythical interpretation of Christian origins against the wider background of Strauss's view of myth. Both aspects received fuller elaboration in the second and third editions of the book when Strauss added new sections, No. 15 ("Definition of the Evangelical Mythus and its Distinctive Characteristics") and No. 16 ("Criteria by which to Distinguish the Unhistorical in the Gospel Narrative").

Without the negative the positive would have lacked cogency, for myth could only be conceived as myth against the background of an understanding of the normal, the possible, and the scientifically feasible. Thus Strauss proposed two negative criteria for recognizing an account as unhistorical:

> *First.* When the narration is irreconcilable with the known and universal laws which govern the course of events....
>
> *Secondly.* An account which shall be regarded as historically valid, must neither be inconsistent with itself, nor in contradiction with other accounts.[22]

Hartlich and Sachs have suggested that Strauss introduced this discussion in order to show that his historical method was independent of Hegelian speculative philosophy. They conclude that his underlying critical presuppositions were of a "purely *empirical-rational* character" as the common property of "science in general especially in the realm of historical science."[23] This last judgment has been both endorsed and questioned.[24] What may be said is that Strauss was using the principle of analogy half a century before it was formulated by Ernst Troeltsch and which had already been used in the seventeenth- and eighteenth-century debates on miracles and the supernatural.[25] In common with the skeptics, he insisted on allowing only those events that were conformable to his understanding of natural laws.[26] Peter C. Hodgson has observed that Strauss was not interested in either critical philosophy or constructive historiography. "Rather he moved from a rationalist historiography to a speculative transfiguration of historical data into philosophical truths. It is difficult to escape the suspicion that a marriage of convenience existed between these operations."[27]

In his application of this negative criterion, Strauss juxtaposed the supernaturalistic and rationalistic accounts of the Gospel stories with a view to showing the untenability of both. He held it to be patently absurd to take the stories at their face value, as the supernaturalists did. But the rationalistic attempts on the part of scholars like Eichhorn and Paulus to save an underlying historical foundation were likewise too far-fetched to be credible.[28] The only viable alternative was

> the mythical view which leaves the substance of the narrative unassailed; and instead of venturing to explain the details, accepts the whole, not indeed as true history, but as a sacred legend. This view is supported by the analogy of all antiquity, political

and religious, since the closest resemblance exists between many of the narratives of the Old and New Testament, and the mythi of profane antiquity. But the most convincing argument is this: if the mythical view be once admitted, the innumerable, and never otherwise to be harmonized, discrepancies and chronological contradictions in the gospel histories disappear, as it were, at one stroke.[29]

Strauss's application of the principle of analogy was thus twofold. On the one hand, he was insisting that reported events of the past should bear analogy to the events of his own experience and understanding, if they were to be admitted as historical. On the other hand, he was contending that the biblical stories bore unmistakable analogy to the known myths of antiquity.

From time to time Strauss professed a certain sympathy with the supernaturalists. For they made no effort to avoid what the text was so obviously saying, whereas the rationalists went to extravagant and absurd lengths in their alternative explanations.[30] On the other hand, Strauss's own position was essentially rationalistic.[31] Not only did he himself offer rational explanations of Jesus' cures[32] and the visions of the risen Lord;[33] his entire mythical explanation was predicated upon an underlying rational view of what must have happened. His mythical explanation was, in fact, a form of rationalism. Both Strauss and Paulus posited rational explanations for what had happened. But whereas Paulus was prepared to give some credence to the historicity of the Gospel stories on the basis of a conjectured rational explanation, Strauss rejected the same stories and offered instead a rational explanation of how the stories arose. There was, however, a major difference. Whereas the rationalism of Paulus was linked to a supernatural, theistic view of the world, that of Strauss was linked to a Hegelian, immanentistic view of God and the world.

The positive aspect of Strauss's method consisted in his identification of the category of myth and his application of it to the Gospels. Strauss observed that the presence of myth had been noted in both sacred and secular history by such scholars as Semler, Eichhorn, Gabler, de Wette, and Schelling. He also noted that G. L. Bauer had published an extensive discussion of mythology in the Old and New Testaments.[34] He endorsed the dictum of the classical scholar, Christian Gottlob Heyne, that, "From myths proceed all the history as well as the philosophy of ancient man."[35] Although in practice he recognized the difficulty of identifying precisely to which category any given myth belonged, he identified three major types of myth recognized by scholars:

1st. *Historical mythi:* narratives of real events coloured by the light of antiquity, which confounded the divine and the human, the natural and the supernatural.

2nd. *Philosophical mythi:* such as clothe in the garb of historical narrative a simple thought, a precept, or an idea of the time.

3rd. *Poetical mythi:* historical and philosophical mythi partly blended together, and partly embellished by the creations of the imagination, in which the original fact or idea is almost obscured by the veil which the fancy of the poet has woven around it.[36]

On this basis Strauss proceeded to define more precisely the types of myth to be found in the Gospels.

> We distinguish by the name *evangelical mythus* a narrative relating directly or indirectly to Jesus, which may be considered not as the expressions of a fact, but as the product of an idea of his earliest followers: such a narrative being mythical in proportion as it exhibits this character. The mythus in this sense of the term meets us, in the Gospel as elsewhere, sometimes in its pure form, constituting the substance of the narrative, and sometimes as an accidental adjunct to the actual history.
>
> *The pure mythus* in the Gospel will be found to have two sources, which in most cases contributed simultaneously, though in different proportions, to form the mythus. The one source is, as already stated, the Messianic ideas and expectations existing according to their several forms in the Jewish mind before Jesus, and independently of him; the other is that particular impression which was left by the personal character, actions, and fate of Jesus, and which served to modify the Messianic idea in the minds of his people. The account of the Transfiguration, for example, is derived almost exclusively from the former source; the only amplification taken from the latter source being—that they who appeared with Jesus on the Mount spake of his decease. On the other hand, the narrative of the rending of the veil of the temple at the death of Jesus seems to have had its origin in the hostile position which Jesus, and his church after him, sustained in relation to the Jewish temple worship. Here already we have something historical, though consisting merely of certain general features of character, position, etc.; we are thus at once brought upon the ground of the historical mythus.
>
> *The historical mythus* has for its groundwork a definite individual fact which has been seized upon by religious enthusiasm, and twined around with mythical conceptions culled from the idea of the Christ. This fact is perhaps a saying of Jesus such as that concerning "fishers of men" or the barren fig-tree, which now appear in the Gospels transmuted into marvellous histories: or, it is perhaps a real transaction or event taken from his life; for instance, the mythical traits in the account of the baptism were built upon such a reality. Certain of the miraculous histories may likewise have had some foundation in natural occurrences, which the narrative has either exhibited in a supernatural light, or enriched with miraculous incidents.[37]

Such myths were all the product of the religious idea or imagery *(Vorstellung)* as the direct expression of the religious imagination in the context of its culture. When such myths were subtracted from the Gospel material, three further categories might remain: *Legends, additions by the author,* and a residual amount of *historical* material. For Strauss *legends* consisted of

> those parts of the history which are characterized by indefiniteness and want of connexion, by misconstruction and transformation, by strange combinations and confusion,—the natural results of a long course of oral transmission; or which, on the contrary, are distinguished by highly coloured and pictorial representations, which also seem to point to a traditionary origin.[38]

Additions by the author were those parts of the narrative which were clearly of an individual character, "designed merely to give clearness, connexion, and climax, to the representation." What was left was a historical core which in fact coincided with a thorough-going rationalism. In the first edition of his book Strauss described

> The simple, historical framework of the life of Jesus, that he grew up at Nazareth, let himself be baptized by John, collected disciples, went about teaching in the Jewish land, opposed Pharisaism everywhere and invited men into the messianic kingdom, but that in the end he fell victim to the hatred and envy of the Pharisaic party and died on the cross.

But immediately Strauss added that

> This framework was enveloped in the most complex and imaginative festoons of pious reflexion and imagination, in which all the ideas which primitive Christianity had concerning its departed Master were transformed into facts and woven into his life.[39]

Strauss did not attempt to elaborate on this. His *Life of Jesus* contained no positive historical statement, though it would be possible to construct out of his account such a statement on the above lines.[40] Instead, he applied his acute mind and tireless energy to the detection of myth in the Gospel stories which were derived chiefly from the thought-world of the Old Testament. At the end of it all, when Strauss came to attempt a positive statement, he did so not in terms of historical reconstruction but of Hegelian philosophy, which he saw as the means of salvaging the true meaning of Christianity from the debris left by historical criticism. The reason for this may have been partly that Strauss had no positive criterion for isolating authentic history.[41] As F. C. Baur saw it, Strauss's method was "negative-critical" and "dialectical."[42] Strauss obtained negative results by analyzing individual stories abstracted from their mythical, literary context. It was dialectical in its method of focusing on opposing interpretations and conflicting accounts, showing them to be mutually exclusive. So far as his historical critical work was concerned, Strauss's interest was largely negative and destructive. What mattered was not the historicity of particular events, but the significance of the meaning of history. And this was to be determined not by the tools of critical history but by philosophical interpretation.

Strauss's detection of myth in the Gospel stories was detailed and relentless. Its presence in the Bible was not motivated by fraudulent attempts to deceive, as the Deists and the Wolfenbüttel *Fragments* insinuated.[43] The myths were by and large the sincere and spontaneous product of the religious imagination. A case in point was the genealogies in Matthew and Luke. These were constructed with hindsight in order to make Jesus fulfill messianic prophecy.

> According to the prophecies, the Messiah could only spring from David. When therefore a Galilean, whose lineage was utterly unknown, and of whom conse-

quently no one could prove that he was not descended from David, had acquired the reputation of being the Messiah; what more natural than that tradition should under different forms have early ascribed to him a Davidical descent, and that genealogical tables, corresponding with this tradition, should have been formed? which, however, as they were constructed upon no certain data, would necessarily exhibit such differences and contradictions as we find actually existing between the genealogies in Matthew and in Luke.

If, in conclusion, it be asked, what historical result is to be deduced from these genealogies? we reply: a conviction (arrived at also from other sources), that Jesus, either in his own person or through his disciples, acting upon minds strongly imbued with Jewish notions and expectations, left among his followers so firm a conviction of his Messiahship, that they did not hesitate to attribute to him the prophetical characteristic of Davidical descent, and more than one pen was put in action, in order, by means of a genealogy which should authenticate that descent, to justify his recognition as the Messiah.[44]

Strauss scorned such rationalistic explanations of the miraculous draught of fishes which attributed the event to prescience or to shrewd knowledge. As the narratives stand, the evangelists clearly believed that a miracle took place. Strauss preferred to see it as an example of how the saying about the disciples henceforth becoming fishers of men took on concrete, historical form. He further claimed that a story related about Pythagoras afforded a secular example of "a common tendency of the ancient legend."[45]

Although Strauss drew from time to time on what he considered to be secular parallels exhibiting similar developments, his main contention was that the Gospel accounts of Jesus were essentially shaped by Jewish beliefs drawn from the Old Testament. The miracles of Jesus were virtually predetermined by popular expectation of how the Messiah should act.

That the Jewish people in the time of Jesus expected miracles from the Messiah is in itself natural, since the Messiah was a second Moses and the greatest of the prophets, and to Moses and the prophets the national legend attributed miracles of all kinds: by later Jewish writings it is rendered probable; by our gospels, certain. When Jesus on one occasion had (without natural means) cured a blind and dumb demoniac, the people were hereby led to ask: *Is not this the son of David?* (Matt. xii. 23), a proof that a miraculous power of healing was regarded as an attribute of the Messiah. John the Baptist, on hearing of the *works* of Jesus *(erga)*, sent to him with the inquiry, *Art thou he that should come (erchomenos)?* Jesus, in proof of the affirmative, merely appealed again to his miracles (Matt. xi. 2 ff. parall.). At the Feast of Tabernacles, which was celebrated by Jesus in Jerusalem, many of the people believed on him, saying, in justification of their faith, *When Christ cometh, will he do more miracles than these which this man hath done?* (John vii. 31).[46]

Not only did messianic expectation predetermine that the Messiah should perform miracles in general; it predetermined the particular kinds of miracles that the Messiah should perform. These included the supernatural dispensation of food (Exod. 16:17), the opening of the eyes of the blind (2 Kings 6), and raising the dead (1 Kings 17; 2 Kings 4). Thus Jesus was made to fulfill the prophecy of Isaiah 35:5–6: "Then shall the eyes of the blind be opened and the ears of the deaf unstopped; then shall the lame man leap as a hart, and the tongue of the dumb shall sing" (cf. Matt. 11:5).

Strauss detected a clue as to whether they really occurred or not in Jesus' reluctance to perform wonders on demand. He found a further clue in the general absence of reference to miracles in the apostolic preaching. Despite their frequent mention in the Gospels, this absence was sufficient to cast doubt upon their authenticity. Strauss then proceeded to question their historicity one by one. This he endeavored to do by rigorous examination of the narratives, searching for minor discrepancies and differences of emphasis that would help him to demonstrate the unreliability of the testimony. But when all else failed, he came back to asserting (as in the case of the paralytic) that it was probably neither a case of "nervous weakness" nor "a rapid psychical cure." Such explanations were "purely arbitrary." Moreover,

> if in the alleged analogies there may be some truth, yet it is always incomparably more probable that histories of cures of the lame and paralytic in accordance with messianic expectation, should be formed by the legend, than that they should really have happened.[47]

The same process of creating myth by reading Old Testament legend into the life of Jesus occurred in the transfiguration narrative. Strauss's concluding remarks on the subject are worth repeating at some length because they illustrate how sharply he differed from the earlier rationalistic biographers of Jesus. Strauss was not concerned with conjectured, naturalistic explanations of the event. His aim was to discover the theological tendency of the narrative.

> According to this, we have here a mythus, the tendency of which is twofold: first, to exhibit in the life of Jesus an enhanced repetition of the glorification of Moses; and secondly, to bring Jesus as the Messiah into contact with his two forerunners,—by this appearance of the lawgiver and the prophet, of the founder and the reformer of the theocracy, to represent Jesus as the perfecter of the kingdom of God, and the fulfilment of the law and the prophets; and besides this, to show a confirmation of his messianic dignity by a heavenly voice.

> Before we part with our subject, this example may serve to shows [sic] with peculiar clearness, how the natural system of interpretation, while it seeks to preserve the historical certainty of the narratives, loses their ideal truth —sacrifices the essence to the form: whereas the mythical interpretation, by renouncing the historical body of such narratives, rescues and preserves the idea which resides in them, and which alone constitutes their vitality and spirit. Thus if, as the natural explanation would have it, the splendour around Jesus was an accidental, optical phenomenon, and the two appearances either images of a dream or unknown men, where is the significance of the incident? where the motive for preserving in the memory of the church an

anecdote so void of ideas, and so barren of inference, resting on a common delusion and superstition? On the contrary, while according to the mythical interpretation, I do not, it is true, see in the evangelical narrative any real event, — I yet retain a sense, a purpose in the narrative, know to what sentiments and thoughts of the first Christian community it owes its origin, and why the authors of the gospels included so important a passage in their memoirs.[48]

In saying this, Strauss was putting his finger on an important critical point which F. C. Baur was to stress. The tendency of a document or narrative must be taken into account in any proper evaluation. But Strauss's last sentence claimed rather more than he had proved. He may have suggested motives for describing an episode in a certain way. What he had not shown was why particular people were prompted by particular motives to apply these particular ideas to a particular person. The naturalists felt obliged to account for the particular phenomena under discussion. Strauss was content to offer a general philosophical interpretation on Hegelian lines and treat it as a sufficient explanation.

Strauss allowed a certain degree of messianic consciousness to Jesus. Otherwise his actions were inexplicable. But this conviction wavered in Jesus' mind. Hence the conflicting descriptions in John and the Synoptics of Jesus' last hours with the disciples.[49] Strauss had his own way of resolving the dilemma of the tensions between John and the Synoptics. Schleiermacher and Hase had detected divergences, and had pronounced in favor of the historicity of John in view of his more precise chronology. Strauss rejected the historicity of both, claiming that John was even more mythical than the Synoptic Gospels.

> Herewith the dilemma above stated falls to the ground, since we must pronounce unhistorical not only one of the two, but both representations of the last hours of Jesus before his arrest. The only degree of distinction between the historical value of the synoptical account and that of John is, that the former is a mythical product of the first era of traditional formation, the latter of the second, — or more correctly, the one is a product of the second order, the other of the third. The representation common to the synoptists and to John, that Jesus foreknew his sufferings even to the day and hour of their arrival, is the first modification which the pious legend gave to the real history of Jesus; the statement of the synoptists, that he even had an antecedent experience of his sufferings, is the second step of the mythical; while, that although he foreknew them, and also in one instance had a foretaste of them (John xii. 27 ff.), he had yet long beforehand completely triumphed over them, and when they stood immediately before him, looked them in the face with unperturbed serenity — this representation of the fourth gospel is the third and highest grade of devotional, but unhistorical embellishment.[50]

It is almost superfluous to add that Strauss treated the resurrection of Jesus as mythical. For him, modern man was confronted by the dilemma that had become acute ever since the publication of the Wolfenbüttel *Fragments:* either Jesus did not really die, or he did not really rise from the dead. The rationalists had largely opted for the former alternative. But while this possibility could not be ruled out altogether, Strauss deemed it improbable. Again he saw his way out of the dilemma, not by reverting to naturalistic explanations involving a resuscitation of Jesus, but by what he considered to be a historical understanding of how myths arise. He took his cue from the direction, given to the disciples in the Gospels, to go to Galilee. Here in relative tranquility they recovered their faith and their poise, and in their enthusiasm for Jesus allowed the myth to build up.

> Here was the place where they gradually began to breathe freely, and where their faith in Jesus, which had been temporarily depressed, might once more expand with its former vigour. But here also, where no body lay in the grave to contradict bold suppositions, might gradually be formed the idea of the resurrection of Jesus; and when this conviction had so elevated the courage and enthusiasm of his adherents that they ventured to proclaim it in the metropolis, it was no longer possible by the sight of the body of Jesus either to convict themselves, or to be convicted by others.[51]

It only remained for the final embellishments to be added, and these were ready to hand in popular Jewish belief.

Strauss's critical investigations raise the question whether there is any place left for Christology in the thinking of modern man. Schleiermacher's solution of an ideal Christ, mediating awareness of God, was rejected as eclectic and unhistorical.[52] Needless to say, so were those of orthodoxy and rationalism.[53] The symbolic interpretations of Kant and de Wette also failed because they lacked substance.[54] However, Hegelianism provided a more comprehensive account of religion and reality, and with it a redefinition of Christology.

> In the most recent philosophy this idea has been further developed in the following manner.[55] When it is said of God that he is a Spirit, and of man that he also is a Spirit, it follows that the two are not essentially distinct. To speak more particularly, it is the essential property of a spirit, in the distribution of itself into distinct personalities, to remain identical with itself, to possess itself in another than itself. Hence the recognition of God as a spirit implies, that God does not remain as a fixed and immutable Infinite encompassing the Finite, but enters into it, produces the Finite, Nature, and the human mind, merely as a limited manifestation of himself, from which he eternally returns into unity. As man, considered as a finite spirit, limited to his finite nature, has not truth; so God, considered exclusively as an infinite spirit, shut up in his infinitude, has not reality. The infinite spirit is real only when it discloses itself in finite spirits; as the finite spirit is true only when it merges itself in the infinite. The true and real existence of spirit, therefore, is neither in God by himself, nor in man by himself, but in the Godman; neither in the infinite alone, nor in the finite alone, but in the interchange of impartation and withdrawal between the two, which on the part of God is revelation, on the part of man religion.

> If God and man are in themselves *one*, and if religion is the human side of this unity: then must this unity be made evident to man in religion, and become in him consciousness and reality.[56]

"The key to the whole of Christology" lay in the recognition of the idea of the unity of divine and human nature in general. In orthodox Christianity it was particularized in the story of the Incarnation. But when seen in the light of Hegelian philosophy, it did not need to be grounded in history but in the truth of philosophy.

> It is Humanity that dies, rises, and ascends to heaven, for from the negation of its phenomenal life there ever proceeds a higher spiritual life; from the suppression of its mortality as a personal, national, and terrestrial spirit, arises its union with the infinite spirit of the heavens. By faith in this Christ, especially in his death and resurrection, man is justified before God; that is, by the kindling within him of the idea of Humanity, the individual man participates in the divinely human life of the species. Now the main element of that idea is, that the negation of the merely natural and sensual life, which is itself the negation of the spirit (the negation of negation, therefore), is the sole way to true spiritual life.[57]

This alone was "the absolute sense of Christology." As Hegel pointed out, faith in its first stages was "governed by the senses." It holds to the external, and treats historical evidence forensically.

> But mind having once taken occasion by this external fact, to bring under its consciousness the idea of humanity as one with God, sees in the history only the presentation of that idea; the object of faith is completely changed: instead of a sensible, empirical fact it has become a spiritual and divine idea, which has its confirmation no longer in history but in philosophy. When the mind has thus gone beyond the sensible history, and entered into the domain of the absolute, the former ceases to be essential; it takes a subordinate place, above which the spiritual truths suggested by the history stand self-supported; it becomes as the faith image of a dream which belongs only to the past, and does not, like the idea, share the permanence of the spirit which is absolutely present to itself.[58]

It remained only for Strauss to suggest how this new understanding could be passed on to the church. The theologian and the minister should not be hypocrites. They should neither avoid the truth nor rudely shatter the faith of the faithful. Rather, the minister will adhere in his discourses to "the forms of the popular conception, but on every opportunity he will exhibit their spiritual significance."[59]

Reaction

Strauss's book brought him instant notoriety. In retrospect it is not immediately clear why it should have been so. The book was not a popular biography but a critical treatise. Its author was comparatively young and unknown. Radical ideas were by no means new when Strauss wrote. Scholars had been producing critical reassessments of Jesus for over half a century. Even the notion of myth was no novelty. Perhaps it was precisely that the ground had been so long and so well prepared, that the great battle could begin. The first skirmish, the *Fragments* controversy, had taken place half a century earlier. Whereas the Fragmentist might be dismissed as an unknown outsider and infidel, Strauss was occupying a theological teaching post, albeit a minor one. Moreover, his book was written with power, style, relentless logic, and a thoroughness which brought together in a concentrated form the negative criticism of his predecessors. Other radical treatments of Christian origins had some historical core and some general resemblance to the Christian faith; Strauss appeared to leave nothing. His unique combination of historical criticism and Hegelian philosophy posed a threat which traditional orthodoxy could not ignore.

Within five years of the publication of Strauss's first volume, some sixty works appeared attacking or supporting Strauss.[60] Nearly thirty years later a writer in the *Westminster Review* could remark, "The name of Strauss has long been a bugbear in the English 'religious world.' High Churchmen and Low Churchmen...hush naughty children with the name of Strauss."[61] About the same time Strauss himself observed that the epoch-making significance of the book was shown by the fact that it cost its author his teaching position and his academic career.[62]

In the van of the attack was Dr. Steudel, with over eighty pages of criticism in the *Tübinger Zeitschrift für Theologie*,[63] and the Tübingen pastor and teacher, C. A. Eschenmayer, with a work entitled *Der. Ischariotismus unserer Tage. Eine Zugabe zu dem jüngst erschienenen Werke: "Das Leben Jesu von Strauss, 1. Theil"* (Tübingen, 1835). Among the others which soon followed were Wilhelm Hoffmann's massive critique of 436 pages, *Das Leben Jesu kritisch bearbeitet von Dr. D. F. Strauss. Geprüft für Theologen* (Stuttgart, 1836). In his review in *Theologische Studien und Kritiken*, the learned "Vermittlungstheologe," Carl Ullmann, wished that Strauss had written in Latin, to avoid doing harm to ordinary people.[64] Professor Adolf Harless of Erlangen published *Die kritische Bearbeitung des Lebens Jesu von D. F. Strauss nach ihrem wissenschaftlichen Werte beleuchtet* (Erlangen, 1837). Harless was one of the founders of the conservative Erlangen school which exerted considerable influence in Lutheran circles in the first half of the nineteenth century. Another conservative writer who joined in the fray was Pusey's friend, the devout August Tholuck. Tholuck's *Die Glaubwürdigkeit der evangelischen Geschichte, zugleich eine Kritik des Lebens Jesu für theologische und nichttheologische Leser* also appeared in 1837. Tholuck was willing to concede that Jesus might not have used powers which transcended the laws of nature, but he suggested that he might have used powers which are largely unknown to us.

Among the replies which attacked Strauss's underlying philosophy was that of the Privatdozent at Halle, Julius Schaller, *Der historische Christus und die Philosophie. Kritik der Grundidee des Werks "Das Leben Jesu" von Dr. D. F. Strauss* (1838). The bluntest of Strauss's critics was E. W. Hengstenberg, the conservative professor of Old Testament at Berlin and founder and editor of the *Evangelische Kirchen-Zeitung*.[65] Hengstenberg commended Strauss's consistency and honesty. He had brought the secular spirit of the age to self-consciousness. Strauss had performed a valuable service by clearly showing where his approach led. The matter was now a straight choice between belief and unbelief. Strauss reciprocated by acknowledging the consistency of this attitude. Whoever, like the editor of the *Evangelische Kirchen-Zeitung*, was willing to take upon himself the yoke of the creeds and dogmas of the church was certainly justified on his own premise in damning those who thought differently.

A work which momentarily caused Strauss to have second thoughts was August Neander's *Das Leben Jesu-Christi*.[66] The work was occasioned by Strauss's study, and it was long regarded as a more positive alternative. By 1872 it had gone into seven editions, and, like Strauss's book, it was subsequently translated into English. Again like Strauss's work, it was not so much a biography as a massive critical examination of various aspects and incidents in the life of Jesus. Neander's approach to the miraculous was rather different from Tholuck's. He denied that miracles were the "results of the *powers of nature intensified*."[67] In them

> We do not see the Divine agency *immediately*, but in a veil, as it were; the Divine causality does not appear in them as coefficient with natural causes, and therefore cannot be an object of external perception, but reveals itself only to Faith. But the miracle, by displaying phenomena out of the ordinary connexion of cause and effect, manifests the interference of a higher power, and points out a higher connexion, in which even the chain of phenomena in the visible world must be taken up.[68]

Like Strauss, Neander tried to piece together the data presented by the Gospels and examine the possibilities and probabilities. But because he was willing to allow the supernatural and miraculous, his interpretation was radically different. The resurrection was a historical event. The alternative explanations were more difficult to believe than the alleged event itself.[69] Neander concluded that unless the events of Christ's life are both supernatural and historical, the Christian faith is empty.

> We make the same remark upon the Ascension of Christ as was made before upon his miraculous Conception. In regard to neither is prominence given to the special and actual *fact* in the Apostolic writings; in regard to both such a fact is presupposed in the general conviction of the Apostles, and in the connexion of Christian consciousness. Thus the end of Christ's appearance on earth corresponds to its beginning. No link in its chain of supernatural facts can be lost, without taking away its significance as a whole. Christianity rests upon these facts; stands or falls with them. By faith in them has the divine life been generated from the beginning; by faith in them has that life in all ages regenerated mankind, raised them above the limits of earthly life, changed them from *glebae adscriptis* to citizens of heaven, and formed the stage of transition from an existence chained to nature, to a free, celestial life, far raised above it. Were this faith gone, there might indeed remain many of the *effects* of what Christianity has been; but as for Christianity in the true sense, as for the Christian Church, there could be none.[70]

In a preface to the American translation, Neander reminded his readers that,

> *Where the Spirit of the Lord is, there is Liberty*....Perhaps the impulse which the American mind has received from the profound Coleridge, who (like Schleiermacher among ourselves) has testified that Christianity is not so much a definite system of

conceptions as a power of life, may have contributed, and may still further contribute,
to prepare the way for a new tendency of scientific theology in your beloved country.[71]

Although Neander hinted at a new approach to theology, the novelty in his case
lay in a less rigid approach to dogma and a stress upon Christianity as a power
and a way of life. He still worked within the framework of theism. In his
Introduction he declared that *"The Truth, that Christ is* GOD-MAN" was
"presupposed."[72] The supernatural presented no insuperable difficulties for him.
Nor, for that matter, did historical criticism. The names of Weisse and Baur
received passing mention,[73] but Neander saw no need to investigate the authorship, date and authenticity of his sources. He took them at face value. What
needed to be done was to examine the credibility of their contents.

One of the byproducts of the controversy provoked by Strauss's book was the
growing alienation between Strauss and F. C. Baur.[74] Baur had been Strauss's
tutor. The two had discussed the work together as Strauss wrote it. But its
publication placed Baur in a difficult position. Already in 1834, the call of Baur
to Schleiermacher's former chair at Berlin had been blocked by Neander and
Hengstenberg. Baur still hoped for a move from Tübingen to a larger Prussian
university, but any defense of Strauss by him would have ruined his chances. For
a time he remained silent. When he finally declared himself in an "Abgenöthigte
Erklärung" published in the third issue of the *Tübinger Zeitschrift für Theologie*
for 1836, he denied any debt to Strauss and insisted that his own methods were
quite different. The background to this was a charge that appeared in the
Evangelische Kirchen-Zeitung that Baur's recently published study of the Pastoral Epistles was influenced by his relationship with Strauss, which came at a
time when Baur was under consideration for Ullmann's former chair at Halle.
Baur denied outright that any of his criticism was based "on the mythical view"
and declared,

> Not only are the basic principles of criticism of another kind, but also the object of
> the critical question under discussion is essentially different, as everyone must
> immediately see. Is the whole objective basis of Christianity called into question
> through my investigation, in the same way as it was through Strauss?[75]

This attempt by Baur to put distance between himself and Strauss was the cause
of some pain to the latter.[76] Their relationship was never quite the same again.

To many people Strauss and Baur seemed to be saying the same thing. Both
were highly critical of the biblical accounts of Christian origins. Underlying the
criticism of both was a common rejection of supernaturalism. But Baur refrained
from attributing the source of New Testament supernaturalism to myth. Both
publicly in his *Kritische Untersuchungen*[77] and privately in his correspondence,
he deplored Strauss's inadequate criticism of sources. As Baur wrote to his
son-in-law, Eduard Zeller, in a letter complaining that Zeller had given undue
prominence to Strauss in his account of the Tübingen School, "Strauss's criticism
is the criticism of history, mine the criticism of the writings which form the

source of the history."[78] Baur resented the suggestion that his own critical method was in any way dependent on Strauss. Moreover, Strauss's work was essentially negative. It failed as a positive account of how Christianity came into being. A few days before his death Baur again protested to Zeller,

> The substance of the matter is still that Strauss carried through the already long present view of the unhistorical reality of miracles methodically and basically to a purely negative historical view, where, however, he also remained; between his *Life of Jesus* and his concluding dogmatic treatment lies an infinite cleft, beyond which, with his standpoint at that time, he could never pass. Only through a completely different criticism can his view descend from its negativity to a base on which there is also a true and real history. I believe that this should have been brought out with even more definite emphasis and should have been designated as the main point of the distinction.[79]

However, as Horton Harris observes,

> Baur never criticised the mythical principle in itself, nor did he ever provide any better answer to the problem of how Christianity originated; on the contrary he steered clear of the whole question and nowhere in his later writings did he deal with it.[80]

The spectral possibility of the mythical origin of Christianity was a question which Strauss's generation did not wish to contemplate. An exception was W. F. Wilcke in *Tradition and Mythe. Ein Beitrag zur historischen Kritik der kanonischen Evangelien überhaupt, wie insbesondere zur Würdigung des mythischen Idealismus im Leben-Jesu von Strauss* (1837).[81] He welcomed Strauss's work as a positive step forward, which clearly demonstrated the advantages of "rationalistic speculation." Wilcke's observation was two-edged. It was intended as a compliment, but it recognized that Strauss's work was at bottom a rationialistic speculation, however much it was decked out as historical investigation. In the meantime, the older rationalism supplied the underlying philosophy for C. F. von Ammon's *Die Geschichte des Lebens Jesu mit steter Rücksicht auf die vorhandenen Quellen* (3 vols., 1842–47). It reemerged in the numerous later lives of Jesus which continued to be written long after Strauss lost his first interest.

The Second "Leben Jesu"

Nearly thirty years elapsed between the publication of Strauss's two *Lives*. Published in one volume, the second was more compact. Although ostensibly designed for more popular consumption—it bore the title of *Das Leben Jesu für das deutsche Volk bearbeitet*[82]—it was prefaced by a lengthy review of over 150 pages, dealing with the views of other scholars and outlining the critical theories underlying his approach. The miraculous was ruled out from the start as being incompatible with scientific history.[83] The concept of myth was again the key concept for interpreting the Gospels. Strauss was willing to modify it in an important detail. In the light of F. C. Baur's criticism, he was now ready to concede a more conscious and intentional element in the creation of myth than hitherto.

> In this new discussion of the life of Jesus, I have, mainly in consequence of Baur's hints, allowed more room than before to the hypothesis of conscious and intentional fiction; but I have seen no reason to change the term. On the contrary, to the question which asks whether conscious fictions of an individual are properly to be called myths, I am bound, even after all the discussions upon the point, to reply: Certainly, as soon as they have gained belief and passed into the legend of a people or a religious sect; for their having done so invariably shews at the same time that they were formed by their author not merely upon notions of his own, but in connection with the consciousness of a majority. Every historical narrative, however it may have arisen, in which a religious community recognises a component part of their sacred origin as being an absolute expression of constituent feelings and conceptions, is a myth; and though Greek mythology may have an interest in separating off from this extended idea of the myth a more contracted one, critical theology, conversely, as against the so-called believers, has an interest in combining all those evangelical narratives to which it attributes only an ideal meaning, under the one common notion of myth.[84]

The word myth has thus become a kind of umbrella term covering anything and everything unhistorical which, in Strauss's case, amounted to most of the Gospel material.

Human happiness has even less to do with history than before.

> No! the happiness of man, or, speaking more intelligibly, the possibility of fulfilling his destiny, developing the powers implanted in him, and thus participating in the corresponding amount of wellbeing—it is impossible—and on this point the saying of Reimarus is an everlasting truth—it is impossible that this can depend on his recognition of facts into which scarcely one man in a thousand is in a position to institute a thorough investigation, and, supposing him to have done so, then to arrive at a satisfactory result.[85]

Not only did Reimarus find endorsement, but so did Spinoza and Kant.

> This is the meaning of the profound saying of Spinoza, that for the purposes of happiness it is not in any way necessary to know Christ after the flesh; but that the case is different with that eternal Son of God, namely the Divine Wisdom, which appears in all things, especially in the human mind, and in Jesus Christ appeared in a pre-eminent degree. Without this, he says, no one can attain to happiness, because it alone teaches what is true and false, good and bad. Kant, like Spinoza, distinguished between the historical person of Jesus and the Ideal of humanity pleasing to God, involved in human reason, or in the moral sense in its perfect purity, so far as is possible in a system of the world dependent upon wants and inclinations. To rise to this ideal was, he said, the general duty of men; and though we cannot conceive of it as existing otherwise than under the form of a perfect man, and though it is not impossible that such a man may have lived, as we are all intended to resemble this ideal, still that it is not necessary that we should know of the existence of such a man

or believe in it, but solely that we should keep that ideal before us, recognise it as obligatory upon us, and strive to make ourselves like it.[86]

The Hegelianism which appeared like a *deus ex machina* at the end of the first *Life of Jesus* was now replaced by the old, enlightened view of the primacy of reason. Strauss was not prepared to go as far as those who argued that "the ideal Christ might have been present within us as much as it is now if a historic Christ had never lived or worked."[87] Each age and culture has produced its own ideals,

> and among these improvers of the ideal of humanity, Jesus stands at all events in the first class. . . . Meanwhile, however high may be the place of Jesus among those who have shewn to mankind most purely and most plainly what it ought to be, still he was not the first to do so, nor will he be the last.[88]

Strauss's closing words underline the critic's obligation to desupernaturalize Jesus and strip him of all the accretions of orthodoxy.

> Therefore the critic is convinced that he is committing no offence against what is sacred, nay rather that he is doing a good and necessary work, when he sweeps away all that makes Jesus a supernatural Being, as well meant and perhaps even at first sight beneficial, but in the long run mischievous and now absolutely destructive, restores, as well as may be, the image of the historical Jesus in its simply human features, but refers mankind for salvation to the ideal Christ, to that moral pattern in which the historical Jesus did indeed first bring to light many principal features, but which as an elementary principle as much belongs to the general endowment of our kind, as its improvement and perfection can only be the problem and the work of mankind in general.[89]

Conclusion

In 1908, Strauss's biographer, Theobald Ziegler, could look back and say, "Rightly and for his sake has the year 1835 been called the great revolutionary year of modern theology."[90] Half a century later Karl Löwith claimed that,

> Strauss's life of Jesus, published in 1835, was a product of the Hegelian philosophy of religion under the influence of Schleiermacher. It marked an application of this philosophy to religion, while Hegel, in contrast, had come to philosophy from theology and his own life of Jesus.[91]

Both these judgments contain an element of exaggeration. The year 1835 did not so much see the opening of hostilities as mark a new phase in a conflict that was already long under way. At the time when Strauss wrote his first *Life* he was a convinced Hegelian. He still claimed to be in the Hegelian tradition in the third part of his *Streitschriften*. But by the time he wrote the second *Life*, the last vestiges of Hegelianism had long disappeared. Moreover, the role played by Hegelianism in the first *Life* was not the most decisive of the numerous factors. Strauss presented his work as a historical and critical study. The decisive category was that of myth. Philosophical considerations came into play at two critical points. The first was Strauss's tacit rejection of a supernaturalistic, theistic framework for his Life, which was a presupposition he took over from his rationalistic predecessors. Like the latter, Strauss examined the Gospel narratives section by section, exploiting whatever differences and discrepancies he could find. But he differed from them in that, instead of offering a series of naturalistic explanations, he ascribed the present form of any given pericope to the mythical reading into it of Old Testament motifs. The idea itself was not new. But Strauss applied it to the Gospels with unprecedented rigor. Nevertheless, this fundamental and characteristic feature of Strauss's work was not derived from Hegel.[92] Hegelianism entered into the account explicitly only at the second of our two critical points, where it figured in Strauss's positive reconstruction of Christology and its significance for the modern reader.

In the *Streitschriften* Strauss explained his debt to Hegel. He made use of the Hegelian distinction between *Vorstellung* (the representation or image) and *Begriff* (the concept or essential idea). But he pointed out that Hegel had little light to shed on the question of historical investigation. Hegel and the Hegelian Right applied their philosophical ideas to the interpretation of the Gospels, but left them intact from the point of view of criticism.

> My criticism of the life of Jesus was from its origin intimately related to Hegelian philosophy. Already in my student years it appeared to me and my friends that the most important point of this system for theology was the distinction between representation *[Vorstellung]* and concept *[Begriff]* in religion which could have various forms yet the same content. In this distinction we found respect for the biblical sources and ecclesiastical dogmas over against freedom of thought brought into harmony in a way to be found nowhere else. Thus the most important question soon became for us that of the relationship of the historical elements of the Bible, particularly the Gospels, to the concept *[Begriff]*. Did the historical character belong to the content, which, for representation *[Vorstellung]* and concept *[Begriff]* itself, demanded recognition even from the latter? Or did it belong to the mere form, with the consequence that understanding was not bound to it? When we sought illumination in the writings of Hegel and his most eminent disciples, we found that it was precisely this point, on which we desired further light above all, that was mostly left in the dark. . . . Sometimes it seemed that history as mere representation was let drop over against the concept *[Begriff]* that had been attained. Sometimes history seemed to have been retained along with the Idea.[93]

In the first *Life of Jesus* Hegelianism provided the philosophical substructure for Strauss's interpretation of the meaning of Christianity. It belonged to his hermeneutic but not to his exegesis. In the second *Life* the exegetical method was more or less the same, but the Hegelian hermeneutic had all but disappeared. It lingered on only in the broadest of broad distinctions between the form of belief and the real significance of Jesus in the history of humanity. But the latter was interpreted more in terms of Kant than of Hegel.

Although Rudolf Bultmann hardly ever referred to Strauss,[94] it is inevitable that the two should be compared. There are certain striking similarities—their historical skepticism and their use of myth as a basic category for interpreting biblical data. Both were concerned with the history of religions. But there are certain important differences. Bultmann specified Gnosticism and Jewish apocalyptic, rather than the Old Testament, as the source of myth in the New Testament. Although Strauss could be said to have used an elementary type of Form Criticism, it was not developed to the level of sophistication that Bultmann's was. Whereas Strauss was hardly interested in sources beyond demonstrating that the Gospels could not have been written by their putative authors, Bultmann combined a study of *forms* with source criticism. Strauss was concerned to eliminate myth in order to expose mistaken beliefs and preserve (at least initially) a Hegelian interpretation of religion. Bultmann sought to demythologize in order to rediscover the kerygma with all its existential power to illuminate life.

Despite all the criticisms, Strauss's book was a *tour de force*. No doubt this contributed to its notoriety. But in the end it was no more than a *tour de force*, and perhaps this is the chief reason why it found so little permanent following. Strauss was soon overshadowed in the theological world by his more methodical and less flamboyant senior, F. C. Baur. Already on April 7, 1837, Strauss could write, "The purely academic life is beginning to be arid to me. I am not made to be a real scholar. I am much too much dependent on moods, and am much too much preoccupied with myself."[95] His historical method had been conceived in a mood of brilliant inspiration, but it did not last. "The mood was no longer there in which I originally wrote the book." Almost a decade later he wrote, "I am no historian; with me everything has proceeded from a dogmatic (or rather anti-dogmatic) concern."[96] The antidogmatic interest, which was perhaps the driving force of the original *Life*, remained with him to the end.

11. BAUR AND THE TÜBINGEN SCHOOL

Current estimates of F. C. Baur (1792–1860)[1] could hardly be more contradictory. In his address at Tübingen commemorating the centenary of Baur's death, Heinz Liebing proclaimed how today, "His name, the results of his research, and especially his method are cited with respect." He went on to acknowledge how many of Baur's ideas "have become common property and which demonstrate the astonishing extent to which we are indebted to his work and live from it . . . . *There has been historical critical theology in the full sense only since Ferdinand Christian Baur.*"[2] Stephen Neill, on the other hand, writing only a year or two after Liebing, could pay tribute to Baur's immense industry, his refusal to take anything for granted, and certain brilliant insights of permanent validity, but then go on to say,

At very few points indeed has subsequent investigation confirmed the rightness of Baur's solutions, even when it has approved his formulations of the questions. This suggests that either the method employed was basically wrong or that there were grave imperfections in the application of it.[3]

Baur's outward life was as unexciting as Strauss's was melodramatic. He was born in 1792, and up to the age of thirteen he was educated at home by his father, the pastor at Blaubeuren. He entered the lower seminary there and later spent two years at Maulbronn. In the autumn of 1809 he enrolled at the Tübinger Stift where he spent the next five years. He then served in a number of minor clerical posts, including appointments at the Stift and Blaubeuren. In 1826 Baur rejoined the reconstituted faculty at Tübingen, where he remained until his death in 1860. His labors were prodigious and his habits regular. He was at his desk by 4:00 a.m. He preached a regular Sunday morning sermon right into old age, when he continued to work a fourteen-hour day. It has been reckoned that his literary output amounted to the equivalent of a four-hundred-page book every year for forty years.[4]

If the outward course of Baur's life was marked only by personal and domestic joys and sorrows, his thought underwent numerous changes over the years. Though he shared to the end the belief of J. C. F. Steudel and the old conservative Tübingen school in objective theological truth in history, his relationship with the school was always tenuous. For a time at least Baur was deeply impressed by Schelling.[5] Although Baur is often said to have developed his characteristic teaching under the influence of Hegel, it has been argued by those who were closest to him that Schleiermacher was the greatest single influence on his thought.[6] It was the influence of Schelling, Fichte, and Schleiermacher, and not that of Hegel, that made itself felt in Baur's early work. Baur's *Symbolik und Mythologie, oder die Naturreligion des Alterthums* (3 vols., 1824–25)[7] revealed his final break with the old supernaturalism. Its introduction contains the celebrated remark, "without philosophy history remains for me eternally dead and dumb."[8] This remark is sometimes taken as proof of Baur's Hegelianism,[9] but the work itself was not an essay in Hegelian philosophy, and it would seem that at the time Baur had not even read Hegel. The work was an early study in the history of religions that was far more exhaustive than anything that Strauss undertook in that field. It antedated by a whole decade Strauss's mythological interpretation of the Gospels. But whereas Strauss was concerned with mythical tendencies within Christianity, Baur was concerned to analyze and describe the mythical forms of ancient religion. At this stage in his career Baur was content to link myths with underlying philosophies. He went on to add that the question whether

in the construction of an individual myth or of an entire religious system any particular subjective arbitrarily limited, philosophical view had been intermingled, can naturally be determined at any given place only on historical grounds.[10]

Baur's first major work was therefore a study in the history of religions. It was followed by other major studies in this area. These touched on Gnosticism, Manicheeism and Apollonius of Tyana,[11] a figure whose apparent parallels with Jesus had attracted the interests of the Deists. To Baur, Philostratus's *Life of Apollonius* was a work of considerable interest "from the standpoint of the comparative history of religion." It presented "a picture analogous to the appearance of Christ" against the background of the syncretism of the age.[12] Baur's comparative historical approach to religion and his massive learning characterized his scholarship throughout his career.

Most of Baur's theological writing was done when he was well past forty. Two dates are generally considered significant turning points—1835 and 1847. The first saw the publication of *Die christliche Gnosis, oder die christliche Religions-Philosophie in ihrer geschichtlichen Entwicklung*[13] in which Baur first evinced a knowledge of Hegel. The second marked the publication of a study "Über Prinzip und Charakter des Lehrbegriffs der reformirten Kirche, in seinem Unterschied von dem der lutherischen, mit Rücksicht auf A. Schweizers *Darstellung de reformirten Glaubenslehre.*"[14] Zeller regarded the article as marking a transition to a stronger interest in the moral and cultural content of religion, as opposed to the philosophical and doctrinal. These dates define the high watermark of Hegel's influence. Between them appeared Baur's major studies on Christian origins and the history of dogma. Baur's chief New Testament studies include the following: *Die sogenannten Pastoralbriefe des Apostels Paulus aufs neue kritisch untersucht* (1835);[15] *Paulus, der Apostel Jesu Christi* (1845);[16] *Kritische Untersuchungen über die kanonischen Evangelien* (1847);[17] and *Das Markusevangelium* (1851).[18] Baur's lectures on New Testament theology were published posthumously.[19] His main works on dogma were these: *Die christliche Lehre von der Versöhnung in ihrer geschichtlichen Entwicklung von der ältesten Zeit bis auf die neueste* (1838);[20] *Die christliche Lehre von der Dreieinigkeit und Menschwerdung Gottes in ihrer geschichtlichen Entwicklung* (3 vols., 1841–43);[21] and *Lehrbuch der christlichen Dogmengeschichte* (1847).[22]

However, Peter C. Hodgson, who has made the most definitive study of Baur by an English-speaking scholar, is unconvinced by this division of Baur's career. He maintains that throughout his days at Tübingen, Baur's fundamental viewpoint remained unchanged, though his emphasis varied. There was a continuity of conviction about the irreducibly historical nature of the Christian church, its Gospel and its faith.[23] Hodgson supports his case by pointing out that Baur's celebrated thesis about a conflict between the Petrine (Judaizing) and Pauline (Hellenizing) parties in the early church, the resultant tendency criticism, and its implications for deciding the authenticity of the New Testament writings were outlined in a monograph on "Die Christuspartei in der korinthischen Gemeinde, der Gegensatz des petrinischen und paulinischen Christenhums in der ältesten Kirche, der Apostel Petrus in Rom" (1831).[24] This was at a time when Baur had possibly not even read anything by Hegel.[25]

Baur turned to the study of methodology in history in *Die Epochen der kirchlichen Geschichtsschreibung* (1852)[26] and continued to lecture on Christian doctrine.[27] His last great work, his *Geschichte der christlichen Kirche* (1853–62) was essentially a continuation and culmination of his life's work.[28]

Baur's Historical Critical Method

In the preface to the first volume of his *Geschichte der christlichen Kirche* Baur drew attention to the approach he had held for many years.

> My standpoint is in one word the purely historical one: namely, that the one thing to be aimed at is to place before ourselves the materials given in the history as they are objectively, and not otherwise, as far as that is possible.[29]

This stance meant exploring the data and examining its unity and diversity with a view to producing "a harmonious picture." Such an enterprise could only be justified by itself. Baur referred the reader who wished to know more to *Die Epochen der kirchlichen Geschichtschreibung*, where he reviewed the techniques and presuppositions of ecclesiastical historians from Eusebius in the fourth century down to scholars like Marheineke and Neander in his own. The difficulty with the latter (as with so many of his predecessors) was his supernaturalism.

> In a single word, Neander adheres to a strictly supernaturalistic conception of the origin and nature of Christianity. If Christianity is an absolutely supernatural miracle, shattering the continuity of history, then history has nothing further to do with it, it can only stand before the miracle and see in it the end of its research and understanding. As miracle, the origin of Christianity is an absolutely incomprehensible beginning.

> The question, however, is simply whether the goal thus set for historical research is not an arbitrary one. If all the attempts made with such great effort in more recent times to illuminate critically the origin of Christianity could have no other result than the firmer establishment of a supernaturalistic view such as Neander's, we must in fact despair of any possible progress in church historiography.[30]

By contrast, Baur defined the task of church history as the understanding of its subject in the context and terms of world history.

Before we look at the results of Baur's researches, it is important to recognize that for Baur the attempt to desupernaturalize Christianity was not merely a matter of assembling data and finding rationalistic explanations for what hitherto had been regarded as miraculous and sacred. The task of the historian was to detect the inner connections—or reason—in events. Otherwise, he fails to penetrate beneath the surface of things. History would be no more than a chance aggregate of happenings. It is precisely here that Hegelianism—or whatever name one cares to call it—comes in.

> Let people call the speculative method Hegelianism or whatever they will, the essence of speculation is and remains the intelligent consideration of the object with

which one has to do, the direction of the consciousness to the place in which things appear as they are, the striving to project oneself into the objective process of the thing itself, in order to follow it in all its moments in which it moves forward. The historical datum should not, therefore, be conceived in a merely external way in relation to this or that accidental connection in which the subject stands. Rather, it should be understood in its inner, essential connections. The sole presupposition that is made here is that history is not merely an accidental aggregate, but a whole entity which hangs together. Where there is connection, there is also reason, and what comes about through reason must also be open to reason, for the intelligent contemplation of the mind *[Geist]*. Without speculation all historical investigation is, with whatever name it may deck itself, a mere dallying on the surface and the outside of things. The more weighty and more comprehensive an object is, with which research is occupied, and the more immediately it belongs to the element of thought, the more it becomes a matter not merely of reproducing in oneself what the individual person has thought and done, but of tracing in thought in oneself the eternal thoughts of the eternal mind *[Geist]*, whose work history is.[31]

This statement is taken from a work written at the time when Hegel's influence over Baur was near its zenith. Even so, it is rather different from the popular conception of Baur's Hegelianism. The dominant thought is not the triadic dialectic which is often supposed to be the outstanding characteristic of Hegel, but (and here Baur does have a genuine link with Hegel) the rationality of history. Hegel did not supply Baur with a preconceived dialectic of thesis, antithesis, and synthesis into which every fact of history must be forced. Baur's view of the dialectical tensions in the early church had been reached independently of Hegel. But, in common with Hegel, Baur acknowledged the need for speculation in order to discern rational connections in history and thus think after him the eternal thoughts of the eternal Mind or Spirit, whose work history is. As with other Idealists, this resolved at one stroke the problem of the supernatural in history, and yet saved the historian from a thorough-going naturalism.

History was a matter of understanding the forward movement of the Spirit in the present through the past. It discovered the activity of the Spirit in temporal and particular forms.

Only when the essence of the Spirit *[Geist]* itself, in its inner movement and development and in its self-consciousness moving forward from moment to moment, is represented in history, only then is the true objectivity of history recognized and grasped. It is in particular the task of the history of Christian dogma to treat Christian dogma as a whole and in its individual aspects, so that all the temporal changes appear as the essential and necessary moments, through which the concept *[Begriff]* moves and passes. Driven ever on by the negativity of every temporal form, to separate the essential from the non-essential by the ever more stringent judgment of pure thought, its goal is to grasp itself, passing through all moments, in its own inmost essence. This standpoint is the basis of the account given here. It is presented in the firm conviction that, only in this way can history be for the thinking spirit *[Geist]* that which it is intended to be in accordance with its divine destiny, the self-understanding of the present out of the past.[32]

It might seem that here Baur was speaking with the voice of Hegel. But whereas the latter was a speculative philosopher, Baur was first and foremost a historian. In later life Hegel receded into the background. He received comparatively scant mention in Baur's last study of his contemporaries in his *Kirchengeschichte des neunzehnten Jahrhunderts* (1862).[33] Even in 1851 when Baur made a résumé of his own theological progress, he stressed historical and critical factors rather than philosophical ones. The account occurs in the context of a discussion of "Die Einleitung in das Neue Testament als theologische Wissenschaft."[34] In it Baur was at pains to set the record straight concerning his relationship with Strauss. His initial ideas were conceived prior to Strauss and independently of him. As he developed them, Baur was led to a fundamental rejection of Strauss's conclusions and methods. Baur saw an organic development in his own thought, beginning with his work on "Die Christuspartei in der korinthischen Gemeinde, der Gegensatz des petrinischen und paulinischen Christenthums in der ältesten Kirche, der Apostel Petrus in Rom" (1831). In it he posited a fundamental conflict between Pauline, Hellenistic Christianity, on the one hand, and Petrine, Jewish Christianity, on the other. This conflict became the key for appraising the historicity and dating of the New Testament epistles. Ultimately it became the basis of his appraisal of the Gospels and his rejection of Strauss's conclusions and method, whom he faulted for his failure to undertake an adequate critical account of the Gospels as historical documents.

> What I summed up in my book on the apostle Paul of the year 1845 and presented in further detail as a unity includes, with the exception of my book on the pastoral Epistles, all my investigations in the letters of Paul and in the book of Acts, a book which stands in such a close relationship to them. The question of the Gospels, which was raised anew by Strauss's *Life of Jesus*, only aroused my acute interest after I had attained an independent view of the relation of the Johannine Gospel to the Synoptics. The basic difference of this Gospel to the Synoptics impressed me so much that at once the view of its character and origin came to me which I developed in the *Theologische Jahrbücher* of 1844. That view furnished a new standpoint both for New Testament criticism and for the study of the gospel history. If the Gospel of John is not, as the others, a historical account, if it actually is not intended to be a historical account, if it has undoubtedly an ideological tendency, then it can no longer stand vis-à-vis the Synoptics in a historical opposition. It is therefore no longer possible to employ Strauss's tactics and methodology with which he now opposes the Johannine account to the synoptic and now the synoptic to the Johannine, and from which only the conclusion can be drawn that we no longer have any idea of what can be retained of the gospel story. To the degree that the historical value of John sinks, that of the Synoptics rises, since there is now no reason to raise doubts of the latter's reliability because of the Johannine Gospel. Since we are able to acknowledge the clear and evident difference and to do so without reserve, we have the key to its very simple explanation. Not by any means do I intend to say by this that in the Synoptic Gospels we have a purely historical account, but only that a definite point of view now emerges by which this whole relationship can be understood. By this route I was led further in my investigations in the Gospel of Luke and summed them

up in the *Theologische Jahrbücher* of 1846 and then expanded this summary in my second main book on the criticism of the New Testament, my *Kritische Untersuchung-en über die kanonischen Evangelien* of 1847.[35]

Baur came to the study of the Gospels via his study of Paul. The common factor running through all Baur's critical work is his use of "tendency" criticism. On the basis of a comparison of the *Tendenzen* presented by Acts and the first two chapters of Galatians, Baur concluded that if the latter be genuine, the former cannot be authentic history.[36] When the same techniques were applied to the epistles generally attributed to Paul, only four—Romans, 1 and 2 Corinthians, and Galatians—were pronounced authentic.[37] The remainder lacked the teaching, style, character, and dynamic of the apostle.[38] These results were presented as the conclusions of careful, historical, critical investigation. On the other hand, when Baur came to interpret Paul's teaching about God and Christ, he did so in terms combining Hegel's philosophical idealism with Schleiermacher's theology. On Paul's view of God, Baur observed,

> What is most remarkable in the apostle's doctrine of God is how he seeks to remove from the idea of God everything particular, limited and finite, and to retain nothing but the pure idea of the absolute. The final result of the whole world-process is that God may be all in all, and this point of view is consistently adhered to throughout.[39]

On the subject of Christ Baur maintained,

> By this time there should surely be little doubt among interpreters that Christ is not called God at Rom. ix. 5. When we consider how absolute the idea of God is to the apostle, how powerfully the absoluteness of God had taken possession of his mind, and how distinctly and consistently he represents the relation of Christ to God as one of subordination, we cannot possibly believe that in this one passage he meant to describe Christ as the absolute God exalted above all.[40]

> Christ is thus essentially man, the archetypal man in whom the higher principle of human nature appears. Did he begin to exist as such only when he was born as a human individual in the person of Jesus of Nazareth? The first is not the pneumatical, as the apostle says, 1 Cor. xv. 46, but the psychical, and the pneumatical follows it; at the same time, however, both of these are momenta of, and are included in, a unity.[41]

> The apostle has nowhere ignored the barrier which separates the Son of God from God, on the contrary, he holds fast to the position that Christ is essentially and substantially man. He is at the same time "the Spirit," the spiritual man untainted by sin. Thus he is the ideal and archetypal man, and in this sense the "Lord of Glory."[42]

The Historical Critical Method and Jesus

Two years after his *magnum opus* on Paul, Baur published his *Kritische Untersuchungen über die kanonischen Evangelien* (1847). He now joined issue in public with Strauss. He rejected the attempt to play off John against the Synoptics, for the former was not a historical Gospel, even though it might be called the "testimony of a genuinely evangelical spirit." Again Baur insisted

upon a thoroughly historical, critical approach which began by trying to discern
the tendency of the documents in question. "The first question which criticism
has to put to these Gospels can therefore only be what each respective author
wanted and intended, and only with this question do we come to the firm ground
of concrete, historical truth."[43] When this technique was applied to the Fourth
Gospel Baur concluded,

> It does not intend to be a strictly historical Gospel, but rather subordinates its
> historical content to an idea imposed upon the whole. In accordance with its basic
> idea, it has interpreted from a different standpoint the eclectic, historical material
> from the Gospel tradition, and set it in different combinations. And precisely for this
> reason it has more or less reshaped it in a manner which could not otherwise occur.
> Thus it appears to be a new, autonomous Gospel, sometimes running parallel to the
> Synoptic Gospels and sometimes departing from them on the same point. However,
> its idea and tendency is something else, but the historical content itself remains the
> same, insofar as we only know how to analyse it and trace it to its elements.[44]

The historical material in John has been adapted and made to serve the Johannine
thesis of the incarnation of the divine Logos, and thus may be said to have a
speculative rather than a historical character.[45] The Logos was presented as the
principle of life and light in a world of darkness. The categories of this Johannine
dualism reflected the conflict with Gnosticism, although John's emphasis was
more ethical than cosmological. There was a certain docetic tendency in John
which stressed the Spirit at the expense of the flesh.[46] Although there were
affinities with Gnosticism, John was really a polemic against the heresy.[47] Because
of this, the Gospel could not be dated before the middle of the second century, its
author being one who saw himself as the heir of the Apostle John, endeavoring to
preserve the spirit of his teaching.[48]

With regard to the Synoptic Gospels, Baur rejected both what he called "the
abstract critical interpretation"[49] and "the negative critical or dialectical interpretation."[50] The latter was represented by Strauss whose work suffered from the
primary error of trying to be a critical history without giving a criticism of the
Gospels.[51] The former was represented by scholars like Eichhorn who defended
"the hypothesis of the *Urevangelium*" on literary grounds.[52] Baur himself rejected
this in favor of the literary interdependence of the Synoptics. With regard to
Mark, Baur contended that,

> As the shortest of the three Synoptic Gospels it can equally well be the first as the
> last of them: equally well the first still hardly developed sketch of gospel history as
> an abstract from already existing more comprehensive Gospels. Storr made it the
> first of all the Gospels, Griesbach the last.[53]

Purely literary criteria were, however, inadequate. The decisive factor was the
theological tendencies of the works in question.[54] Mark's aim was to round off
the Gospel story into a harmoniously ordered and clearly arranged whole. His
method was eclectic, excluding anything abnormal, repetitious and adventitious,

as well as most of the teaching material. He avoided the special interests of Matthew and Luke for the sake of giving what he considered to be the facts of the Gospel story. Evidence of the secondary nature of the work is seen in the freedom with which the author supplies vivid touches of local color which might otherwise suggest an eyewitness account. The author was an unknown writer working during or just after the second half of the second century.[55]

Luke was written in Greek by a Paulinist sometime after the completion of Matthew which he deliberately revised to soften its Judaizing tendency. This must have been after A.D. 70 because of its reference to the fall of Jerusalem but before Marcion (ca. A.D. 139). In *Das Christenthum und die christliche Kirche der drei ersten Jahrhunderte* Baur gave the following assessment of Luke.

> The spirit and tendency of the Gospel of Luke can only be understood by the light of its relation to the Gospel of Matthew; and so the Judaism of the latter supplies a good standard for judging of the Paulinism of the former. Here Jesus is not merely the Jewish Messiah of the Gospel of Matthew: he is the Redeemer of mankind in general, and, in this sense, the Son of God. In accordance with this his universal mission, the whole representation of his personality which this Gospel gives us is a higher and more comprehensive one than that of Matthew. In all his works, in his teaching, in his miracles, especially in the power he exercises over demons, and in the whole of his revelation of himself, his personality appears to be superhuman. And herein lies the reason of the well-marked advance which this Gospel has made in the view which is taken of the Gospel history, and in the execution of its plan. The conception of the Gospel history which we find here is a long way beyond the views on which the Gospel of Matthew is based, and a long way towards the views of the Gospel of John.[56]

Baur arrived at the priority of Matthew on the grounds of his tendency criticism. But this was not the same as saying that Matthew presented authentic history.[57] Behind the canonical Gospel of Matthew lay the Gospel of the Hebrews referred to by Papias and Hegesippus.[58] It was originally written in Hebrew, but translated at an early date. It went through various recensions before reaching its present form around A.D. 130–134.[59]

Matthew's broad outline gives the impression that this

> at least in its essential elements was the historical course of the matter itself. The historical sequence has nothing improbable in the whole. It does not lack a real progress of development. Its individual episodes are motivated in a way which fits. And the catastrophe comes about in the end in a way which it could hardly have otherwise come about after all that has gone before.[60]

On the other hand, many of the details were questionable. This same was true of the teaching recorded in Matthew which was largely authentic, though its form reflected the evangelist's viewpoint.

> Thus we cannot consider the Matthaean Gospel to be a purely historical account of the original factual content of the Gospel history. It has in any case a definite,

individual literary character. As is already indicated by its characteristic pragmatism and in its differences from the other Gospels it can only be designated as the most Judaizing Gospel.[61]

In particular, the author's "dominant interest" is his

endeavor to interpret Gospel history from the viewpoint of the Old Testament Messiah-ideal and its realization in the person of Jesus, and to prove the identity of the now appeared Messiah with him in the light of prophetically interpreted particular criteria.[62]

Baur saw this tendency expressed in the pronouncements on the eternal significance of the Mosaic law, Jesus' concern for the lost sheep of the house of Israel (Matt. 15:24), his reference to himself as the Son of David, and the frequent use of prophecy, especially that applied to Jesus' birth and person.[63]

In the posthumously published *Vorlesungen über neutestamentliche Theologie*, which contain the thought of Baur's last years,[64] Baur expressed the conviction that, while the general outline of Jesus' teaching may be discerned, it was no longer possible to decide on specific points.

Here one still does not have before one anything immediate. Everything is mediated through an account of which one does not know what influence it had on the matter itself, and how much has been added or subtracted by it. On so many points one can only hold to the general, because the special and individual already appear to bear the coloring of a later age. Thus the teaching of Jesus stands at a historical distance from us, in which it is removed from the precision of historical consideration, and can be brought into focus more as a whole than in individual details. Even the very nature of the sources make it impossible to give a precise, consecutive account of the teaching of Jesus. But also the nature of the thing brought it about itself, that the original form in which Christianity emerged as a new religion, when it let itself be clearly enough recognized in its primary significance, was still nevertheless very different from dogmatically developed doctrinal concept. To this belonged the entire historical course of development which Christianity followed beginning with the death of Jesus.[65]

Nevertheless, despite the historical forms which primitive Christianity took as a result of the tensions between its Jewish and Hellenistic forms, Jesus himself remains a figure of decisive historical importance.

The teaching of Jesus is the principal matter, to which everything relates which constitutes the characteristic content of New Testament theology, but only in a derivative and secondary way. It is the foundation and presupposition of all that belongs to the historical development of Christian consciousness. For this reason it is that which lies outside all temporal development. It is that which precedes it, the immediate and original. It is not theology at all but religion. Jesus was the founder of a new religion. But what constitutes the essence of a religion in itself is not a dogmatically religious system, a particular doctrinal concept. It is only fundamental convictions and principles, basic tenets and precepts, as immediate utterances of religious consciousness.[66]

Jesus was, therefore, the founder of a new religion that was not in itself a dogmatic system but the presupposition of later Christian theology. Although Baur's thought here is not worked out in terms of Schleiermacher's "feeling of absolute dependence," it has marked affinities with Schleiermacher's approach, insofar as it treats the "immediate utterances of religious consciousness" as the essence of religion. In the first instance, the religion of Jesus involved a reaffirmation of the Old Testament Law.[67] But when Baur expounded this, he did not do so in terms of Jewish theocracy but in those of philosophical Idealism. Jesus was concerned with absolute moral values. His thought even coincided with that of Kant.

> In his attitude to the Old Testament, both in his affirmative stance on the Law as well as in his polemic against Pharisaism, Jesus placed everything that gives man his moral and religious worth entirely in man's frame of mind *[Gesinnung]*. Thus it is entirely the frame of mind, the immediate consciousness of man that expresses itself in its immanent truth, to which everything is referred in the entire content of the Sermon on the Mount. The frame of mind should be clean and pure, free from all self-seeking, man's entire consciousness directed to the One Thing, in which he recognizes his absolute content, and elevated above everything that ties him to the lower sphere of his sensuous existence with its cares and needs. The inner alone it is by which all value of the external is to be judged. Only when the frame of mind is good in its root can something that is good in itself as fruit grow out of it.... "Love your neighbor as yourself," thus must everything egotistical, subjective and particular be let drop.... It is this formal principle of action which in essentials coincides with the Kantian imperative, "So act that the maxim of your action can be the general law of action."... The same energy of the consciousness, which can grasp the substantial essence of morality only in the innermost center of the frame of mind, declares itself in the demand contained in the aforementioned commandment in its simplest, practical expression. It elevates the individual "I" to the universal, to the "I" of all humanity, identical with itself in all separate individuals.[68]

The above quotation goes beyond Kant in suggesting a cosmic metaphysical identity. Baur went on to explain that the religion of Jesus was concerned with the dialectical union of opposites.

> In the contrast between having and not-having, poverty and wealth, earth and heaven, present and future, Christian consciousness has its purest ideality, as the ideal union of all opposites that press themselves upon empirical consciousness. Everything that the most developed, dogmatic consciousness can embrace is already comprehended in it. And yet it has its entire significance only in the fact that it is still the immediate union of all opposites which developed out of it. All those beatitudes, however different they sound, are always only another expression for the same original basic attitude of the Christian consciousness. It is the pure feeling of the need of redemption, containing the antithesis of sin and grace itself already in itself, but still completely untouched by consciousness of the same, which as such also has already all the reality of redemption in itself.[69]

In what sense was Jesus the founder of this new religion and what role did he play in it? Baur replied that the doctrine of Jesus' person and messiahship was "the most difficult point of New Testament theology."[70] We must turn to the Synoptics rather than John, but even here we cannot simply reproduce their answer. "How easily it could happen that after his death, once his whole life and fate appeared to the disciples of Jesus in a higher light and their messianic faith had its more definite form, even the evangelists themselves read into the pronouncements of Jesus much that was derived only from their later way of looking at things."[71] On the basis of his study of the terms *Son of man, Son of God*, and *Kingdom of God*, Baur concluded that Jesus had a certain messianic consciousness.

> If his teaching consisted of everything that we must regard as essential content in the light of the Sermon on the Mount and the parables, he could only have recognized his messianic vocation in realizing the idea of the Kingdom of Heaven in the sense of all those ethical demands which he made on those who confessed him. Therefore as certainly as he penetrated the religious consciousness of his nation with the concept of the Messiah which was identified with his own person and shared the nation's messianic belief, so certainly on the other hand did he oppose it, in that he wanted to be the nationally expected Messiah only in the spiritual sense in which he conceived the idea of the Messiah. The national messianic faith was indeed the necessary way by which alone he could hope for the realization of his spiritual idea of the Kingdom of Heaven. But if the purity of the idea was not to succumb to the sensual elements of popular messianic expectation, then he had to set himself in continuous opposition to it.[72]

Jesus' language thus involved a certain degree of accommodation. The goal that Jesus set himself was the "spiritual image *[Vorstellung]* of action directed towards the moral reform of the people."[73] This, however, was no mere enlightened moralism. It involved a mystical union in which Jesus played the part of a mediator. In the light of Matthew 11:25–30, Baur observed,

> When he says that all things are delivered to him by his father, he can only mean all that relates to the idea of the Kingdom of Heaven. Thereby he expresses only the consciousness that he was its founder in the sense in which he has explained it chiefly in the Sermon on the Mount. In this consciousness he knows himself to be one with the Father. No one knows the Son except the Father and no one knows the Father except the Son and him to whom the Son reveals it. Everything proceeds from the Son that constitutes a new revelation of God to mankind. He is the highest, immediate emissary of God, through whom everything is mediated.[74]

At this point there are marked affinities with Schleiermacher's concept of Christ.

Certain passages in Baur's writings might give the impression that he regarded the resurrection of Jesus as a historical event, inconsistent with his general approach to history. But in both his *Vorlesungen über neutestamentliche Theologie* and *Das Christenthum* Baur made it clear that the resurrection of Jesus could not be presumed to be a historical event (for as such it lay outside the scope of historical investigation). What was historical fact was the belief of the early church in such an event.

> The question as to the nature and the reality of the resurrection lies outside the sphere of historical inquiry. History must be content with the simple fact, that in the faith of the disciples the resurrection of Jesus came to be regarded as a solid and unquestionable fact. It was in this faith that Christianity acquired a firm basis for its historical development. What history requires as the necessary antecedent of all that is to follow, is not so much the fact of the resurrection of Jesus, as the belief that it was a fact. The view we take of the resurrection is of minor importance for the history. We may regard it as an outward objective miracle, or as a subjective psychological miracle; since, though we assume that an inward spiritual process was possible by which the unbelief of the disciples at the time of the death of Jesus was changed into belief in his resurrection, still no psychological analysis can show what that process was. In any case it is only through the consciousness of the disciples that we have any knowledge of that which was the object of their faith; and thus we cannot go further than to say that by whatever means this result was brought about, the resurrection of Jesus became a fact of their consciousness, and was as real to them as any historical event.[75]

It was this belief that led to the decisive break with Judaism. Beyond this, Baur could only reiterate that it was the Easter faith that was the decisive factor in the causal nexus of history, and ask semi-rhetorically,

> What was it then that invested the belief in the risen one with a higher significance, and made it possible for the principle which had entered into the world in Christianity to develop itself in the great and imposing series of phenomena in which its history was unfolded, and to triumph over every influence which opposed it and threatened to hinder or obscure the all-commanding universalism of its spirit and aims?[76]

Baur's answer to his own question took the form of a descriptive analysis of the forms that the faith of the church took in its subsequent history. But it was not an answer in terms of the question that had been posed. For the question admitted a metaphysical answer and Baur's concept of history precluded metaphysical answers on the level of historical explanation. It was a concept of history which became virtually axiomatic among German critical scholars during the next hundred years.[77]

The Significance of Baur

All too often Baur has been caricatured as a Hegelian disguised as a New Testament scholar. Even *The Oxford Dictionary of the Christian Church* claimed that Baur "developed his characteristic doctrines under the influence of G. W. F. Hegel's conception of history" and then proceeded to describe Catholic Christianity as the synthesis of the conflict between earlier forms.[78] At best such a description is an oversimplification. If Baur was a Hegelian at all, it was not in the appropriation for theology of a dialectic of thesis, antithesis, and synthesis —terms which, in any case were more characteristic of Fichte than Hegel. This formulation is as rare in Baur's reconstruction of the primitive church as it is in Hegel. A term which is, however, characteristic of Baur's historiography is *Gegensatz* (contrast, antithesis), but he had already used the concept in detecting different tendencies and parties in the Corinthian church some years before he studied with Hegel.

It is true that Baur admired Hegel at certain points. But he disclaimed any suggestion that he was a mere disciple of the philosopher, and insisted that his approach to data was rigorously historical. Moreover, both his brother and his son-in-law claimed that Baur was nearer to Schleiermacher than to Hegel.[79] The point at which Baur himself admitted coming closest to Hegel—though even then he insisted that the matter was not the exclusive property of the Hegelians —was in recognizing the need of speculation in order to understand history. It would be possible to take statements from various writings and make a collage which would picture Baur as a thorough-going Hegelian.[80] It would be true to say that when Baur philosophized about the meaning of history, the development and meaning of dogma, or the method of the historian, he spoke like a Hegelian. He thus exposed his flank to critics like Barth and Wolfgang Geiger who accused him of interpreting the Christian revelation in the light of an alien and false meta-physic.[81] Even Ernst Troeltsch, who was anything but unsympathetic to the attempt to understand Christianity in the light of a more general background, saw Baur's work as so rooted in Hegelian dialectic that everything was subordinate to the unfolding of the Christian idea in history. As a consequence, the Incarnation together with "all theology and christology become superfluous."[82]

But to say this is not to say the last word about Baur. Though there is some justice in Troeltsch's premises, Baur himself would certainly have quarreled with the deductions. He was incensed with those of his critics who accused him of ignoring or eliminating Christ. He saw in Hegel the same separation of the historical and ideal in Christ as that produced by Gnosticism, and in both cases it was the result of a speculative comprehension of Christianity.[83] Baur's chief complaint against Strauss was that he reached conclusions without adequate, prior, historical criticism. Before any conclusions could be drawn, Baur insisted on asking first what an author intended, what motivated him, and what was the *Tendenz* of his work. It was in asking—rather than in answering—these questions that Baur made his most positive contribution to theology in general and critical history in particular. Baur's conclusions were often radical, more radical than the consensus of scholarship, even in his own day, would allow. He regularly saw *Gegensätze* in a text where others failed to see disparity or tension. But his exegesis of texts was predominantly concerned with interrogating the text itself, rather than with reading into it a preconceived philosophy. His painstaking discussions of words and phrases were often long and detailed. However, it was in the realm of hermeneutics rather than exegesis that Baur's approach to religion and the figure of Jesus were decided.

The decisive step was the rejection of the supernatural world view of traditional theism in favor of one in which God is seen as the immanent spirit in nature and history. Baur found such a view in Fichte, Schelling, and Schleiermacher before he found it in Hegel. Although he rejected Schleiermacher's subjectivism, Baur welcomed Schleiermacher's innovation in seeing the content of the Christian faith as an expression of human self-consciousness.[84] Consequently, his view of Jesus had affinities with Schleiermacher's, but it also had its own distinctive character. Jesus was the archetypal figure who reconciled all contradictions in his role of unique mediator. But with Baur, moral concern replaced the notion of absolute dependence. Jesus adopted the role of Messiah with a view of transforming it spiritually and morally.

In making this last point Baur placed himself in the mainstream of liberal theology since the Enlightenment, which construed the mission of Jesus in terms of inner, ethical reformation. But in another sense Baur stood apart from the theologians of his day. He was distinguished from most of them in his radical assessments of the New Testament documents. Even more important, however, were his methods. His stress on the importance of the tendency of documents anticipated the methods of Redaction Criticism. It was perhaps the radical conclusions that he drew from this approach which made Baur's contemporaries shy away from the significance of this point. Later on, Wellhausen's Pentateuchal criticism recognized the importance of tendencies within documents, and later Redaction Criticism combined the analysis of tendencies with source criticism in its assessment of New Testament writings. Although Baur posited various recensions of Matthew before it reached its present form, he tended to think in terms of the tendency of the document as a whole rather than to analyze conflicting tendencies within the document.

Rudolf Bultmann has pointed out that Baur's reduction of faith's self-understanding to a consciousness arising out of historical development eliminates the kerygma.[85] Bultmann noted that Baur does this, not out of rationalistic considerations, but in such a way that history itself takes the place of the kerygma. After Baur, however, Bultmann contended that the question of the meaning of history and historical reflection got lost.

In the light of his contributions to theological method, the renewed interest in Baur should cause no surprise. What is perhaps surprising is the comparative neglect of Baur in the second half of the nineteenth century. Although there has been considerable talk of the Tübingen School, and Baur himself wrote in defense of it,[86] it is questionable whether the School ever amounted to more than Baur himself and his immediate circle.[87]

Baur's most famous pupils—D. F. Strauss, Eduard Zeller, and Albrecht Ritschl—each went their separate ways. Strauss had already long been disowned. Zeller was loyal to his father-in-law, but was also loyal to his friend,

Strauss. On being refused a chair in philosophy at Tübingen on account of his attacks on the Christian faith, Zeller moved to Bern, then to Marburg, and finally to Heidelberg. Ritschl openly renounced the Tübingen School.[88] Very few outstanding students held and developed Baur's views, and those who did found difficulties in obtaining academic positions. Among Baur's adherents were Adolf Hilgenfeld, Karl Reinhold Köstlin, Albert Schwegler, and Gustav Volkmar, but none of these enjoyed the prestige or possessed the massive, creative scholarship of Baur. Moreover, dissensions within the School came increasingly to light. Hilgenfeld was perhaps the most dedicated and scholarly upholder of the School. He moved to Jena in 1847, but it was not until Hase's death in 1890 that he obtained a full professorship at the age of sixty-seven. Among the reasons for this was his sweeping rejection of Christian beliefs, his inadequacies as a lecturer and his quarrelsome personality. This contentiousness affected his relations with Baur, whose views on the Gospels he refused to accept.[89] Albert Schwegler wrote an early work in the tradition of Baur on the apostolic age, but thereafter abandoned theology.[90] Baur's views on the Gospels were questioned by Köstlin,[91] and Volkmar adopted a new, if no less skeptical, approach.[92]

After the death of his colleague, Friedrich Kern, in 1842, Baur found himself increasingly isolated within the Tübingen faculty and in German academic theology generally. The Prussian universities were conservative and orthodox, and the Prussian government even more so. On academic grounds the attempt to place the majority of the New Testament writings in the second century was found to be unconvincing. The attempt to give historical explanations for the origins of Christianity found increasing favor in the nineteenth century, but not at the expense of rejecting all supernatural explanations. Perhaps Baur's dogmatic and philosophical pronouncements were too bound up with Hegel and Idealism, so that when men lost interest in Hegel, they also lost interest in Baur. His position was displaced by the anti-metaphysical perspective of the Ritschlians, and his work on Gospel origins was superseded by a multitude of studies on the Synoptic question. Literary criticism reasserted itself, and the priority of Mark gained increasing ascendancy. On a less technical level, public interest in the life of Jesus was captured by Renan and the later liberal lives, including that by Strauss, who outlived his teacher by another thirteen years.

12. LATER CRITICAL STUDY

Gospel Criticism

In the same year that Baur published *Die christliche Gnosis* and Strauss the first volume of his *Leben Jesu,* an apparently insignificant article appeared that in the long run turned out to be no less crucial for subsequent Gospel criticism. Its author was the philologist, Karl Lachmann,[1] and it was written in the decent obscurity of Latin. The title was "De ordine narrationum in evangeliis synopticis,"[2] and its theme was the order of the stories in the Synoptic Gospels. Lachmann dismissed Griesbach's argument as "an absolute frost."[3] His own case rested upon a comparison of order.

> I have therefore decided to consider for the present only their ordering. This is much the simplest element, and no one, to my knowledge, has considered it before. So let us see how much progress can be made from this starting-point.

> The ordering of the gospel stories does not vary as much as people think. The variation appears greatest if all three writers are compared together, or if Luke is compared with Matthew: it is less if Mark is compared with the others one by one.[4]

Lachmann proceeded to set out in tabular form nine sections drawn from Mark 1:21–6:13, and Matthew 4:24–13:58, which contain the same material but in different order. He concluded,

> I hold that no good reason can be found by which we could suppose that Mark was led to alter Matthew's order here, especially as Luke agrees with Mark on almost all these points: but I think I can show why the order of Mark and Luke could not be used in the gospel of Matthew; so it was here, not there, that the order had to be broken by certain devices. Now the gospel of Matthew I regard as originally composed of discourses of the Lord Jesus Christ, collected and woven together, with other stories stuck in afterwards (this view of Schleiermacher's needed expounding only, not arguing, since it is obviously true; so it should be accepted even if you differ from him in interpreting Papias).[5]

Similarly, Lachmann endeavored to show that "Luke hardly ever departs from Mark,"[6] though each evangelist had "compelling reasons for changing the order . . . found in some of these sections."[7] Matthew, for example, desired to give prominence to the Sermon on the Mount.

> It would therefore have seemed more appropriate that the leper should be said to have run and met Jesus when he came down from the mount and before he entered the town of Capernaum, in which he healed the centurion's servant according to the gospel of Matthew, and Peter's mother-in-law according to both evangelists.[8]

Luke's divergences from Mark fall into two classes: two cases where the order is changed but where the words remain much the same; and three cases where sections are set in different positions and differ in matter and wording. The former are best explained by Luke's reluctance to say the same thing twice or take away anything from his account of the journey to Jerusalem; the latter by Luke's possession of other material from reliable sources.[9]

Lachmann did not claim that there were no written or oral sources prior to Mark. Indeed, he believed that he could show how many "molecules" of Gospel history existed and that all three Synoptic Gospels were dependent upon a common written or oral source.[10] But his main point remained that Mark constituted the middle term between Matthew and Luke. Moreover, he urged caution against treating Mark's authority with contempt. Lachmann was the first to treat seriously the order of events in the Gospels as a key to understanding Synoptic relationships. In doing this he made a major contribution to the eventual over-throw of the priority of the Griesbach hypothesis, though he himself did not commit the so-called "Lachmann fallacy" of assuming that the evidence pointed conclusively to the dependence of Matthew and Luke upon Mark.[11] His work was a factor in the eventual widespread acceptance of the two-source theory of Gospel sources, Mark and the sayings source known as Q. Lachmann also made a further contribution toward putting New Testament studies on a scientific basis. His two-volume critical text of the New Testament, *Novum Testamentum Graece et Latine* (1842–50), carried forward the work of Griesbach, getting away from reliance upon printed texts in producing a version based upon manuscripts.

The year after Lachmann's article appeared a similar proposal was made by C. A. Credner in his *Einleitung in das Neue Testament*. Credner identified Papias's Mark with the *Urevangelium* copied by Matthew, Mark and Luke. W. R. Farmer comments,

> Thus, for the first time, the witness of Papias was understood to testify to two primitive sources lying behind our Gospels: an Ur-Marcus and a collection of sayings. Two such hypothetical sources had already been conceived as early as Marsh. But now, for the first time, they were connected with the Apostles Peter and Matthew respectively, through the testimony of Papias.[12]

Three years after Lachmann's article and apparently quite independent of it, the former Protestant pastor and later convert to Roman Catholicism, C. G. Wilke (1786–1854), produced a work on *Der Urevangelist oder exegetisch-kritische Untersuchung über das Verwandtschaftsverhältniss der drei ersten Evangelien*. Wilke claimed that the synoptic agreements could not satisfactorily be explained on the assumption of an oral *Urevangelium* or collections of sayings and other material. The agreement of the Synoptics in the reproduction of con-tents and sequence of material, together with the presence of almost the whole of Mark's substance in Matthew and Luke, could best be explained by positing that Matthew and Luke used Mark as a basis.[13]

Wilke's application of Occam's razor produced a neater solution than any of the previous theories, but this fact was no guarantee of general acceptance. Both Schleiermacher and Lachmann had drawn attention to the apparent looseness and lack of precise chronological arrangement in the Synoptics, but the construction of Mark remained a secondary issue until the twentieth century. Even the priority of Mark was not widely accepted during Wilke's lifetime.[14] However, another contemporary, C. H. Weisse, espoused Lachmann's thesis and carried it further.

Christian Hermann Weisse (1801–66) was a philosopher in the Idealist tradition. He became Professor of Philosophy at Leipzig in 1845 and in later years he also lectured in the theology faculty. In 1838 he published a massive two-volume work entitled *Die evangelische Geschichte kritisch und philosophisch bearbeitet*. At the outset he stressed the need for integrating philosophy and faith. "How, without the organ of philosophy, the Christian faith should be able to win the form in which it will again in our age be acknowledged to be the truth, I acknowledge that I have no idea."[15] Weisse welcomed the appearance of Strauss's *Leben Jesu* as a joyful event that in no way undermined Christian truth. But he felt compelled to join issue with Strauss and attempt "the recovery of the historical picture of Christ."[16] In order to do this, a satisfactory account of Synoptic relationships had to be given. Weisse's solution was the first clear statement of the two-source theory: the priority of Mark and the existence of a common source of sayings that accounted for the teaching material in Matthew and Luke and also the doublets in which two versions of the same material were unconsciously reproduced.

Weisse noticed various linguistic and stylistic indications that pointed to the priority of Mark. It contained more Hebraisms and was apparently less polished and more artless than Matthew and Luke. Mark bore "the stamp of a fresh naturalness and unpresuming vivacity." Where Matthew and Mark give the same stories, the first evangelist appears, with few exceptions, to be "epitomizing." He was at pains to remove harsh expressions and idiosyncracies, especially Mark's frequent use of the word "and" in introducing new stories. Luke was likewise an "epitomizer," but frequently he also paraphrased and added his own comments in order to produce a smooth narrative.[17] Nevertheless, it was the composition and sequence of the whole that had "the final, decisive weight." Despite all deviations, a single thread ran through the narrative. In those passages which Matthew, Mark, and Luke had in common, the first and the third evangelist depart from Mark, but do not agree with each other against Mark. Moreover, where all three agree, the agreement of the other two is "mediated" by Mark.[18]

In addition to their common use of Mark, Weisse detected a second source of material used by Matthew and Luke.

> Particularly in the First Gospel a whole series of so-to-speak doublets of individual sayings of the Lord may be discerned. Indeed they are such that, where the one example belongs to the narrative sequence which this Gospel has in common with Mark, the other proves to have been drawn from that other primary source from which the Gospel derives its name....Less frequent are such repetitions in Luke, although even here they are not entirely absent. For in such cases Luke tends mostly to pass over Mark's report and transmits the apothegm in the form in which he has received it from Matthew, yet in his own free way, inserted in a sequence of his own or presented anecdotally.[19]

Thus Weisse reached the basic conclusion of the two-document hypothesis that, "Not only is Mark the common source of both, but in accordance with our most specific conviction the sayings-collection of Matthew is also."[20]

With regard to the Fourth Gospel, Weisse observed that, "It is less a *picture* of Christ than an *idea* of Christ that John gives; his Christ does not speak from his person but about his person."[21] John was influenced by the Logos teaching that found expression in Gnosticism and in the somewhat wider circle represented by Clement of Alexandria.[22] Weisse felt obliged to posit a connection between the Fourth Gospel and the Apostle John on account of "the authority of the entire Christian church from the second century to the nineteenth."[23] But the connection between John and Jesus was not one of eyewitness reporting but of reflective interpretation.

> The Synoptic discourses are such that they had impressed themselves objectively by their power and unique character on the spirit of the disciples, and because they were there *present* in this spirit, they impelled their repetition. On the other hand, the Johannine discourses are what the spirit of the disciple toiled to summon forth and pour into a new mold. He did this at a time when the form of the Master was threatening to vanish from him in a mist. He was striving to hold fast this picture and recollect the traits that were already dissipating through the means of a theory that was firmly established or borrowed from somewhere concerning the identity and sending of the Master. For the Synoptic picture of Christ, the frame of mind of the disciples giving the report is merely an indifferent channel; for that of John it is a formative force in the making of the picture.[24]

John was thus a theological composition. But this conclusion did not mean that the Synoptics were free from unhistorical elements. Matthew and Luke contain legendary material in their birth and infancy narratives.[25] The resurrection stories also contain myth.

> Only *faith* is historical fact—not the mythical faith in the bodily resurrection of the Lord of the later Christian world, but the personal miraculous faith of the apostles and their companions in the presence of the Risen One in the visions and appearances that they had themselves experienced.[26]

Weisse dismissed eschatology as unworthy of "a spirit of the magnitude of Jesus." It was the product of a "sick brain," too bizarre to be explained as merely accommodation on the part of Jesus for the sake of his hearers.[27]

It was the task of criticism to remove such excrescences from the Master's teaching. When this was done, the resurrection, ascension, and parousia of Jesus would be seen, not as three separate historical events, but as the expression of Christian confidence in the ultimate triumph of Jesus' work and teaching. On Weisse's premises it was only right that the eighth and final book of his work should be devoted to a "concluding philosophical review of the significance of Christ's personality and the Gospel tradition." In the picture that emerged, an altruistic belief in providence and commitment to historical method replaced theistic supernaturalism and evangelical faith.

In the two decades that elapsed after the publication of his *Evangelische Geschichte*, Weisse complained that there had been no one else who had "followed the path laid by the researches of Schleiermacher and Lachmann."[28] The complaint was not entirely justified. It omitted mention of Wilke and it failed to do justice to the work of Ewald who had come down on the side of the priority of Mark, even though he had done so by a somewhat circuitous and eccentric route.

Heinrich Georg August Ewald (1803–75) was a leading Old Testament scholar.[29] His scholarly interests extended into the New Testament and in an article entitled "Ursprung und Wesen der Evangelien"[30] he presented his own solution to the Synoptic problem. In the course of the article he turned on his former colleague, F. C. Baur, whose *Kritische Untersuchungen* had been published the previous year, and accused him of not taking the trouble to understand Christ and the Bible, and of failing to take him into his heart. Half a century later Ewald's famous pupil, Wellhausen, credited him with having defeated the Tübingen school.[31] Nor was the article without influence upon Baur's former pupil, Ritschl, who went on to repudiate Baur's position in an epoch-making article published in 1851.[32]

Ewald adopted the priority of Mark, but did so by dint of an elaborate nine-document hypothesis in which Mark was preceded by an *Urevangelium* and a collection of sayings, which he identified with Papias's *Logia*. Like Herder, he argued that Mark must be the first of the canonical Gospels because it is the simplest and most vivid. Various other works followed, and last in the series came Luke who made use of all previous sources except Matthew. It was not surprising that the complexity of the argument failed to command universal assent, especially when the neater solutions of Wilke and Weisse were already to hand.

In his *Geschichte des Volkes Israel* Ewald saw the goal of history as the discovery of true religion. Jesus' life and teaching fulfilled what the non-Christian religions were striving after. Ewald's thought combined a touch of evolutionary optimism about the steady spiritual progress of mankind with higher criticism and a basically orthodox piety. In *Die Lehre der Bibel von Gott* Ewald wrote the following:

> ...the law as it then was proved itself incapable of coming to Him and making Him its own, and it could now no longer hinder the direct progress to the perfect true revelation and religion He would give to the world, and whose way He broke by all He did, and especially by the death of sacrifice He freely offered for the world. On the other hand also, all that was imperishable in the law and in the community till then, and that had more and more perfectly unfolded its power since the community was established, liberated now from the fatal deficiency which had ultimately led to the worst heathen aberration, could at length be recognised the more distinctly and work the more freely.

> With the death and resurrection of Christ, therefore, was also removed, as by a single quick and sudden stroke, the other deficiency which adhered to the community of the true religion and its law, as they had hitherto existed. The breaking of the hard sheath in which the law had imprisoned the better soul of the true revelation and religion, broke also the limits of its community, and opened to all nations free access to the community, of transfigured revelation and perfected true religion, a community born again by the new law of divine love and redemption one and the same for all men.[33]

This fairly typical example of Ewald's teaching is not so much biblical exegesis as liberal Protestant hermeneutics set in a devout key. It is not surprising that Albert Schweitzer endorsed Weisse's criticism. He paid tribute to the learning that Ewald brought to the study of Christ but accused him of being half-hearted in showing the connection between Jesus and postcanonical Judaism and of failing to detect Jesus' eschatology.[34]

At the close of the period under review there was no consensus of opinion about the Gospels beyond the belief that they had some kind of common origin. The next sixty years produced a different story. In the opinion of W. R. Farmer,

> The history of the Synoptic Problem subsequent to Holtzmann's epoch-making synthesis of 1863 is mainly the history of the triumph of the two-document hypothesis and the transformation of that hypothesis into the form in which Streeter explained and defended it.[35]

The man who brought about the dramatic change was H. J. Holtzmann (1832–1910), who taught at Heidelberg from 1858 to 1875 and then at Strassburg until his retirement in 1904. In 1862 he edited Friedrich Bleek's *Synoptische Erklärung der drei ersten Evangelien*,[36] and in the following year published his own account of *Die Synoptischen Evangelien. Ihr Ursprung und geschichtlicher Charakter*.[37]

Holtzmann saw his critical work as a necessary preliminary to all discussion of the truth of Christianity—a problem made acute since Strauss. He adopted Mark as the oldest Gospel, and posited a common source of teaching and other material upon which Matthew and Luke based their teaching sections.[38] The significance of Holtzmann's work lay not only in the fact that he confirmed and restated Weisse's position. He himself believed that it made untenable the results of the Tübingen School with its tendency criticism. It also helped to establish the liberal Protestant picture of Jesus as a strong, moral, and religious personality. In Holtzmann's pronouncements there are hints of Schleiermacher's God-consciousness. Holtzmann believed that this human picture of Jesus was essentially that of Mark. By establishing the priority of Mark, Holtzmann helped to recover a historical Jesus whose religious personality transcended historical forms.

Nearly half a century later Holtzmann was still arguing for the fundamental historicity of Jesus and his messianic consciousness.

> It is not a matter of banishing Messianism from history, but of correctly determining its relationship to the train of ideas bound up with those terms [Son of God and Son of man]. It can be shown that the concept of the Son of man originally designated the bringer of the Kingdom of God, just as Son of God designated the immediate, untrammeled experience of God in the innermost being *[Gemütsgrund]*. He who, proceeding from the thought of the Kingdom, knew himself to be the chosen organ of its realization, found as a counterpart to the thought of God as Father the complementary idea in his own inner being which constituted his consciousness as Son. Thus these two ideas, Son of man and Son of God, form together in an indivisible, completely closed unity, the messianic thought of Jesus, which leaves behind the

"Messiah of the Jews," even though it was historically conditioned by it and even though it is to be understood only on the basis of premises drawn from the Old Testament and late Judaism.[39]

Holtzmann concluded his account of *Das messianische Bewusstsein Jesu* by remarking that "No significant Protestant theologian today defends the two-natures doctrine of the creeds." Nevertheless, the credal formulas may still serve to present "the relationship of Jewish and human factors in the personal unity of him who speaks to us out of the Gospels—who was the Messiah and more than a Messiah . . . a prophet and more than a prophet."[40]

In recent years the validity of Holtzmann's two-document hypothesis has been vigorously challenged by those who favor a return to Griesbach's hypothesis of the priority of Matthew.[41] W. R. Farmer makes several sharp criticisms of Holtzmann's work.[42] In the first place, he argues that it was not based upon a firm grasp of the primary phenomena of the Gospels themselves, but upon an artificial and deceptive consensus among scholars of differing traditions. Secondly, Farmer sees a structural fault in the idea that Luke did not know Matthew, and hence the need to posit a source for the material common to both. A third fault was his method in reconstructing the source from passages where two or more Gospels agree. Farmer goes on to argue that the two-document hypothesis met a theological need in providing an answer to the Tübingen School by establishing the historicity of Mark against the growing assumption that Matthew was written after the close of the eyewitness period. This coincided with the espousal by Strauss and Baur of the Griesbach hypothesis. "The real enemy," Farmer maintains, "was the Tübingen school and only incidentally the Griesbach hypothesis, which Baur had accepted. But there can be no doubt that the Griesbach hypothesis lost 'popular' support with the collapse of the Tübingen school."[43]

The plausibility of Farmer's thesis has, however, been challenged by C. M. Tuckett who claims that Farmer never gives details of arguments drawn from this period against the Griesbach hypothesis.[44] Moreover, as was noted in the previous chapter, the Tübingen School did not uniformly embrace the Griesbach hypothesis. Nor was the Griesbach hypothesis of prime importance to Strauss or Baur whose historical evaluation of the Gospels was determined on other grounds. Tuckett goes on to claim that there is no evidence that either the adoption of the Griesbach hypothesis by Strauss and Baur or the desire to rescue the eyewitness nature of at least some of the tradition had any influence on the rejection of Griesbach or the adoption of Marcan priority. Griesbach's view had never been universally adopted even before Strauss. And there were in fact cogent arguments against it, not least its failure to explain Mark's motivation and lack of consistency in conflating his sources sometimes with care and at other times with none.[45]

It may be observed with Tuckett that one of Griesbach's strongest arguments against Marcan priority was the common assumption that the author of the First Gospel was the apostle Matthew and the attendant difficulty of thinking that an apostle would have depended on the work of someone who was not even an eyewitness.[46] But where the premise of the argument is not granted, the cogency of the conclusion is lost. The Synoptic question is still keenly debated, though most scholars have followed the path trod by Weisse and Holtzmann. Albert Schweitzer found similarities between the views of his former Strassburg teacher and those of Strauss. Both took much the same view of the development of Jesus' thought. But Holtzmann's capacity to make his view of Jesus seem to arise naturally out of Mark appealed to the climate of opinion. Perhaps it would be more exact to compare Holtzmann's Jesus with that of Schleiermacher. But whereas Schleiermacher's historical Christ was derived from the Fourth Gospel, Holtzmann's was based on Mark, and Mark was perceived to be the Gospel most firmly rooted in history. But as Schweitzer reminded his readers, "The victory . . . belonged, not to the Marcan hypothesis pure and simple, but to the Marcan hypothesis as psychologically interpreted by a liberal theology."[47]

Later Liberal Lives and Studies

In the 1830s, Bruno Bauer (1809–82) made his way from Hegelianism and speculative orthodoxy to radical skepticism, and in the process made a name for himself as an *enfant terrible*.[48] These steps were to cost him his academic career and turn his doubts into bitter hostility. A recent judgment calls him "the anti-theologian *par excellence* long before Nietzsche and the anti-religious long before Lenin, both of whom he towered over in historical expertise and criticism."[49]

Bauer's *Kritik der evangelischen Geschichte des Johannes* represented the Fourth Gospel as the work of a disciple of Philo who produced not a history but a work of art. Bauer's assessment of the Synoptics in his *Kritik der evangelischen Geschichte der Synoptiker* was almost equally negative. He sought to build upon the foundations recently laid by Weisse, Wilke, and Strauss. The abiding merit of Strauss lay in the fact that,

> He has removed the further development of criticism from the danger and trouble of an immediate contact with the earlier orthodox system. . . . After Strauss's great achievement criticism will no longer be in danger of preserving the categories of the older orthodox view. Criticism stands in equally little need of seeking its next, immediate antithesis in the earlier ecclesiastical system. It bears it now in itself. Indeed, in the abstract, pure form in which the matter can be successfully prosecuted, criticism has this inner antithesis to itself in the work of Strauss. And if it succeeds in resolving Strauss's view of the substance and his tradition-hypothesis, it will have thereby resolved the earlier orthodox view in its highest fulfillment.[50]

The implications of these dark, Hegelian hints were unfolded in the next paragraph.

> Thus criticism has to turn upon itself, and direct itself to resolving the mysterious substantiality in which it and its subject were previously held. It is to this that the development of substance itself is driving—the universality and particularity of the Idea and its real existence—infinite self-consciousness.[51]

Alongside Strauss, Bauer placed the work of Weisse and especially Wilke in establishing the priority of Mark.

> After the thorough proof that Wilke adduced for the thesis that the First Evangelist used and copied the text of Luke in addition to that of Mark, he needed only the space of one page in order to add briefly the fact that, e.g., the First Synoptic Evangelist's Sermon on the Mount was "the expanded one of Luke."[52] Thus Wilke has mortally wounded the hypothesis that a sayings collection of the Apostle Matthew was used by the First and Third Synoptic writer. For it is precisely in the text of the First Evangelist that one must come across the most reliable traces of such a collection, if it ever really existed. Wilke also proceeds logically and correctly to the conclusion that a sayings collection must have looked like that "which Papias mentions as the compositions of Matthew which have not survived."[53] But he has not yet delivered the final proof, since he has not yet shown where Luke obtained the sayings with which he enriched the text of Mark.

> Otherwise Wilke, whose work appeared at the same time as Weisse's, has confirmed with extraordinary thoroughness for all time the latter's discovery that the Gospel of Mark was used and copied by the other two. In the moment when the extraordinary discovery was made, Wilke provided the conclusive proof.[54]

But in fact, neither Weisse nor Wilke had gone far enough. It remained for Bauer to complete the task. His own work on the Fourth Gospel had convinced him that "there could be a Gospel of purely literary origin, and finally that we possess in that Gospel a writing of this kind."[55] If this could be true of John, it could also be true of Mark. Moreover, if "artistic composition" could influence contents, it could also create them.

> The task of criticism, the ultimate one that could be given it, is now clearly that of simultaneously examining form and content to determine whether the latter is likewise of literary origin and the free creation of self-consciousness.[56]

Bauer believed that Weisse had shown Strauss to be wrong in concluding that the Gospels were based on "Jewish messianic dogmatics," drawn *a priori* from Old Testament passages.[57] But this conclusion left open the question of how the ideas of the Gospels arose in Christian consciousness. In trying to answer this, the older Hegelians had paid too little attention to criticism. The Hegelian system must be brought to its logical conclusion by asking, "Does not criticism lead precisely to the universality of self-consciousness by recognizing the determinateness of self-consciousness in the letter and in the positive?"[58]

Rather than attempt a survey of Bauer's treatment in general, it will be more illuminating to examine one or two sample specimens of his exegesis and then look at his conclusions. The birth narratives to which he devoted 141 pages are typical of Bauer's approach. He argued that if these stories derived from tradition, they could not differ as they do. They were literary inventions, the product of Christian self-consciousness.

> Luke has placed beautiful, individual pictures in the place of the reports that he found in Mark. Matthew is even more rich in new, fortuitous compositions. But

neither of them have brought into a complete, connected whole their new formations, either among themselves or with what they preserved from Mark. How much more fortunate would they thus have been in outworking of their prehistories! Luke creates initially a rounded whole, which he did not succeed again in doing in his Gospel. Matthew, who takes the germ of his pre-history from that of Luke, is so little affected by it that he makes a new, cogent composition, which likewise was not possible in the remaining part of his work in such great compass. Should they not thus be the authors of these pre-histories? They are and they remain so. Everything has its time. When they wrote, it was precisely the time when Christian self-consciousness went back further to its presuppositions than it did in the time of Mark. It sought to grasp and represent them in the sole form which was available to it, the form of the pre-history of the Lord. For this task the time was a creative one. Matthew and Luke were gripped by the force of a new cultural impetus, and they gave in the fullest form what their age required.[59]

What was true of the birth narratives was also true of the notion of the Messiah. It was the product of Christian self-consciousness.

> In prophecy as in fulfillment, the Messiah was merely an ideal product of religious self-consciousness. As a given, physical individual, he did not exist. Everything of concern to religious self-consciousness is always merely its own act and creation. Even the Dalai Lama is as such the work and creation of his servants.

> The designation of the Messiah as the Son of Man was only created, when the Messiah existed for Christian consciousness, and was thus only created late, since he first occurs in the writing of Mark.[60]

The "external material" of the title Son of Man was derived from Daniel 7 where the Messiah is described as a Son of Man on the heavenly clouds. Bauer contended that it was generally recognized that "out of this material through Christian reworking the figure arose in which, as its most expressive name indicates, human nature brought forth a fruit in which it was itself reborn and transfigured as the true man."[61] Whereas Weisse traced the choice of the expression back to Jesus as a token of "noble modesty," Bauer stressed its supernatural character, but absolved Jesus himself from originating it.[62] He found it incredible that Jesus would want to keep secret his messiahship with all its terrible, supernaturalistic overtones. If he had really been called the Messiah in his lifetime, he would have repudiated it with all his might. The conclusion to be drawn was that the messianic secret was the invention of the First Evangelist, Mark, who found himself embarrassed by contemporary belief which was unjustified by the teaching of Jesus.

The technique which Bauer consistently employed of detecting contradictory, offensive elements, and then pronouncing the whole episode spurious, found expression in the following verdict on the Last Supper.

> The anachronism and contradiction, which arise from putting these words in the Lord's mouth, stand in all their crudity, when it says that this is the blood which is poured out for many. Not to the disciples, who still sat at one table with Jesus, but to the members of the later community could it be said that they should drink the blood which was shed for them. The blood that first really becomes sacrificial blood after it

is shed is not sacrificial blood and can neither be designated as such nor received as such before the sacrifice, before it is shed and served as a sacrifice. In other words, Jesus could not offer before his death the blood that was shed for many.[63]

What was historical about the Christian faith for Bauer was not the Christ of faith but the faith of the early Christians in Christ.

> The Christian dogma of the Redeemer is itself also history—namely, the history of his heavenly descent, his passion and his resurrection. This history is represented in the Gospels as a real, empirical occurrence. We have shown, however, that it is only a dogma, only an ideal product of Christian consciousness. We have, therefore, also criticized the dogma at the point and traced it back to the self-consciousness which appears to be most firmly rooted in reality and least open to doubt.[64]

> We have thus answered the question which has so preoccupied our age, whether this person [i.e., the Redeemer] or Jesus is the historical Christ. We have shown that everything that the historical Christ is, that is said of him, that we know of him, belongs to the world of imagination [Vorstellung] and indeed to Christian imagination [Vorstellung]. Therefore it has nothing to do with a human being who belongs to the real world. The question is answered, so as to be settled for all time.[65]

If there ever was a "historical Jesus," he must have borne a marked resemblance to the Idealist vision of fulfillment in human personality by overcoming "the antithesis of Jewish consciousness" concerning the separation of the divine and the human without causing a new alienation.[66] The question could only be settled by further criticism of the Gospels. However, the real future of humanity lay not in theology but in furthering the interests of humanity itself.[67]

Bauer's references to theology and theologians could hardly have been better calculated to arouse their ire. Their judgment, however, largely took the form of deliberately ignoring Bauer once he had been dismissed from office. Though no less radical than Strauss, there was no demand for a reprint of his critical works and no pamphlet war. Perhaps it was because Bauer ceased to hold an academic appointment. Perhaps it was because F. C. Baur and the Tübingen School appeared to pose a more substantial threat. Perhaps it was because Strauss had said so much of what Bauer was saying less than a decade before. The chief difference between the two was that Strauss explained the beliefs of the primitive church as the mythical application to Jesus of Old Testament prophecy, whereas Bauer put down these beliefs to the creative consciousness of the early Christians. There was a marked similarity of method. Both proceeded by trying to detect discrepancies and difficulties. They then cut the knot by ascribing the episode or idea to myth, in the case of Strauss, or to primitive, creative consciousness, in the case of Bauer. There were also marked affinities with Feuerbach. All three belonged to the Hegelian Left, though of the three it was Bauer who remained the most loyal to Hegel. He was more interested in criticism than Strauss. To Bauer criticism was a tool of Hegelian philosophy, which was to be used in order to discern the historical forms of the manifestation of consciousness.[68] But it was a secularized atheistic Hegelianism which alienated those who thought that Hegel had provided a philosophical basis for Christian beliefs.

Bauer remained obsessed by the religion he sought to undermine. In his *Kritik der Evangelien* he denied the historical existence of Jesus. In his *Kritik der Paulinischen Briefe* he presented a more skeptical alternative to F. C. Baur, which attributed the letters to a late second-century author who read into them the conflicts of the past. Toward the end of his life, in *Christus und die Caesaren*, Bauer saw Seneca and Philo, rather than Jesus and Paul, as the ideological progenitors of Christianity. The work exerted little influence on theology, but its views appealed to Marx and Engels, and it came to be regarded as authoritative in Marxist, Socialist circles. Like Strauss and Feuerbach, Bauer found that his demands for the abandonment of Christianity in favor of humanism were largely ignored by those to whom they were addressed. He had striven long to explain Christianity as a moment in the history of the development of self-consciousness. In turn, he was summarily dismissed by Friedrich Engels, who wrote, "Bauer only achieved something in the field of the history of the origin of Christianity, though what he did here was important."[69]

While the critical battles of the thirties and forties were raging, a number of writers were at work producing books that Schweitzer bracketed together under the unpromising heading of "Further Imaginative Lives of Jesus."[70] Venturini's hypothesis at the turn of the century about an Essene plot was taken up by an anonymous writer who purported to give fresh disclosures from a newly discovered manuscript at Alexandria in *Wichtige Enthüllungen über die wirkliche Todesart Jesu. Nach einem alten zu Alexandria gefundenen Manuskripte von einem Zeitgenossen Jesu aus dem heiligen Orden der Essäer* (5th ed., 1849) and *Historische Enthüllungen über die wirklichen Ereignisse der Geburt und Jugend Jesu. Als Fortsetzung der zu Alexandria aufgefundenen alten Urkunden aus dem Essäerorden* (2nd ed., 1849). At the time they created a stir, and Karl Hase traced the origin of this "frivolity" to Bauer.[71] Also inspired by Venturini was the work of the Jewish author, Joseph Salvador, *Jésus Christ et sa Doctrine. Histoire de la naissance de l'église, de son organisation et de ses progrès pendant le premier siècle* (2 vols., 1838). Salvador portrayed Jesus as the last manifestation of the Jewish mysticism that began in the time of Solomon. Jesus combined mysticism with messianic enthusiasm. Having lost consciousness on the cross, he was resuscitated by Joseph of Arimathea and Pilate's wife, contrary to his own expectation and purpose. Jesus ended his days with the Essenes, and Salvador sought to revive a mystical form of Judaism as a rival to Christianity.

Another writer who found the Essenes a rich source for conjecture was August Friedrich Gfrörer, who wrote a massive *Kritische Geschichte des Urchristentums* (2 vols., 1835–38). Gfrörer had been a Repetent at the Tübinger Stift when Strauss was a student there. After being on the staff of a leading church in Stuttgart for a year, he left the ministry to devote himself to study. At the same time he abandoned orthodox Christianity. The first volume traced the rise of

Jewish theology, culminating with Philo whose "Therapeutae" were identical with the Essenes. The second volume entitled *Die heilige Sage* appeared after the publication of the works of Strauss and Weisse. It changed course in order to join issue with them. Gfrörer maintained that nothing was written down for a generation or more after Jesus' death. Luke was the most trustworthy of the evangelists in view of his attempt to sift the sources. Matthew's lateness was evident from his tendency to carry over the Old Testament into the New. But both Gospels were written long after the destruction of Jerusalem, drawing their material from local Galilean saga which led them to transfer the scene of Jesus' activity to Galilee. Mark was the earliest witness to doubts in the primitive church regarding the credibility of his predecessors. He did not view them as sacred books, but tried to remove their inconsistencies. Thus he omitted most of the discourses, all of the birth and infancy narratives, and retained only those miracles which were firmly embedded in the tradition that he had received. Mark was written between A.D. 110 and 120. Gfrörer was prepared to give greater credence to John, to whose account of miracles he gave rationalistic explanations.

The upshot was that Jesus was portrayed as a spiritual Messiah moving in the realms of Philonic ideas. He did not believe that he would rise from the dead. Joseph of Arimathea, a member of the Essene order, had, unknown to Jesus, bribed the Romans. Two others were crucified with him to distract attention. Joseph had Jesus removed to a tomb of his own in order to resuscitate him. The church grew out of the Essene order by giving further development to its ideas. Although he questioned details of the Gospels and embellished them with imaginative constructions, Gfrörer himself believed in the underlying historical basis of the Christian faith. In 1853 he became a Roman Catholic. He had already been professor of history at Freiburg since 1846. He wrote extensively on the Middle Ages, and strove for the reunion of Catholicism and Protestantism, which he believed to be vital to the leading role of Germany in Europe.

To Albert Schweitzer, the work of Friedrich Wilhelm Ghillany was "incomparably better and more thorough" than that of his predecessors in the genre.[72] Under the pseudonym of Richard von der Alm, he published three massive volumes of *Theologische Briefe an die Gebildeten der deutschen Nation* (1863), followed by *Die Urteile heidnischer und jüdischer Schriftsteller der vier ersten christlichen Jahrhunderte über Jesus* (1864). Ghillany took Gfrörer as his starting point, but rejected his spiritualizing interpretation. Ghillany held that Luke was the first Gospel, and that Mark was based upon the sources of Matthew and Luke. John was unauthentic. Primitive Christian belief was a compound of Judaism, Mithraism (from which it derives the virgin birth, the star of Bethlehem, the wise men, the cross and resurrection, and the cult of eating flesh and drinking blood), and oriental religions generally. Christianity was a species of Gnosticism. Jesus held himself to be the Messiah, and expected the early coming of the Kingdom, but all his ideas have their source in contemporary Judaism. He was the tool of a mystical sect, allied to the Essenes, the head of which was the now notorious Joseph of Arimathea.

Last of the line of those who combined criticism with fiction was the Giessen professor, Ludwig Noack, who published in 1870–71 *Aus der Jordan-wiege nach Golgotha. Vier Bücher über das Evangelium und die Evangelien.* Noack ascribed its failure to attract attention to the Franco-Prussian War, and revised it under the title *Die Geschichte Jesu auf Grund freier geschichtlicher Untersuchungen über das Evangelium und die Evangelien* (1876). But the revised version met with scarcely more success than the first. His approach differed from that of his predecessors in attempting to write a biography of Jesus from the Johannine point of view, though he stripped the Fourth Gospel of all Jewish teaching and miracles. It was written by Judas, "the beloved disciple," who arranged the betrayal on the evening before the Passover, so that Jesus might die, as he desired, on the day of the Passover. Later tradition saw this service of love only as a piece of treachery.

Although Renan's celebrated *Vie de Jésus* does not belong to the same category of imaginative lives as the writings of Venturini and his successors, it was not exactly a critical investigation. Like Strauss's *Leben Jesu*, it was written when its author was beginning to establish himself in the academic world. It created a stir in France, which, if anything, was greater—or at least longer lasting—than Strauss's work did in Germany. Both *Lives* cost their authors their academic posts. But there the similarities begin to fade. For while Strauss's work was a critical study, Renan's was a popular biography. Whereas Strauss was a German Protestant, Renan was a former French Catholic. Both *Lives* were pioneer works, but in different ways. Strauss's novelty lay in his extensive use of myth; Renan's lay in the fact that he was a former seminarian writing a non-supernaturalistic biography of Jesus.

From an early age, Ernest-Joseph Renan (1823–92)[73] had been destined for the priesthood, but by the time he came to write his *Vie de Jésus*, this goal was long behind him. In a sense, Renan was indebted to German Protestant criticism, but it was less for any particular theory than for its stimulus in trying to reconstruct the life of Jesus in non-supernatural terms. The result was a tale told with considerable verve and feeling, which avoided equally the vagaries of the fictitious lives and the painstaking discussions of critical historiography.

In October 1860 Renan sailed for the Middle East in charge of an archaeological expedition to Byblos. The expedition had been commissioned by Louis Napoleon, and Renan, though not a professional archaeologist, was already in the front rank of French Semitic scholars. He was accompanied by his sister, Henriette, who acted as secretary but who died before the mission was completed. The following April, inspired by the scenery of the Holy Land, Renan decided to write a biography of Jesus. It was substantially complete when he left Beirut for Paris the following October. The book was published in June 1863. In the meantime Renan was appointed to the chair of Hebrew, Chaldaic, and Syriac at the Collège de France. He gave his inaugural lecture on February 21, 1862, in the course of which he described Jesus as an incomparable man, so great that he would not contradict those who, struck by the exceptional nature of his achievement, called him God.[74] This intended conciliatory course only made matters worse. The uproar was such that he was suspended from lecturing the following week. At the time, few knew of the existence of his manuscript on the life of Jesus. When it was finally published, it performed the double function of bringing about the termination of Renan's appointment and establishing his popular reputation.

From beginning to end, Renan sought to make the Gospel story credible. Whenever he could, he did not hesitate to splash on local color and evoke a feeling of realism. He pictured Joseph's house at Nazareth, which "no doubt closely resembled those poor shops, lighted by the door, which serve at once as workshop, kitchen, and bedroom, the furniture consisting of a mat, some cushions on the ground, one or two earthenware pots, and a painted chest."[75] From this type of conjecture, Renan moved on to state the original gospel of Jesus, which he expressed with an even greater degree of certainty and even less critical evaluation.

> The revolution that he sought to bring about was a moral revolution; but he had not yet reached the point of trusting to the angels and the last trumpet for its execution. It was only upon men and through men that he wished to act. A visionary, who had no other idea than the approximateness of the last judgment, would not have had this care for the amelioration of human souls, and would not have laid down the finest moral precepts humanity has ever received. There was no doubt still much vagueness in his ideas; and it was exalted sentiment rather than fixed design which urged him on to the sublime work he had conceived, though in a manner quite different from what he imagined.
>
> It is in fact the kingdom of God, I mean, the kingdom of mind, that he founded, and, if Jesus from the bosom of his father sees his work bearing fruit through the ages, he may indeed truly say: "This is what I wished." That which Jesus founded, and which will remain his to all eternity—deductions being made for the imperfections which enter into everything accomplished by mankind—is the doctrine of freedom of mind.[76]

Renan wrote with the calm assurance of a man who has got to the bottom of things. But despite the footnotes added to later French editions, there is an almost complete absence of scholarly exegesis to support his interpretations. Renan's work went through the life of Jesus, explaining incidents and the motives behind them. He wrote with a certainty that was above argument. Throughout he gives the impression that this, if one might borrow Ranke's famous phrase, is how it actually happened.

Jesus' outlook was transformed through his contact with the Samaritans. He received a brilliant illumination when he pointed out that true worship did not depend on places and ritual but upon spirit and truth.

> The day on which he uttered this saying, he was in reality Son of God. He uttered for the first time the sentence upon which will repose the edifice of eternal religion. He founded the pure worship, of all ages, of all lands, that which all elevated souls will

embrace until the end of time. Not only was his religion on this day the best religion of humanity, it was the absolute religion; and if other planets have inhabitants endowed with reason and morality, their religion cannot be different from that which Jesus proclaimed near Jacob's well. Man has not been able to hold to it; for we can attain the ideal but for a moment.[77]

Jesus returned to Galilee "filled with revolutionary ardour." He now expressed his ideas "with perfect clearness." The Law must be abolished and Jesus as the Messiah is the one who will achieve it. The kingdom of God will soon be revealed by Jesus. Although it will not be established without suffering, the Son of man will return in glory after his death, accompanied by legions of angels, and those who have rejected him will be confounded.[78] From this point onwards the legends and extravagant ideas increased until the climax was reached with the death of Jesus.

For the historian, the life of Jesus finishes with his last sigh. But such was the impression he had left in the hearts of his disciples and of a few devoted females, that during some weeks more it was as if he were living and consoling them. Had his body been taken away? Did enthusiasm, always credulous in certain circumstances, create afterwards the group of narratives by which it was sought to establish faith in the resurrection? In the absence of opposing documents this can never be ascertained. Let us say, however, that the strong imagination of Mary Magdalen played in this circumstance an important part. Divine power of love! Sacred moments in which the passion of one possessed gave to the world a resuscitated God![79]

In the final chapter on the "Essential Character of the Work of Jesus" Renan pronounced what was virtually a funeral oration[80] which took up the refrain of his own ill-fated inaugural lecture.

This sublime person, who each day still presides over the destiny of the world, may be called divine, not in the sense that Jesus has absorbed all the divine, but in the sense that Jesus is the person who has impelled his fellow-men to make the greatest step towards the divine. . . . There never was a man—Sakya Mouni alone excepted— who so completely trampled under foot family, the pleasures of this world, and all temporal care. He lived only for his Father and the divine mission with which he believed himself charged.

As to us, eternal children, condemned to impotence, who labour without reaping, and who will never witness the fruit of that which we have sown, let us bow before these demi-gods. They did that which we cannot do—create, affirm, act. Will great originality be borne again, or will the world henceforth content itself by following the paths opened by the bold original minds of antiquity? We do not know. In any case, Jesus will not be surpassed. His worship will constantly renew itself, his history will provoke endless pious tears, his sufferings will subdue the stoutest hearts; all ages will proclaim that, among the sons of men, no one has been born who is greater than Jesus.[81]

Although we have not considered in detail the outline of Renan's construction of the life of Jesus, these same extracts convey better than an analytical précis the mood and tone of the book. In a lengthy preface to the thirteenth edition, Renan explained his underlying philosophy and aims.

> I write for the purpose of promulgating my ideas to those who seek the truth. . . . If the miracle has any reality, this book is but a tissue of errors. If the Gospels are inspired books, and true, consequently, to the letter, from beginning to end, I have been guilty of a great wrong, in not contenting myself with piecing together the broken fragments of the four texts, like as the Harmonists have done, only to construct thus an *ensemble* at once most redundant and most contradictory. If, on the contrary, the miracle is an inadmissible thing, then I am right in regarding the books which contain miraculous recitals as histories mixed with fiction, as legends full of inaccuracies, errors, and of systematic expedients. . . . Criticism does not recognise infallible texts; its first principle is to admit that in the text which is examined there is the possibility of error. Far from being accused of scepticism, I ought to be classed with the moderate critics, since, instead of rejecting *en bloc* weak documents as so much trash, I essay to extract something historical out of them by means of delicate approximation.[82]

Perhaps it is the last sentence here that is the most revealing. In a sense, Renan was right when he insisted on being ranked among the moderate critics. His work was far less skeptical about the main outline and events of Jesus' life than many German contemporaries. Although he hinted about legendary material, there was little to suggest that he was deeply influenced by Strauss on the subject of myth.[83] Nor does he appear to have taken the Synoptic problem very seriously, still less the implication that the later Gospels contain material that is largely unhistorical.[84] Renan's method was characterized by two features. On the one hand, he deliberately set out to exclude the supernatural on the grounds that one just does not encounter miracles today any more than one sees centaurs and winged horses.[85] On the other hand, his reconstruction of events was based upon what is here somewhat euphemistically termed "délicates approximations." Renan had written what was virtually a historical novel—not going beyond the materials in the Gospels like Venturini and his successors—but always suggesting naturalistic explanations and employing a good deal of conjecture in making the narrative fit together. He complained that the Christ of Strauss, Baur, and other German critics was like the Gnostic Christ, an impalpable, intangible creation of their philosophy. His own Christ was rooted in "genuine history."

> Genuine history must construct its edifice out of two kinds of materials, and, if I may so speak, out of two factors: the first, the general state of the human soul in a given age and in a given country; the second, the particular incidents which, uniting with general causes, determined the course of events. To explain history by accidental facts is as false as to explain it by principles which are purely philosophic. . . . In my opinion, the best course to hold is to follow as closely as possible the original narratives, to discard impossibilities, to sow everywhere the seeds of doubt, and to put forth as conjectural the diverse manners in which the event might have taken place.[86]

Although the church in France had suffered some severe body blows from the anti-clericalists since the days of the Revolution, a semi-popular, allegedly critical reappraisal of the central object of its faith by one who was still at least nominally a Catholic and yet who worked in these terms was something new. Reaction was swift. By the end of 1863, the book had gone through ten editions of 5,000 copies each, and by 1864 it had been translated into most European languages. It was still going strong in the 1920s, although by then its literary and antiquarian interest had eclipsed its sensational revelations. In the first few years the rival counterattacks were selling almost equally well. The spate of literature exceeded that provoked by Strauss's first *Life* a generation before,[87] and Strauss himself took note of Renan's work in his second *Life* which appeared the following year. To the end of his life, Renan received a steady stream of letters ranging from hostile abuse to adulation. Among them were a number from priests, plagued by doubt and seeking advice. The Catholic Church mobilized its scholars in a massive counterattack, and Renan's affinities with earlier skeptics were denounced.

While there was clearly a market for Renan's peculiar blend of rationalism and romanticism, the younger generation of French critical scholars were unenthusiastic, if Colani's comments were at all typical. Writing in the *Revue de Théologie* (1864) and claiming to speak on behalf of the new Protestant Strasbourg school, he complained that Renan's Christ was not the Christ of history—that of the Synoptics—but that of the Fourth Gospel, though without his metaphysical halo, and painted in the melancholy blue of modern poetry, the pink of the eighteenth-century idyll, and the grey of a moral philosophy which seemed to derive from La Rochefoucauld.[88]

Renan's *Vie de Jésus* was a book of revenge[89]—revenge on the political and ecclesiastical establishment for terminating his teaching career and revenge on the church at large. It was all the more odious to the Catholic faithful and believers of other communions for its condescending blandness. It was neither the first nor the last work to be so motivated or to damn with the faint praise of assigning to Jesus a place among the great men of history. Such a motif could be detected in the work of the Deists, Reimarus, Lessing, Kant, Strauss, and many others.

In several respects, Renan's work marked the end of one era and the beginning of another. There was little in the book that had not been said long before. Others had developed ideas that were more shocking and with greater display of scholarship. But in this lay the genius of the work. It enjoyed the prestige of scholarship without actually displaying it. Previous studies of Jesus were addressed to the world of learning. They were packed with detailed argument requiring no little background in philosophy, theology, and historical criticism. Renan's book was addressed to a wide public. Most of it had been written during his expedition to Lebanon and the Holy land on the basis of impressions in a mood of continuous inspiration. Renan wrote to Michelin Bertholet,

> I believe that this time one will have before his eyes living beings, and not these pale, lifeless phantoms — Jesus, Mary, Peter, etc., considered as abstract beings, and only typified. I have endeavoured to do the same as he who, by drawing a violin bow, arranges grains of sand in natural waves on vibrating plates.[90]

If F. C. Baur had lived to read it, he would doubtless have dismissed it on the same grounds that he rejected Strauss's work; Renan was setting himself up as a critical historian without undertaking the labor of precise critical work.

Unlike his immediate German predecessors, Renan was not encumbered by the convolutions of Idealism or concerned to restate the meaning of religion and world history in philosophical terms. Owen Chadwick sees Renan's work as the initiation of a new trend in which history began to take precedence over theology and philosophy.

> In the 1860s many educated men wanted a Christ whom they could understand without simultaneously accepting stories which they could no longer understand. Renan gave them such a Christ. It marked a new stage in the link between history and religion.[91]

In this respect Renan soon found counterparts in Germany and England in the shape of Strauss's *Das Leben Jesu für das deutsche Volk bearbeitet* (1864) and Seeley's *Ecce Homo* (1865). If Strauss's *Life* was a work of incomparably more thorough scholarship, all three books were characterized by the elimination of the supernatural and transcendent from history and the attempt to represent Jesus as a great man.

But even in this, it was more a case of *plus cq change, plus c'est la même chose*. For essentially, Renan's work was a return to the outlook of Deism and the Enlightenment. Admittedly it was not the hostile Deism of Woolston, Voltaire, and Reimarus. It was more akin to the view of Lessing and Kant that eliminated God from history and stressed values which could be appreciated by rational, moral men. It was, in fact, a lineal descendant of French skepticism and anti-clericalism, and a form of positivism no less consistent than that of Auguste Comte. If it represented a precedence of history over theology and philosophy, it was in virtue of scarcely veiled commitment to secular philosophy and a rigorous determination to express Jesus in secular terms. Perhaps it was a sign of the times that no need was evidently felt to argue the case for such a philosophy. That it found approval is eloquently attested by the demand for reprints and translations. Renan's book laid the foundation of his fame and fortune. In 1870 he was reinstated to his chair at the Collège de France, and eventually became the Administrator of the Collège. In 1878 he was elected to the Académie Française. He was admitted to the Legion of Honor in 1880 and eventually rose to the rank of Grand Officer. The book's ultimate failure, like that of so many predecessors, to give a satisfying account of Jesus is attested by the continued quest, not only of the historical Jesus, but also of the Christ of faith.

V

ORTHODOXY MODIFIED

13. CONFESSIONAL AND REVIVAL THEOLOGY

The revival of confessionalism, particularly in Lutheranism, was bound up with a number of factors.[1] It was partly a reaction against rationalism, seeking a return to the Bible and the spirit of the Reformation. It was partly a revival movement concerned with personal piety and its bearing on theology. It was also a reaction against Catholicism and schemes for Protestant church union. The tercentenary in 1817 of Luther's *Ninety-Five Theses* was an emotive time. It provoked Claus Harms to reissue the *Theses* together with ninety-five of his own, directed against the modern antichrist, or reason erected into a pope.[2] Deliberately echoing Luther's style, Harms's first thesis declared, "When our Master and Lord, Jesus Christ, says, 'Repent!' He wishes men to form themselves according to His doctrine; He does not formulate His doctrine according to men, as is done now." Rational religion was denounced as "devoid of reason, or of religion, or of both" (No. 32). "If reason in religious matters pretends to be more than secular, it becomes heretical" (No. 47). The Catholic Evangelical and Reformed Evangelical Churches were praised as "magnificent" churches (Nos. 92, 93). But the Lutheran Evangelical Church was "more magnificent than both of them," being maintained by the Sacraments and the Word of God (No. 94). "The two other Churches tend to melt into it, even without the voluntary participation of men. As to the way of the wicked, it shall perish" (No. 95).

At the time when these non-too-subtle words were uttered, union schemes were already afoot in Prussia, Nassau, the Palatinate, and elsewhere.[3] Schleiermacher's *Der christliche Glaube* was conceived as a dogmatics for the united church, ostensibly drawing on the essence of the Reformed and Lutheran Confessions. Schleiermacher's enthusiasm cooled somewhat as royal power increased in church affairs. However, he and the Mediating Theologians *(Vermitt-lungstheologen)* who followed him were in general sympathy. The union schemes led to a polarization of the rationalists, who sought greater doctrinal leniency, and of the conservatives, who objected to the weakening of the confessions of the constituent churches. In 1854, K. R. Hagenbach commented,

> Another new form of supernaturalism is the ecclesiastical positivism and confessionalism, which again asserts itself with power. This tendency, not content with

Biblical orthodoxy, lays stress upon assent to the teachings of symbolical books as the necessary criterion of a correct belief, and aims in Germany to destroy the existing union between protestant denominations.[4]

In the meantime, the revival movement within Lutheranism, which had a long history prior to the nineteenth century, received fresh impetus and attained new heights of social respectability at Berlin through the influence of Baron von Kottwitz and other members of the nobility and *haute bourgeoisie*.[5] Although the movement was by no means confined to Berlin, it was particularly powerful in the Prussian capital, partly because it penetrated the court and higher government and ecclesiastical circles. One result was that after 1820 several important church and university posts were filled by men who had come under the influence of the movement. Among them were Neander, Tholuck, Stier, and Hengstenberg.

Conservative Theologians

Horst Stephan and Martin Schmidt have observed that,

> It is significant for "Erweckungstheologie" that it came as little in Tholuck as it did in Neander to a systematic reflection on the essence of its enthusiastic piety or indeed of Christianity. With its austere faith it lacked self criticism and an open attitude to the reality of life, above all to the difficulties that burden the relationship of living faith to the Bible. In systematic theology it lived entirely upon the achievements of Supernaturalism and Idealism, and for that reason could not transcend them. The undoubted scholarship of its representatives found expression in other areas, in the field of historical research and practice.[6]

The thought of August Neander has already been noted in connection with that of D. F. Strauss.[7] Friedrich August Gottreu Tholuck (1799–1877) came to theology via the study of oriental languages. Kottwitz was instrumental in turning him to evangelical piety and also in obtaining his later appointments. As a student he was more impressed with Neander than with Schleiermacher who resisted his appointment to the faculty at Berlin. Tholuck's first major work was perhaps the most important contribution of revival theology, *Guido und Julius. Die Lehre von der Sünde und dem Versöhner oder die wahre Weihe des Zweiflers* (1823).[8] In 1826 Tholuck was transferred by the Prussian minister of culture, Altenstein, to Halle, where the faculty was predominantly rationalistic. At Halle, Tholuck became widely known as a father-in-God to his students and many others who sought his pastoral advice.[9] As part of his pastoral concern, he joined in the controversies of his day and published a reply to Strauss entitled *Die Glaubwürdigkeit der evangelischen Geschichte, zugleich eine Kritik des Lebens Jesu von Strauss für theologische und nichttheologische Leser* (1837). He edited Calvin's *Institutes* (1834–35) and wrote a *Geschichte des Rationalismus* (1865). Tholuck was the author of numerous commentaries. His exposition of Romans (1824) was followed by works on John (1827), the Sermon on the Mount (1833), Hebrews (1836), and the Psalms (1843). In due course English translations appeared in Clark's *Biblical Cabinet* and *Foreign Theological Library*. Emanuel Hirsch has observed that all Tholuck's commentaries "lie on the boundary between scientific and devotional exposition."[10] While Tholuck could not be accused of propagating a narrow confessionalism and is sometimes even classed among the "Mediating Theologians,"[11] his chief theological significance lay in his influence as a check to rationalism and his summons to personal commitment and holiness. In Hirsch's words, "All these commentaries went through many editions and helped more than anything else to spoil the taste of the parish clergy for rationalistic Bible exposition."[12] Tholuck's legacy might be summed up in the words of his famous pupil, Martin Kähler, concerning *"the historic Christ of the Bible."*

> The real Christ, that is, the Christ who has exercised an influence in history, with whom millions have communed in childlike faith, and with whom the great witnesses of faith have been in communion— while striving, apprehending, triumphing, and proclaiming—*this real Christ is the Christ who is preached*. The Christ who is preached, however, is precisely the Christ of faith. He is the Jesus whom the eyes of faith behold at every step he takes and through every syllable he utters—the Jesus whose image we impress upon our minds because we both would and do commune with him, our risen, living Lord. The person of our living Savior, the person of the Word incarnate, of God revealed, gazes upon us from the features of that image which has deeply impressed itself on the memory of his followers—here in bold outlines, there in single strokes— and which was finally disclosed and perfected through the illumination of his Spirit.[13]

In similar vein to Tholuck, but with more words and less scholarship, was the work of his disciple, Generalsuperintendent Rudolf Stier (1800–82), *Die Reden des Herrn Jesu*.[14] Stier's English translator, W. B. Pope, spoke of "the minute subtilty of its analysis, its keen inquisition into the secret thread of every discourse, with some occasional novelties of theory or exposition."[15] A less charitable, but perhaps more realistic, estimate would be to describe it as a vast, homiletical paraphrase. Although occasional reference was made to Luther, Calvin, Bengel, and contemporary writers, the tone was didactic and rhetorical. The exposition was sprinkled with Greek and Hebrew words and phrases, but their presence added little to the argument. Many of Stier's passages were distinctly purple, though few matched his comment on Luke 2:49: "Solitary floweret out of the wonderful enclosed garden of the thirty years, plucked precisely there, where the swollen bud, at a *distinctive crisis*, bursts into flower."[16]

The most polemical of the theologians associated with the confessional, revival movement was Ernst Wilhelm Hengstenberg (1802–69).[17] Like Tholuck, he had come to theology via classical and oriental languages. He was gradually won over to the revival movement while working on postgraduate studies at Berlin, where in 1826 he assumed the chair vacated by de Wette. He was known to be conservative, but his narrow, militant attitude took many by surprise.[18] Hengstenberg exercised widespread influence in his capacity as founding editor of the *Evangelische Kirchen-Zeitung* in the crucial years from 1827 to his death. Here he waged a relentless war on liberalism in all its forms, sparing neither friend nor foe. Schleiermacher, Hegel, Strauss, and the Mediating Theologians all came under regular fire. An initial sympathy with the Union, which was partly derived from his family background, eventually turned into hostility. "Pure doctrine" became identified with conformity to the Lutheran Confessions. Hengstenberg's "Repristinationstheologie" stood solidly for biblical infallibility and the state's duty to maintain a Christian society. It was said by opponents that he pursued the rationalists with the arts of an advocate.

Hengstenberg was the author of a number of commentaries, chiefly on Old Testament books, but his main theological works were his *Geschichte des Reiches Gottes under dem Alten Bunde*, 2 vols. (1869–71), and his *Christologie des Alten Testaments und Commentar über die messianischen Weissagungen*, 3 vols. (1829–35).[19] Hans-Joachim Kraus dismissed the former work as a highly dogmatic piece of *Heilsgeschichte*, based on the synagogue tradition of teaching rather than history. The latter work shows

> how strongly Hengstenberg ignores the real historicity of the Old Testament. The christological perspectives cause all historical life to shrivel up. The prophet is surely not the messenger of Yahweh, who has to deliver a particular word at a particular time; he is a seer who always looks to nothing but the prophetic and high priestly office of Christ.[20]

As an example of Hengstenberg's method, Kraus cites his comments on Isaiah.

> The Prophet does not confine himself to the events immediately at hand, but in his ecstatic state, the state of an elevated, and, as it were, armed consciousness, in which he was during this whole period, his eye looks into the farthest distances. He sees, especially, that, at some future period, the Babylonian power, which began, even in his time, to germinate, would take the place of the Assyrian,—that, for this oppressor of the world, destruction is prepared by *Koresh* (Cyrus), the conqueror from the East, and that he will liberate the people from their exile; and, at the close of the development, he beholds the Saviour of the world, whose image he depicts in the most glowing colours.[21]

At the other end of the theological scale, C. H. Spurgeon, who by no stretch of the imagination could be accused of inordinate liberalism, described Hengstenberg's commentary on the Psalms as "A masterly work; but about as dry as Gideon's unwetted fleece."[22] His comments on the *Christology* damned with equally faint praise.

> This great work deals with a most vital theme in a masterly manner; it has always been held in high esteem. We confess, however, that we can only read it as a task, for the scholastic style repels us, and it seems to us that in answering a number of sceptical doctors, whose opinions are ridiculous, the author has made much ado about nothing.[23]

The judgments of Kraus and Spurgeon appear to be curiously complementary. No doubt, Spurgeon was right about Hengstenberg's style, but his fault was not that he was too much concerned with history but too little. To read the work today, one feels that Hengstenberg was in too much of a hurry either to cross swords with other scholars or to get to the theology that he wanted to get out of the text. The middle stages of evaluating the documents critically and of trying to project himself back into the circumstances of Old Testament prophecy and New Testament times seem all too often to have been left out. The result was a massive work made up of detailed comments on isolated gobbets. Hengstenberg's major writings were not directly concerned with the Jesus of history, but they helped to defend and preserve with considerable scholarship the pre-critical, christological interpretation of the Old Testament and with it the Christ of orthodox faith.

The Erlangen School

The University of Erlangen stands in a small Bavarian town north of Nuremberg. The town itself was a former Huguenot colony. The University was founded in 1743 by the Markgraf Friedrich von Bayreuth.[24] The foundation statutes tied the university to the Lutheran Confessions and in so doing attempted to exclude pietism. The university of the eighteenth century was a child of the Enlightenment, but the influence of Schelling (who lived at Erlangen and gave occasional lectures there between 1820 and 1827), a renewed interest in historical studies,[25] and an influx of scholars affected by the revival movement helped to break the grip of rationalism and change the religious atmosphere. Among these were the pastor of the Reformed Church in Erlangen and lecturer, Christian Krafft, the philosopher G. H. Schubert, the orientalist J. A. Kanne, and the professor of natural history, Karl von Raumer, whose activities ranged from organizing help for homeless workmen and foreign missions to the study of hymnology and the organization of seminars in his own home on Augustine and Luther. It was from the young men who passed through the hands of these scholars that the Erlangen School emerged in the middle of the nineteenth century.

The first significant theologian of the School was Adolf Harless (1806–79), who helped to found the *Zeitschrift für Protestantismus und Kirche*, which became the organ of the School. The first issue contained a foreword penned by Harless, which set out its program.[26] At the outset, the Erlangen theologians announced their concern for the "holiness" of the Protestant Church, which they saw threatened from many sides. Although they had no desire to allow their journal to dissolve into mere polemics and protests, it was frankly a "protestation" against "Quasi-Protestantism." They rejected pietistic separatism as decisively as they did rationalism. The Erlangen theologians were concerned with the purity of faith within the church as a necessary condition for true Christian living. They repudiated current loose talk about "freedom and Spirit." Above all, they held fast to "the truth and meaning of the Church which has testified to its faith in the

Confessions." The goal of both the journal and the School was edification. Its tone was pastoral and, where necessary, polemical. In all this it sought to be scholarly. Its ethos was definitely ecclesiastical. Its orientation was around the Lutheran Confessions as a sure guide to the contents of the Word of God in Holy Scripture. Nevertheless, the two most distinguished representatives of Erlangen theology, Hofmann and Thomasius, felt it necessary to modify Lutheran orthodoxy, though each in his special way.

J. C. K. Hofmann (1810–77)[27] is widely regarded as the most significant of the Erlangen theologians. As a theological student at Erlangen between 1827 and 1829, he came under the influence of Krafft and Raumer. From Erlangen he moved to Berlin, but was disappointed by the dogmatic approach of Hengstenberg. Though he began Schleiermacher's course on New Testament introduction, he broke off half-way through. He felt hurt by what he called "the manner of his treatment of the factual and historical."[28] He was bored by Marheineke's speculative treatment of dogma. Later on he was to grapple with Schleiermacher, and Hegel was not without some influence, though ultimately he rejected him. But the scholar who most impressed Hofmann at this time was the historian, Leopold von Ranke, whose treatment of the universal significance of Christianity attracted him. Hofmann's early writings were on historical subjects. His first post was that of teacher of history, religion, and Hebrew at the Erlanger Gymnasium (1833).

From 1845, Hofmann held a full chair at Erlangen, attracting large numbers of students from all over Germany and abroad. His writings include *Weissagung und Erfüllung im Alten und im Neuen Testamente, erste und zweite Hälfte* (1841–44); *Der Schriftbeweis. Ein theologischer Versuch*, 3 vols. (1852–56; 2nd ed., 1857–60); and the incomplete *Die Heilige Schrift neuen Testaments zusammenhängend untersucht*, 8 vols. (1862–78). Further parts of this vast compendium of biblical introduction, commentary, history, and theology were published posthumously, as were various other writings.[29]

In his theology Hofmann disclaimed all attempts at system-building. Writing to his friend, the Old Testament scholar and one-time colleague at Erlangen, Franz Delitzsch, he insisted,

> I have not sought the system but the method. . . . But in any case my striving is not directed to system-building but to methodology. . . . Therefore, dearest friend, do not look upon me as a systematician but as a human being who identifies scientific scholarship with method. . . . I prefer to arrange my exegetical lectures so as to teach the method of exposition which I regard as the right one.[30]

A leading contemporary authority, Eberhard Hübner, comments, "Hofmann was above all a biblical exegete and for the sake of biblical exegesis a systematic methodical thinker."[31] Hofmann's approach to salvation history has been compared with Hegel's view of history.[32] But Hofmann himself professed a lack of interest in Hegel,[33] and it would be nearer the mark to say that his approach fell somewhere in between those of Hengstenberg and Schleiermacher. With the former, he read the Old Testament in the light of Christology; with the latter, he insisted upon the primacy of religious experience. But for Hofmann it was not religious experience in general which provided the starting point, but Christian experience formulated in a more traditional—Hofmann himself would have said "objective"—manner.

> Reduced to its simplest expression, Christianity is the living fellowship between God and sinful humanity that is mediated in Christ Jesus and indeed is mediated in the present. If each Christian, who can really give testimony that he participates in the regenerate life, recognizes there his Christianity, everything that constitutes his Christianity is contained in it. The interpretation of this sentence is something different from Schleiermacher's description of the pious self-consciousness. For it is not a state of the Christian that comes to expression, but it is always the factual reality *[Thatbestand]* existing in me which realizes itself.[34]

In making this point, Hofmann aligned himself squarely with the Erlangen emphasis on conversion. But he also took a step away from orthodoxy insofar as he based his theology not on an inductive exegesis of biblical propositions but upon Christian experience. Theology was the scientific, critical understanding of the Christian's relationship with God, "when I the Christian am for me the theologian the most special material of my science."[35]

For Hofmann, salvation history was the concrete embodiment of this experience, and Scripture was the record of this manifestation before and after the coming of Christ.

> What we speak of as history must also appear in Scripture as a sequence. But Scripture itself came into being gradually, and between the Old and New Testament material lies the appearance of Jesus Christ and the emergence of his church. Hence we find now and again in the New Testament reports of events as having happened which were prophesied in the Old, or mention of something as present in the Old which is a past event in the New. And that which is still future even in the New we find prophesied from a very different standpoint from that of the Old Testament. It is now, therefore, a question of seeking out the elements which correspond in the different areas of Scripture, and of recognizing again a fact in all the stages of history, without however neglecting the differences of its forms.[36]

F. W. Kantzenbach sees in this statement the motivation for writing both *Weissagung und Erfüllung* and *Die heilige Schrift*.[37] Hofmann's thought was not so much concerned with the question of the historical Jesus as with the experience of Christ in history. It operated within the framework of traditional, Christian theism, and saw world history rooted in the Trinitarian character of God and the predestination of man.

> The tracing of Christianity as a present factual reality to an eternal reality that lies behind it and beneath it has led us then to a threefold conclusion: to the personality of God, to the inner-divine relationship of the Trinity and to the predestination of

mankind. As the personal God, he is the one who determines himself. His Trinitarian character is his self-determination from within. The predestination of mankind is his self-determination directed outwards.[38]

The eternal will of God, that man should be God's, thus has its eternal object within the inner-divine relationship in order to create for itself its historical object on the basis of it, which is thus a unity included in that eternal will. The eternal will of God is not directed toward the individual man, or to men as individuals, but to man or mankind.[39]

The ultimate goal of the historical process was the union of God and man in Christ. All history was directed toward this.

If it is true that all things, big and small, serve to bring about the uniting of the world under its head, Christ, then there is nothing in world history which is not indwelt by something divine, and nothing therefore that must remain necessarily alien to prophecy.[40]

Indeed—and here Hofmann took another step away from orthodoxy—history was itself prophecy. The latter was never merely prediction. Christ was present in creation and history in a way which pointed forward to the manifestation of Christ.

Since, however, Christ was a Person before he became man, since he is eternal God, his pre-incarnate presentation [Vorausdarstellung] does not occur without him but in virtue of his oneness with that which will beget him in the flesh. The heathen were aware of him in creation but did not distinguish him from it and thus lamented with it on account of its death. They call him Cadmilus, Dionysus, and Adonis, and weep for him too soon, before he died on the cross. He comes in presentation to man, to each according to the lights of his sphere. The heathen detect him, but do not distinguish him from those in whom he manifests features of his image. Therefore they honor them instead of him, and know much too soon about sons of God, long before Jesus the Son of God is exalted and made a Lord over all. They were deceived over the hope which quickened Israel, though Israel called itself and its king Yahweh's Son, even it looked toward a quite different, essential revelation of Yahweh and his anointed.[41]

Hofmann himself regarded his teaching as "a new way of teaching old truth."[42] As such, it was a restatement of orthodoxy that was more concerned with dogmatic than with critical questions. The distinctive features of this restatement have, however, more in common with Karl Barth and Gustaf Aulén in the twentieth century than with the classical expositors of Lutheran orthodoxy. Hofmann's view of the universal significance of Christ anticipated the Christology of the later Barth.[43] He expounded the soteriological significance of Christ in terms closer to Barth's theme of triumphant grace and what Aulén called the "classic" view than the Latin or Western view of Catholic and Protestant orthodoxy.[44] Jesus was "the initiator and originator of complete loving fellowship with God for this very same humanity which in sin initiated opposition to the holiness of God and nullification of God's work of love."[45] The purpose of Jesus' redemptive work was

> that men should cease through him to be the object of the wrath of God on account of their sin, that through him they should become utterly and completely the object of his love, so that their attitude to God through believing appropriation of the act of God should be utterly and completely reciprocal love for God.[46]

As in both Schleiermacher and the "classic" view from Irenaeus onward, Jesus is not merely the example of the ideal relationship between God and man; he is the historical embodiment of it and thus the ground and source of all other relationships between God and man. The historical incarnation of God in Christ is "no longer merely an example *[Vorbild]* of the relationship of God and man, but rather is itself the relationship of God and man."[47] Salvation is conceived primarily in terms of victory and the continuity of the divine saving work which began with creation and culminates in eschatological redemption.

> He suffered this in the certainty that thereby God's wrath against sinful humanity, whose ultimate act was to deliver Jesus' saving work to the enmity of Satan, reached its ultimate end; that with it his own fellowship with the Father conditioned up till now by sin in its historical form was delivered from this conditioning; and that in this way his work, insofar as it stood over against God in the history of his own person, was coming to its completion.[48]

In common with Schleiermacher, Hofmann taught that the cross had nothing to do with penal satisfaction. It was the place where Jesus preserved the ideal union of God and man to the end.[49] "Punishment would have been the denial of the sinner through the self-affirmation of divine holiness."[50] In language evocative of Barth, Hofmann declared,

> But while the inner divine relationship resulted in this extreme opposition *[Gegensatz]* of the Almighty Father and the Son, delivered to the power hostile to God and to death, the history enacted between God and the one who made a second beginning for humanity reached a conclusion which at the same time was the conclusion of the former history of mankind conditioned by sin, making possible a new beginning.[51]

In recent years Hofmann has been criticized for his man-centered orientation of salvation history and for obscuring Luther's dialectic of *simul iustus et peccator* with a doctrine of sanctification bordering on perfectionism.[52] In his own day there was no lack of critics from the orthodox camp, including colleagues at Erlangen.[53] Much of the criticism focused on Hofmann's departure from biblical teaching about the objective satisfaction made by the death of Christ as defined by the Lutheran confessional formulae.

Franz Delitzsch made a comment which struck at the root of Hofmann's position, when he observed that,

> No theologian can produce from the consciousness of his faith and his life of faith such system of doctrine, embracing in all its complexity salvation, past, present and

future—even if only in outline—which, without Scripture playing a causative role in its production, needed only afterwards to verify itself by Scripture's normative authority as being in accord with revelation.[54]

Alongside this may be put the comment of another contemporary, T. Kliefoth,

> We can see in his system—which seeks to express the factuality of Christianity in the categories of a logical, speculative system and which thus gets into the position of being able to do justice neither to the system nor the facts—nothing but a step back in the progress that has been going on for decades from a speculative and common rationalism to positive Christianity.[55]

Hofmann's teaching softened what to many were the harsher features of orthodoxy. It resulted in a Christ-centered, evangelical theology which was based upon Christian experience and which operated within a framework derived from Scripture and orthodoxy. But for all that—or precisely because of it— Hofmann's theology gave the appearance of having fallen between two stools. It lacked the cohesion of a rigorous, exegetical, biblical theology. It appeared to take for granted the validity of the categories within which it operated and the historicity of the facts of salvation history that provided its points of reference. But to base a theology upon experience would have meant following much further along the path trod by Schleiermacher. To work out a valid *Heilsgeschichte* would have required a much more thorough historical and critical approach. Hofmann's work appealed to a public that wanted to be evangelical, Christ-centered, and broadly biblical, but that was content to leave largely to one side the historical questions that engrossed the nineteenth-century biblical critics and the philosophical questions with which Schleiermacher, Feuerbach, and Kierkegaard wrestled.

If Hofmann's distinctive emphases lay in his approach to *Heilsgeschichte* and his restatement of the soteriological significance of Christ, that of Thomasius lay in his restatement of the incarnation in terms of *kenōsis*. A slightly senior contemporary of Hofmann, Thomasius's writings centered on the characteristic Erlangen themes of revival, doctrinal confessionalism and Christ.[56]

Gottfried Thomasius (1802–75) was the son of a Lutheran pastor who had been influenced by Neology. He was educated at home until he was sixteen. He read theology at Erlangen, Halle, and Berlin, where he heard Hegel, Schleiermacher, Marheineke, Neander, and Tholuck. In an autobiographical sketch, penned in 1842, he recalled how all the universities in the 1820s were dominated by the conflict between Rationalism and Supernaturalism.[57] Both appeared to the young Thomasius to be "scientifically untenable." Neither the Idealism of Daub and Marheineke nor the approach of Schleiermacher satisfied Thomasius, who was led "with an almost compulsive power to the historical." He was preoccupied with the historical development of the church and especially of its doctrine. He observed that this preoccupation "led me gradually to a safer, positive standpoint, which I have never since left and which still today appears the safest. Only from there did I come to a thorough knowledge of Holy Scripture and systematic Theology." For seventeen years Thomasius served as a pastor and teacher. This experience gave his theology a definite pastoral stamp. He was called to Erlangen in 1842, where he taught dogmatics, symbolics, historical theology, and practical exegesis.

Thomasius thought of dogma in its traditional sense as "the conceptual expression of the common faith of the church." It was concerned, not with individual, esoteric opinions, but with "what has established itself to the church as scriptural truth and has received sanction through its consensus." In developing his own christocentric dogmatics, Thomasius saw it as his task

> to produce dogma ever new and fresh out of its inmost depths and living roots, and so give it a form in which it appears as the expression of the one biblical and ecclesiastical faith, which by nature is ever both old and young.[58]

The spiritual life of the church depended upon a sound dogmatic foundation, guided by the confessions of the evangelical church.[59] Like Hofmann, Thomasius laid stress upon religious experience, but this was counterbalanced by insistence upon scriptural proof and the ecclesiastical consensus. Thomasius was aware of the need of a restatement of Christology in the light of the teaching of Strauss, Baur, and Dorner. It was they who gave the impetus to Thomasius's *Beiträge zur kirchlichen Christologie*. But significantly enough, it was not so much their historical and critical ideas as the doctrinal implications of their work which provided this prompting.[60]

These attacks upon orthodoxy struck at its belief in the reality of the humanity of Jesus in the light of its two-natures doctrine of Christ. The task was therefore a twofold one: to refute the attacks and to attempt "a *positive account* which would at the same time be a continuation of it."[61] The latter was the aim of the *Beiträge*, the ideas of which were amplified in Thomasius's *magnum opus*, the *Dogmatik*. The first of the *Beiträge* attempted a reappraisal of the Christology of the early church. Chalcedon preserved the church from the twin errors of Ebionism and Gnosticism, which in their various forms undermined the divinity and humanity of Christ. But the formulations of Chalcedon were apt to suggest two abstract natures and thus fail to achieve a view of an integrated person.[62] The orthodox stress on the divinity of Christ tends to destroy his humanity.[63] On the other hand, the specifically Lutheran Confessions, particularly the Formula of Concord, had already taken a step in the right direction with "the tendency of its doctrine of the real communication of attributes."[64] It found expression in the teaching that Christ suffered not only as man but as God, and that in the Lord's Supper we partake not only of his divinity but also of his humanity.

This pointed Thomasius to the next step in the development of Christological doctrine, the doctrine of *kenōsis*, as the possibility of conceiving the orthodox doctrine of the two natures in the face of modern objections. Jesus possessed

> already as man the fullness of God in its *totality,* but divested himself of its use (Phil. 2:7), so that he let it appear only in individual cases, where he wanted (miracles), and for the rest concealed it under the form of a servant. . . . On the other hand, with

> the exaltation he entered also as man into its full possession and use. . . . Consequently the divine characteristics in human nature, although they possessed the same *potentia* already from the conception onwards, only achieved their true actuality in the state of glorification.[65]

For Thomasius, the Incarnation was a fact of Scripture, history, and Christian belief, which could therefore be taken as a basic premise.

> We set against this basic thought of so-called speculative Christology at once the biblical one. The incarnation of God is a *fact*, in which it is not a blessed relationship between God and man that comes to consciousness, but an eternal, divine counsel that is enacted, a historic fact that has entered into a predetermined moment of time (Gal. 4:4), which has its ground in the *free* love of God and its goal in the redemption of the world, fallen away from God (John 3:16; 2 Cor. 5:19).[66]

The doctrine of *kenōsis*, or the self-emptying of the divine fullness during the period of the historical incarnation, was a logical development, posited by christological doctrines that were regarded as axiomatic by Lutheran orthodoxy.[67]

The ideas of the *Beiträge*[68] were further developed in Thomasius's classic attempt to restate Christian dogmatics from the standpoint of Christology: *Christi Person und Werk. Darstellung der evangelisch-Lutherischen Dogmatik vom Mittelpunkte der Christologie aus.*[69] The basic approach was similar to Hofmann's. It started with religious experience, but as with Hofmann it is not the general religious experience of Schleiermacher but Christian experience of God in Christ as defined in a traditional, theistic manner.[70] In discussing the appearance of Christ, Thomasius had certain fixed points which constituted presuppositions for Christology. Among them were the doctrine of the Trinity, the necessity of the incarnation on account of sin, and the eternal counsel of God which decreed the incarnation as the center of salvation history.[71] This led Thomasius to describe the act of incarnation in the following terms.

> If Jesus Christ is divine-human person in the sense designated . . . and if the eternal Son of God is the principle that forms this person, then the act of incarnation may not be conceived as if he, the Son of God, had united with an already existent human individual and thereafter transfigured this individual, by way of gradual penetration, for unity with himself. For that would be merely to say that a man was elevated into communion with God, and not that this man is essentially God. The ego of this person, the proper subject, would always remain merely the human one, and the unity a simply ethical one analogous to that which the Holy Spirit has with believers and saints. The result would be a "God's-man," a deified man, a human person in whom God dwells and works, not a man who is God. But Christ *is* true God.

> Just as little may that act be conceived as if the Son of God had transmuted out of himself, or himself into, the humanity in which he historically appeared. For this definition can only mean, on the one hand, that the eternal Logos is already intrinsically man and now has only brought to complete appearance and actualization that which he is in himself—and that leads back to that same erroneous identity which we have already had to reject; the incarnation presupposes the distinction of divine

essence and human kind. . . . Or else the meaning is that the Logos changed himself into human nature, and here too the mediator would not be true man, or at any rate not actually belonging to us, the members of the humanity who are to be redeemed, because he would not have emerged from the continuity of our race; but also, if the concept of transformation is taken at all strictly, he would no longer be God.[72]

The incarnation means "the assumption of human nature on the part of the second person of the Godhead."[73] It also involves "a self-limitation of the divine."[74] "As the assumption of human nature, the incarnation is at the same time the self-limitation of God the Son; and conversely, the self-limitation of the Son of God mediates the assumption of the flesh."[75] Traditional Christology leads to a double difficulty. On the one hand, it suggests

a twofold mode of being, a double life, a doubled consciousness; the Logos still is or has something which is not merged into his historical appearance, which is not also the man Jesus—and all this seems to destroy the unity of the person, the identity of the ego; thus there occurs no living and complete penetration of both sides, no proper being-man of God. *One* subject, as we postulate it, in which it is God in his totality, the fullness of deity as it subsists in the Son, that has become man—such a subject will not result from this mode of thinking; the great practical interests that we have precisely at this point are not satisfied.

Conversely, however, if the Son of God in assuming human nature had at once imparted to it the unlimited fullness of his divine lordship and transfigured it into his divine mode of being and action, then it would thereby have been stripped of the earthly limitation naturally inherent in it, withdrawn from homogeneity with our present state of life and suffering, and from the outset raised to a perfection from which point on no history, at any rate, would any longer have been possible. In particular, a gradual, naturally human development of life and a naturally human suffering seem incompatible with such a divinization of the human, and a life-movement of the redeemer in the flesh, a conflict with the powers of the world and of wickedness, would be hardly more conceivable.[76]

The way out of this dilemma was to posit

the incarnation itself precisely in the fact that he, the eternal Son of God, the second person of the deity, gave himself over into the form of human limitation, and thereby to the limits of a spatio-temporal existence, under the condition of a human develop-ment, in the bounds of an historical concrete being, in order to live in and through our nature the life of our race in the fullest sense of the word, without on that account ceasing to be God. Only so does there occur an actual entrance into humanity, an actual becoming-one with it, a becoming-man of God; and only so does there result that historical person of the mediator which we know to be the God-man.[77]

Thomasius hastened to add that this "self-limitation" was

certainly not a divesting of that which is essential to deity in order to be God, but it is a divesting of the divine mode of being in favor of the humanly creaturely form of existence, and *eo ipso* a renunciation of the divine glory which he had from the beginning with the Father and exercised vis-à-vis the world, governing and ruling it throughout.[78]

Thomasius claimed, moreover, that his view was grounded in "at least one fully apposite passage" of Scripture (Phil. 2) and that it was supported by "the distinction running through the whole biblical presentation, between the two states of life of the mediator." Additional testimony was found in John 3:13; 6:38; 8:23, 42; 16:27–28, which Thomasius described as "Jesus' own assertions about his appearance in the world."[79] Passages like Hebrews 2:14 and John 1:14 "cannot mean a merely external putting on of human essence." John 17:5 indicates the divesting and resumption of "something proper to the deity of the Son."[80] However, the *locus classicus* was Philippians 2:6ff., where *heauton ekenōsen* means "a self-emptying, a self-divesting of an actual possession, *se expoliare*; every weakening of this concept, such as we find in older writers ... is contrary to the text."[81] This self-emptying did not refer to the divinity itself, but to its form (*morphē*). *"It is thus an act of free self-denial, which has as its two moments the renunciation of the divine condition of glory, due him as God, and the assumption of the humanly limited and conditioned pattern of life."*[82] Thomasius saw further confirmation in those passages in the Gospels that speak of Jesus' growth (Luke 2:40, 52), his need to be in a conscious state in order to still the storm (Matt. 8:23ff.), his ignorance of the future (Mark 13:32), and his suffering and death.[83]

Thomasius was willing to accept the logical corollaries of his position. For the period of the incarnation the Logos ceased to have absolute power over the government of the world.[84] He firmly rejected the *extra Calvinisticum* and at the same time pursued the Lutheran *communicatio idiomatum* to its logical conclusion.

> The Son of God has not reserved a distinct being-for-himself outside the human nature assumed by him, a distinct consciousness, a distinct sphere of activity or possession of power; in no way and at no point does he exist outside the flesh (*nec Verbum extra carnem nec caro extra Verbum* [neither the Word outside the flesh nor the flesh outside the Word]). In the totality of his being he has become man; his form of existence and life is that of a spiritual-corporeal, spatio-temporally conditioned man. On the other hand, and this is only the other side of the same relationship, the human nature is wholly taken up in the divine and completely penetrated by it. It has neither a distinct human consciousness by itself, nor a distinct human movement of the will by itself in distinction from that of the Logos, just as the latter has nothing that was not directly proper to the assumed humanity; what belongs to the Logos is carried forward in the human thought, will and ability. Consequently there can be no question at all here of a dualism of divine and human modes of existence, of divine and human consciousness, of a juxtaposition of divine and human act, any more than there can be any question of a successive molding of the one into the other. All that is excluded from the outset. This is one unitary movement, experience and development of life because it is one ego, one divine-human personality (*unio, communio, communicatio naturarum* [union, participation, impartation of natures]).[85]

The remainder of volume 2 was taken up with a discussion of the relation of this to the states of humiliation and exaltation and a lengthy history of Lutheran Christology. Volume 3 was devoted to the subject of reconciliation, looking back to the atoning work of Christ and forward to the benefits which followed from it. The focal point of everything is the historical incarnation, and Thomasius's special contribution to the understanding of it is his doctrine of *kenōsis*.

Doctrines of *kenōsis* were not new.[86] The early fathers had discussed the meaning of Philippians 2:7, but none went so far as to suggest that it meant the relinquishment of the divine nature or attributes. In post-Reformation Lutheranism, the Tübingen theologians had followed Johann Brenz in his doctrine of *krypsis*, which taught that Christ possessed the divine attributes of omniscience, omnipotence, and omnipresence from birth, and actually used them, though in a concealed manner.[87] The Giessen theologians followed Martin Chemnitz in ascribing possession of the divine attributes of majesty to Christ's human nature, but allowing for his use of them only as he willed.[88] The Formula of Concord drew on both theologians and condemned *kenōsis* in all but name.[89] In the eighteenth century a kind of kenoticism found expression in Herrnhut piety and the teaching of Count Zinzendorf. It found an echo in the line of Charles Wesley's hymn, "Emptied himself of all but love." However, this was the rhetoric of piety and not dogmatic formulation.

Nineteenth-century doctrines of *kenōsis* were advanced by Ernst Wilhelm Christian Sartorius (1797–1859)[90] and Wolfgang Friedrich Gess (1819–91).[91] Sartorius argued that,

> It was not merely some kind of Docetic concealment *(krypsis)* of the Divine glory which took place therein, but an actual deprivation *(kenōsis*, Phil. ii.7), not indeed of his eternal *potentiality,* which was impossible, but certainly of its infinite actuality of finiteness."[92]

Gess went so far as to teach the extinction of the eternal self-consciousness of the Logos in the incarnation, resulting in what A. B. Bruce called "a tolerably complete metamorphosis of the Logos."[93]

Not the least interesting features of kenotic doctrines are the problems that they are intended to solve. A generation after Thomasius, Charles Gore stated a doctrine of *kenōsis* in his symposium, *Lux Mundi* (1889). Initially at least, Gore's doctrine was designed to meet the problem of how Jesus could make factual and historical mistakes, especially concerning matters of biblical criticism.[94] Thomasius and Gore appeal to much the same biblical evidence as proof of the rightness of their teaching. But Thomasius's initial problem was not that of the accuracy of the pronouncements attributed to Jesus in the Gospels, but that of producing a coherent view of the personality of Jesus which was in harmony with orthodoxy and which would answer its critics' charges of abstract, unreal, artificiality. As it developed, Thomasius sought to integrate his Christology into the whole framework of orthodox dogmatics.

Thomasius's method was not unlike that of Anselm's *Cur deus homo*. It started from faith and operated within the premises supplied by faith. Its aim was to reveal the inner logic and define more closely a particular doctrine within the framework of Lutheran orthodoxy. As such it had a certain strength. It produced an answer which had the strength of coherence, given certain premises. To those who shared the premises it might seem to outflank the critics of Lutheran orthodoxy. But it did so at the expense of leading its adherents out on a limb. Thomasius had constructed a massive, dogmatic edifice without reference to critical and philosophical theology. To those who did not share his premises, it was like fighting all over again the battles of Antioch and Alexandria, and Giessen and Tübingen. Thomasius had given an elaborate answer about the Christ of faith at a time when the question which weighed most on the more acute minds of his day concerned the historical Jesus. Thomasius's great concession to the spirit of the age was to show — on dogmatic grounds — how it might be possible to think of the two-natured Christ of faith as a historical Jesus.

A theology of *kenōsis* can only arise within an orthodoxy that is more or less sure of its theistic premises but that feels itself under a certain pressure to give an account of the logicality of its position. A more liberal theology, such as Schleiermacher's, had already cut the knot, and pictured Jesus as a man who was profoundly aware of the divine. But the question remains whether, even on Thomasius's premises, his answer was really satisfactory. It is questionable what factual significance may be attached to the idea that Jesus remained God yet ceased to possess the divine attributes and exercise his divine cosmological functions. E. L. Mascall has described kenoticism as a kind of inverted monophysitism: "Whereas the monophysitism of the Eutychians absorbed the human nature into the divine, that of the kenoticists absorbs the divine nature into the human."[95] Such a procedure might be justifiable within the context of a Lutheranism that freely appealed to the *communicatio idiomatum* when it found itself in difficulties. For others it raised the narrower question of the proper interpretation of the Christ-hymn in Philippians 2[96] and the broader question of the adequacy of traditional incarnational thinking.

14. MEDIATING THEOLOGY

Confessional theology was characterized by the attempt to revive orthodoxy as the answer to modern problems. The theology of the past contained within it whatever was needed to reply to the critics. The kind of concession that a theologian like Thomasius was prepared to make took the form of an adaptation of previous orthodoxy to meet the demands of the hour. The dogmatic edifice remained the same. Alongside confessionalism there emerged a school of thought that professed itself to be positively committed to the Christian faith, but which also sought to build bridges between that faith and modern thought. It was known as Mediating Theology *(Vermittlungstheologie)*.[1] The term came into use as a description soon after the founding of the journal *Theologische Studien und Kritiken* in 1827, which became the organ of the school. Already in the prospectus announcing the journal, which had been compiled by G. C. F. Lücke,[2] the group declared its intention of remaining faithful to the Word while avoiding narrow literalism and false enthusiasm, and of seeking "true mediations" with modern science.[3] The theme was further elaborated in succeeding articles.[4] The school also sought to provide and defend a theological foundation for the Union of the Lutheran and Reformed Churches.

The movement reached its high-water mark in the late sixties, but its basic ideas had already been put forward by Schleiermacher. It was no accident that many of its leading figures were students or friends of the Berlin teacher or scholars who were influenced by him. The large circle of theologians who were associated with the movement included, in addition to those already mentioned, Schleiermacher's successor at Berlin, August Twesten,[5] C. I. Nitzsch,[6] F. W. C. Umbreit,[7] J. K. L. Gieseler,[8] F. Bleek,[9] M. A. Landerer,[10] C. T. A. Liebner,[11] W. Beyschlag,[12] J. Müller, R. Rothe, J. Köstlin,[13] J. P. Lange, and I. A. Dorner. Among its representatives outside Germany were K. R. Hagenbach[14] and A. Schweizer in Switzerland, the Danish scholar and bishop, H. L. Martensen,[15] the Finn, A. F. Granfelt, and the Swedish scholar, Henrik Reuterdahl.[16]

In 1856 Dorner founded the movement's second journal, the *Jahrbucher für Deutsche Theologie*, which continued until 1878. A third organ was the *Deutsche Zeitschrift für christliche Wissenschaft und christliches Leben* which first appeared weekly and thereafter monthly between 1850 and 1861. In the present study we shall not attempt to survey the teaching of all the members of the school, but shall examine a cross section of the writings of those who dealt especially with Christology, making occasional comparisons with those of other writers.

Ullmann

It is possible to distinguish two types or phases of *Vermittlungstheologie:*[17] an older type which was represented by the original founders of *Theologische Studien und Kritiken* in which the influence of Schleiermacher was perhaps more pronounced, and a later, more speculative type, which found expression in the writings of scholars like Rothe and Dorner. Carl Ullmann (1796–1865) belonged to the former type. Like Schleiermacher, he was concerned with stating the essentials of the Christian faith in a way that was credible and relevant to modern man. For Ullmann, Christianity stood or fell with the historic person of Jesus, and much of his writing turned on this point.[18]

Ullmann's presentation of Jesus in *Die Sündlosigkeit Jesu* had marked affinities with that of Schleiermacher. As the title suggests, the salient feature was the thought of an integrated, sinless man set in the context of a religion which is primarily concerned with mankind's spiritual regeneration.

But religion, in its real nature, as no deep thinker of the present day can deny, rests not only objectively on a number of doctrines, laws, and customs, and subjectively on a belief in those doctrines, and on practising those laws and customs: it rests also, objectively, on a real communication of blessing on the part of the living God, regarded as an actual fact, and subjectively on the appropriation on the part of man of this Divine communication, in its deepest relation of Person to Person: it is, on the one hand, the redeeming and sanctifying energy of the personal God working upon sinful man with a view to his being brought back into His blessed fellowship; on the other hand, it is man freely submitting himself to the influence of the Divine power, and voluntarily accepting His salvation; and both in such a way, that the Divine renovating power penetrates into the inmost recesses of the soul, and embraces the whole compass of life. In order to establish a relation such as this, it is above all things necessary that there should exist a personal being in whom the full fellowship between God and men is restored as at the first. He must be capable of forming a medium through which the salvation of God reaches the human race, and possess the power to generate in the soul of man a new life of obedience to God. But a personality able to accomplish this must be perfectly free from all sin—perfectly pure and holy both in heart and life. In this view, therefore, the sinlessness (that is, holiness and perfection of life) of him who is to found the religion, is an indispensable condition, and we should be justified in believing that any religion presented to us was the true one, only where we had indisputable evidence that that condition had been fulfilled in its founder. But then, on the other hand, we can with equal truth assert, that where this has been the case, where we have full reason to recognize in the founder of any given religion an individual of holy and absolutely perfect life, we shall have in this very fact the highest evidence of the actual truth and perfection of that religion itself. For a person of this character must possess the highest religious truth; we will, therefore, expect to find, in connection with him, everything else that is necessary to a perfect religion.

Now, there exists a tradition that a life of sinless perfection has actually been lived.[19]

The answer—or at least the type of answer—to the question here was virtually dictated by the terms in which it was framed. It was certainly not directly lifted out of Schleiermacher. Ullmann's formulation of religion has a more pronounced theistic and ethical character than Schleiermacher's. But the type of Christology that he expounded came from the same mold as Schleiermacher's. It was essentially a view of Jesus as the perfect man who was therefore the founder of the new religion, the archetypal figure who is the source of our communion with God.[20] It was not Ullmann's aim to demonstrate the two-natures Christ of orthodoxy, but to convince his readers of the sinlessness of Jesus and to challenge them to commit themselves to him as "the Son of God."

In this sense it is, that we recognize in the sinless One the only true Mediator between God and man. In Jesus we see Him in whom God is well-pleased with man, and turns to him in grace: Him in whom man may look on the unveiled glory of Divine Love, may zealously apprehend and appropriate that love, and thus be changed into the Divine likeness. But while He thus brings humanity to God, He does not the less draw men more closely together among themselves.[21]

But if you admit the fact of His holiness, you must go still farther; for you must recognize in Him a personal revelation of God, you must own Him as the Reconciler, you must tender Him your homage as the King of the kingdom of God and the Prince of Life.[22]

The proof of religion did not lie in such externals as miracles and fulfilled prophecy—which could conceivably have been read into the life of Jesus—but in the power of his personality.[23] Ullmann's essay proceeded first by examining the idea of sinlessness and its realization in the person of Jesus, and then by considering Christianity itself as a proof of the sinlessness of Jesus. After considering a number of objections, Ullmann finally drew various inferences about Jesus and devotional applications.

In a sense, Ullmann's other apologetic and polemical writings were variations on the themes here sounded. In the article "Über Partei und Schule, Gegensätze und deren Vermittlung" he turned to the question of rationalism and supernaturalism. The supernaturalist saw Christianity "as something utterly new, incomprehensible, miraculous, as stemming immediately from God," whereas the naturalist viewed it "more in its connection with nature and history, as the expression of general human truths, accessible to human thought, as something mediated by human beings."[24] Ullmann insisted that "true mediation" must proceed from "the true mean," and that it was Christ who was "in the highest sense the true mean, the mediator between Godhood and humanity, the mid-point of world history, the inexhaustible source of all higher development of life and spirit." It was, therefore, the task of theology "to develop undisturbed and correctly all the elements which lie in this divine-human manifestation of Christ, and if it does this, it will have the truth, which in the best sense lies in the middle."[25]

In the debate with Strauss, Ullmann conceded that the Gospel narratives must be understood in the light of modern knowledge and that mythical elements might be present.[26] But it was easier to explain the church in the light of Christ than *vice versa*.[27] The "principal content of the Gospel tradition, namely the resurrection of Christ" must be presupposed as "historical and true."[28] Ullmann could agree with Strauss that "the basic idea, the real basic principle of all religion" was "the idea of God's oneness with humanity." But whereas Strauss's "idea become real" was to be found "in the totality of humanity," with Ullmann it was to be found only "in the person of Christ." Ullmann did not wish to deny the idea of a developing union of God and man. Rather, it attained "its zenith and historical fulfillment in Christ."[29] "In Christ, the idea of the Good and the Holy, the idea of religion, God himself, insofar as it is possible within human limitations, has become personal."[30]

Ullmann seems to be following in Schleiermacher's footsteps not only in the substance of his thought but also in his vocabulary when he speaks of Jesus as the "archetype *[Urbild]* of true life in God."[31] But there are also hints of a modified Idealism. Christianity must be grounded in a view which avoids the pitfalls of both pantheism and traditional theism. Strauss failed because all his endeavors were grounded in an "all-consuming, personality-destroying pantheism." To Ullmann, on the other hand, "If ideas are to be realized, it can only come about through persons."[32] The personality of Jesus was to be understood

> out of a new spiritual endowment through the creative Spirit itself, as a creation, which on the one hand was a completion of the original, insofar as that which came to manifestation in Christ lay from eternity in the divine idea of man, but on the other hand was a new creation, insofar as it did not proceed from the nexus of natural and historical data, but flowed from the eternal original Source itself.[33]

This phenomenon was itself miraculous. Indeed, Ullmann takes it as a paradigm for his redefinition of the miraculous that seeks to steer a middle course between the rationalism of Strauss and the supernaturalism of orthodoxy. A miracle is

> that action or event, which we can derive neither from the laws and forces of nature, so far as they are known to us through the most frequent experiences, nor from the historical nexus of human life. Rather, they lead back, on account of their religious significance and their total nexus, to an operation of divine power in nature and history.[34]

In both definitions there is a discontinuity of historical process and normal experience. But the idea of supernatural intervention is also absent. Rather it is a case of a specially gifted individual being able to draw upon reserves of spiritual power. Underlying them was the fact that "through more highly gifted individuals peculiar effects that deviate from the usual are possible in the realm of the spirit and nature."[35] Thus even in cases of walking on water and the miraculous multiplication of loaves "the power of spirit on the organism" cannot be measured by ordinary standards. One should not take one's personal experience and imaginative powers "to be the absolute measure of what has happened or can happen."[36] Miracles were to be understood teleologically in the light of spiritual reality and overall divine purposes. A similar approach was shared by other Mediating Theologians.[37]

The feature that emerges time and again from Ullmann's pronouncements and those of the first generation of Mediating Theologians is the desire to embrace and commend a positive Christian faith that has a recognizable continuity with traditional belief, but that is less rigid than orthodoxy and prefers its own ways of stating its beliefs. Often they expressed admiration for Schleiermacher and taught doctrines which bore marks of his influence, but equally often they felt obliged to stop short of his radicalism and subjectivism.[38] Like Schleiermacher, Ullmann stopped short of identifying Jesus with God. He preferred to speak of God in Christ and of the realization of the union of God and man in him.[39] Like Schleiermacher, Ullmann wished to affirm that this union had taken place in history in the historical person of Jesus. But whereas Schleiermacher endeavored to demonstrate it, making use of biblical criticism, Ullmann appealed to church history to show that unless Jesus had actually lived as he claimed, church history was inexplicable.[40]

As with Schleiermacher, redemption was central to Ullmann's faith. He could even agree with Schleiermacher that redemption was "a matter of feeling." But he wanted to stress, in a way which he felt Schleiermacher did not, that reconciliation

> goes beyond the subject to God, and has thus at the same time something *objective* (forgiveness of sins, justification of the sinner before God, God's turning to the sinner and his divine acquittal), in which there necessarily lies a moment of objective knowledge of the divine being.[41]

Whether we ought with R. Holte[42] to bracket Ullmann's teaching with Aulén's "classic" theory of atonement is open to question. Ullmann seems to have trod a circumspect path between a subjectivism, which would locate the whole action in the consciousness of the individual, and an objective orthodoxy, which would make everything depend upon penal satisfaction. In fact, he seems to be rather vague in his mind as to what constitutes the act of atonement. He was content to say that 2 Corinthians 5:19 "evidently indicates that God's existence in Christ was and is the primary and causal but that the reconciliation which follows from it is the caused."[43] With this observation we are brought back to Ullmann's central theme. *Das Wesen des Christenthums* (from which the above quotation is taken) went on to reaffirm that "the center of Christianity" is "the absolute unity brought into being in Christ and the union of humanity with God that proceeds from him."[44] Everything else was accordingly alloted its place. Doctrine was the expression of the "truly new and creative in the person and appearance of Christ."[45] The union of God and man was effected through faith and love. The former meant the inner appropriation of Christianity; the latter its complete expression in life.[46] The former was not merely intellectual assent, but neither was it mere feeling.[47] The latter arises out of the unity of God and man in Christ.[48]

Even in their own day the Mediating Theologians were accused of being compromising theologians, and the charge has been repeated down to the present.[49] Horst Stephan and Martin Schmidt comment that instead of continuing the creative synthesis begun by Schleiermacher, the movement degenerated into eclecticism.[50] In Ullmann's case this verdict is not without some justice. This is not to deny the learning, the enthusiasm, and the zeal with which he presented his views. There were aspects of his work that both the believing orthodox and the more radical Christian might applaud, but Ullmann frequently left the feeling that he never quite pushed his arguments far enough. He took care not to be caught on the brambles of orthodoxy or fall into the snares of rationalism. But he never strayed from the path followed by Schleiermacher. Although he was concerned with questions of faith and doubt, there was a limit to his questioning beyond which he did not venture.

Müller, Lange, and Schweizer

The union of God and man in the person of Christ and its centrality for Christian faith were themes which figured prominently in the thought of Müller, Lange, and Schweizer. Julius Müller (1801–78)[51] devoted two articles to his "Untersuchung der Frage: Ob der Sohn Gottes Mensch geworden sein würde, wenn das menschliche Geschlecht ohne Sünde geblieben wäre."[52] The question, whether the incarnation would have taken place if man had not fallen, had been made acute by the recent writings of Thomasius, Dorner, and others, including Schleiermacher.[53] Müller's conclusion echoed the thoughts and phraseology of Ullmann.[54] It tended in the same direction as Schleiermacher, but was more objective and definite in its emphasis on the divine initiative in the incarnation.

> Humanity is to be restored from the state of sin to the fellowship of God and led to the full fellowship of God. Now this cannot come about through an isolated fact. Rather, this liberating, sanctifying, fulfilling effect can only proceed from the total revelation of a personality in which the human is completely united with God. But here too it remains the case, that redemption, insofar as its full notion includes the elevation of those freed from the guilt and power of sin to the complete fellowship of God, is the purpose of the incarnation of the Son or the revelation of humanity united with God. On the presupposition of a normal development, which indisputably would have led to the goal essential to man of that complete fellowship with God —even though naturally conditioned by the constant self-communication of God (the Logos)—there is lacking an adequate ground for the incarnation of the Son.[55]

Müller was primarily a dogmatic theologian, and the above conclusion was reached primarily on dogmatic grounds. Johann Peter Lange (1802–84) was a biblical expositor. He was widely esteemed on both sides of the Atlantic for his commentaries, which became an essential feature of the scholarly preacher's library.[56] Lange was among the first to reply to Strauss.[57] The work helped to establish his theological reputation. His later commentaries and studies were comparable with those of Tholuck and Stier. Lichtenberger spoke of him as "the poetical theologian *par excellence* ... clever in finding seductive formulae and ingenious combinations with the view of procuring acceptance for the positive doctrines," and carried away by "the theory of immanence."[58] The Scottish editor of Lange's *Life of the Lord Jesus Christ* hailed the work as "the most complete Life of our Lord" and saw it as a positive answer to the accounts of Hase, Ewald, and Renan.[59] It was, in fact, a vast running commentary, consisting for the most part of paraphrase and reflection on the episodes of the Gospels, making occasional reference to points raised by contemporary scholars. It was prefaced by a lengthy introduction, ranging from the incarnation to modern criticism and the authenticity of the Gospels, and was followed by an even lengthier study of each of the four Gospels, examining their distinctive emphasis.

Lange's outlook was positively supernaturalistic. The individual miracles sprang from the development of Jesus' life and were "nothing but foretokens which must necessarily culminate in the great miracle of His resurrection." The latter was "the culminating point of theocratic history, and the deepest foundation of the Christian view of the world, and so the centre-point of the whole world of living faith in God."[60] Lange was perhaps the most conservative of the Mediating Theologians and the one most concerned with biblical exegesis. He roundly dismissed the questions of the critics in the declaration that,

> The four Gospels, in the form in which we have them, may with perfect justice be pronounced to be credible historical records of the life of Jesus. They are literary representations presenting us with purely objective testimony; they are the products of a perfect, and therefore infinitely tranquil enthusiasm, in entire unison with the object which excited it. No secondary motive is found here, to create a discord or awaken suspicion. Their form is the result of that entire surrender to the manifestations of the perfect image of God which was one with the most powerful subjective appropriation of the same. The purity with which they reflect, as instruments, the rich and glorious reality of the life of Christ, imparts to their moral aspect a nobility which must ever enhance their credibility. With princely magnanimity do they exhibit the essential, while they but very slightly touch upon the non-essential.[61]

The mode in which these sentiments are expressed gives some weight to Lichtenberger's observation, noted above. Lange conceded that the object of the Fourth Gospel was "to describe the life of Jesus Christ in its ideal character."[62] But he insisted that "the material of the first three Evangelists unites harmoniously with the chronological plan of John's narrative, into one rich whole."[63] This conclusion represents a modification of Schleiermacher's position, as was his view of the significance of Jesus, which was essentially on the same lines as that of Ullmann and Müller. It was oriented around the thought of the union of God and man. Jesus was the one who fulfills and mediates this union in his own person. What gave Lange a broader appeal than the other Mediating Theologians was the fact that he spoke the language of conservative pulpit rhetoric.

> The life at once divine and human, however, which was to proceed from the union of God with man, could, from its very nature, be perfected only in the most exalted individuality standing in mutual action with the highest universality.[64]

> Humanity had now, in so far as it was one with Christ, its praise of God in its longing after the righteousness of God, and its Redeemer in Him, according to the whole difference existing between His life and its own. In this glory and redemption of mankind which was manifested in Christ however, the heart and nature of God Himself were most intimately disclosed to the world—the Son of man is the Son of God. He who was certified as the Holy One in the midst of time, is the chosen one from the depths of eternity. His life is the manifestation of the deep things of God, and the deep things of men, in the manifestation of the deep things of His divine-human heart. It is the manifestation of the eternal personality.[65]

Although his chief work falls outside the period under review, mention may be made of Alexander Schweizer (1808–88)[66] who was the leading exponent of *Vermittlungstheologie* in Switzerland. As a dogmatic theologian, he was conscious of the winds of change blowing through the church, and saw in them a significance comparable to the Reformation. A recent writer has observed that Schweizer took for granted as his starting point the position that Schleiermacher labored so much to establish.[67] For him the "burning question" of theology was how "to interpret truly Christ's true humanity with the uniqueness and abiding worth of his personal significance in full harmony with the absolute principle."[68]

The answer lay along the path already marked out by Schleiermacher, but the latter was not entirely satisfactory. He was "without doubt far too one-sided" in the way in which he derived "the doctrine of the person and worth of Christ from our subjective experience."[69] A second source of authority was to be found in the biblical records. But, like Schleiermacher and the other Mediating Theologians, Schweizer saw his work as an endeavor to do justice to the humanity of Jesus, summoning the theology of his time to take full account of the neglected complete humanity of Christ with its human development. Schweizer was prepared to leave to others the work of investigating the historical Jesus. He himself was more concerned with grasping his religious personality as it is known to faith. Jesus' personality was stamped by the idea of redemptive religion that constituted his inner life and vocation as mediator and redeemer.[70]

Rothe

Already in his lifetime, Richard Rothe (1799–1867)[71] had begun to acquire the double image of a saint and a teacher of dangerous speculations.[72] More recently, he has been called "the most original thinker, the system builder among the Mediating Theologians."[73] In his earlier days Romantic literature, especially the poetry of Novalis, made a deep impression on him. In 1817 he went to Heidelberg to study theology. He attended Daub's and Hegel's lectures, but was more attracted to the writings of Schelling. He moved to Berlin in 1819, where he was impressed by Neander. He heard Schleiermacher lecture on the life of Jesus and on ethics. In 1820 he entered the seminary at Wittenberg, where he came under the influence of Kottwitz and Tholuck, who paid regular visits. As chaplain to the Prussian embassy in Rome, he got to know Baron von Bunsen under whose influence his outlook once more changed. He became professor of the seminary at Wittenberg in 1828, where he soon became its director. In 1839 he was appointed professor at Heidelberg, where he spent the remainder of his career apart from five years at Bonn between 1849 and 1854. His main writings were concerned with the early church, ethics, and dogmatics.

Rothe followed Schleiermacher in seeking an approach that would mediate between faith and knowledge, and between Christianity and culture, and also in seeing the locus of religion in awareness of God. Dogmatics was the historical, critical account of teaching followed in certain communities. It presupposed what Rothe termed *philosophia sacra*. This was "a system of truly regenerate, rigorous knowledge—not in the strength of the natural spirit of man but in the strength of the Holy Spirit of God."[74] In it Rothe made "consciousness of God the primary datum and starting point for speculative thought." In contrast with philosophical ethics it did not proceed from "moral consciousness purely as such," but from Christian self-consciousness as the "reflex" of the "historically given ideal of morality in the appearance of the redeemer."[75]

Thus Rothe claimed that his "speculative theology" and ethics took the Bible unreservedly as their norm.[76] But the Bible could no longer be regarded as "the textbook of religion, composed by divine authorship."[77] It was, rather, "the historical source for divine revelation."[78] The latter was not "the supernatural disclosure of religious theorems,"[79] but a "complex of historical facts."[80] Scripture was "precisely what the historian calls a historical source, a historical document—from which he draws his knowledge of historical facts."[81] This was, in fact, demanded by the Protestant principle. "The same ground that requires us Protestants to explain Scripture as the unique source of knowledge of divine revelation, also compels us to demand the most rigorous historical criticism of the same."[82] The New Testament is essentially the *imago Christi*, "the photograph which the historical Christ himself has directly, i.e., without the intermediate step of human, interpretative reflection, projected upon the consciousness of his receptive environment."[83] Such a pronouncement might seem to obviate the need for historical criticism, but for Rothe it was its justification. For the picture of Christ was not given in its totality by any one New Testament document. It emerged only in the light of speculation and criticism.[84] The latter alone allowed Scripture to be what it really is—neither a textbook of religion nor an anthology of sermon texts,[85] but the source of revelation history.

Rothe was not unique in this period in speaking of salvation history, but he virtually inverted the approach of the more orthodox conservatives, like Hofmann. Whereas the latter saw all history as salvation history for which the Bible provided the key, with Rothe it was the speculative understanding of world history that provided the key to the Bible. The alternative was an arbitrary, literalistic exegesis which led to a spiritual gnosticism.[86]

If Rothe learned from Schleiermacher his concept of religious awareness, and from the critics his conviction that biblical theology had to come to terms with critical history, the substance of his speculative theology had no small affinity with Idealist philosophy. The main thrust of his thought was determined by his conception of the union of the personal and spiritual with the material. This, in turn, determined the fundamental character of ethics. Rothe understood the Kingdom of God as the process of the "incarnation in the world [Weltwerdung] of the God of Spirit," in the first instance through the divine act of creation and then through the activity of man.[87] Creation was "an absolutely necessary act of God."[88] It was "the process of his own self-actualizing."[89] However, Rothe stopped short of identifying this with the unfolding of the Absolute Spirit.[90] He was kept on the Christian side of the line by a theism which enabled him to speak of "the divine ordering of the world"[91] and which allowed him to speak of God in personal, purposive terms.[92] In this evolutionary development, man had a special place, for it was the "creaturely person" in which "God as Spirit has his intramundane being."[93]

> Since in man, in virtue of his religious and moral development, a real cosmic existence of God as nature and personality comes into being, the progress of the earthly process of creation can now proceed from this point onwards essentially through the mediation of man. From now on, therefore, God, as divine personality in virtue of divine nature, existing in (spiritual) man, continues the earthly work of creation in its second main stage.[94]

Rothe combines the Idealist thought of the ongoing process of the Spirit in human affairs with Schleiermacher's thought that the *locus* of religion is man's religious awareness. In the narrower sense the church was the sphere where this happened. But the thought is tempered by the Hegelian one, that the state was the ultimate expression of the Spirit's activity. "God utterly wills the state, and indeed the complete state, because he wills complete, normal morality (and piety), but this only has reality in the complete state."[95] In the broader sense this presence of God constitutes the full incarnation of God.

> The fact that in this terminal point of the moral process, human self-consciousness in its complete development is at the same time essentially absolute consciousness of God and human self-activity in its complete development is at the same time essentially absolute divine activity, this is indeed concretely none other than a real existence of God in the human creature, the complete incarnation of God: God is now utterly present in humanity.[96]

Within this scheme it is not surprising that Rothe's teaching on sin and salvation followed the path trod by Schleiermacher. It retained the vocabulary of orthodoxy, but sought to avoid the thornier problems of the fall and original sin.[97] The categories within which Rothe preferred to operate were those of normal and abnormal existence. Sin occurred when the sensuous, natural principle in man got the upper hand and thus created an "abnormal moral function."[98] This situation, in turn, created the need for "redemption." But redemption was not a divine afterthought, occasioned by sin. It was already contained "in the divine world-idea itself," for creation was not a finished act but a "successive" one. Redemption presented more a correction of course in man's development, for the first man or "natural Adam" was not "the true man, i.e., who truly corresponded to his idea."[99]

Creation and redemption thus belong together in the process of human development. The redeemer signifies the realized "Idea of the human as such in its purity and truth."[100] As with Schleiermacher, redemption was not a single propitiatory act; it was a "historical process of development" involving the "actual removal of sin in humanity."[101] "In the kingdom of God redemption enters as a historical force *over against the world*."[102] "What is the work of Christ but simply His realization of the idea for which, and according to which,

God created man?"[103] History prior to and without Christ leads merely to a "mere approximation to the *true* man."[104] The work of the redeemer may thus be described as the "recreation" of humanity "from matter to the good and Holy Spirit."[105] In this respect Jesus is the "mid-point of world history."[106]

Within this scheme the sacraments represent the spiritual renewal that takes place through redemption.[107] The orthodox framework of covenant theology, type and anti-type, and prophecy and fulfillment is replaced by a scheme of cosmic history in which biblical history counts as "the historical preparation for the redeemer."[108] The goal of history and revelation is the "purification and strengthening of the human consciousness of God."[109] To this end God used "new facts"—supernatural events in nature and history—in order to form "the idea of God" and "the picture of God" in human consciousness. Rothe looked forward to a time when the church would have done its work and society would be spiritual. At this time not only would the Redeemer have become identified with mankind, but both would exist as one on a purely spiritual level. For Rothe the eschatological hope was that of a "pure, spiritual, absolute presence" of the Redeemer and the redeemed.[110]

The figure of Christ, the Redeemer, occupied a central place in Rothe's thought. In the second volume of his *Dogmatik* he articulated his Christology on traditional lines, referring to the *communicatio idiomatum*, the two states of Christ, and giving extensive discussion to this restatement of the threefold offices of Christ. He responded to Strauss, Schleiermacher, Martensen, the Erlangen theologians, and numerous other contemporaries. Rather than speak of the sinlessness of Christ, with its negative connotations, Rothe preferred to speak of "an *absolutely complete* normal development of moral being."[111] Moreover, Rothe went beyond other Mediating Theologians in developing the theological significance of the idea within his total theological framework. Thomasius's doctrine of *kenōsis* was irreconcilable with true human development, and it was impossible to conceive of the divine Logos divested of his attributes.[112]

> For Christian piety it remains unshakably firm that only an actual *God-man* can be the redeemer. If the *true God* is not in the redeemer in an essential way, then he can neither be the complete revelation of God, nor can he place us in an absolutely real way in fellowship with God. But he must be likewise essentially *true* man; for only man is the *absolutely adequate* medium for the revelation of God, for us as well as for his drawing nigh to us for the purpose of our fellowship with him.[113]

For Rothe, the two natures of Christ were a necessity posited by his total view of reality, which found empirical confirmation in the New Testament witness to Jesus. What he presented was an extension and reinterpretation of previous orthodoxy. He drew heavily upon previous nineteenth-century philosophical theology, but hardly at all upon the work of critical scholars. The life of the historical Jesus was important theologically. But Rothe was not so much interested in critical history as in the "*central place*, which the second Adam obtains *in humanity:* He is the central individual of the same."[114] As such, Christ was a human being, though he did not possess individuality in himself, but only in relation to others.[115]

> This completion of the second Adam is *in and of itself* not yet the simultaneous completion of the creation of man or the redemption of sinful humanity. The completed second Adam is *of himself alone* not yet the full true man, spiritual *humanity*. He is only now its *principal, individual progenitor*. That is the distinctive feature of *his* individuality. . . .
>
> The personal, human existence of the second Adam thus also goes on growing in the state of exaltation. Finally the individually human existence of God *[das Menschsein Gottes]* becomes an existence of God in humanity *[ein Menschheitsein Gottes]*. Whereby then sin in the old natural humanity is, as a matter of fact, abolished.
>
> Now so far as the second Adam possesses in his personal completion additionally the necessary capacity, he is qualified as the *redeemer* of the human race or the *Christ*.[116]

It is interesting to place alongside each other the comments of Horst Stephan and Peter Meinhold. According to Stephan, Rothe sought to view history and culture with the eye of God. Rothe enjoyed the highest respect on all sides and proved to be a richer source of inspiration than most of his contemporaries, but because of his hasty reading of eschatology into history, his theology as a whole lacked compelling power.[117] According to Meinhold, Rothe "saw in the incarnation not only a unique historical fact, but an idea expressed, according to which God realizes himself generally in the world."[118] Both these judgments are just, but they need to be read in the light of the appeal that Rothe held for so many of his contemporaries. A century earlier Rothe could not have written the way he did. His unique synthesis of Schleiermacher, Idealist philosophy, and traditional orthodoxy made an appeal to minds that were affected by these various elements and that shared a deep longing for a Christian *Weltanschauung* that would make sense of reality at large. To a generation that believed that some form of Idealism held the key to reality and that also believed in the truth of Christian doctrine, Rothe's pronouncements were like the cherished sayings of the fathers. Rothe was not a prophet but a seer. The aphorisms contained in his *Still Hours* spoke to many who did not understand his system but who also wanted more than the conventional wisdom of the traditional evangelical piety. If his understanding of Jesus appears to be only loosely related to historical investigation and precise biblical exegesis, it bore testimony to a perception of the significance of Jesus that others had missed. It rested on a conviction concerning his essential divinity that neither philosophy nor criticism had eroded. Indeed, for Rothe they pointed the way to a broader understanding of the universal significance of Christ.

Dorner

If Rothe was the most speculative of the Mediating Theologians, Isaak August Dorner (1809–84)[119] was their most massive and monumental writer. He studied at Tübingen between 1827 and 1832, where, however, he was more concerned with the thought of Kant, Jacobi, Schelling, Hegel, and Schleiermacher than that of his immediate teachers. He served for two years as assistant to his father before entering the Tübinger Stift in 1834. At the time when Strauss was publishing his *Life of Jesus*, Dorner was writing the first draft of his own Christology in the shape of an article which included a response to Strauss.[120] In 1838 he became an *extraordinarius* at Tübingen. The following year he moved to Kiel, where he became a full professor. Here he published his *Entwicklungs-geschichte der Lehre von der Person Christi von den ältesten Zeiten bis auf die neueste* (1839).[121] During this period began his lifelong friendship with H. L. Martensen.[122] Dorner went on to hold professorships at Königsberg (1843), Bonn (1847), Göttingen (1853), and Berlin (1862), where he was also a member of the Oberkirchenrat. He was a staunch supporter of the Union. He was concerned with the Innere Mission and social reform, and was a founder of the Kirchentag. His writings include a *Geschichte der protestantischen Theologie* (1867),[123] *Gesammelte Schriften aus dem Gebiet der systematischen Theologie, Exegese und Geschichte* (1883), *System der christlichen Sittenlehre* (1885),[124] a brief essay *Ueber Jesu sündlose Vollkommenheit* (1862), and the extensive *System der christlichen Glaubenslehre* (1879–81).[125]

Dorner's two great theological studies—the *Entwicklungsgeschichte* and the *System der christlichen Glaubenslehre*—epitomized the man and his work. They exhibit a familiarity with both German and British thought which far transcended that of most of his contemporaries. In both works Dorner proceeded by way of précis and paraphrase (pausing rarely to give references) through the thoughts of everyone who seemed at all relevant in an attempt to produce his own synthesis. He was more interested in the analysis of ideas than in the technicalities of documentation. It was no accident that his gigantic catalog of thinkers—the *Entwicklungsgeschichte* is still the most exhaustive survey of Christology by a single writer—included both Christian theologians and secular philosophers. Nor was it any less fortuitous that Christology occupied a commanding place in his thought. For Dorner regarded theology as an organic systematic development in which the figure of Christ occupied the central role. Dorner's dogmatic synthesis might be regarded as the climax of Mediating Theology. Perhaps too it was an indication of both Dorner's personal esteem and the prestige of the movement in general that whereas his *Entwicklungsgeschichte* aroused considerable interest, his *System der christlichen Glaubenslehre* exerted little influence.[126]

Dorner divided the history of Christian theology into three great periods. The first, which extended down to the Council of Constantinople (A.D. 381), he termed the "Period of the Settling of the Essential Elements of the Person of Christ on the Divine and Human Sides, Presupposed or Immediate *Unio Perso-nalis.*"[127] In this period, the doctrine of a personal union of the divine and human natures was worked out. Then came a lengthier period, extending to about A.D. 1800, in which first the divine nature of Christ tended to be stressed at the expense of the human (up to about A.D. 1700),[128] and then the human at the expense of the divine (to about A.D. 1800).[129] Finally, the nineteenth century inaugurated the third period which produced a living synthesis of what had gone before in which both the divinity and the humanity are given their proper due.[130]

Perhaps the most interesting and significant feature of this whole analysis is the claim that the foundations of the new Christology were laid by three men: Schelling, Hegel, and Schleiermacher. The appeal of all three lay in their philosophical approach, or, to be more precise, in their vision of an identity philosophy, which made it possible to think of God and man not only as interrelated, but also in terms of personal growth and movement. Schelling was credited with the undying merit not merely of having discerned but also of having taken an important step toward the abolition of the dualism which underlay both the older orthodox "objective" Christologies and the more recent rationalistic "subjective" ones.

> He saw that it is not right to conceive subject and object as mutually exclusive and merely opposed to each other, but that the essential unity of the two must be taken as the principle of all philosophy: this essential unity he terms *Subject-Object*.[131]

Schelling's particular relevance lay in the fact that he saw God as the living organic unity of the many, a unity which is not a static pure being but, like all life, a growth *(ein Werden)*.[132] This was not only an advantage over eighteenth-century Deism and pantheism; it was also compatible with Christian Trinitarianism. It represented an advance upon early Christology which treated Christ as an absolute miracle, utterly separated from the rest of mankind. Schelling's great drawback, however, was his view of mankind in general as a universal incarnation of God and his consequent failure to do justice to the concrete, historic incarnation of Christ.

> The progress made by Schelling consists in his having begun to view *personality* (as the living unity of subject and object, of single and universal) in its infinite worth. According to the "Freiheitslehre," the goal of the entire process of the world is the birth of the perfect humanity, the realization of the idea of the eternal, original, divine man; or, regarded from above, the perfect actualization of the ideal principle, which will one day have become entirely a personal being in the members of His body. . . . But what place does the historical Christ occupy in the midst of this process through which humanity and God are supposed to pass? It is not He who appears as the actor, as the redeemer and perfecter; on the contrary, "the ideal principle" appears to be the soul of history, and that without standing in any necessary relation to His historical manifestation. It is true he gives utterance to the striking principle— "the personal alone can heal the personal"; but he neglects to establish it, and does not allow it a thorough influence. Christ further it is true, according to Schelling, inaugurates a new period, the kingdom of spirit. But is He only the first-born, or also the operative and permanent principle of the regeneration of the world? Is He merely the beginning, or is He also the climax of the new age of the world?[133]

Schelling's underlying failure was a tendency to view God's infinitude quantitatively.

So long as that takes place, the inadequacy between him as substance and as person must remain absolute; and not till God's essence is conceived as absolute personality and love will the relation to the human personality, which, as such, has an infinite susceptibility, assume a different character also for the personal God.[134]

Nevertheless, Schelling's philosophy, not in its actual form, but in its intention of asserting "the true conception of personality as one in which finite and infinite are united," led toward "a higher form of Christology."[135]

Turning to Hegel and Schleiermacher, Dorner observed that,

To Hegel belongs the epoch-making and distinctive merit of having, by a more rigid method, taken more fixed possession of the new land which Schelling had conquered, as it were, by storm; while Schleiermacher began to prepare the way for it especially in a theological direction. Hegel showed, in particular, the untruth of the old determinations of the antagonism between the finite and the infinite, between God and the world, in a manner appreciable by every one who thinks; and thus made the essential unity of the two a matter of universal conviction.[136]

However, Hegel's disciples had fallen short of their master,[137] and Hegel himself was open to question at certain crucial points.

One final conclusion, therefore, is, that with the premises referred to above, the Hegelian system neither did nor could allow that the perfect unity of the divine and human had been realized in Christ in an unique manner, and that His development was sinless.

The ultimate reason of this is, that Hegel conceives God, not as absolute self-consciousness which is reflected in itself, but merely allows Him to become a subject in the endless series or totality of finite spirits; that he arbitrarily, and with an introduction of empirical knowledge into speculation, regards the *world* as the *other*, through and in which God can alone know Himself; that he describes the stages of its history as the stages passed through by the divine self-consciousness in coming to itself; that, in one word, he conceives God, not as an eternal, absolute personality, nor as actually ethical, but as the spirit of the world, for whom the world only exists that it may mediate his own self-consciousness, — somewhat as the nature in and outside of man mediates his self-consciousness.[138]

All this was bound up with the thought of God as merely the *Weltgeist*, which was not only unproved but led to patent absurdities. On Hegel's premises, "the consciousness of God is not complete, so long as that of humanity is still progressing."[139] Either the Idea was eternally real in itself, and thus did not need the world to actualize itself or, since it needed the medium of the world, it was eternally seeking itself but never finding itself.[140] Hegel's system rested upon fundamental "antichristological principles."[141] It fell short of the Christian view which "proclaims that the true reconciliation of the finite and infinite has taken place in the Son of God, and is constantly taking place in those who by faith become children of God and members of the head which is Christ."[142]

Dorner justified his grouping of Schleiermacher together with Hegel and Schelling, despite certain mutual antipathy, on the grounds that he took the essential unity of God and man for his starting point without falling into pantheism. Moreover, Schleiermacher was the most theological and influential of the three.[143] His discussion is based upon a brief look at *Die Weihnachtsfeier* and a more detailed analysis of *Der christliche Glaube*. Schleiermacher differed from Schelling and Hegel in that he based his view, not upon speculative philosophy, but upon his analysis of Christian consciousness in which Christ has the historical role of the archetypal mediator of the consciousness of God.[144]

> His great merit, however, is, to have endeavoured to develop this unity of the divine and human, which to him was solely historical,—that is, which he had not yet understood in its inner necessity,—so clearly, and in such a manner as to secure both the uniqueness and specific dignity of Christ and His brotherhood with men. He believed the perfect being of God to be in Christ; and for this reason regarded Him as the complete man. And so, vice versâ, because He is the complete man, the consciousness of God has become a being of God in Him. In this way he endeavours to conciliate and combine two modes of regarding Him,—that according to which He is an immediate act of God, and that according to which He is the completion of creation.[145]

But among the numerous charges leveled against Schleiermacher there were several that could not be dismissed. One was that "The historical actuality of an archetypal Christ is not satisfactorily deducible from the Christian consciousness."[146] Dorner conceded that Christian consciousness might posit some archetypal cause, but it was not necessary for such a cause to be historical.[147] Schleiermacher did not show "why Christ ought to be considered the *archetypal* embodiment of the new principle, and not merely the first or initiatory embodiment, endowed with power to implant the new principle in humanity."[148] Moreover, "A mere man, however high may be his position, has not the power to bestow the principle of holiness and blessedness, that is, the Holy Spirit."[149]

> If, however, we endeavour to assert for Christ the specific dignity which is demanded by the Christian consciousness, and which Schleiermacher also aims at retaining . . . it is clear that we cannot rest satisfied with the anthropological point of view, from which Christ appears merely as the completed man, as the embodiment of the consciousness of God in its most perfect vigour; but shall be compelled *either to declare less, or more*, concerning Christ than Schleiermacher did.[150]

In the last analysis, the fundamental difficulty with Schleiermacher was his conception of God. Logically, his Sabellian sympathies should have led him to Patripassianism.[151] On the other hand, "Instead of allowing God Himself to pass over into growth and suffering, into finitude or altereity, he rather aims most distinctly at representing God as the eternally complete and absolute spiritual life in its immutability over against the world."[152] The logical outcome of this tendency would be Deism. "We thus find it proved in his case also, that there is no escape from the alternative of Pantheism or Deism, save in a trinitarian conception of God."[153] In practice, Schleiermacher vacillated between these alternatives. Moreover, he could not free himself from this vacillation so long as he did not, on the one hand, ensure the self-assertion of God in the act of self-communication to the world, by asserting Him to be discriminated in Himself; and as, on the other hand, he did not put himself in opposition to Deism, and provide for the capability of God's communicating Himself, by representing Him as an unity discriminated in itself.[154]

Schleiermacher repeated the dilemma of the early church. Abstract Monarchianism was bound to vacillate between Arianism and Sabellianism "until the Church established its doctrine of the trinitarian self-discrimination of God in Himself, in virtue whereof God can be communicative, without losing Himself to the world."[155] It was Dorner's aim to restate this doctrine for his own time.

Dorner could grant that Sabellianism, in both its ancient and modern forms, intended to stress that God had truly revealed himself in Jesus. It presented Jesus as one who walked so close with God that he was sinless and God's being shone through his human personality. The difficulty was that God was not personally in Christ, on this view. The result was an Ebionism that taught that the personality of Christ was "merely human."[156] On the other hand, orthodoxy had fallen into the opposite error of suppressing the human personality of Jesus. "The human nature of Christ was curtailed, in that, after the manner of Apollinaris, the head of the divine hypostasis was set upon the trunk of a human nature, and the unity of the person was thus preserved at the cost of the humanity."[157] The impersonality of Jesus' human nature was an inevitable consequence of the Chalcedonian formula.[158]

Summing up, Dorner expressed satisfaction in his belief that scarcely any theologian of repute ventured to deny the human personality of Christ or to characterize it as impersonal.[159] He was also gratified by the unanimity of contemporary theology as to the sinlessness of Christ, although there was some debate whether Jesus could have attained perfection through free choice or whether he possessed some quality that made it impossible to fall into sin.[160] Dorner saw the way out of this ancient dilemma in his own doctrine of union in growth. These developments were all part of the newer theology—anticipated by the old Lutheran slogan *humana natura capax divinae* ("human nature is capable of the divine")—which refused to see the divine and the human as incompatible exclusives. Even in the Reformed Church there was scarcely a single representative of the old dualism.

> To the theology of the present day, the divine and human are not mutually exclusive, but connected magnitudes, having an inward relation to, and reciprocally confirming, each other; by which view both separation and identification are set aside.[161]

Equally important for Dorner is the agreement of theologians about Christ as the "head and representative of mankind."[162] This view was a truth not derived from philosophical insight but from the faith of Christendom down the ages. Nevertheless, it was one that only in the nineteenth century was really beginning to be understood. It was significant not only for understanding the atonement but also for understanding the nature of the church, moral education, and culture generally. The idea shows that,

> Christ, this divine-human person with soul and body, appropriates to Himself a constantly growing body out of the material of humanity, in that the natural individuals, which, though scattered, belong to and are destined for Him, by their divine idea, are animated by the spirit that proceeds forth from Him, are born again, and are incorporated with Him the Head. Through the idea of the head alone is it possible (but it is also required) to form of humanity, as it is before God, that conception according to which it is not merely a mass, not merely an unity of redeemed individuals, but, taken in conjunction with the world of higher spirits and nature, which is to be glorified for and through it, constitutes the unity of the perfect organism of the world.[163]

This thought led Dorner back to the divinity of Christ and to the doctrine of the Trinity, though significantly the former was conceived not in terms of natures but of revelation.

> Through the medium of this truth, Christology stands in indissoluble connection with the idea of the absolute revelation of God, and with the doctrine of the Trinity. For only on one condition can Christ be regarded as the seat of the central revelation of God, after the movement of the divine heart, to wit, that He is not merely a limited, single individuality, like others, but that He was the meeting point of an universal and absolute susceptibility on the part of human nature to God, and of the absolutely universal or central self-communication of God. Because this man is the centre of the world and absolutely susceptible to God, he is also susceptible to the central, to wit, the personal revelation of God. But also vice versâ: the idea of the head shows that this man can be God.[164]

This situation, in turn, led to a further modification of orthodoxy.

> This is the truth, that the incarnation of God in Christ had not its sole ground in sin; but, besides sin, had a deeper, to wit, an eternal and abiding necessity in the wise and free love of God, so far as this love willed, in general, the existence of a world which should be the scene of its *perfect* revelation, and so far, as consequently, the world is marked by susceptibility to, and need of, this revelation.[165]

This optimistic, christocentric affirmation of the world had an English counterpart in the teaching of F. D. Maurice and his disciples,[166] but Dorner did not develop it with the practical, evangelical fervor of the British Christian Socialists. His interest lay in developing the primacy of the personal union of the divine and human in Christ.

As against the orthodox, with their lack of interest in the humanity of Christ, and the more recent liberals, who treated his divinity as something of which the human was merely conscious, Dorner insisted on the full personality of both.

> In precisely the same manner does the Logos, in power of His love, know humanity as a determination of Himself, to give which to Himself there was in Him the eternal

possibility and will. Whether, therefore, we take our start with the Logos or with man, we find that the self-consciousness (and volition) of each includes the other momentum in itself as a determination of itself. What, consequently, is present on both sides, is nothing but the *divine-human* consciousness, one and the same, which is neither a merely human consciousness of the Logos, nor a merely divine consciousness of man, but a divine-human consciousness of both, that is, as both actually exist, to wit, as united; consequently, divine-human consciousness and volition.[167]

In developing his concept of divine and human personality, Dorner seems to have moved away from the classical, orthodox definition of "person" as "a subsistence in the essence of God,"[168] and toward a modern one of individual, volitional self-consciousness. No less significant are the grounds on which Dorner asserted the personal unity of God and man in Christ.

That in the *state of exaltation* Christ is absolutely complete God-man; that God and man are absolutely united in Him (nay more, that so long as there was self-consciousness in Jesus, there was also a divine-human consciousness, and so forth),—on this point the evangelical theologians of the present day are substantially agreed. The main point, to wit, the image of the exalted God-man as an unity, as required by the needs of the individual believer and of the worshipping Church, is thus secured. For both have to do with the living, exalted Lord.[169]

Such a claim stands squarely in the tradition of Schleiermacher, deducing ontological realities from devotional necessities. Dorner went on to say that "the image of the exalted Lord is based on that of the historical." But neither here nor elsewhere did he do anything to substantiate the latter claim.[170] Instead, he hurried on to a critique of *kenōsis* in which he developed one of the distinctive features of his own Christology.

For Dorner, the union of the two natures was not a static condition following a unique act but a process of growth.

We have no alternative but to assume, that in some way or other the Logos limited Himself for His being and activity *in this man*, so long as the same was still undergoing growth. The divine, therefore, which or so far as it was not yet fully appropriated, owing to the fact of the humanity undergoing a true growth, especially because of its embryonic beginning, did not become man from the very commencement, and certainly did not form a constitutive factor of the initiatory result. The Logos put a limit on His self-communication till human susceptibility had attained more complete development; in such a manner, indeed, that every stage of Christ's existence was divine-human, and that there was never anything human in Christ which was not appropriated by the Logos, and which had not appropriated the Logos, so far as the divine-human perfection at each stage required and allowed of it.[171]

This was a doctrine which was to receive further elaboration in the *System der christlichen Glaubenslehre*, where Dorner went so far as to argue that the incarnation was completed only by the death of Christ.[172] But in the meantime,

Dorner was more concerned with refuting current versions of *kenōsis*[173] and looking forward to overcoming what differences there remained between Lutheran and Reformed Christology.[174]

In his summing up of the Christology of the Mediating Theologians, Ragnar Holte expresses his conviction that its basic tendency was its attempt to grasp the "true humanity of Christ" and to defend the idea of its growth and development.[175] These ideas were certainly present not only in Mediating Theology but also in the kenotic theology of Thomasius. But what is striking is not the presence of these ideas so much as the grounds on which they were stated and defended.

Although he was interested in the humanity of Jesus, Dorner seemed to be almost indifferent to the critical question of the historical Jesus. One would scarcely guess from his major works that Dorner had been a contemporary and colleague of Strauss and Baur. Dorner was interested in the humanity of Jesus as a theological idea within the context of a dogmatic system. He differed from Thomasius not only in his conclusions but also in his method. The latter was concerned with the exegesis of biblical texts within the framework of orthodoxy. Dorner was concerned with the *doctrine* of the person of Christ in the light of doctrinal and philosophical developments. In both cases the figure that emerged was not so much an historical human being as a conjectured rationale for a modified orthodoxy.

In reaching his dogmatic conclusions, Dorner exhibited little awareness of any need to come to terms with Gospel criticism, or indeed to work out a considered view of the relationship between faith and history in the light of historical criticism. The latter's influence on Dorner—as upon Mediating Theologians in general—was largely negative. It prevented them from treating Scripture as a body of revealed truths and helped to direct their concern toward the humanity of Jesus. In all this, Dorner remained very conservative. His Christology was a genuine modification of orthodoxy. The humanity of Christ was not his only concern. It would be nearer the mark to say that his overriding concerns were with the grounding of the incarnation in the nature of God, and the reality of the union of the two natures. In making both these points he saw the key that he was looking for in the notion of personality. But again it must be said that his work was argued on the level of logical implication and compatibility rather than that of historical evidence. Although Dorner made much of the developing personality of Christ, Jesus never comes over as a historical figure, involved in the problems of life in the context of first-century Judaism.

Postscript

By the time Dorner's *System der christlichen Glaubenslehre* appeared, *Vermittlung* was already out of fashion. The positions it was intended to mediate no longer obtained. Those who were interested in speculation had gone beyond the Mediating Theologians in developing a speculative Christianity.[176] But the rising star of the second half of the century was Ritschl, whose philosophical outlook tended to revert to Kant. Sweeping away metaphysical speculation, he proclaimed a Christ whose vocation it was to preach moral righteousness and found the divine, ethical kingdom among men.[177] In due course, Ritschlianism was superseded. Schweitzer with his thorough-going eschatology, the History of Religions School, Bultmann, and Barth and Dialectical Theology came and went.

For Albert Schweitzer, as for many others, the central question of the nineteenth century was the quest of the historical Jesus. In his account of that quest, Schweitzer found no place for men like Dorner, Rothe, Hofmann, Thomasius, and Kierkegaard. In one sense he was right to omit them, for none of them was concerned with what Pannenberg has called Christology "from below,"[178] or "the historical Jesus," as understood by Reimarus, Strauss, Renan, or even Schweitzer himself. But in another sense, these thinkers have just as rightful a place in the history of the quest for the real Jesus. For the Christ that so many of the critics saw, looking back through nineteen centuries of darkness, was the reflection of a liberal, enlightened face, seen at the bottom of a deep well.[179] The work of Dorner, the Mediating Theologians, and the Confessional Theologians was doubtless one-sided and even shortsighted. If it was weak in the field of historical criticism, it maintained a protest against the idea that criticism alone could resolve the question of Christology. For, as F. C. Baur remarked long ago, without philosophy history remains dead and dumb. Historical judgments can only be made within a frame of reference, but this fact in turn raises philosophical and theological questions that cannot be settled *a priori*. The difficulty with Christology "from below," like that of speaking about "the historical Jesus," is the implied suppression of metaphysical and theological values and judgments in the alleged interests of history. The result is either a thorough-going positivism or a temporary positivism, which is arbitrarily suspended at some point when the author wishes to introduce his own metaphysics.

From the Deists and Reimarus to Strauss and Renan, the world view that was brought to the study of the Gospels was decisive in the interpretation of Jesus. The same was true of the Mediating Theologians and the Confessional Theologians. The history of the study of Jesus in European thought in the eighteenth and nineteenth centuries is as much a history of changing philosophies, theologies, and world views, as it is of growing refinements in historical techniques. The Mediating and Confessional Theologians maintained a witness that the historical significance of Jesus could not be perceived without theological insight. It was an insight which provided the frame of reference for understanding his ultimate significance. Although the Mediating and Confessional Theologians were poles apart from Strauss and Renan, they shared a common failing. They came to the question of Jesus with their minds made up, searching in the New Testament for confirmation of their convictions. In common with countless others, they overlooked the Jewishness of Jesus and imposed their own understanding on the fine print of the Gospels. Moreover, few, if any, paid real attention to what the

New Testament said about the Spirit in relation to Jesus. Consequently, the views of Jesus that were put forward in the nineteenth century were set in the contexts of Western, post-Enlightenment philosophy and a theology that oscillated between Deistic Unitarianism and practical tritheism. This virtually ensured that Jesus was seen as a profound religious visionary, a pioneer moral teacher, the human instantiation of the divine principle of the universe, or as the human meta-morphosis of one of three Gods. But if the thinkers of the nineteenth century were at fault in this, it is a fault which they share with many of their counterparts today. If the results seem strained, artificial, and unreal, the reason may lie not in a lack of critical sophistication but in a failure to penetrate the thought-world of the first century and glimpse from within the God whom the first Christians worshiped as Father, Son, and Holy Spirit. For, in the end, the question of Christology is the question of the Trinity.

NOTES

INTRODUCTION

1. Norman Perrin, *The Kingdom of God in the Teaching of Jesus* (London: SCM Press; Philadelphia: Westminster Press, 1963, p. 29). For further reappraisal, see James M. Robinson, *A New Quest of the Historical Jesus and Other Essays* (Philadelphia: Fortress Press, 1983). The work includes a reprint of Robinson's Introduction to the reprint of Schweitzer's *Quest*.

2. *Quest*, p. 403.

3. In 1555 the Peace of Augsburg adopted the principle *cuius regio eius religio*, which permitted the princes of the Holy Roman Empire to determine the religions of their own lands. This determined which states were Protestant and which were Catholic. In the eighteenth and nineteenth centuries the states remained a potent factor in the control of theological appointments. Some were clearly more conservative than others on theological issues.

4. Ludwig Wittgenstein, in private correspondence with M. O'C. Drury, in *Acta Philosophica Fennica* 28, nos. 1–3 (Amsterdam: North Holland Publishing Company); cited from Alastair Hannay, *Kierkegaard* (London: Routledge & Kegan Paul), p. ix.

5. Grand Rapids: Wm. B. Eerdmans Publishing Company, 1984; cf. also the analysis of the factors involved in the trial of Jesus mady by August Strobel, *Die Stunde der Wahrheit. Untersuchungen zum Strafverfahren gegen Jesus*, WUNT 21, (Tübingen: J. C. B. Mohr, 1980).

6. Cf. Gerd Theissen, *The Miracle Stories of the Early Christian Tradition* (Edinburgh: T. & T. Clark; Philadelphia: Fortress Press, 1983); Howard Clark Kee, *Miracle in the Early Christian World: A Study in Sociological Method* (New Haven: Yale University Press, 1983).

7. I have, however, refrained from giving repeated references to standard works and general surveys of the period and have cited them only as specific occasion required. In addition to those works listed in the Abbreviations, mention may here be made of the following: Hans W. Frei, *The Eclipse of Biblical Narrative: A Study in Eighteenth and Nineteenth Century Hermeneutics* (New Haven: Yale University Press, 1974); Paul Hazard, *European Thought in the Eighteenth Century: From Montesquieu to Lessing* (London: Hollis and Carter, 1954); Edgar Hocedez, *Histoire de la Théologie au XIXe Siècle* (Brussels: L'Édition Universelle; Paris, Desclée de Brouwer, 1947–52); Warren S. Kissinger, *The Lives of Jesus: A Bibliography* (New York: Garland Publishing Inc., 1984); F. Lichtenberger, *History of German Theology in the Nineteenth Century* (Edinburgh: T. & T. Clark, 1889); C. C. McCown, *The Search for the Real Jesus: A Century of Historical Study* (New York: Charles Scribner's Sons, 1940); Louis Perriraz, *Histoire de la Théologie Protestante au XIXme Siècle*, 4 vols. (Neuchatel: Éditions Henri Messeiller, 1949–61); Roland N. Stromberg, *Religious Liberalism in Eighteenth-Century England* (London: Oxford University Press, 1945); H. Weinel and A. G. Widgery, *Jesus in the Nineteenth Century and After* (Edinburgh: T. & T. Clark, 1914).

I. THE FRAGMENTS CONTROVERSY: A CHAPTER
IN THE THEOLOGY OF THE ENLIGHTENMENT

1. *Reimarus and His Critics*

1. English trans., *The Quest of the Historical Jesus: A Critical Study of its Progress from Reimarus to Wrede*, with an Introduction by James M. Robinson (1910; reprinted ed., New York: Macmillan, 1968), pp. 13–14; cf. J. Jeremias, "The Present Position in the Controversy Concerning the Problem of the Historical Jesus," *Exp.T.* 69 (1957–58):333–39.

2. *Quest*, p. 23.

3. In the nineteenth century, an English translation was made by Charles Voysey, *Fragments from Reimarus, Consisting of Brief Critical Remarks on the Object of Jesus and His Disciples as Seen in the New Testament* (London and Edinburgh: Williams and Norgate, 1879). New translations have been made by George Wesley Buchanan, *The Goal of Jesus and His Disciples* (Leiden: E. J. Brill, 1970); and Ralph S. Fraser, *Reimarus: Fragments*, ed. Charles H. Talbert (Philadelphia: Fortress Press, 1970; London: S.C.M. Press, 1971). For a reappraisal of Reimarus and bibliography, see *Hermann Samuel Reimarus (1694–1768). Ein "bekannter Unbekannter" der Aufklärung in Hamburg. Vorträge der Tagung der Joachim-Jungius Gesellschaft der Wissenschaften. Hamburg am 12. und 13. Oktober 1972* (Göttingen: Vandenhoeck & Rupprecht, 1973).

4. Hermann Samuel Reimarus, *Apologie oder Schutzschrift für die vernünftigen Verehrer Gottes*, 2 vols., *Im Auftrag der Joachim Jungius-Gesellschaft der Wissenschaften Hamburg herausgegeben von Gerhard Alexander* (Frankfurt: Suhrkamp Verlag, 1972).

5. Three copies of the manuscript are known to exist. The one in the Hamburg Universitäts- und Staatsbibliothek is, according to J. A. H. Reimarus, the final version, written in the author's own hand. It consists of two volumes of 490 and 566 pages respectively. The copy donated by J. A. H. Reimarus to the Universitäts- und Staatsbibliothek in Göttingen, which consisted of 1347 pages, was evidently the work of two secretaries, commissioned by J. A. H. Reimarus, who donated the copy to his alma mater shortly before his death. The latter felt, however, that he was unable to vouch for its fidelity. A third copy, in three volumes of 343, 462 and 502 pages, is preserved in the manuscript collection of the Hamburg Staatsarchiv. Parts of the first draft were in the possession of the Sieveking family which was related by marriage to one of J. A. H. Reimarus's daughters. Several copies appear to be lost, including those used by Lessing. For details see Georges Pons, *Gotthold Ephraïm Lessing et le Christianisme*, Germanica, no. 5 (Paris: Marcel Didier, 1964), pp. 276–78. On Lessing, see also Georges Pons, "Lessings Auseinandersetzung mit der Apologetik," *ZTK* 77 (1980):381–411; Henry E. Allison, *Lessing and the Enlightenment: His Philosophy of Religion and its Relation to Eighteenth-Century Thought* (Ann Arbor: University of Michigan Press, 1966); J. K. Riches, "Lessing as Editor of Reimarus' *Apologie*," in A. E. Livingstone, ed., *Studia Biblica 1978*, vol. 2: *Papers on the Gospels*. JSNT Supplement Series, no. 2 (Sheffield, 1980), pp. 247–54.

Speculation was rife about the identity of the author of the *Fragments*. Numerous candidates were proposed, including Reimarus. An angry letter from Dr. J. A. H. Reimarus drew from the editor of the Altona *Reichs-Postreuther* the disclaimer, "We take this opportunity to deny publicly the very widespread rumor that a certain famous teacher at the Hamburg gymnasium, now deceased, was the author of the *Fragments*" (no. 45, 15 June 1778; cf. Alexander Altmann, *Moses Mendelssohn: A Biographical Study* [London: Routledge and Kegan Paul, 1973], p. 564).

6. Lessing was both the patient and friend of Dr. J. A. H. Reimarus. Although the doctor's sister, Elise, subsequently played down the family's familiarity with Lessing until after 1778 (Letter to von Brinckmann, 12 April 1802, cited by Heinrich Sieveking in "Elise Reimarus 1735–1805 in den geistigen Kämpfen ihrer Zeit," *Zeitschrift des Vereins für Hamburgische Geschichte* 39 [1940]:98), it is evident that he was an intimate of the family during his stay in Hamburg between April 1767 and May 1770. His use of Reimarus's library is clear from the list of books that he returned (cf. notes to J. A. H. Reimarus in the Lachmann-Muncker edition of Lessing's works, vol. 17, dated 22 August 1769, 30 September 1769, 10 April 1770, nos. 236, 240, 258, pp. 269f., 299f., 318f.).

Interesting light on the relationship between Lessing, the Reimarus family and the Jewish leader of the German Enlightenment, Moses Mendelssohn, is shed by Alexander Altmann, op. cit., pp. 253ff., 603–52 and passim. Lessing not only disclosed to Mendelssohn the identity of the author of the *Fragments*, but gave him a copy of the manuscript to take with him to Berlin (Altmann, ibid., p. 254).

7. Lachmann-Muncker, 12:255; cf. *Anti-Goeze*, no. 9, where Lessing declared the identification to be a somewhat hasty speculation. J. L. Schmidt (1702–49) was the author of the so-called *Wertheimer Bibel* which was a free translation with rationalistic notes. Only the Pentateuch actually appeared. It was published anonymously under the title *Die göttlichen Schriften vor den Zeiten des Messie Jesus, der erste Theil worinnen die Gesetze der Jisraelen enthalten sind* (1735). Schmidt sought a new basis for theology, making use of Christian Wolff's rationalism. Like the English Deists, Schmidt rejected the appeal to prophecy and miracles as the vindication of Christianity. By order of the emperor the work was confiscated and the author imprisoned in 1737. He was subsequently allowed to escape, and settled in Hamburg and Altona under the assumed name of Schröt(d)er. Here he translated Spinoza's *Ethics* and Wolff's reply. In 1741 he published a translation of *Christianity as Old as the Creation* by the English Deist, Matthew Tindal. He died in Wolfenbüttel.

8. Lachmann-Muncker, 12:255.

9. *Von der Verschreyung der Vernunft auf den Kanzeln* (Lachmann-Muncker, 12:304–16); *Unmöglichkeit einer Offenbarung, die alle Menschen auf eine gegründete Art glauben könnten* (ibid., pp. 316–58).

10. *Durchgang der Israeliten durchs Rothe Meer* (ibid., pp. 359–68); *Dass die Bücher des A.T. nicht geschrieben wurden, eine Religion zu offenbaren* (ibid., pp. 368–97).

11. Ibid., pp. 397–428.

12. Lachmann-Muncker, 13:221–336. For English translations see above, n. 3. References below are to C. H. Talbert's edition of *Reimarus: Fragments*.

13. *Reimarus: Fragments*, pp. 72–76.

14. Ibid., pp. 76–88.

15. Ibid., pp. 98–102.

16. Ibid., pp. 102–18.

17. Ibid., pp. 118–22.

18. Ibid., pp. 136–38.

19. Ibid., pp. 146–50.

20. Ibid., p. 150.

21. Lachmann-Muncker, 12:402ff.; *Reimarus: Fragments*, pp. 154–61.

22. *Reimarus: Fragments*, p. 260.

23. Ibid., p. 261.

24. Ibid., pp. 174–200. The contradictions that Reimarus detects concern who went to the tomb, in what order, what they found and what they reported. Following second-century views of authorship, Reimarus argues that Matthew and John were apostles and that Mark and Luke wrote from "hearsay." In any case, it is the apostles who "contradict each other most, so much so that I may say frankly that there is almost no single circumstance from the death of Jesus to the end of the story where their accounts might be made to agree" (ibid., p. 197).

25. Ibid., pp. 200–10. Among the passages that Reimarus discussed are Ps. 2:7 (= Matt. 3:17; Acts 13:33; Heb. 1:5; 5:5; 2 Pet. 1:17); Ps. 89:20 (= Acts 13:22); Isa. 55:3 (= Acts 13:34; Heb. 13:20); Ps. 16:10 (= Acts 13:35); Ps. 16:8–11 (= Acts 2:25–28, 31).

26. Ibid., pp. 215–19; cf. Matt. 16:28; Mark 9:1; Luke 9:27.

27. Ibid., pp. 212–15. Reimarus cites Dan. 7:13–14, but is not explicit in his other references. He may have had in mind Justin, *Dialogue with Trypho*, 8, 36, 49, 110. The question of two advents has been examined by A. J. B. Higgins, "Jewish Messianic Belief in Justin Martyr's *Dialogue with Trypho*," *Novum Testamentum* 9 (1967):298–305. Higgins concludes that the doctrine of the two advents is a Christian one and that the only palpable evidence comes from two third-century rabbis, but that they do not offer a genuine parallel. See also Strack-Billberbeck, 2:339f., 488f.; and S. Mowinckel, *He that Cometh* (Oxford: Basil Blackwell, 1959), pp. 304–7. Alongside beliefs in a political messiah, Mowinckel notes notions of a hidden and suffering messiah.

28. Ibid., pp. 223–30.

29. Ibid., pp. 232–35.

30. Ibid., p. 233; cf. David Hume, *An Enquiry Concerning Human Understanding*, sec. 10, no. 95. Richard Swinburne has pointed out that Hume's argument would be valid if conflicting religions adduced miracles of the same kind in support of contradictory doctrines. However, in practice this does not occur (*The Concept of Miracle* [London: Macmillan, St. Martin's Press, 1970], pp. 60f.).

31. Ibid., pp. 235–37.

32. Ibid., pp. 240–48.

33. Ibid., p. 253.

34. Ibid., pp. 265–69. Reimarus found it absurd that over three thousand people should be packed together in one house and that they should be drawn together by a storm (Acts 2:2, 41). He took the account to imply that none of those present were normally resident in Jerusalem. If the noise of the wind filled the city, how did they know to which house to go? In short, he found the whole account improbable.

35. *Quest*, pp. 22–23.

36. A selection of extracts from contemporary criticism is reprinted in *Lessing im Urteile seiner Zeitgenossen. Gesammelt und herausgegeben von Julius Braun*, 3 vols. (Berlin, 1884–97; reprinted in 2 vols., Hildesheim: Georg Olms, 1969). Goeze, Ress, Schumann, Michaelis, Moldenhawer, Kleuker, Mascho, Döderlein, Silberschlag, Schickedanz and Semler were among those who replied (details in *Hermann Samuel Reimarus [1696–1768]*, pp. 155–56).

37. J. M. Goeze (1717–86) studied at Jena and then at Halle under S. J. Baumgarten. He became chief pastor in Hamburg in 1755 and between 1760 and 1770 he was the Lutheran Senior in Hamburg.

Goeze was no stranger to polemics. In 1764 he crossed swords with the enlightened educationist, J. B. Basedow. Between 1765 and 1769 he was engaged in a dispute with J. S. Semler over the Complutensian Polyglot. He criticized Reformed worship (1766), and attacked the immorality of the stage (1768–70). He was involved in disputes with J. G. Alberti (1770), C. F. Bahrdt (1773) and Lessing (1770–80). He repudiated Melanchthon and Philippism (1780) and attacked the heterodoxy of Gottfried Less (1781).

Goeze was something of an authority on the text and editions of the Bible. His scholarship is attested by his *Versuch einer Historie der gedruckten niedersächsischen Bibeln* (1775). During Lessing's stay in Hamburg, the two men had been on amicable terms. But the relationship cooled when Lessing failed to reply to Goeze's questions concerning old Bibles in the library at Wolfenbüttel.

Goeze's writings against Lessing are contained in *Goezes Streitschriften gegen Lessing neu herausgegeben von E. Schmidt* (Stuttgart: G. J. Göschen, 1893).

38. G. Pons notes Lessing's frequent play on words in replying to Goeze *(op. cit., p. 310)*. Lessing was not given to abusing people by their names. but the characters involved in the *Fragments* controversy reappeared in *Nathan the Wise*. For discussion of the identity of the characters in the play, see Hendrik Birus, *Poetische Namengebung. Zur Bedeutung der Namen in Lessings "Nathan der Weise"* (Göttingen: Vandenhoeck and Rupprecht, 1978).

39. Letter to Elise Reimarus, 6 September, 1778. See also letter to his brother, Karl Gotthelf Lessing, 11 August 1778 (Lachmann-Muncker, 13:285–87; cf. Lachmann-Muncker, 16:526–27). Lessing continued the controversy in *Nathan the Wise* (1779), which is discussed in the next chapter.

40. *Fragmente und Antifragmente* (Nüremberg: J. G. Lochner, 1778), p. 199.

41. *ADB*, vol. 40, pt. 2, pp. 408f.; cf. Paul Tillich, *Systematic Theology*, 3 vols. (Chicago: University of Chicago Press, 1957), 2:153–65; Rudolf Bultmann, "New Testament and Mythology," *Kerygma and Myth*, ed. H. W. Bartsch (New York: Harper and Row), 1:1–44.

42. *ADB*, vol. 30, pt. 3; cf. Karl Aner, *Die Theologie der Lessingzeit* (Halle, 1929; reprint ed., Hildesheim: Georg Olms, 1964), pp. 74f. On Jerusalem see Wolfgang Erich Müller, *Johann Friedrich Wilhelm Jerusalem. Eine Untersuchung zur Theologie der "Betrachtungen über die vornehmsten Wahrheiten der Religion"* (Berlin: Walter de Gruyter, 1984).

43. *ADB*, vol. 39, pt. 1, pp. 36ff.; 40, 1, p. 357; 40, 2, pp. 356ff.; 43, 2, p. 385ff.; 47, 2, p. 359; 48, 1, pp. 49, 51; 48, 2, p. 375; 55, 1, p. 102; 60, 2, p. 336; 63, 1, p. 78; 76, 2, p. 366; 78, 2, pp. 375ff.; cf. K. Aner, op. cit., pp. 308–10.

44. *Hamburgische Dramaturgie*, 70 (January 1, 1768; Lachmann-Muncker, 10:83–84).

45. Kümmel, p. 68.

46. Hirsch, 4:49.

47. *Allgemeine Bibliothek der biblischen Literatur* 5 (1793):193, 182f.

48. *D. Joh. Salomo Semlers Lebensbeschreibung von ihm selbst abgefasst* (Halle, 1782), 2:314.

49. Cf. *Institutio Brevio ad Liberalem Eruditionem Theologicam*, 2 vols. (Halle, 1765–66); *Versuch einer freiern theologischen Lehrart, zur Bestätigung und Erläuterung seines lateinischen Buchs* (Halle, 1777).

50. *Lebensbeschreibung*, 2:245.

51. 4 vols. (Halle, 1771–75). References below are to the edition of Heinz Scheible, *Texte zur Kirchen- und Theologiegeschichte*, no. 5 (Gütersloh: Gütersloher Verlagshaus Gerd Mohn, 1967).

52. Op. cit., p. 43.

53. Ibid., p. 42; cf. Gottfried Hornig, *Die Anfänge der historisch-kritischen Theologie. Johann Salomo Semlers Schriftverständnis und seine Stellung zu Luther, FSTR* 5 (Göttingen: Vandenhoeck & Ruprecht, 1961), pp. 225ff. Hornig lists 218 publications by Semler.

54. Ibid., p. 72. Semler argues that 2 Tim. 3:16 applies to the inspiration of the Old Testament only, and in any case it is a pronouncement valid for those with a Jewish background.

55. Ibid., pp. 73, 82.

56. Ibid., pp. 82f.

57. Cf. S. J. Baumgarten, *Untersuchung theologischer Streitigkeiten* (Halle, 1764), 3:181f. Baumgarten mentions J. Clericus, Thomas Burnet and Whiston as advocates of this doctrine. Semler's dissertation was entitled *Vindiciae plurium praecipuarum lectionum codicis graeci Novi Testam. adversus Guilielm. Whiston Anglum atque ab eo latas leges criticas* (Halle, 1750). See further G. Hornig, op. cit., pp. 211–36.

58. Semler was not uncritical of the French Oratorian, Richard Simon (1638–1712), but already in 1757 he was commending to his students Simon's *Histoire critique du texte du Nouveau Testament* (1689), *Histoire critique des versions du Nouveau Testament* (1693) and *Histoire critique des principaux commentaires du Nouveau Testament* (1693). He later provided introductions and notes to H. M. A. Cramer's translation of Simon's *Kritische Schriften über das Neue Testament*, 3 vols. (Halle, 1776–80; cf. Hornig, ip. cit., pp. 182–87, 273). Simon's *Histoire critique du Vieux Testament* (1678) was the cause of heated opposition in the Catholic Church, and led to Simon's expulsion from his order (1678).

59. *Beantwortung*, Vorrede, p. 2.

60. Ibid., p. 9.

61. *Beantwortung der Fragmente eines Ungenannten insbesondere vom Zweck Jesu und seiner Jünger. Andere, verbesserte Auflage. Anhang zur Beantwortung der Fragmente des Ungenannten. Bekant gemacht von D. Joh. Salomo Semler* (Halle, 1780, 432 and 24 pp.) References are to this edition.

62. Ibid., p. 15; cf. p. 26, where Semler arranged synoptically contradictory passages from the *Fragment* on the question of whether the disciples had wittingly or unwittingly distorted the teaching of Jesus.

63. Ibid., pp. 30f.

64. Ibid., pp. 42–45. Semler cited Philo's spiritualizing of the law to show that this was not something invented by the apostles (cf. *De Migratione Abrahami*, ed. T. Mangey, 1742, 1:450). Among rabbinic sources indicating Jewish expectation that the messiah would abolish the law or produce a new one Semler noted Yalkut on Isa. 2:7 and Ps. 2:7; Midrash of R. Albo on Jer. 31:31f.; Targum of Jonathan on Isa. 12:3.

65. Ibid., p. 99.

66. Ibid., pp. 56–61.

67. Ibid., pp. 65ff.

68. Ibid., p. 133.

69. Ibid., p. 161.

70. Ibid., pp. 354f.

71. Ibid., pp. 355f.

72. Ibid., p. 356.

73. Ibid., p. 359.

74. Ibid., p. 267.

75. Ibid., p. 272.

76. Ibid., p. 261.

77. Ibid., p. 262. Johann Christian Edelmann (1698–1767) was an independent thinker who was sharply critical of both orthodoxy and Wolffian rationalism. For a time his name was synonymous with religious skepticism, and his writings which provoked more than 160 replies were banned. He was compared with Reimarus by Carl Mönckeberg in *Herrmann Samuel Reimarus und Johann Christian Edelmann*, Gallerie Hamburgische Theologen, no. 5 (Hamburg: G. E. Nolte, 1867).

78. Ibid., p. 264. This was actually the view of C. F. Bahrdt (1741–92) who taught at Halle and who was opposed by Semler. Goeze had linked Lessing's views with those of Bahrdt, against whom

the Imperial Court Council in Vienna initiated proceedings (*Goezes Streitschriften*, p. 104). Bahrdt's views are discussed below in chapter 9.

79. Ibid.

80. Ibid., p. 264.

81. Ibid., pp. 430ff.

82. *Quest*, p. 26. The Edict was designed to curb the influence of the Enlightenment in Prussia which had become a stronghold of its teaching in the previous half-century. The evangelical theologian, Johann Christian Wöllner (1732–1800), had steadily advanced in political influence and in the favor of Friedrich Wilhelm II (1786–97). The latter made him minister in charge of religious affairs in 1788, replacing the enlightened von Zedlitz. The *Edikt, die Religionsverfassung in den preussischen Staaten betreffend* was based upon Wöllner's *Abhandlung von der Religion*. It bound liturgy, preaching and teaching to the confessions, and sought to make teaching subject to police scrutiny. The establishment of a supervisory commission, the introduction of a catechism and of a dogmatic textbook in the universities, and the steps to control the theological faculty at Halle all failed. The edict was revoked by Friedrich Wilhelm III in 1797, and Wöllner was dismissed the following year.

L. Zscharnack investigated and cleared Semler of the charge of having lost faith in his last years (*Lessing und Semler. Ein Beitrag zur Entstehungsgeschichte des Rationalismus und der kritischen Theologie* [Giessen: Töpelmann, 1905], pp. 357–73).

83. This is partially obscured in the case of Reimarus, as in a sense his entire work was devoted to evaluating the character of the biblical writings. On the other hand, he was more interested in what F. C. Baur called the *Tendenze* of the New Testament writings rather than in questions of authorship, date and authenticity in the light of internal and external evidence.

84. In earlier writings Semler had explained demon possession as a graphic way of depicting physical illness. In the Gospel narratives Jesus had refrained from explaining the correct diagnosis, and thus did not overtly question popular belief. This was an aspect of Semler's theory of accommodation. Semler was interested in the psychosomatic aspect of illness in both biblical and more recent times (cf. L. Zscharnack, op. cit., pp. 340f.). The appearance of a possessed woman at Kemberg prompted Semler's *Abfertigung der neuen Geister und alten Irrtümer in der Lohmannischen Begeisterung zu Kemberg nebst theologischen Unterricht von dem Ungrunde der gemeinen Meinung von leiblichen Besitzungen des Teufels und Bezauberungen der Christen. Zwote Auflage. Mit einem Anhange von den weitern historischen Umständen vermehrt* (Halle, 1760). In the same year he also published his *Widerlegung G. Müller's Nachricht von einer begeisterten Weibsperson* (Halle, 1760). He contributed to the anonymous *Versuch einer biblischen Dämonologie, oder Untersuchung der Lehre der heil. Schrift vom Teufel und seiner Macht. Mit einer Vorrede und einem Anhang von D. Johann Salomo Semler* (Halle, 1776), and wrote a preface to *Hugo Farmers Versuch über die Dämonischen des Neuen Testaments. Aus dem Englischen übersetzt von L. F. A. von Cölln. Nebst einer Vorrede D. Joh. Sal. Semlers* (Bremen and Leipzig, 1776). Hugh Farmer (1714–87) was an English dissenting preacher who proposed psychosomatic explanations for cases of demonology. He wrote a notable reply to Hume on miracles, and his argument appealed to the more rationalistic elements among English dissenters (cf. *DNB*, 6:1075–77). In his *Lebensbeschreibung*, 2:168, Semler spoke of the Old Testament accounts of angels and spirits as "Jewish mythologies of very little worth."

85. Semler declared that Lessing would have done better to have left the manuscript in its dust-covered corner. Lessing was like the lunatic, who, instead of snuffing out the candle, put on straw so that the fire could be more easily seen and extinguished (*Beantwortung, Anhang*, pp. 8ff.). Lessing reciprocated by calling Semler an "impertinent fool of a professor [Professorgans]" (letter to Elise Reimarus, 14 May 1779; cf. L. Zscharnack, op. cit., p. 344).

2. Lessing and the Relevance of History

1. Lachmann-Muncker, 12:428–50.

2. Henry Chadwick, *Lessing's Theological Writings: Selections in Translation with an Introductory Essay* (London: A. & C. Black; Stanford, CA: Stanford University Press, 1956), pp. 17–18.

3. Cf. Avery Dulles, *A History of Apologetics* (New York: Corpus; London: Hutchinson, 1971). A contemporary example is furnished by the Göttingen Professor and Konsistorial-Rath, Gottfried

Less, *Ueber die Religion: Ihre Geschichte, Wahl und Bestätigung*, II, *Beweis der Wahrheit der christlichen Religion* (Göttingen: Verlag der Witwe Vandenhoeck, 1786). The text ran to 1088 pages, and included discussion of Apollonius, the English Deists and their opponents, Voltaire, the Fragmentist, and Lessing himself. The title page bore the quotation, "I speak to the rational: Judge for yourselves what I say" (1 Cor. 10:15).

4. H. Chadwick, op. cit., p. 52; cf. Origen, *Contra Celsum*, 1, 2.

5. *An Enquiry Concerning Human Understanding* (1748), sec. 10.

6. Op. cit., p. 53.

7. Ibid., pp. 55–56.

8. Ibid., p. 54.

9. Ibid. *metabasis eis allo genos* denotes "a switch into another genus." Aristotle observed that "we cannot in demonstrating pass from one genus to another" (*Analytica Posteriora*, 1, 7).

10. *Jesus of Nazareth* (London: Hodder & Stoughton, 1960), p. 180.

11. *History, Sacred and Profane*, Bampton Lectures for 1962 (London: S.C.M. Press, 1964), p. 196.

12. H. Chadwick, op. cit., p. 55.

13. Ibid., p. 56.

14. Ibid., p. 61; cf. Jerome, *In Epist. ad Galatas*, 6.

15. Ibid., p. 59.

16. In a letter to Elise Reimarus, dated 9 August 1778, Lessing gloated over the tactics of his *Nöthige Antwort* to Goeze. The latter had asked him to explain what he understood by the Christian religion, when he declared that it could exist without the Bible. He had expected him to declare himself a Deist and a disciple of Toland and Tindal (*Goezes Streitschriften*, pp. 68–69, 166). Instead, Lessing outlined what he understood by the *regula fidei* without committing himself to what parts, if any, he believed (H. Chadwick, op. cit., pp. 24–25, 62–64).

17. H. Chadwick, op. cit., pp. 104–5. It was first published in 1784, but is variously dated from 1763–64 and even from 1755.

18. Ibid., pp. 202–3. Published in 1795 but dating from ca. 1763.

19. Ibid., pp. 99–101. Published in 1784 but probably written ca. 1752–53 in response to J. W. Hecker's *Das Christentum der Vernunft* (1752).

20. "As reason makes no demands contrary to nature, it demands that every man should love himself, should seek that which is useful to him—I mean that which is really useful to him, should desire everything which really brings man to greater perfection, and should each for himself, endeavour as far as he can to preserve his own being. This is as necessarily true, as that a whole is greater than its part" (*Ethics*, pt. 4, prop. 18, Note; in the translation of R. H. M. Elwes, *The Chief Works of Benedict de Spinoza* [reprint ed., New York: Dover Publications, 1951], 2:201). See further E. M. Curley, "Spinoza's Moral Philosophy," in Marjorie Grene, ed., *Spinoza: A Collection of Critical Essays* (Notre Dame: University of Notre Dame Press, [1973], pp. 354–76).

21. For a survey of the debate see Helmut Thielicke, *Offenbarung, Vernuft und Existenz. Studien zur Religionsphilosophie Lessings*, 4th ed. (Gütersloh: Gütersloher Verlagshaus Gerd Mohn, 1957), pp. 16–28. Friedrich Loofs, for example, believed that no positive Christian construction could be placed on Lessing's thought and that his personal opinions had been concealed beyond discovery ("Lessings Stellung zum Christentum," *ThStKr* [Jahrgang 1913], Heft 1, pp. 31–64). Thielicke, on the other hand, sees him as a Christian "Denker der Anfechtung" (op. cit., p. 141), whose mystery could be unveiled only by approaching him from the standpoint of Kierkegaard (ibid., p. 171).

22. A. Altmann, op. cit., p. 621; cf. idem, "Lessing und Jacobi: Das Gespräch über den Spinozismus," *Lessing Yearbook*, vol. 3 (Munich, 1971), pp. 25–70; R. Schwarz, "Lessings Spinozismus'," *ZTK* 65, no. 3 (July 1968): 271–90; F. Regner, "Lessings Spinozismus," *ZTK* 68, no. 3 (September 1971): 351–75; Kurt Weinberg, "Pantheismusstreit," *EP* 6:35–37.

23. Cf. F. H. Jacobi, *Über die Lehre des Spinoza in Briefen an den Herrn Moses Mendelssohn* (1785; 2nd ed., 1789). Mendelssohn set his view in *Morgenstunden, oder Vorlesungen über das Daseyn Gottes* (1785). The bitter implication for Mendelssohn was that Lessing had kept his thoughts concealed from Mendelssohn and that it was Jacobi, and not Mendelssohn, who had been Lessing's intimate confidant. The painful controversy was continued in Jacobi's pamphlet *Wider Mendelssohns Beshuldigungen* and Mendelssohn's final work *An die Freunde Lessings* (1786). For a detailed account of the controversy, which affected not only Elise and Johannes Reimarus, but Hamann, Goethe and Kant, together with other leading figures of the German Enlightenment, see A. Altmann, op. cit., pp. 582–759.

24. Op. cit., p. 569.

25. Cf. the "Profession de Foi du Vicaire Savoyard" in Rousseau's *Émile, ou de l'Éducation*, bk. 4 (1762).

26. Lachmann-Muncker, 13:23f.

27. Lachmann-Muncker, 12:447. Lessing at first hinted that it was the work of another author which he had discovered. He later wrote to his brother (25 February 1780) that he felt free to publish the whole work, but would never acknowledge its authorship. The work has been attributed to Albrecht Thaer, but Lessing's authorship has been established by A. M. Wagner, "Who is the Author of Lessing's 'Education of Mankind'?" *Modern Language Review* 38 (1943): 318–27, and is now generally accepted.

28. "1. What education is to the individual man, revelation is to the whole human race.... 4. Education gives man nothing which he could not also get from within himself; it gives him that which he could get from within himself, only quicker and more easily. In the same way too, revelation gives nothing to the human race which human reason could not arrive at on its own; only it has given, and still gives to it, the most important of these things sooner" (H. Chadwick, op. cit., pp. 82–83).

29. This view found classic expression in the opening words of Rousseau's *Émile*: "Everything is good leaving the hands of God; everything degenerates in the hands of man."

30. Nos. 9–52 (H. Chadwick, ibid., pp. 83–91).

31. No. 53 (ibid., p. 91).

32. Nos. 59–61 (ibid., p. 92).

33. Ibid., p. 96. No. 86 contained an allusion to Rev. 14:6.

34. Lachmann-Muncker, 13:22.

35. (1) The first concerns the buying of the spices and the visit of the women to the tomb (Mark 16:1; Luke 23:56). Luke appears to mean that the women bought them on the Friday before the sabbath, while Mark says that it was after the sabbath (Lachmann-Muncker, 13:36–40).

(2) In John 19:38–40 Joseph of Arimathea and Nicodemus take the body and bind it with linen cloths with about a hundred pounds of myrrh and aloes, but there is no mention of the women's action narrated in the synoptics (ibid., pp. 40–43).

(3) Matt. 28:1–10 describes the visit of Mary Magdalene and the other Mary. They meet an angel who tells them to go to Galilee where they will see Jesus. Verses 2f. suggest to Lessing that they saw the earthquake, whereas Mark 16:2f. and Luke 24:2f. suggest that it had already happened when they arrived. Mark and Luke mention other women. Luke 24:12 adds that Peter himself ran to the tomb and found it empty. John 20:1–18 mentions only Mary Magdalene who first finds the tomb empty, tells Peter and "the other disciple" who outruns Peter. Both find the tomb empty with the grave clothes folded. Then Mary meets Jesus, supposing him to be the gardener at first. Lessing closes this part of the discussion with a satirical dialogue (ibid., pp. 42–50).

(4) All four evangelists differ over the number of angels, their position and their utterances (ibid., pp. 50–53).

(5) In Luke, Mary Magdalene and the other women tell Peter, John and the other disciples the angels' story of the resurrection; in John it is Mary Magdalene alone who discovers the empty tomb and (without the aid of angels) tells only Peter and John that the corpse has been removed (ibid., pp. 53–66).

(6) Lessing takes Matt. 28:9 to mean that Jesus appeared to Mary Magdalene and the women on their way back to the city; in John 20:11–17 it is as Mary stands weeping outside the tomb (ibid., pp. 66–71).

(7) In Matt. 28:9 the women hold the feet of Jesus; in Luke 24:39 he exhorts the eleven to handle him; John 20:27 invites Thomas to touch him; but John 20:17 forbids Mary Magdalene to hold him (ibid., pp. 71–72).

(8) Matt. and Mark record commands to go to Galilee from the angels (Matt. 28:7; Mark 16:7) and even from Jesus himself (Matt. 28:10). Matt. also records a last encounter in Galilee where Jesus commissions the disciples upon a mountain to preach the gospel and baptize all nations in the triune name; but in Luke Jesus bids the disciples wait in Jerusalem till they receive power (Matt. 28:16–20; Luke 24:49). This and the ascension all appear to happen on the same day. John 21:1–13 has a different episode by the Sea of Galilee. But Luke seems to know nothing of a Galilean appearance (ibid., pp. 73–81).

(9) In Matt. the appearance is on a mountain; in John it is by the lake near Tiberias (ibid., pp. 81–85).

(10) In view of the last point, the Fragmentist was justified in concluding that the accounts were not independent testimonies but conflations produced over a period of many years (ibid., p. 85).

36. Letter to Karl Lessing, 25 February 1778 (Lachmann-Muncker, 18:265f.).

37. The work was written some time in 1778. Lessing stated in his Preface that it was the fruit of many years' thought. It was first published by Karl Lessing in his 1784 edition of his brother's *Theologischer Nachlass*.

38. Nos. 24–25 (H. Chadwick, op. cit., p. 70).

39. Nos. 29–40; cf. Eusebius, *Historia Ecclesiastica*, 3, 24, 5–6; 3, 39, 16 (citing Papias); Jerome, Introduction to his *Commentary on Matthew* (H. Chadwick, ibid., pp. 71–75).

40. H. Chadwick, ibid., p. 72.

41. No. 48 (ibid., p. 78).

42. No. 49 alluding to the prevailing view that Mark abbreviated Matthew which derived from Augustine, *De Consensu Evangelistarum*, 1, 2 (4) (H. Chadwick, ibid., pp. 78–79).

43. H. Chadwick, ibid., pp. 79–81.

44. Ibid., p. 80.

45. Ibid.

46. Cf. C. F. D. Moule, *The Origin of Christology* (Cambridge: Cambridge University Press, 1977), pp. 22–31. The term was used of Adam (Luke 3:38). It is evidently a royal title in Ps. 2:7. It denoted righteousness (Luke 23:47; cf. Mark 15:39) and had messianic connotations (Mark 14:61).

47. No. 58 (ibid., p. 80). According to Justin (*Dialogue*, 47) and Irenaeus (*Adversus Haereses*, 1, 26, 2; 3, 11, 7; 3, 21, 1; 5, 1, 3) this Jewish sect regarded Jesus as the natural son of Mary who was the predestined messiah. They were hardly, as Lessing implies, simply "those Jewish Christians who before the destruction of Jerusalem escaped to Pella on the other side of the Jordan." Fragments of their beliefs preserved by Epiphanius (*Haereses*, 30, 13) are given by P. Vielhauer (Hennecke-Schneemelcher, 1:153–58) who believes that the misnamed Ebionite Gospel of the Hebrews "must have been an abridged and falsified Gospel of Matthew."

48. No. 59 (ibid., p. 80). Cerinthus (fl. ca. A.D. 100) was, as Lessing acknowledged, a gnostic heretic. According to Irenaeus, his views were similar to those of the Ebionites and Carpocrates (*Adversus Haereses*, 1, 26, 2) and John wrote his Gospel to refute him (ibid., 3, 11, 1).

49. No. 60 (ibid., p. 80). Like the Ebionites, Carpocrates accepted only Matthew. Lessing omits to say that he was a second-century gnostic (cf. Irenaeus, *Adversus Haereses*, 1, 25; Hippolytus, *Refutatio*, 7, 32; Eusebius, *Historia Ecclesiastica*, 4, 7, 9).

50. No. 66 (ibid., p. 81).

51. "But that John, last of all, conscious that the outward facts had been set forth in the Gospels, was urged on by his disciples, and, divinely moved by the Spirit, composed a spiritual Gospel" (Clement of Alexandria in Eusebius, *Historia Ecclesiastica*, 6, 14, 7; cf. ibid., 3, 24, 7–13; Origen, *Comm. in Jo.*, 3f.; Epiphanius, *Haereses*, 51; Augustine, *De Consensu Evangelistarum*, 4, 11–20). Recent studies of patristic views of John and the Synoptics include J. N. Sanders, *The Fourth Gospel in the Early Church: Its Origin and Influence on Christian Theology up to Irenaeus* (Cambridge: Cambridge University Press, 1960); F.-M. Braun, *Jean le Théologien dans l'Église Ancienne* (Paris: J. Gabalda et Cie., 1959).

52. No. 1 (ibid., p. 66); cf. Acts 24:5; Epiphanius, *Haereses*, 29, 6, 7 (cited in no. 2).

53. Nos. 3, 16–18 (ibid., p. 69). For a reconstruction of the text of *The Gospel of the Nazaraeans* which is based chiefly on references in Jerome see P. Vielhauer in Hennecke-Schneemelcher, 1:139–53.

54. No. 4 (ibid., p. 66).

55. The nearest that Lessing came to substantiating his point was to claim that, in view of the silence of Irenaeus, the earlier Nazarenes were not yet regarded as heretical, and that they kept the ceremonial law together with Christianity (no. 19). This meant that they could not possibly have believed in a Son of God "who is of the same essence as God" (no. 57). Lessing had no documentary support for his contention that those who were first called Nazarenes held an Ebionite christology. However, he sought to fill this gap by noting the change of mind on the part of J. L. Mosheim (no. 20, ibid., p. 69). In his early attack on Toland, the eminent Göttingen historian, Mosheim, had denied any connection between the earlier and later so-called Nazarenes (*Vindiciae antiquae Christianorum disciplinae contra Tolandi Nazarenum* [1719; 2nd ed., 1722]). For his later opinion see Mosheim's *Historical Commentaries on the State of Christianity during the First Three Hundred and Twenty-Five Years*, Eng. trans. J. S. Vidal, ed. James Murdock (New York: S. Converse, 1854), 1:400–3. In point

of fact, Mosheim lent no support to Lessing who may well have used Mosheim as the source of his information. Mosheim sharply distinguished the Nazarenes from the Ebionites and insisted that they were essentially orthodox Jewish Christians.

56. "So far as can be discovered from the fragments the GN was a gospel of the Synoptic type. Alike in its narratives and discourse material it proves itself for the most part secondary in comparison with Mt. In the narratives a fictional development of the tradition can often be detected....The terminus a quo is accordingly the writing of Mt., the terminus ad quem is Hegesippus (180), who is the first to testify to the existence of the GN. It will have appeared in the first half of the second century. The place of its origin is uncertain. We must think of regions in which Aramaic-speaking Jewish Christian churches continued down to the time of Jerome....The circles in which it arose, those of Syrian Jewish Christians (Nazaraeans), were clearly not "heretical" but belonged, so far as the GN permits us to make out, to the great Church; 'in content and character it was no more Jewish Christian than Mt.' (Waitz, Apokr. 2, 28). A closer characterization of Nazaraean Christianity is not yet possible, since what is dark in the history and theology of Jewish Christianity has not yet been sufficiently cleared up" (P. Vielhauer, Hennecke-Schneemelcher, 1:144, 146).

57. Written in 1780 and published posthumously by Karl Lessing in 1784.

58. Ibid., p. 106.

59. Nos. 7–8 (ibid.).

3. *The Fragments Controversy in Retrospect*

1. *Quest*, p. 26.

2. *Hermann Samuel Reimarus und seine Schutzschrift für die vernünftigen Verehrer Gottes* (Leipzig, 1862), pp. 37–44.

3. Cf. A. C. Lundsteen, *Hermann Samuel Reimarus und die Anfänge der Leben-Jesu Forschung* (Copenhagen: A. C. Olsen, 1939), pp. 108–33; Günter Gawlick, "Der Deismus als Grundzug der Religionsphilosophie der Aufklärung," in *Hermann Samuel Reimarus (1694–1768). Ein "bekannter Unbekannter" der Aufklärung in Hamburg. Vorträge auf der Tagung der Joachim Jungius-Gesellschaft der Wissenschaften, Hamburg am 12. und 13. Oktober 1972* (Göttingen: Vandenhoeck & Rupprecht, 1973), pp. 15–43; Henning Graf Reventlow, "Das Arsenal der Bibelkritik des Reimarus: Die Auslegung der Bibel, insbesondere des Alten Testaments, bei den englishen Deisten," ibid., pp. 44–65. On the influence of Deism generally see Henning Graf Reventlow, *Bibelautorität und Geist der Moderne. Die Bedeutung des Bibelverständnisses für die geistesgeschichtliche und politische Entwicklung in England von der Reformation bis zur Aufklärung, FKD* 30 (Göttingen: Vandenhoeck & Rupprecht, 1980); Eng. tr. *The Authority of the Bible in the Modern World* (Philadelphia: Fortress Press, 1985). On early biblical criticism see Klaus Scholder, *Ursprünge und Probleme der Bibelkritik im 17. Jahrhundert. Ein Beitrag zur Entstehung der historisch-kritischen Theologie, FGLP* 10. Reihe, 33 (Munich: Chr. Kaiser Verlag, 1966); Otto Merk, "Anfänge neutestamentlicher Wissenschaft im 18. Jahrhundert," in Georg Schwaiger, ed., *Historische Kritik in der Theologie. Beiträge zu ihrer Geschichte, STGNJ* 32 (Göttingen: Vandenhoeck & Rupprecht, 1980), pp. 38–59.

4. For accounts of Servetus and his published works see Roland H. Bainton, *Hunted Heretic: The Life and Death of Michael Servetus, 1511–1553*, new edition (Boston: Beacon Press, 1960); B. Becker, ed., *Autour de Michel Servet et de Sebastien Castellion* (Haarlem: H. D. Tjeen Willink & Zoon N.V., 1953).

5. *The Two Treatises of Servetus on the Trinity: On the Errors of the Trinity Seven Books, A.D. MCXXXI; Dialogues on the Trinity Two Books; On the Righteousness of Christ's Kingdom Four Chapters*, trans. Earl Morse Wilbur, Harvard Theological Studies, no. 16 (Cambridge, MA: Harvard University Press; London: Oxford University Press, 1932; reprint ed., New York: Kraus Reprint Co., 1969).

6. Cf. Bainton, op. cit., pp. 43–46.

7. *The Two Treatises of Servetus on the Trinity*, pp. 16–19, 34–37, 92–97, 157, 172–73, 180.

8. Cf. Earl Morse Wilbur, *A History of Unitarianism*, vol. 1, *Socinianism and its Antecedents* (Boston: Beacon Press, 1945); idem, *A Bibliography of the Pioneers of the Socinian-Unitarian Movement in Modern Christianity, in Italy, Switzerland, Germany, Holland* (Rome: Edizioni di Storia e Letteratura, 1951); George H. Williams, *The Radical Reformation* (London: Weidenfeld and

Nicolson, 1962). On the Socinian approach to Scripture and dogma see Klaus Scholder, op. cit., pp. 34–55.

9. *The Racovian Catechism, with Notes and Illustrations*, trans. Thomas Rees (London, 1818; reprint ed., Lexington, KY: The American Theological Library Association, 1962), sec. 4, chap. 1, pp. 52–53.

10. Ibid., p. 66.

11. Ibid., sec. 3, chap. 1, p. 43.

12. Ibid., sec. 4, chap. 1, p. 159.

13. Cf. Earl Morse Wilbur, *A History of Unitarianism*, vol. 2, *In Transylvania, England, and America* (Cambridge, MA: Harvard University Press, 1952). The Deists receive only passing mention from Wilbur who notes that the Arians and Unitarians of the early eighteenth century saw themselves as quite different from the Deists. Nathaniel Lardner, James Foster, George Benson (who had contacts with continental scholars and whose work was translated into German by Michaelis) and Samuel Chandler were among those who controverted the Deists (ibid., pp. 264–66).

14. For analyses of the religious philosophy of the Enlightenment, see Karl Aner, *Die Theologie der Lessingzeit* (Halle, 1929; reprint ed., Hildesheim: Georg Olms, 1964); Wolfgang Philipp, *Das Werden der Aufklärung in theologiegeschichtlicher Sicht*, FSTR 3 (Göttingen: Vandenhoeck & Ruprecht, 1957). Wolfgang Philipp has edited an anthology of Enlightened theological writings, *Das Zeitalter der Aufklärung, Klassiker des Protestantismus*, 7 (Bremen: Carl Schünemann Verlag, 1963). On the Enlightenment and history see Peter Hanns Reill, *The German Enlightenment and the Rise of Historicism* (Berkeley, Los Angeles and London: University of California Press, 1975).

15. Cf. Richard H. Popkin, *The History of Scepticism from Erasmus to Descartes*, rev. ed. (New York: Harper and Row, 1968). The age saw a renewed interest in the writings of Sextus Empiricus, the codifier of Greek skepticism. Another important influence on post-Reformation thought was Cicero's *De Natura Deorum*, with its account of the conflict between the Epicurean and Stoic views of God. Prior to 1564 there were no less than forty-three editions. Günter Gawlick claims that every scholar of the time was familiar with its argument and that it exerted a considerable influence on the Enlightenment ("Cicero and the Enlightenment," in *Studies on Voltaire and the Eighteenth Century*, no. 25, 1963, pp. 657ff.).

16. H. S. Reimarus, *Programma de Instinctu Brutorum, Existentis Dei eiusdemque sapientissimi Indice* (Wismar, 1725); idem, *Programma quo Fabula de Apibus Examinatur* (Wismar, 1726); idem, *De Vita et Scriptis Joann. Albert Fabricii Commentarius* (Hamburg, 1737); idem, *Die vornehmsten Wahrheiten der natürlichen Religion in 10 Abhandlungen auf eine begreifliche Art erläutert und gerettet* (Hamburg, 1754; 4th ed., 1772); idem, *Allgemeine Betrachtungen über die Triebe der Thiere, hauptsächlich über ihre Kunsttriebe zur Erkenntnis des Zusammenhangs der Welt, des Schöpfers und unser selbst* (Hamburg, 1760, 3rd ed. 1772); idem, *Angefangene Betrachtungen über die besonderen Arten der thierischen Kunsttriebe. Mit einem Anhange über die Natur der Pflanzen-thiere begleitet* (Hamburg, 1773); idem, *Die Vernunftlehre als eine Anweisung zum richtigen Gebrauche der Vernunft in dem Erkenntnis der Wahrheit aus zwoen ganz natürlichen Regeln der Einstimmung und des Widerspruchs hergeleitet* (Hamburg, 1756; 5th ed., 1790).

17. *Die vornehmsten Wahrheiten der natürlichen Religion*, 4th ed., pp. 587–90.

18. For fuller discussion see R. M. Burns, *The Great Debate on Miracles, From Joseph Glanvill to David Hume* (Lewisburg: Bucknell University Press, 1981); Colin Brown, *Miracles and the Critical Mind* (Grand Rapids: Eerdmans, 1984).

19. *Tractatus Theologico-Politicus*, chap. 6, in *The Chief Works of Benedict de Spinoza*, trans. R. H. M. Elwes (reprint ed., New York: Dover Publications, 1955), 1:81. On Spinoza's view of religion generally see Leo Strauss, *Spinoza's Critique of Religion* (New York: Schocken Books, 1982).

20. Ibid., p. 83.

21. Ibid., p. 86.

22. Ibid., p. 91.

23. Pierre Bayle, "Spinoza," in his *Historical and Critical Dictionary*, trans. with an Introduction and Notes, Richard H. Popkin (Indianapolis: Bobb-Merrill Co., 1965), pp. 288–338. Hume referred to Spinoza's "hideous hypothesis" and asserted that, "the doctrine of the immateriality, simplicity, and indivisibility of a thinking substance is a true atheism, and will serve to justify all those sentiments, for which Spinoza is so universally infamous" (*A Treatise of Human Nature*, bk. 1, pt. 4, sec. 5, ed. L. A. Selby-Bigge [reprint ed., Oxford: Clarendon Press, 1967], pp. 240–41).

24. See Chapter 2, notes 21–23.

25. Cf. Copleston, 4:260–62.

26. G. W. F. Hegel, *Lectures on the History of Philosophy*, trans. E. S. Haldane and F. H. Simson (New York: The Humanities Press; London: Routledge and Kegan Paul, 1896; reprint ed., 1968), 3:252–90.

27. Cf. *Leviathan*, chap. 37.

28. On the attitudes of British seventeenth-century scientists to miracles see R. M. Burns, op. cit., pp. 19–69. On British thought on science and religion see R. S. Westfall, *Science and Religion in Seventeenth-Century England* (New Haven: Yale University Press, 1958); Henry G. van Leeuwen, *The Problem of Certainty in English Thought, 1630–1690*, International Archives of the History of Ideas, no. 3 (The Hague: Martinus Nijhoff, 1963).

29. From an extract cited by Burns, op. cit., p. 55, from the Boyle Manuscripts, Royal Society, London, vol. 7, fol. 120–22.

30. Sir Isaac Newton, *Theological Manuscripts*, selected and edited by H. McLachlan (Liverpool: Liverpool University Press, 1950), pp. 44–47.

31. Ibid., pp. 61–118.

32. Ibid., p. 54.

33. Ibid.

34. Ibid., pp. 54f.

35. *Opticks* (1704), III, 1, Q. 28.

36. Cf. G. Buchdahl, *The Image of Newton and Locke in the Age of Reason* (London and New York: Sheed and Ward, 1961); H. G. Alexander, ed., *The Leibniz-Clarke Correspondence, Together with Extracts from Newton's Principia and Opticks* (New York: Philosophical Library Inc., 1956). Voltaire's *Lettres sur les Anglais* (1733) popularized English thinkers. His *Élements de la Philosophie de Newton* (1738) and sundry other pieces enthusiastically lauded Newton at the expense of Descartes. Voltaire who was in England between 1726 and 1729 was also an enthusiastic advocate of Locke's sensationalism, though not of his views of God (cf. Norman L. Torrey, "Voltaire," *EP* 8:262–70).

37. *Essay Concerning Human Understanding*, bk. 2, chap. 1, sec. 2, ed. A. S. Pringle-Pattison (1924; reprint ed., Oxford: Clarendon Press, 1967), p. 42.

38. Ralph Cudworth (1617–88) declared, "I perswade myself, that no man shall ever be kept out of heaven, for not comprehending mysteries that were beyond the reach of his shallow understanding; if he had but an honest and good heart, that was ready to comply with Christ's commandments" (A *Sermon before the House of Commons*, March 31, 1647). Benjamin Whichcote (1609–83) went even further: "To go against Reason is to go against God; it is the selfsame thing, to do that which the Reason of the case doth require; and that which God Himself doth appoint: Reason is the Divine Governor of Man's Life; it is the very Voice of God" (*Aphorism*, 76).

39. *Essay Concerning Human Understanding*, bk. 4, chap. 17, sec. 23, p. 354.

40. Ibid., bk. 4, chap. 19, sec. 4, p. 360.

41. *A Discourse of Miracles*, in I. T. Ramsey, ed., *The Reasonableness of Christianity with a Discourse of Miracles, and Part of a Third Letter Concerning Toleration* (London: A. & C. Black, 1958), p. 79.

42. Ibid., p. 82. In making this point Locke clearly differentiated himself from Deism. For comparison of Locke with the Deists see S. G. Hefelbower, *The Relation of John Locke to English Deism* (Chicago: University of Chicago Press, 1918); Maurice Cranston, *John Locke: A Biography* (London: Longmans, 1957).

43. Viret alluded to Deists in his *Instruction Chrétienne*, 2 vols. (1564), in the "Epistre" signed, Lyons, December 12, 1563. See further E. C. Mossner, "Deism," *EP* 2:326–27; Günter Gawlick, op. cit., p. 41. In the *Apologie oder Schutzschrift für die vernünftigen Verehrer Gottes* (Alexander's edition, 1:134), Reimarus mentioned Gabriel da Costa (born ca. 1585) who was born and raised a Catholic but became a convert to Judaism, taking the name Uriel. He was twice expelled for his rationalism, before being reconciled in 1640. His account of his life and view was published posthumously by the Dutch theologian Philipp van Limborch, *Urielis Acosta Exemplar humanae vitae. Addita est brevis refutatio argumentorum quibus Acosta omnem religionem impugnat, per Philippum a Limborch* in an appendix to *Philipi a Limborch De veritate Christianae amica collatio cum reuditio Judaeo* (Gouda, 1687), pp. 341–64. See further, Gawlick, op. cit., pp. 16–17, 38.

Gawlick also notes that Reimarus could have included among previous rational worshipers of God Geoffrey Vallée who was executed in 1574. Only a single copy of his *La Béatitude des*

Chrestiens (1573) survived the attempt to eradicate it. The earliest known German anti-Christian polemic dates from 1587, but was not published until the nineteenth century: *"Origo et fundamenta religionis Christianae. Eine bisher noch unbekannte deistische antichristliche Schrift aus dem sechzehnten Jahrhundert Mitgeteilt von D. August Gfrörer," Zeitschrift für die historische Theologie* 6 (1836):2. Stück, pp. 180–259. A further anonymous work which denounced the founders of the three great revealed religions, Moses, Jesus and Mohammed, was *Liber de tribus Impostoribus. Anno MDIIC*, ed. Gerhard Bartsch, with Latin text and German translation by Rolf Walther (Berlin: Akademie Verlag, 1960).

44. *Toleranz und Gewissensfreiheit* (Berlin, 1774), p. 204.

45. *The Works of Richard Bentley,* ed. Alexander Dyce (1838; reprint ed., New York: AMS Press, 1966), 3:25. The words were printed in the first edition but dropped from later editions and restored by Dyce in a footnote. The context suggests that Bentley thought of the Deists in this way because he judged them opposed to sanctity and worship. In preparing later lectures for publication Bentley consulted Newton concerning his use of Newton's views.

46. Cf. Thomas Halyburton, *Natural Religion Insufficient, and Revealed Necessary to Man's Happiness in his Present State* (1714), which contains a detailed account of Lord Herbert's position and that of his disciple, Charles Blount (see *The Works of Thomas Halyburton* [Glasgow: Blackie and Son, 1837], pp. 253–501).

47. F. C. Baur took up the question in "Apollonius von Tyana und Christus, oder das Verhältnis des Pythagoreismus zum Christentum. Ein Beitrag zur Religionsgeschichte der ersten Jahrhunderte nach Christus," *Tübinger Zeitschrift für Theologie* 4 (1832):3–235. D. F. Strauss saw parallels in *The Life of Jesus Critically Examined* (reprint ed., Philadelphia: Fortress Press, 1972), p. 495. Recent studies include G. Petzke, *Die Traditionen über Apollonius von Tyana und das Neue Testament, Studia ad Corpus Hellenisticum Novi Testamenti,* no. 1 (Leiden: E. J. Brill, 1970); and E. V. Gallagher, *Divine Man or Magician: Celsus and Origen on Jesus,* SBL Dissertation Series, no. 64 (Chico, CA: Scholars Press, 1982), pp. 157–165. *Philostratus: The Life of Apollonius,* 2 vols., was edited by F. C. Conybeare, Loeb Classical Library (Cambridge, MA: Harvard University Press; London: William Heinemann, 1912). John Ferguson sees the life of Apollonius as the result of counter propaganda, encouraged by the empress Julia Domna, based upon a source which was "the stock-in-trade of historical romances" and upon which no credence may be placed (*The Religions of the Roman Empire* [London: Thames and Hudson, 1970], p. 182). Alexander Severus set Apollonius alongside Orpheus, Alexander the Great, Abraham and Christ in his private *lararium*.

48. References below are to the facsimile reprint of the first edition (New York and London: Garland Publishing, 1978). Toland closed his preface with the refusal to be known by any other title than "that most glorious one of being a Christian" (p. xxx). Nevertheless, his book was regarded by the orthodox as an attack on the Christian faith. It was condemned by the Irish Parliament, and the Lower House of the Convocation of Canterbury was prevented by the Upper House from taking proceedings against its author only on a technical point of law. It was attacked by Leibniz in his *Annotatiunculae Subitaneae ad librum Christianismo mysteriis carente* (1701), but the first full German translation was the edition of L. Zscharnack (1908). Toland is the subject of a recent study by Robert E. Sullivan, *John Toland and the Deist Controversy: A Study in Adaptations,* Harvard Historical Studies, no. 101 (Cambridge, MA: Harvard University Press, 1982). Sullivan draws attention to the influence of English Socinianism and anti-Trinitarianism on Toland and the Deists in general. See also Stephen H. Daniel, *John Toland: His Methods, Manners and Mind* (Kingston and Montreal: McGill-Queen's University Press, 1984).

49. Toland insisted that no doctrine "of the *Gospel* is still a *Mystery*" (op. cit., p. 102). Though he ridiculed "the *Partizans* of *Mystery*" who "fly to *Miracles* as their last Refuge" (ibid., p. 150), he expressed his belief that "Miracles are produc'd according to the Laws of Nature, tho above its ordinary Operations, which are therefore supernaturally assisted" (ibid., pp. 156–57).

50. Ibid., p. 158.

51. Ibid., pp. 158–73.

52. Ibid., p. 168.

53. Op. cit., 2nd ed., (1718), p. 73; cf. pp. 65ff.

54. "Since the Nazarens or Ebionites are by all Church-historians unanimously acknowledg'd to have been the first Christians, or those who believ'd in CHRIST among the Jews, with which his own people he liv'd and dy'd, they having been the witnesses of his actions, and of whom were all the Apostles: considering this, I say, how it was possible for them to be the first of all (for they are made to

be the first Heretics) who shou'd form wrong conceptions of the doctrine and designs of JESUS? and how came the Gentiles, who believ'd on him after his death, by the preaching of persons who never knew him, to have truer notions of these things; or whence they cou'd have their information, but from believing Jews?" (ibid., p. 76).

55. Ibid., p. 78.

56. Ibid., p. 4; cf. pp. 83–84, where Toland rejected "Apostolick Tradition" and argued that Mohamet did not invent his teaching about Jesus, but drew on existing, valid tradition.

57. A. C. Lundsteen argues that parts of Reimarus's treatment of the passage of the Israelites through the Red Sea were lifted directly from Toland's *Tetradymus* (op. cit., p. 116; cf. Lachmann-Muncker, 12:359ff.). Lundsteen refers to an observation in Reimarus's manuscript that, "The notorious Toland, who far surpasses in learning and acuteness all other opponents of revelation, has to be sure brought for the first time this mystery from ancient obscurity to light, and I would not know that he could rightly be answered" *(Apologie,* bk. 1, chap. 3, sec. 4). In footnote f., Reimarus added, "I have made use of the same with profit." (See *Apologie,* ed. Gerhard Alexander, 1:299ff.).

58. E. C. Mossner, *EP* 8:142. The *Pantheisticon* was discussed in *Fortgesetzte Sammlung von alten und neuen theologischen Sachen* (1720), p. 284; cf. G. V. Lechler, *Geschichte des englischen Deismus* (Stuttgart and Tübingen, 1841; reprint ed., with bibliography, ed. G. Gawlick [Hildesheim: Georg Olms, 1965]), p. 473.

59. Richardson, *History,* p. 273. On Collins, see James O'Higgins, *Anthony Collins: The Man and His Works* (The Hague: Martinus Nijhoff, 1970).

60. (Reprint ed., New York and London: Garland Publishing, 1978), p. 32. This edition also contains Richard Bentley's *Remarks upon a Late Discourse of Free Thinking: In a letter to F. H. D. D. by Phileleutherus Lipsiensis* (1713) and Collins's *Philosophical Inquiry concerning Human Liberty* (1717).

61. Reimarus discussed Collins in bk. 1, chap. 4, secs. 11f. (cf. A. C. Lundsteen, op. cit., p. 117).

62. The full title reads: *A Discourse of the Grounds and Reasons of the Christian Religion. In two Parts: The first containing some CONSIDERATIONS of the Quotations made from the Old in the New Testament, and particularly on the Prophesies cited from the former and said to be fulfill'd in the latter. The second containing an EXAMINATION of the Scheme advanc'd by Mr. WHISTON in his* "Essay towards restoring the true Text of the Old Testament, and for vindicating the Citations thence made in the New Testament." *To which is prefix'd an Apology for free debate and liberty of writing.*

63. In the preface to *The Scheme of Literal Prophecy* (pp. vii-xii), Collins listed some twenty-eight replies. Among them were Edward Chandler's *Defence of Christianity from the Prophecies of the Old Testament* (1725) and Samuel Chandler's *Vindication of the Christian Religion* (1725). Thomas Sherlock modified the traditional predictive argument in *The Use and Intent of Prophecy in the Several Ages of the World; in Six Discourses, Delivered at the Temple Church in April and May, 1724.* Sherlock acknowledged that prophecy was not necessarily predictive in a specific, literal way: "The argument from prophecy therefore is not to be formed in this manner: All the ancient prophecies have expressly pointed out and characterised Christ Jesus; but it must be formed in this manner: All the notices which God gave to the fathers of his intended salvation are perfectly answered by the coming of Christ" *(Discourse,* 3; in *The Works of Bishop Sherlock,* ed. T. S. Hughes [London: A. J. Valpy, 1830], 4:56).

64. *A Discourse of the Grounds of the Christian Religion,* p. 27, where Collins observes that more weight is given in the New Testament to fulfillment of the words of Moses and the prophets than to miracles (cf. Matt. 24:23–24; Mark 13:21–22; Luke 16:31; 2 Pet. 1:19). Cf. *The Scheme of Literal Prophecy,* pp. 334, 337.

65. Ibid., pp. 50–61.

66. Ibid., pp. 61–78; cf. *The Scheme of Literal Prophecy,* pp. 298ff.

67. Ibid., p. 53. Wilhelm Surenhuis or Surenhusius (1666–1729) was Professor of Greek and Hebrew at the University of Amsterdam. He was a friend of the Hamburg Hebraist, J. C. Wolf (1683–1739). Collins noted Surenhusius's *Tractatus in quo secundum Veterum Theologorum Hebraeorum formulas allegandi, & modus interpretandi, conciliantur loca ex V. in Nov. Test. allegata* (Amsterdam, 1713), p. 712.

68. Ibid., p. 71; cf. Surenhusius, Thesis 9, 1, 1.

69. Ibid., p. 92.

70. William Whiston (1667–1752) succeeded Sir Isaac Newton as Lucasian Professor of Mathematics at Cambridge, but was deprived of his appointment in 1710 for unorthodox views on the Trinity. His translation of Josephus appeared in 1737 (cf. *DNB*, 61:10–14). His essay featured in S. J. Baumgarten's *Hallische Bibliothek*, 4:420ff.

71. First *Discourse* (1727), p. 1.

72. Ibid., p. 3.

73. Ibid.

74. Ibid., p. 55.

75. Woolston examined in the first *Discourse* the cleansing of the Temple, the demoniac and the Gadarene swine, the transfiguration, the changing of water into wine at Cana, the man with the palsy and the man born blind. In the second he considered the woman with a hemorrhage, the woman in Luke 13, and the woman by the well of Samaria. In the third he discussed the cursing of the fig tree and the man by the Pool of Bethesda. In the fourth he discussed the man born blind in John 9, the miracle at Cana again, and the paralytic in Mark 2 and parallels. The fifth *Discourse* was devoted to the raising of Jairus' daughter, the widow of Nain's son and Lazarus. The sixth *Discourse* examined the resurrection of Jesus.

76. Ibid., p. 51.

77. Ibid., p. 56.

78. Second *Discourse* (1727), p. 27.

79. Ibid., p. 31.

80. Ibid., p. 55.

81. Third *Discourse* (1728), p. 5.

82. Ibid., p. 49.

83. Ibid., p. 58.

84. Fourth *Discourse* (1728), p. 11.

85. Ibid., p. 23.

86. Ibid., p. 28, cf. pp. 29–43; Fifth *Discourse* (1728), pp. 42–55.

87. Sixth *Discourse* (1729), p. 31.

88. Ibid., p, 27.

89. Ibid., pp. 10–15.

90. Ibid., pp. 19–20.

91. Ibid., pp. 22–25.

92. Ibid., pp. 33–37.

93. Ibid., p. 26.

94. Ibid., p. 38.

95. Under the Rules of the King's Bench Woolston enjoyed considerable freedom, and he died in his own house.

In *Woolston's Case* (1 Fitzg. 64) in 1728 Lord Raymond said, "We do not meddle with any difference of opinion, we interfere only where the very root of Christianity is itself struck at." This view was confirmed by Lord Mansfield in *Evans v. Chamberlain of London* (1762) (2 Burn's Ecc. Law, 207), "The common law of England knows no prosecution for mere opinions," and by Justice Thomas Erskine in *Shore v. Wilson* (1842) (9 Cl and Fin, 534), "It is indeed still blasphemy, punishable at common law, scoffingly or irreverently to ridicule or impugn the doctrine of the Christian faith; yet any man may, without subjecting himself to penal consequences, soberly and reverently examine and question the truth of those doctrines which have been essential to it." In Scottish law the penalty for blasphemy was death, but by an act of 1825, amended in 1837, this was reduced to a fine or imprisonment or both. On the subject of the blasphemy laws see H. H. L. Bellot in *EB*, 3:701.

In 1703 the Presbyterian minister, Thomas Emlyn (1663–1741), was tried for blasphemy in Dublin and was found guilty of "writing and publishing an infamous and scandalous libel declaring that Jesus Christ is not the supreme God." He had defended his Arian views in a tract entitled *An Humble Inquiry in the Scripture Account of Jesus Christ* (1702). He was imprisoned for two years before payment of a fine of £20 secured his release. See E. M. Wilbur, op. cit., 2:244–46.

96. Thomas Sherlock (1678–1761) enjoyed a notable career at Cambridge, where he became Master of St. Catherine's Hall and Vice-Chancellor of the University. He was successively Bishop of Bangor (1728), Salisbury (1734) and London (1748), and Master of the Temple (1704–53). He

declined the see of York and possibly also that of Canterbury. References to the *Tryal of the Witnesses* are to the edition with modernized spelling in T. S. Hughes's edition of his *Works*, 5 vols. (1830), pp. 152–223. By 1765 it had reached a 14th edition in England. A French version was produced by Le Moine and La Haie (1732) and a German one by Schier (1751) (cf. G. V. Lechler, op. cit., p. 312). The French version was widely used by Catholic apologists. A less popular but weighty reply to Woolston was Richard Smallbroke's *Vindication of our Saviour's Miracles*, 2 vols. (1729). Woolston had dedicated his third *Discourse* to him. Various replies were discussed by Thomas Stackhouse in *A Fair State of the Controversy between Mr. Woolston and his Adversaries* (1730).

97. *Works*, 5:180.

98. Ibid., p. 181.

99. Ibid., p. 208.

100. Ibid., p. 219.

101. Ibid., p. 190; cf. Locke, *An Essay Concerning Human Understanding*, bk. 4, chap. 15, par. 5; Joseph Butler, *The Analogy of Religion* (1736), Introduction, no. 3; David Hume, *Enquiry Concerning Human Understanding*, sec. 10, no. 89; J. S. Mill, *A System of Logic*, 8th ed. (London: Longmans, 1925), p. 411.

102. "But the doctrines which are to be proved by miracles are the new revealed doctrines of Christianity, which were neither known or knowable to the reason of man: such are the doctrines of salvation and redemption by Christ, of sanctification and regeneration by the Spirit of God" (*Discourse* X, on Acts 2:22; *Works*, 1:204).

103. Leslie Stephen, *History of English Thought in the Eighteenth Century* (1876; reprint of 3rd ed., [1902], New York: Harcourt Brace and London: Rupert Hart-Davis, 1962), 1:113.

104. This, together with other quotations, was printed on the title page. Sherlock's sermon was preached before the Society for the Propagation of the Gospel in Foreign Parts on February 17, 1715 (*Works*, 3:346, 348).

105. *Christianity as Old as the Creation: Or, the Gospel, A Republication of the Religion of Nature* (1730; facsimile reprint ed., New York and London: Garland Publishing, 1978), p. 3.

106. Ibid., p. 375.

107. Ibid., p. 159.

108. Ibid., p. 373.

109. Ibid., p. 13.

110. Ibid., p. 186.

111. Ibid., pp. 44–57.

112. Ibid., p. 20.

113. Ibid., p. 339.

114. Ibid., p. 342.

115. Cf. L. Stephen, op. cit., 1:113–37. Stephen regards as all but indistinguishable from Tindal the replies of the Dissenter, James Foster, *Usefulness, Truth, and Excellency of the Christian Revelation* (1731; 3rd ed., 1734), and the Anglican, A. A. Sykes, *Principles and Connection of Natural and Revealed Religion* (1740, op. cit., 1:122f). John Conybeare's *Defence of Revealed Religion* (1732) played down the capacities of reason, claiming that revelation provides man with a "telescope" to bring into focus what previously was dim and vague. Stephen regards John Leland's *Answer to Tindal* (1733), and *View of the Principal Deistical Writers* (1754), as largely a repetition of Conybeare (op. cit., 1:130). Even William Law's *The Case of Reason, or Natural Religion, Fairly and Fully Stated* (1731) adds little to the position of Locke. The work that is generally regarded as the greatest of the replies was Bishop Butler's *The Analogy of Religion, Natural and Revealed, to the Constitution and Course of Nature* (1736), which argued that, "though natural Religion is the foundation and principal part of Christianity, it is not in any sense the whole of it" (pt. 2, chap. 1, ed. W. E. Gladstone [Oxford: Clarendon Press, 1896], p. 188).

116. Annet was a schoolmaster, but lost his employment in 1744 for his attacks on Christianity. In 1739 he published *Judging for Ourselves: Or Free Thinking, the Great Duty of Religion*. He attacked Sherlock in *The Resurrection of Jesus Consider'd: In Answer to the Tryal of the Witnesses. By a Moral Philosopher* which went through three editions in 1744; *The Resurrection Reconsider'd* (1744); *The Sequel of the Resurrection Consider'd* (1745); and *The Resurrection Defenders stript of all Defence* (1745). He replied to his critic, Gilbert West's *Observations on the Resurrection of Jesus Christ* (1747), in *Supernaturals Examined* (1747). He attacked George Lyttleton's *Observations on*

the Conversion and Apostleship of St. Paul in a Letter to Gilbert West (1747), in *The History and Character of St. Paul, examin'd in a Letter to Theophilus* (1748). Annet is also widely thought to be the author of the anonymous *The Conception of Jesus Consider'd, As the Foundation of the Christian Religion* (1744), which impugned the birth narratives of Matthew and Luke. He pleaded for a more liberal attitude to divorce in *Social Bliss Consider'd* (1749). Annet argued that all miracles were incredible, and in nine numbers of a paper entitled *The Free Enquirer* (1761–62) he urged that Moses was an imposter and that much of the Pentateuch was false invention. He was convicted of blasphemy in 1762. His sentence included a year's hard labor, a fine, and sureties of £100 to guarantee good conduct for life. However, in 1766 Annet published *A Collection of Tracts of a Certain Free Enquirer noted by his Sufferings for his Opinions* which contained all the above.

117. Op. cit., 1:208.

118. Hirsch, 1:320.

119. Ibid.; cf. Annet, *A Collection of Tracts*, pp. 265–362.

120. Ibid., pp. 302ff.

121. Ibid., pp. 209, 271.

122. Cf. Mark 15:44.

123. John 19:34–36.

124. Ibid., p. 296.

125. Sir George Lyttleton's *Observations* had argued that the truth and divine character of Christianity could be proved entirely from Paul, who must have either been telling the truth or have been an imposter. Annet's reply opted for the latter alternative. Lyttleton's work was translated into German (1748), Dutch (1748), and French (1754 and 1758) (cf. Lechler, op. cit., p. 315).

126. West's *Observations on the History and Evidences of the Resurrection of Jesus Christ* (1747) earned him the degree of Doctor of Laws from Oxford. It harmonized the narratives taking their contents as eyewitness testimony. It was translated into German by Sulzer ([Berlin, 1748]; cf. G. V. Lechler, op. cit., pp. 314f., 450, who notes that a French version was made by the Abbé Guené in 1757). Other replies included S. Chandler's *Witnesses of the Resurrection* (1744), and the anonymous *Sequel of the Tryal of the Witnesses* (1749).

127. *Gegensätze des Herausgebers* (Lachmann-Muncker, 12:449).

128. *Nachrichten von einer Hallischen Bibliothek*, 5:136ff.

129. *The True Gospel of Jesus Asserted*, p. 27.

130. Ibid., pp. 43ff.

131. Ibid., pp. 141–42.

132. Morgan was the author of *The Moral Philosopher, in a Dialogue between Philalethes a Christian Deist and Theophanes a Christian Jew* (1737). Two further volumes were published in 1737 and 1739. They were followed by *A Vindication of the Moral Philosopher* (1741) against the attacks of Samuel Chandler. Morgan's work and the replies to him were made known in Germany through S. J. Baumgarten's *Hallische Bibliothek*, 5:331f., 349–62; 6:181; and C. G. Jöcher's *Primae Lineae Historiae controversarum a Thoma Morgano excitarum* (Leipzig, 1745).

133. Op. cit., 1:71.

134. Ibid., pp. 379ff.

135. Middleton's *Miscellaneous Works* were edited in four volumes by R. Manby in 1752. A fifth volume was published in 1755, and a German version of *Vermischte Abhandlungen* appeared in 1793.

136. *Miscellaneous Works*, 2:73–74.

137. Ibid., p. 74.

138. The work was actually printed in 1748, but due to the inclement weather the ink took a long time to dry, and the book did not appear until the following year. It was preceded by an *Introductory Discourse* (1747) and *Remarks on Two Pamphlets* (1748), and was followed by a posthumous *Vindication* (1751). I have discussed Middleton's argument in more detail in *Miracles and the Critical Mind*.

139. Cf. Calvin, *Institutes of the Christian Religion*, Prefatory Address to King Francis of France, no. 3, ed. J. T. McNeill (Philadelphia: Westminster Press, 1960), 1:14–18; B. B. Warfield, *Miracles: Yesterday and Today, True and False* (1918; reprint ed., Grand Rapids: Wm. B. Eerdmans, 1954). Warfield leaned heavily on Middleton's work in his discussion of the cessation of miracles in the early church.

140. *Journal*, January 28, 1749; cf. also August 12, 1771; and Wesley's letter to Middleton (1749) in *The Letters of the Rev. John Wesley, A.M.*, ed. J. Telford (London: Epworth Press, 1931), 2:312–88.

141. Op. cit. (reprint ed., London: Sherwood & Co., 1925), pp. 225–27. A recent study of the miracles and their background is B. Robert Kreiser, *Miracles, Convulsions, and Ecclesiastical Politics in Early Eighteenth-Century Paris* (Princeton: Princeton University Press, 1978).

142. Op. cit., pp. 219–20; cf. Middleton's discussion of J. Chapman, *Miscellaneous Tracts*, pp. 175–76 (ibid., pp. 176–77).

143. Op. cit., 1:227.

144. Cf. E. Troeltsch, "Ueber historische und dogmatische Methode in der Theologie," *Gesammelte Schriften* (reprint ed., Aalen: Scientia Verlag, 1962), 2:729–53.

145. I have attempted a fuller discussion of Hume's essay in *Miracles and the Critical Mind* which contains references to philosophical and historical studies of Hume. There is reason to think that Hume conceived his argument while staying at La Flèche during the 1730s in the course of discussion with Jesuits at the Seminary there. If so, his argument could be seen as a response to both Catholic and Protestant apologetics, made at the height of the Deist controversy. Although Hume was a skeptic, professing no religious beliefs and not a Deist, his arguments were anticipated, as R. M. Burns has shown, in one form or another by the Deists (op. cit., pp. 70–95).

146. Hume made the observation in his account of *My Own Life*, dated April 18, 1776 (text in E. C. Mossner, *The Life of David Hume*, 2nd ed. [Oxford: Clarendon Press, 1980], pp. 611–15, see p. 612).

147. Op. cit., no. 96, pp. 122–25.

148. Ibid., no. 87, p. 110.

149. Ibid., no. 91, p. 116.

150. Ibid., no. 90, p. 114.

151. Ibid., no. 92, p. 116.

152. Ibid., no. 93, p. 117.

153. Ibid., no. 94, pp. 119–20.

154. Ibid., nos. 95–98, pp. 121–27.

155. Ibid., no. 100, p. 130.

156. *Gesammelte Schriften* (Leipzig and Berlin: Teubner, 1927), 3:131.

157. *Gesammelte Schriften*, 4:339–40.

158. Ibid., p. 429.

159. *The Idea of History* (London: Oxford University Press, 1946), p. 76.

160. Cf. op. cit., vol. 1, chs. 3 and 4.

161. Günter Gawlick observes that Spinoza's *Tractatus Theologico-Politicus* was perceived by contemporaries as a Deistic work and exercised influence on the Deists (op. cit., p. 41). Gawlick draws attention to the letter of Lambert de Velthuysen to Jacob Ostens, dated January 24, 1671 (Spinoza, *Opera*, ed. Carl Gebhardt [Heidelberg, 1924], 4:207); Matthias Earbery, *Deism Examin'd and Confuted. In an Answer to a Book Intitled, Tractatus Theologico Politicus* (London, 1697); Rosalie L. Colie, "Spinoza and the Early English Deists," *Journal of the History of Ideas* 20 (1959):23–46; idem, "Spinoza in England, 1665–1730," *Proceedings of the American Philosophical Association* 107 (1963):183–219; Paul Vernière, *Spinoza et la Pensée française avant la Révolution* (Paris: Presses Universitaires de France, 1954), 1:38–219.

162. Cf. Norman L. Torrey, *Voltaire and the English Deists* (New Haven: Yale University Press, 1930; reprint ed., Archon Books, 1967). Rousseau took a somewhat different view from the English Deists, seeing Jesus as a divine man, and assigning sentiment a greater role in religion. However, he was hardly more disposed to orthodox Christianity than the Deists (cf. Ronald Grimsley, *Rousseau and the Religious Quest* [Oxford: Clarendon Press, 1968]; and Rousseau, *Religious Writings*, ed. Ronald Grimsley [Oxford: Clarendon Press, 1970]).

163. Cf. G. V. Lechler, op. cit., pp. 446, 450. For details of translations of English books into German and reviews of English works in German see Mary Bell Price and Lawrence Marsden Price, *The Publication of English Humaniora in Germany in the Eighteenth Century*, University of California Publications in Modern Philology, no. 44 (Berkeley, 1955). This complements their earlier bibliography which was confined to purely literary works, *English Literature in Germany* (Berkeley: University of California, 1934).

164. Cf. G. V. Lechler, op. cit., p. 448; Henning Graf Reventlow, in *Hermann Samuel Reimarus*, p. 45.

165. Lechler observed that it was no accident that J. L. Schmidt was a Wolffian (op. cit., p. 448). Many theologians of the day disapproved of Wolffianism, but Wolff himself came to dominate German philosophy in the middle of the eighteenth century.

166. M. Schmidt, *RGG*[3], vol. 5, col. 265.

167. Stück 134 (cf. Lachmann-Muncker, 5:443–45).

168. The visit is referred to by J. B. Büsch in his *Memoriae Immortali H. S. Reimari* appended to J. A. H. Reimarus, *De Vita Sua Commentarius* (Hamburgi, 1815), p. 9. The view that Reimarus became acquainted with Deism on his travels is shared by Reventlow, op. cit., p. 45.

169. Cf. Reventlow, op. cit., p. 59. Reimarus alluded to Middleton's *Free Inquiry* in his *Schutzschrift*, bk. 2, chap. 4, sec. 3, and Notes m and p (cf. G. Alexander's edition, 2:377, 383).

170. Reventlow, op. cit., p. 60, who notes the observation of M. Loeser in his dissertation on *Die Kritik des Hermann Samuel Reimarus am Alten Testament* ([Berlin, 1941], p. 29, cf. p. 43) that the catalog in the Hamburger Staats- und Universitätsbibliothek of Reimarus's library indicates that he possessed most of the Deists' writings. The critical notes in G. Alexander's edition of Reimarus confirm the latter's familiarity not only with post-Reformation critics of Christianity but also with Jewish and Islamic thought.

171. Loeser observed that "Reimarus raised hardly any objection to the religion of the Old Testament, its writings and characters in its stories, that the English Deists had not already anticipated. His merit lies in the fact that he brought all previously raised objections into a system of criticism" (ibid., p. 112; cf. Reventlow, op. cit., p. 59). A. C. Lundsteen went so far as to say that in many places we cannot avoid the thought that Reimarus's work was "a plagiarism of English Deistic authors to the point of verbal reproduction" (op. cit., p. 138).

172. The *Qu'rān* 4, 156/157; cf. G. Parrinder, *Jesus in the Qu'rān* (London: Faber and Faber, 1965), pp. 105–21.

173. Cf. Matt. 28:12–15 with Justin, *Dialogue with Trypho*, 108; Tertullian, *De Spectaculis*, 30; Origen, *Contra Celsum*, 2, 56–63; 6, 56–58. A crude but elaborate version was perpetuated until modern times by the medieval *Tol'doth Jesu*, in J. C. Wagenseil's *Tela ignea Satanae* (Altdorf, 1681), which was known to Reimarus (G. Alexander, op. cit., 2:677). Cf. Joseph Klausner, *Jesus of Nazareth* (London: Allen and Unwin, 1925), pp. 47–54; J. Jocz, *The Jewish People and Jesus Christ: A Study of the Controversy between Church and Synagogue* (reprint ed., with revisions, London: S.P.C.K., 1962), pp. 57–65; Günther Schlichting, *Ein jüdisches Leben Jesu. Die verschollene Toledot-Jesehu-Fassung Tam ū-mūʿād. Einleitung, Text, Übersetzung, Kommentar, Motivsynopse, Bibliographie, WUNT* 24 (Tübingen: J. C. B. Mohr, 1982).

174. Cf. H. Heppe, *Reformed Dogmatics, Set Out and Illustrated from the Sources* (London: Allen and Unwin, 1960), pp. 695–712; James P. Martin, *The Last Judgment in Protestant Theology from Orthodoxy to Ritschl* (Grand Rapids: Eerdmans, 1963), pp. 1–86.

175. Leibniz concluded his *Monadologie* (1714; German version, 1720) with a vision of the universe working as a perfect mechanism in which sins carried their own punishment and virtue its own reward (no. 89; cf. *Théodicée* [1710]). Eschatology was inevitably excluded by the deterministic pantheism of Spinoza's *Ethica*. See further, J. P. Martin, op. cit., pp. 87–128.

176. Cf. Schweitzer, *Quest*, pp. 330–403, with J. Moltmann, *Theology of Hope* (London: S.C.M. Press, 1967), pp. 38–39. On the significance of Reimarus's discussion of the political aspects of the kingdom see Ernst Bammel, "The Revolution Theory from Reimarus to Brandon," in Ernst Bammel and C. F. D. Moule, eds., *Jesus and the Politics of His Day* (Cambridge: Cambridge University Press, 1984), pp. 11–69.

177. *Ursprünge und Probleme der Bibelkritik im 17. Jahrhundert*, FGLP 10. Reihe 33 (Munich: Chr. Kaiser Verlag, 1966), p. 12.

178. *Axiomata* (1778), Introduction (Lachmann-Muncker, 13:109).

179. Arthur von Arx observed that this applied not only to Lessing's view of religious history but to his approach to literature and art (*Lessing und die geschichtliche Welt* [Frauenfeld and Leipzig: Huber, 1944], pp. 36–68). Among the passages to which he draws attention is the following: "We see then that the poet, while he distances himself from his own particular truth, imitates all the more faithfully general truth.... For while the poet abstracts from being everything that uniquely concerns and distinguishes the individual, his conception *[Begriff]* leaps over, as it were, all the particular

objects that lie in among and rises, so far as possible, to the divine original image, in order to become the immediate copy of the truth" (*Hamburgische Dramaturgie*, Stück 94, March 25, 1768). In the passage, Lessing compared his views with those of Plato, Aristotle and Sophocles.

II. PHILOSOPHICAL IDEALISM AND RATIONAL RELIGION

4. *From Kant to Goethe*

1. "Der deutsche Idealismus," in *GS*, (Tübingen: J. C. B. Mohr, 1925; reprint ed. Aalen: Scientia Verlag, 1981), 4:532–33.

2. *Geist der Goethezeit. Versuch einer ideelen Entwicklung der klassisch-romantischen Literaturgeschichte*, 6th ed. (Leipzig: Koehler & Amelang, 1964), 4:367–68.

3. Kant's essay "Beantwortung der Frage: Was ist Aufklärung?" appeared in the December 1784 edition of the *Berlinische Monatsschrift*, 4, 12, pp. 481–94. It was reprinted in Kant's *GS*, 8:35–42. The above translation is that of Lewis White Beck in his edition of Kant's *Foundations of the Metaphysics of Morals and What is Enlightenment?* (Indianapolis and New York: Bobbs-Merrill, 1959), p. 85.

The motto *Sapere aude!*, "Dare to be wise," occurs in Horace, *Ars Poetica*, 40. It had been adopted by the *Gesellschaft der Wahrheitsfreunde* which was founded in 1736 to spread the principle of Wolffian rationalism. The members pledged themselves not to accept or reject any belief except for a "sufficient reason"; cf. Lewis White Beck, *Early German Philosophy: Kant and His Predecessors* (Cambridge, MA: The Bellknap Press of Harvard University Press, 1969), p. 260.

The question of Enlightenment was a much debated topic of the day. As Kant noted at the end of his essay, Moses Mendelssohn also addressed the topic in the *Berlinische Monatsschrift* (cf. A. Altmann, op. cit., pp. 660–666).

4. Op. cit., pp. 90–91.

5. Preface to the First Edition (*Critique of Pure Reason*, Eng. trans. Norman Kemp Smith [London: Macmillan, 1927; reprint ed. with corrections, 1973], p. 9). This translation contains the second edition of 1787, with material from the first which was omitted or changed.

6. Ibid., p. 8.

7. Ibid., p. 9.

8. Kant agreed with the empiricists that "all our knowledge begins with experience," but differed from them in his insistence that "it does not follow that it all arises out of experience" (ibid., Introduction, p. 41). The "raw material" of "sensible impressions" is processed by the mind which employs "two pure forms of sensible intuition, serving as principles of *a priori* knowledge, namely, space and time" (ibid., Transcendental Aesthetic, p. 67). Kant concluded his discussion of the "Transcendental Aesthetic" (or "science of all principles of *a priori* sensibility," p. 66) with the observation, "When in *a priori* judgment we seek to go out beyond the given concept, we come in the *a priori* intuitions upon that which cannot be discovered in the concept but which is certainly found *a priori* in the intuition corresponding to the concept, and can be connected with it synthetically. Such judgments, however, thus based on intuition, can never extend beyond objects of the senses; they are valid only for objects of possible experience" (p. 91). In his discussion of "Transcendental Analytic" (or "the dissection of all our *a priori* knowledge into the elements that pure understanding by itself yields," p. 102), Kant analyzed four classes of "Categories" or "Pure Concepts of the Understanding": Quantity, Quality, Relation, and Modality (ibid., pp. 111–119).

9. Kant saw four main Antinomies, corresponding to the four main types of Categories: that the world is both finite and infinite; that every substance is made up of simple parts and that nothing is made up of simple parts; that there is a need to assume freedom, but that the laws of nature require the denial of freedom; that the existence of the world posits "a being that is absolutely necessary," but that no such being exists ("Transcendental Dialectic," pp. 396–421).

10. *Transcendental Dialectic*, p. 528. Kant argued that there were only three rational proofs of the existence of God: the ontological, cosmological, and teleological. However, the two latter were dependent upon the former which turned out to be a fallacious, tautological argument (pp. 495–524).

11. Ibid., pp. 566–67.

12. *Foundations of the Metaphysics of Morals*, p. 39; cf. *The Critique of Practical Reason*, trans. Lewis White Beck (Indianapolis and New York: Bobbs-Merrill, 1956), p. 30.

13. *Foundations of the Metaphysics of Morals*, p. 51.

14. Letter dated May 4, 1793 (*GS*, 11:429, no. 574).

15. *Op. cit.*, pp. 126–36.

16. *Critique of Practical Reason*, p. 137.

17. *Religion within the Limits of Reason Alone*, trans. with an Introduction and Notes by Theodore M. Greene and Hoyt H. Hudson, with a new essay "The Ethical Significance of Kant's *Religion*" by John R. Silber (La Salle: Open Court, 1934; New York: Harper and Brothers; reprint ed., 1960), p. 3.

18. Ibid., p. 5.

19. Ibid., pp. 4–5.

20. Kant left a great number of unpublished notes and manuscripts which have been edited and included in the later volumes of the *GS*. They form the subject of the study by Erich Adickes, *Kants Opus Postumum, dargestellt und beurteilt, Kant-Studien Ergänzungschefte im Auftrag der Kant-Gesellschaft*, no. 50 (Berlin, 1920). Adickes claimed that Kant eventually abandoned the moral proof of the existence of God which introduced an alien heteronomy and hedonism into his system (op. cit., 846ff.). Moral experience itself was experience of the divine. Theodore M. Greene saw in this "the germ of a theism very different from the deism of his published writings" (op. cit., p. lxvi). Although N. Kemp Smith, A. H. Dakin, C. C. J. Webb and others have followed Adickes, his views have been challenged by G. A. Schrader in "Kant's Presumed Repudiation of the 'Moral Argument' in the *Opus Postumum*: An Examination of Adickes' Interpretation," *Philosophy* 26 (1951):228–41 (cf. John R. Silber, op. cit., pp. cxl–cxlii). See further Keith Ward, *The Development of Kant's View of Ethics* (New York: Humanities Press, 1972), pp. 160–77; W. H. Werkmeister, *Kant: The Architectonic and Development of his Philosophy* (La Salle and London: Open Court, 1980).

21. Ibid., p. 32.

22. Ibid., p. 123.

23. Ibid., p. 55.

24. John 1:1–2.

25. John 1:3.

26. Hebrews 1:3.

27. John 3:16.

28. John 1:12.

29. Philippians 2:6–8; cf. the discussions in Reformed and Lutheran theology on the state of Christ's humiliation (H. Heppe, *Reformed Dogmatics* [London: Allen and Unwin, 1950], pp. 488–94; H. Schmid, *The Doctrinal Theology of the Evangelical Lutheran Church*, 3rd ed. [Minneapolis: Augsburg Publishing House; reprint ed. of 1899 ed., no date], pp. 381–85).

30. Ibid., pp. 54–55. On Kant's view of Christ and its influence on Hegel, see Horst Renz, *Geschichtsgedanke und Christusfrage. Zur Christusanschauung Kants und seiner Fortbildung durch Hegel im Hinblick auf die allgemeine Funktion neuzeitlicher Theologie. STGNJ* 29 (Göttingen: Vandenhoeck & Rupprecht, 1977).

31. Ibid., p. 56.

32. Ibid., pp. 7–10, 100–105.

33. Ibid., p. 78.

34. Ibid., p. 77.

35. "Yet the good principle has descended in mysterious fashion from heaven into humanity not at one particular time alone but from the first beginnings of the human race (as anyone must grant who considers the holiness of this principle, and the incomprehensibility of a union between it and man's sensible nature in the moral predisposition) and it rightfully has in mankind its first dwelling place" (ibid.).

36. Ibid., p. 56; cf. pp. 79–84, where Kant discusses the apologetic role of miracles. Unlike Thomas Woolston, Kant did not call in question the biblical miracles. Kant entertained the theoretical

possibility of events deemed miraculous. But he insisted on judging them in the light of moral principles. He reserved the right of the scientist to seek explanations in terms of natural laws, "even though he must renounce knowledge of what it is in itself that works according to these laws, or what it might be for us if we had, possibly, another sense" (ibid., p. 82). "Sensible men, while not disposed to renounce belief in them, never want to allow such belief to appear in practice" (ibid., p. 80).

37. Ibid., p. 58.

38. Ibid., p. 59.

39. Ibid., p. 78; cf. pp. 119, 125, 146–51.

40. In a lengthy footnote Kant attributed the idea of a virgin birth to the need to explain how a person could be free from man's innate disposition to evil. Natural generation is always tainted by sinful pleasure. But to exclude the possibility of inheriting evil, one would have to exclude the mother's part in conception. "Yet of what use is all this theory pro and con when it suffices for practical purposes to place before us as a pattern this idea taken as a symbol of mankind raising itself above temptation to evil (and withstanding it victoriously)?" (ibid., p. 75).

41. Ibid., p. 76. Carl Friedrich Bahrdt (1741–92) discussed the authority of Jesus from a rationalist, philosophical standpoint in his *System der moralischen Religion zur endlichen Beruhigung für Zweifler und Denker* (Berlin, 1787). On Bahrdt see below, chap. 9.

42. Ibid., p. 77.

43. Ibid., pp. 108–9.

44. Ibid., p. 145.

45. Ibid., p. 146.

46. Ibid., pp. 146–47.

47. Ibid., p. 148; cf. Matt. 22:34–40; Mark 12:28–34; Luke 10:25–28.

48. Ibid., pp. 105–14.

49. Ibid., p. 115. In an earlier article, "Idee zu einer allgemeinen Geschichte in weltbürgerlicher Absicht" (*Berlinische Monatsschrift*, November 1784, 4:385–411; *GS*, 8:15–31), Kant saw world history as the eventual triumph of rationality and morality. But in *Die Religion* he contented himself with reflections "Concerning Service and Pseudo-Service under the Sovereignty of the Good Principle, or, Concerning Religion and Clericalism" (pp. 139–90). Discussions of Kant's views on history include R. G. Collingwood, *The Idea of History*, pp. 93–104; Michel Despland, *Kant on History and Religion, With a Translation of Kant's "On the Failure of all Attempted Philosophical Theodicies"* (Montreal and London: McGill-Queen's University Press, 1973; G. E. Michalson, Jr., *The Historical Dimensions of a Rational Faith: The Role of History in Kant's Religious Thought* (Washington, D.C.: University Press of America, 1979); Yirmiahu Yovel, *Kant and the Philosophy of History* (Princeton: Princeton University Press, 1980).

50. In obedience to Wöllner's edict, Kant obtained approval from the official censor for the publication of the first of the four books of *Die Religion* in 1791. It appeared in the April 1792 issue of the *Berlinische Monatsschrift*. But the second book failed to pass the Berlin censor because it controverted the teachings of the Bible. However, Kant submitted it together with the remaining books to the philosophical faculty at Jena, which together with other universities had the right to authorize publication, and the whole work was duly published. On the circumstances see G. Wobbermin in *GS*, 6:497–501 and Theodore M. Greene, op. cit., pp. xxxii-xxxvii.

51. Letter dated October 1, 1794, signed *ad Mandatum* by Wöllner (*GS*, 11:525–26, no. 640).

52. Kant replied to the King in a letter dated October 12, 1794 (*GS*, 11:527–30, no. 642). The correspondence was reprinted in the preface to *Der Streit der Fakultäten* (1798; *GS*, 7:316ff.). Here Kant claimed that he was writing for scholars. He intended no disrespect for the Christian religion but sought to exhibit the "Vernunftreligion" which underlies all true religion. He concluded with a promise to make no further pronouncements on revealed and natural religion. However, a second edition of the book was published at Neuwied in 1793 and a third at Frankfurt and Leipzig in 1794. An abbreviated version *Kants Theorie der rein moralischen Religion mit Rücksicht auf das reine Christentum. Kurz dargestellt* was published at Riga in 1796.

53. *The Life of Jesus Critically Examined*, ed. Peter C. Hodgson (Philadelphia: Fortress Press, 1972), pp. 50–52.

54. Julius Kaftan, *Die Religionsphilosophie Kants in ihre Bedeutung für die Apologetik* (1874); Friedrich Paulsen, *Kant, der Philosoph des Protestantismus* (1899); cf. Werner Schultz, *Kant als*

Philosoph des Protestantismus, Theologische Forschung 22 (Hamburg-Bergstedt: Herbert Reich, 1961), pp. 19–20.

55. Cf. Paul Wrzecionko, *Die philosophische Wurzeln der Theologie Albrecht Ritschls. Ein Beitrag zum Problem des Verhältnisses von Theologie und Philosophie im 19. Jahrhundert, Theologische Bibliothek* 9 (Berlin: Verlag Alfred Töpelmann, 1964).

56. *Critique of Pure Reason*, p. 668.

57. Herder's *Sämtliche Werke* were published by his widow, M. C. von Herder, in 45 volumes (1805–20). But this and other collections were superseded by the critical edition of Bernhard Suphan, *Herders Sämtliche Werke*, 33 volumes (Berlin: Weidmann, 1877–1913), to which reference is made below. Important studies include Rudolf Haym, *Herder*, 2 volumes (Leipzig, 1880–85; reprint ed., Berlin: Aufbau Verlag, 1954); August Werner, *Herder als Theolog. Ein Beitrag zur Geschichte der protestantischen Theologie* (Berlin, 1871); Alexander Gillies, *Herder* (Oxford: Blackwell, 1945); G. A. Wells, *Herder and After: A Study of the Development of Sociology* ('S-Gravenhage: Mouton, 1959); Robert T. Clark, Jr., *Herder: His Life and Thought* (Berkeley and Los Angeles: University of California Press, 1955); E. Fülling, *Geschichte als Offenbarung. Studien zur Frage Historismus und Glaube von Herder bis Troeltsch* (Berlin: Töpelmann, 1956).

58. *Quest*, pp. 27–34.

59. *PT*, p. 339.

60. *EB*, 11:482. Kant introduced Herder to Rousseau and the British empiricists (cf. R. T. Clark, op. cit., 46). Herder's enthusiasm for the influence of British thinkers is attested by the following comment: "Has it profited or injured Germany that Spalding, Felix Hess, Sack, Bamberger and others have made us acquainted with Foster and Shaftesbury, Butler and Law, Beson and Locke? At first it was all the cry, 'Naturalism! Deism! Arians! Socinians!' Christianity will sink if the translators are not steered with firmness! The outcome has shown otherwise" (*SW*, 11:205).

Hamann's religious immediacy and Spinoza's pantheism proved to be more influential than Kant's critical philosophy. Among Herder's last works were two attacks on Kant, *Metakritik zur Kritik der reinen Vernunft* (1799) and *Kalligone* (1800). In a letter to Herder dated May 10, 1781, Hamann described Kant as "a Prussian Hume" whose "enthusiasm for the intellectual world beyond space and time is worse than Plato's." Kant had made "a new leap from Locke's *tabula rasa* to *formas et matrices innatas*" (cf. Ronald Gregor Smith, *J. G. Hamann, 1730–1788: A Study in Christian Existence with Selections from his Writings* [London: Collins, 1960], p. 244.)

61. Cf. R. Haym, op. cit., 1:196; 2:222; G. A. Wells, op. cit., p. 14.

62. The work was the fruit of more than twenty years of study. In the preface Herder claimed to have read pretty well everything that had been written on the subject (*SW*, 13:5). Suphan claimed that what *Faust* was to Goethe the *Ideen* were to Herder (*SW*, 14:653). It was published in four parts. Ill health prevented a fifth part. Herder's republican sympathies antagonized the Weimar court, but he himself was horrified by the bloodshed of the French Revolution. Moreover, the increasing popularity of Kant's transcendentalism tended to isolate him. This was aggravated by the attitude of the theological students whom he examined in the course of his duties as Generalsuperintendent. He found himself confronted by young upstarts who "postulated" a God out of their own freedom or consciousness with a grimace as if they had created him themselves (Haym, op. cit., 2:703). At first he directed his polemic against Kant's disciples. Instead of treating the existence of God as a postulate of pure practical reason, Herder sought to base belief on history.

The *Ideen* were translated by T. O. Churchill with the title *Outlines of a Philosophy of the History of Man*, 2 volumes (London, 1803). However, references below are to Suphan's text in the present writer's translation.

Kant wrote several negative reviews of Herder's works which have been translated in Immanuel Kant, *On History*, ed. Lewis White Beck (Indianapolis and New York: Bobbs-Merrill, 1963), pp. 27–52.

63. *Ideen*, 3, 12, 6 (*SW*, 14:83); cf. 1, 2, 3 (*SW*, 12:62).

64. Cf. Letter 47 in *Briefe das Studium der Theologie betreffend* (*SW*, 11:73–83) and *Vom Geist der Ebräischen Poesie. Eine Anleitung für die Liebhaber derselben und der ältesten Geschichte des menschlichen Geistes* (1783; *SW*, 11 and 12). These contained Herder's views on picture language, personification, fable, saga and poetry. He returned to the theme in the *Ideen*, 3, 12, 3 (*SW*, 14:58–67).

65. Eng. trans. *God, Some Conversations, A Translation with a Critical Introduction and Notes*

by Frederick H. Burkhardt (New York: Hafner Publishing Company, 1949). On the background see also A. C. M'Giffert, "The God of Spinoza as Interpreted by Herder," *The Hibbert Journal* 3 (1904–5):706–26; R. T. Clark, op. cit., pp. 339–47.

66. Op. cit., Eng. trans., p. 96; cf. Spinoza, *Ethica*, vol. 1, Definitions 3 and 5.

67. Ibid., pp. 97–98.

68. Ibid., pp. 98–99.

69. Ibid., p. 26.

70. Ibid., pp. 102–3.

71. On the background of these works see R. T. Clark, op. cit., pp. 384–412. The first collection of *Christliche Schriften* (1794) contained essays on subjects which had figured in the Fragments controversy: *Von der Gabe der Sprachen am ersten christlichen Pfingstfest* and *Von der Auferstehung, als Glauben, Geschichte und Lehre*. The fourth and fifth collections were entitled *Vom Geist des Christenthums. Nebst einigen Abhändlungen verwandten Inhalts* (1798) and *Von Religion, Lehrmeinungen und Gebräuchen* (1798).

72. Op. cit., 1, 2 (*SW*, 19:139); cf. Rudolf Bultmann, "New Testament and Mythology" in *Kerygma and Myth*, ed. H.-W. Bartsch, Volumes 1 and 2 combined (London: S.P.C.K., 1972), pp. 1–44.

73. Ibid., 1, 11 (*SW*, 19:143).

74. Ibid., 1, 12 (*SW*, 19:143).

75. Ibid., 1, 5 (*SW*, 19:140).

76. Ibid., 1, 8 (*SW*, 19:141–42).

77. Ibid., 1, 9–10 (*SW*, 19:142–43).

78. Ibid., 4, 4–5 (*SW*, 19:195–96).

79. *Regel*, 1, 5 (*SW*, 19:382).

80. *Von Gottes Sohn*, 1, 16 (*SW*, 19:272).

81. *Vom Erlöser der Menschen*, 4, 18 (*SW*, 19:213–14); cf. *Regel*, 3, 15 (*SW*, 19:417).

82. Kümmel, p. 82.

83. Herder and F. A. Wolf (1759–1824) were acquainted. Weimar and Halle, where Wolf taught philology, were only a day's journey apart. The celebrated *Prolegomena* argued that Homer was not a single historical author and that the work attributed to him was the product of oral tradition. Having eagerly awaited and read Wolf's work, Herder published an article of his own on "Homer, ein Günstling der Zeit." Wolf accused Herder of plagiarism, but Herder claimed that the points at issue had been already widely accepted since Blackwell and Wood (Letter to Heyne, May 13, 1795; cf. R. Haym, op. cit., 2:647). Herder's own ideas went at least as far back as an unpublished essay on Homer and Ossian dating from 1775. Goethe, Schiller and Humboldt all stood by Herder in the controversy (see further, R. T. Clark, op. cit., pp. 375ff.).

84. *Von Gottes Sohn*, 3, 1 (*SW*, 19:305–6).

85. Ibid., 5, 55 (*SW*, 19:378–79).

86. Ibid., 5, 56 (*SW*, 19:379).

87. *SW*, 20:95.

88. Op. cit., 5, 4 (*SW*, 19:248–49).

89. Ibid., 5, 4 (*SW*, 19:239).

90. Ibid.; cf. Adolf Harnack, *What is Christianity?* (New York: G. P. Putnam's Sons, 1901), pp. 51, 144.

91. Ibid., 5, 4 (*SW*, 19:240).

92. Ibid., 5, 4 (*SW*, 19:242).

93. Ibid., 5, 4 (*SW*, 19:250).

94. Preface to the 13th edition in *The Life of Jesus* (London: Mathieson and Company, no date), p. xxii.

95. *SW*, 11:7.

96. *Logik*, 2:2 (Stuttgart, 1895), p. 423. G. A. Wells observes that "German intellectual activity between 1790 and 1850 was confined almost entirely to university circles, and university scholars were indifferent to Herder's work because it was that of a non-academic" (op. cit., p. 149). In 1832 F. C. von Savigny noted that "in no other nation does such an important section of intellectual activity fall to the lot of public teachers" ("Wesen und Werth der deutschen Universitäten," *Vermischte Schriften* [Berlin, 1850], 4:284). Mark Pattison commented on Herder's response to Wolf that "Herder

might possess the ear of the public, but among the learned he counted for nothing" (*Essays* [Oxford: Oxford University Press], 1:387).

97. *Quest*, p. 36.

98. For a brief survey and literature see F. Götting in RGG[3], vol. 2, columns 1668–75. His thought has been examined at length in relation to the literature of his day by H. A. Korff in *Geist der Goethezeit*, 5 volumes (Leipzig: Koehler & Amelang; reprint ed., 1964). His theology is discussed by Hirsch, 5:247–71. Studies of his religious views include Karl Aner, *Goethes Religiosität* (Tübingen: J. C. B. Mohr, 1910); Heinrich Hoffmann, *Goethes Religion* (Bern: P. Haupt, 1940); and in more detail Peter Meinhold, *Goethe zur Geschichte des Christentum, Deutsche Klassik und Christentum* (Freiburg and Munich: Verlag Karl Alber, 1958). References below are to the Weimar edition of Goethe's *Werke*.

99. H. Hoffmann, op. cit., pp. 3–4; cf. H. A. Korff, op. cit., 4:367–68.

100. In 1773 he wrote an anonymous pamphlet on the two versions of the Decalogue, *Zwo wichtige bisher unerörtete biblische Fragen*. Goethe returned to biblical criticism in his semi-autobiographical *Dichtung und Wahrheit* (1811–33), Book 12.

101. This was in his last months as a student at Leipzig, which terminated in an illness which forced him to return home to Frankfurt in 1770. He was deeply impressed by the pietistic friend of his mother, Susanne Katherine von Klettenberg. Goethe's letters of this time were sprinkled with expressions of evangelical piety: "You were the first person who has preached to me the true gospel." "The Savior has finally snatched me." "My soul is now still, quite still" (cf. H. Hoffmann, op. cit., pp. 5, 29; P. Meinhold, op. cit., pp. 16–18). Goethe visited the Herrnhut community at Marienborn, near Frankfurt, and even considered joining them. But as Fräulein von Klettenberg constantly found, Goethe was never a true pietist.

102. Op. cit., p. 9.

103. *Ueber den Granit* (1784; *Werke*, 2, 9, p. 174).

104. Letter to F. H. Jacobi, June 9, 1785 (*Werke*, 4, 7, pp. 63–64).

105. Cf. Hoffmann, op. cit., p. 9.

106. A recent evaluation of Herder's influence is given by Walter Kaufmann, *Discovering the Mind*, vol. 1, *Goethe, Kant, Hegel* (New York: McGraw Hill, 1980), pp. 59–64. Herder's influence on Goethe was at its greatest in his earlier period (cf. Haym, op. cit., 2:197–207). Kaufmann argues that "it was Goethe and not Herder who exerted the decisive anti-Kantian influence on subsequent German thought" (op. cit., p. 62). He suggests that Lessing may have had a decisive influence on Goethe's *Faust* (ibid., pp. 65–69).

107. Revue of Vaucher, *Histoire physiologique des Plantes* (cf. Hoffmann, op. cit., pp. 12, 30).

108. Letter to Jacobi, May 5, 1786 (*Werke*, 4, 7, p. 214). Earlier he declared to Jacobi, "He does not prove the Being of God, Being *is* God. And if for this reason others scold Spinoza for being an atheist, I should like to name him and praise him as *theissimum*, indeed, *christianissimum*" (letter, June 9, 1785, ibid., p. 62). On Goethe and Spinoza see H. A. Korff, op. cit., 2:21–31; Werner Danckert, *Goethe. Der mystische Urgrund seiner Weltschau* (Berlin: W. de Gruyter, 1951), pp. 455–59; Kurt Weinberg, "Pantheismusstreit," *EP*, 6:35–37.

109. *Parilipomena I zu Goethes naturwissenschaftlichen Schriften* (*Werke*, 2, 11, p. 374; cf. p. 163).

110. *Dichtung und Wahrheit* (*Werke* 1, 26, p. 320; cf. Hoffmann, op. cit. pp. 16–17).

111. Op. cit., p. 17.

112. *Zahme Xenien*, 7. Reihe. For Goethe's attitude to the church see P. Meinhold, op. cit., pp. 43–109, 233–82.

113. "Mysteries are still no wonders" (*Maximen und Reflexionen*, no. 210, p. 36).

114. Letter dated August 9, 1782 (*Werke*, 4, 6, pp. 35–38). The tension between the eternal laws by which man completes his course and his moral freedom is graphically expressed in the poem *Das Göttliche*.

115. *Venetianische Epigramme* (1790), 66 (*Werke*, 1, 1, p. 323).

116. Ibid., 79 (*Werke*, 1, 1, p. 325).

117. *Nachlass*, 11 (*Werke*, 1, 53, p. 10).

118. Letter dated September 4, 1788, expressing Goethe's appreciation of Herder's *Ideen* (*Werke* 4, 9, p. 18).

119. *Italienische Reise*, October 12, 1787 (*Werke*, 1, 32, p. 110).

120. *Werke*, 1, 6, p. 288.

121. Similar pronouncements are noted by W. Danckert, op. cit., p. 418. In the *Brief des Pastors zu* *** (1773) he wrote, "For since God became man, so that we poor sensuous creatures may grasp and understand him, one must guard against nothing more than making him into God again." In conversation with F. W. Riemer on October 19, 1823, he observed that, "The doctrine of the divinity of Christ, first decreed by the Council of Nicea, was very useful to despotism, indeed it was a necessity." In 1830 he confessed to Kanzler Müller, "To me Christ always remains a highly significant, but problematic being."

122. *Werke*, 1, 14, pp. 62–63; translation of Anna Swanwick, in Kuno Francke, ed., *The German Classics* (New York: German Publication Society, 1913), 1:288.

123. Alexander Gillies argues that many of Goethe's ideas here and elsewhere are to be found in Herder (*Goethe's Faust: An Interpretation* [Oxford: Blackwell, 1957], p. 40). This is supported by R. T. Clark, who notes that precedence for this translation is given by Herder's *Buch von der Zunkunft des Herrn des Neuen Testaments Siegel* (1779; op. cit., p. 262). However, in *Vom Gottes Sohn* (*SW*, 19:274, 296) Herder retained "word" as the translation of *logos*. Arnold Ehrhardt sees affinities between Faust's translation and Neo-Pythagoreanism and Orphism (*The Beginning: A Study in the Greek Philosophical Approach to the Concept of Creation* [Manchester: Manchester University Press, 1968], pp. 1–14). Herder had introduced Goethe to Orphism through J. M. Gesner's *Orphica* (1764).

124. *Werke*, 1, 15, p. 337. Part 1 of *Faust* appeared in 1808; Part 2 was completed shortly before the author's death.

125. Conversation on March 11, 1832 (Johann Peter Eckermann, *Gespräche mit Goethe in den letzten Jahren seines Lebens*; cf. *Goethe, Gedenkausgabe der Werke, Briefe und Gespräche*, ed. Ernst Beutler [Zürich: Artemis Verlag, 1949], 24:769–70).

126. Ibid., pp. 770–71.

127. Goethe's description of himself to Lavater (July 29, 1782) remained valid half a century later: "no anti-Christian, no un-Christian, but yet a dedicated non-Christian" (*Werke*, 4, 6, p. 20). But it may be supplemented by the fact that he called himself a "Hypsistarian" (letter to S. Boisserée, March 1831, *Werke*, 4, 48, pp. 155–56; cf. P. Meinhold, op. cit., pp. 278–82). The term derives from the Greek *hypsistos*, "highest." In the 1820s Carl Ullmann and Wilhelm Böhmer published conflicting accounts of this fourth-century sect, which aroused the interest of Goethe and others because of its non-confessional, anti-dogmatic attitude, which united elements of Judaism, Christianity and paganism. They professed to worship God as Father, "All Ruler and Highest."

5. *Absolute Idealism*

1. Cf. H. B. Acton, "Idealism," *EP*, 4:110–18.

2. Fichte's *Sämmtliche Werke*, in eight volumes, were edited by I. H. Fichte (Berlin: Veit, 1845–46), who also produced three volumes of *Nachgelassene Werke* (Bonn: R. Marcus, 1834–35), and two of *Briefwechsel* (Berlin, [1830] 1862). A more critical, but less complete, edition of *Werke* was edited by Fritz Medicus, 6 vols. (Leipzig: Felix Meiner Verlag, 1914; 2nd ed., 1922). A critical edition of *Briefwechsel* was edited by Hans Schulz, 2 vols. (Leipzig: H. Haessel, 1925). For details of reprints and other literature see H. H. Baumgartner and W. Jacobs, eds., *Johann Gottlieb Fichte-Bibliographie in Zusammenarbeit mit der J. G. Fichte-Gesamtausgabe der Bayerischen Akademie der Wissenschaften* (Stuttgart-Bad Canstatt: F. Frommann, 1968). Mention may also be made of Günter Bader, *Mitteilung göttlichen Geistes als Aporie der Religionslehre Johann Gottlieb Fichtes* (Tübingen: J. C. B. Mohr, 1975).

3. The work has been translated by Garret Green, *Attempt at a Critique of all Revelation* (Cambridge: Cambridge University Press, 1975).

4. See below, chapter 9.

5. Cf. *Fichte: Science of Knowledge (Wissenschaftslehre)*, ed. and trans. Peter Heath and John Lachs (New York: Meredith Corporation, 1970), p. 3.

6. *Ueber den Begriff der Wissenschaftslehre oder der sogenannten Philosophie* (Weimar, 1794; 2nd ed., Jena and Leipzig, 1798); *SW*, 1:41f.

7. *Die Thatsachen des Bewusstseyns. Vorlesungen gehalten an der Universität zu Berlin im Winterhalbjahre 1810–11* (1817; *SW*, 2:607).

8. Heath and Lachs, eds., op. cit., p. 110 (cf. *SW*, 1:110).

9. Ibid., pp. 225–26 (*SW*, 1:255).

10. *SW*, 5:403.

11. *SW*, 5:539; cf. *Die Wissenschaftslehre in ihrem allgemeinen Umrisse* (1810; *SW*, 2:696). For Fichte's attitude to Spinoza see, e.g., Heath and Lachs, eds., op. cit., pp. 81, 83, 101–2, 117–19, 146, 226.

12. *Die Thatsachen des Bewusstseyns* (*SW*, 2:685).

13. Ibid. (*SW*, 2:696).

14. *SW*, 5:5.

15. *Die Anweisung zum seligen Leben* (*SW*, 5:475–76).

16. Ibid. (*SW*, 5:476).

17. Ibid. (*SW*, 5:476–77).

18. Ibid. (*SW*, 5:477).

19. Ibid. (*SW*, 5:480).

20. Copleston, 7:88.

21. Op. cit. (*SW*, 5:569). This view may be compared with Fichte's earlier *Attempt at a Critique of All Revelation*, where Jesus is mentioned only in footnotes (pp. 144, 159–60). Fichte's earlier statement was more in line with Kant's purely moral interpretation of Jesus. Fichte spoke of the "maxims" of Jesus. He identified two conditions for faith in revelation: "Namely, that one partly wants to be good and partly needs the representation of a revelation having occurred as a means for producing the good in himself" (p. 159). Fichte's later interpretation encompassed the moral, but could not be reduced to a purely moral interpretation of Jesus as an ethical archetype and teacher.

22. Op. cit. (*SW*, 5:570–72).

23. Ibid. (*SW*, 5:572).

24. Ibid. (*SW*, 5:568).

25. Ibid. (*SW*, 5:569).

26. Heath and Lachs, eds., op. cit., p. 4.

27. "So far as content is concerned, therefore, there are no judgments purely analytic; and by them alone we not only do not get far, as *Kant* says; we do not get anywhere at all. . . . The celebrated question which Kant placed at the head of the *Critique of Pure Reason:* How are synthetic judgments *a priori* possible?—is now answered in the most universal and satisfactory manner. . . . we have established a synthesis between the two opposites, self and not-self, by postulating them each to be divisible; there can be no further question as to the possibility of this, nor can any ground for it be given; it is absolutely possible, and we are entitled to it without further grounds of any kind" (Heath and Lachs, eds., op. cit., p. 112; cf. Kant, *Critique of Pure Reason*, trans. Norman Kemp Smith, Introduction, pp. 48, 55).

28. Schleiermacher was influenced by Fichte, but at the same time presented alternative answers to the questions which Fichte wrestled with (cf. M. Redeker, *Schleiermacher: Life and Thought* [Philadelphia: Fortress Press, 1973], pp. 30, 38, 74–75, 154, 175–76).

29. According to Baur's brother, F. A. Baur, F. C. Baur made a special study of Fichte and Schelling (Letter to E. Zeller, January 12, 1861; cf. Horton Harris, *The Tübingen School* [Oxford: Clarendon Press], p. 144; cf. also pp. 16, 169).

30. Cf. Paul Tillich, *On the Boundary: An Autobiographical Sketch* (New York: Scribner's, 1966), pp. 46–47, where Tillich describes the Fichte renaissance under his mentor, Fritz Medicus, and his own debt to Fichte and Schelling.

31. For a survey of Hegel's thought and relevant literature see H. B. Acton, "Hegel," *EP,* 3:435–51. The older edition of Hegel's *Sämtliche Werke. Jubiläumsausgabe*, ed. Hermann Glockner, 26 vols. (Stuttgart: F. Frommann, 1927–39; reprint ed., 1957–68), was based on the collected posthumous edition of his works compiled by colleagues and pupils (Berlin, 1832–40). A critical edition incorporating unpublished material was begun by G. Lasson in 1905 and continued by Johannes Hoffmeister and others with the title *Sämtliche Werke, Neue Kritische Ausgabe* (Hamburg: F. Meiner, 1952–). English translations are noted below.

Studies relevant to the present inquiry include E. Brito, *Hegel et la tâche actuelle de la christologie* (Paris: Éditions Lethielleux, 1979); idem, *La christologie de Hegel: Verbum Crucis* (Paris: Beauchesne, 1983); A. Chapelle, *Hegel et la Religion*, 3 vols. (Paris: Éditions Universitaires,

1963–67; A. Chapelle, A. Leonard, C. Bruaire, L. Rumpf et al., *Hegel et la théologie contemporaine* (Paris: Delachaux et Niestlé, 1977); S. Crites, *In the Twilight of Christendom: Hegel vs. Kierkegaard on Faith and History.* American Academy of Religion Studies in Religion, 2, (Chambersburg, Pa.: American Academy of Religion, 1972); Emil L. Fackenheim, *The Religious Dimension in Hegel's Thought* (Bloomington and London: Indiana University Press, 1967); J. N. Findlay, *Hegel: A Re-examination* (London: Allen & Unwin, 1958); Hayo Gerdes, *Das Christusbild Sören Kierkegaards. Verglichen mit der Christologies Hegels und Schleiermachers* (Düsseldorf-Cologne: Eugen Diderichs Verlag, 1960); H. S. Harris, *Hegel's Development*, vol. 1: *Toward the Sunlight, 1770–1801;* vol. 2: *Night Thoughts, Jena, 1801–1806* (Oxford: Clarendon Press, 1972, 1983); M. J. Inwood, *Hegel,* (London: Routledge and Kegan Paul, 1983); W. Kaufmann, *Hegel: Reinterpretation, Texts and Commentary* (London: Weidenfeld & Nicolson, 1966); Quentin Lauer, *Hegel's Concept of God* (Albany: State University of New York Press, 1982); Karl Löwith, *From Hegel to Nietzsche: The Revolution in Nineteenth-Century Thought* (New York: Holt, Rinehart and Winston, 1964); A. MacIntyre, ed., *Hegel: A Collection of Essays* (Notre Dame and London: University of Notre Dame Press, 1976); M. J. Petry, *Hegel's Philosophy of Objective Spirit*, 3 vols. (Dordrecht: D. Reidel Publishing Company, 1978; B. M. G. Reardon, *Hegel's Philosophy of Religion* (London: Macmillan, 1977); Leroy S. Rouner, ed., *Meaning, Truth and God*, Boston University Studies in Philosophy and Religion, no. 3 (Notre Dame and London: University of Notre Dame Press, 1982); Erik Schmidt, *Hegels Lehre von Gott* (Gütersloh: Gütersloher Verlagshaus, 1952); idem, *Hegels System der Theologie* (Berlin: Walter de Gruyter, 1974); Jörg Splett, *Die Trinitätslehre G. W. F. Hegels, Symposion* 20 (Freiburg-Munich: Verlag Karl Alber, 1965); Charles Taylor, *Hegel* (Cambridge: Cambridge University Press, 1975); James Yerkes, *The Christology of Hegel*, American Academy of Religion Dissertation Series, no. 23 (Missoula: Scholars Press, 1978); R. K. Williamson, *Introduction to Hegel's Philosophy of Religion* (Albany: State University of New York Press, 1984). See also Kurt Steinhauer and Gitta Hansen, *Hegel: Bibliography—Bibliographie* (Munich: K. G. Saur Verlag, 1980).

32. (Tübingen: J. C. B. Mohr, 1970); partial Eng. trans., *On Christianity: Early Theological Writings*, trans. T. M. Knox, with an introduction and fragments trans. by Richard Kroner (Chicago: Chicago University Press, 1948; reprint ed., New York: Harper Torchbook, 1961). Other early fragments are given by H. S Harris, op. cit., pp. 481–516, who also gives a comprehensive list of Hegel's early works (pp. 517–27). New German editions of Hegel's early writings include E. Moldenhauer and K. M. Michel, eds., *Werke*, 1, *Frühschriften* (Frankfurt: Suhrkamp Verlag, 1971) and W. Hamacher, ed., *"Der Geist des Christentums:" Schriften 1796–1800, Mit Bislang unveröffent-lichten Texten* (Frankfurt, Berlin, Vienna: Ullstein Verlag, 1978).

33. Op. cit., I p. 103. Hölderlin adopted the phrase as a motto. It was inscribed in an album presented to Hegel by friends at the end of February, 1791. Hegel was already reading Spinoza and the controversial writings about him. Despite the tendency of scholars to associate the phrase with Holderlin rather than Hegel, Harris thinks that it aptly describes Hegel's understanding of natural science and his hopes for universal liberty, equality and fraternity following the French Revolution. Harris's work presents a detailed account of Hegel's studies and interests at this period.

34. Eng. trans. by H. S. Harris and Walter Cerf, *The Difference between Fichte's and Schelling's System of Philosophy* (Albany: State University of New York Press, 1977).

35. The translation used below is that of A. V. Miller with an analysis and foreword by J. N. Findlay, *Phenomenology of Spirit* (Oxford: Oxford University Press, 1977).

36. Eng. trans. by E. B. Spiers and J. B. Sanderson, *Lectures on the Philosophy of Religion* (1895; reprint ed., London: Routledge and Kegan Paul; New York: Humanities Press, 1962). The lectures dealing with Christianity have been edited and translated by Peter C. Hodgson from the critical edition of Georg Lasson, *The Christian Religion: Lectures on the Philosophy of Religion, Part III. The Revelatory, Consummate, Absolute Religion*, American Adacemy of Religion Texts and Translations Series, no. 2 (Missoula: Scholars Press, 1979). A critical edition is in preparation. To date only the first volume has been published: *Lectures on the Philosophy of Religion*, 1, *Introduction and The Concept of Religion*, ed. P. C. Hodgson, trans. F. Brown, P. C. Hodgson and J. M. Stewart, (Berkeley, Los Angeles, London: University of California Press, 1984). Hodgson has reviewed the shifts in Hegel's views in "Hegel's Christology: Shifting Nuances in the Berlin Lectures" in *American Academy of Religion: The Currents in Contemporary Christology Newsletter* 4/5 (1984): 1–12.

37. Eng. trans. by E. S. Haldane and E. H. Simson, *Lectures on the History of Philosophy*, 3 vols. (1892–96; reprint ed., New York: Humanities Press and London: Routledge and Kegan Paul,

1968); cf. Q. Lauer, *Hegel's Idea of Philosophy. With a new Translation of Hegel's Introduction to the History of Philosophy* (New York: Fordham University Press, 1971).

38. Eng. trans. by J. Sibree, *The Philosophy of History* (1857; reprint ed., with an introduction by C. J. Friedrich, New York: Dover Publications, 1956).

39. Cf. H. Nohl, ed., op. cit., pp. v, 402–5; H. S. Harris, op. cit., 1:211–33, 330–99. *Das Leben Jesu* was probably written between May 9 and July 24, 1795. The first two parts of *Die Positivität* were written when Hegel was living at Bern between November 2, 1795 and April 29, 1796. The third part was written at Frankfurt probably between September 14 and 24, 1796. *Der Geist des Christentums* seems to have been written at Frankfurt between 1798 and 1799, and the fragment in 1800.

40. Introduction to *On Christianity*, pp. 4–5.

41. Text in H. Nohl, ed., op. cit., pp. 73–136. Knox omitted to translate this work on the grounds that "it is little more than a forced attempt to depict Jesus as a teacher of what is in substance Kant's ethics" (op. cit., p. v.). See further above, chap. 4, n. 30. It is included, however, in G. W. F. Hegel, *Three Essays: The Tübingen Essay, Berne Fragments, The Life of Jesus*, edited and translated with introduction and notes by Peter Fuss and John Dobbins, Notre Dame: University of Notre Dame Press, 1984. Unfortuunately this work appeared when the present study was already in press.

42. H. Nohl, ed., op. cit., p. 75.

43. Ibid., p. 87.

44. Hegel's acquaintance with Lessing, especially his *Nathan*, is demonstrated by various allusions and quotations (op. cit., pp. 156, 170, 183, 190, 218, 175; cf. Eng. tr., pp. 72, 92, 107, 116, 150, 175).

45. H. Nohl, op. cit., p. 87; cf. *The Magic Flute*, libretto by Emanuel Schikaneder, music by Wolfgang Amadeus Mozart. It was first performed in Vienna on September 30, 1791. The central theme of Act II is the testing of the virtues of Tamino and Pamina by various trials to see whether they are fit to enter the Temple of Wisdom. The work was an allegory of Freemasonry and its rituals. Its ideals were extolled by Lessing in *Ernst und Falk*. Both Freemasonry and Lessing's work attracted Hegel at this time (cf. H. S. Harris, op. cit., 1:105, 114, 156, 244). Hegel enjoyed Mozart. A letter from his Frankfurt period records his visit to the opera to hear *The Magic Flute* (Letter 23, *Briefe* 1:52; cf. Harris, op. cit., I p. 262). Hegel could well have been familiar with the opera before that date.

46. Ibid., p. 97.

47. *On Christianity*, p. 68.

48. Ibid., p. 69.

49. Ibid., p. 75.

50. Ibid., pp. 75–76.

51. Ibid., p. 77.

52. Ibid., pp. 71, 78–79; 165–66; cf. H. S. Harris, op. cit., 1:94, 199–203, 226–27, 376–78.

53. Ibid., p. 85.

54. Ibid., pp. 82–84.

55. Ibid., p. 82. Over half a century later J. R. Seeley made the same comparison in *Ecce Homo* (1865), but drew the opposite conclusion. Jesus' strength lay precisely in his power to enthuse men to lead moral lives (chap. 9). Kierkegaard's comparison of Christ and Socrates is discussed below in chapter 8.

56. Ibid., pp. 162–63.

57. Ibid., p. 8.

58. Ibid., p. 187.

59. Ibid., p. 205.

60. Ibid., pp. 206–7.

61. Ibid., p. 209; cf. p. 191.

62. Ibid., p. 225.

63. Ibid., p. 239.

64. Ibid., p. 260. This follows an exposition of John 1:1–14.

65. Ibid., p. 266; cf. p. 268. Hegel saw this point exemplified in Matt. 16:13–17; John 6:29, 65; 7:38–39; 12:36. It was symbolized by the rite of baptism (ibid., p. 275).

66. Ibid., pp. 281–82.

67. Ibid., p. 282; cf. H. Nohl, ed., op. cit., p. 325.

68. Ibid., pp. 285–86.

69. Ibid., p. 288.

70. Ibid., p. 290.

71. Ibid., p. 291.

72. Ibid., p. 292.

73. Ibid., p. 301.

74. Op. cit., p. 64.

75. Cf. Paul Tillich, *Systematic Theology* (Chicago: University of Chicago Press, 1951), 1:163–210; (1957), 2:161–80.

76. *Enzyklopädie*, no. 33 (*SW,* 6:46).

77. Cf. Richard Kroner, *Von Kant bis Hegel*, 2nd ed. (Tübingen: J. C. B. Mohr, 1961), 1:16.

78. *Enzyklopädie*, no. 161 (*SW,* 6:128).

79. *Enzyklopädie*, no. 162 (*SW,* 6:130).

80. *Phenomenology of Spirit*, p. 14.

81. Op. cit., p. 70.

82. *The Christian Religion*, pp. 2–4.

83. Ibid., p. 10.

84. See above, n. 31.

85. Ibid., p. 11.

86. Ibid., p. 82.

87. *Lectures on the Philosophy of Religion*, 1:146.

88. Ibid., pp. 142–43; cf. Paul Ricoeur, "The Status of *Vorstellung* in Hegel's Philosophy of Religion," in L. S. Rouner, ed., op. cit., pp. 70–88; and J. N. Findlay, "Hegel as Theologian," ibid., pp. 177–96.

89. *The Christian Religion*, p. 190.

90. Ibid., p. 181.

91. Ibid., pp. 193, 215–16.

92. Ibid., p. 212.

93. *Phenomenology of Spirit*, p. 476.

94. In his *Siebenkäs* (1796–97) the Romantic poet Jean Paul gives a discourse by the dead Christ on the loneliness and meaninglessness of the world without God. In *Die fröhliche Wissenschaft* (1882) Nietzsche explored the nihilistic, existential consequences of the death of belief in God which left man free to devise his moral values and destiny (cf. *The Joyful Wisdom*, no. 343). See further R. Bultmann, "The Idea of God and Modern Man," in R. Gregor Smith, ed., *World Come of Age: A Symposium on Dietrich Bonhoeffer* (London: Collins, 1967), pp. 256–73; Christian Link, *Hegels Wort "Gott selbst ist tot"*, *Theologische Studien* 114 (Zürich: Theologischer Verlag, 1974).

95. *The Gospel of Christian Atheism* (London: Collins, 1967), pp. 110–11.

96. *PT*, p. 391.

97. Op. cit., p. 493.

98. Ibid.

99. Cf. F. C. Copleston, "Hegel and the Rationalisation of Mysticism," in *Talk of God, Royal Institute of Philosophy Lectures, II, 1967–1968* (London: Macmillan and New York: St. Martin's Press, 1969), pp. 118–132; James Yerkes, op. cit., p. 309.

100. *Critique of Pure Reason*, trans. Norman Kemp Smith, p. 507.

101. The response to Hegel by Schleiermacher, Feuerbach, Kierkegaard, Strauss, F. C. Baur, Bruno Bauer, and others will be examined below. For contemporary views of Hegel see the anthology edited by Günther Nicolin, *Hegel in Berichten seiner Zeitgenossen* (Hamburg: Felix Meiner Verlag, 1970).

102. Schelling's *Sämmtliche Werke* were edited by K. F. A. Schelling, *Erste Abteilung*, 10 vols., *Zweite Abteilung*, 4 vols. (Stuttgart and Augsburg: J. G. Cotta'scher Verlag, 1856–61). His *Werke, Nach Original-Ausgabe in neuer Anordnung* were edited by M. Schroter, 8 vols. (Munich: C. H. Beck, 1927–59). Studies include J. Watson, *Schelling's Transcendental Idealism: A Critical Exposition* (Chicago: S. C. Griggs, 1892); Robert F. Brown, *The Later Philosophy of Schelling: The Influence of Boehme on the Works of 1809–1815* (Lewisburg: Bucknell University Press and London:Associated University Press, 1977); Thomas F. O'Meara, *Romantic Idealism and Roman Catholicism: Schelling and the Theologians* (Notre Dame and London: University of Notre Dame Press, 1982); P. C. Hayner, *Reason and Existence: Schelling's Philosophy of History* (Leiden: E. J. Brill, 1967); Horst Fuhrmans, *Schellings letzte Philosophie* (Berlin: Junker and Dünnhaupt Verlag,

1940); idem., *Schellings Philosophie der Weltalter* (Düsseldorf: L. Schwann, 1954); Walter Schulz, *Die Vollendung des deutschen Idealismus in der Spätphilosophie Schellings* (Stuttgart: Kohlhammer Verlag, 1955); Xavier Tilliette, *Schelling, Une Philosophie en Devenir*, 2 vols. (Paris: J. Vrin, 1970); Paul Tillich, *Mysticism and Guilt-Consciousness in Schelling's Philosophical Development* (Lewisburg: Bucknell University Press; London: Associated University Presses, 1974); and Alan White, *Schelling: An Introduction to the System of Freedom* (New Haven and London: Yale University Press, 1983). For further writings see Guido Schneeberger, *Friedrich Wilhelm Joseph von Schelling. Eine Bibliographie* (Bern: Francke Verlag, 1954).

103. *Either/Or* (Princeton: Princeton University Press, 1944; reprint ed., 1971), 1:31; cf. W. Lowrie, *Kierkegaard*, rev. ed. (New York: Harper & Brothers, 1962), 1:234.

104. Walter Kaufmann, *Hegel*, p. 64.

105. *Darstellung meines Systems der Philosophie* (*SW*, 1, 4, p. 113).

106. Ibid., pp. 114–15, 117–18, 129.

107. *Critique of Pure Reason*, Introduction, pp. 48–55.

108. Cf. Schelling's *System of Transcendental Idealism (1800)*, trans. Peter Heath, with an Introduction by Michael Vater (Charlottesville: University of Virginia Press, 1978); *Philosophie und Religion* (*SW*, 1, 6, p. 21); *Philosophie Untersuchungen* (*SW*, 1, 7, pp. 358–89); *Bruno Or On the Natural and the Divine Principle of Things (1802)*, edited and translated with an introduction by Michael G. Vater (Albany: State University of New York Press, 1984).

109. *Darlegung* (*SW*, 1, 7, p. 50).

110. *History of the Development of the Doctrine of the Person of Christ*, Eng. trans. P. Fairbairn (Edinburgh: T. & T. Clark, 1863), 2, 3, p. 100.

111. Ibid., pp. 120–21.

112. Ibid., p. 106; cf. Ragnar Holte, *Die Vermittlungstheologie: Ihre theologischen Grundbegriffe kritisch untersucht* (Uppsala: Acta Universitatis Upsaliensis, 1965), p. 122.

113. *SW*, 1, 5, p. 297; cf. p. 304, where Schelling observed that, "The essential in the study of theology is the relation of the speculative and historical construction of Christianity and its principal doctrines."

114. *SW*, 1, 5, p. 294.

115. Copleston, 7:127–29; cf. the similar comment made by Reinhold Niebuhr of Paul Tillich, whose thinking was much indebted to Schelling ("Biblical Thought and Ontological Speculation," in Charles W. Kegley, ed., *The Theology of Paul Tillich*, rev. ed. [New York: Pilgrim Press, 1982], pp. 252–63).

116. *SW*, 1, 7, pp. 377–78, 405–6.

117. *SW*, 1, 7, p. 380.

118. "Description is merely negative and *never* brings the *Absolute itself* in its true being before the soul" (*Philosophie und Religion, SW*, 1, 6, p. 22).

119. *SW*, 1, 6, p. 67.

120. *Philosophie der Offenbarung* (*SW*, 2, 4, p. 3).

121. *SW*, 2, 4, p. 135.

122. *SW*, 2, 4, p. 153.

123. *SW*, 2, 4, p. 172. "Potency denotes the relationship between the objective and the subjective by means of which the Absolute manifests itself."

124. *SW*, 2, 4, p. 201.

125. Cf. *Defensio Fidei Catholicae de Satisfactione Christi* (1617), chap. 5.

126. Ibid.

127. *SW*, 2, 4, p. 202.

128. Dorner's *Entwicklungsgeschichte der Lehre von der Person Christi* first appeared in 1839. The second edition was published in 1845–56. T. F. O'Meara's study (see above, n. 102) indicates Schelling's influence on Catholic thinkers was at its height when Schelling was living in Catholic South Germany. See also, Wayne Leroy Fehr, *The Birth of the Catholic Tübingen School: The Dogmatics of Johann Sebastian Drey*, American Academy of Religion Academy Series, no. 37 (Chico, CA: Scholars Press, 1981).

129. Cf. T. F. O'Meara, op. cit., p. 186.

130. Letter to F. C. Sibbern, December 15, 1841 (Kierkegaard, *Letters and Documents*, trans. H. Rosenmeier, *Kierkegaard's Writings*, vol. 25 [Princeton: Princeton University Press, 1978], no. 55, p. 107).

131. Letter to Emil Boesen, February 6, 1842 (ibid., no. 68, p. 138).
132. Letter to Boesen, February 27, 1842 (ibid., no. 69, p. 139).
133. Letter of February, 1842 (ibid., no. 70, p. 141).
134. *Systematic Theology,* 1:71–79.
135. Ibid., p. 79.

III. NEW PERSPECTIVES ON RELIGION

6. *Schleiermacher and Religious Awareness*

1. *Maximen und Reflexionen*, ed. Max Hecker (Weimar: Goethe Gesellschaft, 1907), no. 899, p. 196.

2. Although Schleiermacher had supported the call of Hegel, the two men enjoyed little rapport at Berlin. Hegel was at the height of his powers and prestige, but was not elected to the Academy until shortly before his death. Hegel stood somewhat aloof from other thinkers, recognizing only Goethe. Moreover, Schleiermacher enjoyed greater popularity in his classes on philosophy than Hegel (cf. Martin Redeker, *Friedrich Schleiermacher. Leben und Werk* [Berlin: Walter de Gruyter, 1968], pp. 268–69, 308–9. The German original of this work gives statistics of class attendances at Schleiermacher's lectures which are omitted from the English translation noted below in note 3).

3. Schleiermacher's *Sämmtliche Werke* were published in three parts: I. *Theologie*, vols. 1–11; II. *Predigten*, vols. 12–21; III. *Philosophie*, vols. 22–31 (Berlin: G. Reimer, 1835–64). A *Kritische Gesamtausgabe*, edited by H.-J. Birkner, G. Ebeling, H. Kimmerle, H. Fischer and K.-V. Selge, is in process of publication. Details of editions and translations are given below in connection with the works discussed. For works prior to 1964, see Terence N. Tice, *Schleiermacher Bibliography. With Brief Introductions, Annotations and Index*, Princeton Pamphlets, no. 12 (Princeton: Princeton Theological Seminary, 1966). In addition note may be made of the following: Karl Barth, *PT*, pp. 425–73; idem., *The Theology of Schleiermacher: Lectures at Göttingen, 1923–24*, ed. Dietrich Ritschl (Grand Rapids: Eerdmans, 1982); Albert L. Blackwell, *Schleiermacher's Early Philosophy of Life: Determinism, Freedom, and Phantasy*, Harvard Theological Studies, no. 33 (Chico, CA: Scholars Press, 1982); Wilfried Brandt, *Der Heilige Geist und die Kirche, SDST* 25 (Zürich-Stuttgart: Zwingli Verlag, 1968); Wilhelm Dilthey, *Leben Schleiermachers*, ed. Martin Redeker, in Dilthey's *Gesammelte Schriften*, XIII/1 and 2, XIV/1 and 2 (Göttingen: Vandenhoeck & Rupprecht, 1966); Robert W. Funk, ed., *Schleiermacher as Contemporary, Journal for Theology and Church*, no. 7 (New York: Herder and Herder, 1970); B. A. Gerrish, *Schleiermacher and the Beginnings of Modern Theology* (Philadelphia: Fortress Press, 1984); Friedrich Hertel, *Das theologischen Denken Schleiermachers untersucht an der ersten Auflage seiner Reden "Über die Religion", SDST* 18 (Zürich-Stuttgart, 1965); Emanuel Hirsch, *Schleiermachers Christusglaube* (Gütersloh: Gütersloher Verlagshaus Gerd Mohn, 1968); Richard R. Niebuhr, *Schleiermacher on Christ and Religion* (New York: Scribners, 1964; London: S.C.M. Press, 1965); Erwin H. U. Quapp, *Christus im Leben Schleiermachers. Vom Herrnhuter zum Spinozisten* (Göttingen: Vandenhoeck & Rupprecht, 1972); Martin Redeker, *Schleiermacher: Life and Thought* (Philadelphia: Fortress Press, 1973); Gerhard Spiegler, *The Eternal Covenant: Schleiermacher's Experiment in Cultural Theology* (New York: Harper & Row, 1967); Robert Stalder, *Grundlinien der Theologie Schleiermachers*, vol. 1: *Zur Fundamentaltheologie* (Wiesbaden: Franz Steiner Verlag, 1969); Stephen Sykes, *Friedrich Schleiermacher* (London: Lutterworth Press; Richmond, VA: John Knox Press, 1971); John E. Thiel, *God and World in Schleiermacher's Dialektik and Glaubenslehre: Criticism and the Methodology of the Dogmatics* (Berne: Peter Lang, 1981); Klaus Eberhard Welker, *Die grundsätzliche Beurteilung der Religionsgeschichte durch Schleiermacher* (Leiden: E. J. Brill, 1965); Robert R. Williams, *Schleiermacher, the Theologian: Construction of the Doctrine of God* (Philadelphia: Fortress Press, 1978).

4. Letter to his friend and publisher, Georg Reimer, April 30, 1802 (L. Jonas and W. Dilthey, eds., *Aus Schleiermachers Leben in Briefen* [Berlin: Reimer, 1860–63; reprint ed., Berlin: Walter de Gruyter, 1976], 1:294–95; Eng. trans. F. Rowan, *The Life of Schleiermacher as Unfolded in his*

Autobiography and Letters [London: Smith, Elder & Co., 1860], p. 284). It should be noted that Rowan's two volumes correspond only to the first two of the four German volumes (1858–63). These early years were the subject of E. R. Meyer's *Schleiermachers und C. G. von Brinkmanns Gang durch die Brüdergemeinde* (Leipzig, 1905).

5. W. Dilthey, "Friedrich Daniel Ernst Schleiermacher," in *Gesammelte Schriften*, 3rd ed. (Göttingen: Vandenhoeck & Rupprecht, 1963), p. 355. In an undated letter probably written in his first term, Schleiermacher's father commended to him Kant's *Kritik der reinen Vernunft* and *Prolegomena* as a safe guide in the boundless desert of transcendental ideas (F. Rowan, op. cit., 1:66).

6. *SW*, 2, 7, pp. 3–12.

7. Cf. Jack Forstman, *A Romantic Triangle: Schleiermacher and Early German Romanticism*, American Academy of Religion Studies in Religion, no. 13 (Missoula: Scholars Press, 1977).

8. The translation cited below is that of John Oman (1893), Schleiermacher, *On Religion: Speeches to its Cultured Despisers*, with an introduction by Rudolf Otto (New York: Harper & Brothers; reprint ed., 1958).

9. Eng. trans. by H. L. Friess, *Soliloquies* (Chicago: Open Court, 1926).

10. *Briefe*, 4:60.

11. Work on the translation occupied Schleiermacher until 1828. In its day it was regarded as the standard German edition.

12. The second edition appeared in 1805 under the author's name. A third edition with "Erläuterungen" appeared in 1821 and a fourth in 1831.

13. *SW*, 1, 2, pp. 221–30.

14. Eng. trans. W. Hastie, *Christmas Eve: A Dialogue on the Celebration of Christmas* (Edinburgh: T. & T. Clark, 1890).

15. Eng. trans. Terence N. Tice, *Brief Outline on the Study Of Theology* (Richmond: John Knox, 1966). On the theology faculty at Berlin, see Walter Elliger, *150 Jahre Theologische Fakultät Berlin: Eine Darstellung ihre Geschichte von 1810 bis 1960* (Berlin: Walter de Gruyter, 1960).

16. Eng. trans. S. MacLean Gilmour, edited with an introduction by Jack V. Verheyden, *The Life of Jesus* (Philadelphia: Fortress Press, 1975).

17. The idea had been cherished since the time of the Great Elector. It was seen by Friedrich Wilhelm III as a bond uniting his Eastern and Western provinces. By an order in cabinet of 1817, he enjoined the "Vereinigung" of the two churches into "a new, lively, Evangelical Christian Church in the Spirit of its holy founder." However, confessional unity was not attained, as was acknowledged by a further order of 1834. For documents, see G. Ruhbach, ed., *Kirchenunionen im 19. Jahrhundert*, 2nd ed., *TKT* 6 (Gütersloh: Gütersloher Verlagshaus Gerd Mohn, 1968); cf. also Walter Elliger et al., *Die Evangelische Kirche der Union. Ihre Vorgeschichte und Geschichte* (Witten: Luther-Verlag, 1967).

18. Eng. trans., ed. H. R. Mackintosh and J. S. Stewart, *The Christian Faith* (Edinburgh: T. & T. Clark, 1928). Since the publication of the English translation, critical editions of the German text have been prepared by Martin Redeker, based upon the second edition, *Der christliche Glaube*, 2 vols., 7th ed. (Berlin: Walter de Gruyter, 1960); and Hermann Peiter, *Der christliche Glaube*, based on the first edition, in three parts as vol. 7 of the *Kritische Gesamtausgabe* (Berlin: Walter de Gruyter, 1980–81).

19. Text in G. Ruhbach, ed., op. cit., p. 35. The passage was omitted from the second edition.

20. Eng. trans. of the latter by James Duke and Francis Fiorenza, *On the Glaubenslehre: Two Letters to Dr. Lücke*, American Academy of Religion Texts and Translations Series, no. 3 (Chico, CA: Scholars Press, 1981).

21. Second Speech, Eng. trans., p. 39.

22. Ibid., p. 101.

23. Ibid., p. 40. In his subsequent "Explanations" Schleiermacher defended himself against the charge of Spinozism, and pointed out that his claim that Spinoza was full of the Holy Spirit should not be taken in a specifically Christian sense (ibid., pp. 104–5). See further, E. H. U. Quapp, op. cit.

24. Ibid., p. 94.

25. Marginal note in Schleirmacher's own handwriting in the first edition of *Das Christliche Glaube*, sec. 8, p. 29 (cf. W. Dilthey, *GS*, XIV/1, pp. v-vi). The English translation of this sentence fails to do justice to the pithiness of the original: "Faith is especially the certainty set in the self-consciousness of what is set along with it."

26. Second Speech, ibid., p. 95.
27. Ibid., p. 40.
28. First Speech, ibid., p. 16.
29. Second Speech, ibid., pp. 89–90.
30. Fifth Speech, ibid., p. 241.
31. Ibid., p. 242.
32. Ibid., p. 246.
33. First Speech, ibid., p. 6.
34. Fifth Speech, ibid., p. 247.
35. Ibid., p. 251.
36. Ibid., p. 248.
37. *Types*, p. 60.
38. Op. cit., p. xii.
39. Op. cit., p. 41.
40. *TC*, p. 147.
41. Barth, *TC*, p. 142; cf. Schleiermacher, *SW*, 1, 1, p. 525; F. Rowan, op. cit., 2:57.
42. *Christmas Eve*, pp. 73–74.
43. Letter to Reimer dated February 10, 1806 (*Briefe*, 4:122; cf. W. Dilthey, *GS*, XIII/2, p. 152). Schleiermacher was an active member of the Berlin Academy of Singing.
44. *SW*, 1, 1, p. 469.
45. *Christmas Eve*, pp. 25–26; cf. pp. 27, 40, where music is linked with the Romantic poetry of Jean Paul and Novalis.
46. Ibid., p. 73.
47. Ibid., p. 9; cf. pp. 12–22, 72.
48. Ibid., p. 54.
49. Ibid., pp. 56–57.
50. Ibid., pp. 57–58.
51. Ibid., p. 58.
52. Ibid., pp. 58–59.
53. Ibid., p. 59.
54. Letter to Henrietta Herz, January 17, 1806 (*Briefe*, 2:50); Barth, *TC*, p. 149.
55. *TC*, p. 149.
56. *Christmas Eve*, p. 60.
57. Ibid., p. 61.
58. Ibid., p. 62.
59. Ibid., p. 73.
60. *GS*, 4:373.
61. Ibid., p. 69.
62. Ibid., pp. 71–72.
63. *SW*, 1, 1, pp. 463f.
64. Barth notes the occurrence of the term in Schleiermacher's first sermon of 1794 (*TC*, p. 139).
65. *The Christian Faith*, Thesis of sec. 3, p. 5.
66. Ibid., pp. 8–9.
67. Ibid., Thesis of sec. 4, p. 12.
68. *History of Christian Doctrine*, 2nd ed. (Edinburgh: T. & T. Clark, 1897), pp. 503ff.
69. The point is brought out by R. Hermann in *RGG*[3], V, col. 1430, who insists that "Gefühl" is not a "Sentiment" but the "Innewerden" or awareness of man as a whole. "Schlechthinnig" (which Schleiermacher acknowledged to be borrowed from F. Delbrück, cf. *Der christliche Glaube*, ed. M. Redeker, 1:23, note) might be translated as "unbedingt" or "unconditioned." See also M. Redeker's edition of Dilthey's *Leben Schleiermachers*, where it is noted that Schleiermacher's meaning was elastic and at times confused (*GS*, XIV/2, pp. 581–83). Schleiermacher himself attempted further clarification in his letter to Dr. Lücke (*On the Glaubenslehre*, pp. 38–46). See further Christel Keller-Wentorf, *Schleiermachers Denken: Die Bewusstseinslehre in Schleiermachers philosophischer Ethik als Schlüssel zu seinem Denken* (Berlin: Walter de Gruyter, 1984).
70. Ibid., Thesis of sec. 32, p. 131.
71. Ibid., Thesis of sec. 33, pp. 133–34.

72. Ibid., Thesis of sec. 34, pp. 137–38.

73. Ibid., Thesis of sec. 19, p. 88; cf. *Brief Outline on the Study of Theology,* nos. 1–31, pp. 19–27.

74. Ibid., Thesis of sec. 30, p. 125.

75. Ibid., Thesis of sec. 50, p. 194. Schleiermacher goes on to say that our sense of absolute dependence points to one of "Absolute Causality" (sec. 51, p. 200), which in turn gives rise to the thought of God's eternity, omnipresence, omnipotence and omniscience (secs. 52–55, pp. 203–28).

76. Ibid., Thesis of sec. 66, p. 271. "Flesh" is subsequently defined as "the totality of the so-called lower powers of the soul" (p. 272).

77. Ibid., p. 271.

78. Ibid., p. 273. In footnotes Schleiermacher found support for his view in Augustine's allusion to the will that turns away from God (*Confessions*, 19). He instanced Johann Gerhard's *Loci Communes Theologici*, 5:2ff. as an example of the contrary view of sin.

79. Ibid., sec. 72, pp. 299–304.

80. Ibid., Thesis of sec. 11, p. 52.

81. Ibid., p. 54.

82. Cf. Irenaeus, *Adversus Haereses*, 3, 18, 6–7; 5, 1, 1, etc.

83. *Cur Deus Homo*, 1, 11ff.

84. Cf. Calvin, *Institutes of the Christian Religion*, 2, 15–17; Luther, *Commentary on St. Paul's Epistle to the Galatians*, ad Gal. 3:10–13.

85. Ibid., p. 54.

86. Ibid., sec. 94, p. 385.

87. Ibid., pp. 387–88.

88. Ibid., sec. 95, p. 389.

89. Cf. secs. 10, Postscript, 55.1, 93, 94.2, 125.1, pp. 47–52, 219–22, 377–85, 386–88, 578–80; W. Dilthey, *GS*, XIV/2, pp. 481–91.

90. Ibid., Thesis of sec. 95, p. 389.

91. Ibid., secs. 96–99, pp. 391–424.

92. Ibid., secs. 100–5, pp. 425–75.

93. Ibid., Thesis of sec. 94, p. 385.

94. Ibid., sec. 95, p. 389.

95. Ibid., p. 390.

96. Ibid., sec. 95, p. 390.

97. Ibid., sec. 96, pp. 392–93.

98. Ibid., p. 394.

99. Ibid., p. 397.

100. For Schleiermacher's discussion of the virgin birth, see sec. 97, pp. 398–413.

101. Ibid., Thesis of sec. 100, p. 425.

102. Ibid., p. 427.

103. Ibid., Thesis of sec. 103, p. 441.

104. Ibid., pp. 446–47.

105. Ibid., p. 449.

106. Ibid., p. 448.

107. Ibid., p. 449.

108. Ibid., sec. 104, p. 460.

109. Ibid., pp. 461–62.

110. Ibid., Thesis of sec. 105, p. 466.

111. Ibid., Thesis of sec. 107, p. 478.

112. Ibid., sec. 99, p. 420; cf. pp. 417–21.

113. Ibid., Thesis of sec. 170, p. 738.

114. Ibid., p. 739.

115. Ibid., pp. 738–39.

116. Ibid., p. 739.

117. Ibid., sec. 172, pp. 747–51; cf. the essay which followed the first edition *Ueber den Gegensatz zwischen der sabellianischen und der athanasianischen Vorstellung von der Trinität* (1822; *SW,* 1, 2, pp. 485–574).

118. Ibid., p. 750.

119. Ibid., p. 751.

120. Cf. Heinz Kimmerle, "Hermeneutical Theory or Ontological Hermeneutics," *Journal for Theology and Church*, no. 4 (New York: Harper & Row, 1967), pp. 107–21.

121. Schleiermacher, *Hermeneutics: The Handwritten Manuscripts*, ed. Heinz Kimmerle, trans. James Duke and Jack Forstman, American Academy of Religion Texts and Translation Series, no. 1 (Missoula: Scholars Press, 1977), p. 9.

122. Ibid., p. 95 (marginal note of 1828).

123. *SW*, 1, 7, p. 157.

124. *SW*, 1, 2, pp. 1–220. Eng. trans. Connop Thirlwall, *A Critical Essay on the Gospel of St. Luke* (London: James Taylor, 1825).

125. Johann Leonhard Hug (1765–1846) was a Catholic biblical scholar who taught at Freiburg. He was an authority on text and canon. His most important work was his *Einleitung in die Schriften des Neuen Testaments* (1808–9; 4th ed., 1847; Eng. trans., 1827 and 1836). Eichhorn's views are discussed below in chapter 9.

126. *SW*, 1, 2, p. 6.

127. *SW*, 1, 2, pp. 7–11.

128. Schleiermacher detected four such blocks which he examined in detail: Luke 1 and 2 (pp. 15–37); Luke 3:1–9:50 (pp. 37–115); Luke 9:51–19:48 (pp. 116–182); Luke 20:1–24:53 (pp. 182–220).

129. *SW*, 1, 2, pp. 219–20.

130. Op. cit., sec. 61 (*SW*, 1, 8, pp. 218–23).

131. Op. cit., sec. 62 (*SW*, 1, 8, p. 219).

132. Op. cit., secs. 64, 67, 68 (*SW*, 1, 8, pp. 230–33, 241–54); cf. also *Ueber die Zeugnisse des Papias von unsern beiden ersten Evangelien* (*ThStKr* 5 [1832]:735–68; reprinted in *SW*, 1, 2, pp. 361–92). Schleiermacher found in Papias's utterances in Eusebius, *H.E.*, 3, 36, 39, confirmation for his fragmentary theory of Gospel origins. What Papias was alluding to were not the Gospels' sources. The *Einleitung* proceeded to examine the life of Jesus under three divisions: the Galilean elements, other elements and the Jerusalem material (pp. 254–315). It then treated John (pp. 315–44).

133. *The Life of Jesus*, p. 37. Schleiermacher first lectured on this in 1819 and repeated his series four times in the next twelve years. He appears to have been the first scholar to give academic lectures on the life of Jesus.

134. Ibid., p. 433.

135. Ibid., p. 43.

136. Eng. trans. Leander E. Keck, *The Christ of Faith and the Jesus of History: A Critique of Schleiermacher's Life of Jesus* (Philadelphia: Fortress Press, 1977). See further, D. Lange, *Historischer Jesus oder mythischer Christus. Untersuchungen zu den Gegensatz zwischen Friedrich Schleiermacher und David Friedrich Strauss* (Gütersloh: Gütersloher Verlagshaus, 1975).

137. Op. cit., pp. 45–74.

138. Ibid., p. 227.

139. Ibid., p. 229.

140. I have discussed this question more fully in *Miracles and the Critical Mind* (Grand Rapids: Eerdmans, 1984).

141. Ibid., pp. 94–95. Cf. D. M. Baillie, *God Was in Christ: An Essay on Incarnation and Atonement* (London: Faber & Faber, 1956), pp. 106–32. Baillie was one of the translators of *The Christian Faith* but he scarcely alluded to Schleiermacher in *God Was in Christ*, perhaps because he was writing at a time when Schleiermacher was out of fashion.

142. Op. cit., p. 62.

143. Op. cit., p. 160.

144. Schleiermacher was aware of problems of chronology with regard to the Last Supper. He conceded that he could not explain why John omitted it. On the basis of the synoptic accounts Schleiermacher argued that it was "a symbolic institution that was in a special way to bind the participants together and all the participants with him and his unique life" (ibid., p. 394). Schleiermacher acknowledged the violent attacks that had been made on the resurrection narratives, but explained that the "contradictions" were no greater than elsewhere in the Gospels (ibid., p. 432). He proceeded to discuss the accounts with reference to the Wolfenbüttel Fragments (p. 445) and J. A. Brennecke's *Biblischer Beweis, dass Jesus nach seiner Auferstehung noch siebenundzwanzig Jahr leibhaftig auf Erden gelebt und zum Wohl der Menschheit in der Stille fortgewirkt habe* (1819) (pp.

451–52). Schleiermacher himself spoke of Jesus' "state of revivification *[Wiederbelebtsein]*" (p. 464; cf. *SW*, 1, 6, p. 493) and of return "to a truly human life" (p. 469).

145. Ibid., p. 415.

146. Ibid., pp. 416–17.

147. Ibid., pp. 415–16.

148. Karl Barth, *PT*, p. 425, citing Schleiermacher's address to the Academy of Sciences "Ueber den Begriff des grossen Mannes" (1826; *SW*, 3, 3, p. 83).

149. *Schleiermachers Briefwechsel mit Joachim Christian Gass* (Berlin, 1852), p. 195.

150. Eduard Zeller, *David Friedrich Strauss in his Life and Writings* (London: Smith, Elder & Co., 1874), p. 33.

151. Cf. M. Redeker, *Der christliche Glaube*, 1:xxxiii-xl; F. Flückiger, *Philosophie und Theologie bei Schleiermacher* (Zollikon-Zürich: Evangelischer Verlag, 1974); R. R. Niebuhr, op. cit., pp. 6–17.

152. Redeker, who regards this as a malicious exaggeration, concedes some grounds for it in Schleiermacher's argument for divine omnipotence and omniscience (op. cit., 1:xxxv-xxxvi; cf. nos. 54–55; D. F. Strauss, *Die christliche Glaubenlehre* [Tübingen: C. F. Osiander, 1841], 2:175ff.).

153. F. C. Baur, *Primae rationalismi et supranaturalismi historiae* (Tübingen, 1827); idem., *Die christliche Lehre von der Versöhnung* (Tübingen: C. F. Osiander, 1838), pp. 614ff.; cf. Schleiermacher's response to Baur's early comments in *On the Glaubenlehre*, pp. 76–77. Hengstenberg's criticisms appeared in the *Evangelische Kirchen-Zeitung* which he edited.

154. There appears to be a veiled allusion in the Preface to *Phenomenology of Spirit* (p. 43): "The anti-human, the merely animal, consists in staying within the sphere of feeling, and being able to communicate only at that level." In his introduction to Hermann Hinrichs, *Die Religion in ihrem Verhältnis zur Wissenschaft* (Heidelberg, 1822), Hegel wrote, "If the feeling of absolute dependence is the essence of religion and of the Christian faith, the dog would be the best Christian, for he bears this the strongest in himself and lives predominantly in this feeling. The dog has even feelings of release *[Erlösungsgefühle]*, if satisfaction is brought to his hunger by a bone. Only the free spirit has religion and can have religion." For comparison of the two thinkers, see Robert R. Williams, "Hegel and Schleiermacher on Theological Truth," in Leroy S. Rouner, ed., *Meaning, Truth and God*, pp. 52–69.

155. *On the Glaubenlehre*, p. 82.

156. Ibid., p. 87.

157. Ibid., p. 63.

158. "For I do not seek to understand in order that I may believe, but I believe in order that I may understand" (*Proslogion*, 1). "For he who shall not have believed shall not experience, and he who will not have experienced does not understand" (*De Fide Trinitatis*, 2).

159. Cf. R. R. Niebuhr, op. cit., pp. 141–42, who also compares Schleiermacher's approach with that of Jonathan Edwards in the latter's *Treatise Concerning the Religious Affections* (1746).

160. Letter, August 4, 1832 (F. Rowan, op. cit., 2:326).

161. *Types*, p. 100.

162. *Quest*, pp. 62–63.

7. Feuerbach and the Reduction of Theology to Anthropology

1. Jacques Barzun, *Romanticism and the Modern Ego* (Boston: Little, Brown and Co., 1943), pp. 21–22.

2. Cited from "The Romantic School," *The Works of Heinrich Heine*, trans. Charles Godfrey Leland (London: Heinemann, 1906), 5:313. Cf. also Heine's discussion of Idealism in *Religion and Philosophy in Germany*, trans. John Snodgrass with a new introduction by Ludwig Marcuse (Boston: Beacon Press, 1959).

3. D. F. Strauss, *Streitschriften zur Verteidigung meiner Schrift über das Leben Jesu*, no. 3 (Tübingen: C. F. Osiander, 1837). The distinction was further amplified by K. L. Michelet in his *Geschichte der letzen Systeme der Philosophie in Deutschland* (Berlin: Duncker und Humblot, 1838), 2:654ff., and has been widely used ever since. See further, S. D. Crites, "Hegelianism," *EP*, 3:451–59; W. J. Brazill, *The Young Hegelians* (New Haven: Yale University Press, 1970); Karl

Löwith, *From Hegel to Nietzsche: The Revolution in Nineteenth-Century Thought* (New York: Holt, Rinehart and Winston, 1964), pp. 53–135; D. McLellan, *The Young Hegelians and Karl Marx* (London: Macmillan, 1969).

4. *Theology and the Church: Shorter Writings 1920–1928* (London: S.C.M. Press; New York: Harper Brothers, 1962), p. 217. Barth's lecture on Feuerbach given here (pp. 217–37) appears in a different translation as an introduction to Feuerbach, *The Essence of Christianity*, trans. George Eliot (1854), reprint ed. with a foreword by H. Richard Niebuhr (New York: Harper Torchbook, 1957). Barth also discussed Feuerbach in *PT*, pp. 534–40.

5. *Lectures on the Essence of Religion*, trans. R. Manheim (New York: Harper & Row, 1967), p. 5.

6. Feuerbach's *Sämtliche Werke* were edited by Wilhelm Bolin and Friedrich Jodl in ten volumes (Stuttgart: Frommann Verlag, 1903–1910). They were republished in facsimile together with three supplementary volumes edited by Hans-Martin Sass. A critical edition in sixteen volumes of his *Gesammelte Werke* (Berlin: Akademie Verlag), was begun in 1967 under the editorship of Werner Schuffenhauer. Studies include (in addition to those noted above): H. Arvon, *Ludwig Feuerbach ou la Transformation du Sacré* (Paris: Presses Universitaires de France, 1957); Klaus Erich Bockmühl, *Leiblichkeit und Gesellschaft. Studien zur Religionskritik und Anthropologie im Frühwerk von Ludwig Feuerbach und Karl Marx*, *FSTR* 7 (Göttingen: Vandenhoeck & Rupprecht, 1961); F. Jodl, *Ludwig Feuerbach*, 2nd ed. (Stuttgart: Frommann Verlag, 1921); E. Kamenka, *The Philosophy of Ludwig Feuerbach* (New York: Praeger, 1970); H. Lübbe and H.-M. Sass, eds., *Atheismus in der Diskussion: Kontroversen um Ludwig Feuerbach* (Munich: Chr. Kaiser Verlag; Mainz: Matthias Grünewald Verlag, 1975); S. Rawidowicz, *Ludwig Feuerbachs Philosophie. Ursprung und Schicksal* (1931; reprint ed., Berlin: Walter de Gruyter, 1964); E. Schneider, *Die Theologie und Feuerbachs Religionskritik. Die Reaktion der Theologie des 19. Jahrhunderts auf Ludwig Feuerbachs Religionskritik mit Ausblicken auf das 20. Jahrhundert und einem Anhang über Feuerbach*, *STGNJ* 1 (Göttingen: Vandenhoeck & Rupprecht, 1972); Uwe Schott, *Die Jugendentwicklung Ludwig Feuerbachs bis zum Fakultäts-Wechsel 1825. Ein Beitrag zur Genese der Feuerbachschen Religionskritik mit einem bibliographischen Anhang zur Feuerbach-Literatur*, *STGNJ* 10 (Göttingen: Vandenhoeck & Rupprecht, 1974); Marx W. Wartofsky, *Feuerbach* (Cambridge: Cambridge University Press, 1977); Marcel Xhaufflaire, *Feuerbach et la Théologie de la Sécularisation* (Paris: Éditions du Cerf, 1970; German version, *Feuerbach und die Theologie der Säkularisation* [Munich: Chr. Kaiser Verlag; Mainz: Matthias Grünewald Verlag, 1972]).

7. Letter written from Heidelberg in 1824 to his father who had urged him to study under Paulus (*SW*, 2:359).

8. *Thoughts on Death and Immortality from the Papers of a Thinker, along with an Appendix of Theological-Satirical Epigrams, Edited by One of his Friends*, trans. James A. Massey (Berkeley, Los Angeles, and London: University of California Press, 1980), p. 192.

9. Undated letter written four weeks after beginning lectures at Berlin (*SW*, 2:361).

10. Letter to Hegel, dated November 22, 1828, which accompanied the work (*SW*, 4:361). A German version appears in *SW*, vol. 4, and the Latin original in *SW*, vol. 11.

11. For Eng. trans. see above, n. 8.

12. The First part appeared in the *Hallesche Jahrbücher*. The full work containing the rejection of Hegel was published separately the same year.

13. For Eng. trans. see above, n. 4.

14. Eng. trans. with introduction by M. H. Vogel, *Principles of the Philosophy of the Future* (Indianapolis: Bobbs-Merrill, 1966).

15. Eng. trans. M. Cherno, *The Essence of Faith According to Luther* (New York: Harper & Row, 1967).

16. Abridged Eng. trans. A. Loos, *The Essence of Religion* (New York: A. K. Butts & Co., 1873).

17. For Eng. trans. see above, n. 5.

18. Cf. M. Xhaufflaire, op. cit. German edition, pp. 158–96; Marx W. Wartofsky, op. cit., pp. 196–252, 341–431.

19. *SW*, 2:410–11.

20. *The Essence of Christianity*, p. xxxv. It may be noted that George Eliot has used Latin to express technical terms *(ego, Ens realissimum)*, whereas Feuerbach himself used non-technical German ("Ich = "I"; "das allerwirklichste Wesen" = "the most real Being").

21. Ibid., p. 80.
22. Ibid., p. 83. On Feuerbach's *I-Thou* concept, its ambiguities and shifts in meaning, see Marx W. Wartofsky, op. cit., pp. 1, 10, 34–37, 188, 310–11, 314, 346, 385–86, 425; M. Xhaufflaire, op. cit., pp. 182–84.
23. Cf. M. Xhaufflaire, op. cit., p. 159.
24. *The Essence of Christianity,* p. 207.
25. *Lectures on the Essence of Religion,* p. 17.
26. D. F. Strauss, *The Life of Jesus Critically Examined* (reprint ed., Philadelphia: Fortress Press, 1972; London: S.C.M. Press, 1973), p. 777.
27. *The Essence of Christianity,* p. 121.
28. Ibid., p. 50.
29. Ibid., p. 51.
30. Ibid., p. 269.
31. Ibid., p. 134.
32. Ibid., p. 135.
33. Ibid., p. 276.
34. Ibid., p. 277.
35. *Thoughts on Death and Immortality,* pp. 239–42.
36. *The Essence of Christianity,* pp. 67–68.
37. Ibid., p. 44.
38. Cf. Karl Barth, *Theology and Church,* p. 227; Copleston, 7:299–300.
39. A shift in attitude is apparent when his *Grundsätze der Philosophie der Zukunft* is compared with *Das Wesen des Glaubens im Sinne Luthers* (cf. also Marx M. Wartofsky, op. cit., pp. 59, 292).
40. Cf. *Lectures on the Essence of Religion,* p. 25; Wartofsky, op. cit., pp. 215–20.

8. Kierkegaard and the Reentry of Transcendence

1. Kierkegaard's *Samlede Vaerker,* 15 vols., were edited by A. B. Drachmann, J. L. Heiberg and H. O. Lange (Copenhagen: Gildendals, 1901–36). A definitive edition of *Kierkegaard's Writings,* 26 vols., under the direction of Howard V. Hong, is being produced by the Princeton University Press. Among the volumes that have so far appeared is Vol. 25, *Letters and Documents,* trans. with introduction and notes by Henrik Rosenmeier (1978). *Søren Kierkegaard's Journals and Papers,* 7 vols., have been edited and translated by Howard V. Hong and Edna H. Hong, assisted by Gregor Malantschuk (Bloomington and London: Indiana University Press, 1967–78). For other works see the appropriate references below. An analytical overview of individual writings is given by George E. Arbaugh and George B. Arbaugh, *Kierkegaard's Authorship* (London: George Allen and Unwin, 1968). For bibliography see Jens Himmerlstrup and K. Birket-Smith, eds., *Søren Kierkegaard. International Bibliografi* (Copenhagen: Nyt Nordisk Forlag, Arnold Busck, 1962); Aage Jørgensen, *Søren Kierkegaard-litteratur. 1961–1970* (Aarhus: Akademsk Boghandel, 1971). For discussion of various aspects of Kierkegaard's thought see the following: Wilhelm Anz, *Kierkegaard und der deutsche Idealismus, Sammlung gemeinverständlicher Vorträge und Schriften aus dem Gebiet der Theologie und Religionsgeschichte,* 210/211 (Tübingen: J. C. B. Mohr, 1956); R. H. Bell and R. E. Hustwit, eds., *Essays on Kierkegaard and Wittgenstein* (Wooster: College of Wooster, 1978); Conrad Bonifazi, *Christendom Attacked: A Comparison of Kierkegaard and Nietzsche* (London: Rockliff, 1953); Frithiof Brandt, *Søren Kierkegaard, 1813–1855: His Life, His Works* (Copenhagen: Det danske Selskab, 1963); Hinrich Buss, *Kierkegaards Angriff auf die bestehende Christenheit, TF 49* (Hamburg: Herbert Reich, 1970); E. J. Carnell, *The Burden of Søren Kierkegaard* (Grand Rapids: Eerdmans; Exerter: Paternoster Press, 1965); James Collins, *The Mind of Kierkegaard* (Chicago: Regnery, 1953); Hermann Diem, *Kierkegaard's Dialectic of Existence* (Edinburgh: Oliver and Boyd, 1959); idem., *Kierkegaard: An Introduction* (Richmond: John Knox Press, 1966); Louis Dupré, *Kierkegaard as Theologian* (London and New York: Sheed & Ward, 1963); John W. Elrod, *Being and Existence in Kierkegaard's Pseudonymous Works* (Princeton: Princeton University Press, 1975); idem., *Kierkegaard and Christendom* (Princeton: Princeton University Press, 1981); C. Stephen Evans, *Kierkegaard's "Fragments" and "Postscript": The Religious Philosophy of Johannes Climacus,* (Atlantic Highlands, N.J.: Humanities Press. 1983); Henning Fenger, *Kierkegaard, The*

Myths and their Origins: Studies in the Kierkegaardian Papers and Letters (New Haven: Yale University Press, 1980); Hayo Gerdes, *Das Christusbild Sören Kierkegaards, Verglichen mit Hegels und Schleiermachers* (Dusseldorf and Cologne: Eugen Diederichs Verlag, 1960); idem., *Das Christusverständniss des jungen Kierkegaards* (Itzehoe: Die Spur, 1962); idem., *Sören Kierkegaard. Leben und Werk* (Berlin: Walter de Gruyter, 1966); Jerry H. Gill, ed., *Essays on Kierkegaard* (Minneapolis: Burgess, 1969); Alastair Hannay, *Kierkegaard* (London: Routledge & Kegan Paul, 1982); Emanuel Hirsch, *Kierkegaard-Studien*, 2 vols. (Gütersloh: C. Bertelsmann, 1930–33); Howard A. Johnson and Niels Thulstrup, eds., *A Kierkegaard Critique* (Chicago: Regnery, 1962); Ralph Henry Johnson, *The Concept of Existence in the Concluding Unscientific Postscript* (The Hague: Martinus Nijhoff, 1972); E. D. Klemke, *Studies in the Philosophy of Kierkegaard* (The Hague: Martinus Nijhoff, 1976); Christa Kühnhold, *Der Begriff des Sprunges und der Weg des Sprachdenkens. Eine Einführung in Kierkegaard* (Berlin: Walter de Gruyter, 1975); Walter Lowrie, *Kierkegaard*, 2 vols., rev. ed. (New York: Harper & Brothers, 1962); idem., *A Short Life of Kierkegaard* (reprint ed., Princeton: Princeton University Press, 1963); Louis Mackey, *Kierkegaard: A Kind of Poet* (Philadelphia: University of Pennsylvania Press, 1971); Gregor Malantschuk, *Kierkegaard's Thought*, ed. H. V. Hong and E. H. Hong (Princeton: Princeton University Press, 1971); Denzil G. M. Patrick, *Pascal and Kierkegaard: A Study in the Strategy of Evangelism*, 2 vols. (London: Lutterworth Press, 1947); Hans Rudolf Schär, *Christliche Sokratik. Kierkegaard über den Gebrauch der Reflexion in der Christenheit, Basler und Berner Studien zur historischen und systematischen Theologie*, no. 34 (Bern: Peter Lang, 1977); Joseph H. Smith, ed., *Kierkegaard's Truth: The Disclosure of the Self*, Psychiatry and the Humanities, no. 5 (New Haven: Yale University Press, 1981); Frederick Sontag, *A Kierkegaard Handbook* (Atlanta: John Knox Press, 1979); Paul Sponheim, *Kierkegaard on Christ and Christian Coherence* (New York: Harper and Row; London: S. C. M. Press, 1968); Brita K. Stendahl, *Søren Kierkegaard* (Boston: Twayne Publishers, 1976); Mark C. Taylor, *Kierkegaard's Pseudonymous Authorship: A Study of Time and the Self* (Princeton: Princeton University Press, 1975); idem., *Journeys to Selfhood: Hegel and Kierkegaard* (Berkeley and Los Angeles: University of California Press, 1980); J. Heywood Thomas, *Subjectivity and Paradox* (Oxford: Basil Blackwell, 1957); Josiah Thompson, ed., *Kierkegaard: A Collection of Critical Essays* (New York: Doubleday, 1972); Reidar Thomte, *Kierkegaard's Philosophy of Religion* (Princeton: Princeton University Press, 1948); Niels Thulstrup, *Kierkegaard's Relation to Hegel* (Princeton: Princeton University Press, 1980); Niels Thulstrup and Marie Mikulová Thulstrup, *Bibliotheca Kierkegaardiana*, 16 vols. planned (Copenhagen: C. A. Reitzel, 1978–); N. Viallaneix, *Écoute, Kierkegaard. Essai sur la Communication de la Parole*, 2 vols. (Paris: Éditions du Cerf, 1979); Jean Wahl, *Études Kierkegaardiennes* (Paris: Fernand Aubier, 1938).

2. Cf. Aage Henriksen, *Methods and Results of Kierkegaard Studies in Scandinavia: A Historical and Critical Survey* (Copenhagen: Ejnar Munksgaard, 1951); *Bibliotheca Kierkegaardiana*, vol. 8: *The Legacy and Interpretation of Kierkegaard* (1981); W. Anz, "Zur Wirkungsgeschichte Kierkegaards in der deutschen Theologie und Philosophie," *ZTK* 79 (1982), 450–82.

3. *Journals and Papers*, no. 6073 (n.d. 1847), 5:415; cf. W. von Kloeden, "The Home and the School," *Bibliotheca Kierkegaardiana*, vol. 1: *Kierkegaard's View of Christianity* (1978), pp. 11–16. For a time in his early career, J. P. Mynster (1775–1854) had been a Kantian, but he returned to a more orthodox position. He came to Copenhagen in 1811, where he established his reputation as a preacher. He held numerous positions in the church and university, becoming a court preacher in 1826. It was only in the 1840s, as Kierkegaard came to relinquish hopes of ordination and the bishop became increasingly perturbed over Kierkegaard's writings, that the relationship became one of estrangement. Kierkegaard came to regard the bishop as the personification of formal, compromising religion, especially in view of the agreement that Mynster made with the democratic party following the year of revolutions in 1848, in an endeavor to secure the place of the church in Danish national life.

4. In an undated entry written in 1838, Søren wrote of "the great earthquake" which drove him to "a new infallible principle for interpreting all phenomena," including his father's longevity, the gifts of his family and the deaths of his mother, brothers and sisters. "A guilt must rest upon the entire family, a punishment of God must be upon it" (*Journals and Papers*, no. 5430, 5:140–41). In 1796 Michael Pedersen's first wife died childless. The following year he was obliged to marry his servant who later became Søren's mother. In an undated fragment of 1846 Søren observed, "How appalling for the man who, as a lad watching sheep on the Jutland heath, suffering painfully, hungry and exhausted, once stood on a hill and cursed God—and the man was unable to forget it when he was

eighty-two years old" (no. 5874, 5:310). The father was eighty-two when he died. When Peter Christian Kierkegaard read the passage in old age, having himself resigned the see of Aalborg and being himself afflicted with a melancholy sense of unworthiness, he acknowledged that this was the story of the father and his family (H. P. Barfod, *Til Minde om Biskop Peter Christian Kierkegaard* [Copenhagen, 1888], pp. 13–15).

5. *Journals and Papers*, no. 6164 (n.d. 1848), 6:12. The *Journals and Papers* contain numerous references to Michael Pedersen Kierkegaard, to whom Søren also dedicated several of his discourses.

6. Eng. trans. by Lee M. Capel (Bloomington: Indiana University Press; London: Collins, 1966). The examiners accepted the work on the strength of the candidate's knowledge and scholarship, but concern was expressed about the author's style and method of presentation. In 1854 the Magister degrees were officially regarded as doctoral degrees.

7. Hans Lassen Martensen (1808–84) was academically only slightly senior to Kierkegaard, when he became his tutor in 1834. He spent two years travelling abroad (1834–36), where he met among others the sons of Hegel, and also Paulus, Strauss, Baur and Schelling. In 1840 he was appointed professor of systematic theology at Copenhagen. He became a court preacher in 1845, and succeeded Mynster in 1854. Although he used Hegelian categories, he was never simply a Hegelian (cf. *Christian Dogmatics* [1849; Eng. trans. Edinburgh: T. & T. Clark, 1898], pp. 108–27). Martensen's *Christian Ethics* (3 vols. [1871–78; Eng. trans. Edinburgh: T. & T. Clark, 1873–81]) enjoyed considerable prestige. Martensen became the leading representative in Denmark of *Vermittlungstheologie*, seeking to combine faith and culture, seeing Christ as the head of humanity. He maintained a long friendship with I. A. Dorner. Their *Briefwechsel*, 2 vols. (Berlin, 1888) touched on many aspects of theology. See further Hermann Brandt, *Gotteserkenntnis und Weltentfremdung. Der Weg der spekulativen Theologie Hans Lassen Martensens* (Göttingen: Vandenhoeck und Rupprecht, 1971).

8. H. Brandt, op. cit., pp. 63–65; cf. *Aus Schleiermachers Leben in Briefen*, 2:502–6. On Kierkegaard's differences with Schleiermacher see P. H. Jørgensen, "Feeling of Absolute Dependence," in *Theological Concepts in Kierkegaard, Bibliotheca Kierkegaardiana* (1980), 5:51–54.

9. H. Brandt, op. cit., p. 32, who cites Martensen's recollections of Kierkegaard's penchant for "Sophistik" and exhausting capacity for argument (Martensen, *Aus Meinem Leben* [1883], 1:91–92).

10. *Journals and Papers*, no. 3245 (October 17, 1835), 3:496–97.

11. *Journals and Papers*, no. 1096 (n.d. 1836), 2:3. Kierkegaard possessed the third edition of *Der christliche Glaube*. The Hegelian approach to faith was exemplified by Philipp Marheineke, *Die Grundlehren der christlichen Dogmatik als Wissenschaft*, 2nd ed. (Berlin, 1827), pp. 6ff. Hegelianism was introduced to Denmark by J. L. Heiberg in 1824 (cf. N. Thulstrup, op. cit., pp. 17–33, 83–96). Kierkegaard's attitude to Hegel, Fichte and Schelling is further discussed in *Bibliotheca Kierkegaardiana*, vol. 4: *Kierkegaard and Speculative Idealism* (1979).

12. Cf. Ronald Gregor Smith, "Hamann and Kierkegaard," in *Zeit und Geschichte. Dankesgabe an Rudolf Bultmann zum 80. Geburtstag herausgegeben von* Erich Dinkler (Tübingen: J. C. B. Mohr, 1964), pp. 671–83. To Kierkegaard, Hamann was "still the greatest and most authentic humorist" (*Journals and Papers*, no. 1699, August 4, 1837, 2:358). Smith holds that they shared a common view of "the Christian mystery of the condescension of God in Christ in terms of irony, of a Christian-Socratic ignorance, and of humility. The contrast between Christianity and the wisdom of the world runs through all that he [Hamann] thought and was" (op. cit., pp. 674–75). However, Smith holds that over the years Kierkegaard drifted from Hamann's essentially Lutheran position.

13. *Fortegnelse over Dr. Søren A. Kierkegaards efterladte Bogsamling* (1856); critical edition, ed. Niels Thulstrup, *Katalog over Søren Kierkegaards Bibliothek* (Copenhagen: Munksgaard, 1957); cf. Hayo Gerdes, *Sören Kierkegaard*, pp. 19–21.

14. *Journals and Papers*, no. 5324, 5:120.

15. Cf. Theodor Haecker, *Kierkegaard—The Cripple* (London: Harvill Press, 1948).

16. Cf. Ib Ostenfeld, *Søren Kierkegaard's Psychology*, trans. and ed. Alastair McKinnon (Waterloo: Wilfrid Laurier University Press, 1978); H. Fenger, op. cit., pp. 63–80. Kresten Nordentoft, *Kierkegaard's Psychology*, trans. B. H. Kirmmse (Pittsburgh: Duquesne University Press, 1978), explores Kierkegaard in connection with psychological analysis.

17. H. Fenger, op. cit., pp. 1–31, 213–20, and passim.

18. Cf. W. Lowrie, op. cit., 1:116–49, especially pp. 132ff.

19. Carl Saggau, *Skyldig—Ikke Skyldig? Ett par Kapitler af Michael og Søren Kierkegaards*

Ungdomsliv (Copenhagen: E. Munksgaard, 1958); Henning Schmidt, "Where Did Venus Go When She Went Out?" (*Nyt fra Odense Universitet,* May 25, 1976); cf. H. Fenger, op. cit., pp. 62–80, 228.

20. Cf. G. E. and G. B. Arbaugh, op. cit., pp. 40–43, 227–230.

21. Written in 1848 and published by Peter Christian Kierkegaard in 1859; Eng. trans. Benjamin Nelson, *The Point of View for my Work as an Author: A Report to History, and Related Writings* (New York: Harper & Row, 1962).

22. Ibid., p. 43.

23. Plato, *Theaetetus,* 149 B, 150, 161 E. Socrates' mother was a midwife and he professed skill in midwifery.

24. *The Concept of Irony,* pp. 215–16.

25. *Journals and Papers,* no. 649 (n.d. 1847), 1:273. For Kierkegaard's reflections on communication see nos. 649–681, pp. 267–319.

26. Cf. *Philosophical Fragments,* pp. 13–27; *Works of Love,* p. 257.

27. Eng. trans. David F. Swenson, Lilian Marvin Swenson, and Walter Lowrie (1944), with revisions and foreword by Howard A. Johnson, 2 vols. (Princeton: Princeton University Press, 1959). The work was an apologia for his broken engagement. It presented a choice between the aesthetic and the ethical which could not be combined in a Hegelian manner. In later writings Kierkegaard developed the religious as a third category which transcended the ethical.

28. Eng. trans. W. Lowrie (1941), revised by Howard A. Johnson and published together with *The Sickness unto Death* (1849) (New York: Doubleday, 1954). Kierkegaard speaks of "the teleological suspension of the ethical" and presents Abraham's offering of Isaac as a paradigm of faith.

29. Eng. trans. David E. Swenson (1941), revised with introduction and commentary by Niels Thulstrup, trans. Howard V. Hong (Princeton: Princeton University Press, 1962). The name of the pseudonymous author is taken from the seventh-century monk of the monastery on Sinai who wrote the *klimax tou paradeisou (Ladder of Paradise).* Already in 1839 Kierkegaard ironically described Hegel as a Johannes Climacus who entered heaven "by means of his syllogisms" (*Journals and Papers,* no. 1575, 2:209–10). Hegel himself described "Science" as a "ladder" (*Phenomenology,* p. 14).

30. Eng. trans. W. Lowrie (1944), revised by Howard A. Johnson (Princeton: Princeton University Press, 1957).

31. Eng. trans. W. Lowrie (Princeton: Princeton University Press, 1940).

32. Eng. trans. D. F. Swenson and W. Lowrie (1941).

33. *Journals and Papers,* no. 5873 (February 7, 1846), 5:310.

34. *Journals and Papers,* no. 6131 (April 19, 1848), 5:443.

35. *Journals and Papers,* no. 6133 (April 24, 1848), 5:444.

36. Eng. trans. Howard Hong and Edna Hong (New York: Harper and Brothers; London: Collins, 1962).

37. Eng. trans. W. Lowrie (1940; reprint ed., New York: Oxford University Press, 1961).

38. Eng. trans. W. Lowrie (Princeton: Princeton University Press, 1941).

39. Among the numerous references to Mynster in the *Journals and Papers,* those written in March, 1854, after the Bishop's death are particularly revealing (nos. 6853–55, 6:491–98).

40. Eng. trans. W. Lowrie (1944); new ed. with supplement by Howard A. Johnson (Princeton: Princeton University Press, 1968).

41. Op. cit., pp. 275–76.

42. Op. cit., pp. 12–13, 380–81.

43. Op. cit., pp. 292–93; cf. *Journals and Papers,* no. 649 (n.d. 1847), 1:267. However, Kierkegaard rejected Kant's view of human autonomy (no. 188, n.d., 1:76–77).

44. *Concluding Unscientific Postscript,* pp. 67–113; cf. R. J. Campbell, "Lessing's Problem and Kierkegaard's Answer," *SJT* 19 (1966):35–54.

45. Ibid., p. 86.

46. Ibid., p. 112.

47. Cf. Niels Thulstrup's notes in *Philosophical Fragments,* pp. 149–51; cf. pp. xlix-xl. However, in *Kierkegaard's Relation to Hegel,* Thulstrup observes, "Through the reading of Jacobi's *Ueber die Lehre des Spinoza, in Briefen an Herrn Moses Mendelssohn,* Kierkegaard became seriously interested in Lessing, whom he put in a place of honor in the *Postscript*" (pp. 316–17). This was evidently in 1844. Danish readers were kept abreast of foreign theology, including the debate about

Strauss's *Leben Jesu*, by the *Tidskrift for undenlansk theologisk Litteratur*, edited by H. N. Clausen and M. H. Hohlenberg from 1833 onwards. The views of Strauss and Feuerbach were advocated in Denmark by A. F. Beck and Hans Bröchner. Strauss's *Leben Jesu* was translated into Danish by F. Schaldemose on the basis of the fourth edition, 2 vols. (1842–43). Kierkegaard does not appear to have owned a copy. Rather than address the critical debate directly, he sought to undercut it by his theological and philosophical considerations.

48. *Philosophical Fragments*, p. 11; cf. Plato, *Meno*, 80.
49. Ibid., p. 13.
50. Ibid., pp. 19–22.
51. Ibid., pp. 46–67.
52. Ibid., p. 49.
53. Ibid., pp. 51–52.
54. Ibid., pp. 53–54.
55. *Concluding Unscientific Postscript*, p. 296.
56. *Philosophical Fragments*, pp. 57–58.
57. "If the difference is infinite between God who is in heaven and thee who art on earth, the difference is infinitely greater between the holy One and the sinner" (*The High Priest* from *Three Discourses at the Communion on Fridays* [1849], in *Christian Discourses*, p. 368; cf. p. 72).
58. *Philosophical Fragments*, pp. 58–59.
59. Ibid., p. 59.
60. Ibid., p. 76.
61. Ibid.
62. Ibid., pp. 38–45.
63. Ibid., p. 26.
64. Ibid., p. 78.
65. Ibid., p. 79.
66. Ibid., p. 80.
67. Ibid.; cf. 1 John 1:1.
68. Ibid., pp. 83–84; cf. Luke 13:26.
69. Ibid., pp. 130–31.
70. Cf. Rudolph Bultmann's contention that we can know *that* Jesus lived but not *what* he was like in "The Primitive Christian Kerygma and the Historical Jesus," in Carl E. Braaten and Roy A. Harrisville, eds., *The Historical Jesus and the Kerygmatic Christ* (New York and Nashville: Abingdon, 1964), pp. 15–42.
71. Cf. Hayo Gerdes, *Das Christusbild Sören Kierkegaards*, p. 31. Kierkegaard's *Journals and Papers* contain passing references to the thought of D. F. Strauss (no. 3262), F. C. Baur (no. 4243), and Bruno Bauer (nos. 1233, 2211, 3605, 3998, 5222, 5355). But Kierkegaard was more concerned with their philosophical ideas than with their critical work. W. von Kloeden gives a brief but detailed account of the works that Kierkegaard studied as a student and subsequently ("Bible study" in *Bibliotheca Kierkegaardiana*, vol. 1: *Kierkegaard's View of Christianity*, pp. 16–38). This supports the view that, while Kierkegaard was concerned to understand Scripture making use of modern writers, he was not interested in the critical debate about the historicity of Jesus and the Gospel records. The modern writers that he studied included Tholuck, Rückert, Olshausen and Neander. During the winter term of 1832–33 he read the moderate rationalist H. N. Clausen, whose *Quatuor Evangeliorum Tabulae Synopticae* had been published in 1827. This may have led him to purchase W. M. L. de Wette's *Kurze Erklärung des Evangeliums Matthäi*, 2nd ed. (Leipzig, 1838).
72. *Concluding Unscientific Postscript*, p. 31.
73. Ibid., p. 173, from chap. 2 on "The Subjective Truth, Inwardness: Truth is Subjectivity."
74. Ibid., p. 178.
75. Ibid., p. 540.
76. *Training in Christianity*, pp. 28–29.
77. Ibid., p. 135.
78. *Journals and Papers*, nos. 73–75, 1:27–29. The reference to Lessing alludes to the point discussed in the *Postscript*, p. 86. The first marginal note alludes to John 7:17; cf. 8:31; Matt. 7:24; Luke 6:47. In his defense of his dissertation Kierkegaard put forward as his first thesis, "The similarity between Christ and Socrates consists essentially in dissimilarity" (*The Concept of Irony*, p. 349). In 1837 the *Tidskrift for undenlansk theologisk Litteratur* published an extract from F. C. Baur's

Das Christliche des Platonismus, oder Sokrates und Christus. Kierkegaard owned a copy and also Baur's *Die christliche Gnosis* (1835) and *Die christliche Lehre von der Versöhnung* (1838). By this time Baur had become the leading Hegelian historian of theology.

79. *The Present Age and Two Minor Ethico-Religious Treatises*, Eng. trans. Alexander Dru and Walter Lowrie (London: Oxford University Press, 1940), p. 99.

80. Ibid., p. 151. Kierkegaard has in mind the contrast between Christ and Magister Adler, his contemporary, who claimed divine inspiration.

81. Cf. his reflections on Luther in *Journals and Papers*, nos. 2456–556, 3:62–104.

82. For Luther's views see Ian D. Kingston Siggins, *Martin Luther's Doctrine of Christ* (New Haven: Yale University Press, 1970); Paul Althaus, *The Theology of Martin Luther* (Philadelphia: Fortress Press, 1970), pp. 179–98; Philip S. Watson, *Let God Be God! An Interpretation of the Theology of Martin Luther* (London: Epworth Press, 1947), pp. 102–37.

83. *Christian Discourses*, p. 273; *Philosophical Fragments*, pp. 39–40. On Christ generally see *Journals and Papers*, nos. 273–370, 1:123–52.

84. *Works of Love*, p. 115.

85. *The Gospel of Suffering*, Eng. trans. D. F. Swenson and L. M. Swenson (Minneapolis: Augsburg Publishing House, 1948), pp. 73, 86; *Christian Discourses*, p. 273; *The Present Age*, p. 91; *For Self-Examination and Judge for Yourselves!*, Eng. trans. W. Lowrie (Princeton: Princeton University Press, 1941; reprinted., 1974), pp. 84–85; *Journals and Papers*, no. 288 (September 11, 1838), 1:125.

86. *Journals and Papers*, 1:125, no. 186 (September 11, 1838); *The Gospel of Suffering*, Eng. trans. D. F. Swenson and L. M. Swenson (Minneapolis: Augsburg, 1948), pp. 73, 86; *Christian Discourses*, p. 273; *For Self-Examination*, Eng. trans. W. Lowrie (New York: Oxford University Press, 1941); Cf. H. Gerdes, *Das Christusbilds Sören Kierkegaards*, p. 33.

87. "The incarnate Son of God is, therefore, the covering *[involucrum]* in which there is the Divine Majesty presents Himself to us with all His gifts, and does so in such a manner that there is no sinner too wretched to be able to approach Him with the firm assurance of obtaining pardon. This is the one and only view of the Divinity that is available and possible in this life" (Luther, *Luther's Works*, vol. 2: *Lectures on Genesis, Chapters 6–14*, [Saint Louis: Concordia Publishing House, 1960], p. 49; cf. WA, 42:296, lines 22ff.).

88. *Journals and Papers*, no. 3110 (n.d. 1850), 3:421. Pascal figured comparatively frequently in Kierkegaard's papers of 1850 (nos. 3105–22, pp. 418–24).

89. *Philosophical Fragments*, pp. 39–40.

90. Op. cit., p. 177.

91. Cf. Charles Gore, "The Holy Spirit and Inspiration," in *Lux Mundi* (London: John Murray, 1889), pp. 357–62. On Thomasius's doctrine of *kenōs*is see below, chap. 13.

92. *Journals and Papers*, no. 4651 (n.d. 1850), 4:395.

93. *Training in Christianity*, pp. 128–31.

94. *Journals and Papers*, no. 327 (n.d. 1849), 1:138. On Barth's relation to Kierkegaard see Egon Brinkschmidt, *Sören Kierkegaard und Karl Barth* (Neukirchen-Vluyn: Neukirchener Verlag, 1971).

95. *Training in Christianity*, pp. 142–43.

96. *Christian Discourses*, p. 87.

97. Cf. L. Dupré, op. cit., pp. 147–81. Dupré argues that the figure of Christ oscillates constantly between that of a model and that of redeemer. But from 1849 onwards Kierkegaard gradually integrated his soteriology with his ascetic theology of the imitation of Christ (ibid., p. 180). Cf. also N. H. Søe, "Christ," W. von Kloeden, "Die Leidensgeschichte Christ" and Mark C. Taylor, "Christology," in *Bibliotheca Kierkegaardiana*, vol. 5: *Theological Concepts in Kierkegaard* (1980), pp. 55–70, 71–75, 167–206.

98. *Journals and Papers*, no. 697 (n.d. 1849), 1:324.

99. *Christian Discourses*, p. 308; cf. p. 368; *Training in Christianity* etc., p. 270.

100. Cf. Dietrich Bonhoeffer, *The Cost of Discipleship* (New York: Macmillan; London: S. C. M. Press, 1959), pp. 35–47.

101. Anselm, *Proslogion*, 1; cf. above, chap. 6, n. 158. The *credo ut intelligam* precedes Anselm's ontological argument which Kierkegaard ironically reflected on in his papers (*Journals and Papers*, no. 20 [n.d. 1853], 1:11; no. 3615, [n.d. 1851], pp. 667–68).

102. *Philosophical Investigations*, trans. G. E. M. Anscombe, 2nd ed. (Oxford: Blackwell, 1958), Part 1, nos. 124, 127, pp. 49e, 50e.

103. Cf. *Journals and Papers*, vol. 2, nos. 2233–39, pp. 515–17.

IV. THE LIFE OF JESUS AND CRITICAL HISTORY

9. *Early Gospel Criticism*

1. The work ran to three volumes and was published in Zürich by Orell, Gessner and Füssli (1768–72). A seventh edition appeared in 1822–23. Hess wrote various other popular biblical histories.

2. Cf. the German text cited by Schweitzer, *Geschichte*, p. 30.

3. Eng. trans. Oliver A. Taylor, from the fifth edition (1830), *Plan of the Founder of Christianity* (New York: G. & C. & H. Carvill, 1831).

4. Bahrdt was born into an eminent clerical family. He taught at Leipzig, Erfurt, and Giessen. On the recommendation of the enlightened educationist, J. B. Basedow, Bahrdt became director of the Philanthropinum Marschlin (1775). The following year he became General-Superintendent, Dürkheim. However, he was dismissed on account of heresy. His appointment to a lectureship at Halle was opposed by Semler, but his eloquence attracted large numbers of students. His ridicule of Wöllner's religious edict brought him a year's imprisonment. He ended his days as an innkeeper near Halle, where he founded the Masonic "Deutsche Union." He wrote voluminously. His views on Jesus were noted but rejected by Kant (see above, chap. 4, n. 41). His *Geschichte seines Lebens, seiner Meinungen und Schicksale* (4 parts, 1790–91) was edited by Felix Hasselberg (Berlin, 1922), and abbreviated by T. Hagenmeier, *C. F. Bahrdt, Ein Abenteurer der Aufklärungszeit* (Heidenheim: Heidenheimer Verlagsanstalt, 1972); ct. S. G. Flygt, *The Notorious Dr. Bahrdt* (Nashville: Vanderbilt, 1963).

5. *Quest*, pp. 38–44.

6. Venturini was a Privatdozent in Helmstedt and a teacher in Copenhagen. In 1799 he failed to secure the posts of professor at Helmstedt and librarian at Wolfenbüttel, despite the good will of the Duke of Brunswick. In 1807 he accepted the living at Hordorf. His biographical novel about Jesus was first published anonymously at Copenhagen. It shows some dependence on the work of H. E. G. Paulus on exegetical details.

7. Schweitzer, *Quest*, p. 44.

8. *Quest*, p. 47, though this is questioned by Hirsch, 5:32.

9. (Heidelberg: C. F. Winter, 1828). Each of the two volumes had two parts numbered separately. I. *Die Geschichtserzählung nach den vier vereint geordneten Evangelien in Beziehung auf eine wortgetreue, erklärende, synoptische Uebersetzung derselben;* II. *Die wortgetreue, eklärende, synoptische Uebersetzung der vier vereint geordneten Evangelien in Beziehung auf die Geschichtserzählung derselben.*

10. *Quest*, p. 48.

11. Op. cit., 1, 1, p. x.

12. Ibid., 1, 1, p. xi.

13. Ibid., 2, 2, p. 206; cf. the verses in 1, 2, pp. 245–52.

14. Ibid., 1, 1, pp. 65–67.

15. Ibid., 1, 1, pp. xii-xiii.

16. Ibid., 1, 1, pp. 357–59.

17. Ibid., 1, 1, pp. 349–56.

18. Ibid., 1, 1, pp. 244, 281; 1, 2, p. 55.

19. Ibid., 1, 2, pp. 266–315.

20. Ibid., 1, 2, p. 268; cf. John 20:15.

21. Ibid., 1, 2, pp. 270–71; cf. Luke 24:13–45.

22. Ibid., 1, 2, p. 304; cf. Acts 2:24.

23. Ibid., 1, 2, p. 303.

24. Ibid., 1, 2, pp. 306–17.

25. Ibid., 1, 2, p. 331.

26. Ibid., 1, 2, pp. 331–32.

27. *The Life of Jesus Critically Examined*, pp. 49–50, where Strauss notes both the commentaries and *Das Leben Jesu*.

28. *Quest*, pp. 56–57.

29. Eng. trans. from the fourth edition by James Freeman Clarke, *Life of Jesus. A Manual for Academic Study* (Boston: Walker, Wise & Co., 1860), p. xvi. References below are to this version. Hase's interpretation has been the subject of a dissertation by G. Fuss, *Die Auffassung des Lebens Jesu bei...Karl von Hase* (Jena, 1955).

30. Martin Schmidt, *RGG*³, 3, col. 85.

31. Op. cit., no. 3, p. 3.

32. Ibid., no. 5, p. 7.

33. Ibid., no. 5, p. 10.

34. Ibid., no. 118, p. 232. Hase's review of treatments of the life of Jesus (nos. 21–23, pp. 30–40) and his bibliography which expanded with the successive editions of his work (pp. 240–59) indicate a comprehensive familiarity with publications in Britain and Europe.

35. Ibid., p. xiv.

36. Ibid., no. 7, p. 12.

37. Ibid., no. 7, pp. 12–13.

38. Ibid., no. 7, pp. 13–14.

39. Ibid., no. 87, pp. 175–76.

40. Ibid., no. 48, pp. 98–99.

41. Ibid., no. 50, p. 103.

42. Ibid., no. 74, pp. 151–54.

43. Ibid., no. 120, p. 236. August Friedrich Gfrörer (1803–61) was the author of a great number of historical works. Educated at Tübingen, he later became a Roman Catholic. Hase noted his view that the friends of Jesus prevented his limbs from being broken, and managed to control his burial in the hope of rendering him aid.

44. Ibid., no. 116, p. 228.

45. Ibid., no. 116, p. 229.

46. Ibid., no. 120, pp. 236–37.

47. Ibid., no. 26, p. 43.

48. Ibid., no. 121, p. 238.

49. Ibid., no. 239, p. 240.

50. Ibid., no. 58, p. 119. Cf. also his discussion of the sinlessness of Christ (no. 32, pp. 54–57) with its affinities to Schleiermacher.

51. Ibid., no. 62, pp. 131–32; no. 65, pp. 137–39; no. 79, pp. 160–62; no. 82, pp. 164–66.

52. *Quest*, p. 61. Schweitzer also claimed that Hase was the first to distinguish two different periods in the life of Jesus and that this distinction, especially through the influence of Holtzmann and Keim, prevailed until Johannes Weiss. However, it may be observed that Reimarus also noted two phases and corresponding ways of speaking. But in his case the order was reversed, and Jesus' Jewish language about the kingdom took on an increasingly political significance.

53. Hirsch, 5:31.

54. J. N. D. Kelly, *Early Christian Doctrines*, rev. ed. (New York: Harper and Row; London, A. & C. Black, 1978), p. 60.

55. *Hypotyposis* cited by Eusebius, *Historia Ecclesiastica*, 6, 14, 5.

56. *De Consensu Evangelistarum*, 1, 2, 3–4.

57. Eusebius, *Historia Ecclesiastica*, 3, 39, 15–16.

58. The first known Gospel harmony was Tatian's *Diatessaron* in the second century. It was still in use at the time of Eusebius, who commented on Tatian's daring in correcting the style of the apostles and altering their expressions (ibid., 4, 29, 6). Translations included one into Old High German. Augustine's *De Consensu Evangelistarum* (ca. 400) was also a harmony.

59. Calvin produced his commentary on John in 1553 and followed it with *Commentarii in harmoniam ex Matthaeo, Marco et Luca* (1555). Other harmonies dating from the Reformation

period include Osiander's *Harmoniae evangelicae libri quattuor* (1537) and M. Chemnitz, *Harmonia quattuor evangelistarum* (1593). See further B. M. Metzger, "Evangelienharmonie," *RGG*[3], 2, cols. 769–70; D. Wünsch, "Evangelienharmonie," *TRE*, 10:626–36. F. C. Baur discussed harmonies in his *Kritische Untersuchungen über die kanonischen Evangelien* (Tübingen: L. F. Fues, 1847).

60. Eng. trans. *Introduction to the New Testament. By John David Michaelis, Late Professor in the University of Göttingen, &c. Translated from the Fourth Edition of the German, and Considerably Augmented with Notes, and a Dissertation on the Origin & Composition of the Three First Gospels by Herbert Marsh, D.D., F.R.A.S., Lord Bishop of Peterborough*, 4 vols. (London: F. C. & J. Rivington, 1793–1801; cited from the fourth edition, 1823). Marsh was a Fellow of St. John's College, Cambridge, and studied in Germany under Michaelis. His own essay on the mutual relations between the Gospels, which posited a Greek narrative source and a sayings source, was attacked by the more conservative English theologians. His lectures on biblical criticism at Cambridge (1809–16) were among the first to popularize German methods in England. He became Lady Margaret Professor of Divinity in 1807, holding the post until his death. He was successively Bishop of Llandaff (1816) and Peterborough (1819).

61. Kümmel, p. 69.

62. Op. cit., 1:72.

63. Ibid., 1:87.

64. Ibid., 1:23–30.

65. Ibid., 3/1:154.

66. Ibid., 3/1:94.

67. Ibid., 3/1:281–82.

68. Ibid., 3/1:278, 285.

69. Kümmel, p. 69.

70. Eichhorn set out his ideas in his youthful "Urgeschichte" which he published anonymously in 1779 in his journal *Repertorium für biblische und morgenländische Literatur*. The work was subsequently edited and annotated with the author's permission by Gabler who had studied with Eichhorn at Jena (3 vols, 1790–93). See further Christian Hartlich and Walter Sachs, *Der Ursprung des Mythosbegriffes in der modernen Bibelwissenschaft* (Tübingern: J. C. B. Mohr, 1952), pp. 20–38. Eichhorn was a friend of Goethe to whom the poet dedicated a number of verses in his *West-Östlicher Divan* (see "Eichhorn" in *Goethe-Handbuch*, 1916).

71. J. LeClerc, *Historia Ecclesiastica* (Amsterdam, 1716), 1, 64, 11, p. 429; J. D. Michaelis, op. cit., 3/1:92–95.

72. The two winners, Halfeld and Russwurm, had studied with Eichhorn but neither made any significant impact on the course of further study (cf. W. R. Farmer, op. cit., p. 10).

73. *Allgemeine Bibliothek der biblischen Literatur* (1794), 5:759–996.

74. Cf. Kümmel, p. 78.

75. *Einleitung in das Neue Testament* (Leipzig: Weidmann, 1804), 1:406, 411, 458–59 (cited in the translation of S. MacLean Gilmour and Howard Clark Kee in Kümmel, pp. 78–79).

76. On Griesbach see Bernard Orchard and Thomas R. W. Longstaff, eds., *J. J. Griesbach: Synoptic and Text-Critical Studies*, SNTS Monograph Series, no. 34 (Cambridge: Cambridge University Press, 1978). The revived interest in Griesbach's work is attested by W. R. Farmer, *The Synoptic Problem: A Critical Analysis* (1964; reprint ed., Macon, GA: Mercer University Press, 1976); idem, "Modern Developments of Griesbach's Hypothesis," *NTS* 23 (1977):275–95; Hans-Herbert Stoldt, *History and Criticism of the Marcan Hypothesis*, trans. Donald L. Niewyk, introduction by William R. Farmer (Macon, GA: Mercer University Press and Edinburgh: T. & T. Clark, 1980); and Bernard Orchard's edition of *A Synopsis of the Four Gospels in a New Translation, Arranged according to the Two-Gospel Hypothesis* (Macon, GA: Mercer University Press, 1982). It has, however, been criticized by C. M. Tuckett in *The Revival of the Griesbach Hypothesis: An Analysis and an Appraisal*, SNTS Monograph Series, no. 44 (Cambridge: Cambridge University Press, 1983). Tuckett also questions the claim that the hypothesis fell into neglect through adverse publicity acquired through its adoption by the Tübingen School ("The Griesbach Hypothesis in the 19th Century," *JSNT* 3 [1979]:29–60).

77. "Abriss einer Geschichte der Umwälzung, welche seit 1750 auf den Gebiet der Theologie in Deutschland statt gefunden," (*Vermischte Schriften grösstenteils apologetischen Inhalts* [Hamburg: F. Perthes, 1839], 2:1–147, see pp. 134–35; cited by G. Delling in B. Orchard and T. R. W. Longstaff, eds., op. cit., p. 15).

78. G. Delling, ibid.; cf. Griesbach, *Anleitung zum Studium der populären Dogmatik, besonders für künftige Religionslehrer* (Jena, 2nd ed. 1786, 4th ed. 1789).

79. Griesbach used the Received Text as the basis of his version, but recognized the importance of classifying manuscripts into families. He saw three main groups, Alexandrian, Western, and Byzantine. Of these only the first two were valuable. For an appraisal see G. D. Kilpatrick, "Griesbach and the Development of Text Criticism" (Orchard and Longstaff, eds., op. cit., pp. 136–53).

80. Kümmel, p. 75, translated from the fourth edition (1822), pp. viii-ix.

81. F. C. Baur's use of terms like "die Synoptiker" ("the synoptics") and "die synoptische Darstellung" ("the synoptic account") in his *Kritische Untersuchungen* (p. 129 and often) is indication of their common acceptance. The term "synoptic" became current in English in this sense around 1841 (*A New English Dictionary* [Oxford: Oxford University Press, 1919], 9/2:385).

82. Cf. W. R. Farmer, op. cit., pp. 6–7. The view that the Gospels were based upon the work of a predecessor who had undertaken to draw up a narrative (*diēgēsis;* cf. Luke 1:1) came to be known as the *Diegesentheorie* (cf. F. C. Baur, op. cit., p. 36; Schweitzer, *Quest*, p. 89).

83. Enlarged edition in *Commentationes Theologicae*, ed. J. C. Velthusen, C. T. Kuinoel and G. A. Ruperti, (Leipzig, 1794), 1:360–434; reprinted in *Opuscula academica*, ed. J. P. Gabler (Jena, 1825), 2:358–525. Latin text with English translation by B. Orchard in Orchard and Longstaff, eds., op. cit., pp. 68–135. This is prefaced by an introduction by Bo Reicke who also discusses "Griesbach's Answer to the Synoptic Question" (pp. 50–67).

84. Henry Owen, *Observations on the Four Gospels* (London, 1764); Anton Friedrich Büsching, *Die vier Evangelisten mit ihren eigenen Worten zusammengesetzt und mit Erklärungen versehen* (Hamburg, 1766).

85. Op. cit., p. 106.

86. Ibid., pp. 106–7.

87. Ibid., pp. 108–13.

88. Ibid., pp. 114–33.

89. Ibid., p. 135.

90. Cf. H.-H. Stoldt, op. cit., p. 6, who also notes the tendency criticism of the "Anonymous Saxon," Christian Adolf Hasert, *Die Evangelien, ihr Geist, und ihre Verfasser, in Verhältnis zu einander*.

91. *Einleitung in das Neue Testament*, 1/8, no. 79.

92. Eng. trans. from the fifth edition by F. Frothingham, *A Historico-Critical Introduction to the Canonical Books of the New Testament* (Boston: Crosby, Nichols & Co., 1858). De Wette was the author of a widely used Old Testament introduction (1817; 8th ed., 1869), Eng. trans. T. Parker, *A Critical and Historical Introduction to the Canonical Scriptures of the Old Testament*, 2 vols. (Boston: Little and Brown, 1843). Other writings include *Kurzgefasstes exegetisches Handbuch zum Neuen Testament*, 3 vols. (1836–48); and *Das Wesen des christlichen Glaubens* (1846). See further C. Hartlich and W. Sachs, op. cit., pp. 91–120; Ernst Staehelin, *Dewettiana. Forschungen und Texte zu Wilhelm Martin Leberecht de Wettes Leben und Werk* (Basel: Helbing und Lichtenhahn, 1956); Rudolf Smend, *Wilhelm Martin Leberecht De Wettes Arbeit am Alten und am Neuen Testament* (Basel: Helbing und Lichtenhahn, 1958).

93. Eng. trans. William Urwick, *An Introduction to the New Testament*, 2 vols. (Edinburgh: T. & T. Clark, 1869; 4th rev. ed. by W. Mangold, 1886). Schleiermacher is reputed to have observed of his student that he had a charisma for introduction to Holy Scripture (ibid., p. v). Bleek's *Beiträge zur Evangelienkritik* were published in 1846. His *Synoptische Erklärung der drei ersten Evangelien* was edited by H. J. Holtzmann in 1862.

94. Cf. W. R. Farmer, op. cit., pp. 19–20, who maintains that the theory that Matthew and Luke were unknown to each other continued long after it had been demolished by E. von Simons, *Hat der dritte Evangelist den kanonischen Matthäus benützt?* (Bonn, 1880).

95. Ibid., p. 21.

96. Ibid., p. 22.

97. Cf. Karl Barth, *PT*, p. 484.

98. *Biblische Dogmatik Alten und Neuen Testaments. Oder kritische Darstellung der Religionslehre des Hebraismus, des Judenthums und Urchristenthums. Zum Gebrauch akademischer Vorlesungen*, (1813; cited from the second improved edition, Berlin: Realschulbuchhandlung, 1818). Its companion volume was entitled *Dogmatik der evangelisch-lutherischen Kirche nach den symbolischen*

Büchern und den älteren Dogmatikern. Zum Gebrauch akademischer Vorlesungen (Berlin: Realschulbuchhandlung, 1816).

99. Especially in the opening sections de Wette cited Fries's *Neue Kritik der Vernunft* (Heidelberg, 1807), and his *Wissen, Glauben und Ahnung* (Jena, 1805). He also appealed to Kant's *Kritik der reinen Vernunft* (op. cit., p. 7). Jakob Friedrich Fries (1773–1843) was a fellow pupil with Schleiermacher at Niesky, and retained religious affinities with him. He became a friend of de Wette at Heidelberg. His three volume *Neue Kritik der Vernunft* appeared in a second edition (1828–31). He regarded himself as a Kantian, and sought to free theology from mythology.

100. *Biblische Dogmatik*, nos. 4–8, pp. 4–7.

101. Ibid., no. 28, p. 17.

102. Ibid., no. 31, p. 19.

103. Ibid., no. 50, p. 30.

104. Ibid., no. 227, p. 209, citing the support of Karl Gottlob Bretschneider, *Historisch-dogmatische Auslegung des Neuen Testaments*, pp. 257ff. Bretschneider became General-Superintendent at Gotha in 1816. His *Probabilia de evangelii et epistolarum Joannis apostoli indole et origine* (1820) questioned the historicity of the Fourth Gospel on the grounds of its divergence from the Synoptics. He was a rationalistic supernaturalist. A scholar in various fields, he edited Melanchthon and founded the *Corpus Reformatorum*.

105. Ibid., no. 228, p. 210. In a footnote de Wette drew attention to the following writings on "the rise of Christianity and the history of its founder" which he named in addition to the works that he had previously noted: J. J. Hess, *Vom Reiche Gottes;* idem., *Lebensgeschichte Jesu*, 7th ed. (1794); idem., *Lehre, Thaten und Schicksale unsers Herrn*, 2 parts (1806); idem., *Geschichte und Schriften der Apostel*, 3rd ed., 3 vols. (1809); J. J. Keller, *Das Leben Jesu nach den vier Evangelisten* (Stuttgart, 1802); *Jesus von Nazareth, wie er lebte und lehrte etc.* (Halle, 1799); Leonhard Meister, *Jesus von Nazareth, sein Leben und Geist, nach dem Matthäus* (Basel, 1802); H. C. Bergen, *Denkwürdigkeiten aus dem Leben Jesu, nach den vier Evangelien etc.* (Giessen, 1789); J. L. N. Hacker, *Jesus der Weise von Nazareth etc.*, vol. 1 (Leipzig, 1800); G. L. Horn, *Die Lebensgeschichte Jesu nach den drey ersten Evangelien* (Nuremburg, 1803); J. C. Greiling, *Das Leben Jesu von Nazareth* (Halle, 1813); J. A. Jacobi, *Die Geschichte Jesu etc.* (Gotha, 1816). De Wette observed that, "All these works correspond to the idea of a history composed in a genuinely historical-religious spirit in a more or less incomplete way." However, he dismissed as "verwerflich" Venturini's writings on the *Natürliche Geschichte des grossen Propheten von Nazareth, Geschichte des Urchristentums etc.* (p. 211).

Earlier de Wette noted works by the following writers who defended the historicity of the resurrection against the objections of the Wolfenbüttel *Fragment:* Döderlein, Less, Michaelis, Griesbach, Friedrich (ibid., no. 224, pp. 205–6). However, not all took proper note of "the true historical character of the Gospels."

Although de Wette frequently abbreviates titles and fails to give full information, his work is a unique conspectus of critical work in the relevant fields and in this respect could serve as an important source for research into German theology in the early nineteenth century. It shows, *inter alia*, familiarity with the ideas of Lord Herbert of Cherbury, Blount, Hobbes, Collins, Woolston, Morgan, Toland, and Tindal, even though he may have known them at second-hand via John Leland's *Abriss der vornehmsten Deistischen Schriften*, 3 vols. (Hanover, 1755), and the writings of Less, Baumgarten, and Henke (*Dogmatik der evangelisch-lutherischen Kirche*, no. 10, p. 18).

106. Ibid., no. 55, pp. 35–36.

107. First edition, p. 212, cited from the translation in Kümmel, p. 107. It may be noted that de Wette published a third edition (Berlin: Reimer, 1831) and also some explanatory comments *Ueber Religion und Theologie. Erläuterung zu seinem Lehrbuche der Dogmatik*, 2nd ed. (Berlin: Reimer, 1821). Here de Wette stressed the symbolic character of Christianity, provoking the critical comments of D. F. Strauss, *The Life of Jesus Critically Examined*, Eng. trans. (Philadelphia: Fortress Press, 1972), no. 149, pp. 775–76.

108. Ibid., no. 220, p. 200.

109. First edition, p. 252, cited from Kümmel, ibid.

110. Ibid., no. 256, pp. 232–33.

111. Kümmel, p. 106.

112. Ibid., no. 281, p. 255.

113. Ibid., no. 289, p. 261; cf. no. 242, p. 211.
114. Ibid., no. 239, p. 219.
115. Ibid., no. 249, p. 225, nos. 289–296, pp. 261–67.
116. Ibid., no. 238, p. 218; cf. no. 267, p. 241.
117. Ibid., no. 230, p. 213.
118. Ibid., no. 255, p. 232.
119. *PT*, p. 490.

10. *Strauss and the Question of Myth*

1. Strauss's *Gesammelte Schriften* were edited by Eduard Zeller, 12 vols. (Bonn: E. Strauss, 1876–78). Zeller also edited his *Ausgewählte Briefe* (Bonn: E. Strauss, 1895), and wrote *David Friedrich Strauss in his Life and Writings*, Eng. trans. (London: Smith, Elder & Co., 1874). Strauss's *Leben Jesu kritisch bearbeitet* was published in 2 vols, each with 2 parts (Tübingen: C. F. Osiander, 1835–36). The edition used below is the translation by George Eliot (Marian Evans) from the fourth German edition of 1840, 3 vols. (London, 1846); reprinted with a critical introduction and bibliography, edited by Peter C. Hodgson (Philadelphia: Fortress Press, 1972; London: S.C.M. Press, 1973).

Studies include T. Ziegler, *David Friedrich Strauss*, 2 vols. (Strassburg: K. J. Trübner, 1908); Christian Hartlich and Walter Sachs, *Der Ursprung des Mythosbegriffes in der modernen Bibelwissenschaft* (Tübingen: J. C. B. Mohr, 1952); Gunther Backhaus, *Kerygma und Mythos bei David Friedrich Strauss und Rudolf Bultmann* (Hamburg-Bergstedt: Herbert Riech, 1956); Gotthold Müller, *Identität und Immanenz. Zur Genese der Theologie von David Friedrich Strauss. Eine theologie- und philosophiegeschichtliche Studie* (Zürich: EVZ-Verlag, 1968); R. S. Cromwell, *David Friedrich Strauss and his Place in Modern Thought* (Fair Lawn, NJ: R. E. Burdick, 1974); Franz Courth, *Das Leben Jesu von David Friedrich Strauss in der Kritik Johann Evangelist Kuhns. Ein Beitrag zur Auseinandersetzung der Katholischen Tübinger Schule mit dem Deutschen Idealismus*, STGNJ 13 (Göttingen: Vandenhoeck & Rupprecht, 1975), idem, "Die Evangelienkritik des David Friedrich Strauss im Echo seiner Zeitgenossen. Zur Breitenwirkung seines Werkes," in Georg Schwaiger, ed., *Historische Kritik in der Theologie*, STGNJ 32 (Göttingen: Vandenhoeck & Rupprecht, 1980), pp. 60–98; and Horton Harris, *David Friedrich Strauss and his Theology, Monograph Supplements to the Scottish Journal of Theology* (Cambridge: Cambridge University Press, 1973). Harris includes a bibliography listing both published and unpublished material by Strauss and selected works concerning Strauss. On Strauss's relations with the Hegelians, see William J. Brazill, *The Young Hegelians* (New Haven and London: Yale University Press, 1970); and Lawrence S. Stepelevich, *The Young Hegelians: An Anthology* (Cambridge: Cambridge University Press, 1983).

2. E. Zeller, op. cit., p. 25. J. C. F. Steudel (1779–1837) became a professor at Tübingen in 1815. The faculty was reconstituted in 1826 on the death of E. G. Bengel, the grandson of the famous J. A. Bengel. The other three full professors were Baur, Kern and C. F. Schmid (cf. Peter C. Hodgson, *The Formation of Historical Theology: A Study of Ferdinand Christian Baur* [New York: Harper and Row, 1966], p. 16). On the Catholic School see Wayne L. Fehr, *The Birth of the Catholic Tübingen School: The Dogmatics of Johann Sebastian Drey*, American Academy of Religion Series, no. 37 (Chico, CA: Scholars Press, 1981).

3. H. Harris, op. cit., p. 22.

4. "Die Lehre von der Wiederbringung aller Dinge in ihrer religionsgeschichtlichen Entwicklung" in G. Müller, op. cit., pp. 50–82.

5. Ibid., p. 261.

6. Other professors at Berlin were the historian and convert from Judaism, Johann August Wilhelm Neander (1789–1850), the Hegelian, Philipp Konrad Marheineke (1780–1846), and the conservative professor of Old Testament, Ernst Wilhelm Hengstenberg (1802–69), who edited the *Evangelische Kirchen-Zeitung* from 1827 to 1869, which he used as a vehicle from which to attack Schleiermacher and all unorthodox teaching. At Berlin Strauss found a kindred spirit in Johann Karl Wilhelm Vatke (1806–82) who had become a Privatdozent in Old Testament in 1830. He was an enthusiastic Hegelian, who aroused the opposition of Hengstenberg. He developed and transcended

de Wette's teaching. Strauss enjoyed a lifelong friendship with Vatke, and during his studies in Berlin took up lodgings with him.

7. Translation in Harris, op. cit., pp. 32–35.

8. H. Benecke, *Wilhelm Vatke in seinem Leben und Schriften* (Bonn: E. Strauss, 1883), p. 75.

9. Cf. T. Ziegler, "Zur Biographie von David Friedrich Strauss," *Deutsche Revue* 2 (1905):343ff. From a series of forty-six letters of which Ziegler published extracts (2:196–208, 342–51; 3:99–108).

10. *Streitschriften zur Vertheidigung meiner Schrift über das Leben Jesu und zur Charakteristik der gegenwärtigen Theologie. (Erster Band), Erstes bis drittes Heft* (Tübingen: C. F. Osiander, 1837; reprint ed. in 1 vol. Hildesheim: G. Olms, 1980). Further volumes did not appear. Part 1 replied to the criticism of Steudel. Part 2 dealth with C. A. Eschenmayer's *Der Ischariotismus unserer Tage* (1835) and the literary critic, Wolfgang Menzel. Part 3 was divided into three parts, dealing respectively with Hengstenberg, the Hegelians, and finally Julius Müller and Carl Ullmann. For a summary see H. Harris, op. cit., pp. 75–84. See also D. F. Strauss, *In Defense of my* Life of Jesus *Against the Hegelians*, ed. and tr. by Marilyn Chapin Massey, (Hamden: Archon Books, 1983).

11. *The Life of Jesus Critically Examined*, p. lviii. On the various editions see Peter C. Hodgson, ibid., pp. xxiv-xxv, xxxvi-xlvii.

12. Eng. trans. *A New Life of Jesus*, 2 vols. (London: Williams and Norgate, 1865; 2nd ed., 1879).

13. Eng. trans. Leander E. Keck, *The Christ of Faith and the Jesus of History: A Critique of Schleiermacher's Life of Jesus* (Philadelphia: Fortress Press, 1977).

14. Eng. trans. M. Blind, *The Old Faith and the New* (New York: H. Holt & Co., 1873).

15. E. Zeller, op. cit., p. 154.

16. Op. cit., no. 13, p. 71.

17. *A New Life of Jesus*, 1:169–83. In the preceding pages Strauss reviewed previous lives of Jesus and theories of Gospel origins.

18. *Kritische Untersuchungen über die kanonischen Evangelien* (Tübingen: L. F. Fues, 1847), p. 42.

19. Eusebius, *Historia Ecclesiastica*, 3, 39.

20. "The Griesbach Hypothesis in the 19th Century," *JSNT* 3 (1979):32.

21. Op. cit., pp. xxv-xxix; cf. C. Hartlich and W. Sachs, op. cit., pp. 121–47.

22. Ibid., no. 16, p. 88.

23. Op. cit., p. 147.

24. It is endorsed by Van Harvey, "D. F. Strauss' *Life of Jesus* Revisited," *Church History* 30 (1961):191–211, but questioned by Hodgson, op. cit., p. xxix.

25. Cf. above, chap. 3, n. 144.

26. This rigid application of analogy is challenged by Wolfhart Pannenberg in "Redemptive Event and History," *Basic Questions in Theology* (Philadelphia: Fortress Press; London: S.C.M. Press, 1970), pp. 15, 81.

27. Op. cit., p. xxix.

28. Ibid., no. 6, pp. 46–50.

29. Ibid., no. 8, pp. 56–57.

30. E.g., ibid., no. 25, p. 130; no. 29, pp. 140–43.

31. Ibid., no. 43, pp. 201–5.

32. Ibid., nos. 92–96, pp. 415–57.

33. Ibid., no. 140, pp. 735–44.

34. Ibid., no. 8, p. 52. In 1802, G. L. Bauer published in two parts his *Hebräische Mythologie des Alten und Neuen Testaments, mit Parallelen aus der Mythologie anderer Völker, vornehmlich der Griechen und Römer*. In it he claimed that the earliest records of all nations were mythical. See further, Hartlich and Sachs, op. cit., pp. 69–87. Other precursors discussed by Hartlich and Sachs include Eichhorn, Gabler, Herder, and Schelling.

35. Ibid.; cf. C. G. Heyne, *Apollodori bibliothecae libri tres et fragmenta* (1783; 2nd ed., 1803), pp. 3–4.

36. Ibid., no. 8, p. 53.

37. Ibid., no. 15, pp. 86–87.

38. Ibid., no. 15, p. 87.

39. Ibid., first edition, no. 12, p. 72 (author's translation).

40. Cf. Peter C. Hodgson, op. cit., pp. xxviii, xxxii-xxxiv.

41. Cf. Hodgson, ibid., p. xxvii.

42. Op. cit., pp. 41–46.

43. Ibid., no. 5, pp. 44–46.

44. Ibid., no. 22, pp. 117–18.

45. Ibid., no. 71, pp. 315–19, citing Porphyry, *Vita Pythagorae*, no. 25, and Iamblichus, *Vita Pythagorae*, no. 36, ed. Kiessling. His treatment may be compared with that of R. Bultmann in *The History of the Synoptic Tradition*, Eng. trans. John Marsh (Oxford: Blackwell, 1963), p. 217. Ludwig Bieler cited the same sources with similar intent in *Theios Aner*, 2 vols. in 1 (reprint ed., Darmstadt: Wissenschaftliche Buchgesellschaft, 1976), 1:105. For further discussion see H. van der Loos, *The Miracles of Jesus* (Leiden: Brill, 1965), pp. 670–79.

46. Ibid., no. 91, p. 413.

47. Ibid., no. 96, p. 457.

48. Ibid., no. 107, pp. 545–46. Strauss noted that de Wette treated the story as a myth, and others entertained the possibility. He drew attention to the Shekinah glory in the Old Testament, and saw a parallel in Plato's *Symposium*, where Socrates was glorified, though in a natural manner.

49. Ibid., no. 126, pp. 640–49.

50. Ibid., no. 126, p. 649.

51. Ibid., no. 140, p. 743.

52. Ibid., no. 148, pp. 768–73.

53. Ibid., nos. 146, 147, pp. 764–67, 767–68.

54. Ibid., no. 149, pp. 773–77.

55. In a footnote Strauss referred to Hegel's *Phänomenologie des Geistes*, pp. 561ff.; Hegel's *Vorlesungen über die Philosophie der Religion*, 2:234ff.; Marheineke's *Grundlehren der christlichen Dogmatik*, pp. 174ff.; Rosenkranz's *Enzyklopädie der theologischen Wissenschaften*, pp. 38ff., 148ff.; and the third of his own *Streitschriften*, pp. 76ff.

56. Ibid., no. 150, p. 777.

57. Ibid., no. 151, p. 780.

58. Ibid., no. 151, pp. 780–81.

59. Ibid., no. 152, p. 783.

60. The sixth German edition of Schweitzer's *Geschichte der Leben-Jesu-Forschung* contains an appendix listing sixty works (nineteen of them anonymous). Schweitzer pointed out that the list made no claims to completeness. It consisted mainly of works in the University Library in Strasbourg.

61. Vol. 82, July, 1864, p. 83.

62. *GS*, 1:5.

63. The article *Vorläufig zu Beherzigendes bey Würdigung der Frage über die historische oder mythische Grundlage des Lebens Jesu* (1835) was also printed separately. Strauss replied in the first of his *Streitschriften* which Steudel answered in his *Kurzer Bescheid auf Herrn Dr. David Friedrich Straussens Streitschriften* in two parts in the *Tübinger Zeitschrift für Theologie* (1837) with separate reprint.

64. *ThStKr* 9 (1836):770–816. Strauss gave serious consideration to this suggestion, but concluded that nothing would have been gained by it (*Streitschriften*, 3. Heft, pp. 129ff.). Later Ullmann published *Historisch oder Mythisch? Beiträge zur Beantwortung der gegenwärtigen Lebensfrage der Theologie* (Hamburg, 1838; 2nd ed., 1866).

65. Cf. Schweitzer, *Quest*, pp. 106–7; H. Harris, op. cit., pp. 78–79 *et passim*.

66. Eng. trans. from the fourth German edition by John M'Clintock and Charles E. Blumenthal, *The Life of Jesus Christ in its Historical Connexion and Historical Development* (London: Henry G. Bohn, 1851). Previously Neander had counseled against banning Strauss's work in his *Erklärung in Beziehung auf einen ihn betreffenden Artikel der Allgemeinen Zeitung nebst dem auf höher Veranlassung von ihm verfassten Gutachten über das Buch des Dr. Strauss "Leben-Jesu"* (1836).

67. Op. cit., no. 86, p. 136.

68. Ibid., no. 87, p. 137.

69. Ibid., no. 297, pp. 472–76.

70. Ibid., no. 308, p. 487.

71. *The Life of Jesus Christ*, p. ix.

72. Ibid., no. 2, p. 2.

73. Ibid., nos. 4–5, pp. 7–8.

74. On this see H. Harris, op. cit., pp. 85–116; Peter C. Hodgson, *The Formation of Historical Theology*, pp. 73–84.

75. *Tübinger Zeitschrift für Theologie* 3 (1836):207–8; cited from Harris, op. cit., p. 92.

76. Letter by Strauss to Baur, August 19, 1836; cf. Harris, op. cit., pp. 92–93.

77. See above, notes 18 and 42.

78. Letter of October 19, 1860 (Harris, op. cit., p. 111). The occasion of the letter was Zeller's "Die Tübinger historische Schule," *Historische Zeitung* 4 (1860):356–73.

79. Letter of November 6, 1860; cited from Harris, op. cit., p. 115.

80. Op. cit., p. 90.

81. In the first edition of *The Quest of the Historical Jesus*, Schweitzer confused the author with C. G. Wilke, and this error has been perpetuated in subsequent English editions. Julius Wellhausen drew attention to the mistake in his *Einleitung in die drei ersten Evangelien*, 2nd ed. (Berlin: Georg Reimer, 1911), p. 34. This was subsequently corrected by Schweitzer (*Geschichte*, 6th ed., p. 114, n. 4). The question of myth was subsequently taken up by Emanuel Marius, *Die Persönlichkeit Jesu mit besonderer Rücksicht auf die Mythologien and Mysterien der alten Völker* (1879); and Otto Frick, *Mythos und Evangelium* (1879). Bruno Bauer and, later on, A. Drews also questioned the historical basis of the Gospels and spoke of the Christ-myth.

82. Eng. trans, *A New Life of Jesus*, 2nd ed., 2 vols. (London: Williams and Norgate, 1879). The title of the German original indicated Strauss's desire to do for the German people what Renan had done for the French. He considered Renan to be appropriate for the French but not the Germans (op. cit., 1:xviii).

83. Op. cit., 1, no. 24, pp. 195–201.

84. Ibid., 1, no. 25, pp. 213–14.

85. Ibid., 2, no. 100, p. 435.

86. Ibid., 2, no. 100, pp. 435–36; cf. Spinoza's letter of Oldenburg, no date, ca. December, 1675, in *The Chief Works of Benedict de Spinoza*, trans. R. H. M. Elwes (reprint ed., New York: Dover, 1955), 2, no. 21, pp. 298–99; Kant, *Religion within the Limits of Reason Alone*, chap. 2.

87. Ibid., 2, no. 100, p. 436.

88. Ibid., 2, no. 100, p. 437.

89. Ibid., 2, no. 100, p. 439.

90. Op. cit., 1:197; cf. also H. Harris, op. cit., p. 41.

91. *From Hegel to Nietzsche*, p. 334.

92. Cf. Hartlich and Sachs, op. cit., pp. 122–34.

93. *Streitschriften*, 3. Heft, pp. 57–58.

94. While Bultmann acknowledged his debt to many scholars in his "Autobiographical Reflections," Strauss was not one of them (C. W. Kegley, ed., *The Theology of Rudolf Bultmann* [London: S.C.M. Press, 1966], pp. xix-xxv). See further Roger A. Johnson, *The Origins of Demythologizing: Philosophy and Historiography in the Theology of Rudolf Bultmann* (Leiden: Brill, 1974), pp. 138–41.

95. *GS*, 1:6.

96. Letter of July 22, 1846 (cf. Barth, *PT*, p. 543).

11. *Baur and the Tübingen School*

1. There is no complete edition of Baur's works, but several have been reprinted in the five-volume edition of Baur's *Ausgewählte Werke in Einzelausgaben*, ed. Klaus Scholder (Stuttgart-Bad Castatt: Friedrich Fromann Verlag, 1963–75). Recent studies containing bibliographies include Wolfgang Geiger, *Spekulation und Kritik. Die Geschichtstheologie Ferdinand Christian Baurs* (Munich: Chr. Kaiser Verlag, 1964); Peter C. Hodgson, *The Formation of Historical Theology: A Study of Ferdinand Christian Baur* (New York: Harper & Row, 1966); Peter Friedrich, *Ferdinand Christian Baur als Symboliker*, STGNJ 12 (Göttingen: Vandenhoeck & Rupprecht, 1975); and Horton Harris, *The Tübingen School* (Oxford: The Clarendon Press, 1975). Details of other works are given in the notes below, and in Klaus Scholder, "Baur, Ferdinand Christian," *TRE*, 5:352–59.

2. Heinz Liebing, "Historical Critical Theology. In Commemoration of the Death of Ferdinand Christian Baur, December 2, 1960," *JTC* 3 (1967):55–69 (esp. 55–56).

3. *Interpretation*, p. 27.

4. S. Neill, *Interpretation*, p. 19; cf. P. C. Hodgson, op. cit., pp. 285–91 for a complete list. I am informed by Professor Peter Stuhlmacher that a substantial collection of Baur's sermons have been

preserved at Tübingen but have not yet been edited and published. They would doubtless throw light on Baur's beliefs and personal faith.

5. Cf. P. C. Hodgson, op. cit., p. 11; H. Harris, op. cit., pp. 143–46.

6. This was the view of his brother, Friedrich August Baur, in a letter to Eduard Zeller dated January 12, 1861. But see the discussion in Heinz Liebing, "Ferdinand Christian Baurs Kritik an Schleiermachers Glaubenslehre," *ZTK* 54 (1957):225–45; P. C. Hodgson, op. cit., pp. 13–14; H. Harris, op. cit., pp. 146–54. In his early career Baur was most impressed by *Der christliche Glaube*. However, he was critical of Schleiermacher's relative supernaturalism and pantheism, as he wrote to his brother, Friedrich August Baur (July 26, 1823). The letter contained the following observation on Schleiermacher's christology:

> When the principal doctrines concerning the Person of the Redeemer are themselves deduced from the religious selfconsciousness, with the result that the external history of Jesus is viewed as a history of the inner developments of the religious self-consciousness, then I can think of the Person of Christ as the Redeemer only as a certain form and capacity of the self-consciousness which appeared in an external history merely because the natural development of the selfconsciousness in its highest perfection must necessarily at some time take this form. Christ is thus in every man and the external appearance of Jesus is here also not the original form of Christ; but in the historical form only the archetypal, ideal form is supposed to be demonstrated and the inner consciousness brought to clear view. It is abundantly clear how precisely this view hangs together with the pantheistic-idealistic basic view of the whole system (cf. H. Harris, op. cit., p. 149).

7. Facsimile reprint of the original Stuttgart edition, published by J. B. Metzler (Aalen: Scientia Verlag, 1979).

8. Op. cit., 1:xi.

9. Cf. Karl Barth, *PT*, p. 503.

10. Op. cit., pp. xi-xii.

11. *Das manichäische Religionssystem nach den Quellen neu untersucht und entwickelt* (Tübingen: Hopfer de l'Orme, 1831); *Die christliche Gnosis, oder die christliche Religions-Philosophie in ihrer geschichtlichen Entwicklung* (Tübingen: C. F. Osiander, 1835); and his study of "Apollonius von Tyana und Christus, oder das Verhältniss des Pythagoreismus zum Christentum," *Tübinger Zeitschrift für Theologie* 6 (1832):40–124, reprint in F. C. Baur, *Drei Abhandlungen zur Geschichte der alten Philosophie und ihres Verhältnisses zum Christentum*, ed. E. Zeller (Fues's Verlag, 1876; facsimile reprint ed., Aalen: Scientia Verlag, 1978).

In his early years Baur was also influenced by Ernst Gottlieb Bengel, who stimulated Baur's interest in historical theology, Barthold Niebuhr's *Römische Geschichte*, the methods of the classical scholar, F. A. Wolf, and Schleiermacher's Plato research (cf. P. C. Hodgson, op. cit., p. 9).

12. *Drei Abhandlungen*, p. 227.

13. Tübingen: C. F. Osiander, 1835; reprint ed., Darmstadt: Wissenschaftliche Buchgesellschaft, 1967.

14. *Theologischer Jahrbücher* 6 (1847):309–89.

15. Stuttgart and Tübingen: J. G. Cotta'schen Verlagshandlung, 1835.

16. *Paulus, der Apostel Jesu Christi. Sein Leben und Wirken, seine Briefe und seine Lehre. Ein Beitrag zu einer kritischen Geschichte der Urchristentums* (Stuttgart: Becher und Müller, 1845); 2nd ed. edited by E. Zeller, 2 vols. (Leipzig: Fues's Verlag, 1866–67); Eng. trans. A. Menzies, *Paul the Apostle of Jesus Christ, His Life and Work, His Epistles and His Doctrine. A Contribution to a Critical History of Primitive Christianity* (London and Edinburgh: Williams and Norgate, 1875).

17. *Kritische Untersuchungen über die kanonischen Evangelien, ihr Verhältniss zu einander, ihren Charakter und Ursprung* (Tübingen: L. F. Fues, 1847).

18. *Das Markusevangelium nach ihrem Ursprung und Charakter. Nebst einem Anhang über das Evangelium Marcions* (Tübingen: L. F. Fues, 1851).

19. *Vorlesungen über neutestamentliche Theologie*, ed., Ferdinand Friedrich Baur (Leipzig: Fues's Verlag, 1864; reprint ed., with new introduction by Werner Georg Kümmel [Darmstadt: Wissenschaftliche Buchgesellschaft, 1973]).

20. Tübingen: C. F. Osiander, 1838.

21. Tübingen: C. F. Osiander, 1841–43.

22. Stuttgart: Bechers Verlag, 1847; 2nd ed. (Tübingen: L. F. Fues, 1858).

23. Op. cit., p. 22.

24. *Tübinger Zeitschrift für Theologie* 5 (1831):61–206; reprint in *AW*, 1:1–146.

25. Hodgson (op. cit., p. 23) believes that it was in connection with his work on *Die christliche Gnosis* (1835) that Baur first read Hegel's *Vorlesungen über die Philosophie der Religion* which Marheineke had published in 1832. It was probably his first direct contact with Hegel's thought, and it may have come about through the agency of Strauss who had spent the winter of 1831–32 in Berlin with a view to learning more of Hegel. He had returned an enthusiastic Hegelian, and had introduced Hegelianism into his lectures at Tübingen. Baur's first mention of Hegel is in a letter to F. A. Baur, where he says that Hegel's *Religionsphilosophie* had occupied him throughout the winter of 1834–35. It attracted him in many respects, and he has not been able to find in it the "atrocities customarily attributed to it" (February 15, 1835). Later on Baur commended Hegel in an address he delivered as rector of the university in 1841 which aroused opposition (cf. Hodgson, op. cit., p. 18). Baur testified to Hegel's influence in *Die christliche Gnosis* in his survey of "Die evangelische theologische Fakultät vom Jahr 1812 bis 1848" in K. Klüpfel, ed., *Geschichte und Beschreibung der Universität Tübingen* (1847), p. 407.

Because of his sympathetic treatment of Hegel in *Die christliche Gnosis* and his silence about the contents of Strauss's *Leben Jesu*, Baur came to be associated with the Hegelians in the minds of some contemporaries like Hengstenberg in the *Evangelische Kirchen-Zeitung*. This drew from Baur his "Abgenöthigte Erklärung gegen einen Artikel der *Evangelischen Kirchen-Zeitung*, herausgegeben von D. E. W. Hengstenberg, Prof. der Theol. an der Universität zu Berlin, Mai 1836," (*Tübinger Zeitschrift für Theologie* 3 [1836]:179–232; reprint in *AW*, 1:267–320). Here he testified to the "blessing for church and state and the abiding fruit for all" of the work of "men like Schleiermacher and Hegel" (*AW*, 1:313–14). But in a footnote to this seal of approval, Baur was careful to qualify his position. "I do not shun to mention here also Hegel. I am not dependent on any philosophical system, because I well know how deceptive it is to make oneself dependent on human authority, but equally I have the conviction that much can be learned in theology from Hegel too, and I also believe that many of those who are so quick and ready to denounce him would judge otherwise, if they could bring themselves to become more closely acquainted with his writings" (*AW*, 1:313). Baur went on to defend Hegel's alleged pantheism and "Satanic teaching," claiming that there was "an immanent relation of God to the world that is unjustly denounced as pantheistic, and everything that is denounced as pantheistic is not pure and simply pantheistic" (ibid., p. 318).

26. Tübingen: L. F. Fues, 1852; reprint in *AW*, 2:1–282, and also Hildesheim: Georg Olms, 1962; Eng. trans. in Peter C. Hodgson, ed., *Ferdinand Christian Baur on the Writing of Church History* (New York: Oxford University Press, 1968), pp. 41–257.

27. *Vorlesungen über die christliche Dogmengeschichte*, ed. Ferdinand Friedrich Baur, 3 vols. (Leipzig: Fues's Verlag, 1865–67); Eng. trans. of introduction in P. C. Hodgson, ed., op. cit., pp. 259–366.

28. 5 vols. (Tübingen: L. F. Fues, 1853–62). The last three volumes were edited by F. F. Baur and E. Zeller. Reprint of vol. 1, *Das Christentum und die christliche Kirche der drei ersten Jahrhunderte* in *AW*, vol. 3. Eng. trans. of vol. 1 by A. Menzies, *The Church History of the First Three Centuries*, 2 vols. (London: Williams and Norgate, 1878–79). Reprint of vol. 5, *Die Kirchengeschichte des neunzehnten Jahrhunderts* in *AW*, vol. 4.

29. Eng. trans. 1:x.

30. P. C. Hodgson, ed., op. cit., p. 213, commenting on Neander's *Leben Jesu Christi in seinem geschichtlichen Zusammenhang* (1837) and his *Geschichte der Pflanzung und Leitung der christlichen Kirche durch die Apostel* (1832). Cf. also *The Church History of the First Three Centuries*, 1:1–2.

31. Preface to *Die christliche Lehre von der Dreieinigkeit und Menschwerdung Gottes*, pp. xviii-xix (*AW*, 2:298).

32. Preface to *Die christliche Lehre von der Versöhnung*, p. vii (*AW*, 2:285–86).

33. Hegel received only eight pages and was ambiguously referred to as "the most important philosopher next to Schelling who has become for the great public at least almost completely silent" (*AW*, 4:348). Kant, Fichte, and Schelling all received more attention, while Schleiermacher had fifty-three pages devoted to him.

34. *Theologische Jahrbücher* 10 (1851):294–96, Eng. trans. in Kümmel, pp. 127–29.

35. Kümmel, pp. 128–29 (slightly adapted).

36. *Paul the Apostle*, 1:105.

37. Ibid., 1:245–365.

38. Ibid., 2:106–111.

39. Ibid., 2:237. On the question of Paul and Jesus, see Friedemann Regner, *"Paulus und Jesus" im Neunzehnten Jahrhundert. Beiträge zur Geschichte des Themas "Paulus und Jesus"*, STGNJ 32 (Göttingen: Vandenhoeck & Ruprecht, 1977).

40. Ibid., 2:240–41.

41. Ibid., 2:247.

42. Ibid., 2:253 (with Baur's Greek translated); cf. *Vorlesungen über neutestamentliche Theologie*, pp. 186–95.

43. *Kritische Untersuchungen über die kanonischen Evangelien*, p. 74.

44. Ibid., p. 108.

45. Ibid., p. 310.

46. Ibid., p. 233; cf. John 7:10; 8:59; 10:39.

47. Ibid., pp. 373–74.

48. Ibid.; cf. *The Church History of the First Three Centuries*, 2:79–85. Baur also saw reflections of the Montanist and Paschal controversies.

49. Ibid., pp. 22–40.

50. Ibid., pp. 40–70.

51. "The greatest characteristic of the work is that it gives a critique of Gospel history without a critique of the Gospels" (ibid., p. 41).

52. Ibid., p. 23.

53. Ibid., p. 36.

54. Ibid., pp. 535–67. Baur returned to deal with Mark at greater length in *Das Markusevangelium* (1851) and current theories in "Rückblick auf die neuesten Untersuchungen über das Markusevangelium," *Theologische Jahrbücher* 12 (1953):54–93.

55. Baur rejected the theory of a proto-Mark as well as the Papias tradition concerning Mark and Peter (Eusebius, *Historia Ecclesiastica*, 3, 39). He saw no evidence of such a relationship in the Gospel itself (ibid., pp. 536ff.; *Das Markusevangelium*, pp. 133–52).

56. *The Church History of the First Three Centuries*, 1:78.

57. *Kritische Untersuchungen*, p. 571.

58. Ibid., pp. 571–72; cf. Eusebius, *Historia Ecclesiastica*, 3, 39; 4, 22.

59. Ibid., pp. 605–9; cf. *Vorlesungen über neutestamentliche Theologie*, p. 45.

60. Ibid., p. 600.

61. Ibid., pp. 606–7.

62. Ibid., p. 609.

63. Ibid., pp. 609–15.

64. The work was based on Baur's lectures between 1852 and 1860 (op. cit., p. iii).

65. Op. cit., pp. 122–23.

66. Ibid., pp. 45–46; cf. *The Church History of the First Three Centuries*, 1:23–26. In *Die Tübinger Schule*, 2nd ed. (1860), pp. 12–13 (*AW*, 3:306–7) Baur expressed surprise that critics like Uhlhorn, Hase, and Ritschl could suppose that he traced the origin of Christianity back only to Paul, the Fourth Gospel, or some early Christian group.

67. Ibid., pp. 44–60.

68. Ibid., pp. 60–62.

69. Ibid., pp. 63–64.

70. Ibid., p. 75.

71. Ibid.

72. Ibid., p. 93. Baur's last journal article was devoted to "Die Bedeutung des Ausdrucks *ho huios tou anthrōpou*," *Zeitschrift für wissenschaftliche Theologie*, no. 3 (1860), pp. 274–92. For comparison of Baur's views with more recent scholarship, see P. C. Hodgson, op. cit., pp. 228–34.

73. Ibid., p. 90.

74. Ibid., pp. 113–14; cf. pp. 94–95, 105, 109–10.

75. *The Church History of the First Three Centuries*, 1:42–43; cf. *Vorlesungen*, pp. 126–27.

76. Ibid., p. 43.

77. See chapter 2, notes 10 and 11.

78. *ODCC*, p. 144.

79. See above, n. 6.

80. In addition to passages already noted containing affinities with Hegel, see his "Conclusions and Suggestions" in his *Epochen der kirchlichen Geschichtschreibung* (Eng. trans. in P. C. Hodgson,

ed., op. cit., pp. 241–57) and the introduction of Baur's *Lehrbuch der Dogmengeschichte* (*AW,* 2:303–10).

81. Barth, pp. 499–507; W. Geiger, op. cit., pp. 225–47.

82. E. Troeltsch, "Adolf von Harnack und Ferdinand Christian Baur," in *Festgabe für D.Dr. A. Von Harnack, zum siebzigsten Geburtstag* (Tübingen: J. C. B. Mohr, 1921), p. 284.

83. *Die christliche Gnosis,* pp. 710–11, 717, 720–21; cf. P. C. Hodgson, op. cit., pp. 60–66.

84. "Its essential character consists in the fact that it makes Christian consciousness its principle, and develops the entire content of Christian faith from the pronouncements of Christian consciousness" (*Kirchengeschichte des neunzehten Jahrhunderts,* 2nd ed. [1877], p. 219). "Schleiermacher's *Christian Faith* has its great historical significance in the fact that it is the first attempt that has been carried through to demonstrate the Christian faith as the original property of the human spirit, as something that has not come to it from outside, but rather as something that has sprung from its own innermost depths." However, it was too subjectively based. There was need of a "progression from the standpoint of the subjectivity of consciousness, upon which Schleiermacher remains standing, to the standpoint of objectivity" (*Vorlesungen über die christliche Dogmengeschichte,* 3:351, 349; cf. W. Geiger, op. cit., p. 159).

85. *Theology of the New Testament,* Eng. trans. K. Grobel (New York: Scribner's, 1955), 2:244–45.

86. *AW,* 5 is devoted to writings for and against the Tübingen School, dated between 1855 and 1862. They include Karl Hase, *Die Tübinger Schule. Ein Sendschreiben an Herrn Dr. Ferdinand Christian Baur* (Leipzig: Breitkopf und Härtel, 1855); F. C. Baur, *An Herrn Dr. Karl Hase. Beantwortung des Sendschreibens "Die Tübinger Schule"* (Tübingen: Fues, 1855); G. Uhlhorn, "Die älteste Kirchengeschichte in der Darstellung der Tübinger Schule," *Jahrbücher für Deutsche Theologie* 3 (1838):280–349; F. C. Baur, *Die Tübinger Schule und ihre Stellung zur Gegenwart,* 2nd ed. (Tübingen: Fues, 1860); Albrecht Ritschl, "Ueber geschichtliche Methode in der Erforschung des Urchristenthums," *Jahrbücher für Deutsche Theologie* 6 (1861):430–59; Heinrich von Sybel, "Die historische Kritik und das Wunder," *Historische Zeitschrift* 6 (1861):356–73; A. Ritschl, "Einige Erläuterungen zu dem Sendschreiben: 'Die historische Kritik und das Wunder,'" *Historische Zeitschrift* 8 (1862):85–99.

87. Cf. P. C. Hodgson, op. cit., pp. 6–7. In his study of *The Tübingen School* Horton Harris lists as members the following whose careers and thought he sketches: Baur, Eduard Zeller, Albert Schwegler, Karl Christian Planck, Karl Reinhold Köstlin, Albrecht Ritschl, Adolf Hilgenfeld, and Gustav Volkmar. Although Strauss was associated with Baur and Tübingen in the minds of many, Baur was at pains to dissociate himself from Strauss. Harris argues that there were two qualifications which constituted membership of the School and which ensured that there were ultimately only eight genuine members: acceptance of the principle of a purely historical interpretation of Christianity and the New Testament, and the making of an essential contribution to the historical development of the School itself (op. cit., p. 247).

88. In the year following Baur's death Ritschl criticized Baur's christology and method (see above, n. 86). In his study of *Die Entstehung der altkatholischen Kirche* (1850; 2nd ed., 1857) Ritschl offered an alternative account of Christian origins. He rejected metaphysical speculation and stressed Christian order for living *Lebensführung.* Later on Ritschl expounded the person and work of Jesus in terms of his "vocation" (using Baur's term *Beruf*) to found and maintain the kingdom of God (*Die christliche Lehre von der Rechtfertigung und Versöhnung,* 3 vols. [1870–74]). There were marked similarities with Baur but also important differences, including the claim that Mark was the first Gospel. On Ritschl and Baur see Philip Hefner, *Faith and the Vitalities of History: A Theological Study Based on the Work of Albrecht Ritschl* (New York: Harper and Row, 1966), pp. 12–44.

89. Cf. H. Harris, op. cit., pp. 113–26, 238–48. In 1849 Hilgenfeld published *Das Evangelium und die Briefe Johannis, nach ihrem Lehrbegriff dargestellt,* in which he attacked the main tenets of orthodoxy. This was followed by *Das Markus-Evangelium, nach seiner Composition in der Evangelien-Literatur, seinem Ursprung und Charakter* (Leipzig: Breitkopf und Härtel, 1850). Baur described it as "completely weak, untenable and without principle." His own study of *Das Marcusevangelium* (1851) was in part a reply. Hilgenfeld further annoyed Baur by his attempt to defend the authenticity of 1 Thessalonians. Personal relations became increasingly strained, and Hilgenfeld developed his own positions, notably in *Das Urchristentum in den Hauptwendepunkten seines Entwicklungsganges, mit besonderer Rücksicht auf die neuesten Verhandlungen der Herren Hase und Baur* (Jena, 1855).

90. Schwegler wrote a massive, two-volume study of *Das Nachapostolische Zeitalter in den*

Hauptmomenten seiner Entwicklung (Tübingen: Fues, 1846), in which he sought to fill in the details which Baur had not as yet done. Investigation of the historical Jesus was excluded in the belief that the sources were too unreliable to permit positive conclusions. Thereafter, Schwegler turned to history and philosophy.

91. Köstlin responded to Baur's views on the Gospels in *Der Ursprung und die Komposition der synoptischen Evangelien* (Stuttgart: Mächen, 1853). In it he argued that tendency criticism was insufficient to determine literary relationships, and that literary criticism must be resorted to. Köstlin now argued that, though Mark was the youngest of the canonical Gospels, both Matthew and Luke had made use of a proto-Mark.

92. In *Die Religion Jesu* (Leipzig: Brockhaus, 1857) Volkmar put forward new proposals concerning the origin of the Gospels. He acknowledged that there was a person called Jesus who was crucified but little beyond that. He traced the Gospel stories to the apostolic and post-apostolic ages and the controversy between the Paulinists and Jewish Christians, maintaining Baur's basic framework, but with a very different explanation (cf. H. Harris, op. cit., pp. 233–37). Volkmar's later writings include *Der Ursprung unserer Evangelien nach den Urkunden, Laut den neuern Entdeckungen und Verhandlungen* (Zürich: J. Herzog, 1866); *Die Evangelien, oder Marcus und die Synopsis der kanonischen und ausserkanonischen Evangelien nach dem ältesten Text, mit historisch-exegetischem Commentar* (Leipzig: Fues, 1870); *Jesus Nazarenus und die erste christliche Zeit, mit den beiden ersten Erzählern* (Zürich: Caesar Schmidt, 1882).

12. *Later Critical Study*

1. Karl Lachmann (1793–1851) studied theology briefly before turning to classical philology. He became a full professor at Berlin in 1827. He established a reputation for his editions of classical and Middle High German texts.

2. *Theologische Studien und Kritiken* 8 (1835):570–90; reprinted in Lachmann's *Novum Testamentum Graece et Latine*, vol. 2 (1850). The key sections have been translated by N. H. Palmer in "Lachmann's Argument," *NTS* 13 (1966–67):368–78. Palmer also touches on the argument in *The Logic of Gospel Criticism* (London: Macmillan; New York: St. Martin's Press, 1968).

3. *NTS*, 13:372.

4. Ibid., p. 370.

5. Ibid., pp. 372–73.

6. Ibid., p. 374.

7. Ibid., p. 373.

8. Ibid.

9. Ibid., pp. 374–75.

10. Ibid., p. 376.

11. Cf. B. C. Butler, *The Originality of Matthew: A Critique of the Two-Document Hypothesis* (Cambridge: Cambridge University Press, 1951), pp. 62–71; W. R. Farmer, "'The Lachmann Fallacy,'" *NTS* 14 (1967–68):441–43. Farmer suggests that the term originated with Wellhausen.

12. *The Synoptic Problem: A Critical Analysis* (Macon, GA: Mercer University Press, 1976), p. 17.

13. Op. cit. (Dresden and Leipzig: G. Fleischer, 1838), pp. 293, 684; cf. Kümmel, p. 148.

14. An anonymous reply by "Philosophotos Aletheias" appeared under the title *Die Evangelien, ihr Geist, ihre Verfasser, und ihr Verhältnis zur einander* (Leipzig, 1845); cf. Schweitzer, *Quest*, p. 124. It saw Paul as an evil genius and urged that criticism should be directed at weeding out the Pauline elements in the Gospels. See above, ch. 9, n. 90.

15. Op. cit. (Leipzig: Breitkopf und Härtel, 1838), 1:viii.

16. Ibid., 1:iii–iv.

17. Ibid., 1:67–68.

18. Ibid., 1:71–73.

19. Ibid., 1:82–83.

20. Ibid., 1:83.

21. Ibid., 1:115.

22. Ibid., 2:192. In a footnote Weisse refers to F. C. Baur, *Die christliche Gnosis*, pp. 502ff.

23. Ibid., 1:98.

24. Ibid., 1:110.

25. Ibid., 1:139–232.

26. Ibid., 2:427; cf. pp. 305–438.

27. Ibid., 1:594.

28. *Die Evangelienfrage in ihrem gegenwärtigen Stadium, Über den gegenwärtigen Standpunkt der Evangelienkritik und H. Ewalds "Geschichte Christus und seiner Zeit"* (Leipzig: Breitkopf und Härtel, 1856), p. 85.

29. Ewald became a professor at Göttingen in 1827, but was dismissed ten years later as one of the "Göttingen Seven" professors who objected to the unconstitutional behavior of the King of Hanover. He obtained a chair at Tübingen (1838), where he soon quarreled with Baur. He returned to Göttingen in 1848. His study of the prophets inspired him to enter politics, but his opposition to the Prussian government led to his dismissal in 1867. He produced a Hebrew grammar and wrote extensively on the Old Testament. His *Geschichte des Volkes Israel* (1858–59), Eng. trans. *The History of Israel*, 7 vols. (London: Longmans, Green, 1876–88), dealt with *The Life and Times of Christ* in vol. 6, and *The Apostolic Age* in vol. 7.

30. *Jahrbücher der biblischen Wissenschaft* (1848), 1:113–54.

31. J. Wellhausen, "Heinrich Ewald," in *Festschrift zur Feier des Hundertfünfzigjährigen Besetehens der Königlichen Gesellschaft der Wissenschaften zu Göttingen* (Berlin, 1901), pp. 61–88, see especially p. 66.

32. See chapter 11, notes 86 and 88.

33. Eng. trans. of vol. 1 by T. Goadby, *Revelation: Its Nature and Record* (Edinburgh: T. & T. Clark, 1884), p. 256.

34. *Quest*, p. 135. In *Die Evangelienfrage in ihrem gegenwärtigen Stadium*, Weisse faulted Ewald for not going far enough in dissociating Jesus from the ideas of his time. To Schweitzer, his fault lay in failing to see the full significance of the eschatological thought world of Jesus.

35. Op. cit., p. 48.

36. 2 vols. (Leipzig: Wilhelm Engelmann, 1862).

37. (Leipzig: Wilhelm Engelmann, 1863); translation of extracts in Kümmel, pp. 152–55. Holtzmann's later works include *Lehrbuch der historisch-kritischen Einleitung in das Neue Testament* (Freiburg: J. C. B. Mohr, 1885; 3rd ed., 1892); *Lehrbuch der neutestamentlichen Theologie*, 2 vols. (Tübingen: J. C. B. Mohr, 1896–97), revised by A. Jülicher and W. Bauer (1911); *Das Johannesevangelium untersucht und erklärt* (Darmstadt: Waitz, 1887; 3rd ed., 1908); *Die Entstehung des Neuen Testaments* (Halle: Gebauer-Schwetschke, 1904); *Das messianische Bewusstsein Jesu. Ein Beitrag zur Leben-Jesu-Forschung* (Tübingen: J. C. B. Mohr, 1907).

38. Holtzmann posited the existence of a primary source behind Mark which he called "A." He believed that Mark shortened it by eliminating much of its teaching material. However, in his *Lehrbuch der historisch-kritischen Einleitung*, pp. 351–57, the idea of an *Urevangelium* received less prominence. Holtzmann maintained that no essentially new solution had appeared in the meantime. It was only later that the sayings source came to be designated as Q, probably meaning *Quelle*, source (cf. F. Neirynck, "The Symbol Q (= Quelle)" and "Once More: The Symbol Q," in *Evangelica: Gospel Studies—Études d'Évangile, Bibliotheca Ephemeridum Theologicarum Lovaniensium* 60 [Leuven: Leuven University Press, 1982], pp. 683–89, 689–90).

39. *Das messianische Bewusstsein Jesu*, p. 98.

40. Ibid., p. 100.

41. See above, chap. 9, n. 76.

42. Op. cit., pp. 38–40.

43. Ibid., p. 58.

44. "The Griesbach Hypothesis in the 19th Century," *JSNT* 3 (1979):29–60; idem., *The Revival of the Griesbach Hypothesis: An Analysis and Appraisal*, SNTS Monograph Series, no. 44 (Cambridge: Cambridge University Press, 1983), pp. 3–7.

45. C. G. Wilke, *Der Urevangelist*, p. 446; H. J. Holtzmann, *Die synoptischen Evangelien*, p. 113.

46. *The Griesbach Hypothesis*, p. 7.

47. *Quest*, p. 204.

48. Bauer went to Berlin in 1828 to study theology and philosophy, especially under Hegel. He obtained his habilitation in 1834 and began teaching as a right wing Hegelian. He also came under the

influence of Hengstenberg. His review of Strauss's *Leben Jesu* in the *Jahrbücher für wissenschaftliche Kritik* 9 (1835) criticized Strauss from the standpoint of speculative orthodoxy. Strauss had failed to see the absolute necessity of divine and human nature in Jesus as the culmination of previous development of the spirit. From 1836 to 1838 Bauer edited the *Zeitschrift für spekulative Theologie*.

Bauer's break with orthodoxy was marked by his *Herr Dr. Hengstenberg. Ein Beitrag zur Kritik des religiösen Bewusstseins. Kritische Briefe über den Gegensatz des Gesetzes und des Evangeliums* (1839). It was followed by numerous other works including his *Kritik der evangelischen Geschichte des Johannes* (1840); *Kritik der evangelischen Geschichte der Synoptiker*, 2 vols. (Leipzig: O. Wigand, 1841; reprint ed., Hildesheim: G. Olms, 1974); *Kritik der evangelischen Geschichte der Synoptiker und des Johannes*, vols. 1 and 2 (Leipzig: O. Wigand, 1841); vol. 3 (Braunschweig: F. Otto, 1842); *Kritik der Evangelien und Geschichte ihres Ursprungs*, 3 vols. (Berlin, 1850–51); *Kritik der Paulinischen Briefe*, 3 vols. (Berlin, 1850–52; reprint ed. in 1 vol., Aalen: Scientia Verlag, 1972); *Philo, Strauss und Renan und das Urchristenthum* (Berlin, 1874); *Christus und die Caesaren. Der Ursprung des Christenthums aus dem römischen Griechenthum* (Berlin, 1877; reprint ed., Hildesheim: G. Olms, 1968); *Das Urevangelium und die Gegner der Schrift: "Christus und die Caesaren"* (Berlin, 1880).

Tensions in Berlin led to his transfer to Bonn (1839). His interpretation of Hegel as an atheist led to increased opposition, especially through his paper *Die Posaune des jüngsten Gerichts über Hegel den Atheisten und Antichristen* (Leipzig, 1841; Eng. trans. of extract, "The Trumpet of the Last Judgment over Hegel," in L. S. Stepelevich, ed., *The Young Hegelians: An Anthology* [Cambridge: Cambridge University Press, 1983], pp. 177–86). The Prussian education minister circulated the Prussian universities for reports on whether Bauer should be allowed to retain his right to teach. Bonn replied in the negative, and the right was revoked (1842). The Bonn faculty did not want a professional Hegelian and an outspoken critic of Schleiermacher and Neander. In later life, Bauer entered politics as a radical, though somewhat conservative, atheist.

See further Ernst Barnikol, *Bruno Bauer. Studien und Materialen. Aus dem Nachlass ausgewählt und zusammengestellt von Peter Reimer und Hans-Martin Sass* (Assen: Van Gorcum, 1972); Ferdinand Berger, "Bruno Bauers Auseinandersetzung mit David Friedrich Strauss," *NZSTh* 16 (1974): 131–45; William J. Brazill, *The Young Hegelians* (New Haven and London: Yale University Press, 1970), pp. 175–226; Peter Cornehl, *Die Zukunft der Versöhnung. Eschatologie und Emanzipation in der Aufklärung bei Hegel und in der Hegelschen Schule* (Göttingen: Vandenhoeck & Rupprecht, 1971); David McLellan, *The Young Hegelians and Karl Marx* (London: Macmillan, 1969), pp. 48–84; Joachim Mehlhausen, "Die religionsphilosophische Begründung der spekulativen Theologie Bruno Bauers," *ZKG* 78 (1967):102–29; idem., "Bauer, Bruno," *TRE* 5:314–17; idem., "Der Umschlag der theologischen Hegelinterpretation dargetan an Bruno Bauer," in Georg Schwaiger, ed., *Kirche und Theologie im 19. Jahrhundert*, *STGNJ* 11 (Göttingen: Vandenhoeck & Rupprecht, 1976), pp. 175–97; Schweitzer, *Quest*, pp. 137–60.

49. *RGG*³, 1, col. 924.

50. Op. cit., 1:viii.

51. Ibid.

52. C. G. Wilke, *Der Urevangelist*, pp. 685–86.

53. Ibid., p. 691.

54. *Kritik der evangelischen Geschichte der Synoptiker,* 1:xi-xii.

55. Ibid., 1:xiv.

56. Ibid., 1:xv.

57. Ibid., 1:xviii.

58. Ibid., 1:xxi.

59. Ibid., 1:127.

60. Ibid., 3:14.

61. Ibid., 3:14–15.

62. Ibid., 3:15–17; cf. C. H. Weisse, *Die evangelische Geschichte*, 1:324–25, 530.

63. Ibid., 3:241; cf. p. 311.

64. Ibid., 3:307.

65. Ibid., 3:308.

66. Ibid., 3:315.

67. Ibid., 3:313.

68. Cf. W. J. Brazill, op. cit., pp. 198–207.

69. "Ludwig Feuerbach and the End of Classical Philosophy," (1888), chap. 4; cf. Karl Marx and Frederick Engels, *Selected Works* (London: Lawrence and Wishart; New York: International Publishers, 1968), p. 618; cf. p. 602.

70. *Quest*, pp. 161–79.

71. Cf. Schweitzer, *Quest*, p. 162, who questions whether the author had ever read a line of Bauer's work.

72. *Quest*, p. 166, where Schweitzer notes that he was the first to place the eschatology recognized by Reimarus and Strauss in an eschatological setting (albeit that of Venturini) and to write a life of Jesus governed by the idea of eschatology.

73. Between 1843 and 1845 Renan studied at the seminary of Saint-Sulpice. His personal unhappiness, his distaste for Catholic philosophy and theology, and his interest in Kant and German scholarship caused growing doubts about his vocation and about the existence of God. In 1852, Renan produced a doctoral thesis on *Averroës et l'Averroîsme*. However, it was in the realm of philology that his professional expertise lay. Renan's *Vie de Jésus* became the first volume of his *Histoire des Origines du Christianisme*, 7 vols. plus index vol. (Paris: Calmann-Lévy, 1863–83; Eng. trans. *The History of the Origins of Christianity* [London: Mathieson Co., 1890]). References to Renan's *Life of Jesus* are to this English translation. Numerous other translations were also made. Despite his skepticism, Renan could not let go of religion. He continued to write on religious subjects to the end of his life, including a five-volume *History of the People of Israel*, Eng. trans. (Boston: Roberts Brothers, 1888–96). Renan's *Oeuvres Complètes* were edited by Henriette Psichari, 10 vols. (Paris: Calmann-Lévy, 1947–61). See further, Owen Chadwick, *The Secularization of the European Mind in the Nineteenth Century*, Gifford Lectures of 1973–74 (Cambridge: Cambridge University Press, 1975); Vytas V. Gaigalas, *Ernest Renan and his French Catholic Critics* (North Quincy, MA: The Christopher Publishing House, 1972); Jean G. H. Hoffmann, *Les Vies de Jésus et le Jésus de l'Histoire. Étude de la valeur historique des Vies de Jésus de langue française, non catholiques, d'Ernest Renan à Charles Guignebert, Acta Seminarii Neotestamentici Upsaliensis*, no. 17 (Paris: Messageries Évangeliques Distributeur, 1947); M.-J. Lagrange, *Christ and Renan: A Commentary on Ernest Renan's "The Life of Jesus"*, Eng. trans. Maisie Ward (London: Sheed and Ward, 1928); Schweitzer, *Quest*, pp. 180–92; W. H. Wardman, *Ernest Renan: A Critical Biography* (London: University of London, The Athlone Press, 1964).

74. Cf. W. H. Wardman, op. cit., p. 77.

75. *The Life of Jesus*, p. 14.

76. Ibid., pp. 70–71. This translation conveys perhaps a slightly more intellectualistic sense than the French original. It translates both "esprit" and "âme" by "mind."

77. Ibid., p. 136.

78. Ibid., p. 137.

79. Ibid., p. 249.

80. Cf. *Quest*, p. 187.

81. *The Life of Jesus*, pp. 264–66.

82. Ibid., pp. x-xi. It was written four years after the book's first appearance. Renan had revised the work in the meantime, and responded in the preface to his critics.

83. In the course of the preface, Renan mentioned Strauss, Baur, and numerous other German writers whom he discussed in general terms. Before the book had even been published, the liberal Protestant, Albert Réville, urged Renan to delay until Strauss had finished revising his own *Life of Jesus*. He wanted Renan to have the last word and write a history, not "un plaidoyer." But Renan was in no mood for delays. He later corresponded with Strauss on the subject of the Franco-Prussian War (Wardman, op. cit., pp. 80, 117–19).

84. The Introduction contained a general discussion of documents (pp. xxxiiilvi), but the *Life* was not based on careful evaluation of sources.

85. Ibid., p. xi.

86. Ibid., pp. xxii.

87. The Everyman's Library edition of *The Life of Jesus* (London: J. M. Dent; New York: E. P. Dutton, 1927) noted some 180 titles of works in the British Museum Catalogue. Schweitzer, *Geschichte*, pp. 647–51, contains an appendix listing eighty-five works. V. V. Gaigalas refers to seventeen volumes in the Library of Congress containing a collection of *Réfutations de la "Vie de*

Jésus'' (op. cit., p. 29). He also notes a collection of some 300 books and pamphlets in the University of Strasbourg on the subject and Philibert Milsand, *Bibliographie des publications relatives au livre de M. Renan, "Vie de Jésus," de juillet 1863 à juin 1864* (Paris: Dentu, 1864).

88. Colani's article was subsequently published separately, *Examen de la Vie de Jésus de M. Renan* (Strasbourg: Treutel et Würtz, 1864). Colani developed his own views in *Jésus Christ et les Croyances Messianiques de son Temps* (Strasbourg: Treutel et Würtz, 1864; 2nd. ed. also 1864). He argued that there was no connection between Jesus and Jewish messianic beliefs, and that the apocalyptic teaching of Mark 13 was an interpolation.

E. de Pressensé attacked Renan from a more orthodox standpoint in *L'École critique et Jésus-Christ, à propos de la Vie de Jésus par M. Renan* (Paris: C. Meyrueis, 1863). He gave his own account, Eng. trans. *Jesus Christ: His Times, Life and Work* (New York: Scribner, 1868). Renan was defended by Albert Réville, *La Vie de Jésus de Renan devant les Orthodoxes et devant la Critique* (Paris: J. Cherbuliez, 1864).

89. Cf. Wardman, op. cit., p. 80.

90. *Renan's Letters from the Holy Land. The Correspondence of Ernest Renan with M. Bertholet while gathering the material in Italy and the Orient for "The Life of Jesus"*, Eng. trans. L. O'Rourke (New York: Doubleday, 1904), pp. 176–77.

91. Op. cit., p. 223.

V. ORTHODOXY MODIFIED

13. *Confessional and Revival Theology*

1. Cf. H.-J. Birkner, H. Liebing, and K. Scholder, *Das konfessionelle Problem in der evangelischen Theologie des 19. Jahrhunderts* (Tübingen: J. C. B. Mohr, 1966); H. Fagerberg, *Bekenntnis, Kirche und Amt in der deutschen konfessionellen Theologie des 19. Jahrhunderts* (Uppsala: Lundequistska Bokhandeln, 1952); M. Schmidt, "Die innere Einheit der Erweckungsfrömmigkeit im Übergangstadium zum Lutherischen Konfessionalismus," *TLZ* 70 (1949):17–28; F. W. Kantzenbach, *Gestalten und Typen des Neuluthertums. Beiträge zur Erforschung des Neokonfessionalismus im 19. Jahrhundert* (Gütersloh: Gütersloher Verlagshaus Gerd Mohn, 1968); H. Weigelt, *Erweckungsbewegung und konfessionelles Luthertum im 19. Jahrhundert, untersucht an Karl von Raumer* (Stuttgart: Calwer Verlag, 1965).

2. *Das sind die 95 Thesen oder Streitsätze Dr. Luthers zum besonderen Abdruck besorgt, und mit andern 95 Thesen...in 1817 begleitet* (Kiel, 1817); partial Eng. trans. in F. Lichtenberger, *History of German Theology in the Nineteenth Century*, Eng. trans. W. Hastie (Edinburgh: T. & T. Clark, 1889), pp. 209–10. Claus Harms (1778–1855) was drawn away from rationalism partly by Schleiermacher's *Reden*. He enjoyed an influential ministry at Kiel, and was the author of a widely esteemed *Pastoraltheologie* (3 vols., 1830–34). He declined a call to succeed Schleiermacher at the Dreifaltigkeitskirche in 1835. Together with A. Twesten he published *Die ungeänderte Augsburgische Confession* (Kiel, 1819). In contrast with the Erlangen School, he regarded the Confession as definitive and rejected philosophical speculation. His *Ausgewählte Werke* were edited in two volumes by Peter Meinhold (Flensberg: C. Wolf, 1955).

3. See chap. 6, n. 17.

4. *Enzyklopädie und Methodologie der theologischen Wissenschaften*, 4th ed. (1854); Eng. trans. George R. Crooks and John F. Hurst, *Theological Encyclopaedia and Methodology on the Basis of Hagenbach* (New York: Hunt and Eaton; Cincinnati: Cranston and Stowe, 1889), pp. 104–5.

The initial support of conservatives like Hengstenberg turned into hostility, when it began to appear that the union involved a weakening of doctrinal orthodoxy. In Silesia the opposition was led by the Breslau professor, J. G. Scheibel. The Marburg scholar, A. F. C. Vilmar (1800–68) became the leader of the conservative church party in Kurhessen. He combined an emphasis on "the objective facts" of salvation and Christian experience with a high view of the church. Vilmar's *Die Theologie der Tatsachen wider die Theologie der Rhetorik. Bekenntnis und Abwehr* (1856) went through several editions (reprint ed., Darmstadt: Wissenschaftliche Buchgesellschaft, 1968).

5. Cf. L. Tiesmeyer, *Die Erweckungsbewegung in Deutschland während des 19. Jahrhunderts,* 4 vols. (Kassel: Ernst Rötger, 1903–12); F. W. Kantzenbach, *Die Erweckungsbewegung. Studien zur Geschichte ihrer Entstehung und ersten Ausbreitung in Deutschland* (Neuendettelsau: Freimund-Verlag, 1957); idem, *Baron Hans Ernst von Kottwitz und die Erweckungsbewegung in Berlin, Pommern und Schlesien. Briefwechsel* (Ulm: Verlag Unser Weg, 1963); G. A. Benrath, "Erweckung/Erweckungsbewegungen, I Deutschland," *TRE,* 10:210–20.

6. Stephan-Schmidt, p. 114.

7. See above, chap. 10, nn. 66–73.

8. Eng. trans. J. E. Ryland, *Guido and Julius; or, Sin and the Propitiator Exhibited in the True Consecration of the Sceptic* (Boston: Gould and Lincoln, 1854). By 1871 the work had seen nine editions. It was partly a reply to de Wette's *Theodor oder des Zweiflers Weihe* (1822).

9. Tholuck enjoyed an international reputation. E. B. Pusey's *Historical Enquiry into the Probable Causes of the Rationalistic Character lately dominant in the Theology of Germany* (1828) was indebted to him. In 1831 an American visitor, Professor Robinson, recorded, "To the American Christian who travels on this part of the Continent, Tholuck is undoubtedly the most interesting person whose acquaintance he will make. He possesses a greater influence and reputation than any other theologian in Germany" (*Biblical Repository,* 1:29, reprinted in Tholuck's *Commentary on the Gospel of John* [Edinburgh: T. & T. Clark; Philadelphia: Smith, English, 1860], p. iii).

10. Hirsch, 5:104.

11. Cf. Martin Schmidt, *RGG*[3], 6, col. 854; *ODCC,* p. 1369. Although Tholuck was aware of the intellectual movements of his time and sought to respond, his thought remained within the parameters of evangelical piety and he did not support the Union.

12. Hirsch, 5:103.

13. *The So-Called Historical Jesus and the Historic, Biblical Christ,* Eng. trans. of the 1896 edition translated and edited with an introduction by Carl E. Braaten (Philadelphia: Fortress Press, 1964), pp. 66–67. Kähler was also influenced by the Erlangen theologian, J. C. K. von Hofmann, whom he credited with breaking through Schleiermacher's immanentism and with recovering the motif of salvation history. See further, Johannes Wirsching, *Gott in der Geschichte, Studien zur theologiegeschichtlichen Stellung und systematischen Grundlegung der Theologie Martin Kählers* (Munich: Chr. Kaiser Verlag, 1963); Johannes Heinrich Schmid, *Erkenntnis des geschichtlichen Christus bei Martin Kähler und bei Adolf Schlatter, Theologische Zeitschrift* Sonderband, 5 (Basel: Friedrich Reinhardt Verlag, 1978).

14. 7 vols. (1843–48; 3rd ed., 1870–73); Eng. trans. W. B. Pope from the second edition, *The Words of the Lord Jesus* (Edinburgh: T. & T. Clark, 1863).

15. Op. cit., 1, Translator's Preface.

16. Op. cit., 1:18.

17. Cf. J. Bachmann and T. Schmalenbach, *Ernst Wilhelm Hengstenberg. Sein Leben und Wirken nach gedruckten und ungedruckten Quellen,* 3 vols. (Gütersloh: C. Bertelsmann, 1876–92); A. Kriege, *RGG*[3], 3, cols. 219–20; idem, *Geschichte der Evangelischen Kirchen-Zeitung unter der Reaktion Ernst Wilhelm Hengstenbergs* (Dissertation, Bonn, 1958).

18. Cf. W. Elliger, *150 Jahre Theologische Fakultät Berlin. Eine Darstellung ihrer Geschichte von 1810 bis 1960 als Beitrag zu ihrem Jubiläum* (Berlin: Walter de Gruyter, 1960), pp. 26–29.

19. Eng. trans. T. Meyer and J. Martin, from the second edition, *Christology of the Old Testament and a Commentary on the Messianic Predictions,* 4 vols. (Edinburgh: T. & T. Clark, 1854–58; reprint ed., with preface, Merrill F. Unger [Grand Rapids: Kregel Publications, 1956]).

20. Kraus, p. 223.

21. Ibid.; cf. Hengstenberg, op. cit., 2:3.

22. *Commenting and Commentaries* (London: Passmore and Alabaster, 1876), p. 86.

23. Ibid., p. 44.

24. For an account of the Erlangen School and literature, see F. W. Kantzenbach, *Die Erlanger Theologie. Grundlinien ihrer Entwicklung im Rahmen der Geschichte der Theologischen Fakultät, 1743–1877* (Munich: Evangelischer Presseverband für Bayern, 1960).

25. Erlangen became a center of historical study, especially of Lutheranism. Among the scholars associated with this were J. G. V. Engelhardt, Theodosius Harnack and Heinrich Friedrich Ferdinand Schmid, the author of *Die Dogmatik der evangelischlutherischen Kirche* (Erlangen: C. Heyder, 1843;

Eng. trans. C. A. Hay and H. E. Jacobs, *The Doctrinal Theology of the Evangelical Lutheran Church* [reprint ed., Minneapolis: Augsburg, 1961]). The Erlangen Ausgabe of Luther, 67 vols. (1826–57) was the standard edition prior to the Weimarer Ausgabe.

26. Vol. 1, 1, July, 1838; text reprinted in Kantzenbach, op. cit., pp. 245–61.

27. On Hofmann see P. Wapler, *Johannes von Hofmann. Ein Beitrag zur Geschichte der theologischen Grundprobleme der kirchlichen und politischen Bewegungen im 19. Jahrhundert* (Leipzig: A. Deichert, 1914); J. Wach, *Das Verstehen. Die theologischen Hermeneutik von Schleiermacher bis Hofmann*, vol. 2 (Tübingen: J. C. B. Mohr, 1929); Christoph Senft, *Wahrhaftigkeit und Wahrheit. Die Theologie des 19. Jahrhunderts zwischen Orthodoxie und Aufklärung, BHT* 22 (Tübingen: J. C. B. Mohr, 1956), pp. 87–123; Eberhard Hübner, *Schrift und Theologie. Eine Untersuchung zur Theologie Joh. Chr. K. von Hofmanns, FGLP* 10. Reihe, No. 7 (Munich: Chr. Kaiser Verlag, 1956); J. Haussleiter, ed., *Grundlinien der Theologie Joh. Christ. K. v. Hofmanns in seiner eigenen Darstellung* (Leipzig: A. Deichert, 1910).

28. F. W. Kantzenbach, op. cit., p. 181.

29. Hofmann's works were published in Nördlingen by C. H. Beck. Posthumous works included *Theologische Ethik* (1878); *Enzyklopädie der Theologie*, ed. H. J. Bestmann (1879); *Biblische Hermeneutik*, ed. W. Volck (1880; Eng. trans. C. Preus, *Interpreting the Bible* [Minneapolis: Augsburg, 1959]). Volck edited three further volumes of *Die heilige Schrift* (1881–86).

30. *Theologische Briefe der Professoren Delitzsch und von Hofmann*, ed. W. Volck (Leipzig: J. C. Hinrich'sche Buchhandlung, 1891), pp. 14ff.

31. Op. cit., p. 9.

32. "What comprehended history is for Hegel, salvation history is for Hofmann" (E.-W. Wendebourg, "Die heilsgeschichtliche Theologie des J. Chr. K. von Hofmanns in ihrem Verhältnis zur romantischen Weltanschauung," *ZTK* 52 [1955]:64–104, quotation is from p. 80).

33. Writing of his student days in Berlin, Hofmann recorded, "Even at that time I read Hegel's *Phenomenology,* but only to become acquainted with it, and his philosophy of history ruined for me all taste for his philosophy" (ibid., pp. 37–38). However, Eberhard Hübner urges that Hofmann's thought should be seen against the broader background of the Idealist philosophy of history (op. cit., p. 101; and also in personal correspondence with the author).

34. *Enzyklopädie der Theologie*, p. 51; cf. *Interpreting the Bible*, pp. 48–49. In *Der Schriftbeweis*, 1:8, Hofmann defined Christianity as "the factual reality of fellowship of God and man mediated in Jesus Christ."

35. *Der Schriftbeweis*, 1:10.

36. Ibid., 1:29.

37. Op. cit., p. 196.

38. *Enzyklopädie der Theologie*, p. 60.

39. *Der Schriftbeweis*, 1:36.

40. *Weissagung und Erfüllung*, 1:7.

41. Ibid., 1:39.

42. Cf. the title of Hofmann's defense of his teaching, *Schutzschriften für eine neue Weise, alte Wahrheit zu lehren*, 4 vols. (Nördlingen: C. H. Beck, 1856–59).

43. For an account of Barth's teaching in the later volumes of the *Church Dogmatics*, see C. Brown, *Karl Barth and the Christian Message* (London: Tyndale Press, 1967), pp. 99–137. Barth discussed Hofmann in *PT*, pp. 607–15, where he acknowledged its strengths but detected tensions between Hofmann's biblicism and his appeal to experience. *PT* was based on lectures dating from 1932–33. Barth's later position appears to have come closer to Hofmann. Barth served as a Referent for Hübner's work on Hofmann.

44. G. Aulén, *Christus Victor*, Eng. trans. A. G. Hebert (London: S.P.C.K., 1931).

45. *Schutzschrift*, 3:9.

46. *Theologische Ethik, p. 57.*

47. *Der Schriftbeweis*, 1:45.

48. *Schutzschrift*, 3:16.

49. *Der Schriftbeweis*, 1:47.

50. *Schutzschrift*, 3:25.

51. *Der Schriftbeweis*, 2/1, 212–13.

52. E. Hübner, op. cit., pp. 132–39.

53. In his introduction to the second edition of his *Commentar über den Brief an die Römer* (Frankfurt and Erlangen: Heyder & Zimmer, 1856), F. A. Philippi attacked the subjective treatment of

"the objective biblical and ecclesiastical doctrine of reconciliation and justification." He followed it with a paper on *Herr Dr. von Hofmann gegenüber der lutherischen Versöhnungs- und Rechtfertigungslehre* (Frankfurt and Erlangen: Heyder & Zimmer, 1856). In the same year Heinrich Schmid published *Dr. von Hofmanns Lehre von der Versöhnung in ihrem Verhältnis zum kirchlichen Bekenntnis und zur kirchlichen Dogmatik geprüft*. The following year Thomasius published *Das Bekenntnis der lutherischen Kirche von der Versöhnung und die Versöhnungslehre Hofmanns, mit einem Nachwort von Dr. Th. Harnack* (Erlangen: T. Bläsing, 1857). Hofmann replied in his various *Schutzschriften*. See further, Philipp Bachmann, *J. Chr. K. von Hofmanns Versöhnungslehre und der über sie geführte Streit. Ein Beitrag zur Geschichte der neueren Theologie*, Beiträge zur Förderung christlicher Theologie, 14. Jahrgang, Heft 6 (Gütersloh: C. Bertelsmann, 1910); F. W. Kantzenbach, *Gestalten und Typen*, pp. 154–76.

54. *Theologische Briefe*, p. 45.

55. T. Kliefoth, *Der Schriftbeweis des Dr. J. Chr. K. von Hofmann* (1860); cited by F. W. Kantzenbach, *Die Erlanger Theologie*, p. 202.

56. Thomasius's writings include *Origines. Ein Beitrag zur Dogmengeschichte des dritten Jahrhunderts* (Nuremberg, 1837); *Beiträge zur kirchlichen Christologie*, reprint of articles in the *Zeitschrift für Protestantismus und Kirche* (Erlangen: T. Bläsing, 1845); *Dogmatis de obedientia Christi activa historia et progressiones inde a confessione Augustana ad formulam usque concordia* (Erlangen, 1845–46); *Das Bekenntnis der evangelisch-lutherischen Kirche in der Konsequenz seines Prinzips* (Nuremberg: A. Recknagel, 1848); *Christi Person und Werk. Darstellung der evangelisch-lutherischen Dogmatik vom Mittelpunkte der Christologie aus*, 2 vols. (vol. 2 in two parts) (Erlangen: T. Bläser; 2nd ed. 1856–63, cited here below; 3rd ed. rev. by F. Winter [Erlangen: A. Deicher, 1886–88]); *Das Wiedererwachen des evangelischen Lebens in der lutherischen Kirche Bayerns. Ein Stück süddeutscher Kirchengeschichte, 1800–1840* (Erlangen: A. Deichert, 1867); *Die Christliche Dogmengeschichte als Entwicklungsgeschichte des kirchlichen Lehrbegriffs*, 2 vols. (Erlangen: A. Deichert, 1874–76; vol. 2 completed by G. L. Plitt; 2nd ed. prepared by N. Bonwetsch and R. Seeberg [Leipzig, 1886–88]). See also above, n. 52. Extracts from *Christi Person und Werk* are given by Claude Welch in *God and Incarnation in Mid-Nineteenth Century German Theology: G. Thomasius, I. A. Dorner, A. E. Biedermann*, Library of Protestant Thought (New York: Oxford University Press, 1965).

57. Reproduced by Hermann Jordan, *Beitrag zur bayerischen Kirchengeschichte*, 24, 4–5, pp. 141–43, cited by F. W. Kantzenbach, *Die Erlanger Theologie*, pp. 165–67.

58. *Christi Person und Werk*, 1:iv-v.

59. Cf. also *Das Wiedererwachen*, p. 304.

60. Thomasius was particularly concerned with D. F. Strauss, *Die christliche Glaubenlehre*, 2 vols. (1840–41); F. C. Baur, *Die christliche Lehre von der Dreieinigkeit und Menschwerdung Gottes*, 3 vols. (1841–43); and I. A. Dorner, *Entwicklungsgeschichte der Lehre von der Person Christi* (1839). In the foreword to *Christi Person und Werk*, 1:vi, Thomasius explained that the work was written to display the true nature of Christian dogma, as opposed to Strauss's view.

61. *Beiträge*, p. 4.

62. Ibid., p. 15.

63. Ibid., p. 25.

64. Ibid., p. 32.

65. Ibid., p. 42.

66. Ibid., pp. 77–78.

67. The final part of the *Beiträge* reviewed certain key christological dogmas with a view to outlining a program. *1. Unio hypostatica.* "According to it the *Son of God has not assumed this or that individual, but sarx [flesh], the human nature common to all individuals (the general)* (John 1:14: Heb. 1:14; 1 Tim. 3:16; Col. 2:9; etc.)" (ibid., p. 90). *2. Communio naturarum.* From this follows "the truth of his human and divine nature." His human nature is "fully homogeneous with ours." But this means "divesting, self-limitation, self-determination" (ibid., pp. 97–98). In the incarnation there is not merely an external union of the natures, a *synapheia* in an "external or merely ethical manner." Nor can there be an "absorption" or "transformation into the divine." "They equally contradict Scripture and furthermore rob the entire work of redemption of its significance" (ibid., p. 99). *3. Communicatio idiomatum.* The union must extend to Christ's conscious life and activity (Heb. 3:17; 5:8; 1 Cor. 2:8; 1 Pet. 4:1). *"What the Redeemer does as man, he also does as God."* "So far as the Logos possesses and exercises the divine glory, so far he possesses and exercises it also as man" (ibid., pp. 103–4). *4. Status exinanitionis.* The Redeemer's life falls into two stages.

The first is the state of humiliation which necessarily affects his "use of power," "omnipresence," and "knowledge" (ibid., pp. 106–7). All his acts were acts of "self-denial" (ibid., p. 109). *5. Status exaltationis.* This second stage is also an essential part of his work. Again, the unity of his person is stressed. "For our nature, assumed by him, *remains* henceforth his own. In him our sinful race is made eternally acceptable to the Father, and with it is given the possibility to each individual to be taken up into that fellowship with God which is the destiny of humanity. *Jesus Christ* brings it to the goal and thus brings its idea to fulfilment" (ibid., p. 116).

68. Prior to *Christi Person und Werk*, Thomasius sought to clarify his position in *Zeitschrift für Protestantismus und Kirche* 11 (1846):284–93; 19 (1850):1–42.

69. The intention of the work is reflected in its structure. Part 1 bracketed together the doctrines of God, man, and sin under the heading of "The Presuppositions of Christology." Each major section concluded with a summary of "consequences for Christology." Part 2 dealt with the person of Christ, and Part 3 with the Holy Spirit, church, sacraments, and final consummation.

70. Cf. C. Welch, op. cit., sec. 35, p. 34.

71. Ibid., sec. 34, pp. 31–33; cf. also *Christi Person und Werk*, 1:60, 68.

72. Ibid., sec. 38, pp. 42–43.

73. Ibid., sec. 39, p. 44.

74. Ibid., sec. 40, p. 46.

75. Ibid., sec. 40, p. 49.

76. Ibid., sec. 40, p. 47.

77. Ibid., sec. 40, p. 48.

78. Ibid.

79. Ibid., sec. 40, p. 50.

80. Ibid., sec. 40, p. 51.

81. Ibid., sec. 40, p. 52.

82. Ibid., sec. 40, p. 53.

83. Ibid., sec. 40, pp. 53–56.

84. Ibid., sec. 40, p. 55.

85. Ibid., sec. 41, pp. 58–59. Calvin taught that "the Son of God descended from heaven in such a way that, without leaving heaven, he willed to be borne in the virgin's womb, to go about the earth, and to hang upon the cross; yet he continuously filled the world even as he had done from the beginning!", *Institutes*, 2, 13, 4; Eng. trans. F. L. Battles (Philadelphia: Westminster Press, 1961), 1:418; cf. E. D. Willis, *Calvin's Catholic Christology: The Function of the so-called Extra Calvinisticum in Calvin's Theology* (Leiden: E. J. Brill, 1966). The Formula of Concord (1576) rejected the teaching, "That, according to the humanity, he is not at all capable of omnipotence and other properties of the divine nature. And this they dare to assert against the express testimony of Christ (Matt.xxviii.18): 'All power is given unto me in heaven and in earth.' And they contradict Paul, who says (Col.ii.9): 'In him dwelleth all the fullness of the Godhead bodily'" (Epitome 8, Negativa 15).

86. For reviews of kenotic christology, see A. B. Bruce, *The Humiliation of Christ* (1876; 2nd ed., Cincinnati: Jennings and Graham; New York: Eaton and Mains, no date); D. G. Dawe, *The Form of a Servant: A Historical Analysis of the Servant Motif* (Philadelphia: Westminster Press, 1963); W. Pannenberg, *Jesus—God and Man*, Eng. trans. L. L. Wilkins and D. A. Priebe (London: S.C.M. Press, 1968), pp. 307–23. For interpretations of Philippians 2, see R. P. Martin, *Carmen Christi: Philippians 2:5–11 in Recent Interpretations and in the Setting of Early Christian Worship*, SNTS Monograph Series, no. 4 (Cambridge: Cambridge University Press, 1957; rev. ed. [Grand Rapids: Eerdmans, 1983]).

87. J. Brenz, *De divina maiestate Domini nostri Jesu Christi* (1562).

88. M. Chemnitz, *De duabus naturis in Christo* (1570).

89. Epitome 8, Negativa 20.

90. Sartorius taught at Marburg and Dorpat before becoming Generalsuperintendent and Senior Court Preacher at Königsberg. He revived the doctrine in his Dorpat *Beiträge* (1832) to which Thomasius expressed his debt (op. cit., 2:483). He developed his teaching in *Die Lehre von Christi Person und Werk* (1831; 6th ed., 1853; Eng. trans. O. S. Stearns, *The Person and Work of Christ* [Boston: Gould, Kendall and Lincoln, 1848]); and *Die Lehre von der heiligen Liebe* (1840; 4th ed., 1864; Eng. trans. Sophia Taylor, *The Doctrine of the Divine Love; or, Outlines of the Moral Theology of the Evangelical Church* [Edinburgh: T. & T. Clark, 1884]).

91. *Die Lehre von der Person Christi entwickelt aus dem Selbstbewusstsein Christi und aus dem Zeugnisse der Apostel* (Basel, 1856; Eng. trans., *The Scripture Doctrine of the Person of Christ, Freely Translated from the German of W. F. Gess, with many additions by J. A. Reubelt* [Andover, MA: W. F. Draper, 1870]); expanded in *Christi Person und Werk nach Christi Selbstzeugnis und den Zeugnisse der Apostel*, 3 vols. (Basel: Bahnmeier, 1870–87).

92. *The Doctrine of the Divine Love*, p. 140.

93. Op. cit., p. 149.

94. "The Holy Spirit and Inspiration," Charles Gore, ed., in *Lux Mundi: A Series of Studies in the Religion of the Incarnation* (London: John Murray, 1889), pp. 313–62, especially, pp. 358ff. Gore developed his teaching in his Bampton Lectures on *The Incarnation of the Son of God* (London: John Murray, 1895; 2nd ed., 1907). As with Thomasius, whom he alluded to, Gore came to regard the doctrine as crucial for understanding the nature of God. He saw it as the supreme example of divine selfrestraining love which is active in all God's works (cf. *Dissertations*, pp. 94–95, 172). For literature and discussion, see C. Brown, "Charles Gore," in P. E. Hughes, ed., *Creative Minds in Contemporary Theology* (Grand Rapids: Eerdmans; 2nd ed., 1969), pp. 341–74.

95. *Christ, the Christian and the Church* (London: Longmans, 1946), p. 12.

96. Among the attractive alternative interpretations of Philippians 2:7 is the view that it refers to Isaiah 53:12 ("he poured out his soul to death") and thus it is an allusion to the death of the Servant of the Lord. Another interpretation sees in the passage a reference to the temptations of Jesus in which the Son of God refused to grasp at supernatural power and went the way of humble servanthood.

14. Mediating Theology

1. For surveys and literature, see Werner Elert, *Der Kampf um das Christentum. Geschichte der Beziehung zwischen dem evangelischen Christentum in Deutschland und dem allgemeinen Denken seit Schleiermacher und Hegel* (Munich: C. H. Beck, 1921); Hirsch, 5:364–414; Ragnar Holte, *Die Vermittlungstheologie. Ihre Grundbegriffe kritisch untersucht, Acta Universitatis Upsaliensis Studia Doctrinae Upsaliensia 3* (Uppsala, 1965); Max Huber, *Jesus als Erlöser in der liberalen Theologie. Vermittlung, Spekulation, Existenzverständnis* (Winterthur: Verlag P. G. Keller, 1956); Johannes Wirsching, ed., *Christologische Texte aus der Vermittlungstheologie des 19. Jahrhunderts, TKT* 8 (Gütersloh: Gütersloher Verlagshaus Gerd Mohn, 1968). In English the school is generally referred to as Mediating Theology, but F. Lichtenberger and his translator preferred "School of Conciliation" (op. cit., p. 467).

2. G. C. F. Lücke (1791–1855) was a student of Schleiermacher and he was a friend of both him and de Wette. He became a professor at Bonn (1818) and Göttingen (1827). Schleiermacher addressed his *Sendschreiben* to him (see above, chap. 6, nn. 20, 155–57).

3. The prospectus, dated June 1, 1827, was signed by Lücke, Gieseler, Nitzsch, Ullmann, and Umbreit. It was reprinted in the first issue the following year. See text in Jörg Rothermundt, *Personale Synthese. 189 Isaak August Dorners Dogmatische Methode, FSOT* 19 (Göttingen: Vandenhoeck & Rupprecht, 1968), p. 12.

4. Among these were Carl Ullmann's "Über Partei und Schule, Gegensätze und deren Vermittlung," *ThStKr* 9 (1836):5–61; and "Vierzig Sätze, die theologische Lehrfreiheit innerhalb der evangelisch-protestantischen Kirche betreffend," *ThStKr* 16 (1843):7–35. In the former article he declared that, "Mediation is the tracing back, completed in a scientific manner, of relative antitheses to their original unity, whereby an inner reconciliation and a higher standpoint are attained in which they are resolved. The scientific state, which emerges as the result of this mediation, is the true, sound mean" (op. cit., p. 41). The latter article discussed whether scholars like Bruno Bauer and Strauss should be allowed to teach within the universities. Ullmann believed in a relative, but not absolute, freedom, because the evangelical church desired both unity and freedom (op. cit., p. 7).

5. August Twesten (1789–1876) was one of the first students at the University of Berlin. He became professor of philosophy at Kiel (1814), where he remained until 1835, when he assumed Schleiermacher's chair. He became an influential figure in church circles in Berlin, where he opposed the speculative theology of Marheineke and the conservatism of Hengstenberg. In the tradition of Schleiermacher he stressed the ecclesiastical character of theology and the importance of the Union. In addition to his works on logic, he published his *Vorlesungen über die Dogmatik der evangelischen-*

lutherischen Kirche nach dem Compendium des Herrn Dr. W. M. L. de Wette, 2 vols. (Hamburg: Perthes, 1826; 4th ed., 1838).

6. Carl Immanuel Nitzsch (1787–1868) came to Mediating Theology via Kantianism. For two decades beginning in 1822 he taught at Bonn. His *System der christlichen Lehre* (Bonn: Adolph Marcus, 1829; 6th ed., 1851), has been described as the classic dogmatics of the school (K. Scholder, *RGG*[3], 4, col. 1500). He had strong practical and church interests and was a supporter of the Union. Together with Julius Müller and Neander, he founded the *Deutsche Zeitschrift für christliche Wissenschaft und christliches Leben* (1850) in opposition to confessionalism. The chief work of his Berlin period was his *System der praktischen Theologie*, 3 vols. (1847–67). Though personally irenic, Nitzsch emerged as the leader of the movement.

7. F. W. C. Umbreit (1795–1860) was a professor of Old Testament exegesis at Heidelberg from 1823. A founder of *ThStKr*, he assisted in editing it until the late fifties.

8. Johann Karl Ludwig Gieseler (1792–1854) held chairs at Bonn (1819) and Göttingen (1831). He was an advocate of oral tradition. His support of academic freedom aroused the enmity of Hengstenberg. His *Lehrbuch der Kirchengeschichte*, 3 vols. (1824–30) was valued by F. C. Baur (*AW*, 2:244). It was later expanded and translated into English.

9. See above, chap. 9, nn. 93–96; chap.12, n. 36.

10. M. A. Landerer (1810–78) taught at Tübingen, where he adopted a mediating position between the conservatism of J. T. Beck and the radicalism of F. C. Baur.

11. Carl Theodor Albert Liebner (1806–71) taught at Göttingen, Kiel, and Leipzig. His incomplete *Die christliche Dogmatik aus dem christologischen Princip dargestellt* (1849) combined the idea of Christ as the archetypal man with a doctrine of *kenōsis*.

12. Willibald Beyschlag (1823–1900) became professor at Halle in 1860, where he led the mediating party. In *Die Christologie des Neuen Testaments. Ein biblisch-theologischer Versuch* (Berlin: Rauh, 1866) he claimed that none of the biblical writers treated Christ merely as a creature, but all of them distinguished him from God. In common with other Mediating Theologians, he viewed Christ as the archetype of humanity. He was the author of a widely-read *Leben Jesu*, 2 vols. (Halle: E. Strien, 1885), and of a *Neutestamentliche Theologie*, 2 vols. (Halle: E. Strien, 1891; 2nd ed., 1895; Eng. trans. N. Buchanan, *New Testament Theology* [Edinburgh: T. & T. Clark, 1895]). He wrote appreciations of Ullmann and Nitzsch. His autobiographical *Aus meinem Leben*, 2 vols. (Halle: E. Strien, 1896–99), is a mine of information concerning the period.

13. J. Köstlin (1816–1902) taught at Halle and was an editor of *ThStKr*.

14. Karl Rudolph Hagenbach (1801–74) came under Schleiermacher's influence at Berlin. He returned to Basel in 1823, where he became a full professor in 1828. His views matured under the influence of de Wette on whom he wrote a *Denkschrift* (1850). He edited the *Kirchenblatt für die reformirte Schweiz*. His numerous writings include *German Rationalism, its Rise, Progress and Decline*, Eng. trans. W. L. Gage and J. H. W. Stuckenberg (Edinburgh: T. & T. Clark, 1865); *A Text-Book of the History of Doctrines*, Eng. trans. H. B. Smith, 2 vols. (New York: Sheldon; Boston: Gould & Lincoln, 1862); and *History of the Church in the Eighteenth and Nineteenth Centuries*, Eng. trans. J. F. Hurst, 2 vols. (New York: Scribner, 1869). See also chap. 13, n. 4.

15. See chap. 8, n. 7.

16. On Reuterdahl and the influence of Schleiermacher, see Aleksander Radler, *Religion und kirchliche Wirklichkeit. Eine rezeptionsgeschichtliche Untersuchung des Schleiermacherbildes in der Schwedischen Theologie, Studia Theologica Lundensia*, 36 (Lund: C. W. K. Gleerup, 1977).

17. J. Wirsching, ed., op. cit., p. 5.

18. Carl Ullmann (1796–1865) was influenced by Schleiermacher and Neander in his student days. He held chairs at Heidelberg (1821), Halle (1829), and Heidelberg again (1836). He helped to found *ThStKr*. In 1853 he became Prälat and in 1856–61 director of the Oberkirchenrat at Karlsruhe. His attempts to reconcile the pietists and introduce a new liturgy and catechism led to liberal opposition and his ultimate downfall.

Ullmann's *Die Sündlosigkeit Jesu. Eine apologetische Betrachtung* first appeared in *ThStKr* 1 (1828). It was reprinted separately and subsequently expanded (Hamburg-Gotha: Perthes, 1828; 7th ed., 1863; Eng. trans. R. C. L. Brown, of 6th ed., *The Sinlessness of Jesus: An Evidence for Christianity* [Edinburgh: T. & T. Clark, 1858]; Eng. trans. of 7th ed., Sophia Taylor [1901]). The work was originally intended for student use, but later revisions had a wider readership in mind.

Other writings include *Historisch oder Mythisch? Beiträge zur Beantwortung der gegenwärtigen Lebensfrage der Theologie* (Hamburg: Perthes, 1838; 2nd ed., 1866; reprint of a review of Strauss's *Leben Jesu* in *ThStKr* 9 [1836]:770–816, also containing "Noch ein Wort über die Persönlichkeit

Christi und das Wunderbare an der evangelischen Geschichte," *ThStKr* 11 [1838]:277–369); "Der Cultus des Genius," ThStKr 13 (1840):7–62, replying to Strauss: "Über den unterscheidenden Charakter des Christentums, mit Beziehung auf neuere Auffassungsweisen," *ThStKr* 18 (1845):7–61; reprinted in *Das Wesen des Christentums, Mit Beziehung auf neuere Auffassungsweisen desselben von Freunden und Gegnern* (Hamburg-Gotha: Perthes, 1845; 5th ed., 1865); "Was setzt die Stiftung der christlichen Kirche durch einen Gekreuzigten voraus?" in Theodor von Hanffstengel, ed., *Zwei wichtige theologische Abhandlungen* von Dr. C. Ullmann (Braunschweig and Leipzig, 1896), pp. 77–125; reprinted in J. Wirsching, ed., op. cit., pp. 13–37. Although he wrote several biblical studies, his main work was as a church historian. He published a monograph on Gregory of Nazianzus in 1825. His *magnum opus* was *Die Reformatoren vor der Reformation,* 2 vols. (Hamburg: Perthes, 1841–42; 2nd ed., 1866; Eng. trans. R. Menzies, *The Reformers before the Reformation* [Edinburgh: T. & T. Clark, 1855]).

19. Op. cit., R. C. L. Brown's translation. The 7th ed. expanded the thought in still broader terms.

20. Op. cit., pp. 9–13.

21. Ibid., p. 266.

22. Ibid., p. 288.

23. Ibid., p. 8.

24. *ThStKr* 9 (1836):36.

25. Ibid., p. 58.

26. *ThStKr* 9 (1836):787–88.

27. Ibid., pp. 792–93.

28. Ibid., p. 791.

29. Ibid., p. 812.

30. Ibid., p. 813.

31. Ibid., p. 812.

32. Ibid., p. 813.

33. "Noch ein Wort über die Persönlichkeit Christi und das Wunderbare in der evangelischen Geschichte," *ThStKr* 11 (1838), 324–25.

34. Ibid., p. 327.

35. Op. cit., p. 332.

36. Ibid., pp. 333–34.

37. "But indeed, the miracles of revelation... must be regarded partly in relation to the higher ordering of the things to which they belong... partly in the light of their similarity with common nature... finally on their teleological completeness as truly in accordance with law, and even... in its own way as the natural" (C. I. Nitzsch, *System der christlichen Lehre,* 6th ed., p. 85; cf. R. Rothe, *Zur Dogmatik* [Gotha: Perthes, 1863], pp. 102–3, though Rothe allowed for free divine intervention without "creaturely secondary causes," pp. 96ff.). See further R. Holte, op. cit., pp. 84–85.

38. August Twesten referred to Schleiermacher's *Reden* and *Der christliche Glaube* as "the works with which we are in essential agreement," and went on to say that "faith has no other source than feeling and no other law than that of expressing this completely" (*Vorlesungen über die Dogmatik,* 4th ed., [Hamburg: Perthes, 1838], pp. 2, 22). But he insisted that faith is not mere knowledge of subjective feeling-states. It involved the apprehension of objective reality. Similarly, Nitzsch defined religion as "a way of life determined by relationship with God or by conscious dependence on God" (op. cit., p. 7). "With consciousness of God is posited the idea of God" (ibid., p. 30). Nitzsch's work was much more biblically oriented than Schleiermacher's. His arguments were buttressed by appeals to biblical texts and were couched in more orthodox language. See further, R. Holte, op. cit., pp. 48–68.

39. Nitzsch's position was similar. He concluded his review of Jesus' sonship with the comment, "Accordingly we have to honor in the Son the self-conceiving self-mediating love which is God" (op. cit., p. 193). His treatment of the incarnation was set in the context of the section on salvation. The nearest that he came to an affirmation of divinity was in Section 127 on "The God-man, his Self-Renunciation and Humiliation" (ibid., pp. 258–63). He proceeded by offering a paraphrase of New Testament texts. He concluded with a note on recent developments, which pointed out that, while one must not cease to value orthodox formulae, "the threads of inner development" demanded "a still more complete fabric. There is still much work to be done; this dogmatics is still young and tender" (ibid., p. 263).

40. The argument which figured in Die *Sündlosigkeit Jesu* was elaborated in "Was setzt die

Stiftung der christlichen Kirche durch einen Gekreuzigten voraus?" The argument began with two fixed points: "The one, Christ has lived and was crucified; the other, there exists a Christian church" (J. Wirsching, ed., op. cit., p. 13). To demonstrate the former point, he did not examine the Gospels but appealed to secular historians like Tacitus (*Annales*, 15, 44) and Suetonius (*De vita Caesarum*, 5, 25). On the premise that every effect has an antecedent sufficient cause (ibid., p. 17), Ullmann looked for the sufficient cause of the church. He concluded, "the church, as it stands before us as a fact of world history, could only thus be constituted by someone who had been crucified, if the latter had bound his followers to him by a towering spiritual, morally pure, godly personality, by a mighty all-conquering love, and by a teaching full of truth and power, and had laid the ground for a new, higher development of the moral, religious life" (ibid., p. 34).

41. *Das Wesen des Christentums*, p. 46. For fuller discussion of this work, see R. Holte, pp. 101–13.

42. Op. cit., pp. 107–8; cf. G. Aulén, *Christus Victor* (London: S.P.C.K., 1931).

43. Op. cit., p. 26.

44. Ibid., p. 72.

45. Ibid., pp. 80–81.

46. Ibid., p. 92.

47. Ibid., p. 105.

48. Ibid., p. 74.

49. J. Wirsching, ed., op. cit., p. 5.

50. Stephan-Schmidt, p. 189.

51. Julius Müller taught at Göttingen, Marburg, and Halle (1839), where he succeeded Ullmann and was preferred over the candidacy of F. C. Baur. He followed Neander and Tholuck rather than Schleiermacher, and waged a polemic against Hegelianism and Baur's criticism.

His most important work was *Die christliche Lehre der Sünde*, 2 vols. (Breslau: J. Max; Stuttgart: A. Heitz, 1839–44; 6th ed., 1877; Eng. trans. *The Christian Doctrine of Sin*, W. Pulsford, of the 3rd ed. [Edinburgh: T. & T. Clark, 1852]; Eng. trans. W. Urwick, of the 5th ed., containing responses to various contemporary writers including members of the Erlangen School [1877]). The work was the most detailed treatment of a subject which was central to the concerns of Mediating Theology. There were marked affinities with Schleiermacher in seeing sin as selfishness and guilt in relation to the question of man's dependence on God. However, Müller's work was more historically and theistically oriented. He agreed with Schleiermacher's "superstructure" but rejected "the theoretic foundation of his doctrine" (1:359). He traced the origin of sin to an extra-temporal act (2:357–66). Against Schleiermacher, he insisted on the virgin birth as a precondition of Christ's sinlessness and of man's redemption. "In order that His life might be human he must be conceived and developed and born of a woman; but that it might be from its commencement sinless, a divine creative act must supplant the human act on which the commencement of any new life ordinarily depends" (2:379; cf. Neander, *Leben Jesu*, pp. 16–17). For an analysis and critique of the work, see Barth, *PT*, pp. 588–96.

Müller was a staunch supporter of the Union. Much of his work appeared in the *Deutsche Zeitschrift für christliche Wissenschaft und christliches Leben*, which he helped to found.

52. The articles first appeared in the *Deutsche Zeitschrift* (1850), nos. 40–43, and were revised in Müller's *Dogmatische Abhandlungen* (Bremen, 1870), pp. 66–126; reprinted in J. Wirsching, ed., op. cit., pp. 39–80.

53. J. Wirsching, ed., op. cit., pp. 39, 50.

54. Müller himself saw a similarity between his conclusion and that of Nitzsch (ibid., p. 79; cf. Nitzsch, op. cit., sec. 127, see above, n. 39). On Ullmann and Müller, see W. Pannenberg, *Jesus —God and Man*, pp. 359–60.

55. Ibid., pp. 79–80.

56. Lange studied at Bonn, where he became a professor in 1854 after a previous appointment at Zürich (1841). He published a *Christliche Dogmatik*, 3 vols. (Heidelberg: K. Winter, 1849–52). His multi-volume *Theologisch-homiletisches Bibelwerk* (Bielefeld: Velhagen & Klasing, 1856 onwards), covered the Old and New Testaments. It was published in Edinburgh by T. & T. Clark and in New York by Charles Scribner. The American version was entitled *Theological and Homiletical Commentary on the Old and New Testaments. Specially Designed for the use of Ministers and Students. Translated, enlarged and revised under the general editorship of Dr. Philip Schaff, assisted by leading Divines of the various Evangelical Denominations*. Its continued popularity is evidenced by

the Zondervan, Grand Rapids reprint in the mid-twentieth century. Among his other works was a *Leben Jesu*, 3 vols. (Heidelberg: K. Winter, 1844–47); Eng. trans. *The Life of the Lord Jesus Christ: A Complete Examination of the Origin, Contents, and Connection of the Gospels...Edited, with Additional notes by Marcus Dods* (Edinburgh: T. & T. Clark, 1864).

57. *Ueber den geschichtlichen Charakter der kanonischen Evangelien, insbesondere der Kindheitsgeschichte Jesu mit Beziehung auf das Leben Jesu von D. F. Strauss* (Duisberg, 1836). At the time, Lange was a pastor in Duisberg.

58. Op. cit., p. 481.

59. Op. cit., 1:ix-xxxi.

60. Ibid., 5:119.

61. Ibid., 1:125.

62. Ibid., 6:249.

63. Ibid., 1:293. Lange appealed to B. Jacobi's article for data on chronology in John in *ThStKr* 3 (1831), ibid., 1:290.

64. Ibid., 1:32.

65. Ibid., 1:34.

66. Alexander Schweizer became *ordinarius* professor at Zürich (1835), which was the center of Swiss radicalism. He subsequently became Pfarrer of the Grossmünster and a member of the Zürich Church Council. A disciple of Schleiermacher, he strove for a renewal of Protestant dogmatics which would show the fundamental unity of the central dogmas of the past with current free thought. His writings include *Die Glaubenslehre der evangelisch-reformirten Kirche dargestellt und aus den Quellen belegt*, 2 vols. (Zürich: Orell & Füssli, 1844–47); *Die protestantischen Centraldogmen, innerhalb der reformirten Kirche*, 2 vols. (1854–56); *Die christliche Glaubenslehre nach protestantischen Grundsätzen dargestellt*, 2 vols. (Leipzig: S. Hirzel, 1863–69; 2nd ed., 1877); *Die Zukunft der Religion* (Leipzig: S. Hirzel, 1878). See further, Karl Barth, *PT*, pp. 569–76; M. Huber, op. cit., pp. 65–77.

67. M. Huber, op. cit., p. 66.

68. M. Huber, op. cit., p. 69; cf. A. Schweizer, *Die christliche Glaubenslehre*, 2nd ed., 2, sec. 116, 2.

69. Op. cit., 2, sec. 115, 2; cf. Huber, op. cit., p. 70.

70. Op. cit., 2, sec. 117; cf. secs. 119, 123.

71. Rothe's writings include *Die Anfänge der christlichen Kirche*, 3 vols. (Wittenberg: Zimmerman, 1837; reprint ed., Frankfurt: Minerva, 1963); *Theologische Ethik*, 3 vols. (Wittenberg: Zimmermann, 1845–48; 2nd ed., 5 vols. [vols. 3–5, Wittenberg: H. Koeling, with foreword by H. Holtzmann, 1867–71]); *Zur Dogmatik* (Gotha: Perthes, 1863; 2nd ed., 1869; reprint ed., Braunschweig and Leipzig: G. Reuter; with foreword by Th. von Hanfstengel, 1898; consisting of articles in *ThStKr* which Rothe helped to edit); *Dogmatik. Aus dessen handschriftlichen Nachlasse herausgegeben von Dr. D. Schenkel*, 2 vols. (vol. 2 in two parts) (Heidelberg: J. C. B. Mohr, 1870); *Der erste Brief Johannis praktisch erklärt* (Wittenberg: Roelling, 1875); *Stille Stunden. Aphorismen* (1872; 2nd ed., 1888); Eng. trans. J. T. Stoddart, with introduction by J. MacPherson, *Still Hours* (London: Hodder and Stoughton, 1886); *Gesammelte Vorträge und Abhandlungen aus seinen letzten Lebensjahren, eingeleitet von* Friedrich Nippold (Elberfeld: Friderichs, 1886); *Nuchgelassene Predigten*, vols. 1 and 2 ed. D. Schenkel, vol. 3 ed. J. Bleek (Elberfeld: Friderichs, 1868–69). Studies include F. W. F. Nippold, *Ein christliches Lebensbild auf Grund der Briefe Rothes entworfen* (Wittenberg: H. Koelling, 1877); Adolph Hausrath, *Richard Rothe und seiner Freunde*, 2 vols. (Berlin: G. Grote, 1902–6); C. Walter, *Typen*, pp. 117–36; Hans-Joachim Birkner, *Spekulation und Heilsgeschichte. Die Geschichtsauffassung Richard Rothes*, FGLP 10. Reihe, 17 (Munich: Chr. Kaiser, 1959, containing further bibliography).

72. The liberal Protestantenverein, which Rothe had helped to found, was accused by the *Evangelische Kirchen-Zeitung* of trying to make capital out of their solitary saint (84 [1869]:149; cf. Birkner, op. cit., p. 11). A. Hausrath compared him with the best saints of the Middle Ages (op. cit., 2:564).

73. E. Schott, *RGG*[3], 5, col. 1197; cf. Barth, *PT*, pp. 597–98.

74. From Rothe's foreword to C. A. Auberlen, *Die Theosophie Friedrich Christoph Oetingers* (1837), p. xvi.

75. *Theologische Ethik*, 1:14–15.

76. Ibid., p. 43.

77. *Zur Dogmatik*, p. 122.

78. Ibid., p. 294; cf. Birkner, op. cit., pp. 41–42, comparing the development of Rothe's thought in the two editions of *Theologische Ethik*, 1:26–27; 2nd ed., p. 50–51.

79. *Zur Dogmatik*, p. 32.

80. Ibid., p. 127.

81. Ibid., p. 295.

82. Ibid., p. 304.

83. Ibid., pp. 300–1. Birkner draws attention to the frequency of the idea of the "picture" (op. cit., p. 44; cf. *Stille Stunden*, 2nd ed., p. 155; *Gesammelte Vorträge*, p. 106; *Nachgelassene Predigten*, 1:146, 251, 292–93; 2:33–34, 38, 56, 96–97, 100–1, 124, 287; 3:16, 65–66, 70, 85, 198, 304, 364).

84. It was on this score that J. C. K. von Hofmann joined issue with Rothe ("Richard Rothes Lehre von der heiligen Schrift," *Zeitschrift für Protestantismus und Kirche*, Neue Folge 42 [1861]:129ff.; reprinted in *Die heilige Schrift*, 1:25ff.; cf. *Vermischte Aufsätze zusammengestellt von H. Schmid*, [1878], pp. 95ff.). Rothe replied in *Zur Dogmatik*, pp. 125ff., 299ff. (cf. Birkner, op. cit., p. 44).

85. "The Bible was not written to furnish texts for sermons" (*Still Hours*, p. 220).

86. The exegesis of "scribes" like Stier, Beck, and Hofmann, which failed to take into account other sources of knowledge, was essentially rabbinic (ibid., p. 219).

87. *Theologische Ethik*, 1:98–99; cf. pp. 188, 217.

88. Ibid., 1:91.

89. Ibid., 1, secs. 10 and 11.

90. Ibid., 1:59.

91. Ibid., 1:124.

92. Cf. *Still Hours*, pp. 113–126.

93. *Theologische Ethik*, 1:98–99; see note on p. 98.

94. Ibid., p. 232.

95. Ibid., 2:136.

96. Ibid., 2:155.

97. Rothe had no place for a historical fall. He was also critical of Julius Müller's work and the Erlangen School (ibid., 3:12–20, 51–55). See also *Still Hours*, pp. 185–92. His approach may be compared with John Hick's "Irenaean Theodicy" in *Evil and the God of Love* (London: Macmillan, 1966).

98. Ibid., 2:170; cf. 3:41ff.

99. Ibid., 2:263.

100. Ibid., 2:315.

101. Ibid., 3:163:cf. pp. 146, 174, 335.

102. Ibid., 3:176.

103. *Still Hours*, pp. 215–16.

104. Ibid., 3:47.

105. Ibid., 3:160; cf. pp. 119, 133, 157–58.

106. *Gesammelte Vorträge*, p. 167; cf. *Theologische Ethik*, 5:407; Birkner, op. cit., p. 63.

107. *Theologische Ethik*, 3:322.

108. Ibid., 3:120: cf. *Still Hours*, pp. 217–23, 301–2.

109. *Zur Dogmatik*, p. 60; cf. *Theologische Ethik*, 3:120–21, 133–34.

110. *Theologische Ethik*, 3:192.

111. *Dogmatik*, 2/1, p. 84.

112. Ibid., pp. 154–58.

113. Ibid., p. 159.

114. Ibid., p. 181.

115. *Still Hours*, p. 207. John Henry Newman held a similar view of Christ's impersonal humanity, which likewise affirmed Christ's perfect humanity, though it was based more consciously on the christology of Cyril of Alexandria (cf. Roderick Strange, *Newman and the Gospel of Christ* [Oxford: Oxford University Press, 1981], p. 57). Newman's view prompted D. M. Baillie to question the propriety of the idea (*God Was in Christ* [London: Faber, 1956], p. 15–16). Interestingly, both Newman and Rothe spoke of Jesus as "the second Adam" instead of the Pauline phrase, "the last Adam" (1 Cor. 15:45), and in so doing substantially altered Pauline thought.

116. *Dogmatik*, 2/1, pp. 181–82. 201

117. Stephan-Schmidt, p. 198.

118. "Die Bewertung der Inneren Mission bei Richard Rothe," *ZKG* 60 (1941) :483.

119. On Dorner, see August Dorner, "Isaak August Dorner," *ADB* 48 (1904):3 7–47 (containing bibliography); J. Bobertag, *Isaak August Dorner. Sein Leben und seine Lehre, mit besonderer Berücksichtigung für Theologie und Kirche* (Gütersloh, 1906); John M. Drickamer, "Higher Criticism and the Incarnation in the Thought of I. A. Dorner," *Concordia Theological Quarterly* 43 (1979):197–206; Jorg Rothermundt, *Personale Synthese. Isaak August Dorners dogmatische Methode* (Göttingen: Vandenhoeck & Rupprecht, 1968); idem, "Personalismus und Ontologie bei I. A. Dorner," *Kerygma und Dogma* 14 (1968):331–55; idem, "Dorner, Isaak August," *TRE* 9, pp. 155–58.

120. "Über die Entwicklungsgeschichte der Christologie, besonders in der neueren Zeiten," *Tübinger Zeitschrift für Theologie*, 7/4 (1835):81–204; 8/1 (1836):96–240.

121. 2 vols. (Stuttgart: S. G. Liesching; 2nd ed., Berlin: G. Schlawitz, 1845–56; Eng. trans. W. L. Alexander, P. Fairbairn, and D. W. Simon, *History of the Development of the Doctrine of the Person of Christ*, Vol. 1 in two parts, Vol. 2 in three parts [Edinburgh: T. & T. Clark, 1861–63]).

122. *The Briefwechsel zwischen H. L. Martensen und I. A. Dorner, 1838–1881. Herausgegeben aus deren Nachlass*, 2 vols. (Berlin, 1888), contains material not only on the thought of both authors but on the whole German theological scene.

123. Munich: J. G. Cotta, 1867; Eng. trans. G. Robson and S. Taylor, *History of Protestant Theology*, 2 vols. (Edinburgh: T. & T. Clark, 1887).

124. Ed. A. Dorner (Berlin, 1885; Eng. trans. C. M. Mead and R. T. Cunningham [Edinburgh: T. & T. Clark, 1887]).

125. 2 vols. (Berlin: W. Hertz, 1879–81; 2nd ed., 1886; Eng. trans. A. Cave and J. S. Banks, *A System of Christian Doctrine*, 4 vols. [Edinburgh: T. & T. Clark, 1880–82]). Extracts from the section on christology are given by Claude Welch in his own translation in *God and the Incarnation in Mid-Nineteenth Century German Theology: G. Thomasius, I. A. Dorner, A. E. Biedermann*, Library of Protestant Thought (New York: Oxford University Press, 1965), pp. 103–284.

126. R. Seeberg, *Die Kirche Deutschlands im neunzehnten Jahrhundert*, 3rd ed. (Leipzig: Deicher, 1910), p. 291; Barth, *PT*, p. 577. Dorner himself predicted that his *System* would not be acclaimed by the rising generation of theologians (Letter to Martensen, July 3, 1878, *Briefwechsel*, 2:353). Later he wondered whether Martensen's dogmatics would make his own superfluous. Although he believed that he was biblical in a proper sense, the Confessionalists and the "Biblicists" would not be satisfied. Nor would he find favor with men like Lipsius or Ritschl (May 11, 1879, ibid., 2:390).

127. *History of the Development of the Doctrine of the Person of Christ*, 1/1, p. xix; cf. 1/1, p. 92 through 1/2, p. 429.

128. Ibid., 2/1 and 2/2, pp. 1–362.

129. Ibid., 2/2, pp. 363–82 and 2/3, pp. 1–69. Dorner summed up his position with the observation, "On the one hand, the pernicious effects on the doctrine of the Person of Christ of allowing the divine to have the predominance which had been conceded to it from A.D. 451 till 1700, with the sole exception of the age of the Reformation, were now exhibited to all times; and, on the other hand, it was made no less clearly evident, that the sole dominion of subjectivity, leaving as it did to the divine in Christ a merely accidental position alongside of His personal humanity, involved the total loss of Christology" (ibid., 2/3, p. 71). The task was to achieve a balance, allowing both natures to stand "in their integrity and entirety." Dorner observed that "distinguished men of freer and deeper mind," like Lessing, Semler, Herder, Tersteegen, Claudius, Hamann, Lavater, Stilling, Kleuker, Crusius, and Oetinger "were unable either to feel at home in the old orthodox system, or to overlook its inner unsoundness" (ibid., p. 73).

130. Ibid., 2/3, pp. 71–260. A similar series of divisions was expounded in the *System*, 3:199–279.

131. Ibid., 2/3, p. 100.

132. Ibid., 2/3, pp. 101–3. Dorner's account of Schelling rested on his earlier works, his *Darlegung des wahren Verhältnisses der Naturphilosophie zu der verbesserten Fichteschen Lehre* (1806); *Vorlesungen über die Methode des akademischen Studiums* (1803); and *Philosophische Untersuchungen über das Wesen der menschlichen Freiheit* (1809). Cf. also J. Rothermundt, *Personale Synthese*, pp. 138–39.

133. Ibid., 2/3, pp. 117–18.

134. Ibid., 2/3, p. 120.

135. Ibid., 2/3, p. 121.

136. Ibid., 2/3, p. 139. Dorner's account is based chiefly on Hegel's *Vorlesungen über die Philosophie der Religion* (1832); but reference is also made to *Phänomenologie des Geistes* (1807); *Vorlesungen über die Geschichte der Philosophie* (1833); and *Vorlesungen über die Philosophie der Geschichte* (1837).

137. Ibid., 2/3, pp. 121–31, where Dorner reviews the teaching of Marheineke, Rosenkranz, and Conradi.

138. Ibid., 2/3, pp. 147–48.

139. Ibid., 2/3, p. 153.

140. Ibid., 2/3, p. 155.

141. Ibid., 2/3, p. 148.

142. Ibid., 2/3, p. 160.

143. Ibid., 2/3, p. 174.

144. Ibid., 2/3, pp. 176, 179.

145. Ibid., 2/3, p. 194.

146. Ibid., 2/3, p. 200.

147. Ibid., 2/3, p. 201.

148. Ibid., 2/3, p. 203.

149. Ibid.

150. Ibid., 2/3, p. 206, noting Alexander Schweizer as a theologian who declared less than Schleiermacher (cf. his *Geschichte der reformirten Dogmatik* [1847], 2:275ff.).

151. Ibid., 2/3, p. 208.

152. Ibid., 2/3, p. 211.

153. Ibid.

154. Ibid., 2/3, p. 212.

155. Ibid., 2/3, pp. 212–13.

156. Ibid., 2/3, p. 227.

157. Ibid., 2/1, p. 220.

158. Ibid., 2/1, pp. 114–19.

159. Ibid., 2/3, pp. 229–30.

160. Ibid., 2/3, pp. 230–32; cf. W. Pannenberg, *Jesus—God and Man*, pp. 354–64, who notes that under the influence of Müller, Ullmann eventually dropped the idea of *peccare non potuit* ("he was not able to sin") in favor of the simple assertion of Jesus' factual freedom from sin.

161. Ibid., 2/3, pp. 231–32. Dorner added that insight into this truth depended on whether God's essence was seen as ethical, and the ethical conceived as ontological. Among those he noted as sharing this insight were S. T. Coleridge, F. D. Maurice, Julius Hare, Thomas Arnold, E. B. Pusey, E. de Pressensé, Hagenbach, and Osterzee.

162. Ibid., 2/3, p. 232.

163. Ibid., 2/3, p. 233.

164. Ibid., 2/3, p. 234.

165. Ibid., 2/3, p. 236. As a corollary, Dorner claimed that, if we do not attribute to Christ a significance for humanity reaching beyond the time of sin, he would become superfluous after the accomplishment of his work of redemption. The thought was further elaborated in the *System*, Section 62, 2:205–20. See also J. Rothermundt, op. cit., pp. 161–68.

166. Cf. A. R. Vidler, *F. D. Maurice and Company* (London: S.C.M. pp. 38–61); F. Olofsson, *Christus Redemptor et Consummator: A Study in the Theology of B. F. Westcott* (Uppsala: *Acta Universitatis Upsaliensis, Studia Doctrinae Christianae Upsaliensia* 19, 1979).

167. Ibid., 2/3, p. 249.

168. Calvin, *Institutes*, 1, 13, 6; cf. Karl Barth, *Church Dogmatics*, 2nd ed. (Edinburgh: T. & T. Clark, 1975), 1/1, pp. 353–68.

169. Ibid., 2/3, p. 249.

170. Even in his introduction which reviewed biblical thought, Dorner made little attempt to grapple with the questions of history. His passing references to Strauss were more concerned with the latter's theological and philosophical ideas than with answering his historical criticism. This observation is further substantiated by John M. Drickamer's article (see n. 119) which, despite the reference to "higher criticism" in its title, is concerned with the theological stance of Dorner rather than strictly critical questions.

171. Ibid., 2/3, p. 250.

172. "With Christ's death not merely is His earthly work finished, but also the inner, primarily spiritual consummation of His person established. Hence, the lowest stage of His outward Humiliation is in itself the beginning of His Exaltation" (*System of Christian Doctrine*, 4, sec. 123, p. 125). "In the ascension of Christ, or His absolute exaltation, His resurrection finds its conclusion, inasmuch as the complete spiritualization and transfiguration of His earthly into pneumatic personality is presented therein in perfected form. The exalted God-man is raised above the limits of time and space, the humanity of Jesus having become the free, adequate organ of the Logos. This state of consummation itself is figuratively expressed as the *Session at the right hand of the Father*, and denotes, on the one hand, divine repose and blessedness in the certainty of His eternal glory and majesty (for He is now personally Lord of glory and King of kings), and on the other, his relation to His office" (ibid., sec. 126, p. 138). See further, J. Rothermundt (op. cit., pp. 192–200), who rejects the criticisms of E. Hirsch (5:386–87) and others, that Dorner's doctrine of a developing incarnation is self-contradictory. He holds that the alternative of a full, complete union from the very first instant would be quasi-magical, and that Dorner was trying to think of the union of divine and human nature as both personal and historical. This requires growth, and is more satisfactory than the supposition that God divested himself altogether of certain attributes.

173. "...*But precisely the kenōsis of self-depotentiation fails to perform that at which it aims.* For if the Logos, professedly in love, has given up His eternal, self-conscious being, where is His love during that time? Love without self-consciousness is an impossibility. *Nay more: What necessity can there be for the eternal Logos accomplishing this unethical sacrifice of Himself? ...Nay more, on such a supposition the incarnation of the Logos is of no advantage whatever to humanity.* It does not allow of the Logos communicating Himself in ever increasing measure, and in such a manner as to direct the development of the man assumed....

"...It does *not even, with its kenōsis, help the question of the unity of the divine and human,* unless we should say that the depotentiation was in itself incarnation, that is, conversion into an human existence. This, the strongest form of Theopaschitism, would reduce the God-man to a theophany, which must necessarily cease of itself as soon as the human drama had been played out, and the Logos had been reconverted to Himself. If, however, no conversion be supposed to have taken place (as by Thomasius), and yet the *kenōsis* be assumed for the purpose of the Unio (out of regard to which, the assimilation of the two natures through the *kenōsis* of the Logos is supposed to take place), we should have nothing but two homogenous magnitudes in or alongside of each other....

"That mythologizing theory of the *kenōsis* of the Logos which perturbs the conception of God and suspends the Trinity, is invented for the purpose of securing an unity of the divine-human life, which shall be absolutely immoveable and complete from the very beginning" (ibid., 2/3, pp. 253–56).

174. Ibid., 2/3, p. 259–60.

175. Op. cit., p. 129.

176. The chief representatives of late speculative theology were A. E. Biedermann (1819–85), R. A. Lipsius (1830–92), and H. Lüdemann (1842–1933). The christology of all three is described by M. Huber, op. cit., pp. 123–96, and extracts from Biedermann's *Christliche Dogmatik* (1869; 2nd ed., 1884–85) are given by C. Welch, op. cit., pp. 285–382.

177. Cf. Paul Wrzecionko, *Die philosophischen Wurzeln der Theologie Albrecht Ritschls. Ein Beitrag zum Problem des Verhältnisses von Theologie und Philosophie im 19. Jahrhundert* (Berlin: Töpelmann, 1964); Rolf Schäfer, *Ritschl. Grundlinien eines fast verschollenen dogmatischen Systems,* BHT 41 (Tübingen: J. C. B. Mohr, 1968); G. Lundström, *The Kingdom of God in the Teaching of Jesus: A History of Interpretation from the Last Decades of the Nineteenth Century to the Present Day* (Edinburgh: Oliver and Boyd, 1963). See also chap. 11, n. 88.

178. *Jesus—God and Man*, pp. 33–37; cf. Colin Brown, *Miracles and the Critical Mind*, pp. 289–90, for criticism of this idea.

179. Cf. George Tyrrell, *Christianity at the Cross-Roads* (1909; reprint ed ., London: Allen and Unwin, 1963), p. 49, speaking of Harnack.

Index

Numbers in italics refer to pages in the endnotes